AYN RAND

Ayn Rand, 1905–1982.

AYN RAND

THE RUSSIAN RADICAL

Public Library San Mateo, CA

Chris Matthew Sciabarra

The Pennsylvania State University Press
University Park, Pennsylvania

Library of Congress Cataloging-in-Publication Data

Sciabarra, Chris Matthew, 1960–
    Ayn Rand : the Russian radical / by Chris Matthew Sciabarra.

        p.   cm.
    Includes bibliographical references and index.
    ISBN 0-271-01440-7 (cloth)
    ISBN 0-271-01441-5 (paper)
    1. Rand, Ayn.   2. Objectivism (Philosophy)   3. Dialectic.
    4. Philosophers—Russia.   5. Philosophers—United States.
    I. Title.
    B945.R234S35   1995
    191—dc20   94-34071
                                                                      CIP

It is the policy of The Pennsylvania State University Press to use acid-free paper for the
first printing of all clothbound books. Publications on uncoated stock satisfy the
minimum requirements of American National Standard for Information Sciences—
Permanence of Paper for Printed Library Materials, ANSI Z39.48–1992.

Frontispiece: Ayn Rand at Warner Brothers during the filming of the Warner Brothers'
movie version of *The Fountainhead,* 1948. (From the Warner Bros. release, *The
Fountainhead* © 1949 Warner Bros. Pictures, Inc. Courtesy of Turner Entertainment)

To the memory of my Uncle Sam,
for his guidance, loyalty, support, and love.

Contents

Acknowledgments

This book is the product of many years of research and dialogue. I owe a debt of gratitude to many individuals.

For their constructive comments on my earlier article, "Ayn Rand's Critique of Ideology": Walter Block, the late Roy Childs, Douglas Den Uyl, Howard Dickman, Antony Flew, Jeff Friedman, Robert Hessen, Robert Hollinger, Greg Johnson, Don Lavoie, Eric Mack, and Wallace Matson.

For aiding my historical research: N. O. Lossky's sons Boris and Andrew, and grandson Nicholas; Brian Boyd; Helene Sikorski, sister of the late Vladimir Nabokov; Father Makarios Rigo; the late dean Father John Meyendorff and librarian Eleana Silk, of St. Vladimir's Orthodox Theological Seminary; Bernice Rosenthal; James McClelland; and George Kline. Professors Kline and Rosenthal were also kind enough to share their meticulous comments on sections of this book. Special thanks to Robin Katz and Irina Kushnerik for their translations of letters and historical documents.

My acknowledgments also to the Ayn Rand Institute, Lectures on Objectivism, and Second Renaissance Books for giving me the opportunity to purchase and lease materials, including hundreds of hours of audio and video lectures by Ayn Rand and other Objectivists, and to Leonard Peikoff, Diane LeMont, and the Estate of Ayn Rand for timely correspondence on several issues of historical and legal significance to the current project.

For their financial and moral support: the Earhart Foundation, including

David Kennedy and Antony Sullivan, and William O'Boyle and the Institute for Humane Studies, including Walter Grinder, Leonard Liggio, Jeremy Shearmur, and Chris Blundell.

For his conviction, perseverance, and belief in the importance of my work: Sandy Thatcher. For her assistance in the preparation of this book, Cherene Holland. For their painstaking copyediting and proofreading efforts: Andrew B. Lewis and Kerime Toksu. For their marketing efforts, Lisa Bayer, Alison Reeves, and Karen Walker. And for the jacket design, Steve Kress.

For giving me the opportunity to interact with many scholars and students in an electronic forum: Svein Olav Nyberg's Hegel study group; Paul Vixie's "Objectivist" study group; and Jimmy Wales's "Moderated Discussion of Objectivist Philosophy."

Thanks also to David Kelley and the Institute for Objectivist Studies for sponsoring a 1993 colloquium on my book, which elicited helpful comments from Debra Cermele, Roger Donway, Elisa George, Laurence Gould, Karen Reedstrom, Joan Kennedy Taylor, Francisco Villalobos, and Michael Young. Thanks to Donald Heath and Jamie Dorrian for their assistance and delightful demeanor no matter how many times I interrupted them.

Thanks also to Ed Crane and David Boaz of the Cato Institute; Andrea Rich of Laissez-Faire Books; Ralph Volpicella and the Mil-rite Printing staff; Angela Carannante, Lorraine DaTello, Nadine Goldstein, Michael Lipner, Ron Mangano, Mary Morse, and Kathy Sharp from New Dorp High School; the late James Bennett; Kathy Lendech and Turner Entertainment Company, and the folks at Robert's One-Hour Photo; my New York University friends and colleagues, including Steve Faulkner, Farhad Kazemi, Kenneth King, Marilyn LaPorte, Richard Randall, Mario Rizzo, and Gisbert Flanz and Bertell Ollman, both of whom have greatly influenced my approach to political theory; Mary Toledo of the Reason Foundation; Barbara Branden, for her constructive comments and guidance; Nathaniel Branden for his insightful comments and for sharing *The Six Pillars of Self-Esteem* prior to its publication; Joe Cellantano; William Dale; John and Marsha Enright; Oz Garcia; Scott Gordon; Mike Hardy; Don Hauptman; Howard Kainz; Irfan Khawaja; Gema LaBoccetta, E. Frederic Mirer; David Ross; Tim Starr; and Fred Weiss.

For commenting on this manuscript in whole or in part: Bill Bradford, John Hospers, Tibor Machan, Victor and Susan Niederhoffer, David Oyerly, Peter Saint-Andre, David Ramsay Steele, George Walsh, Charles Wieder, and several anonymous readers. An earlier draft of this book was reviewed by Allan Gotthelf. Though Professor Gotthelf strongly disagrees with my arguments concerning the sources and dialectical character of Ayn Rand's thought, my final presentation benefited nonetheless from his helpful criticism.

I owe a very special debt of gratitude to five people: Stephen Cox and Douglas Rasmussen, for their long-term support of and critical commentary on my work; Murray Franck, for his comments, indispensable legal advice, and friendship; and Michelle Marder Kamhi and Louis Torres, for their encouragement of my efforts in countless ways on an almost daily basis.

Thanks also to my aunts, uncles, cousins, and friends, too numerous to mention, and also, to my immediate family, all of whom have been a source of personal and spiritual support, especially: my late mother, Ann; my sister, Elizabeth; my brother, Carl; my sister-in-law, Joanne; Tom Beck; Pamela Bolen; Matthew Cappabianca; Robert ("A-W") Crammer; Mark Cwern; Michelle Ely; Annette Memon; Hiromi Shinya; Michael Southern; Elaine Thompson; Peter Vigliarolo; Ira Zornberg; and Blondie, who during some of my most difficult days, gave me firsthand evidence of the "Muttnik Principle" in action.

In acknowledging the above parties, I do not mean to suggest their implicit or explicit endorsement of any of the ideas herein expressed. What appears in this book is my own interpretation of Ayn Rand's legacy and philosophy for which I take full responsibility. I do not speak for a group or a movement, but only for myself.

Introduction

Ayn Rand is one of the most widely read philosophers of the twentieth century. Yet despite the sale of nearly thirty million copies of her works, and their translation into many languages (Landrum 1994, 302),[1] there have been few book-length, scholarly examinations of her thought. This is hardly surprising since academics have often dismissed her "Objectivist" ideas as "pop" philosophy.[2] As a best-selling novelist, a controversial, flamboyant polemicist, and a woman in a male-dominated profession, Rand remained outside the academy throughout her life. Her works had inspired passionate responses that echo the uncompromising nature of her moral vision. In many cases, her audiences were either cultish in their devotion or savage in their attacks. The left was infuriated by her anticommunist, procapitalist politics, whereas the right was disgusted by her atheism and civil libertarianism.

Since her death in 1982, interest in her thought has not abated. Respondents to a joint Library of Congress–Book of the Month Club survey of "lifetime reading habits" indicated that *Atlas Shrugged* was second only to the Bible in its significant impact on their lives.[3] Rand's influence on American political thought has been acknowledged by Martin Anderson, Reagan's chief domestic and economic adviser; Hillary Rodham Clinton; Alan Greenspan, chairman of the Federal Reserve; John Hospers, philosopher and one-time Libertarian Party presidential candidate; Charles Murray, author of *Losing Ground*; Robert Nozick, Harvard philosopher and National Book Award winner; and Clarence Thomas, associate justice of the Supreme Court. Most important, there has been a steady growth in Rand scholarship. In the past decade, a number of collections of her writings were published for the first time, as were several studies of her career and impact.[4] The number of reference guides and journals dedicated to the examination of Objectivist ideas continues to grow.[5] Discussions of her thought and excerpts from her essays appear regularly in journals and college textbooks.[6] In addition, several professional scholarly organizations have been founded to promote the serious study of Rand's philosophy.[7] A new generation of thinkers schooled in the Objectivist, classical liberal, and libertarian traditions has extended and refined the Randian legacy. They include Leonard Peikoff, heir to the Estate of Ayn Rand, who continues to lecture and write on Objectivism; Nathaniel Branden, who despite his separation from Rand in 1968, continues to develop the interconnections between neo-Objectivist philosophy and psychology; David Kelley, who has presented a sophisticated realist theory of perception based largely on Rand's epistemological contributions; Douglas Den Uyl and Douglas Rasmussen, who have combined Randian and Aristotelian insights in their own unique defense of a free society; and Tibor Machan, whose many books reflect a deep appreciation of Rand's philosophy.

Nevertheless, the growth in Rand scholarship and influence has generated few comprehensive, book-length examinations of her thought. Three earlier attempts at extended critique, by Albert Ellis (1968), William F. O'Neill ([1971] 1977), and John W. Robbins (1974), were published eight to twelve years before Rand's death and, hence, did not assess her full contribution. *The Philosophic Thought of Ayn Rand*, edited by Den Uyl and Rasmussen (1984), is an important anthology of essays written by several scholars who examine aspects of Rand's epistemology, ethics, and politics, from different perspectives. Peikoff's *Objectivism: The Philosophy of Ayn Rand* (1991b) is the first systematic statement of Rand's philosophy, albeit from an orthodox, noncritical vantage point. And Ronald Merrill's *Ideas of Ayn Rand* (1991) presents some original theses, though with a more popular orientation.

This book is the first scholarly attempt to trace Rand's roots and assess her place in intellectual history. My central theme is captured by the title: *Ayn Rand: The Russian Radical*, for in this book I address two questions:

1. In what sense can Rand's philosophy be understood as a response to her Russian past?

2. In what sense can Rand's philosophy be understood as a contribution to twentieth-century radical thought?

The answers to these questions provide a new interpretation of Rand's Objectivism in terms of its intellectual origins and its significance for the history of social theory. I contend that Rand achieved a unique synthesis by rejecting—and absorbing—key elements in the Russian tradition. She rejected the Marxist and religious content of Russian thought. She accepted the dialectical revolt against formal dualism. Her distinctive integration of a libertarian politics with a dialectical method forges a revolutionary link. She projected a dialectical sensibility while formulating a fundamentally non-Marxist, radical critique of statism.

In this book, I do not focus on Ayn Rand's personal life or on the controversial movement she inspired. I reconstructed certain biographical elements, especially concerning Rand's Russian education, in an effort to trace her early intellectual development. In a few instances, I could not ignore circumstances in Rand's public and private life, particularly those events which divided sympathetic and critical commentators alike and led to interpretive modifications, or distortions, of her overall project. It is my hope that this book will contribute to a much-needed scholarly appreciation of Rand's profoundly original theoretical system.

Rand Scholarship: Problems and Perspectives

I must admit that Rand's deeply controversial public persona has left for the present generation of scholars two major, related problems: (1) the need to distinguish Rand's personality from her philosophical legacy; and (2) the task of determining what (and who) defines Objectivism as a distinct school of thought.

The first problem is not peculiar to Rand scholarship. It is a truism that in studying any philosophy, one must never lose sight of the personal, cultural, and historical context of the originating philosopher. Yet the study of philosophy cannot be reduced to exploring this or that philosopher's idiosyncrasies. That would be psychologism at its worst. One should not judge Schopenhauer's philosophy by his penchant for sleeping with loaded pistols or Nietzsche's by the fact that he died insane. Similarly, one should not judge Rand's philosophy by her intolerance toward dissenters, her penchant for moralizing, her style of polemical exposition, or the "cult of personality" that she inspired.

Perhaps even more than her status as an iconoclastic thinker, a novelist, or a woman, Rand's truculent temperament and cultic following severely hampered serious scholarship on her work. Indeed, the fledgling Objectivist movement in the 1960s contributed to a second major problem: the difficulty in pinpointing the "genuine" representatives of her philosophy. Echoing the sectarianism and authoritarianism within the left academy, Objectivists have tended to engage in philosophical "purges" and personal disputes that have led some to disavow the contributions of others still working largely within the broad framework defined by Rand. The first such schism occurred in 1968, when Rand ended her personal and professional relationship with her chief associate, psychologist Nathaniel Branden.[8]

In my view, there are distinctions between the "orthodox" interpreters of Rand's thought and those who can be termed "neo-Objectivists." The orthodox thinkers see Rand's philosophy as closed and complete. The neo-Objectivists accept certain basic principles, while expanding, modifying, or revising other aspects of Rand's thought. The "neo-Objectivist" label is not employed critically; for history, I believe, will describe all these thinkers simply as "Objectivists." Nevertheless, Rand did not sanction all of the developments proceeding from her influence. In the case of Nathaniel Branden, for instance, although Rand enthusiastically approved his theoretical work while he was her associate, she repudiated his subsequent efforts.[9] A later dispute between Leonard Peikoff and David Kelley centered on the question of what *precisely* constitutes the philosophy of Objectivism.

Adopting an orthodox, "closed-system" approach, Peikoff (1991b) has stated: " 'Objectivism' is the name of Ayn Rand's philosophy as presented in the material she herself wrote or endorsed" (xv). Peikoff excludes from "official Objectivist doctrine" both his own work after Rand's death and Rand's unedited, unpublished lectures and journals, since she "had no opportunity to see or approve" of the material.[10]

Peikoff follows Rand's own pronouncements. At the time of the Branden schism, Rand maintained (in 1968) that she was a theoretician of Objectivism, which she characterized as "a philosophical system originated by me and publicly associated with my name."[11] She claimed that it was her "right and responsibility" to defend the system's integrity, and she renounced any "organized movement" in her name.

Twelve years after this "statement of policy," when a magazine called *The Objectivist Forum* was established, Rand approved the journal as "a *forum* for students of Objectivism to discuss their ideas, each speaking only for himself." Rand stated that the magazine was neither the "official voice" of her philosophy nor her "representative" or "spokesman."

Rand explained further that those who agree with certain tenets of Objectivism but disagree with others should give proper acknowledgment "and then indulge in any flights of fancy [they] wish, on [their] own." Anyone using the name of "Objectivism" for his own

> philosophical hodgepodge . . . is guilty of the fraudulent presumption of trying to put thoughts into *my* brain (or of trying to pass his thinking off as mine—an attempt which fails, for obvious reasons). I chose the name "Objectivism" at a time when my philosophy was beginning to be known and some people were starting to call themselves "Randists." I am much too conceited to allow such a use of my name.[12]

Upholding the consistency of her system as one of its virtues, Rand opposed the practice of those philosophers who "regard philosophy as a *verb*, not a noun (they are not studying or creating philosophy, they are *'doing'* it)" (2). Thus Peikoff's interpretation of Objectivism as a "closed system" clearly mirrors Rand's own view.

By contrast, David Kelley (1990) views Objectivism as an "open system": "A philosophy defines a school of thought, a category of thinkers who subscribe to the same principles. In an open philosophy, members of the school may differ among themselves over many issues within the framework of the basic principles they accept" (57).

The evolution of academic Marxist thought illustrates Kelley's point clearly. In defining the essence of contemporary Marxism, it is impossible to disconnect the statements of Karl Marx from the multiple interpretations constructed over the past century. These interpretations are as much a logical development of Marx's methods and theories as they are a reflection of the particular historical, social, and personal contexts of his interpreters. The interpretations also reflect different periods in Marx's own development. Some scholars stress the earlier, more "humanistic" Marx, whereas others argue for an economistic interpretation based on his mature works. Most scholars would agree, however, that one cannot detach Marx's unpublished writings from the corpus of his thought. Indeed, the great bulk of Marx's work was issued posthumously. For example, Marx's *Grundrisse*, composed of seven unedited workbooks, was first published in the twentieth century. It provides a cornucopia of material from which one can reconstruct his method of inquiry as a distinct "moment" (or aspect) of his dialectical approach. The *Grundrisse* is an essential complement to and reflection on Marx's published exposition in *Capital*.

In addition, a Marxist scholar cannot neglect the plethora of interpretive twists resulting from the combination of Marx's theories with compatible approaches in psychology, anthropology, and sociology. What has emerged is a scholarly industry that must take account of structuralist, phenomeno-logical, critical, and analytical approaches, to name but a few. Finally, we have been presented with different philosophical interpretations of the "real" Karl Marx: the Aristotelian Marx, the Kantian Marx, the Hegelian Marx, and the Leninist Marx.[13]

None of these developments alter the essential body of theory that Marx proposed in his lifetime. One can empathize with the innovative theorist who, jealously guarding his discoveries, aims to protect the "purity" of the doctrine. Ironically, Rand suggests a spiritual affinity with Marx on this issue. She remembers that upon hearing the "outrageous statements" made by some of his "Marxist" followers, Marx exclaimed: "But I am not a Marxist."[14]

Nevertheless, although one can debate whether a particular philosophy is "closed" or "open," scholarship must consider the many theoretical developments emerging over time directly or indirectly from the innovator's authentic formulations. Much of current intellectual history focuses not on the ideas of the innovator, but rather, on the evolution of the ideas and on the context in which the ideas emerged and developed. As W. W. Bartley argues, the affirmation of a theory involves many logical implications that are not immediately apparent to the original theorist. In Bartley's words, "The informative content of any idea includes an infinity of unforeseeable non-trivial statements." The creation of mathematics for instance, "gener-ates problems that are wholly independent of the intentions of its cre-ators."[15]

In this book, I have adopted a similarly hermeneutical approach. The principles of this scholarly technique were sketched by Paul Ricoeur in his classic essay, "The Model of the Text."[16] Ricoeur maintains that a text is detached from its author and develops consequences of its own. In so doing, it transcends its relevance to its initial situation and addresses an indefinite range of possible readers. Hence, the text must be understood not only in terms of the author's context but also in the context of the multiple interpretations that emerge during its subsequent history.

I do not mean to suggest that Rand's ideas lack objective validity, that is, validity independent of the interpretations of others. Ultimately, one must judge the validity of any idea by its correspondence to reality and/or its explanatory power. But to evaluate the truthfulness of a philosophic formulation is not the only legitimate task of scholarship. Indeed, my primary purpose in this study as an intellectual historian and political theorist is *not* to demonstrate either the validity or the falsity of Rand's ideas. Rather, it is to shed light on her philosophy by examining the context in which it was both formulated and developed.

In this book I attempt to grasp Rand's Objectivism as a text developing over time. As a concept, "Objectivism" is open-ended; it *contains* its history and its future. It must be understood in terms of both its historical origins and its post-Randian evolution. The existential conditions from which it emerged and to which it speaks are in large part what give it its very significance. So, too, its meaning continues to unfold through a clash of interpretations offered by followers and critics alike. By clarifying these conditions and factors, I hope to provide an enriched appreciation of Rand's contributions.

Such an assertion might imply that I claim to have grasped the implications of Objectivism even more thoroughly than did Rand herself.[17] Although I would never presume to such intellectual hubris, it is true, nonetheless, that Rand could not have explored the full implications of her philosophy in her lifetime. Such a task is reserved necessarily for succeeding generations of scholars.

First and foremost then, this is a book about ideas. I discuss Rand's ideas as she expressed them in her published and unpublished works, in her written essays and spoken lectures, from the earliest available material to the last. I consider *all* these sources important to a comprehensive understanding of her thought and legacy. Unfortunately, because Rand never wrote an exhaustive treatise, her system must be pieced together from her novels, essays, and lectures. Furthermore, many of Rand's journals and private papers are not yet available to the scholarly community. Since Rand agreed to place these papers with the Library of Congress, it is hoped that future scholars will have more information at their disposal than I have had.[18]

I also discuss Rand's thought as it has been interpreted, modified, or extended by those she influenced. This book is as much an analysis of the tradition that Rand's philosophy has sparked as it is of the ideas she herself expressed, and I include substantive analysis of work by Barbara Branden,

Nathaniel Branden, Douglas Den Uyl, David Kelley, Tibor Machan, Leonard Peikoff, Douglas Rasmussen, George Walsh, and others. Even for those works not officially sanctioned by Rand, there is significant textual evidence to support their continuity and consistency with Objectivism. Some of these authors in fact, have written more for a scholarly than for a popular audience. Hence, their alternative formulations of Objectivist positions are characterized by scholarly rigor and precision appropriate to that context. I do not hesitate to use these materials, although this must be done with care, always remembering that the best source for evaluating their consistency is the writing of Rand herself. Ultimately, I argue that there is an essential unity in Rand's legacy and that this unity is *both* philosophical and methodological.

Before proceeding, however, I feel compelled to assert that Rand's philosophy should be taken seriously and treated with respect. The mere mention of Ayn Rand's name in academic circles can evoke smirks and a rolling of the eyes. Most often she is dismissed, without discussion, as a reactionary, a propagandist, or a pop-fiction writer with a cult following. The fact that her work often appeals to the young seems proof that her ideas are immature or simplistic.

From my own experience, I can attest that Rand's work does inspire youthful admiration. I was first exposed to her ideas when I was a senior in high school. Captivated by the starkness of her essays and the benevolent heroism of her fictional protagonists, I consumed all of Rand's available works. I gradually discovered a rich classical liberal and libertarian literature that provided a fundamental alternative to mainstream social science.

Although my interest in Rand never abated during my college years, I was far removed from the dogmatic, cult-like devotion of fans who seemed to worship her every pronouncement. Moreover, I witnessed the hostile reaction to her work by many academic professionals. Although Rand provided an insightful, moral defense of capitalism, I found it difficult to imagine that she could ever gain scholarly acceptance.

Not until I was in graduate school did I discover something else in Rand's work. As a doctoral student, I was engaged in a comprehensive study of dialectical method with two distinguished scholars of the left academy, Bertell Ollman and Wolf Heydebrand. Much to my amazement, I discovered provocative parallels between the methods of Marxian social theory and the philosophic approach of Ayn Rand. Both Marx and Rand traced the interconnectedness of social phenomena, uncovering a startling cluster of relations between and among the institutions and structures of society. Both

Marx and Rand opposed the mind-body dichotomy, and all of its derivatives. But unlike Marx, Rand was virulently anticommunist. Unlike Marx, Rand viewed a genuinely capitalist social system as a necessary condition for the achievement of truly integrated human being. Paradoxically, Rand seemed to embrace a dialectical perspective that resembled the approach of her Marxist political adversaries, even while defending capitalism as an "unknown ideal."

In 1984, recognizing these parallels and distinctions, I was encouraged by Ollman and Heydebrand to undertake my first systematic study of the dialectical aspects of Rand's philosophy. In the process, I rediscovered elements in Objectivism that challenged my entire understanding of that philosophy and its place in intellectual history.

Rand was notorious for maintaining that her intellectual debt to other thinkers was very limited. And yet in my own research, I discovered similarities between Rand's approach and the dialectical approach of Hegelians and Marxists. Rand would have vehemently denied such a link. She viewed Hegel and Marx as heirs to the destructive Platonic and Kantian philosophic traditions. I grew certain, however, that at some point in her intellectual development, Rand had absorbed, perhaps unwittingly, crucial dialectical methods of analysis. My preliminary study compelled me to look further.

The Study in Brief

Rand was born and reared during a revolutionary period in Russian history. That context is the key to understanding the peculiar character of her Objectivism, her essentially dialectical mode of inquiry, and her radical critique of contemporary society. By the time she graduated from the University of Leningrad in 1924,[19] she had been exposed to a dialectical revolt against formal dualism that would profoundly influence her literary craft and philosophical project.

In this book, I explore Objectivism on three distinct levels: (1) its intellectual roots, (2) its formal structure, and (3) its radical social implications.

All too often, Rand's philosophy is presented as a deductive formulation from first principles. This approach prevails in the work of both her followers and her detractors. Objectivism is defined in a logically derivative manner:

Rand allegedly begins with an ontological view of the law of identity and then proceeds to enunciate a doctrine of epistemological realism, ethical egoism, individualist-libertarian-capitalist social philosophy, and a "Romantic-Realist" literary credo. Each of these branches is integrated in a hierarchy of interrelated abstractions.

I do not deny that such a relational structure exists within Objectivism as a formal totality, but I depart from established perspectives by exploring Rand's philosophy as a phenomenon with a history and as a system.

From a historical vantage point, I examine Rand's philosophy in "the process of its becoming." I approach Objectivism diachronically, as an evolved response to the dualities that Rand confronted in Soviet Russia. Although she rejected both the mysticism of Russia's religious traditions[20] and the secular collectivism of the Russian Marxists, she nonetheless remained a profoundly *Russian* thinker. Rand's Russian nature was not reflected merely in her heavy foreign accent or in the length of her novels. She was Russian in more fundamental ways. In the sweeping character of her generalizations, and in her passionate commitment to the practical realization of her ideals, Rand was fully within the Russian literary and philosophic tradition. Like most of Russia's great literary figures, she was an artist, social critic, and nonacademic philosopher who constructed a broad synthesis in her battle against the traditional antinomies in Western thought: mind versus body, fact versus value, theory versus practice, reason versus emotion, rationalism versus empiricism, idealism versus materialism, and so on. And like most of Russia's indigenous philosophers, she presented an exhaustive, all-encompassing theoretical totality. Her system is as much defined by what she *accepted* in Russian thought as by what she *rejected*. In her intellectual development, Rand reflects the very Hegelian *Aufhebung* she ridiculed as a violation of the law of identity. In her intellectual evolution, Rand both absorbed and abolished, preserved and transcended, the elements of her Russian past.

I do not mean to imply that Rand's ideas can be wholly explained by—or reduced to—the context from which they emerged. People have free will; innovation and creativity are possible. But free will does not mean that people can step outside of their own skin. No human being can adopt a perspective on the whole that is external to all personal, cultural, social, or historical context. We are as much the creatures of history as its creators. Though Rand used genuinely inductive and deductive techniques in fashioning her unique synthesis, she also responded to real, concrete circumstances.

Abstracting Rand's philosophy from this context damages our understanding of its historical importance.

Part One partially recovers the lost world of revolutionary Russia and evokes the oppressive conditions that prompted Rand to emigrate to the United States. I concentrate on the intellectual traditions that dominated Russian culture during Rand's formative years. Living in Russia during its celebrated Silver Age, she witnessed a burst of Nietzschean and neo-Hegelian thought: the Symbolist movement, Russian Religious Renaissance, and Russian Marxism each attempted the resolution of various forms of dualism. I focus in greater detail on the contributions of Nicholas Onufrie-vich Lossky, Rand's philosophy teacher at Petrograd University. Lossky, who encapsulated many of the significant dialectical methods prevalent in Russian thought, was the most significant of Rand's professors and perhaps the one who most influenced her early intellectual development. I explore the historical connection of Rand and Lossky. As the dean of contemporary, pre-Bolshevik, Russian philosophy,[21] Lossky viewed the world as an organic totality in which each part is internally related to every other. This dialectical conception reappears in many forms in the writings of Lossky's student, Ayn Rand. I conclude Part One, with a developmental study of Rand's intellectual maturation from the moment of her arrival in the United States until her death in 1982. My focus here is not on Objectivism as an integrated system, but on Rand's intellectual groping toward synthesis.

Historically, Rand's revolt against dualism animated her project.[22] In Part Two, I switch from the historical to the synchronic. I reconstruct Rand's system to show how it is an inherently dialectical and nondualistic formulation that differs considerably from conventional alternatives.

Since the hierarchical structure of Objectivism cannot be ignored, I present the basic tenets of Rand's perspective in a logically progressive manner to emphasize their more specific applications. It would be an error, for example, to begin with Rand's politics and proceed to her ontology. Because each branch and principle depend on their antecedents, one must first enter the lofty domain of metaphysics and work methodically toward Rand's epistemology, philosophical psychology, aesthetics, ethics, and politics.

In Part Three, I show how Rand's mode of analysis culminates in a radical assessment of the nature of power as manifested in all social practices and institutions. I scrutinize her attempt to trace the interrelationships of culture, education, sex, race, and the neofascist welfare-warfare state. I also examine her theory of history, her vision of the Objectivist society, and her communitarian impulse.

In this book I also make explicit comparisons and distinctions between Rand and other social thinkers. This is often a difficult task, owing partly to Rand's myopia concerning both her intellectual debts and her assessment of other philosophers. In bravura fashion, Rand once said that in the history of philosophy, she could only recommend the "3 A's"—Aristotle, Aquinas, and Ayn Rand.[23] According to Barbara Branden's biography, Rand's formal study of philosophy was limited to just a few college courses. She studied Plato, Aristotle, and Nietzsche in some depth, but read only excerpts from—or summaries of—the work of other key figures. She often learned about different schools of thought in conversation with friends and colleagues who were themselves students of philosophy.[24] Though Rand recognized some positive elements in the thought of Nietzsche, Spinoza, the classical liberals (such as Locke), and the Founding Fathers, though she celebrated the work of such twentieth-century individualists as Ludwig von Mises, John T. Flynn, and Isabel Paterson, she failed to see that many of the philosophers whom she attacked shared a similarly integrated perspective.

Nathaniel Branden (1982T) has observed that her wholesale rejection of other viewpoints was a by-product of her theatrical, emotional, and abrasive style. According to Branden, Rand did little to build bridges to those who operated in different intellectual contexts. As a polemicist, she often dismissed her opponents on moralistic or psychologistic grounds. Moreover, her broad generalizations often lacked the rigor of scholarly analysis.[25] Branden does not fault Rand for this; he argues that it was not Rand's goal to work out the details of a full philosophical system. Rand offered important ideas in perception, epistemology, metaethics, politics, and aesthetics, but left it to her followers to defend Objectivism in the realm of technical philosophy (N. Branden 1989, 417–18).

This is not to deny the sophistication or originality of Rand's thought. But an enriched appreciation of her philosophy cannot emerge unless we compare her ideas to the ideas of the thinkers she celebrated or disparaged. Rand's place in intellectual history will very much depend upon how effectively she responded to these other traditions and to the central problems with which they have grappled. These comparisons are essential. As Robert Hollinger suggests, we can utilize contrasting doctrines to enhance our understanding of Rand's project, "even if they come from the pens of people whom Rand would consider anathema."[26]

I do not make these comparisons either to challenge Rand's originality or to bolster her credentials as a grand social theorist. Rand synthesized a number of elements in her philosophic system that have been explored previously by other thinkers. She is neither qualified nor disqualified as a serious thinker simply because what she says about any particular issue resembles what other thinkers have said about that issue in the past. The integrity and seriousness of her work cannot be established by merely pointing out its similarity to or difference from the works of more "respected" philosophers such as Aristotle, Hegel, Marx, Nietzsche, Lossky, Hayek, or Habermas.

Comparison promotes confrontation and communication not merely between those who celebrate Rand and those who criticize her but also between the traditions that are being engaged. As Richard Bernstein (1971) puts it, "The provincialism that is so fashionable among 'true believers' of different philosophic orientations can blind us to a serious, sympathetic understanding of other philosophers who are working in different idioms" (4). The dialogue that may result can help us to comprehend not only the perspectives of those we oppose but the implications of our own beliefs as well.

For many reasons, such a dialogue has been slow to develop with Objectivism. Nathaniel Branden, Barbara Branden, and David Kelley all suggest that the Objectivist movement of the 1960s fostered a cult-like reverence toward Rand. Ironically, a movement dedicated to freedom and individual autonomy engendered disputes over ideological purity.[27] Some devout followers attempted to model themselves on Rand's fictional characters. If John Galt, the protagonist of *Atlas Shrugged*, smoked cigarettes, this behavior was to be emulated. If Rand's heroines had a penchant for rough and explosive sex, this was also to be admired.[28] Many of Rand's disciples accepted each of her pronouncements as if they were intrinsic to the system of Objectivism. If Rand equated horror movies with depravity, or argued against electing a woman president on principle, or expressed distaste for the music of Beethoven, the works of Shakespeare, or the paintings of the Impressionists, or abhorred the practice of homosexuality, or disliked facial hair,[29] her personal, aesthetic, and sexual preferences were elevated to the status of dogma.

Kelley (1990) writes that many of Rand's followers failed to distinguish between the ideas essential to her philosophy and those that were not. For Kelley, Rand offers "the foundation and outline of a system" within which different interpretations are likely to develop (61).

Nevertheless, one cannot simply dismiss the authoritarian, sometimes downright foolish, aspects of the organized Objectivist movement. That these aspects exposed Rand's philosophy to ridicule and caricature cannot be denied. Of course, from the vantage point of intellectual history, Rand has no monopoly on folly. Of greater importance, however, is the charge that authoritarianism is inevitable in any grand system of philosophy. Since Rand posits a cultural revolution as necessary to the establishment of a genuinely free society, she seems to mimic the totalistic approach of the Marxists. In the twentieth century, Marxist ideology linked its organic, integrative methodology with its sanction of the total state. Hence, it is legitimate to examine the connection between what Karl Popper has called political and methodological totalitarianism. According to Popper ([1962] 1971), the totalistic attempts by Hegel and Marx to transcend the dualism of facts and standards underlies the inexorable totalitarianism of their worldviews. Popper argues that the fact-value distinction is a necessary one, for it bars people from attempting to enforce their own normative prescriptions on society as if these values were divinely dictated. Popper's "open society" is liberal and capitalist; it opposes totalistic central planning, but sanctions limited social engineering.

And yet by identifying dialectics with Marxism and dualism with capitalism, Popper agrees with Marx. Marx argued that dualism was both *essential* and *historically specific* to the capitalist mode of production. For Marx, capitalism both reflected and generated the dualities in the modern world. His historical project points toward a communist society that would transcend these dualities and the capitalist system on which they depend.

Rand proposes a resolution transcending the Popperian and Marxian alternatives. She links her defense of capitalism to a strong, dialectical sensibility. Her vision of the free society rejects traditional antinomies, but embraces the morality and practicality of the capitalist system. Given the collapse of Marxism as a theoretical paradigm and political force, Rand's alternative is particularly compelling. In many ways, it redeems the integrity of dialectics as a radical method by rescuing it from its mystical, collectivist, and statist incarnations.

Dialectics and Dualism

Yet Rand would have been the first to deny her status as a "dialectical" thinker. Rand's own view of "dialectics" was based on her experiences in the Soviet Union. In Rand's mind, the very word "dialectics" must have raised a "red flag" of sorts. In 1959, she saw Nikita Khrushchev on American television. As she later recounted, he recited "the credo of dialectic materialism in the exact words and tone in which I had heard it recited at exams, in my college days, by students at the University of Leningrad."[30] This credo was branded into the minds of students as an ideological tool of Soviet repression. Barbara Branden (1986) writes that Rand "understood the theory of dialectical materialism—and had on her body and spirit the scars of its practice" (42). For Rand, "dialectics" was pure Heraclitean nonsense; it was the view "that *contradictions* are the law of reality, that A is non-A."[31] In this sense, Rand, like Popper, interprets dialectics as an endorsement of *logical* contradiction, embodying a view of the universe based on nonidentity.[32]

Certainly dialectical language at times obscures a strictly logical understanding of contradiction and identity. Some writers are guilty of claiming that dialectical "logic" transcends the so-called formal, static, or one-dimensional logic of Aristotle.[33] The question is, in part, one of semantics. Unless I clarify my own understanding of "dialectics," I am vulnerable to at least two criticisms: (1) that in reconstructing Objectivism, I utilize categories and distinctions foreign to Rand's own system (Kelley, 20 August 1989C); and (2) that, in focusing on "dialectics" as a key component of the Objectivist approach, I have linked Rand to her Russian predecessors on the basis of a nonessential characteristic (Kelley in Kelley 1993T).

I reject both criticisms as follows:

Throughout the history of philosophy the term "dialectics" has been used in many different senses. Aristotle recognized dialectic and rhetoric as counterparts of each other; for him, rhetoric was the art of public speaking, or the "faculty of observing in any given case the available means of persuasion," whereas dialectic was the art of logical discussion and argumentation.[34] In dialectic, the interlocutor proceeds from accepted (or specific) propositions and argues toward a more basic (or general) conclusion.[35] Although mastery of this dialectic technique was the hallmark of Socratic and Platonic philosophy, Aristotle argued that it was insufficient for establishing scientific truth.[36] Nevertheless, he valued the dialectic because it demanded the study of questions from multiple vantage points. It is for this reason, perhaps, that Marx, Engels, and Lenin recognized Aristotle as the father of dialectical inquiry. Engels, in fact, called Aristotle "the Hegel of the ancient world," who "had already analyzed the most essential forms of dialectic thought."[37] And Lenin argued that within Aristotle lies "the living germs of dialectics *and inquiries* about it."[38]

More than two thousand years after Aristotle's death, Hegel developed a conception of dialectics as an ontological and historical process. Hegel's dialectical method affirms the impossibility of logical contradiction and focuses instead on *relational* "contradictions" or paradoxes revealed in the dynamism of history. For Hegel, opposing concepts could be identified as merely partial views whose apparent contradictions could be transcended by exhibiting them as internally related within a larger whole. From pairs of opposing theses, elements of truth could be extracted and integrated into a third position.[39] Other philosophers saw this form of dialectics as a triadic movement in which the conflict of "thesis" and "antithesis" is resolved through "synthesis."[40] Dialectical materialists placed this process on an economic foundation and used it as the basis for a philosophy of history.

The best way to understand the dialectical impulse is to view it as a technique to overcome formal dualism and monistic reductionism. Dualism attempts to distinguish two mutually exclusive spheres, though it often leads theorists to emphasize one sphere to the detriment of another. Thus one can differentiate between genuine philosophical dualists, who see two coequal principles at work, and philosophical monists, who accept the dichotomies defined by dualists and reduce one polarity to an epiphenomenon of the other.[41] Wolf Heydebrand (1981) explains that these dualistic forms can be found in nearly every branch of philosophy: in ontology, in the radical separation of body and mind, or matter and consciousness; in epistemology, in the radical separation of the real object and the datum present to the knowing mind; in ethics, in the radical distinction between good and evil (92).

Dialectical method is neither dualistic nor monistic. A thinker who employs a dialectical method embraces neither a pole nor the middle of a duality of extremes. Rather, the dialectical method anchors the thinker to both camps. The dialectical thinker refuses to recognize these camps as mutually exclusive or exhaustive.[42] He or she strives to uncover the common roots of apparent opposites. He or she presents an integrated alternative that examines the premises at the base of an opposition as a means to its transcendence. In some cases, the transcendence of opposing points of view provides a justification for rejecting *both* alternatives as false. In other cases, the dialectical thinker attempts to clarify the genuinely integral relationship between spheres that are ordinarily kept separate and distinct.[43]

In Rand's work, this transcendance of opposites is manifest in every branch of philosophy. Rand's revolt against formal dualism is illustrated in her rejection of such "false alternatives" as materialism and idealism, intrinsicism and subjectivism, rationalism and empiricism. Rand was fond of using what Thorslev has called a "Both-And" formulation in her critique of dualism.[44] Typically, Rand argues that Both X And Y share a common premise, Z. Her characteristic expression is: "Just as X depends upon Z, so too does Y depend upon Z." Moreover, Rand always views the polarities as "mutually" or "reciprocally reinforcing," "two sides of the same coin." This is not merely an expository technique. Rand was the first to admit that a writer's style is a product of his or her "psycho-epistemology" or method of awareness.[45] By her own suggestion, one can infer that such an expository style reflects a genuinely dialectical methodology.

It must be emphasized, however, that Rand does not literally *construct* a synthesis out of the debris of false alternatives. Rather, she aims to *transcend* the limitations that, she believes, traditional dichotomies embody. In some instances, Rand sees each of the opposing points of view as being half-right and half-wrong. Consequently, at times, her resolution contains elements from each of the two rejected positions.

Rand's dialectical approach is also illustrated in her recognition of such integral relationships as that between mind and body, reason and emotion, fact and value, theory and practice. For Rand, these factors are distinctions within an organic unity. Neither can be fully understood in the absence of the other, since each is an inseparable aspect of a wider totality.

It is this emphasis on the totality that is essential to the dialectical mode of inquiry. Dialectics is not merely a repudiation of formal dualism. It is a method that preserves the analytical integrity of the whole. Although it recommends study of the whole from the vantage point of any part, it eschews reification, that is, it avoids the abstraction of a part from the whole and its illegitimate conceptualization as a whole unto itself. The dialectical method recognizes that what is separable in thought is not separable in reality.

Moreover, dialectics requires the examination of the whole both systemically (or "synchronically") and historically (or "diachronically"). From a synchronic perspective, it grasps the parts as systemically interrelated, as both constituting the whole, and constituted by it. For example, a dialectical thinker would not disconnect any single theoretical issue, such as the problem of free will, from its broader philosophic context. He or she would necessarily examine a host of connected issues, including the efficacy of consciousness, the nature of causality, and the reciprocal relationships between epistemology, ethics, and politics.

Diachronically, dialectics grasps that any system emerges over time, that it has a past, a present, and a future. Frequently, the dialectical thinker examines the dynamic tensions within a system, the internal conflicts or "contradictions" that require resolution. He or she refuses to disconnect factors, events, problems, and issues from one another or from the system they jointly constitute. He or she views social problems not discretely but in terms of the root systemic conditions they both reflect and sustain.

The dialectical thinker seeks not merely to understand the system, but to alter it fundamentally. Hence, a dialectical analysis is both critical and revolutionary in its implications. A dialectical thinker would not analyze a specific racial conflict, for example, without examining a host of historically constituted epistemic, ethical, psychological, cultural, political, and eco-nomic factors that both generate racism and perpetuate it. In such a view, it is the system that permits racism that must be transcended.

The dialectical sensibility is readily apparent in every aspect of Rand's project, in her literary credo, philosophic approach, and social analysis.

From a literary standpoint, Rand recognized her own novels as organic wholes in which every event and character expresses the central theme. Moreover, her fiction was integral to the evolution of her grand philo-sophic synthesis.

Philosophically, Rand recognized Objectivism as a coherent, integrated *system* of thought, such that each branch could not be taken in isolation from the others. Her theories provide a basis for both critical analysis and revolutionary social transformation.

And from the perspective of social theory, Rand's analysis of contempo-rary society was multidimensional and fully integrative. Rand focused on relationships of power, examining their historical genesis and their long-term deleterious effects on the stability and cohesiveness of the social order. She refused to view societal problems as separate from one another, and proposed a resolution that was comprehensive and fundamentally radical in its implications.

Thus Rand's dialectical method was dynamic, relational, and contextual. It was dynamic because it viewed specific factors in terms of their movement over time. It was relational because it traced the interrelations between and among factors. It was contextual because it related these factors to their wider context. In a strictly formal sense, such a method has been employed to various degrees by thinkers as diverse as Aristotle, Kant, Hegel, Marx, Solovyov, Lossky, and those in the hermeneutic and analytic traditions.[46]

I did not discover any historical evidence that would suggest that Rand was influenced methodologically or substantively by modern hermeneutic or analytic philosophers. Indeed, in her lifetime, Rand did not read much formal philosophy except while she attended the University of Leningrad. There she would have been exposed to many thinkers in the Russian dialectical tradition, the most prominent of whom was N. O. Lossky. It was Lossky who first engaged Rand in the serious study of philosophy. And it was under Lossky's tutelage that Rand was most probably introduced to a formal, dialectical method of thinking, even if she did not characterize it as such.

Significantly, it was Lossky who introduced Rand to the work of Aristotle. If Aristotle was the father of dialectical inquiry, as Marx, Lenin, and Engels maintained, then Rand was profoundly correct to view her own system as the heir to Aristotelianism. Ultimately, it might be said that her debt to Aristotle concerns *both* the form and the content of her thought.

Nevertheless, if it is true that Rand and her Russian predecessors shared a dialectical revolt against formal dualism, it would be very difficult to dismiss such an affinity as pure coincidence. One could infer legitimately, and independently of Rand's own explicit self-descriptions, that there are important connections between her thought and the ideas and methods of her Russian teachers. In the context of any other thinker in intellectual history, such a claim seems innocuous. That someone *might be influenced* by his or her teachers is a rather uncontroversial thesis. Yet when placed within the context of Rand scholarship, this thesis has been criticized by some who believe that the mere consideration of Rand's possible predecessors constitutes an assault on her originality.[47]

I strongly disagree with such sentiment. By placing Rand's thought in its proper historical and intellectual context, we can better appreciate its most distinctive characteristics. Although I cannot substantiate all of my historical claims beyond *any* reasonable doubt, I believe that herein I offer the best explanation yet published for the origins of Rand's unique approach to philosophic and social analysis.

I must reject also the criticism that I have reconstructed Rand's Objectivism by utilizing categories and distinctions foreign to it. True, my terminology sometimes differs from Rand's own, but this does not erase the fact that dialectics is her essential mode of inquiry. And even though she formulated most of her philosophical contributions relatively late in life,[48] her dialectical sensibility informed her earliest writings. On many methodological and substantive issues, Rand's approach converges with the Russian synthesis and with other dialectical traditions as well.

In addition, I must reject the criticism that I have linked Rand to her Russian ancestors on the basis of a characteristic that is "nonessential" to Objectivism. Although it is certainly true that the use of dialectical method is not distinctive to Rand's approach, one could argue too, that the *content* of Rand's Objectivism *taken in its separable parts*, is not distinctive either.[49] Other thinkers have defended comparable doctrines of epistemological realism, ethical egoism, individual rights, and libertarian political theory. What must be recognized here is that Rand's use of dialectical method was as essential to her historic formulation of Objectivist principles, as was her original synthesis in the realm of content. In constructing a philosophy, every philosopher develops a certain content through the use of a specific method. *In the seamless conjunction of a realist-individualist-libertarian content with a radical, dialectical method, Rand forged a new system of thought worthy of comprehensive, scholarly examination.* In many significant ways, she was fully justified to characterize herself as a veritable "radical for capitalism."[50]

This is not to deny the dialectical savvy of other non-Marxist social thinkers.[51] But Rand's perspective is unique—both in its historical roots and in its political implications. Rand proposed a fully integrated defense of capitalism and of the constituent epistemological, psychological, ethical, social, cultural, political, and historical conditions required for its emergence and survival.

Nietzsche once observed that some writers are prone to muddy the waters to make them appear deep.[52] One can easily read the work of Ayn Rand and emerge with a clear sense of her polemical abilities. As an artist and an essayist, Rand painted in broad strokes. In her exposition of Objectivism, she traced connections between seemingly unrelated events, institutions, and cultural forces as if these links were self-evident. Underlying her "popular" style and stark presentation was a mode of analysis based on the conviction that all social phenomena are interrelated.

My discussion of Rand's ideas and the ideas of those whom she has influenced is much less colorful. I do not intend to muddy the waters of Ayn Rand's crystalline ocean by reconstructing her words in the style of academic jargon; rather, I hope to show just how deep that ocean actually is.

Part One

The Process of Becoming

1 Synthesis in Russian Culture

In her autobiography *The Italics Are Mine* (1992), Nina Berberova, one of the most important writers in twentieth-century Russian literature, describes a struggle that is at once profoundly personal and profoundly suggestive of the Russian character. She describes "one of the most important themes of [her] inner life," as she aims for the "fusing of opposites" in her very being:

> All dualism is painful for me, all splitting or bisecting contrary to my nature. . . . My whole life has been the reconciliation within myself of the old dichotomy. . . . [D]iverse and often contrasting traits fuse in me. Long ago I stopped thinking of myself as being composed of two halves. I feel physically, that a *seam*, not a *cut*, passes through me, that I myself am a seam, that with this seam, while I am alive, something has united in me, something has been soldered, that I am one of many examples in nature of soldering, unification, fusion, harmonization, that I am not living in vain, but there is sense in that I am as I am, an example of synthesis in a world of antitheses. (23–24, 36)

No theme has been more central to the history of Russian thought than this struggle against dualism. It emerges from a desire to transcend the dichotomies that fragment human existence: spirit versus flesh, reason versus emotion, the moral versus the practical. This yearning to achieve synthesis in the human condition was fully absorbed by Ayn Rand and became one of the earmarks of her Objectivist philosophy.

Ayn Rand was born Alissa Zinovievna Rosenbaum,[1] in St. Petersburg on 2 February 1905, during the Silver Age of Russian cultural history. Though she later attributed much of Russia's cultural brilliance to its Westernized elements, she reveled in the beauty of the epoch:

> As a child, I saw a glimpse of the pre–World War I world, the last afterglow of the most radiant *cultural* atmosphere in human history (achieved not by Russian, but by Western culture). So powerful a fire does not die at once: even under the Soviet regime, in my college years, such works as Hugo's *Ruy Blas* and Schiller's *Don Carlos* were included in theatrical repertories, not as historical revivals, but as part of the contemporary esthetic scene.[2]

Rand's recollection reflects her abiding contempt for the specifically "Russian" aspects of the culture. By emphasizing the achievements of the period as distinctly "Western," Rand disowned the Slavic mysticism and collectivism that she considered characteristic of the Russian psyche. This fact is crucial to our understanding of Rand's early intellectual development. It helps us to grasp why Rand could never admit that she was a child of her Russian past. For Rand, Russian culture *meant* hatred for the individual and the rational mind. Russian thought stressed emotion and intuition, not logic and reason; it rejected individualism and embraced communal organicism as expressed in the concept of *sobornost'* (conciliarity);[3] it was antimaterialist and, above all, anticapitalist. Each aspect of this Russian totality was a natural extension of the other. In Rand's view, the rejection of reason required the renunciation of individual freedom, material wealth, and capitalism. When Rand tied her defense of the free market to her celebration of the free mind, she was establishing an inseparable link between reason, freedom, individualism, and capitalism, all elements that were absent from the Russian culture that she despised.[4]

Tatyana Tolstaya (1991) echoes much of Rand's own view of the constituent elements in the Russian psyche:

> In Russia, in contrast to the West, reason has traditionally been seen as a source of destruction, emotion (the soul) as one of creation. How many scornful pages have great Russian writers dedicated to

Western pragmatism, materialism, rationalism! They mocked the English with their machines, the Germans with their order and precision, the French with their logic, and finally the Americans with their love of money. As a result, in Russia we have neither machines, nor order, nor logic, nor money. (6)

It was perhaps in reaction to this Russian hostility toward reason and individualism that the mature Rand seemed to overemphasize the rational and individuating aspects of human nature.[5] But inherent in Rand's view is an integration of reason and emotion, individual and community. By explicitly rejecting conventional rationalism and atomistic individualism, Rand implicitly affirms important elements in the Russian critique of "Western" dualism.

This is not to say that the struggle against dualism is an exclusively Russian project. To distinguish between Russian and Western culture does not imply that each is hermetically sealed from the other. The history of Russian philosophy is replete with intermingling between Russian and European, especially German, thought. What has emerged, especially since the time of Peter the Great, is a complex amalgam of multiethnic and Western influences. Many Russian thinkers in fact were schooled in European universities; they absorbed the integrated constructions of such Western philosophers as Aristotle, Leibniz, Spinoza, Hegel, and Marx, among others.[6]

The Character of Russian Philosophy

One of the most startling characteristics of Russian philosophy has been its nonacademic, noninstitutional orientation (Edie, Scanlan, and Zeldin 1965, ix). Until the end of the nineteenth century, most creative Russian thinkers worked outside the university. Even Vladimir Solovyov, the father of systematic Russian philosophy, withdrew from academia at an early point in his life, because of serious disputes with government authorities (Kline 1967, 258).

Russian thought has always been human-centered, intimately connected to the literary arts, and immoderately passionate (ibid.). In fact, most of the great Russian thinkers—Tolstoy, Dostoyevsky, Pasternak, Gogol, Blok,

Bely, and Solovyov—were literary artists and social critics, whose zeal was partially responsible for their exclusion from academic life.

Russian philosophy throughout the eighteenth and nineteenth centuries was considered suspect by the government. In fact, philosophy as a separate discipline was banned from the Russian university curriculum for considerable periods. And until 1889, only the study of certain Platonic and Aristotelian texts was permitted (ibid.).

The lack of formal philosophical instruction led to the genesis of informal intellectual groups during the 1830s. Many university students studied German metaphysics and French social theory in such group settings. They rejected the view of philosophy as pure contemplation and saw it as a tool in the struggle for truth, justice, and freedom. The whole notion of philosophy as a strictly theoretical discipline is alien to Russian culture. Marxists would later emphasize the unity of theory and practice, but such a social commitment has always been deeply ingrained in the Russian psyche (Copleston 1986, 1). As Kline (1967) explains: "The Russian intelligentsia subordinated theoretical truth (istina) to practical truth-justice (pravda). Russian thinkers were engaged in the 'quest for truth-justice' (iskaniye pravdy)" (258).

This integration of the theoretical and the practical suggests a dialectical theme in Russian philosophy. In the 1840s, Russian intellectuals were deeply influenced by the Idealism of Schelling, Kant, Fichte, and Hegel. In particular, Hegel's impact on Russian intellectual life was immeasurable. Even Hegel's dialectical language found a home in Russia. Hegel stressed Aufhebung, a process in which one evolutionary state is transcended and abolished, while being simultaneously absorbed and preserved in the motion of the succeeding state. In Russian, the Hegelian Aufhebung is captured by the term snyatiye, which connotes "sublation," "cancellation," the "raising to a higher level," and "preservation" (Edie, Scanlan, and Zeldin 1965, xii). The Hegelian domination of Russian philosophy set the stage for a Marxist infusion in the 1890s and beyond.

The Slavophiles

The movement toward dialectical transcendence of opposites is manifested especially in the 1840s in Khomyakov's critique of Western religion. Alexey Khomyakov embraced the Slavophile devotion to Orthodox Christianity and personal mystical experience. He viewed Russian Orthodoxy, with its Byzantine roots, as the reconciliation of Catholicism and Protestantism. N. O. Lossky, Rand's teacher and author of the indispensable *History of Russian Philosophy*, explains that for Khomyakov, "the rationalism of Catholicism which established unity without freedom gave rise, as a reaction against it, to another form of rationalism—Protestantism which realizes freedom without unity" (1951, 37). Khomyakov saw the necessity for a communal, conciliar unity that transcended the Catholic emphasis on the individual judgment of the pope and the Protestant emphasis on the individual judgment of the believer.[7] Russian Orthodoxy bound the Church and the state much more closely than was the case in the West. It was the original organic union, in Khomyakov's view, a freedom-in-unity and a unity-in-freedom.

The whole theme of transcending opposites is both a Kantian and Hegelian inheritance. Lossky (1951) explains: "Many Russian philosophers in dealing with the essential problems of world interpretation like to have recourse to antinomies; i.e., like to express the truth by means of two mutually contradictory judgements, and then seek ways of reconciling the contradiction" (190). This Hegelian streak in Russian philosophy made a deep impact on both Slavophiles and Westernizers, and even on those thinkers who turned to materialism and positivism (134).

Ivan Kireevsky followed in this dialectical tradition. He was among the first of the Slavophiles to trace the "intimate *internal* relations in the world" (Lossky 1951, 21). Kireevsky rejected Western dualism and its inherent fragmentation of spirit, science, state, society, and family. He strove "for wholeness of the internal and external mode of life" (24).

But in celebrating the holistic worldview of Eastern Orthodoxy and Russian culture, Kireevsky did not reject the Western Hegelian and Aristotelian traditions. Surprisingly, whereas some critics have derided Hegelian dialectics as a violation of the Aristotelian law of contradiction, Kireevsky argued that the genuine Aristotelian spirit "reappeared with Hegel." Kireevsky saw Aristotle's basic views as identical with Hegel's. Hegel's system was "as Aristotle himself would have constructed, if he had been born in our time." Especially in his celebration of reason as the "sole arbiter of truth," and in his emphasis on the relational and logical connections between concepts, Hegel had, in Kireevsky's view, carried on the Aristotelian project.[8]

Following the Hegelian model, Kireevsky departed from the one-sidedness of the Slavophile tradition. The typical Slavophile appealed to the Russian national character and Eastern Orthodox Christianity, arguing that Russian culture must avoid the influence of the Western secular enlightenment. The Westernizers, by contrast, advocated that Russia assimilate European science and commit itself to secular reason. Kireevsky aimed for integral knowledge, a wholeness in the human spirit, a synthesis of the two worldviews and a transcendence of the gap between reason and faith. Isolated from each other, the Slavophile and the Westernizer presented incomplete perspectives. For Kireevsky, unity was of prime importance.

Such unity was also expressed in Kireevsky's elaboration of Khomyakov's concept of *sobornost'*, a doctrine accepted in varying forms by most Russian philosophers. Lossky (1951) explained that *sobornost'* involved "*the combination of freedom and unity of many persons on the basis of their common love for the same absolute values*" (41). In Kireevsky's view, "The wholeness of society, combined with the personal independence and the individual diversity of the citizens, is possible only on the condition of a free subordination of separate persons to absolute values and in their free creativeness founded on love of the whole, love of the Church, love of their nation and State, and so on" (Lossky 1951, 26).

The struggle against dualism and fragmentation is manifested in the ontological and ethical theories of other Russian philosophers in the nineteenth century, such as Nicholas N. Strakhov, Nicholas G. Cherny-shevsky, and Nicholas F. Fedorov.[9] Like Kireevsky, the Slavophile Strakhov viewed the world as a "harmonious organic whole." His book, *The World as a Whole* conceptualizes the parts as constituents of the totality, even as the totality constitutes the parts. The parts submit to one another; they "serve each other, informing one whole" with "man" at the center (Lossky 1951, 72).

Rejecting the mysticism and altruism of the Slavophiles, Chernyshevsky embraced a materialist, atheistic, and democratic socialist world view that greatly influenced Lenin. He valued the Hegelian dialectical method and proposed an organic union of spiritual and material dimensions (Shein 1973, 223). His ethics is a form of psychological egoism, where each person always acts selfishly. In his novel *What is to be done?* Chernyshevsky's main character, Lopuhov, states: "I am not a man to make sacrifices. And indeed there are no such things. One acts in the way that one finds most pleasant."[10] But for Chernyshevsky, each person's happiness and self-interest coincides with the common good, and hence, there is no conflict between the individual and society. His ethical ideal approaches a secular-ized *sobornost'*.

Fedorov utilized the Hegelian category of "relatedness" in his conception of mankind as a constituted whole. He criticized Western positivism for its "separation of theoretical and practical reason" (Edie, Scanlan, and Zeldin 1965, 30). Like Chernyshevsky, however, Fedorov attempted to eliminate the distinction between egoism and altruism. Whereas egoists live only for themselves, and altruists only for others, Fedorov argued that this was a false dichotomy. He envisioned a moral world in which each individual lived with and for others.

The Impact of Vladimir Solovyov

Vladimir Solovyov was the first and most original of Russia's systematic philosophers. Like Leibniz, he exhibited a genius for absorbing and synthesizing the contributions of many varied thinkers and traditions (Zenkovsky 1953, 484–85). From Hegel, Solovyov learned to use a formal dialectical method. He was also influenced by the mystic Slavophiles, as well as by Fichte, Kant, Schelling, Schopenhauer, and Spinoza. Having received his doctorate from St. Petersburg University, Solovyov proceeded to develop an organic synthesis of religion, philosophy, and science. His impact was widespread; he influenced nearly every Russian thinker who succeeded him, including Trubetskoy, Frank, Bulgakov, Berdyaev, and Lossky. Each of these thinkers elaborated on Solovyov's doctrine of intellectual intuition.

In 1874, Solovyov wrote *The Crisis of Western Philosophy*. He criticized positivism and the empiricist-rationalist dichotomy. Empiricists, according to Solovyov, have embraced a form of sensualism that reduces everything to simple and subjective sense-experience. In the end, empiricism dissolves into subjectivism. So, too, positivism excludes metaphysics and "cuts itself off from reality." Rationalism, by contrast, identifies being with pure thought (Copleston 1986, 220). Thus each tradition fails to grasp the integrated nature of real being. Frederick Copleston argues that, in Solovyov's view, "we cannot understand reality without sense-experience, and we cannot understand it without ideas or concepts and the rational discernment of relations. What is needed is a synthesis of complementary truths, of distinct principles" (213).

Lossky (1951) grasped that this Solovyovian synthesis was at root, profoundly Hegelian:

The final results of empiricism and of rationalism are somewhat similar: empiricism leaves us with nothing but appearances, without an object of which they are appearances and without a subject to whom they appear; rationalism ends with pure thought; i.e., [quoting Solovyov:] "thought without a thinker and without anything to think of." Neither in experience nor in thought does man transcend his subjective relation to the object and become aware of the object as an existent, that is, as something which is more than his sensation or his thought. Neither experience nor thought can, then, lead to truth, since truth means that which is—i.e., existence. [Quoting Solovyov:] "But only the whole exists. *Truth, then, is the whole* [emphasis added]. And if truth be the whole, then that which is not the whole—i.e., every particular thing, being or event taken separately from the whole—is not truth, because in its separateness it does not even exist: it exists with all and in all. Truth then is all in its unity or as one." (96)

Solovyov's synthesis of experience and reason, empiricism and rationalism, echoes Hegel's dictum, "The True is the whole" as expressed in *The Phenomenology of Spirit* (Hegel [1807] 1977, 11). For Solovyov, as for Hegel, no particular thing can be grasped if it is cut off from the totality, which gives it meaning. And yet Solovyov rejected Hegel's metaphysics for its one-sided rationalism.[11] Solovyov argued that by dichotomizing experience and reason, practice and theory, Western philosophy embraces alternatives that are equally one-sided and partial. Both experience and reason are essential to the comprehension of objective reality. Experience provides the sensory data for knowledge, as reason apprehends relations. But in uniting experience and reason, Solovyov embraced a third means of knowledge, exemplified in faith and mystical intuition.

Like Kant, Solovyov attempted to reconcile science and religion. He sought to unite the true, the good, the beautiful, the philosophical, and the theological. Recognizing that no philosopher could escape from examining his own premises, Solovyov attempted to achieve a synoptic grasp of reality. Lossky (1951) explained that Solovyov gave clear expression to the "characteristic features of Russian philosophical thought—the search for an exhaustive knowledge of reality as a whole and the concreteness of metaphysical conceptions" (95).

Following in the footsteps of his Slavophile ancestors, Solovyov saw religion as providing this synoptic "total unity." Each branch of philosophy echoes this unity. In metaphysics, the world is conceived as an organic whole. In ethics, Solovyov attacked both moral subjectivism and social realism. The subjectivist stresses the realization of individual good, and the social realist views the individual's moral will as subordinate to society's institutions. Solovyov integrated the essential moral will of the individual with the necessity of social life. As morality is both public and private, politics bridges the gap between individual and social good. In the perfect, ideal society, a Slavophile messianism will achieve a free theocracy that unites all people.

That such a system might deteriorate into totalitarianism was one of the chief objections raised by the Russian Hegelian philosopher, B. N. Chicherin.[12] But Chicherin accepted Solovyov's universalist aim to transcend both rationalism and empiricism. Deeply influenced by Hegel, Chicherin argued that dialectical logic is ontological; the laws of reason are then identical with the laws of being. Like Solovyov, Chicherin was highly critical of the dichotomy of reason and experience. He advocated their integrated unity.

The Silver Age

In the post-Solovyovian period, Russian philosophy entered a Silver Age. But the Silver Age was much more than a philosophical renaissance. It was an era of cultural flourishing that had begun in the final decade of the nineteenth century and had culminated by 1924, in the aftermath of the Bolshevik Revolution. The Silver Age was the historical context of Rand's formative years. It was marked by a burst of creativity in the literary arts, coupled with a renewed interest in religion, mysticism, and the occult. Artists and philosophers reacted strongly against positivism and materialism, examining the nature of freedom, art, beauty, truth, and the dignity of the individual. They precipitated a revolution of the spirit, heralding the radical changes that were to consume Russian society.

The Influence of Nietzsche in Russia

The Russian Symbolists constituted one of the most important cultural movements of the age.[13] Writers such as Dmitri Merezhkovsky, Andrey

Bely, Aleksandr Blok, and Viacheslav Ivanov attempted to transcend the polarity in Russian culture between Westernizers and Slavophiles. Paradoxically, they embraced the Christian messianism of the Slavophiles and Solovyovian mysticism, while simultaneously absorbing the Dionysian aspects of Nietzsche's philosophy. They challenged both materialism *and* asceticism, positivism *and* rationalism, Marxists *and* czarist authoritarians. As nihilists, emotionalists, and subjectivists they were hostile toward reason and science. They rejected urbanization and industrialization, and envisioned a new anarchic culture of freedom, love, and *sobornost'*.[14]

Central to the Symbolist movement was the absorption of key Nietzschean themes. The Symbolists answered Nietzsche's critique of Christianity by cultivating a new religious morality of cultural creativity, Promethean individuality, and sexual pleasure.[15] Symbolist artists aimed to embody the characteristics of Nietzschean supermen and to achieve a transformation of values by integrating Christian mysticism and Dionysian revelry.[16]

Like Nietzsche, the Symbolists rejected dualistic interpretations of the world. In Nietzsche's view, as in Hegel's, one cannot isolate the elements of opposition, which are often "insidiously related, tied to, and involved" with one another ([1886] 1966, 10). For Nietzsche, as for Hegel, historical evolution develops through such opposition. But Nietzsche refused to embrace monistic idealism. Monism merely emphasizes one aspect of a dualist distinction at the expense of the other. Nietzsche aimed to transcend the very language of duality.

One of the distinctions that Nietzsche attempted to transcend was the opposition of good and evil. These ethical constructs are problematic, in Nietzsche's view, because their meaning is deeply dependent on the moral system in which they are expressed. The Christian "slave morality" views altruistic self-sacrifice as the good. According to Nietzsche, it achieves submission and conformity by appealing to resentment, guilt, jealousy, and envy. However, the achievement of human mediocrity is not the ethical goal of "master morality." Instead of appealing to the herd mentality of the mob, master morality elevates self-responsibility and nobility as an ethical ideal, stamping out the weak and uncreative elements of humanity.

Like his distinction between master morality and slave morality, Nietzsche's conceptualization of the Apollonian and Dionysian duality also made a deep impact upon the Russian Symbolists. The Symbolists embraced the Dionysian principle as a corrective for the excessive rationalism of Western philosophy. Rosenthal argues that the Apollonian-Dionysian dualism gave the Symbolists "a conceptual framework for esthetic and psychological reflection and fueled their opposition to positivism and utilitarianism, sanctioning their demand that the needs of the inner man (the soul or the psyche) be heard. The Dionysian became a symbol of interrelated esthetic, psychological and religious impulses."[17]

For Nietzsche, Apollo and Dionysus embodied opposing metaphysical principles. In 1969, Rand would reiterate this Nietzschean symbolism in her assessment of New Left counterculture. In Rand's view, Nietzsche had used the symbols of Greek tragedy to express a false dichotomy between reason and emotion. But Rand saw Nietzsche's archetypes as appropriate symbols for what happens when reason and emotion *are* disconnected. Apollo embodies individuation and is "the symbol of beauty, order, wisdom, efficacy . . . —i.e., the symbol of reason." By contrast, Dionysus's drunkenness is characterized by a loss of self, "wild, primeval feelings, orgiastic joy, the dark, the savage, the unintelligible element in man—i.e., the symbol of emotion."[18] Though Nietzsche saw power in the integration of Apollo and Dionysus, he embraced the superiority of the uninhibited, unfettered Dionysian impulse.

Rand argued that the New Left counterculture exhibited this Dionysian loss of self. Though Rand sympathized with the New Left's rejection of the Establishment, she condemned its flagrant irrationalism, its drug-induced emotionalism, and its anti-industrialism. Perhaps Rand had recognized in the New Left the elements that she had observed in the Russian Symbolist movement of her youth. Rand may have appreciated some of the Nietzschean undertones of Symbolism; she cites Aleksandr Blok as one of her favorite poets.[19] But Rand was quick to recognize the antirational, antiself, and anticapitalist components of the Dionysian principle. Ultimately, her rejection of Dionysian subjectivism would separate her from Nietzsche and his "counterfeit" individualism.

As for Aleksandr Blok, he was the dominant literary figure in the St. Petersburg of Rand's youth. Educated at St. Petersburg University in the Juridical and Philological colleges (*fakul'tety*), he emerged as the supreme Russian Symbolist poet of his generation.[20] He gave regular readings of his poetry at the university until his death in 1921. Like his fellow Symbolists Ivanov and Bely, Blok conjoined fierce Dionysian imagery with Solovyovian Christian mysticism, putting forth an image of "a Nietzscheanized Christ, a Christ-Dionysus archetype."[21] Blok envisioned an anarchistic *sobornost'* unifying all believers in the mystical body of Christ.[22] He aimed to resolve the tension between individualism and social cohesion, between culture and civilization.

Blok argued that there was an inherent contradiction between culture and civilization. Culture, in his view, is Dionysian; it is spontaneous, creative, organic, and whole. Civilization is Apollonian; it is mechanical, abstract, rational, and materialistic. Blok opposed bourgeois society because it fragmented culture and civilization and gave one-dimensional emphasis to the Apollonian principle. Ultimately, Blok envisioned a society that inte-grated Apollonian structure and Dionysian process.

Envisioning a similar transcendence was Dmitri Sergeyevich Merezhkov-sky. Merezhkovsky was a prolific Symbolist writer who argued that the highest unity would be achieved through the sex act, since each body is interpenetrated and expressive of all other bodies. Merezhkovsky's rejection of the split between men and women led him to embrace the androgyne, or man-woman, as the ideal personality. Each man and each woman would freely express both the masculine *and* the feminine characteristics they each embody. Merezhkovsky aimed not for the artificial merging of two selves but for an organic and indivisible sexual whole within each human being. His aesthetic sought to synthesize the polarities of the external world that reflected the splits within him (Rosenthal 1975, 36). To bridge the gap between real and ideal, Merezhkovsky embraced a form of mysticism that "absorbed all dichotomies, softened the hard edges of reality into a beautiful and harmonious unity" (226).

Though some Symbolists opposed the Bolshevik Revolution and its Marxist materialism, their attempt to reconcile Nietzsche with Russian mysticism had contributed to the erosion of the old values and institutions. The Symbolists had uncovered a dimension in Nietzsche's thought that served their cultic and collectivist desires to liberate the instincts and transcend the self. Their attacks on Christian slave morality would ulti-mately reinforce the atheism of their Bolshevik rivals.[23]

The impact of Nietzschean philosophy on Russian Symbolism was signifi-cant. But Nietzsche's thought also influenced the Marxism of the Silver Age. The interpenetration of Nietzschean and Marxist thought was facilitated by their common Hegelian roots. Four important Nietzschean Marxists of the period were Stanislav Volsky, Anatoly V. Lunacharsky, Aleksandr A. Bogdanov, and Vladimir A. Bazarov. Even Maxim Gorky, the father of Socialist Realism, underwent a Nietzschean phase.

The Nietzschean Marxists stressed the individual's free will, desire, and creativity. They rejected Kant's deontological ethics and viewed the proletariat as beyond good and evil. As George Kline (1969) explains, "The Nietzschean collectivists maintained that under socialism individuals would *freely* desire to subordinate their individual creativity to the creativity of the collective" (171).

Stanislav Volsky argued that bourgeois society alienated the individual. Genuine individualism would not emerge until socialism was achieved. In the new society, "*All* obligatory norms . . . will eventually disappear" (172). Lunacharsky, Bogdanov, and Bazarov shared the same concern for the free individual. Like their philosophic predecessors, however, they embraced a Russian *sobornost'* in which the individual is liberated through his dissolution "in an impersonal social collective" (177). These thinkers espoused a humanist religion in their early years and were known, appropriately, as the "God-builders." Elevating human strength and potential to God-like status, they argued that in socialism, "man" would be the master of his own fate. Though Lenin rejected their secular religion, they had fully incorporated the Nietzschean-Dionysian principle of self-transcending collectivism into the corpus of their thought.[24]

Neo-Idealism and the Russian Religious Renaissance

Nietzsche's influence extended also to the Russian religious renaissance of the neo-Idealists. But it is more likely that the neo-Idealists absorbed Nietzschean and existentialist ideas from Dostoyevsky. Mihajlo Mihajlov suggests that Dostoyevsky had, in fact, made an impact on Nietzsche himself. Nietzsche's notes and drafts in the winter of 1886–87 constantly refer to Dostoyevsky. Nietzsche also wrote abstracts of several of Dostoyevsky's works.[25]

The neo-Idealists praised Dostoyevsky for his dialectical literary method. Each of Dostoyevsky's characters embodies particular ideas. In their interplay, collisions, and encounters, certain of these ideas emerge victorious (Copleston 1986, 142). It is this literary method that deeply influenced Rand.[26]

Though traces of Dostoyevsky and Nietzsche may be found in the work of the neo-Idealists, it is also true that the ideas of these two seminal thinkers were preserved in the Russian tradition of philosophical synthesis. Such thinkers as Kozlov, Shestov, Bulgakov, Berdyaev, Florensky, Frank, and Lossky had all been influenced by the thought of Kant, Fichte, Schelling, Hegel, and Solovyov. Many of the neo-Idealists studied in Germany, working in the seminars of philosophers who represented the Freiburg and Marburg schools of Transcendental Idealism. Most of them strove to overcome Kant's phenomenalism by attempting to link the knowing subject and the world in an organic unity.[27] They followed Hegel in seeking the identity of thought and being.

The neo-Idealists had attempted to provide a genuine philosophical basis for religion. They began not with religious presuppositions, but with some of the more advanced ontological and epistemological theories of their day. They had accepted Solovyov's critique of Western positivism and rationalism and his intuitivist theory of knowledge. In the words of Father Pavel Florensky, they grasped that "Truth as a living wholeness" could emerge only through the direct rational intuition of the objects of the external world. Florensky affirmed that the essence of religious experience was love, "because love means that an entity passes from the isolated separateness of A into the other, non-A, establishes its consubstantiality with it and consequently finds itself, i.e., A, in it" (Lossky 1951, 179–80).

The neo-Idealists included in their number two genuinely original, systematic intuitivists, Semyon Frank and N. O. Lossky. I discuss Lossky's thought in Chapter 2. At this point, it is valuable to examine some of the contributions of Frank, who was Lossky's colleague at St. Petersburg University from 1912 to 1915. By 1921, Frank took the position of Chair of Philosophy at Moscow University.[28]

Like Lossky, Frank called his philosophical system "ideal-realism," symbolic of his attempt to integrate apparent opposites. Rather than embracing a dualistic vision, Frank saw three levels of existence: the physical world of objects, the spiritual world of ideas, and an unobservable, mysterious sphere in which both the material and the spiritual were fully united.[29] True to the Hegelian tradition, Frank presented this vision of the world as a "metalogical unity." He argued that this unity encompasses both A and not-A. It does not violate the law of contradiction; the law is "simply inapplicable to it" (Lossky 1951, 267). In this organic whole, both unity and plurality are subsumed. Frank preserved the Hegelian *Aufhebung* by advocating an "*antinomic monodualism.*" He argued that in negation, we both destroy and preserve "the connection between distinct, differentiated entities, and thus ascend to the universal 'yea,' to the all-embracing acceptance of being, including the negative relation as well as that which is negated" (271).

The vision of the world as an organic whole was not restricted to the religious Russian philosophers. Naturalists such as V. Karpov and K. Starynkevich saw each organism as connected to a whole. In analyzing a beehive, a forest, or a marsh, these thinkers viewed *all* life as part of an organic unity on earth stretching even into the cosmos (330). Other organicist visions were proposed by Gustav G. Shpet and Alexey F. Losev, who combined Hegelian and Husserlian insights to defend dialectical phenomenology and philosophical realism (Zenkovsky 1953, 834).

Russian Marxism

Most significant of all the nonreligious organicist conceptions however, was Russian Marxism.[30] The Russian Marxist intellectual movement drew from the messianic tradition of the Slavophiles, putting forth a secularized, proletarianized version of *sobornost'*.[31] This ideological amalgam had inherent problems of internal consistency but it did not depart from any of the essential organicist and antidualist characteristics of Russian philosophy.

Part of the reason for the fundamental agreement of Marxism with its Russian counterparts is their common philosophical roots. Marx, like many Russian thinkers, was influenced by Leibniz, Spinoza, and Hegel. Bertell Ollman (1993) argues that these thinkers shared a belief "that the relations that come together to make up the whole get expressed in what are taken to be its parts. Each part is viewed as incorporating in what it is all its relations with other parts up to and including everything that comes into the whole" (35). Leibniz, Spinoza, and Hegel had differing conceptions of the parts. For Leibniz, the parts were monads. For Spinoza, the parts were modes. For Hegel, the parts were ideas. But the logical form of the relation between the parts and the whole was the same (ibid.).

Marx inherited this dialectical tradition. But he transcended the tendency to dissolve all things into their relations. As Sidney Hook observes, Hegel had embraced a strict organicity, in which "all of existence becomes relevant in considering the nature of any part of it." Thus, "piecemeal knowledge is impossible; since if everything must be known before anything can be known, nothing can be *adequately* known" (Hook [1936] 1950, 53). For Hegel, Truth is indeed the Whole; error emerges in the one-sided abstraction of any single part from the totality.

Although Marx accepted the spirit of Hegel's dictum, he departed from strict organicity in several significant ways. Marx argued that no whole could be studied from a synoptic vantage point. The totality is studied through the abstracted parts. Marx varied the scope of his abstractions by altering the relational units, the perspective, and the level of generality. By focusing on the mutual determination of structure and function, Marx concretized knowledge of the whole. As Ollman (1979) argues, Marx refused to separate "events from their conditions, people from their real alternatives and human potential, social problems from one another, and the present from the past and the future" (126). Marx viewed each part of the totality as a cluster of relations. Each part is in organic conjunction with every other part such that each expresses the sum of its interrelations. The conditions of each thing's existence are taken to be part of what it is (Ollman 1976, 15–16). Ollman (1993) explains further that the Marxian dialectic replaces "the common sense notion of 'thing,' as something which *has* a history and *has* external connections to other things, with notions of 'process,' which *contains* its history and possible futures, and 'relation,' which *contains* as part of what it is its ties with other relations" (11).

This emphasis on internal relations was equally important to the Russian Marxists. But Marxist scholarship in Russia underwent several transformations. From the earliest moments of the Bolshevik Revolution, Marxism was hardening into a state ideology that legitimated repression and dictatorship. During the Silver Age, however, Marxist thought was being supplemented in a variety of ways. Such thinkers as Berdyaev, Bulgakov, and Struve integrated Marxism with Kantian ethics.[32] The Nietzschean Marxists explored the provocative synthesis of quasi-individualist and socialist ideas. And Lenin utilized a naive realist epistemology to answer Machian neo-Kantians, as well as more popular revisionist and positivist interpreters of Marx. By the following decade, professional scholars had probed the limited editions of Marx's *Grundrisse*, which appeared in the Soviet Union as early as 1939 and 1941 in two successive volumes published by the Marx-Engels-Lenin Institute.[33] Throughout this period, however, the entrenchment of Stalinist dogmatism ultimately quelled all theoretical debate and dissent.

Though Lenin's writings suffered at times from simplistic diatribe, his influence on Russian Marxism made a significant impact during the Silver Age. Despite Lenin's failure to develop his realist perspective adequately, his polemics were extremely effective in shaping the character of Marxist ideology.[34]

Lenin began with a realist ontology. He saw objective conditions as prior to consciousness. He asserted the primacy of the material world and the objectivity of space and time. He wrote in *Materialism and Empirio-Criticism* that "things exist independently of our consciousness, independently of our perceptions, outside of us." Epistemologically, he adopted a reflection theory of knowledge. He disputed the Kantian distinction between the phenomenon and the noumenal thing-in-itself. "The only difference," in Lenin's view, "is between what is known and what is not known."[35]

Like Plekhanov, the father of Russian Marxism, Lenin rejected dualism, since it failed to grasp the internal relatedness of mind and matter. Lenin recognized the supreme importance of the Hegelian dialectic to Marx's method. His writings feature scathing attacks on subjectivists and empiricists who divorced cognition from the object. He believed that the reduction of the world to pure sense perception led inexorably to a subjectivist, solipsistic idealism. Like Nietzsche, he condemned such empiricism as a philosophy of immaculate perception.[36] But Lenin rejected rationalism as equally one-sided, and proposed a resolution of the age-old dichotomies. His attempt at an organic synthesis was entirely within the tradition of Russian philosophy.[37]

The appeal of Russian Marxism, however, had little to do with Lenin's critique of dualism. The Russian Marxists had strategically merged Western dialectical categories of explanation with the indigenous concept of *sobornost'*. They secularized the concept, and aimed not for Oneness in the mystic body of Christ, but for a collective unity that was One with the Proletariat. Evgeny Ivanovich Zamiatin warned that this would lead to the establishment of the One State. Ultimately, the voluntarist *sobornost'* had been replaced by the Bolsheviks' administrative machinery for massive statist repression.

By 1919–20, anti-Bolshevik writings enjoyed limited circulation throughout Russia. One of these works, *We*, written by Zamiatin,[38] depicted a totalitarian society in which peoples' names were replaced by numbers, and the distinction between public and private life was all but obliterated, except for two hours a day when the "mighty uni-personal organism" was allowed to disintegrate "into separate cells."[39]

> Each morning, with six-wheeled precision, at the very same minute and the very same second we, in our millions, arise as one. At the very same hour we monomillionedly begin work—and, when we finish it, we do so monomillionedly. And, merging into but one body with multimillioned hands, at the very second designated by The Tables of Hourly Commandments we bring our spoons up to our mouths; at the very same second, likewise, we set out for a walk, or go to an auditorium, or the Hall of Taylor Exercise, or retire to sleep. (177)

The One State forbade romantic love and the free conduct of sexual life, for

> isn't it an absurdity that the State . . . could allow sexual life without
> any control whatsoever? Anybody, any time, and as much as one
> wanted to. . . . Completely unscientifically, like brutes. And, like
> brutes, they bred offspring gropingly. Isn't it laughable—to know
> horticulture, poultry culture, pisciculture . . . and yet be unable to
> reach the last rung of this logical ladder: child culture. (178)

Like Zamiatin, Rand rejected the One State. In the 1930s, having
escaped to America, she would author a number of anticollectivist writings
of her own, including the "semi-autobiographical" novel, We the Living, and
a futuristic novelette called Anthem. These works would portray Rand's
rejection of the intellectual trends during America's so-called Red Decade,
when many writers and artists embraced the promise of collectivism
(B. Branden 1986, 95). But Rand's early works can also be read as a
passionate reaction against the dominant philosophic and cultural trends of
the Silver Age. Rand would reject the Slavophile and Symbolist denigration
of reason and their cultic commitment to the dissolution of self in a
collective whole. She would reject the neo-Idealist defense of religion. She
would reject Russian Marxism as a legitimating ideology for the newly
emerging totalitarian state.

In her rejection of Russian mysticism, altruism, collectivism, and statism,
Rand began to identify a philosophic conjunction that was not as apparent
to others of her generation. Perhaps this unity was clearer to Rand because
she had lived in a laboratory that had enabled her to make such grand
inductive generalizations.

But in repudiating these traditions, Rand had absorbed the tendency
toward synthesis so prevalent in Russian philosophy. Wherever the young
Alissa Rosenbaum had turned, she would have encountered a nondualistic,
formal commitment to the dialectic. This mode of inquiry was apparent in
Nietzsche's philosophy, which had influenced the philosophic and cultural
movements of the Silver Age. It was also prevalent in the works of the
Slavophiles, Solovyov and his successors, the Symbolists, the Russian
Marxists, and the neo-Idealists of the religious renaissance. And the most
important philosopher of this neo-Idealist tradition was Nicholas Onufrievich Lossky, Rand's teacher.

2   Lossky, the Teacher

No study of Rand's Objectivism would be complete without a consideration of the life and thought of N. O. Lossky, her philosophy professor at Petrograd University. The relationship between these two is of paramount historical importance because it was probably Lossky who introduced Rand to dialectical methods of analysis.

It has been said that Rand read little philosophy in her mature years. But as a student at the university, she would have been required to study many philosophic texts in depth. It is very likely that at no time in her life did Rand *read* as much philosophy and literature as she did while being educated in Russia. Hence, one cannot discount Lossky's impact: as Rand's first philosophy teacher, he laid the basis for a highly integrated view of the philosophic disciplines.

In his lectures, Lossky presented broad methodological tools with which to analyze the contributions of important thinkers in intellectual history. According to Rand, Lossky introduced her to the thought of Plato and Aristotle. Since Rand paid homage to Aristotle as her philosophical forefather, this first encounter with his work was of prime significance to her intellectual development. It is quite possible too that Rand's interpretation of Aristotle may have taken root in Lossky's.

It is nearly impossible to establish with certainty that Rand actually studied Lossky's writings. But Lossky's conception of the history and method of philosophy—his intuitivist epistemology and organicist ontology—permeated his lectures and seminars. He was famous for teaching several Petrograd courses that explicitly reflected his antimaterialist and anti-Marxist orientation. And about the time that Rand entered the university, he published two of the most important works of his career, *The Intuitive Basis of Knowledge* and *The World as an Organic Whole*. It is very likely that she would have been presented with significant Losskyian themes within the context of the course she attended.

An Extraordinary Life

Nicholas Onufrievich Lossky was born in the village of Kreslavka in Vitebsk, a province west of Moscow, on 6 December 1870. He was educated at the classical gymnasium in Vitebsk, but was expelled for his socialistic and atheistic beliefs.[1] Continuing his studies in Switzerland, Lossky returned to Russia in 1889 and entered St. Petersburg University two years later. Lossky graduated from the college of History and Philology and the college of Natural Science. His mentor at the university was the distinguished Kantian philosopher, Aleksandr Ivanovich Vvedensky. It was through his interactions with Vvedensky that Lossky developed a passion for philosophy. Eventually, Lossky became privatdocent of philosophy and delved deeply into the thought of Vladimir Solovyov.[2]

In 1899, Lossky went abroad to study with Wundt, Muller, and Windelband. These three helped Lossky to prepare for a full-time professorship, while also influencing his emerging religious idealist perspective. Wilhelm Wundt, who occupied the Chair of Philosophy at Leipzig from 1875 to 1918, shared Lossky's view of the world as a totality of individual agents. Wilhelm Windelband, who occupied the chairs of Philosophy at Zurich, Strasbourg, and Heidelburg, was a post-Hegelian, neo-Kantian thinker of the Baden school. It was from thinkers such as Windelband that Lossky further developed his mastery of philosophic integration. Rand's protégé, Leonard Peikoff, reviewing Windelband's classic *History of Philosophy*, praises its structure, coherence, and logic. Windelband was known for his uncanny ability to trace interrelationships between seemingly disconnected topics[3] and must have marveled at his student, Nicholas Lossky, who was learning to do the same.

Lossky received his master's in 1903 and completed his doctorate in 1907

Fig 1. Nicholas Onufrievich Lossky (1870–1965), Ayn Rand's philosophy teacher at Petrograd University. Photo taken in the United States, 1950. (Courtesy of Boris Lossky)

with a dissertation titled "The Foundations of Intuitivism" (*Obosnovanie intuitivizma*), which was later published.[4] During this period, Lossky contributed to several Russian journals, including *Novaia zhizn'* in 1905, *Poliarnaia zvezda* in 1906, and *Russkaia mysl'* in 1909 (Kline, 18 August 1993C). In that same year, 1909, many Russian intellectuals, including Berdyaev, Bulgakov, Gershenzon, Struve, and Frank, contributed to the publication of a famous symposium, *Vekhi* (Signposts). As ex-Marxists, these thinkers warned prophetically of revolutionary excesses and proclaimed a manifesto for Russia's spiritual reawakening. (Rosenthal and Bohachevsky-Chomiak 1990, 4, 22–23). Like several of his contemporaries, Lossky was moving toward a synthesis of neo-Idealism and religion.

But Lossky also owed a debt to German scholarship and philosophy, which was reflected in his sustained efforts to bring German works to a Russian audience (Kline 1985, 265–66). He translated Kant's *Critique of*

Pure Reason, Kant's dissertation of 1770, and Friedrich Paulsen's monograph on Kant. He also edited two translations of Fichte in 1905 and 1906 and was a cotranslator of works by Fischer in 1901–5 (ibid.).[5]

Lossky became a lecturer at St. Petersburg University and held a professorship from 1916 until 1921. During this period, he wrote several works that firmly established his reputation in Russian philosophy. Throughout his career, he published such distinguished books as *The Fundamental Doctrines of Psychology from the Point of View of Voluntarism* (1903); *The Intuitive Basis of Knowledge* (1906); *The World as an Organic Whole* (1917); *The Fundamental Problems of Epistemology* (1919); *Logic* (1922); *Freedom of Will* (1927); *Value and Existence* (1931); *Dialectical Materialism in U.S.S.R.* (1934); *Sensuous, Intellectual and Mystical Intuition* (1938); his acclaimed *History of Russian Philosophy* (1951); and *Dostoyevsky and His Christian Understanding of the World* (1953).

Lossky's works eventually were published in many languages. His student, English interpreter, and lifelong friend, Natalie Duddington, was the first to read one of his articles on intuitivism before the Aristotelian Society in England in 1914. Her translations of *The Intuitive Basis of Knowledge* and *The World as an Organic Whole* were the first presentations in English of a bona fide technical work by any twentieth-century Russian philosopher (Edie, Scanlan, and Zeldin 1965, 315). Throughout the 1930s, 1940s, and 1950s, Lossky continued to publish in many journals worldwide, including the *Personalist*, for which he served as a foreign advisory editor. Coincidentally, the *Personalist* would later become the first forum in which professional philosophers would debate the ethical theories of Lossky's student, Ayn Rand.

Lossky's life was severely disrupted in 1921–22, when despite his adherence to Fabian socialism, he was denounced by the regime as a religious counterrevolutionary. Under the guidance of Father Pavel Florensky, Lossky had reentered the Russian Orthodox Church in 1918 after having miraculously survived an elevator accident. His religious views cost him his professorship in philosophy and eventually led to his exile from Russia.

Lossky left the Soviet Union in August 1922 and settled in Prague, where at the invitation of Thomas Masaryk he began teaching at the Free Russian University. He also taught at Charles University and the University of Bratislava, where he was appointed professor in 1942. When the Soviets entered the city toward the end of World War II, Lossky escaped to the United States. His son Vladimir became a theologian and historian of religion. His son Andrew, a graduate of Yale University, went on to teach history at UCLA. His son Boris became a distinguished art historian.

In 1946, Lossky was appointed professor of philosophy at St. Vladimir's Orthodox Theological Seminary and Academy in New York City.[6] Lossky taught and lived at the Union Theological Seminary building on 121st Street and Broadway, before St. Vladimir's moved to Crestwood in 1963. By the early 1950s, Ayn Rand was also living in New York City. Some thirty years after their initial encounter, Rand and Lossky were neighbors again, a fact which neither realized.

In October 1961, Lossky entered a Russian nursing home near Paris, closer to his son Boris, and in 1965, died.

More than twenty-five years after Lossky's death, a postcommunist Russia is beginning to rediscover the richness of its prerevolutionary intellectual heritage. Starting in 1989, such journals as *Voprosy filosofii* and *Voprosy literatury* began publishing the first of a projected thirty-five to forty volumes on Russian philosophy and literature, featuring the works of the Symbolists, Solovyov, Frank, Shestov, Bulgakov, Berdyaev, Florensky, and Lossky, among others.[7] *Voprosy filosofii* began publishing Lossky's memoirs, *Vospominaniia*, in 1991.[8]

Lossky's Philosophy: An Eclectic Synthesis

Lossky characterized his intuitivist philosophy as an integration of idealism and realism. He rejected "one-sided idealism" and "one-sided materialism," and proposed an "ideal-realist" perspective that sought a "unity of opposites."[9] He was influenced by Fichte, Schelling, Hegel, Solovyov, Külpe, Bergson, and most important, Leibniz.[10] The intellectual debt that Lossky owes to Leibnizian monadology and Bergsonian intuitionism is expressed in his dictum that "everything is immanent in everything else" (Shein 1967, 86). Though Lossky was more rationalistic than most of his Russian predecessors, he combined Leibnizian and Platonic realism with a deeply organic view of the world.

As part of the Russian religious renaissance, Lossky, like Solovyov, rejected the Thomistic separation of philosophy from theology (Copleston 1988, 60). Like Semyon Frank, Lossky conceptualized three hierarchical levels of existence: the physical/real, the spiritual/ideal, and the mystical/

metalogical in which both material and spiritual elements are united.[11] Real being has a spatiotemporal character. Ideal being, which has a nonspatio-temporal character, includes the apprehension of relations, number, unity, and plurality. Metalogical being corresponds to the Absolute. To apprehend each of these three levels, human cognition engages three corresponding types of intuition: sensory, intellectual, and mystical. Each of these forms is organically linked to the others.

Lossky's philosophy aims to overcome both Humean skepticism and Kantian rationalism. Acclaimed as "a great master of the word" (Zenkovsky 1953, 662), Lossky defended a pluralistic, though organic, view of the world. He saw his epistemological theory as a form of intuitivism. Rejecting Cartesian dualism and subjectivism, he insisted on the integrity of knowledge. His intuitivism is a doctrine of "epistemological coordination," in which "the cognized object, even if it forms part of the external world, enters the knowing subject's consciousness directly, so to speak in person, and is therefore apprehended as it exists independently of the act of knowing" (Lossky 1951, 252). Hence, we do not perceive the mere stimulation of sensory organs. We perceive and apprehend real existents. Even though our perceptions are selective and fragmentary and may differ based upon each individual's subconscious choices, the knowing subject directs his or her attention on the actual objects of the external world (ibid.).

Relational contemplation becomes possible because the world is an organic whole of constituent elements. Like Leibniz, Lossky argued that the world consisted of monads, or "substantival agents," of which human beings were of prime importance. But for Lossky, these agents were not "windowless." Lossky rejected metaphysical atomism. He insisted that substantival agents were not self-contained and independent, but interacted in an organic system of "hierarchical personalism" (Zenkovsky 1953, 659, 662, 666). He argued that "the whole world consists of actual or potential persons."[12] In Lossky's view, every agent in the universe, even an electron, is a potential person. These agents enter into relations with one another to form a single systemic whole. But as a religious idealist, Lossky asserted that the highest agent is the World Spririt. By conceptualizing an organic system united by an Absolute, Lossky attempted to avoid the radical plurality of the atomists, while making the universe intelligible (Shein 1973, 146).

Lossky opposed what he described as the "extremes" of both "universal-istic" and "individualistic" systems of philosophy. In the former, the individual is granted no independent value, whereas in the latter, the individual is totally independent of the whole. Although it aims to promote human diversity, individualism constructs a social system of undifferentiated atoms and culminates in a crude solipsism.[13] The truly organic system is neither wholly collectivistic nor atomistic, but interweaves unity and plurality.

However, Lossky achieved such organicism through a mystical union. Deeply influenced by his Russian philosophic predecessors, Lossky was part of a pre-Bolshevik religious renaissance. He incorporated mystical and communitarian notions into the corpus of his thought. He opposed ethical relativism, and presented an absolutist morality. He argued that existence and value are mutually related through a Supracosmic principle discoverable by mystic intuition (Shein 1967, 86–87). This Absolute is God, the perfect, almighty, omnipotent, omniscient, omnipresent, and omnibenevolent being. All substantival agents and all intrinsic values (e.g., Being, Love, Beauty, Truth, Freedom) emanate from God. As an adherent of Russian Orthodoxy, and in quasi-Hegelian fashion, Lossky argued that the gulf between God and Man is bridged by Christ, the God-Man of the Trinity.

Like most Russian philosophers, Lossky (1951) also embraced the notion of *sobornost'*, such

> that the creativeness of all beings that live in God must be completely unanimous, *soborny* (communal). Every member of the kingdom of God must make his individual, i.e., unique, unrepeatable and unreplaceable contribution to the communal creativeness: only in that case will the members' activity be mutually complementary, creating a single and unique beautiful whole, instead of being a repetition of the same actions. (259)

In the Kingdom of Harmony, each part exists for the whole, just as the totality exists for each part. For Lossky ([1917] 1928), in the Kingdom of Harmony, there is "a complete interpenetration of all by all, the distinction between part and whole disappears: every part is a whole. The principles of organic structure are realized in the completest way possible. It is a wholly perfect organism" (81). In the Kingdom of Harmony, there are no egoistic "acts of repulsion." For Lossky, as for Solovyov before him, selfishness separates us from God, and is the primary evil. Because human beings have free will, they must choose the purity of moral perfection by embracing the path to God. In Lossky's view, only "Goodness and beauty can exist in their pure form without any admixture of evil or ugliness." But the evil must depend upon the good in order to survive, for "evil and ugliness can have no reality without having some element of beauty and goodness in them."[14]

Lossky and Aristotle

It is easy to see why, in later years, Rand characterized Lossky as a Platonic philosophical adversary (B. Branden 1986, 42). Given Lossky's mystical and Ideal notions, Rand's depiction is certainly not without merit. Yet, though Lossky had much in common with Platonists, he argued that his "ideal-realism" was rooted in the "concrete ideal-realism" of Aristotle. For Lossky, Aristotle offered the first version of the concrete ideal-realist perspective. It is here that we can begin to appreciate Lossky's method of analysis, despite the explicitly mystical content of his formal philosophy. It is here that we can begin to dissect the dialectical kernel in Lossky's mystical shell. For in his dialectical methodology, Lossky has integrated a Russian tendency toward synthesis with complementary elements in Aristotelian, Leibnizian, and Hegelian thought. Lossky ([1917] 1928) writes:

> According to Aristotle, every particular thing and being in the world is the result of the combination of matter and form. . . . Abstraction being made of these definite characteristics of concrete things, matter is conceived of as the *possibility* of any one of these forms or characteristics. . . . Aristotle was a naturalist who never lost sight of living reality . . . [forming] abstractions without separating from living reality that which is abstracted from it, but merely mentally emphasizing it for the sake of observing it more carefully against the whole background of real existence. (193–94)

By tracing his own position to the "concrete ideal-realism" of Aristotle, Lossky suggested that the classical Greek thinker was a forerunner of the intuitivist perspective. This is not to say that Lossky's epistemology is essentially Aristotelian. In later years, Lossky claimed that he shared the Aristotelian realist view that people directly apprehend their own mental states *and* the objects in the external world. But for Lossky, this realist tradition fails because it accepts the Aristotelian distinction between form and matter. Lossky (1957) explained that in the Aristotelian epistemology,

Man can cognize objects of the external world because human reason is the potential form of all objects which becomes actual when those objects are perceived. . . . When a man perceives a stone, the form of the stone is present in his mind, but he does not become a stone because only the form, and not the matter, of the stone enters his mind. Since, however, the form is the essence of an object, we may say that in a certain sense knowledge of an object implies the identity between the thought and the object of thought. This identity is but partial, because only the essence of an object, and not its existence, is present in the human mind. (38)

This is not sufficient, in Lossky's view, because in Aristotle's realism, the mind grasps *only* the metaphysical essence but not the existence of the object. In Lossky's intuitivism, the "conditions of direct perception" allow for the immanent presence of the object "in the knowing subject's consciousness" (42). It is this insistence on direct intuition that also leads Lossky to reject the "causal theory of perception," which states that "the action of external objects upon the sense organs and through them on the cortex is the *cause* that produces in the subject's mind the contents of sense perception." Although the causal theory assumes that there *are* external objects, it inevitably regards everything in human consciousness as "mental and subjective."[15] Rejecting the causal theory as subjectivist, and Aristotle's theory as insufficiently intuitivist, Lossky (1955) argued that genuinely "direct intuition" preserves the objectivity of the existents it perceives; the mind processes information through an "immediate contemplation of reality" (139). We perceive existents *as they exist*, not as distorted copies.

Rand would have applauded her teacher's rejection of the subjectivist theory, but she would have viewed Lossky's approach as nonobjective and "intrinsicist."[16] Rand argued that although the subjectivists view concepts as products of consciousness apart from existence, the intrinsicists view concepts as intuitively grasped products of reality apart from any "distortions" of consciousness. For Rand, the subjectivists attempt to circumvent reality, and the intrinsicists try to circumvent the *identity* of consciousness. Rand would have argued that Lossky had merely embraced intrinsicism as a means of fighting subjectivism, and that neither approach is genuinely *objective*.

But for Lossky, objectivity is preserved through direct intuition in which the metaphysical existence of the object is "given to" the mind, thus collapsing the distinction between form and matter, essence and existence.

Epistemologically, people achieve a coordination between subject and object that provides for a direct insight into both the essential and existential reality of the thing. And yet, because we are not omniscient, we are never able to know completely and exhaustively the infinite complexity of an object in its organic wholeness. Each act of discrimination and comparison is an attempt to resolve the fragmentation and incompleteness of human knowledge (Lossky 1957, 43). As a neo-Leibnizian personalist, Lossky argues that every substantival agent in the universe grasps a fragment of the whole. From the smallest electron to the Absolute World Spirit, all substantival agents are "consubstantial" and "welded into a single whole" (41). Hence it is in the Whole that the Truth is to be found.

This variation on Hegel's dictum is more a metaphysical proposition than it is an epistemological one. For Lossky assumed the existence of substantival agents on levels lower and higher than the human. These are metaphysical assertions which Rand would have rejected categorically. And yet it must be remembered that Lossky presented an intuitivist perspective that he believed owed much to the concrete ideal-realism of Aristotle. Though he rejected aspects of the Aristotelian epistemology, Lossky saw Aristotle as a philosophical intuitivist. In later years, Rand would present an interpretation of Aristotle that linked the Greek philosopher to a similar metaphysical-intuitivist tradition. Rand explained that Aristotle affirmed the existence of essences in concretes.[17] Aristotle "held that definitions refer to metaphysical *essences*, which exist in concretes as a special element or formative power, and he held that the process of concept-formation depends on a kind of direct intuition by which man's mind grasps these essences and forms concepts accordingly" (*Introduction*, 52).

She argued that Objectivism departs from Aristotle's theory by regarding "essence" as epistemological and contextual, rather than as "metaphysical." One can speculate that Lossky's lectures on Aristotle provided Rand with an intuitivist interpretation of Aristotelian philosophy.[18] This might explain her insistence that Aristotle's theory was a form of intuitivism with an emphasis on metaphysical "essence."[19]

It is clear, however, that Lossky saw Aristotle as a spiritual ally in his struggles against dualism and atomism. After all, Aristotle had opposed both the eleatic monists and the Heracliteans. As Tibor Machan (1992) explains: "Eleatic monism is the affirmation of identity to the exclusion of difference and the affirmation of stasis to the exclusion of change. The Heraclitean flux is the affirmation of difference to the exclusion of identity and the affirmation of change to the exclusion of stasis" (48).

Embodying both change and identity, being and becoming, Aristotle's notion of identity is profoundly ontological. Becoming presupposes Being, change presupposes identity. Like Rand after him, Lossky praised Aristotle's ability to integrate these facts of identity and change, the basic axioms of existence and mind. Lossky endorsed an ontological interpretation of the laws of logic.[20] For Lossky ([1917] 1928), "Logical and metaphysical principles fundamentally coincide: they are the expression of the same general structure of the world, considered in its different aspects (viz. in its significance for knowledge and for being)" (173). Like Aristotle, Lossky viewed the laws of logic as "therefore, no less a real than . . . a logical necessity."[21] A *is* A, but this logical identity is not a static tautology; it too is an expression of a metaphysical fact.

Lossky appreciated Aristotle's attempt to transcend the one-sided traditions of his predecessors. Aristotle's emphasis on the concrete led him to condemn both the Platonic idealists and the Democritean atomists. For Aristotle, Plato had committed the fallacy of reification; he had inferred the existence of (specific) things from a (general) Ideal abstraction. Aristotle aimed to comprehend the universal through the part, grasping the abstraction through an apprehension of the particular.[22] It is Aristotle's dedication to the real concrete that enabled him to bridge the gap between universals and particulars. Thus Aristotle sought to transcend the polarity between ideas *and* sensory objects, mind *and* body. Unlike the Platonists, he saw a closer affinity between mind and body, arguing that it is only through the corporeal functions of the body, that the mind can exercise its distinctive faculties.[23] But in contrast to the atomists, Aristotle maintained the integrity of the whole as a whole.

Like Aristotle before him, Lossky did not isolate an abstracted particular from its context, a part from the whole. In Aristotle's teleology, the actualization of an organism's potential cannot be reduced to the potentiality of each of its elements taken separately. Allan Gotthelf explains that for Aristotle,

> The development, structure, and functioning of living organisms cannot be wholly explained by—*because it is not wholly due to*—the simple natures and potentials of the elements which constitute these organisms. No sum of actualizations . . . 'element-potentials' is sufficient by itself for the production of those complex living structures and functionings for which Aristotle offers teleological explanations.[24]

Thus, for Aristotle, everything is part of a system of related things:

> When any one of the parts or structures, be it which it may, is under
> discussion, it must not be supposed that it is its material composition
> to which attention is being directed or which is the object of the
> discussion, but the relation of such part to the total form. Similarly,
> the true object of architecture is not bricks, mortar, or timber, but
> the house; and so the principal object of natural philosophy is not
> the material elements, but their composition, and the totality of the
> form, independently of which they have no existence. . . . [A] house
> does not exist for the sake of bricks and stones, but these materials
> for the sake of the house, and the same is the case with the materials
> of other bodies. [25]

Like Aristotle, Lossky rejected mechanistic conceptions in favor of teleological explanations. Mechanism sees events in simple temporal sequence and views causality as an external relation between disconnected elements. It implicitly accepts a vision of the whole that is inorganic and atomistic. By contrast, Lossky (1934a) argued that "the whole conditions its elements and is not the sum of them" (149). His teleological conception suggests that "a new event is conditioned not only by the preceding events but also by the future, namely, by the purpose for the sake of which the change is produced. Thus, e.g., the structure of the eye is partly conditioned by the purpose of having an organ of vision" (Lossky [1917] 1928, 154–55).

It is this Aristotelian emphasis on the integrity of the whole that was furthered by thinkers such as Leibniz and Hegel, modern philosophers who made a huge impact on Lossky. [26] Lossky regarded Hegel as a great philosophical intuitivist, another in the grand tradition of concrete ideal-realism. Hegel "makes logic subordinate to the metaphysics of concretely speculative being—his logic is metaphysical." [27] Moreover, like Aristotle, Hegel argued against those who refused to grasp organic unity. He repudiated "conventional opinion," which saw things as disconnected, atomistic elements. In a now famous passage, Hegel ([1807] 1977) explains:

> The bud disappears in the bursting-forth of the blossom, and one
> might say that the former is refuted by the latter; similarly, when the
> fruit appears, the blossom is shown up in its turn as a false manifesta-
> tion of the plant, and the fruit now emerges as the truth of it instead.
> These forms are not just distinguished from one another, they also

supplant one another as mutually incompatible. Yet at the same time their fluid nature makes them moments of an organic unity in which they not only do not conflict, but in which each is as necessary as the other; and this mutual necessity alone constitutes the life of the whole. (2)

Whereas some would criticize this formulation as a rejection of Aristotle's law of identity, Lossky argued that the Hegelian dialectic posited an "*interpenetration* between different and even opposite processes (inner and outer) . . . not an identity of opposites, but only their *unity*." For Lossky, the identity of opposites is a meaningless phrase, because nothing can violate the law of contradiction. Lossky thought it far more likely that every change embodied a unity of opposing movements.[28] Hence, just as motion is not a contradiction of identity, so too, we must grasp that "both movement and rest belong to the body in different respects" (Lossky 1951, 288).

Lossky's Epistemology

In his theory of knowledge, Lossky carried on the Aristotelian and Hegelian revolt against partial or one-sided perspectives. But his attempts to transcend dualities were also fully within the Russian tradition of philosophical synthesis. In *The Intuitive Basis of Knowledge* (1906), Lossky's first major book on epistemology, there is a sustained polemic against rationalism and empiricism. Lossky argued that empiricism must inevitably dissolve into sensationalism and subjectivism. Though rationalism and empiricism are "diametrically opposed," they share a commonality, "the supposition that subject and object are isolated from one another" (Lossky [1906] 1919, 68). In Lossky's view, epistemology

> must relinquish the assumption made by both rationalists and empiricists that subject and object are isolated from one another, that the object lies outside the boundaries of knowledge, and that what can be known of it is either its effect or its copy innate in the subject. The new theory of knowledge must destroy the barriers thus erected between subject and object, recognise their fundamental unity, and in this manner bring about their reconciliation. (69)

Both rationalism and empiricism lead to one-sidedness, such that they exaggerate the importance of one subjective activity or another. Whereas empiricism emphasizes the subject's sensory data, and rationalism stresses the subject's reason, Kant's critical philosophy attempted to resolve the opposition by accentuating "the structure of the cognitive faculty as a whole (sensibility, understanding and reason)" (Lossky [1906] 1919, 402). In effect, however, Kant's resolution is equally one-sided and subjectivist. Kant's approach attempts to connect phenomenal reality with the cognitive process, but this is achieved "at the expense of subordinating existence to knowledge . . . by resolving phenomena, or the world of our experience, into processes of knowledge." Kant put forth an unsubstantiated assertion that the relations in the world were constructed by the mind, and not inherent in the structure of reality. Likewise, post-Kantian Idealists reconciled knowledge (i.e., consciousness) and existence in a similarly rationalistic manner by suggesting "that existence is nothing else than an evolution of thought." Thus in each case, the rationalist, empiricist, and Kantian critical alternatives "institute an impassable gulf between knowledge and existence" (403).

Lossky's intuitivism (or "intuitionalism") aimed not to discard the old systems, but to "free them from the old exclusiveness, and so prepare a way for their reconciliation and union" (402). He refused to collapse the polarity of knowledge and existence by adopting a rationalist or empiricist perspective. His intuitivism challenged the basis of the dispute by exposing its fallacious premises, showing that each school is both "partly right and partly wrong." Lossky rejected any "antitheses between knowledge and existence, the rational and the non-rational, the *a priori* and the *a posteriori*, the universal and the particular, the analytic and the synthetic" (403).

Though Lossky repudiated dualism, he argued that the subject and the object are independent of each other, and that in reality, there is no subordination of either to the other. Their existence is objective. Their relation is one of coordination. Lossky proposed that the subject and object be reconciled by an "epistemological coordination," such that "although each retains its independence in respect of the other, they yet form an indissoluble unity" (69).

Citing the influence of Leibniz, Schelling, Hegel, Solovyov, and S. N. Trubetskoy, Lossky viewed this coordinating process as a "union of opposed principles . . . an act of fertilisation" (221). In Lossky's view, knowledge emerged through relational comparison, *"a process of differentiating the real world by means of comparison"* (226). Investigation of reality requires careful differentiation, a process in which the individual abstracts "a fresh aspect" from reality in order to make the world humanly knowable (231).

Knowledge, then, is neither copy, nor symbol, nor appearance of reality, but *"reality itself,"* a part momentarily abstracted from the whole, but retaining its organic existential validity. Phenomena are neither "mere presentations" nor distorted copies of reality. The relations we perceive are not the artificial constructions of human cognition. They are real. According to Lossky's intuitivism, "the relation of the phenomenal to the real is . . . a metaphysical and not an epistemological question" (404). Thinking is not metaphysically creative (409). Knowledge *"contains"* reality, it "does not *create* real existence." For Lossky, the "known object is immanent in the process of cognition" (225).

This "immanent interpenetration" of the subject and the object leads to a "coordination" between them.[29] Epistemological coordination links the object, the act of knowing, and the content of knowledge. Though the act of knowing is "subjective," in that it is performed by the subject, Lossky argues that the object and the content of knowledge are "objective," not constructed or distorted by the cognitive faculty.[30] What we perceive is *in* the object, not a construction of our imagination. "Greenness," like shape and density, is an aspect of the object, an aspect singled out through our mental analysis. Unlike Kant, Lossky ([1906] 1919) attempted to defend epistemological objectivity by insisting that knowledge consists of "elements of the real world. The cognitive activity merely subjects this content to a process of discrimination and comparison; it does not introduce any qualitatively new elements into the content known. It neither creates nor reproduces the real world" (405).

Lossky's struggle against Kantian subjectivism was not merely an assertion of the objectivity of knowledge but also a defense of the necessity for a metaphysical foundation for philosophy. For Lossky, "Metaphysics is the science about the world as a whole, containing the knowledge *of things as they are in themselves."* Immanuel Kant's critical philosophy had denied that such a metaphysical science was possible. For Kant, the subject could only apprehend "the objects immanent in his consciousness." These objects are subjective presentations, "they are things, as they *seem* to me, but not things as they are in themselves." Thus Kant claimed that "a science of things as they are in themselves is impossible" and epistemologically illegitimate. In Lossky's view (1934c), Kant erroneously equated immanence in the consciousness of the subject with immanence in the subject of consciousness (265).

The specifically human component of the cognitive process then is abstraction and differentiation. The act of knowing does not alter the character of the object. The act of differentiating does not create distinctions; it merely detects "such peculiarities as already exist" (Lossky [1917] 1928, 11). But abstraction presupposes a real, complex whole. Copleston (1986) writes: "According to Lossky, the whole is prior to its parts, not constructed out of them. We can designate points in a line, but a line does not consist of juxtaposed points. If it is objected, for example, that a given atom is certainly different from any other atom, Lossky's reply is that neither can exist apart from the system of atoms" (364).

The World as an Organic Whole

Having presented an intuitivist theory of knowledge in 1906, Lossky knew that he would be compelled to write a sequel to his epistemology that would focus on its underlying metaphysic. In *The World as an Organic Whole*, published in 1917, Lossky continued to discuss many of the same themes, sustaining his opposition to the one-dimensionality of contemporary philosophy. He rejected "mechanistic" and "inorganic" conceptions as one-sided and partial. He argued vociferously for an organic view of the world that complemented his intuitivist epistemology.

Lossky began his metaphysical treatise by explaining that there are two basic, opposing conceptions of the world: the organic and the inorganic. Lossky's characterization ([1917] 1928) is deeply significant, and it is worth quoting at length:

> Those who take the inorganic view conceive of a complex whole with distinguishable parts A, B, C, D, as made up of elements A, B, C, D, capable of existing on their own account independently both of each other and of the whole in which they are found. The elements are taken to be self-subsistent to such an extent that if B, C, D completely disappeared A would go on existing as before. Coming together in space, these elements may form a group and thus give rise to a complex whole. According to this view, the elements are absolute, primordial, and exist unconditionally. The whole is, on the contrary, relative, derivative, and entirely deter-

mined by its parts. In other words, plurality is regarded as primary and unity as secondary and as conditioned by the plurality. (1)

Lossky distinguishes this inorganic, reductive conception of the world, from the organic view:

Those who take the organic view understand plurality and wholeness in a diametrically opposite way. It is the whole that exists primarily, and the elements can exist and come into being only within the system of the whole. The world cannot be explained as the result of adding A to B, then to C, and so on: plurality cannot give rise to wholeness, but is, on the contrary, generated by it. In other words, the whole is prior to its parts; the absolute must be sought in the domain of wholeness or, rather, beyond it, and certainly not among the elements; the elements are in any case derivative and relative, i.e., they can only exist in relation to the system of which they are members. (2)

Lossky argued that the inorganic view was the basis for mechanistic and reductive materialism. It perpetuated a philosophy of external relations, while bolstering a vulgar empiricist, atomistic worldview. The organic conception, by contrast, is teleological, integrative, internally relational, and reflective of the nature of reality.[31]

This formulation is crucial because it exhibits Lossky's dedication to the doctrine of internal relations, his conviction that in an organic unity, nothing is "constructed out of its elements in an external manner" (Lossky [1917] 1928, 17). Every element in the whole, every atom in the world, every note in a musical composition is an internal "*aspect* of the world discoverable by means of analysis and existing, not independently, but only on the basis of a world-whole, only within a universal system." The organic view sees A and B in an internal "relation to each other as one whole, each aspect of which subsists together with the others, on the basis of the whole." The internal relations between the elements of the whole are *objective* relations of difference and similarity, of quantity and quality, of temporality and spatiality, of causality and interaction, of ends and means. The "network of relations is all-embracing and all-pervading" (19).

The doctrine of internal relations involves vast issues of ontology and epistemology and could be the subject of a book in itself. In order to grasp the full depth of Lossky's thought, it is necessary to examine, however briefly, some of the major questions concerning the internalist-externalist debate. These issues are significant for two reasons:

First, internalism permeates all of Russian thought and Lossky's thought in particular. It is, in fact, central to the theme of synthesis in Russian philosophy. But the debate is not distinctively Russian. The internalist-externalist debate is as old as the speculative metaphysics of Parmenides. Ironically, during the Russian Silver Age, in the period from 1890 to 1920, Western, post-Hegelian, Idealist philosophers, such as Bradley, Royce, and Bosanquet, were raising some of the very same internalist issues as their Russian counterparts. The internalist-externalist dispute has continued throughout the twentieth century in the writings of such distinguished philosophers as A. J. Ayer, Brand Blanshard, Thomas Nagel, Richard Rorty, Bertrand Russell, and thinkers in the Marxist tradition. No discussion of the flavor of Russian thought, or of Lossky's thought, would be complete without a grasp of these important issues.

Second, the internalist-externalist debate is crucial to our understanding of Rand's philosophy. In Part 2, I argue that Objectivism exhibits an organic, internalist orientation, even as it seeks to transcend the very dichotomy of the internal versus the external. Rand was a rare philosophic phenomenon: she was an epistemological realist who recognized the relational character of existence and knowledge. The radical thrust of Rand's cultural criticism lies ultimately in its ability to trace the *internal* relationships between and among the various constituents and institutions in social reality. Although Rand diverges considerably from the strict organicity of the Hegelian Idealists, there is an element of internalism and organic unity which pervades the very fabric of Objectivism.

In exploring the full significance of Lossky's internalism, it would be valuable to discuss complementary developments in the thought of other philosophers. Lossky's perspective itself is an outgrowth of his own appropriation of Leibnizian, Spinozian, and Hegelian insights. One modern expositor of the internalist orientation who shares many of Lossky's philosophical premises, is Brand Blanshard. As an Absolute Idealist, Blanshard, like Lossky, rejects the distinctions between necessary and contingent and between analytic and synthetic. Significantly, Blanshard's work has been acclaimed in Objectivist publications and lectures.[32]

To begin, it is important to ask what exactly is meant by "internal" as opposed to "external" relations. According to Blanshard ([1962] 1964): "A given term is internally related to another if in the absence of the relation it could not be what it is. A term is externally related to another if the relation could equally be present or absent while the term was precisely the same" (475).

Richard Rorty (1967) dramatizes this distinction between internal and external relations by describing two extreme positions. The internalist orientation is associated with idealism and monism. It sees all the properties of a thing as "essential to its being what it is (and, a fortiori, that all its relations are internal to it)." This theory views every property of every element as profoundly significant such that the alienation or deprivation of a single aspect would mean, "in a nontrivial sense," that the element was no longer what it once was (125).

If I say: "I am a young American male of Greek and Sicilian descent," each one of the terms I have used to describe myself is "internal" to who I am. "Young" indicates that I still consider myself youthful while being thirtysomething. "American" designates not only my citizenship, but indicates that I have grown up in a society that is freer and more democratic than most. "Male" identifies my gender, while "Greek" and "Sicilian" suggest family traditions that were crucial to my upbringing. Indeed, they might even conjure up an image of a swarthy, "Mediterranean" complexion. In any event, the internalist would say no element of this self-description can be altered without changing the *essential* quality of who and what I am today. If I were older, my description might be different. When I was younger, I *know* that some of my attitudes were markedly different than they are today. If I were female, or a Russian citizen, or of African descent, my experiences, not to mention my physical appearance, would be correspondingly different. That is not to say that I might not hold some of the same values that I hold today. But the simple fact is that none of the attributes I have noted in the above description, namely, "young," "American," "male," "Greek," and "Sicilian," can be separated from the person that is me. And if it were possible to alter any of these characteristics, then I would be a different person!

According to Rorty, the externalist orientation "holds that none of a thing's properties are essential to it (and thus, a fortiori, that no relations are internal to it). This view is put forward by those who make a firm distinction between the thing itself and a description of it." The externalists argue that although certain properties of the thing enable us to describe it, the absence of these properties does not mean that the thing is no longer the same. Such a proposition is "trivial" or "misleading," according to the externalists. For in one sense, the alteration of one single aspect of a thing makes it different from what it once was. But in another sense, the modification of a single element would merely change our description of the thing. The externalists argue that "there are an infinity of equally correct descriptions, and nothing in the thing itself determines which of these is *the* description." The externalists assert that the specification of "essential properties" is thus a nominal exercise and completely arbitrary (Rorty 1967, 125). Thus, to say that "I am a young, American male of Greek and Sicilian descent" is merely to describe what I am. I could have provided an equivalently correct description by saying that I was a man in my thirties, with several birthmarks on my face, working at an American college, and living in Brooklyn, New York. Or I could have said that I was 5'7½", 145 pounds, with a size 8½ shoe. The point is that I can provide endless self-descriptions and not one of them is truer than any other. To say that one attribute is more "essential" than any other attribute is to place an arbitrarily privileged distinction on one to the exclusion of others.

But common sense tells us that some things are more important than others. If I were to remove one tiny birthmark from my face, this would have less of an effect on my essential "personhood" than, say, a sex-change operation. What is the something in "maleness" that is more significant to my self than "birthmark-ness"? Would a new "female" appearance alter any of the fundamental "me"? Externalism does not deny that there is this thing called me, but it rejects the claim that there is anything about "me" that we can consider more *essential* than any other thing. Hence, it views the designation of essence as a purely linguistic, nominal, and arbitrary exercise.

Curiously, both the internalist and the externalist deny Aristotle's distinction between essence and accident. The externalists claim that the characterization of a thing's "essence" is a purely conventional practice, and the internalists also argue that the distinction between "essential" and "nonessential" is arbitrary. They believe that every thing has an intrinsic nature, which is organic and integrated. Though the internalists accept that essence-accident distinctions are inevitable in a world of imperfect knowledge, they seem to imply that such division is ontologically illegitimate, for *every* aspect is as important as every other.[33] By extension, the internalists also seem to imply that there *can* be a world of perfect knowledge.

This helps us to focus on one of the fundamental problems inherent in the most extreme form of internalism: a problem of individuation arising from excessive integration. In Hegel and Blanshard, as in Lossky, there is a tendency toward strict organicity.[34] Every part of the totality must be considered when assessing the significance of any other part. Expanding the discussion beyond the mere consideration of an object's relational properties, Blanshard argues, for instance, that every object has a certain shape, and that this shape is the result of two factors: the object's nature *and* its interaction with other objects.[35] Blanshard ([1962] 1964) writes that a thing's "ultimate elements are engaged in manifold interactions, by way of attraction and repulsion, with things around it, and these almost certainly determine its shape down to the last detail. This particular shape, like this degree of malleability, is not externally related to its other characters; they are bound up with these causally and therefore . . . necessarily" (481).

Although Blanshard recognizes that different entities have parts that are "more obviously interdependent" than others, still he claims that no element is external to the totality. A thing is what it is by virtue of "lines of demarcation"—causal, logical, or both—running out into an illimitable universe" (485). Thus, the thing is affected in varying degrees by its relations, "no matter how external they may seem." Since "everything is related in *some* way to everything else, no knowledge will reveal completely the nature of any term until it has exhausted that term's relations to everything else" (Blanchard 1940, 2:452). This would suggest that *everything* must be known before anything can be analyzed.

To transcend this problem, both Hegel and Lossky hypothesized an Absolute standpoint, whereby the Truth lies in a Metaphysical Whole as grasped by an omniscient consciousness. In such a whole, all relations are internal and simultaneous. The main problem for such an internalist orientation is individuation: trying to abstract and define the nature of an individual entity such that it is not dissolved in the relationships that it embodies. It is this dilemma of individuation that prompted Lossky to assert the ontological priority of concrete particulars within the whole. He calls his system *concrete* ideal-realism and sees both Hegel and Aristotle as his philosophic forebears. He argues that relations are not disembodied; just as no object is external to its relations, relations have no existence except between objects. Lossky ([1917] 1928) explains: "Relations are not independent; they cannot exist on their own account, apart from the elements they relate" (37). And yet if each thing is constituted by a cluster of relations, and the relations themselves can be extended to include the organic whole itself, we are still faced with an unresolved individuation problem.

Externalists such as Thomas Nagel and A. J. Ayer reject internalist organicism because they correctly perceive that it fails to resolve this issue of individuation. Nagel argues further that any search for the real "nature" or "essence" of a thing is incoherent. As Rorty (1967) explained it,

Blanshard's "essence" of X depends on a metaphysical "X-as-known-by-an-ideal-knower," that is, a Being who can grasp all of the relational interactions between and among all of the constituent properties of the totality (129). The externalists reject organic internalism because such a system ultimately depends on omniscience as a standard of certainty.

Issues of individuation and omniscience are not inherent in externalism. The externalist orientation claims to oppose the internalism of the Idealists with a hard-boiled philosophic realism. Things are what they are and cannot be defined in terms of their relations to anything else. A thing has an identity and its nature cannot "be constituted by the nature of the system to which it belongs" (Copleston 1966, 405). But the externalist argues that there is a sharp dichotomy between what an entity really *is*, something which cannot be known completely, and our linguistic descriptions of what an entity is, something which is entirely arbitrary. The externalist perpetuates the Kantian distinction between a noumenal and phenomenal world, necessity and contingency, analysis and synthesis. The externalist's "realism" dissolves into a crude, dualistic, and atomistic perspective on reality. Its fundamental problem is a lack of integration, owing to excessive differentiation. Every thing is self-subsistent and logically independent of every other thing.[36] Relations and systems are arbitrary constructs of the mind.

It is for this reason that Lossky rejected externalism as a vestige of Kantian dualism. Kant argued that relations are added to the data of our senses by the constructive activity of the mind. The subject creates or constructs the object and its relations. But according to Lossky ([1917] 1928), the mind contemplates relations that exist in the world. The relations we conceive "presuppose relations that obtain within organic being" (24). They are "objective elements which can be *perceived*" (33). They exist "in the very nature of the object" (34).

As an organic internalist, Lossky denied both dualism and atomism. Like Blanshard and other internalists, Lossky saw an intimate connection between the necessary and the contingent, the analytic and the synthetic, the causal and the logical. Human knowledge cannot be bifurcated because reality is an integral whole.

Within this organic totality, the elements can enter into opposition and conflict with one another, but they are still interconnected and interrelated by virtue of their presence within a systemic context. Organicism recognizes the interaction of elements as more than "the mere sum of two actions of which the first follows the second as a response." The nature of interaction lies in the fact that it involves the "*simultaneous* determination" of two or more elements, such that "there is no meaning in drawing a distinction between the agent and the patient" (5–6). Lossky recognized metaphysical plurality in the world, but refused to view the world's many elements as independent of the whole. Each of the mechanical elements of the system is conditioned by the totality itself (6–7).

Lossky argued further that "not a single knowable element" of the totality "exists on its own account, apart from a necessary relation to other elements." Every object of knowledge has distinguishable aspects, but none of these can be grasped in isolation from the total context. Metaphysical plurality does not discount the importance of causal connections and internal relations (11–12).

Thus the elements of the whole may be separated in one respect, but "in another respect they have the same basis and belong to the same whole. Their very separateness necessarily demands that in some other respect they should be united and interdependent" (13). Those who subscribe to the inorganic, mechanistic, and atomistic perspective conceive of atoms as independent of one another. Yet the atoms themselves belong to one universe in which they interact. The "single whole space" of the universe constitutes "the one all-embracing basis" that is common to all of its constituent elements. Hence the position and movement of an atom is relative within the broader context of the whole.

Lossky argued that not even the atomist can deny the essentially organic structure of the world. For even in the atomist's denial is the retention of wholeness with every judgment made. Every philosophical theory presumes the idea of a whole that constitutes and is constituted by its elements. Thus the idea of an organic "whole lies at the root of every judgement we make concerning any object whatsoever" (8). If we deny such an organic, relational structure to reality, we forfeit the conditions that make the world knowable.

Lossky's organicism and internalism proliferate throughout his works, even in his less than fully developed aesthetics. Though Lossky lacked a formalized philosophy of art, he viewed each work of art as a totality, "the successive parts of which exist in consequence and for the sake of one another as well as of the whole: the parts of such a whole are not only a means but also an end for one another" (159–60). In this regard, Lossky appropriated a notable Aristotelian theme. In *De Poetica*, Aristotle wrote:

> The truth is that, just as in the other imitative arts one imitation is always of one thing, so in poetry the story, as an imitation of action,

must represent one action, a complete whole, with its several incidents so closely connected that the transposal or withdrawal of any one of them will disjoin and dislocate the whole. For that which makes no perceptible difference by its presence or absence is no real part of the whole.[37]

Lossky ([1917] 1928) expresses this same organicist sentiment with regard to musical composition: A piece of music is a complex whole in which its constituent elements form an organic unity. Each part is in harmony with the other, and all parts exist for the whole (48).

And yet, despite the ultimate necessity of holding an organic view on all ontological, epistemological, and aesthetic issues, Lossky is compelled to explain the prevalence of inorganic and atomistic conceptions. If organicism and internalism are true of reality and of knowledge, then why do fragmented perspectives endure?

Lossky argued that since knowledge requires comparison, differentiation, and analysis, it can disintegrate into atomistic elements. Like all entities on earth, humans are beings of finite capabilities. At any given moment, they focus on "some one part of the world" and abstract this part from the whole in a particular respect. Since knowledge expands with the addition of information, they can conclude falsely "that knowledge consists in *constructing* in our minds a complex whole out of *independent* elements." This is the Kantian error which fails to discriminate "our acts of knowing from that which is known." Such a mistake must inevitably "ascribe the characteristic of fragmentariness to the objects of knowledge and to the whole knowable world" (15).

Lossky believed, however, that the analysis that is performed by the mind yields a partial and incomplete picture of the whole. Lossky was unable to attain a fully integrative and organic view without the infusion of mystical elements. As a religious philosopher, Lossky hypothesized that an Absolute "being whose powers of attention and discrimination were infinite would be capable of contemplating everything at the same time, both as connected with and as distinguished from everything" (16). Such an omniscient being would be incapable of error, but He would be able to see the organic whole "in its differentiated aspect at once, without being broken up in time" (ibid.).

In his analysis of the persistence of fragmentation, Lossky seems oblivious to institutional or historical explanations. Marx maintained, for instance, that it was the capitalist mode of production that made such fragmentation possible, and inevitable. And it was Lossky's student, Ayn Rand, who proposed that social fragmentation was a constituent element of a broader systemic irrationality: statism.

The thought of N. O. Lossky was a fusion of complementary organicist and internalist tendencies in Russian and Western philosophy. Lossky's ideal-realism exhibited a Russian proclivity to synthesize opposites and resolve antagonisms. He rejected the dualistic obsession with dichotomies of rationalism or empiricism, idealism or materialism, knowledge or existence. These alternatives were, for him, partial and incomplete. Like other thinkers in Russian philosophy, however, Lossky achieved the ultimate integration through a mystical Absolute. His system of hierarchical personalism embraced a vision of the world as an organic whole, a unity of *sobornost'* achieved in God's Kingdom of Harmony.

Ayn Rand's philosophical project embodies this same struggle against dualities, the same powerful propensity toward synthesis. But although she appears to have inadvertently accepted her teacher's formal dialectical insights, she adamantly opposed his mysticism.

3 Educating Alissa

In 1945, Rand wrote:

> When I am questioned about myself, I am tempted to say, paraphrasing Roark [the protagonist of *The Fountainhead*]: "Don't ask me about my family, my childhood, my friends or my feelings. Ask me about the things I think." It is the content of a person's brain, not the accidental details of his life, that determines his character. My own character is in the pages of *The Fountainhead*. For anyone who wishes to know me, that is essential. The specific events of my private life are of no importance whatever. I have never had any private life in the usual sense of the word. My writing is my life.[1]

In this passage, Rand suggests that she is "tempted" to adopt an "essence-accident" distinction in the definition of her own life. The *essential* Rand is the *thinking* Rand. What she has written and what she thinks are what she considers most fundamental to answering the question, "Who is Ayn Rand?" The events and life experiences that shaped her thought are "accidental details" and "of no importance whatever" in grasping the significance of her character.

Although I perforce distinguish the philosophy from the philosopher, I believe that Rand's self-portrait here verges on the reification of her intellect as a disembodied abstraction. One cannot focus exclusively on the philosopher's character or, more important, on the philosopher's body of work as if either were generated and developed in a vacuum. Rand herself often paid close attention to context and history in the analysis of philosophical and cultural trends. And yet she paints an oddly flat portrait of her own being. By concentrating on her ideas to the exclusion of her developmental psychology, social interactions, and experiences, she achieves a one-sidedness that is in stark contrast to the richness and complexity of her own mode of analysis.

What Rand wished to emphasize was that *ideas mattered.* She never would have discounted completely the influence of social relationships on a person's thinking. Nor was she apt to create a dichotomy between a person's thought and emotions. But at times, she did exhibit a problematic tendency to view ideas as the sole means for understanding human behavior or for judging an individual's moral worth. In her novels, characters often serve as embodiments of ideas; they are one-sided expressions of specific philosophic principles. In her theory of history, this tendency to emphasize the importance of ideas could translate into a crude form of philosophical determinism.

But within the present context, I cannot accept Rand's self-evaluation. Her ideas cannot be fully understood without an appreciation of their historical context. That context includes some of her most important life experiences. Certainly Rand's ideas are not knee-jerk, emotional responses to personal trauma. But an assessment of her philosophy and her place in intellectual history cannot be complete without a *contextual* and *developmental* foundation. Rand would be the first to admit that "the content of a person's brain" derives from experiential, objective reality.[2] One can no more divorce experience from thought than one can separate body and mind. The two are inseparably linked. Emphasizing Rand's ideas to the exclusion of her life experiences or, alternatively, Rand's private life to the exclusion of her ideas, leads to a predictably distorted view of her historical significance.

Here I attempt to fill some of the major gaps in our knowledge of Rand's formative years of development, perhaps to discover an experiential link between Objectivist philosophy and its Russian antecedents. There is not much information available on Rand's education in Russia. I have been obliged to combine significant factual evidence with a certain degree of reasonable speculation.

The Early Years

In an early biographical essay, Barbara Branden portrays Ayn Rand the child exhibiting a desire to integrate facts and values. Echoing the yearning for synthesis ever-present in the Russian psyche, the young Alissa Rosenbaum learned to reject "any such inner dichotomy."[3] Though Branden's characterization was garnered from her subject's mature self-reflections, it is clear that the integration of traditional polarities was the leitmotif of Rand's lifelong philosophical project. Rand argued that she had always held the same basic philosophic convictions from the time of childhood, and that it was only her applications and knowledge which expanded over time.[4]

But as the young Alissa Rosenbaum, she *learned* to think with a rigorous methodology. She mastered the art of tracing philosophic interconnections. And she achieved these intellectual feats within the context of her growing passion for literary writing.

From her earliest school days in St. Petersburg, Alissa fell in love with arithmetic.[5] Her intelligence was manifested initially as she began to master the logic and precision of the mathematical sciences. However, she despised the rote learning and drill techniques of her early teachers. She read her textbooks, staying ahead of her lessons, never needing to invest great effort in the comprehension of any discipline.[6] In later years, Rand (1979bT) recalled that she would sit in the back row of the class and write short stories when she was bored with the subject matter. Disappointed with the tragic plots of Russian children's books, Rand was writing screenplays from age eight and adventure novels from age ten.

With the first shots of World War I, Alissa's universe was transformed dramatically. By 1916, under the mounting pressures of war, Petrograd was disintegrating. Starvation, inflation, labor strikes, crime, and czarist tyranny would bring forth the Russian Revolution. In February–March of 1917, Petrograd workers precipitated mass food riots.[7] Czarist troops mutinied rather than fire on their comrades. In retaliation the czar dissolved the Duma. But it was too late. In Petrograd two authorities were vying for political legitimacy: a Duma committee of liberal constitutionalists, and a Soviet of Workers' and Soldiers' Deputies. Under pressure from the Petrograd Soviet, the Duma committee established a provisional government headed by Prince Lvov. Alexander Kerensky, a moderate social revolutionary, was granted admittance to the government. Within three days, Czar Nicholas had abdicated (Palmer and Colton 1971, 781–92).

Alissa was dazzled by this popular revolt against the czar, and she was initially impressed by Kerensky's republican impulses, but she rarely articulated her political attitudes in front of her family. Zinovy, Alissa's father, a nonobservant Jew, tried to shelter his three daughters from the growing disorder; he strongly discouraged the discussion of politics at home. Only after the Revolution could no longer be ignored did he share his views with his family. It was only then that Alissa realized that her faith in the dignity of the individual reflected his own intense belief in the struggle for human freedom.[8] In her father Alissa had found a spiritual ally.

The Stoiunin Gymnasium

It was during this time that Alissa began more advanced gymnasium studies. There are no records of exactly where she undertook these studies,[9] but the circumstantial evidence suggests that in the academic year 1916–17, and quite possibly in 1915–16 and 1917–18 as well, she was enrolled in the gymnasium of Maria Nikolaievna Stoiunina.

According to Nicholas Lossky (12 February 1992C) this famous gymnasium for girls and young ladies was founded by Maria Stoiunina and her husband, Vladimir Stoiunin, for the distinctive purpose of furthering their "very much *avant-garde* ideas in the field of education for women." As a secondary or middle school, the Stoiunin Gymnasium aimed to prepare female students for university instruction. It accepted girls from ages ten and eleven and brought them through a college preparatory program by age seventeen. Alissa, aged ten, could have entered the Stoiunin Gymnasium as early as the fall semester of 1915–16. One interesting piece of evidence to confirm her presence in this gymnasium emerges from her adult recollections. Barbara Branden, quoting from an interview with Rand, writes:

> Alice did make one girlfriend, also a classmate, shortly after the February revolution [February 1917]. The girl was a sister of Vladimir Nabokov; her father was a cabinet minister in the Kerensky government. "She was very interested in politics, as was I, and this brought us together. It was a friendship based on conscious common interest." . . . The two girls discussed their ideas on the revolution— the Nabokov girl defended constitutional monarchy, but Alice believed in a republic, in the rule of law. They exchanged political pamphlets which were sold on the streets of Petrograd but which

were forbidden by their parents: they read the pamphlets secretly, and discussed them. The friendship lasted only a short time. The girl's father, realizing that conditions were getting worse and that it was dangerous to remain, left Russia with his family at the end of the year. Alice never saw her friend again.[10]

Presently in her eighties, Helene Vladimirovna Sikorski, sister of Vladimir Nabokov, confirms that both she and her sister, Olga, were enrolled in the Stoiunin Gymnasium during the period in question.[11] Olga Vladimirovna was born in January 1903 and Helene Vladimirovna in March 1906.[12] In 1915–16, Olga began studying at the Stoiunin school in the second class (for children aged twelve and thirteen). Helene began school the following year. Both of these sisters were in attendance at the Stoiunin Gymnasium in 1916–17. Although Rand was correct to note that the Nabokovs left Petrograd near the end of 1917, she was mistaken in thinking that they left Russia at this time. In fact, the Nabokovs left Petrograd in mid-November 1917, and Russia only in April of 1919.

Helene does not remember Alissa Rosenbaum, but she confirms that her sister Olga was deeply interested in politics at the time, favoring constitutional monarchy because she was influenced by her father's opinions. Born in 1905, Alissa was a contemporary of both Nabokov sisters. In February of 1917, Olga was fourteen, Alissa was twelve. Though there was a two-year difference between Olga Nabokov and Alissa Rosenbaum, it is still quite possible that the young girls were indeed classmates. In 1921, Alissa entered college when she was sixteen, at least a year ahead of others in her class. This suggests that she was more advanced than other girls her age. At the Stoiunin Gymnasium, the school year lasted from mid-September to late May. Olga and Alissa were probably in the same class for at least three months in the spring semester and two months in the fall 1917 semester.[13]

In later years, Rand never mentioned the name of the gymnasium in which she was enrolled. But some of her most vivid scholastic memories were of the academic year, 1917–18. She remembered that one teacher influenced her in classical language when she was twelve or thirteen years old. Alissa read Pushkin's *Eugene Onegin: A Novel in Verse* and wrote a paper on the book's characters. The teacher gave her a lesson in literary causality, teaching her to judge characters by specific incidents or actions.[14]

Also in these years, Alissa began to formulate a conscious philosophy by "thinking in principles." She questioned every idea she held. She attempted "to name her path, to grasp it, to conceptualize it, and, most important, to put it under her conscious control" (B. Branden 1986, 22). Alissa began to keep a personal journal and philosophical diary as she entered a period of self-critical, "wonderfully intense intellectual excitement" (ibid.).

While in school, Alissa studied the works of Turgenev, Chekhov, Tolstoy, and many of the classic Russian poets. She did not care much for Russian literature. Alissa's mother, Anna Rosenbaum, who was a language teacher in several Petrograd high schools,[15] introduced her daughter to the works of the great French Romantic, Victor Hugo. Hugo's heroic visions profoundly inspired Alissa. She credited Hugo as being the single greatest literary influence on her work (B. Branden 1986, 24).

All of these significant intellectual events took place in Alissa Rosenbaum's world of 1917–18, the very period in which she probably can be placed at the Stoiunin Gymnasium, with its rich, college-preparatory program. Alissa's presence in this school has some importance. Maria Nikolaievna Stoiunina and Vladimir Stoiunin, the founders of the famous gymnasium, were the parents of N. O. Lossky's wife. As his in-laws, they invited Lossky to teach at the gymnasium. He taught both logic and psychology to select classes of young women from 1898 through 1922. Usually, Lossky gave instructions to the graduating class, those who were at least seventeen, but it is not impossible that Alissa could have learned of the great Lossky while at the Stoiunin Gymnasium. It is not impossible that she could have enrolled in one of his college preparatory courses. It is certainly possible that in her typically disciplined manner, Alissa was charting a future educational direction which would include further study with the distinguished Lossky at Petrograd University.

The Crimean Gymnasium

Unfortunately, however, Alissa was living during a time when goals were not easily realized. In the aftermath of the October revolution, the Rosenbaum family was terrorized by the Bolsheviks. Zinovy's pharmacy was nationalized, and his family's situation grew worse by the day. Their savings dwindled. They had little to eat. The political climate in Petrograd was grave. With no end to food and fuel shortages, street violence, and sabotage, the Rosenbaum family, like the Nabokov family before them, fled to the Crimea.

Alissa continued her studies in the fall of 1918, while in the Crimea.

Crimean schools were still beyond the ideological control of the Bolsheviks. Many of the instructors in Alissa's gymnasium were "old-fashioned, pro-Czarist ladies," who kept teaching despite the rise of communism (B. Branden 1986, 32). By this time, Alissa was expanding upon her own learning methods. Those principles, which seemed self-evident to her, were subjected to a more rigorous process of understanding and analysis. Barbara Branden writes that despite Alissa's "remarkable memory, memory never was the tool she employed for learning" (ibid.). She was taught to use both inductive and deductive methods of analysis.

Following the pedagogical impulses of her mother Anna, Alissa tutored her classmates in geometry. Her mathematics teacher hoped she would become a professional mathematician. Though Alissa broadened her study of mathematics and logic, she knew that the study of pure method would not be sufficient. Always suspicious of the purely abstract, she exhibited a continuing desire to merge the theoretical and the practical, the technical and the artistic. She sought out the classics of foreign literature, works by Rostand, Hugo, and Sienkiewicz. She even enrolled in American history classes, an odd elective for a Russian. It was during this same period that Alissa became an atheist. Much like the victorious Bolsheviks, Alissa saw the concept of God as rationally unprovable and deeply degrading.[16] But unlike the Russian Marxists, Alissa rejected both the God of Christianity and the equally mystical, collectivist, God-state of the Communists.

In the spring of 1921, as the Red Army solidified control of the Crimea, Alissa graduated from high school. In dire financial straits, Alissa and her mother Anna began teaching illiterate Red Army soldiers to read and write (B. Branden 1986, 38).

As material conditions grew worse in the Crimea, Zinovy decided to return to Petrograd with his family. It was a fateful decision, for instead of seeking exile from Russia, the Rosenbaums returned to a city firmly under Red control. Although Alissa would eventually emigrate to the United States, her mother and father would later be denied permission to leave the Soviet Union and would die during the siege of Leningrad (125, 375).

A Revolution in Education

Petrograd was a city that Alissa had loved. As she later wrote in *We the Living*:[17] "It was St. Petersburg; the war made it Petrograd; the revolution made it Leningrad" (226). In her first novel, Rand wrote of Petrograd as a tribute to human achievement, even as she hinted at an underlying tragedy:

> Cities grow like forests, like weeds. Petrograd did not grow. It was born finished and complete. Petrograd is not acquainted with nature. It was the work of man. . . . Petrograd's grandeur is unmarred, its squalor unrelieved. Its facets are cut clearly, sharply; they are deliberate, perfect with the straight-forward perfection of man's work. . . . Petrograd did not rise. It came to be at the height. It was commanded to command. It was a capital before its first stone was laid. It was a monument to the spirit of man. (229)

But Petrograd had changed, and its revolutionary transformation was no less visible in the area of university instruction. The Red government introduced sweeping educational reforms that reflected the changes that had taken place in the character of society.

In the days immediately following the Revolution, freedom of expression in the arts lasted for a while. Lenin was even prepared to allow the dissemination of works with which he disagreed. By 1918, a group of writers, poets, and artists had formed the *Proletkult* (Proletarian Cultural Movement) to encourage workers to develop a distinctively "proletarian culture."

These agencies sought to attract people of pure proletarian class origins. In the beginning, they operated three hundred literary workshops with an enrollment of 84,000. At its peak in 1921, membership reached 500,000. But by 1922, following Lenin's denunciations, the number of agencies had dwindled.[18] The organization was effectively disbanded in 1923, its functions gradually absorbed by the trade unions and the "Commissariat of Enlightenment."[19]

Lenin himself was rather suspicious of the *Proletkult* for two major reasons: First, it was a non-Party organ. Second, it advocated the creation of a new "pure" proletarian culture by suppressing every last remnant of traditional aristocratic and bourgeois culture. Lenin believed that such an ahistorical state-of-nature would be illusory; the *Proletkult* did not recognize the new society's need to appropriate significant aspects of the existing culture.[20] Though many bourgeois cultural trends were renounced as counterrevolutionary, it was clear that the new regime could not survive without absorbing some of the very values and institutions it abhorred. In the universities, this meant that many of the "old guard" or "bourgeois specialists" had to be employed during the transition to socialism—as long as they remained politically neutral (Fitzpatrick 1979, 3).

Though the Bolsheviks closed the ecclesiastical schools in 1917–18 (Zernov 1963, 206), many of the remaining religious and Idealist professors retained their university positions. A number of thinkers of the religious renaissance, such as Berdyaev and Bely, continued to deliver public lectures on theology, philosophy, and ethics (McClelland 1989, 261). Gradually, the regime began to establish its own network of ideological agencies. Philosophy was subordinated to social science. A national Philosophical Institute was created in the Academy of Sciences, on a level with the Marx-Engels-Lenin Institute of the Central Government, and under the supervision of the state authorities.

The Bolsheviks also began to formulate new principles of educational and arts policy set forth by Narkompros, the Commissariat of Enlightenment. Narkompros was headed by Anatoly V. Lunacharsky between 1917 and 1929. During the early years, distinct schools of thought united by their progressive and Marxist orientation, coexisted within Narkompros. The most progressive of these schools was the Petrograders. These anti-authoritarian educators advocated so-called activity methods of teaching, which included pupil-participation and informal student-teacher relationships within a less traditional, nonscholastic curriculum. Many hoped to integrate a Marxist emphasis on the polytechnical school (Fitzpatrick 1970, 29). The Petrograd educators were influenced heavily by Deweyite progressivism (30). But despite their best efforts, many academic institutions were not willing to cooperate with Narkompros. They wished to function with full autonomy, having struggled to attain such independence for many years in their opposition to czarist control. Narkompros asserted that it would defend the independence of scholarship, but in practice it aimed to limit the influence of professors who were anti-Bolshevik and non-Marxist (68). Apparently, in defending "Enlightenment," "autonomy," and "progressive education," the Commissariat had become adept at using euphemisms to conceal its growing domination of intellectual life.

In actuality, the regime viewed academic freedom as a "bourgeois prejudice" (Sorokin [1924] 1950, 246–47). Private publishing houses were closing, hurt primarily by paper shortages. Initially, Petrograd seemed to escape the more severe censorship measures being implemented in Moscow. Despite its intention to preserve the utility of the "old guard," while promoting the values of the new, the regime began to destroy a whole generation of intellectuals.

With the coming of the New Economic Policy (NEP) in 1921, the state simultaneously acted to check any revival of "bourgeois" values. The sovietization of Russian intellectual life meant greater administrative control over the universities through Narkompros, the trade unions, and the Communist Party organs (McClelland 1989, 261). During the early 1920s, however, academic institutions "underwent a period of wild experimentation and extreme anarchy." Many of the older professors could not adapt to progressive methods; many of the newer professors lacked academic expertise. Indeed, the effects were disastrous for both instructors and pupils.[21]

In a far-reaching reorganization of university structure, Narkompros united the existing schools of history, philology, and law under a social science college, or *fakul'tet obshchestvennykh nauk*, within each university (Fitzpatrick 1979, 68). The new social science program aimed to introduce concepts of Marxist methodology and scientific socialism. Though the non-Marxist professors resented these innovations, they were not required to demonstrate proficiency in Marxist studies. In fact, many of them continued to teach courses that had a subtle anti-Soviet bias. A continued shortage of Marxist teachers led the Central Committee to abolish many of the social science colleges that had been established, though Petrograd University was unaffected by this policy change (69–71).

The Narkompros policy innovations fundamentally altered the organization of the university. The original university structure contained three major colleges (Kline, 20 October 1992C):

1. The *istoriko-filologicheskii fakul'tet*, or College of History and Philology, broadly defined to include philosophy.
2. The *fiziko-matematicheskii fakul'tet*, or College of Mathematics and Physics, which included geology, chemistry, and other hard sciences.
3. The *iuridicheskii fakul'tet*, or law school.

The new university structure placed the College of History and Philology under the social science banner. A leftist academician, N. Ya. Marr, brought to the newly organized social science college a greater emphasis on ethnology and linguistics studies. Archaeology and anthropology were also included. The law school was officially dissolved since it lacked Marxist professors. It continued to function unofficially, under the title of "former law department," until its reestablishment in the autumn of 1926. Later, the economics department was absorbed by the Leningrad Polytechnical

Institute, and the social-pedagogical department was made part of the Herzen Pedagogical Institute (Fitzpatrick 1979, 72–73).

Within the social science colleges, the regime did not require the teaching of atheism, but instruction did have to be nonreligious. Marxist studies and politically correct textbooks were hastily introduced in the early 1920s. There was an emphasis within these Marxist courses on political economy and historical materialism. Students in the engineering schools and universities were required to spend four hours per week on these subjects.[22] Petrograd University did not establish an official course on Party history and Leninism until the mid-1920s, when it was renamed Leningrad University.

There were other innovations. Lunacharsky required that students of proletarian descent graduate without examination. Special classes were organized for their instruction, but many of these pupils were ridiculed by established academics as "zero students" (Sorokin [1924] 1950, 226–27). The Soviets also lifted admission restrictions on women and Jews as early as 1918, and abolished tuition, all in an effort to democratize the student body.[23] There was less emphasis on scheduled classes, periodic examinations, homework, and discipline. Without preparation or proper orientation to new pedagogical techniques, teachers were encouraged to adopt the "laboratory" and "project" methods (Shteppa 1962, 29). The chaotic results were predictable. In any event, most changes in academic policy were somewhat beside the point; the cataclysmic conditions throughout Petrograd had dramatically affected the quality of university life. As James McClelland (1989) writes:

> The period from the fall of 1918 to the spring of 1921 was one of terrible material deprivation in central Russia and chaos, bloodshed, and fighting on the periphery. Universities and institutes remained open, but despite an initial flood on students taking advantage of the new open admissions policy, the number of those actively attending lectures soon dwindled to an abnormally low level. Some professors remained at their posts throughout the period, while many others fled, either in search of warmth and food or out of political sympathy for the Whites. (258)

There was one final innovation introduced into Petrograd University. Effective at the beginning of the academic year 1920–21, the length of a university education was reduced from five years to three.

As a young woman of sixteen, Alissa Rosenbaum took advantage of the new educational reforms. She did not have to face the institutional bias against women and Jews. She entered the university on 2 October 1921, in the three-year course of the *obshchestvenno-pedagogicheskoe otdelenie*, the Department of Social Pedagogy, which contained the historical and philosophical disciplines and was designed presumably to prepare students for careers as teachers of the social sciences.[24]

Nearly three years later, in May 1924, and two months prior to her graduation, the student purges began. The authorities began ruthlessly to expel and exile those students who could not prove their proletarian class background. A regime that had ostensibly dedicated itself to the democratization of education was now creating new distinctions and privileges. But the purge commission decided to pass over those students who were on the verge of graduating. Had the traditional five-year program still been in effect, Alissa would not have been a graduating senior, and as the daughter of a "petit-bourgeois" pharmacist, she would have been expelled, or worse. She later remarked that it was "sheer accident that I escaped that purge."[25]

Majoring in History

Alissa was disgusted by the "mystical chaos" of Russian academic philosophy. She was uninterested in the study of Russian literature. She decided to major in history.[26] She later wrote that her systematic study of history in college was crucial "in order to have a factual knowledge of men's past." She minored in philosophy, "in order to achieve an objective definition of my values." Ultimately, Alissa discovered that she could learn history, but that philosophy "had to be done by me."[27]

University life in those years was primitive. The school lacked heat and light. Reports of death by starvation, disease, and suicide proliferated. Students and professors met for lectures and discussions in cold classrooms, dormitories, and auditoriums illuminated by flickering candles (McClelland 1989, 260–61). For a period, some lectures were scheduled in the evening because professors were engaged in compulsory manual labor during the day, and students were struggling to earn a living (Sorokin [1924] 1950, 223).

Alissa's university had become an intellectual battleground between the "old guard" and their Soviet antagonists. The social science college was, by far, the most conflict-ridden of the newly established schools. Older professors were the targets of growing academic repression (Fitzpatrick 1979, 68). The Party had allowed many of these professors to continue with their "bourgeois-objectivist" scholarship, but this period of coexistence between these groups ended once and for all in 1928–29, when many established scholars were purged from the Academy of Science for attempting to block the election of communist scholars. Many historians were arrested, exiled, or executed.[28]

In the early 1920s, the study of history was slowly supplemented by courses designed to increase *politgramota* or political literacy. Social science curriculums in the pedagogical institutes were modified to include new Marxist subjects and requirements. Hence, many of the history courses Alissa took initially were probably condensed to include themes in political economy, dialectical method, and historical materialism (Shteppa 1962, 29, 36). Among these courses were specific "Soviet subjects." Rand recollected in 1971 that the ideological conditioning prevalent in U.S. educational institutions was mild in comparison to the ideological bludgeoning she had experienced (Rand 1971T). She proudly proclaimed that though there were only a very few good professors still actually teaching during this period, she remained stalwart and unaffected by the propaganda to which she was subjected (Rand 1974aT).

In *We the Living*, Kira, Rand's fictional alter ego, is compelled to take Marxist lectures and courses not unlike those Rand herself had probably attended. These included courses on the history of communist philosophy and the doctrine of historical materialism. Rand lists lectures with titles such as "Marxism," "Proletarian Women and Illiteracy," "The Spirit of the Collective," "Proletarian Electrification," "The Doom of Capitalism," "The Red Peasant," "The ABC of Communism," "Comrade Lenin and Comrade Marx," and "Marxism and Collectivism," and Komsomol discussions on the problems with the New Economic Policy (134). The endless attacks on individualism that Alissa Rosenbaum heard in lectures of this type led her to formulate a futuristic vision in which the word "I" is lost to a collectivistic world. This was the basis of her poetic novelette, *Anthem*, written in 1937.[29]

The predominance of propaganda in many of her courses did not make a high-quality education impossible. In retrospect, Rand recognized that it was under the Soviet educational system that she developed her method of "thinking in principles." She stated that she "learned in reverse." The system generated within her a deeply critical outlook which she carried into her adulthood. She grasped: "No matter what you are taught, listen to it critically, whether you agree or not. And if you disagree, formulate your reasons. . . . Under the Soviets . . . I learned a great deal, but only in that way."[30]

Though Marxism had been a serious presence in her history and social science courses, it did not have a monopoly on the curriculum during this period. Most of the historians in the department were non-Marxist scholars who taught from texts that featured diverse historical methodologies.[31] Yet between 1919 and 1925, general approaches to ancient, medieval, and modern history were underemphasized, and studies of "socioeconomic formations" became more prominent. Marxist historiography in the study of antiquity was evident in such works as A. I. Tiumenev's *Essays on the Socioeconomic History of Ancient Greece*, published in three volumes between 1920 and 1923. Tiumenev's books greatly influenced academic scholarship and university teaching during this period. In 1923, Tiumenev also authored *Did Capitalism Exist in Ancient Greece?* In that same year, V. S. Sergeev's *History of Rome* appeared.

By contrast, several major works in medieval and early modern history were used that had a distinctly "bourgeois" orientation. Included in the history curriculum were such books as P. Vinogradov's *Book of Readings on the History of the Middle Ages*, D. N. Egorov's anthology *The Middle Ages through Their Monuments*, and D. M. Petrushevsky's *Essays on Medieval Society and State* and *Essays on the Economic and Social History of Medieval Europe*. The Soviets criticized Petrushevsky's works for having little relation to established Marxist doctrine. In time, the curriculum was supplemented by texts that were much closer to the new spirit of Marxist historiography, including works by N. M. Pakul and I. I. Semenov on the Dutch and English revolutions (Shteppa 1962, 36–38).

General Russian history was taught with the assistance of S. I. Kovalev's *General History Course*. However, the most important textbook in this period was written by M. N. Pokrovsky. Pokrovsky, in league with Lunacharsky and Krupskaya, formed part of the Bolshevik triumvirate in charge of Narkompros, between 1918 and 1929.[32] His *Russian History in Briefest Outline* (*Russkaia istoriia v samom szhatom ocherke*), published in 1923, was a very popular text that earned Lenin's praise. Pokrovsky's history was profoundly Marxist in its orientation, containing much important material.

Thus, although Alissa was probably exposed to a variety of historical perspectives, her course of study was moving gradually in the direction of Marxist historiography. Even if she had rejected the materialist bias of the

Marxist texts, she was learning typically dialectical modes of historical inquiry, which emphasized the interconnections between economic, political, social, and intellectual factors. However, as the scholarly atmosphere was chilled by Soviet repression, it is quite probable that most of Alissa's teachers in the last year of her university education were at least *pro forma* Marxists, if not dogmatic Marxist-Leninists (Kline, 28 February 1992C).

Still, during the early Soviet period most of Petrograd's historians were non-Marxist in their political orientation. Unfortunately, an exhaustive search of the Leningrad archives by the university archivists, N. T. Dering and L. V. Guseva, did not uncover any specific information on Alissa Rosenbaum's coursework, grades, or teachers.[33] Yet it is clear that Alissa would have encountered a history department dominated by some of the finest Russian scholars of the twentieth century.[34] Among them were:

- L. S. Berg, the author of *Theories of Evolution*. Berg's quasi-teleological approach emphasized that evolutionary changes had definite direction.
- Nikolai Ivanovich Kareev, who taught courses on the French Revolution, and authored a number of theoretical works attacking Marxism. Though Lenin had criticized him sharply, he was not dismissed in the early Soviet period.
- E. V. Tarle, who taught a Marxist historiography and surpassed even Kareev in importance in Petrograd's history department.
- Sergei Fyodorovich Platonov, who specialized in sixteenth- and seventeenth-century Russian history and taught at Petrograd through 1925. Platonov offered a conservative-monarchist historical interpretation.[35]

Pitirim Sorokin, who received his doctorate from Petrograd University in 1922, also taught in the College of Social Sciences and in the Sociological Institute as a sociologist-historian. In later years, as a renowned Harvard sociologist, Sorokin spearheaded "creative altruism" as a means of conquering the human "predatory instincts" he had witnessed in the Soviet Union. Perhaps remembering him from Petrograd, Rand later derided Sorokin as "a thoroughly Russian mystic-altruist."[36]

The Petrograd history department was also graced by the presence of the renowned Ivan Mikhailovitch Grevs. Grevs was a specialist in medieval European history. He taught on the fathers of the Latin Church and the medieval humanists (including Dante and Petrarch). Grevs pioneered the seminar system and field trips in Russian higher education. He was a leading advocate for higher education for women.

Perhaps the most important historian in the department at this time was L. P. Karsavin, who was a student of Grevs (Zenkovsky 1953, 843). Until 1922, Karsavin was the chair of the department. As a history major, Alissa would have met with Karsavin in some formal or informal capacity, either as his student, or in search of course-selection advice and general curriculum guidance.[37] Karsavin was well known in Petrograd intellectual circles. Along with Platonov, Tarle, and Grevs, Karsavin gave regular talks in public forums, such as the Petrograd House of Scholars, the House of Literary Men, and the Theological Institute. He also participated in the workers' council of faculty members as a representative from the university, lecturing at gatherings of Red Army soldiers and workers' clubs (Shteppa 1962, 24–28). Like his colleague, N. O. Lossky, Karsavin advocated a philosophy of history that was conjoined to a general Christian worldview (Copleston 1988, 56). As a historian of the Church, he specialized in the theology and mysticism of the Middle Ages. He was a speculative and religious thinker in the tradition of Solovyov. He built his system on a religious metaphysic (Lossky 1951, 299). Karsavin applied the doctrine of the coincidence of opposites to the issue of the Trinity. Like Hegel, he saw historical development as holistic and organismic, an immanent process of becoming. As Lossky explains, in Karsavin's system,

> The development of the subject is the transition from one of its aspects to another, conditioned by the dialectical nature of the subject himself and not by impacts from without. Karsavin rejects external relations in the domain of historical being. Every historical individual (a person, a family, a nation, etc.) is in his view the world-whole itself in some one of its unique and unrepeatable aspects; thus, the domain of historical being consists of subjects that interpenetrate one another and nevertheless develop freely, since each of them contains everything in an embryonic form, and there are no external relations before them. (307)

Karsavin and many of the other distinguished historians who taught at Petrograd perpetuated the Russian yearning for synthesis. Whether she was reading her Marxist texts or attending the lectures of her non-Marxist professors, Alissa Rosenbaum was fully exposed to the dialectical methods distinctive to Russian thought and scholarship.

Minoring in Philosophy

In addition to her studies in history, Alissa enrolled in several philosophy and literature courses surveying the works of Schiller, Shakespeare, and Dostoyevsky. She would recollect for Barbara Branden (1986) a special admiration for Dostoyevsky's brilliant literary technique: "For a long time, I studied his plots carefully, to see how he integrated his plots to his ideas. I identified, in his work, what kind of events express what kind of theme, and why. He was very valuable for my subconscious integration concerning plot and theme" (45).

As if sensing a natural spiritual affinity between Dostoyevsky and Nietzsche, Alissa moved on to the works of the famous German philosopher. She had first discovered Nietzsche's *Thus Spake Zarathustra* upon the advice of an older cousin. She was captivated by its exaltation of the heroic, its defense of the individual, and its dismissal of altruism as slave morality.[38] But as she read further, Alissa was troubled by Nietzsche's defense of psychological determinism. In her reading of *The Birth of Tragedy*, Alissa discovered that Nietzsche had embraced Dionysian, drunken, orgiastic emotionalism over Apollonian reason (B. Branden 1986, 45).

Certainly, this interpretation of Nietzsche was widespread throughout the Silver Age of Russian philosophy. The Symbolists, among others, celebrated Nietzsche precisely because he exalted a Dionysian cultic loss of self. Alissa would have been exposed to this particular Nietzschean theme in the work of Aleksandr Blok, one of her favorite poets. But she could have also incorporated such interpretations of Nietzsche from the lectures of Faddei Frantsevitch Zielinsky, another social science teacher at Petrograd University and one of the greatest classical scholars of the twentieth century.

Zielinsky taught at the university from 1885 through 1921. Alissa may not have entered the university in time to register in one of his courses, but he had had a huge impact on many other Russian scholars and poets of his generation. Editor of the journal *Vestnik vsemirnoi istorii* (Herald of universal history), Zielinsky was a specialist on ancient Greece. He translated the works of Herodotus and Thucydides into Russian and wrote on Greek and Roman mythology.

Zielinsky viewed Nietzsche's philosophy as "the last major contribution of antiquity to contemporary thought."[39] He believed that the resurgence of the Dionysian impulse was a necessary requirement to curb the "highly moralistic influence of Judaism in Christianity."[40] His celebration of the Dionysian was consistent with the views of other Silver Age thinkers who were integrating the works of Nietzsche with a mystical Christian worldview.

Alissa was probably among the last students at the university to study Nietzsche's philosophy formally. Lenin's wife, Nadezhda Krupskaya, began a campaign to remove ideologically dangerous books from the People's Libraries. Nietzsche's works were foremost among the banned materials. They were removed from libraries in factories, trade union halls, and universities, and were placed on closed reserve in major research centers along with other "counterrevolutionary" tracts (Rosenthal and Bohachevsky-Chomiak 1990, xiii). In 1923–24, some of Nietzsche's books were burned by the authorities.[41] Apparently, where the Symbolists had recognized a cultic collectivism in Nietzsche's work, the Soviet regime could see only a preoccupation with the heroic, creative, and the solitary.[42]

Alissa's exposure to formal philosophy was probably limited to a few university courses. But included in nearly every history course she took, there was a significant dose of "intellectual" history. As a philosophy minor, she would have been required to take several courses offered by philosophy department faculty.[43]

Petrograd's philosophy department was dominated by neo-Kantians, including Ivan Ivanovich Lapshin, Sergei Alexeevitch Alexeev (who wrote under the name Askoldov), and Aleksandr Ivanovich Vvedensky (B. Lossky 1991, 74–77, 89, 158 n. 116). Lapshin rejected metaphysical speculation, whereas Alexeev criticized the doctrine of dialectical materialism. These two thinkers were greatly influenced by their mentor, Aleksandr Vvedensky. An elderly master who survived the deportations and the purges, Vvedensky taught from 1890 to 1925. He was a genuine Kantian, offering courses in logic, psychology, and the history of philosophy. As an exceptionally gifted teacher, Vvedensky touched the lives of many thousands of students who attended his lectures and were inspired by his ideas (Lossky 1951, 164). Among his students was N. O. Lossky. Vvedensky advocated a deontological morality, faith in God, the immortality of the soul, and the necessity of free will.

Yet it does not seem that Alissa had any extensive exposure to the teachings of Kantian philosophers at Petrograd University. Rand never mentioned Kantian philosophy as a subject she studied extensively in college, though she probably had light exposure to Kant's ideas.[44] Despite the presence of all of these world-renowned historians, philosophers, and scholars, Rand never publicly acknowledged the names of any of her teachers—except one. This is not atypical of Rand; in fact, in keeping with her own visions of self-creation, she concedes only a limited literary and philosophical debt to Hugo, Dostoyevsky, and Aristotle.[45] The one teacher whose name she mentioned in any context, was Nicholas Onufrievich Lossky.

Lossky and Rand

Any investigation of the links between Lossky and Rand is fraught with problems. It is almost impossible to establish with certainty the exact circumstances of their relationship. None of Rand's early journal writings survived her Russian years. Rand burned her philosophic diaries and fictional outlines long before she came to the United States. She knew that if discovered, such writings would implicate her as an anticommunist (B. Branden 1986, 38). Very little of Rand's American journals have been made public, and none of the published entries date prior to 1934. In any event, it is unlikely that the unpublished diaries of Rand would include extensive comments, if any, on Lossky.

The first mention of Lossky occurs in a single paragraph of Barbara Branden's biographical essay, "Who is Ayn Rand?" This personal recollection is drawn from over forty hours of interviews that Branden conducted with Rand.[46] Lossky is the only one of her professors whom Rand mentioned in these interviews. Branden nearly duplicates this Lossky reference from her early essay, in her best-selling, book-length biography, *The Passion of Ayn Rand*. Because of its historical importance, I quote this passage at length:

> Despite her doubts about the value of formal philosophy, she chose as an elective a course on the history of ancient philosophy. The course was taught by Professor N. O. Losky [sic], a distinguished international authority on Plato. To her surprise, the course turned out to be her favorite. She was profoundly impressed by Aristotle's definition of the laws of logic, and rejected completely, "the mysticism, and collectivism" of Plato. . . . Professor Losky [sic] was a

stern, exacting man, contemptuous of all students, particularly of women. It was said that he failed most students the first time they took his examination, and that he was especially hard on women. In the spring, his students went to his home for their oral examination; a long line of them stood outside his study, nervously awaiting their turn. Alice had hoped that she would be questioned on Aristotle. But when she entered his study, he questioned her only about Plato. She had studied carefully, and she answered easily and precisely. After a while, although she had not stated any estimate, Professor Losky [sic] said sardonically: "You don't agree with Plato, do you?" "No, I don't," she answered. "Tell me why," he demanded. She replied, "My philosophical views are not part of the history of philosophy yet. But they will be." "Give me your examination book," he ordered. He wrote in the book and handed it back to her. "Next student," he said. He had written: Perfect.[47]

There are only three subtle differences between this passage and the one that appears in "Who is Ayn Rand?" In the earlier biographical essay, Branden tells us that Lossky gave Alissa a "Perfect" grade, out of three possibilities: Perfect, Passing, or Failure. She adds that Lossky believed that female students "had no business in philosophy." She also spells Lossky's name correctly.[48] None of these distinctions alters the essential intellectual chutzpa that Rand exhibited in her final examination session with the famed professor.

The authenticity of Rand's reminiscences has been challenged in some respects by at least four scholars, three of whom are relatives of Lossky. Boris and Andrew, Lossky's surviving sons, and Nicholas, his grandson, have all objected to the characterization of N. O. Lossky as contemptuous of female philosophy students. They point out that their family has had a history of strong women, including Maria Stoiunina, who established the famous gymnasium for girls and young ladies, attended by Alissa Rosenbaum, and in which Lossky actually taught. One of Lossky's female students during the Russian period of his life, Natalie Duddington, became a lifelong friend and the English translator of his important works. Andrew recollects that his father demanded a basic competence in the subject matter of his courses from both men and women, making no distinctions between them. His examinations were forthright, neither tricky nor especially difficult. The distinguished philosopher George Kline was a regular auditor of two of Lossky's courses at St. Vladimir's Orthodox Theological Seminary. He too vouches for the professor's fairness and nonsexist attitudes. Kline enjoyed a friendly correspondence with Lossky and recalls that the professor "always treated his students with respect and kindness." Lossky's contempt was reserved only for dogmatic, simplistic, Marxist-Leninists who attacked speculative and idealist thought.[49]

As an expert in the history of Russian philosophy, Kline has also taken issue with the characterization of Lossky as a scholar of Plato. Lossky knew his Greek philosophy well and would have been more than qualified to teach a course on the ancients. But as a specialist in German philosophy from Kant to Husserl, N. O. Lossky published nearly three hundred works, and not one of them even mentions Plato in the title.

Some of the interpretive differences regarding Lossky's attitudes toward female philosophy students can be attributed to subjective factors. The evidence indicates that Lossky was not particularly unfair to his students. However, it is impossible to grasp the mental strain under which Lossky lived in the 1921–22 academic year. This may very well have affected his demeanor and otherwise affable personality. Certainly it cannot be discounted that to a sixteen-year-old student, any professor in a bad mood could be the source of great personal consternation. It is also quite possible that as a fiction writer, Rand has merely embellished the story by intensifying the conflict between its major characters.[50]

But there is a greater problem of historical authenticity that requires some elucidation.

In 1920–21, Lossky was at the top of his profession. He had already published a number of significant philosophical treatises, and continued to lecture at the university, and at the Stoiunin Gymnasium. He succeeded in earning a few extra black bread rations by teaching an "Introduction to Philosophy" course in the National University, a school of adult education, in the Shlissel'burg district of Petrograd.[51] He gave speeches on the subject of God in the system of organic philosophy to the Free Philosophical Association.

Lossky's courses at the university were in the grand intuitivist tradition of philosophy he spearheaded. In 1916, he taught on Fichte, Schelling, and Hegel and on Leibniz. In 1917, he offered classes on the theory of judgments, and an introduction to philosophy. In 1918–19, he lectured on the problems of free will, the problem of the trans-subjectivity of sensual qualities, logic, contemporary epistemology, and an introduction to metaphysics. In 1919–20, Lossky again offered his course on Fichte, Schelling, and Hegel, followed in 1920–21 by a seminar on materialism, hylozoism, and vitalism from an antimaterialist perspective.[52] None of his listed university courses dealt specifically with Plato, Aristotle, or the ancient philosophers.

More important, something happened in the summer of 1921 that would alter Lossky's life forever, ending his illustrious career at the university and ultimately leading to his exile from the Soviet Union. In Moscow, a meeting of the State Scientific Council was called to discuss the future of university professors. The regime was becoming increasingly suspicious of those non-Marxist professors and intellectuals who had continued to oppose the Revolution. M. N. Pokrovsky chaired the meeting. The Council removed many of Petrograd's privatdocents. Professor Lapshin was also barred from teaching. Only Aleksandr Vvedensky was allowed to remain.

When the Council addressed the issue of the celebrated Lossky's presence at the university, they were compelled to censure him for his defense of the Trinity. But it was brought to the attention of Pokrovsky that Lossky, to his credit, had once been expelled from the Vitebsk Gymnasium for his propagandistic views in favor of atheism and socialism. The Council decided to remove him from his Petrograd teaching position, but allow him to serve in the Institute of Scientific Research, an annex to the university. Consequently, in 1921, Lossky—officially—taught no university courses.

Pitirim Sorokin, another of the ousted professors, knew that the autonomy of the university was being destroyed. Elected deans were replaced by Communists, and a Red student was given a special commissary position over the rector of the university. He observes that the research the barred professors conducted at the Historical and Sociological Institutes, kept them away from teaching responsibilities "where they would not be harmful to students" ([1924] 1950, 247, 284). With many Petrograd positions vacated, students were subjected to the amateur scholarship of newly appointed Bolshevik professors. One such professor, Borichevsky, taught a course in logic which competed with Vvedensky's. Borichevsky's expertise was limited to Spinoza, Epicurus, and materialism. His embarrassing mistakes in the presentation of Plato's philosophy were the subject of the student's ridicule. Sorokin adds that those professors who were barred from teaching were also barred from organizing special alternative courses.

When Lossky learned of his dismissal from the university, he was devastated. Around the middle of August 1921, he came down with a gallstone illness. The doctors prescribed bed rest, and between September and December, Lossky spent most of his time in convalescence. Around the Christmas holidays, his health began to improve. Undeterred by threats from the Bolsheviks or heckling by Komsomoltsy in the audience, Lossky joined Sorokin, Grevs, Karsavin, and others in public forums that praised Christianity and the Kingdom of God.

But in January 1922, Lossky experienced a relapse in his illness. He lost weight, developed jaundice, and was on the verge of having gallbladder surgery. In March, on the day of the Annunciation of the Virgin Mary, Lossky went with his wife to donate some of their valuables to the Church. From the moment of their sacrifice, Lossky (1969) writes, his jaundice and his illness were cured (215–16).

The Bolshevik leadership was becoming more fearful of the continued strength exhibited by prerevolutionary scientists, writers, and other public figures. On 16 August 1922, Lossky was summoned to the offices of the Cheka. He thought it was in response to a passport inquiry he had made to travel to Czechoslovakia. Instead, he was arrested, along with other Petrograd scholars, including Lapshin and Karsavin. Under forced interrogation, Lossky was compelled to agree that he had been involved in counterrevolutionary activities that were punishable by death. Under Bolshevik reprieve, partly due to Trotsky's intervention, the sentenced intellectuals were released on the condition that they would leave the country at once. They could travel with small amounts of linen and clothing and were instructed to leave their books behind. By 15 November 1922, Lossky, his wife, three sons, and his mother-in-law, Maria Nikolaievna Stoiunina, boarded a German steamer. Stopping in Berlin, the Losskys applied for and received visas allowing them into Czechoslovakia on 13 December 1922.

So, the question is, How could Lossky have taught Rand if he was barred from teaching at the university, and if he was intermittently sick throughout the period, only to be exiled by the end of 1922? Could it be that the relationship between Lossky and Alissa Rosenbaum was a product of Rand's imagination?[53]

An assessment of all the available evidence in this perplexing case is not as damning to the integrity of Rand's recollections as might appear at first glance. There are two basic possibilities: (1) Rand mistook, hallucinated, or lied about her contact with the distinguished professor; or (2) Lossky may have taught a course connected to Petrograd University that was not fully documented by school or personal records.

Let's consider the circumstances of both Rand and Lossky:

In 1961, when Rand had told her future biographer of her encounters with Lossky, she had already achieved a worldwide following. Though she was not taken seriously by many academics, it is unlikely that the mere mention of Lossky's name would have created a stir of excitement in the United States,[54] where, until the latter part of 1961, the elderly professor had been living in relative obscurity. In fact, as I indicated in Chapter 2, Lossky had entered a French-Russian nursing home by October 1961. He was weak and very ill until his death in 1965.[55]

But any fabrication on the part of Rand could have been easily debunked by a search of the historical record. Except for this brief passage in the 1962 essay, duplicated, for the most part, in Branden's 1986 biography, the Lossky-Rand experience has not been written about or discussed in any interviews, public forums, articles, or books. Although Rand's recollection of her final examination experience with Lossky is predictably self-complimentary, it was *not* Rand's style to bolster her credentials by fabrication, name-dropping, or by acknowledging a professor whose religious philosophy she would have adamantly opposed.

Barbara Branden (1986) writes: "During the years of my friendship with Ayn Rand, I was always impressed with the range and exactitude of her memory" (13). Branden never found Rand to make a mistake about a date or time and could not imagine that Rand would have fabricated the Lossky experience.[56] In fact, Branden claims that although Rand's recollections of other teachers were partial and incomplete, Lossky remained "very memorable."[57] There were no other professors whom Rand acknowledged as having made an impact on her in any positive way.[58] Furthermore, Branden argues, Rand seemed to know the ancient philosophers very well. What she gained from this single course was enormous.[59]

I find it very difficult to believe that Rand was mistaken or that she lied about her experiences with the celebrated professor. Lossky's circumstances, however, are somewhat more complex. Though Lossky's son, Boris, characterizes the relationship between his father and Rand as quite possibly historical fiction, he makes "an extenuating caution in this judgment."[60] Lossky's appointment to the Institute of Scientific Research on the fringe of the university was different from most. The Council allowed Lossky to teach philosophical disciplines at the Institute with the provision that they not be tainted with spiritualist ideology. He could have lectured in logic, epistemology, psychology, and similar areas of study. Quite possibly among these other areas would have been a course in ancient philosophy, or a course in epistemology, surveying Plato, Aristotle, and other classical thinkers. Lossky would have lectured his students throughout the semester and followed the traditional procedure of testing his students' proficiency by written and oral examination. In this manner, the students would have received credit for the course, even though it was offered at the annex (B. Lossky, 29 May–4 June 1992C).

But to speculate on Lossky's activities at the Institute of Scientific Research poses a further problem: the courses are untraceable. Any such "elective" course, taught by a censured professor at the university annex, would not have received "official" academic visibility. Alissa Rosenbaum must have been aware of Lossky's eminent reputation as an exceptional educator, since he had taught at the Stoiunin Gymnasium. She might have been pleasantly surprised to discover him at the Petrograd annex. She would have expended a deliberate, conscious decision to enroll not merely in *a* philosophy course, but specifically in *Lossky's* class. She would have needed permission to attend his lectures. The considerable effort she would have had to make to arrange this suggests that she knew of Lossky's reputation as a brilliant philosopher or, perhaps, as a dedicated anticommunist. Boris Lossky does not deny these possibilities. Unfortunately, there are no institute listings in the family "red book" of Lossky's publication and pedagogical activities (B. Lossky, 27 October 1992C).

Another aspect of Barbara Branden's passage might provide a clue to the peculiar circumstances surrounding Lossky and Rand. Rand's recollections of her oral examinations in the spring indicate that she went to Lossky's home, rather than to an office or university classroom. This would have been unusual, but entirely within the realm of possibilities, given the appalling conditions at the university and its related institutes. Boris remembers that there was an acute shortage of firewood. It was so cold at the university that the office ink would freeze up (B. Lossky 1991, 77). The general lack of fuel led his father to schedule a number of student meetings in the enlarged dining room of his residence. These meetings may have been more frequent due to Lossky's illness, which kept him at home, intermittently, from the fall of 1921 through March of 1922. Final examinations were held in June. Boris Lossky recollects that several of his father's students visited their home during the period in question to discuss philosophy. He does not remember seeing a long line of nervous students waiting outside his father's study in the spring, nor does he remember Alissa Rosenbaum (B. Lossky, 29 May–4 June 1992C).

Aside from the unlikely possibility that Rand lied, one of the worst-case scenarios, then, is that she colored her recollections of the spring examination with a certain theatricality. There is another hypothesis that one could suggest: Rand may have remembered the examination incident perfectly, but not which professor was involved.[61] But I doubt this, given Barbara

Branden's insistence that Rand's recollections of Lossky were "very memorable." This is not to imply that Rand could never make a mistake; there is evidence that Rand did not remember every detail and date correctly. For instance, in my discussion of her relationship with the Nabokov sister, I discovered that Rand was mistaken regarding the date of the Nabokovs' departure from Russia. Boris Lossky also questions a number of Rand's reminiscences. Having read Branden's biography, he suggests for instance, that she slightly exaggerated the harshness of the 1917 Petrograd winter. He also notes some discrepancies in Rand's recollections of particular dates caused by the differences between the "old style" and "new style" calendars.[62]

But discrepancies in dates or temperatures are minor compared to a mistake in the recollection of a human being. Given the extenuating circumstances surrounding Lossky's annex activities, it is my conviction that Rand has accurately described an actual event. Though I cannot prove this judgment, I firmly believe that it is the best explanation of the facts. The evidence suggests that Rand genuinely appreciated the privilege of studying with such a distinguished scholar. She remembers that in her freshman year at Petrograd, "many students and professors were fairly open." After the government crackdown, "all the better professors from pre-revolutionary times were exiled to Europe."[63] Lossky was one of them. By another "accident" of historical circumstance, young Alissa Rosenbaum had been among the very last students taught by Lossky in his native homeland.

A Reign of Terror

But Lossky was not alone in his fate. Academic freedom was slowly eradicated in the years after the Revolution. The government had created *rabfaks* (workers' colleges), which offered workers a kind of general equivalency diploma in preparation for attending the university. The professors were told to pass these students even if they fell below established academic standards (Fitzpatrick 1979, 65).

This was not the only hardship university academics faced in Petrograd. Typhus, influenza, pneumonia, cholera, and starvation were becoming commonplace. Sorokin recalls that in the cafeterias of Petrograd, discussion was monopolized by reports of secret police arrests and executions. Some scholars chose suicide. Faculty meetings became ongoing memorials to the dead. The rector of Petrograd University asked his colleagues not to die so quickly because there was a lack of coffins and graves. In time, coffins had to be rented to transport bodies to the collective ditches. Sorokin ([1924] 1950) remarked: "Not even in death can we escape Communism!" (231).

In the face of such inhumanity, and in the aftermath of the NEP, new liberal scholarly journals were founded. Satirical writings, such as Zamiatin's *We*, began to circulate. Monuments to socialism and to Marx were desecrated, and many people returned to the Church. The Central Committee of the Communist Party feared the "growing influence of a revitalized bourgeois ideology" and chose "to apply decisive measures of struggle against this evil."[64] The expulsion of the intellectuals was the first step in the ideological "cleansing" of Soviet education. In addition to Lossky, more than one hundred leading Russian intellectuals and philosophers were exiled, including Aikhenvald, Alekseyev, Berdyaev, Bulgakov, Frank, Gurvich, Ilyin, Izgoyev, Karsavin, Kistyakovsky, Kizevetter, Lapshin, Melgunov, Myakotin, Novikov, Osgorgin, Ovchinnikov, Peshekhonov, Prokopovich, Sorokin, Stepun, Stratonov, Troshin, Vysheslavtsev, Yasinsky, and Yuskova. Anti-Marxist philosophical activity was declared illegal.[65]

Academic independence at Petrograd University was suddenly crushed. University faculty meetings were forbidden, and noncommunist journals were suppressed. In the face of growing state repression, protest was both ineffective and dangerous. Alissa learned "that it was useless to attempt political protests in Soviet Russia."[66] At home, Alissa's father, in league with other pharmacists, had attempted to reopen his chemist shop, only to face government nationalization of his business for a second time. The Rosenbaum family was starving.

Clashes between communist and noncommunist students became more violent. Eventually, a purge commission was established to remove nonproletarians from the student council and from the university at large. The student purge began in Alissa Rosenbaum's senior year, two months before her graduation from the newly renamed University of Leningrad. She would reconstruct the atmosphere of the student purge in her novel, *We the Living*. In an effort to cleanse the university of "all socially undesirable persons," the purge commission asked students to name the respective occupations of both parents before 1917, and from 1917 to 1921. Trade union and Communist Party members were saved from the wrath of the commission (*We the Living*, 198). In later years, Alissa recollected that "great numbers of students were sent to Siberia, young boys and girls I knew."[67]

The excesses of this purge were later denounced by Party leaders. Several Leningrad professors petitioned the authorities for the successful reinstatement of fifty purged students. In their efforts to democratize the student body, the authorities had merely shifted the student population from the social science colleges to the engineering schools. Fitzpatrick (1979) explains that the purge had the effect of "removing a great many of the women who had entered higher education after the revolution, since most of the women were of 'bourgeois' origin. In 1923/24, 38% of all students in higher education were women; but in 1928, with a smaller total number of students, women made up only 28%" (99).

As a graduating senior, Alissa Rosenbaum escaped the student purge. On 15 July 1924, she received her diploma, having successfully completed the University of Leningrad's requirements for a social science degree.[68] But she was deeply scarred by the reign of terror the Communists had inflicted on students and professors, on family and friends.

Coming to America

In the days following her graduation from Leningrad University, Alissa Rosenbaum, with a degree from the department of social pedagogy, was

Fig. 2. The Peter and Paul Fortress, St. Petersburg. In 1924, Ayn Rand lectured tourists on the fortress's history. (Courtesy of Boris Lossky)

more than qualified to lecture in history. Her family was starving, and her mother Anna, who was working as a language teacher in several Leningrad high schools, managed to get Alissa a job. She worked as a tour guide and lecturer at the Peter and Paul Fortress. Instructing tourists on the horrors of czarist Russia and on the fortress's history, Alissa spoke "to excursion groups—to silent rows of peasants and workers." She hated her job, but she was thankful that it helped pay for food and clothing.[69]

Yearning to leave Russia and join her American relatives in Chicago, Alissa began the difficult process of trying to secure a passport. Her mother made several inquiries regarding the rules and regulations governing foreign travel. Letters were exchanged, couched in euphemisms intended to avoid arousing suspicion. The mail was interminably slow. Alissa would be allowed to leave Russia only on the condition that she return. A letter was required from her relatives, confirming that she was only visiting, and that they would be responsible for her financial welfare. After months of waiting, Alissa received her Russian passport in the fall of 1925. She traveled to Latvia, only to risk the denial of her visa by the U.S. consulate. After she swore that she intended to return to Russia to marry, the consulate gave her permission to enter the United States. She traveled to Berlin and Paris, where she boarded a French steamer bound for New York. In mid-February 1926, she arrived.[70] She was twenty-one.

Alissa had left Russia because she believed that the rule of force was destroying all that was good in human beings.[71] She had an undiluted hatred for the communist system, which stayed with her for the rest of her life. In later years, this anticommunism led her to cooperate with the House Un-American Activities Committee as a friendly witness in the "Hearings Regarding Communist Infiltration of the Motion Picture Industry." She had written a well-received "Screen Guide for Americans" (1947), which had described how communist propaganda could be fought; however, Rand's cooperation with the committee was a source of great personal consternation. As a civil libertarian, she believed that it was improper for a government agency to engage in the ideological exposure of communists. But she had hoped that the HUAC would offer her a public forum in which she could voice her opposition to communist tyranny; in the end, she thought that she had probably made a mistake.[72]

And yet, very few passages in Rand's novels can convey the genuine pain she felt on the day of her testimony, thinking back to her experiences in the Soviet Union. On 20 October 1947, speaking before the HUAC, Rand, now a successful novelist and screenwriter, criticized the movie, *Song of*

Russia, because it painted a false portrait of Soviet life. In an episode immortalized in Lillian Hellman's *Scoundrel Time*, Congressman John Mc-Dowell ridiculed Rand's contention that nobody smiled in Russia. Rand explained that Russian life was not prosperous, open, or pleasant. She attested to the food shortages, the fear of state terror, the tyranny of the secret police. She testified:

> It is almost impossible to convey to a free people what it is like to live in a totalitarian dictatorship. . . . [The Russian people] try to live a human life, but you understand it is totally inhuman. Try to imagine what it is like if you are in constant terror from morning till night and at night you are waiting for the doorbell to ring, where you are afraid of anything and everybody, living in a country where human life is nothing, less than nothing, and you know it. You don't know who or when is going to do what to you because you may have friends who spy on you, where there is no law and any rights of any kind.[73]

But in climbing out of Russia's ideological quagmire, Rand could not rid herself of every last drop of her past. For even though she rejected the mystic, collectivist, and statist *content* of Russian philosophy, she had adopted its dialectical *methods*. Living in the United States, she began to articulate the organic principles that were necessary for the achievement of a genuinely *human* existence.

4 The Maturation of Ayn Rand

Not long after her arrival in America, Alissa Rosenbaum renamed herself Ayn Rand. In her early writings, she engages in a concerted effort to understand and critique polarities she had confronted in the Russia of her youth. She focuses primarily on the dialectical unity of religion and statism. She gropes toward a philosophical synthesis that rejects faith and force, but integrates the splits within human existence, between mind and body, fact and value, theory and practice.

Novelist and Philosopher

Rand was once asked if she was primarily a novelist or a philosopher. In typically dialectical fashion, she responded, "Both" ([1961] 1992T):

> In a certain sense, every novelist is a philosopher, because one cannot present a picture of human existence without a philosophical framework; the novelist's only choice is whether that framework is present in his story explicitly or implicitly, whether he is aware of it or not, whether he holds his philosophical convictions consciously or subconsciously. (*New Intellectual*, vii)

Rand's literary and philosophical goals were *internally related*. She could not pursue her literary project without gradually articulating a philosophical framework. And she could not apply her philosophy without expressing its values concretely in stories, screenplays, dramas, and novels. Thus Rand transcended the dualism between philosophy and art, social thought and entertainment. As she stated in a journal entry dated 4 May 1946, she had no interest in presenting newly discovered knowledge "in its abstract, general form."[1] She wished to apply her knowledge "in the concrete form of men and events, in the form of a fiction story." Such a fusion of the abstract and the concrete led Rand to wonder if she represented "a peculiar phenomenon." Like Nina Berberova and other Russian writers, Rand believed, with no show of modesty, that she had achieved "the proper integration of a complete human being" (xiv).

Rand's goal in writing was "the projection of an ideal man." This literary portrayal was, for her, "an end in itself—to which any didactic, intellectual or philosophical values contained in a novel are only the means."[2] But the "ideal man" was not a pure abstraction. He had to be related to "the conditions which make him possible and which his existence requires."[3] By defining the values such an ideal man would have and by delineating the social conditions that would make it possible for him to exist and flourish, Rand slowly moved from best-selling novelist to public philosopher. She shifted from the specifically anticommunist political themes of her first novel, *We the Living,* to the broad metaphysical and epistemological themes of *Atlas Shrugged.* She eventually boasted that she was "challenging the cultural tradition of two-and-a-half-thousand years."[4] Her formal philosophy, "untainted by any Kantian influence," aimed to reconnect the elements in human existence "which Kant had severed."[5]

Digesting the Past

There is no evidence to suggest that Rand explicitly criticized the works of Russian philosophers. No journals from her Russian period are extant, and the journal entries currently available date a full dozen years after her university encounters with Lossky. But in the late 1920s and early 1930s, Rand drew from her own experiences in Russia to compose a number of short stories and plays. Many of these unpublished stories appear in *The Early Ayn Rand,* among them, "Good Copy," "Escort," "The Night King,"

"Her Second Career," and "The Husband I Bought."[6] This last tale of unrequited love was based on Rand's first romantic experiences in Russia with a man who was probably exiled to Siberia.[7]

In 1931–32, she wrote a film treatment and screenplay called "Red Pawn," which dealt specifically with the evil of Soviet communism. Of greater philosophical importance, however, is the secondary theme of this work. For the first time, Rand dealt with "the philosophic identity of Communism and religion."[8] In Rand's Russia, religion offered the only organized opposition to the Bolsheviks. Religion was viewed as communism's natural enemy. Whereas communism was atheistic and materialistic, religion celebrated God's existence and human spiritual redemption.

Rand examined this opposition between two dominant Russian cultural forces and refused to accept their apparent hostility as evidence for their mutual exclusivity. She recognized that something fundamental united the communists and the believers. Tracing their essential similarities became one of Rand's earliest philosophical preoccupations.

For Rand, communism was a secular substitute for religion. Like the Church before it, communism subjugated the individual to an allegedly higher power. In this respect, religion and communism were *identical*. The main difference between them was their respective agencies of domination. For believers, it was God; for the communists, it was the state.[9]

Though Rand had not yet mastered English, she created tantalizing images in "Red Pawn" to dramatize the organic conjunction of religion and communism. Much of the movie action is situated on Strastnoy Island, a "bit of land in the Arctic waters off the Siberian coast."[10] In the czarist days, a monastery occupied the island. But since the Revolution, the monastery had been converted into a Soviet prison.[11]

Rand writes that the island's library occupied the former chapel of the old monastery. In the library, a sacred mural remained, depicting Christ's walk to Golgotha. But above the mural, the communists had scrawled, in red letters, "Proletarians of the World Unite!" Red flags were sketched into the raised hand of St. Vladimir. A hammer and sickle were superimposed on Moses' tablets. The fresh paint dripped down the chapel walls.

> Tall candles in silver stands at the altar had to be lighted in the daytime. Their little red flames stood immobile, each candle transformed into a chandelier by the myriads of tiny reflections in the gilded halos of carved saints; they burned without motion, without noise, a silent, resigned service in memory of the past— around a picture of Lenin.[12]

Others would have seen the superimposed communist symbols as a defilement of a Christian sanctuary; Rand saw an organic conjunction of corresponding worldviews. Her mixture of religious and communist images suggests that the two cultural forces had interpenetrated one another, serving similar goals, if not the same master.

We the Living

Comparable imagery is evident in Rand's first published novel, *We the Living*. In a passage ultimately deleted from the original 1936 edition, Rand presents a fairy tale about a mighty Viking who is hated by both the King and the Priest.[13] While the King despises the Viking for his refusal to bow to royal authority, the Priest hates the Viking because he "looked at heaven only when he bent for a drink over a mountain brook, and there, overshadowing the sky, he saw his own picture."[14]

The enraged King promises his royal subjects a material reward for the Viking's head. Similarly, the Priest assures his parishioners that their sins will be forgiven if they kill the Viking. When the Viking embarks on a quest for the sacred city, however, his anticipated triumph prompts his adversaries to be more conciliatory. The King offers the Viking a royal banner to plant in the sacred city. The Priest offers the Viking a temple banner. But the Viking refuses to take either. For on the mast of his ship "was his own banner, that had never been lowered." He conquers the sacred city, and toasts, "To a life . . . which is a reason unto itself." Rand writes: "A Viking had lived, who had laughed at Kings, who had laughed at Priests, who had laughed at Men, who had held, sacred and inviolable, high over all temples, over all to which men knew how to kneel, his one banner—the sanctity of life" (180).

This tale was but another symbolic way for Rand to say that statism and religion are at war with the sovereign individual. The King, a symbol of statism, is no different from the Priest, a symbol of religion; both are fundamentally opposed to the independent Viking who refuses to worship either.

Rand wrote *We the Living*, originally entitled, *Air Tight: A Novel of Red Russia*, between 1930 and 1933, "to get Russia out of her system."[15] Far simpler in its structure than her later novels, *We the Living* offered, in Rand's view, the most classic plot progression of any of her works. Moreover, it was, Rand said, the closest to an autobiography that she would ever write.[16] Despite differences between Rand and the main character, Kira Argounova, Kira is clearly a stand-in for Rand. In fact, throughout her fiction, it was never Rand's custom to distance herself from the views of her central protagonists. In this sense, they are all Rand.

Kira is a young engineering student enrolled at Petrograd University. The novel chronicles her personal struggle under the harsh conditions of Soviet dictatorship. The plot centers on a fatal romantic triangle between Kira and the two men who love her. Kira falls in love with a counterrevolutionary, Leo Kovalensky. When Leo develops tuberculosis, Kira becomes the mistress of a heroic communist revolutionary, Andrei Taganov, in order to gain access to food and money for Leo's welfare.

Andrei is a virtuous, if misguided, character—much more admirable than Leo, Kira's true love. Andrei epitomizes the idealism of the revolution, refusing to be corrupted by the growing tyranny of the regime. But the regime *is* corrupt, and it gradually destroys the best of its citizens. In the end, Kira is alienated from both men. Leo becomes a self-destructive alcoholic, and Andrei, confronting the utter bankruptcy of his ideals, commits suicide. With nothing left for her in Russia, Kira attempts to escape across the border, but is shot by the border patrol and left to bleed to death in the snow. In a last shining moment, she sees that "Life, undefeated, existed and could exist."[17]

In *We the Living*, Kira, unlike Rand herself, did not escape communism. Rand wanted to show how dictatorship thwarts escape, crushes values, crushes life itself. Escape from such a system is a fluke, in Rand's view. Totalitarianism necessarily perpetuates an "airtight" environment of brutality and repression; spiritual and physical death are its *essential* by-products.[18]

A "Nietzschean" Phase?

In 1936, *We the Living* was issued by Macmillan in a limited edition of three thousand copies. It was not reissued until 1959, after Rand had established herself as a best-selling author. In the second edition, Rand made several revisions, which she described as "editorial line-changes." In the original edition, Rand claimed that her writing "reflected the transitional state of a mind thinking no longer in Russian, but not yet fully in English."[19] Hence, she wished to correct "awkward" and "confusing" formulations.

However, a number of scholars have reviewed Rand's modifications and concluded that these were not strictly linguistic. The most compelling case is offered by Ronald Merrill, who argues that Rand excised those references in the first edition which implied an endorsement of Nietzsche's ethical principles, that the weak may be sacrificed for the sake of the strong. The second edition reflects the attitudes of the more mature Rand.[20]

In the first edition, there is a scene in which Kira and Andrei debate the meaning of communism. Andrei assumes that Kira admires the communist ideal, but rejects its methods. But she surprises him. She states: "I loathe your ideals. I admire your methods. If one believes one's right, one shouldn't wait to convince millions of fools, one might just as well force them. Except that I don't know, however, whether I'd include blood in my methods."[21]

Andrei retorts, "Why not? Anyone can sacrifice his own life for an idea. How many know the devotion that makes you capable of sacrificing other lives? Horrible, isn't it?"

"Not at all," Kira answers. "Admirable. If you're right. But are you right?"

In the second edition, Rand has removed this entire exchange. Kira merely states, "I loathe your ideals." She keeps her own counsel concerning his methods.

The conversation between these two characters continues in the first edition, when Kira argues that there are things which are sacred to the individual that cannot be touched by the state or the collective. Andrei rejects Kira's claims, declaring "that we can't sacrifice millions for the sake of the few." Kira answers:

> "*You can! You must. When those few are the best.* Deny the best its right to the top—and you have no best left. What are your masses but mud to be ground underfoot, fuel to be burned for those who deserve it? What is the people but *millions of puny, shrivelled, helpless souls* that have no thoughts of their own, no dreams of their own, no will of their own, who eat and sleep and chew helplessly the words others put into their mildewed brains? And for those you would sacrifice the few who know life, who *are* life? I loathe your ideals because *I know no worse injustice than justice for all. Because men are not born equal and I don't see why one should want to make them equal.* And because I loathe most of them." [Emphasis added except in fifth sentence.]

In the revised edition, Kira states:

> "*Can you sacrifice the few? When those few are the best?* Deny the best
> its right to the top—and you have no best left. What are your masses
> but *millions of dull, shrivelled, stagnant souls* that have no thoughts of
> their own, no dreams of their own, no will of their own, who eat
> and sleep and chew helplessly the words others put into their brains?
> And for those you would sacrifice the few who know life, who *are*
> life? I loathe your ideals because *I know no worse injustice than the
> giving of the undeserved. Because men are not equal in ability and one
> can't treat them as if they were.* And because I loathe most of them."
> [Emphasis added except in the fourth sentence.]

In the original passage, Kira has contempt for the masses and is inclined
to see them destroyed. In response to Andrei, Kira shows an unquestioning
resolve to side with the exalted few in any conflict with the "puny,
shrivelled, helpless" masses. She rejects the credo of "justice for all" when
it becomes a euphemism for any attempt to make all human beings
metaphysically equal.

In the comparable passage from the 1959 revised edition, Kira expresses
a similar contempt for the masses. But here, Kira's language is less vitriolic.
She answers Andrei with a question, not a protest. She rejects those who
would attempt to achieve metaphysical egalitarianism through the injustice
of granting values to those who have no right to them. Yet in *both* editions
of the novel, Kira follows her exchange with Andrei by stating: "I don't
want to fight for the people, I don't want to fight against the people, I don't
want to hear of the people. I want to be left alone—to live!" Even Ronald
Merrill agrees that in this belief, Rand's Kira has moved away from a
stark "Nietzschean" ethos. Merrill argues that Kira's sentiment foreshadows
Rand's mature Objectivist position. In fact, Merrill believes that Rand's
conception of egoism developed largely as a reaction to the Nietzschean
orientation of her youth.

Stephen Hicks, in a review of Merrill's book, argues that Merrill's
conclusion is premature, since only a full disclosure of Rand's early journals
will settle the issue of her alleged Nietzschean phase. Rand finished her
novel in 1933, and published it in 1936. Hicks argues correctly that there is
evidence in one of her published journal entries that Rand rejected the
"Nietzschean" ethos as early as 1934. In this entry, foreshadowing the

character of Gail Wynand in *The Fountainhead*, Rand condemns those who would achieve power through the masses. If Rand had rejected Nietzsche in 1934, it is likely that she would have revised those passages which could have been interpreted as Nietzschean, before the book was actually published.[22]

Hicks states further that Rand may have allowed Andrei to set the terms of the debate, much as the communist state sets the terms for each of the characters in *We the Living*. Rand had not yet constructed a full theoretical response to the ethics of altruism, and Kira reflects this void. Having fully developed her own rational egoist ethic in later years, it may have been easier for Rand to eliminate the ambiguous passages, rather than to have provided a full philosophical explanation of their actual meaning.[23]

There may be some merit to Merrill's contention that Rand went through a "Nietzschean" phase, but I tend to agree with Hicks that the evidence for such a provocative thesis is inconclusive. However, there are two important issues which must be emphasized because they shed much light on Rand's attitudes toward the Nietzschean worldview:

First, in my discussion of the Silver Age of Russian philosophy, it was clear that Russian writers had stressed the Dionysian aspects of Nietzsche's thought. Rand was probably exposed to this particular interpretation of Nietzsche from a very early age. Though Rand was most impressed by Nietzsche's critique of altruism and Christianity, she concretized his grand, abstract metaphors with her own images. Despite her initial attraction to Nietzsche's work, Rand necessarily rejected his Dionysian impulses. And though she continued to draw from Nietzschean imagery as late as *The Fountainhead*, she was probably already moving *away* from Nietzsche as early as her student years.

Second, and more important, Rand was moving *toward* a nondualistic philosophical framework. While she was exploring the philosophic identity of religion and communism, she was also beginning to see that both forces perpetuated a social dualism that forced the individual to choose between two sides of the same false coin.

In the religious realm, the fraud was obvious to Rand. For instance, in 1934 she wrote a play, *Ideal*, which depicted religion as causing hypocrisy and opposing integrity. Religion, for Rand, divorces ideals from life on earth, by viewing "this world [as] of no consequence." An evangelist in *Ideal* proclaims: "Whatever beauty [the world] offers us is here only that we may sacrifice it—for the greater beauty beyond."[24] Religion tells people that beauty is unreachable and that nobility emerges from the *sacrifice*, not the achievement, of values.[25] It condemns people for not achieving unreachable ideals, ideals they do not really wish to attain because their very realization would demand self-annihilation.

This recognition of religion as a source of social dualism reappears in Rand's journal entries during this same period. Rand argued that religion engenders a metaphysical split between this world and the next, between human existence on earth and an illusory life after death.[26] In Rand's view, religion declares war on the human ability to think, and it is consequently "the root of all human lying and the only excuse for suffering." It fragments living and thinking, and sees "ideals as something quite abstract and detached from one's everyday life. The ability of *living* and *thinking* quite differently, in other words eliminating thinking from your actual life" (2).

It is for this reason that Rand saw "*Faith as the worst curse of mankind*, as the exact antithesis and enemy of *thought*." But at this point in her intellectual development, Rand was not certain about why people have abdicated the use of logical reasoning in the governance of their lives. She asked if reason is impossible to individuals, or if individuals have merely been taught that it is futile. If people have been taught such, then "the teacher is the church." Rand hoped "to be known as the greatest champion of reason and the greatest enemy of religion."[27]

Just as religion was a source of social dualism, so too was statism. The theme of *We the Living*, according to Rand, was the "individual against the State" (*New Intellectual*, 60). Rand did not believe that there was a necessary incompatibility between the individual and all forms of government. She was not an anarchist; she rejected neither government per se, nor truly *human* social relationships. What she opposed was *statism* in all its incarnations.

Communism both constituted and perpetuated a social dichotomy between the individual and the masses. Under communism, the masses are collectively organized by the coercive state. In such a system, the individual has no alternative but *conflict* with the society at large. Hence, it is quite possible that in the early edition of the novel, Kira's call to sacrifice the masses for the sake of the few is the only alternative she can advocate *within* the context of communism, which sacrifices the few for the sake of the many. Just as religion pits thinking against living, communism pits the individual against the community. Within this context, Kira is forced to choose between two poles of a deadly duality. When she is able to remove herself briefly from this context, she exclaims that indeed, she does not wish to fight for or against the people. She wants only "to be left alone."

Like Rand, Kira lived in a society which had no developed concept of the individual. *The Russian language does not even have a word for "privacy."*[28] This peculiarity of Russian might have motivated Rand to write, several years later, in *The Fountainhead*: "Civilization is the progress toward a society of privacy" (684). Russian religious and political culture did not recognize the sphere of the private. Kira knew that it was "an old and ugly fact that the masses exist and make their existence felt." But under communism, "they make it felt with particular ugliness" (*We the Living*, 49). She protests to Andrei, that it is "a rare gift, you know, to feel reverence for your own life and to want the best, the greatest, the highest possible, here, now, for your very own. To imagine a heaven, and then not to dream of it, but to demand it" (107).

Hence, Kira may not be expressing a Nietzschean contempt for the masses, as much as she is expressing a desire to break free of a system that crushes the individual under the weight of an undifferentiated collective. It is a system that compels Kira to see the world dualistically, in terms of herself versus everyone else. Soviet communism had appropriated the essence of Russian *sobornost'*, the fusion of the individual and the collective whole. But instead of preserving the uniqueness and privacy of its members, it sought to annihilate their individual identities. For Rand, communism is a system that defeats "the living" by robbing them of the very qualities that make them human. It institutionalizes a war of the masses against the solitary person.

After she wrote *We the Living*, Rand knew that she had more work to do. By 1934, she began to view her writing as part of a broader project. In her own words, "These are the vague beginnings of an amateur philosopher. To be checked with what I learn when I master philosophy—then see how much of it has already been said, and whether I have anything new to say, or anything old to say better than it has been said."[29]

She intended that her journals would be *only* for her own use and did not worry if her thoughts appeared "disjointed." Despite her humility in characterizing herself as "an amateur philosopher," Rand's musings are much more articulate and self-conscious than she intimates.

Rand hoped that once her ideas were fully developed, she would be able to present them as a "Mathematics of Philosophy." She aimed to "arrange the whole in a logical system, proceeding from a few axioms in a succession of logical theorems" (7). But it was clear to her that such a project would take time and effort.

In her journals, Rand dealt critically with the writings of other thinkers, such as Albert Jay Nock, H. L. Mencken, Peter Kropotkin, and José Ortega y Gasset. Having rejected both religion and communism, both the worship of God and the idolatry of the collective, Rand wanted to grasp *why* people allowed themselves to obey standards set by others. Reading Ortega y Gasset's *Revolt of the Masses*, she was perplexed by the actions of "the *mass* man." Mass men are not those who obeyed their own standards. Rather, they submit to the dictates of others. They are not genuine individuals, in Rand's view. Since they lack internally generated ideals, they cannot be free. Rand believed that no human quality such as freedom could be "disconnected from its content." She asked: "Isn't there a terrible mistake of abstraction here? Isn't it as Nietzsche said, 'not freedom *from* what, but freedom *for* what'?"[30]

For Rand, the "mistake of abstraction" is the social division of ideals and action, theory and practice, morality and practicality. No human value can be separated from the conditions that make its achievement possible. Rand was developing a view of the individual that included not merely negative notions of freedom, but positive notions of autonomy and self-responsibility. Autonomy demands that individuals achieve values by their own effort, not by a mystical alliance with God or a selfless union with the collective. The person who attains values and power by pandering to the masses is to be rejected as "a slave to those masses." A genuine selfishness, an "exalted egoism," demands that the individual achieve his or her "own theoretical values and then apply them to practical reality," for it is one's "*actual living*" that must take priority "over all other considerations."[31]

Seeing "history as a deadly battle of the mass and the individual" (8), Rand was poised to begin working on a mammoth literary project whose "first purpose . . . is *a defense of egoism in its real meaning*."[32] Her working title for the book was *Second-Hand Lives*. Ultimately, it would be called *The Fountainhead*.

The Fountainhead

In 1935, Rand began to outline the plot and characters of the book that would be her first, genuine commercial success. In these early outlines, Rand continues in her quest for a nondualistic, integrated view of human being.

The Fountainhead follows the exploits of Howard Roark, Rand's first, fully formed "ideal man."[33] Roark is a brilliant architect, a man of integrity expelled from school for his unwillingness to conform to traditional architectural styles. One of Roark's classmates is Peter Keating, a man who always relied on Roark's assistance to complete school projects. While Roark is destitute and looking for work, Keating becomes a professional success by manipulating those around him, and by imitating old and tired architectural standards. He lives a "second-hand" life, in which "the source of his actions is scattered in every other living person" (*Fountainhead*, 607).

Throughout the novel, we meet other characters, such as Dominique Francon, Gail Wynand, and Ellsworth Toohey. Dominique is Roark's beloved, and one of the more bizarre characters in the novel. She separates herself from the things that she grows to love, including Roark. She is convinced that no man of integrity can succeed in a world ruled by the mob. Wynand, the most tragic figure in Rand's fiction, is a newspaper magnate who boasts that he has the power to mold the tastes of the masses. His belief that everyone can be corrupted is challenged by his encounters with Roark. Toohey, a critic writing for Wynand's newspaper, is an arch collectivist. He organizes public protests against Roark's "arrogant" architectural stylings. Through Toohey's intervention, Roark is prevented from winning many important building contracts.

But Roark continues his struggle to create buildings in a distinctive and brilliantly imaginative style. In the final sequences of the novel, the ambitious Peter Keating seeks to exploit Roark's expertise to secure a lucrative contract for the design of a public housing project. Knowing that he will never get the opportunity to implement some of his most cost-effective plans for housing, Roark agrees to submit designs for the project—in Keating's name—on the condition that the blueprints not be altered. Toohey senses that these plans are not Keating's creation; he recognizes Roark's impeccable technique. When the plans are altered significantly and distorted, and the project is built, Roark is outraged. He dynamites the public housing project, is arrested, and brought to trial.

During the trial, Wynand, now Roark's friend, decides to embark on a press campaign to build support for the indicted architect. For the first time in his life, Wynand finds the strength to stand for a principle not dictated by the masses. To his grief, he discovers that he cannot alter public opinion. He faces the realization that he has created a vast business empire by pandering to the tastes of the mob; he is its slave and not its master.

Roark defends himself in court by enunciating the principles of individualism. He asserts that the authorities had no right to alter his plans. In one of Rand's characteristically romantic endings, Roark is vindicated of criminal charges. He agrees to rebuild the project according to his own specifications. The novel concludes with Howard Roark triumphant.

Though *The Fountainhead* is fiction, in it Rand articulates a far more integrated—and specifically Randian—view of human existence than she had presented in any previous book. Yet in her portrayal of Howard Roark, the influence of Nietzsche can still be detected.[34] Rand had wanted to place a quotation from Nietzsche at the beginning of *The Fountainhead* when it was first issued in 1943, but she removed the passage before the manuscript went to publication. In 1968, she quoted it in the introduction to the twenty-fifth anniversary edition of *The Fountainhead*. She explained that despite her profound disagreement with Nietzsche's metaphysics and epistemology, she remained impressed by his ability to project man's greatness in beautifully poetic and emotional terms. She quoted from *Beyond Good and Evil*, in which Nietzsche celebrates the "fundamental certainty which a noble soul has about itself, something which is not to be sought, is not to be found, and perhaps also, is not to be lost. *The noble soul has reverence for itself.*"[35]

In her outlines of 26 December 1935, Rand had this same imagery in mind when she described Howard Roark as "the noble soul par excellence." Rand stated that Roark is "man as man should be. The self-sufficient, self-confident, the end of ends, the reason unto himself, the joy of living personified. . . . A man who *is* what he should be."[36] At this time, Rand did not provide a full philosophical articulation of what human beings "should be." But she did present, in fictional form, her own understanding of the nature of the genuine individualist as distinguished from the mass man. For Rand, the individualist transcends dualism, whereas the mass man is split between the dictates of his own conscience and the demands of society. Ultimately, the mass man, or "second-hander," abdicates his own soul.

The individualist, symbolized in the character of Roark, was not a spiritual abstraction disconnected from material reality. Rand presented Roark as a fully integrated being of mind and body. She matched Roark's integrity of spirit with a consummate physical strength. Roark's egoism is not boastful, conceited, or ostentatious. In her outline of 9 February 1936, she wrote that Roark is "natural" in his selfishness. "He has the quiet, complete, irrevocable calm of an iron conviction. No dramatics, no hysteria." This spiritual tranquility is matched by Roark's "tall, slender, somewhat angular" appearance. His passionate sensuality is captured in the hardness of his muscles. He walks swiftly, with ease, "as if movement requires no effort whatever, a body to which movement is as natural as immobility, without a definite line to divide them, a light, flowing, lazy ease of motion, an energy so complete that it assumes the ease of laziness."[37]

Roark is the exact opposite of the mass man, for "he was born without the ability to consider others." This does not mean that Roark is incapable of social relationships, or that he would trample on the rights of others to achieve his goals. For Rand, Roark's egoism entailed a cohesion of self. Roark is not a solipsist or a brute. His self is the focal point of responsibility, decision making, and value. It is Roark's own happiness that is his "basic, primary consideration." Roark owes nothing to others, nor does he seek to impose obligations on them. As a Randian hero, Roark is an atheist. He was "born without any 'religious brain center.'" His intransigent mind "does not understand or even conceive of the instinct for bowing and submission. His whole capacity for reverence is centered on himself" (699).

By contrast, Rand portrays most of the other characters in *The Fountainhead* as variations of the mass man. Keating, like so many other secondary characters in the novel, tries to achieve greatness as defined by others. He is the "perfect example of a selfless man who is a ruthless, unprincipled egotist—in the accepted meaning of the word." He is vain and greedy, a "mob man at heart," who sacrifices everything for the sake of a professional success that lacks personal significance. Keating "has no self and, therefore, cannot have any ethics." He exists in an empty shell, never achieving the full distinction of what an individual "should be."

Whereas Keating attempts to live through others by submitting to social conventions, Wynand attempts to rule others by forcing them to submit to *his* dictates. But as a publishing magnate, Wynand "rules the mob only as long as he says what the mob wants him to say." *The Fountainhead* depicts what happens when Wynand attempts to stand on principles that are genuinely his own. For Rand, Wynand is "a man who could have been."

By contrast, Toohey achieves distinction by extolling humanitarian causes and glorifying collectivism. He is unable to attain values through productive effort and can only achieve greatness in the eyes of others by crushing and ridiculing the heroic. Rand describes him as "a man who never could be—and knows it" (698). Toohey seeks domination by diminishing the value of all things so as to reflect his own inferiority.[38]

Continuing the use of Nietzschean imagery in her notes, Rand explains that Toohey's character has "an *insane will to power*, a lust for superiority that can be expressed *only through others*" (700). Toohey is a parody of this Nietzschean will to power; he exhibits a superior intellect and force of personality entirely directed toward the inversion and obliteration of values.[39] But Rand also uses Toohey to subtly celebrate Nietzsche in her finished novel. Nietzsche becomes a persistent target of Toohey's derision. For instance, in one of his newspaper columns denouncing Roark's architectural design of the Enright House, Toohey states: "It is not our function—paraphrasing a philosopher whom we do not like [Nietzsche]—to be a fly swatter, but when a fly acquires delusions of grandeur, the best of us must stoop to do a little job of extermination."[40]

When a photograph of Roark appears in *The Banner*, Toohey mocks Rand's protagonist for his exalted expression of admiration toward the Enright House that he has created. With obvious Nietzschean overtones, Toohey writes, in the newspaper caption below the photo, "Are you happy, Mr. *Superman?*" (343).

More important than all of these subtle allusions to Nietzsche is Rand's portrait of Toohey. Through Toohey's character, Rand presents the thesis "that only mental control over others is true control." Toohey seeks primarily, a *spiritual* communism, in which each individual is spiritually subordinated "to the mass in every way conceivable." He hopes to achieve social domination through "the tremendous power of numbers." Stressing the metaphysical equality of all men as a means of obliterating any "consideration given to the content of their character," Toohey is a genuine mass man. For Toohey, individuals are valuable only in relation to the masses they serve. Voicing contempt for his betters "*because* they are better,"[41] Toohey encapsulates all that is evil in modern politics.

But Toohey also symbolizes the essence of the Russian *sobornost'* against which Rand was reacting. In Russian thought, *sobornost'* signified a mystic or spiritual union of all people in society. Individuals would allegedly retain their uniqueness, but in practice, the Russian ideal involved the dissolution of the individual into an organic totality. The communists merely secularized this vision of conciliarity; they retained the Russian impulse toward the material *and* spiritual subordination of the individual, but substituted the State for the body of Christ.

Toohey's newspaper column, "One Small Voice," features endless attacks against individualism that reek of Russian *sobornost'*. In many ways, he extols the virtue of the cultic loss of self, a theme that was prominent in the writings of the Nietzschean Russian Symbolists. But Toohey goes further: he advocates the sacrificing and subordinating of the individual to the almighty One. Rand uncovers this pretentious use of altruistic language as an ideological tool to conquer the human spirit, to make men small and insignificant, to rule the masses by elevating mediocrity and ridiculing greatness.

In her portrayal of Toohey, Rand also continues her literary policy of integrating the traits of mind and body. She depicts her chief villain as a repulsive swine. She writes in her outline, that Toohey's "puny physical appearance seems to be a walking testimonial to the spiritual pus filling his blood vessels."[42]

Despite her emphasis on the individual's ego as the fountainhead of human progress, Rand had provided a far more complex psychological portrait of the mass men as fragmented and incomplete. In opposition to this splintered picture of a human being, Rand began to articulate a nondualistic, nonatomistic view of the genuine individual.

While writing *The Fountainhead*, Rand continued her paean to individualism in her novelette, *Anthem*, originally titled *Ego* (Reedstrom 1993b). Written in 1937, first published in England in 1938, Rand's futuristic story offers an alternative to Zamiatin's visions of a technologically advanced collectivist dystopia. Rand projects the primitive conditions that *must* predominate in any social order that destroys the individual. In *Anthem*, total collectivism has led to the obliteration of industry and the distortion of human relationships. Peoples' names have been replaced by euphemistic code words and numerical notations. Even the word "I" has been lost. The rediscovery of this word by the protagonist of the story is one of Rand's most poetic tributes to individualism. Foreshadowing the egoistic ethical credo of *Atlas Shrugged*, uniting body and soul through secular means, Equality 7-2521 proclaims:

> "I am. I think. I will. What must I say besides? These are the words. This is the answer. . . . This—my body and spirit—this is the end of the quest. I wished to know the meaning of things. I am the meaning. I wished to find a warrant for being. I need no warrant for being, and no word of sanction upon my being. I am the warrant and the sanction. . . . My happiness is not the means to any end. It is the end. It is its own goal. It is its own purpose. Neither am I the means to any end others may wish to accomplish. I am not a tool for their use. I am not a servant of their needs. I am not a bandage for their wounds. I am not a sacrifice on their altars. I owe nothing to my brothers, nor do I gather debts from them. I ask none to live for me, nor do I live for any others. I covet no man's soul, nor is my soul theirs to covet."[43]

At the end of the novelette, Rand's protagonist has renamed himself Prometheus. He escapes the collectivist society with the woman he loves to build a new individualist culture. In her elevation of Promethean individuality, Rand inherits the Nietzschean-Symbolist leitmotif, without its penchant for Dionysian emotionalism, organic collectivism, or the cultic loss of self.[44] The genuine individual is neither slave nor master; he does not submit to, or seek self-assertion through, the rule of the collective.

Early Nonfiction

Mixed reviews of The Fountainhead did not block Rand from achieving commercial success. In the early 1940s, Rand was planning to write her first nonfiction work, "The Moral Basis of Individualism." She wrote a condensed version called, "The Only Path to Tomorrow," which appeared in Reader's Digest. Rand considered the essay a "bromide" to serve as the credo for a broad union of Old Right intellectuals committed to capitalism. The group never materialized primarily because of its ideological diversity (B. Branden 1986, 163). Nevertheless, during this period, Rand had the opportunity to interact with several conservative and libertarian thinkers and activists, including Channing Pollock, Albert Jay Nock, Ruth Alexander, Rose Wilder Lane, Isabel Paterson, Henry Hazlitt, and Ludwig von Mises, the father of the contemporary Austrian school of economics and the teacher of the renowned Nobel laureate F. A. Hayek (163, 188). Rand championed the Austrian school of economics in her later nonfiction essays. Though she shared much in common with her procapitalist political contemporaries, she was often disappointed by what she perceived as their cynicism, subjectivism, and mysticism.

Despite its political clichés, "The Only Path to Tomorrow" provides a first peek at Rand as a public philosopher. In the essay, Rand argues that totalitarian ideology is the greatest threat to civilization. She posits a historical antagonism between "Active Man" and "Passive Man." "Active Man" is another name for Howard Roark. "Active Man" is the individualist. He is a producer, creator, and originator. He requires independence and "neither needs nor seeks power over other men—nor can he be made to work under any form of compulsion" (Rand 1944, 89).

"Passive Man" was another name for Peter Keating. He dreads independence and "is a parasite who expects to be taken care of by others, who wishes to be given directives, to obey, to submit, to be regulated, to be told" (90). Collectivism breeds upon such passivity. It is an ideology that unites the masses through "the ancient principle of savagery."

Interestingly, Rand does not argue that the needy are parasites on the wealthy. She states emphatically that "Passive Man" can be rich or poor. Coming from all social classes, the "Passive Man" is a parasite on the genuine productive achievements of the "Active Man." This theme reappears in much more sophisticated form in Rand's mature critique of contemporary statism.

Rand's well-known antipathy for Soviet collectivism enabled her to contribute an anticommunist tract to the Motion Picture Alliance for the Preservation of American Ideals. Written in 1946, the "Screen Guide for Americans" followed the same form as her earlier *Reader's Digest* article. Rand supported the communists' right to express their ideas, but argued that moviegoers and producers should not be obligated to patronize and sanction projects that aimed to corrupt American institutions.

In the pamphlet, Rand posited a stark battle between Freedom and Slavery, between republican government and dictatorship. Of greatest philosophical relevance is Rand's contention that the dictator is not an individualist. He is "by definition . . . the most complete collectivist of all, because he exists by ruling, crushing and exploiting a huge collection of men" (Rand 1947, 49). Rand had transferred her insights on the "soul of the collectivist" into a successful piece of political propaganda for the Hollywood film industry.

Throughout the 1940s, Rand wrote several screenplays, including the film version of *The Fountainhead*, which starred Gary Cooper, Patricia Neal, and Raymond Massey; *You Came Along*, starring Robert Cummings and Lizabeth Scott; and an especially romantic *Love Letters*, with Jennifer Jones and Joseph Cotten.[45] These works adumbrate typically Randian themes, but they are of little or no independent philosophical interest. The 1940s were marked by something much more important to Rand's intellectual maturation. The celebrated author began working on the magnum opus of her literary career.

Atlas Shrugged

In *The Fountainhead*, Rand focused on the principles of individualism and collectivism as manifested within the individual's soul. The personal conflicts faced by each of her characters are primarily internal. Each character is a mixture of two extremes symbolized by Howard Roark and Ellsworth Toohey. The characters are defined not by their relations to one another, but by their specific natures. Their social ties were secondary and derivative of the central theme.

In 1945, Rand began to outline a new novel, initially called *The Strike*. She wanted to change her focus radically by delving deeply into the dialectical interrelationships between characters, social structures, and institutional processes. She wished to proceed "from persons, in terms of history, society, and the world." Her emphasis was not on Active Man or Passive Man, not on prime movers or second-handers. Rather, "the story must be primarily a picture of the whole," Rand stated in her journal.[46] For Rand, *Atlas Shrugged* was "to be much more a 'social' novel than *The Fountainhead*." First and foremost, the novel had to focus on the cluster of relationships that constitute the social totality:

> Now, it is this *relation* that must be the theme. Therefore, the personal becomes secondary. That is, the personal is necessary only to the extent needed to make the relationships clear. In *The Fountainhead* I showed that Roark moves the world—that the Keatings feed upon him and hate him for it, while the Tooheys are out consciously to destroy him. But the theme was Roark—not Roark's relation to the world. Now it will be the relation. (x)

As a novel, *Atlas Shrugged* explores these relations in every dimension of human life. Rand traces the links between political economy and sex, education and art, metaphysics and psychology, money and moral values. She concentrates extensively on the union of spiritual and physical realms, on the specific, concrete means by which certain productive individuals move the world, and by which others live off of their creations. She attempts to show the social importance of the creative act by documenting what would happen if the prime movers, the "men of the mind," were to go on strike.[47]

No summary of *Atlas Shrugged* could possibly unravel its intricacies. The book boasts a long list of protagonists and villains, but it centers around the exploits of Dagny Taggart and Hank Rearden, two industrialists who attempt to keep their respective businesses afloat in a global economy plagued by extensive government intervention and growing social chaos. The economic devastation wrought by growing statism is made worse by a conspiracy of omission. As the state becomes more intrusive, creative thinkers and producers from every profession begin to disappear. They unite secretly behind John Galt, a brilliant inventor, who leads a "strike of the men of the mind." These people of creative ability desert their businesses and leave the statists nothing to loot. They retire to a capitalist utopia in the mountains of Colorado known as Galt's Gulch.

It takes Dagny a long time to realize that she is fighting to keep her transcontinental railroad alive in a parasitical society that is slowly consuming her. As the world heads toward cataclysm, the leader of the United States government takes to the airwaves to issue a call for calm. Using specially developed technology, Galt interrupts the broadcast and proceeds to explain the cause of the decline of civilization. His speech touches on nearly every major branch of philosophy; it is the essence of Rand's Objectivist worldview. Galt asks the remaining producers to stop permitting their own victimization and join the strike. When the strike succeeds in stopping the motor of the world, the people of creative ability return on their own terms, to rebuild a truly human society.

Integrating science fiction and fantasy, symbolism and realism, philosophy and romance, Rand's novel inspires passionate responses from admirers and critics alike. Admirers see the book as the credo of a new intellectual movement, but critics from both ends of the political spectrum are repulsed. Left-leaning reviewers abhorred Rand's preoccupation with capitalism, whereas conservative columnists were sickened by Rand's atheism. Granville Hicks (1957) asserted that "the book is written out of hate." He condemned Rand for "cheerfully" celebrating "the destruction of civilization." And Whittaker Chambers, writing for *National Review*, sensed that Rand was heavily indebted to Nietzsche. But he believed that in her atheism and "materialism," Rand had greater affinity with Marx. Chambers wrote: "Thus, Randian Man, like Marxian Man, is made the center of a godless world." Chambers believed that in the "dictatorial tone" and "overriding arrogance" of the book, one can hear a voice "from almost any page . . . commanding: 'To a gas chamber—go!' "[48]

These hostile reviews from the left and the right partially reflected Rand's own belief that she had finally achieved a genuine philosophical synthesis that was neither Marxist nor religious. In her philosophic journals, Rand explained that her novel had to "*vindicate* the industrialist" as "the author of material production." Rand wished to secularize the spiritual, and spiritualize the material:

> The material is only the expression of the spiritual; that it can neither be created *nor used* without the spiritual (thought); that it

has no meaning without the spiritual, that it is only the means to a spiritual end—and therefore, any new achievement in the realm of material production is an act of *high spirituality*, a great triumph and expression of man's spirit. And that those who despise "the material" are those who despise man and whose basic premises are aimed at man's destruction.[49]

For Rand, the "spiritual" did not pertain to an otherworldly faculty, but rather to an activity of human consciousness. Reason, as "the highest kind of spiritual activity," was required "to conquer, control, and create in the material realm" (ibid.). Rand did not limit material activities to purely industrial production. She wished to "show that *any* original rational idea, in any sphere of human activity, is an act of creation and creativeness" (ibid.). This applies equally to the activity of industrialists and artists, businessmen and intellectuals, scientists and philosophers. Each of these spheres is accorded epistemological significance.

By connecting reason and production, thought and activity, theory and practice, Rand intended to uncover the "deeper, philosophical error" upon which these dichotomies were based. As such, *Atlas Shrugged* was designed to "*blast* the separation of man into 'body' and 'soul,' the opposition of 'matter' and 'spirit.'" Rand rejected the metaphysical dualists who had bifurcated human existence. She proclaimed in her journals that "man is an indivisible entity." Mind and body "can be considered separately only for purposes of discussion, not in actual fact." In reality, the human individual is an integrated whole.

This vision is central to Galt's sixty-page speech, which took Rand two years to complete (B. Branden 1986, 266). It abounds with ideas and principles that served as the basis for Rand's formal philosophical totality. But Rand's transcendence of dualism is just as obvious in those sections of Galt's speech which were edited out of the final manuscript. Rand writes:

> You had set every part of you to betray every other, you believed that your career bears no relation to your sex life, that your politics bear no relation to the choice of your friends, that your values bear no relation to your pleasures, and your heart bears no relation to your brain—you had chopped yourself into pieces which you struggled never to connect—but you see no reason why your life is in ruins and why you've lost the desire to live?[50]

Rand's revolt against dualism was motivated by a profound desire to exalt a heroic and integrated view of human existence. Even in the sex act, Rand's characters show a passionate spirituality that is not cut off from intense physical pleasure. In her journals, Rand explained that she wanted to dramatize the "*essential*, unbreakable tie between sex and spirit—which is the tie between body and soul." The religionists damned human beings for the sins of the flesh, whereas the materialists divorced man's mind from the functions of his body. Rand proclaimed that her morality of rational selfishness was designed for human life on earth. In her ethos, sex is as much a spiritual celebration as it is a physical one.[51]

Rand projects this mind-body synthesis in a fictional representation of the "ideal man." She explains that her chief protagonist, John Galt, "*has no intellectual contradiction and, therefore, no inner conflict.*" He experiences a joy in living that is not determined by pain or fear or guilt.[52] Each of Rand's heroes reflects this same "worship of joy" to a lesser degree, but all are united by Galt's oath, one that is similar to the credo enunciated by Equality 7-2521 in *Anthem*. Galt states: "I swear—by my life and my love of it—that I will never live for the sake of another man, nor ask another man to live for mine" (1069).

After years of literary and philosophic integration, Rand published *Atlas Shrugged* in 1957. She credited herself with having created a new, nonreligious morality through an aesthetic medium. She aimed to bridge the gap between art and entertainment. She wrote in her journal that traditional morality sees "art" and "entertainment" as polar opposites. Art is supposed to be "serious and dull." Entertainment is enjoyable, but superficial. No serious work of art, in such a traditional view, could possibly be both entertaining and "true to the deeper essence of life."[53] Rand rejected this distinction, and presented her novel as an organic totality, a work that fused action, adventure, and sensuality with philosophy, contemplation, and spirituality.

The Public Philosopher

After *Atlas Shrugged*, Rand turned toward a more systematized presentation of her philosophy in essays, books, and lectures. As early as 1958, a year after the publication of the novel, she was planning a book on her philosophy, which she had named Objectivism.[54] Its subtitle was to be "A

Philosophy for Living on Earth." In her journal, Rand wrote: "The purpose of this book is to make its sub-title redundant."[55] Though Rand never authored such a systematic formal treatise, much the same could be said about the subtitles of her anthologies, particularly *The Virtue of Selfishness: A New Concept of Egoism,* and *Capitalism: The Unknown Ideal.* Rand sought to make these books' subtitles redundant too. She labored for many years as the champion of both "rational selfishness" and "laissez-faire capitalism." Her concept of egoism conjoined the adjective "rational" to the noun "selfishness" in such a way to collapse their distinctions. Human beings are most selfish when they are pursuing their own rationally defined values and interests. Human beings are most rational when their values and interests are self-motivated. Likewise, Rand sought to collapse the distinction between the adjective "laissez-faire" and the noun "capitalism." Capitalism was an unknown ideal for Rand, because it had yet to be discovered in its purest and *only* legitimate form.

It could be said that for Rand, the notion of rational self-interest was *internal* to the concept of egoism; the notion of laissez-faire was *internal* to the concept of a genuinely capitalist social system. She and others explored many of these principles with increasing breadth and depth in such publications as *The Objectivist Newsletter* (1962–65), *The Objectivist* (1966–71), and *The Ayn Rand Letter* (1971–76). Important essays from these periodicals were anthologized in such nonfiction works as *The Virtue of Selfishness* (1964), *Capitalism: The Unknown Ideal* (1967), *The New Left: The Anti-Industrial Revolution* (1971), *The Romantic Manifesto* (1971), *Introduction to Objectivist Epistemology* (1979), and Rand's posthumously published works, *Philosophy: Who Needs It* (1982) and *The Voice of Reason* (1989). However, Rand's first nonfiction work to appear in book form was the lead essay of *For the New Intellectual,* which presented philosophical passages culled from the body of Rand's fiction. Rand's harsh and polemical tone, coupled with her caricaturing of many philosophers, led Sidney Hook to denounce the book for its sloganeering: "This is the way philosophy is written in the Soviet Union. In a free culture there must always be room for vigorous polemic and controversy but civility of mind is integral to the concept of a civilized society."[56]

Despite pinpointing a very real lack of civility in Rand's exposition, Hook did not realize that Rand's impulse toward synthesis was indeed the way philosophy had been written in Russia for many generations. Rand provoked the wrath of academicians partially because, like her Russian philosophical ancestors, she was an outcast, a social critic writing with a passionately

Fig. 3. Nathaniel and Barbara Branden at their wedding, 1953. (Courtesy of Nathaniel Branden)

Fig. 4. Members of Rand's inner circle, at the wedding of Nathaniel Branden's sister, Elayne, to Harry Kalberman. *From left:* Joan Mitchell, Alan Greenspan, Nathaniel Branden, Barbara Branden, Leonard Peikoff, Elayne Kalberman, Harry Kalberman, Ayn Rand, Frank O'Connor (Rand's husband), and Allan Blumenthal. (Courtesy of Barbara Branden)

immoderate tone that was far more accessible to the general public and far less considerate of scholarly give-and-take.

As her sales increased, so did her impact. She electrified audiences on television and radio, and in newspapers and magazines. With the establishment of the Nathaniel Branden Institute (N.B.I.), Rand's philosophy was mass marketed through the rental of taped courses. Rand made personal appearances at Columbia, Princeton, Harvard, Yale, New York University, and other college campuses across the country. On 2 October 1963, she received an honorary degree, Doctor of Humane Letters (L.H.D.), from Lewis and Clark College in Portland, Oregon, in recognition of her growing influence (Gladstein 1984, ii).

But in 1968, the Objectivist movement was torn asunder in a schism between Rand and two of her closest friends and associates, Nathaniel and Barbara Branden. In later years, it became apparent that the schism was inextricably tied to a collapsing love affair between Rand and Nathaniel

Branden.[57] Even though Rand continued to publish and lecture in the ensuing years, her fractured movement disintegrated under the weight of charges and countercharges. Eventually, Rand's disillusionment with the state of the world led to her virtual retirement from public life.

Ayn Rand died on 6 March 1982 and was buried in Valhalla, New York.

In the years since her death, Objectivist philosophy has emerged as a veritable tradition of thought.

Flowing almost directly from what remained of Rand's inner circle are the "orthodox" Objectivists, led by Leonard Peikoff. The orthodox school consists of thinkers such as Harry Binswanger, Edwin Locke, Edith Packer, George Reisman, John Ridpath, and Peter Schwartz, among others.

Leonard Peikoff received his doctorate in philosophy at New York University in 1964 under the direction of Sidney Hook. Peikoff's dissertation was titled "The Status of the Law of Contradiction in Classic Logical Ontologism."[58] His mentor criticized him as a "monist" and a "Hegelian," but this did not deter Peikoff from his Objectivist predilections.[59] Yet like a genuine Hegelian, Peikoff argues that no philosophic problems can be resolved in a vacuum, since all issues are interconnected.[60] Admitting to a tendency toward rationalism, Peikoff never tires of quoting Hegel's dictum that "The True is the Whole."[61] He repeats this credo in his books, articles, and courses, warning of the danger of "one-sided distortions" (1983T, lecture 7). His presentation has always been more deductive than inductive, more synthetic than analytic.[62] But in many ways, the Peikoff-Rand link parallels the relationship between Engels and Marx. Like Engels, Peikoff has continued to publish and edit many of his mentor's previously unavailable writings. He has also made an important contribution to the formalized presentation of Rand's philosophy in his most recent book, which derives from both the written and oral tradition of Objectivism.

In contrast to the Randian orthodoxy, there are those neo-Objectivist thinkers who are generally associated with the Institute for Objectivist Studies (I.O.S.), a scholarly organization headed by David Kelley. Kelley's *Evidence of the Senses* is a realist defense of perception in the Objectivist tradition. Other thinkers who have spoken at Institute forums or written for its journal, include Joan and Allan Blumenthal, Stephen Hicks, George Walsh, and the late Kay Nolte Smith.

There is also a group of "libertarian" neo-Objectivists, consisting of such theorists as Tibor Machan, Eric Mack, Douglas Den Uyl, and Douglas Rasmussen. This group of thinkers relates Rand's work to the Aristotelian, classical liberal, and modern libertarian traditions.

Finally, one cannot discount the contributions of Nathaniel and Barbara Branden. Despite leaving Rand's inner circle in 1968, the Brandens have each moved in the direction of "revisionism."[63] Nathaniel Branden in particular has emerged from his years with Rand as an important theorist and practitioner of "biocentric" psychology. As the so-called father of the self-esteem movement, Branden has emphasized the role of self-esteem in nearly every aspect of human life. His books include *The Psychology of Self-Esteem* (1969), *The Disowned Self* (1971), *The Psychology of Romantic Love* (1980), *Honoring the Self* (1983), and *The Six Pillars of Self-Esteem* (1994). Even though he departs from some of Rand's formulations, he continues to build on the Objectivist approach.[64]

Part Two

The Revolt
Against Dualism

5   Being

N. O. Lossky (1951) once wrote: "Philosophy is a science and therefore, like every other science, it seeks to establish truths that have been strictly proved and are therefore binding for every thinking being and not only for a particular people or nation." Operating at the highest level of generality, the philosopher traces the interconnections between the entities, elements, and aspects of reality. The philosopher must unite "two opposed and not easily combinable faculties: the highest degree of abstract thinking and a high degree of concrete contemplation of reality" (402). In Lossky's view, however, people have not developed these faculties to the degree required for the truly stupendous tasks of the examined life. That many opposing schools of philosophy exist illustrates that philosophy is at a much more primitive level of development than either mathematics or physics (403). But for Lossky, philosophy was paving the way for a more unified, nondualistic conception of being and knowing.

Though Rand rejected much of the content of Lossky's philosophy, her own system retained an exhaustive and dialectical form that reflected her Russian roots. Just as significant, however, was Rand's profound respect for *philosophy* as essential to human being. Like her teacher, Rand perpetuated a distinctive tradition of philosophizing that stretched back to the days of the ancient Greeks. For Rand, it was the culture of classical antiquity that marked the beginning of humankind's intellectual maturity. The classical thinkers contributed to humanity the very concept of philosophy as a secular discipline in which the mind strove to achieve "a comprehensive view of existence." Rand believed that this authentic, nonreligious commitment to the examined life was rarely duplicated in the history of thought: "The grandeur, the reverence, the exalted purity, the austere dedication to the pursuit of truth, which are commonly associated with religion, should properly belong to the field of philosophy. Aristotle lived up to it and, in part, so did Plato, Aquinas, Spinoza—but how many others?"[1]

Like her teacher, Rand argued that philosophy requires the greatest level of abstraction *and* concretization, "the integration of factual data, the maintenance of a full context, the discovery of principles, the establishment of causal connections and thus the implementation of a long-range vision" (108). Every aspect of Rand's thought—from her social ontology to her politics—concentrates on the specifically *conceptual* nature and needs of human consciousness.

Like most systematic visions, Rand's Objectivism cannot be fully appreciated until it is grasped as a totality. No totality, however, can be presented as such. Peikoff argues correctly that the whole can only be examined through the parts. Every part of a philosophical system implies both the whole and every other part.[2] Furthermore, Peikoff understands that Objectivism is structured as an *internally related* system, such that any "change in one element redounds throughout the network." Indeed, for Peikoff, as for Rand, Objectivism mirrors the very interrelationships that are present in existence and knowledge. Peikoff maintains: "*Human knowledge on every level is relational.* Knowledge is *not* a juxtaposition of independent items; it is a unity . . . a total, a sum, a single whole." The relational character of knowledge is a reflection of the metaphysical fact that "there is only one universe." In the universe, "everything . . . is interconnected." Peikoff writes:

> Every entity is related in some way to the others; each somehow affects and is affected by the others. Nothing is a completely isolated fact, without causes or effects; no aspect of the total can exist ultimately apart from the total. Knowledge, therefore, which seeks to grasp reality, must also be a total; its elements must be interconnected to form a unified whole reflecting the whole which is the universe.[3]

Peikoff stresses also that no mind can disregard the relationships among its contents because the discovery of such relationships is inherent in the identity of consciousness. Thus every tenet of a philosophy, just like every aspect of knowledge, "must be judged in the light of the total picture, i.e., of the full context." Since every element of knowledge "is potentially relevant to the rest," a genuinely integrated philosophy must transcend fragmentation and subdivision. Peikoff (1991b, 125) suggests that Rand's achievement lies partially in her methodical consistency within the context of available knowledge.

Ultimately, then, one cannot analyze any of Rand's isolated philosophical insights by disconnecting them from the corpus of her thought. Taken together, each part generates and is generated by the totality. Rand's approach is so thoroughly integrated that her philosophical beginnings seem to presuppose the results of her entire system.[4]

Yet, as I have demonstrated, Rand's philosophy was not a mere deduction from first principles. It was a historical product of her revolt against formal dualism. Ironically, Rand has been criticized for the reverse evolution of her thought, for its movement from political to metaphysical themes. William O'Neill ([1971] 1975) suggests, for instance, that Rand's philosophy really began with ethics and terminated, as an afterthought, with a theory of truth and knowledge: "Her epistemology and her metaphysical assumptions—indeed, the vast bulk of her philosophy—are essentially an *a posteriori* rationalization for a fervent *a priori* commitment to the ethics of laissez-faire capitalism" (175).

In a certain sense, of course, O'Neill is correct. Rand's literary project began with a political dynamic and concluded with ontological and episte-mological themes. In *We the Living*, Rand focused on the central question of the individual against the state. By the time she had written *Atlas Shrugged*, she was examining the role of the mind in human existence and making explicit connections between epistemic and political themes.

But it is ahistorical for O'Neill to suggest that *any* thinker could develop a system of thought by merely deducing it from metaphysical principles. It is true that many Objectivists imply that the morality of capitalism flows logically from the law of identity. Rand herself wrote with such a polemical flair that many of her ontological and political insights seem self-evident. The fact is, however, that Rand's system is less a rationalization of her belief in capitalism than it is an articulation of the underlying, interconnected ontological, epistemological, and ethical premises on which capitalism depends.

Rand could never have begun with metaphysics and merely deduced her political ideas. She did not emerge full-grown from the head of Zeus as a modern goddess of wisdom. Her entire philosophical project was a historical product from its genesis to its formal presentation. Indeed, Rand had to develop her thought quite extensively before she could present it as an organic *system* of philosophical integration.

She begins with ontology and epistemology, breaking up the world into humanly knowable, relational units. This analytical moment of Rand's method encapsulates a process of intellectual "chewing," of breaking down the whole into graspable elements. By tearing these elements apart, Rand makes them intellectually digestible (Peikoff 1983T, lecture 1). Her mode of inquiry traces the interconnections between these units on a social scale, reconstructing the totality as an organic whole. Her ethics and her politics are grounded in her teleological and biological insights. Though Rand is known for her polemics, she was quite adept at theoretical integration, expanding and synthesizing the units of her analysis to encompass the whole of reality.

A central aspect of Rand's exposition is her ability to trace the dialectical relationships between apparent opposites. Rand was never misled into accepting her opponents' definition of a specific philosophical or social problem. She aimed to "go to the root of the issue," claiming that the essential aspects of any question often could not be grasped by relying on the static premises and traditional frames of reference in mainstream thought (N. Branden 1989, 215).

Toward this end, Rand analyzed the antinomic "paradoxes" in modern philosophy. For Rand, a paradox had the appearance of a logical contradiction, which is at root, impossible (Peikoff 1974T, lecture 2). Hence, it was incumbent upon her as a dialectical thinker, to trace the links between apparent opposites, to show that the alternatives offered by contemporary schools of thought were false.[5]

Though Rand aimed to document the fundamental links uniting such opposites, she also attempted to show that many contemporary thinkers had merely settled for embracing reductionist monism rather than finding a remedy for the various forms of dualism. They emphasized one pole of a duality as a means of reconciling opposition. In Rand's view, dualism could not be conquered through the absorption of one polar principle by another. Just as Rand's philosophy attempts to transcend alleged polarities as a means of providing an integrated view of human existence, so her critique of opposing traditions in Western thought seeks to uncover the fundamental errors they share. In most cases, Rand shows that each of the opposing schools of philosophy is half right *and* half wrong.

Since Rand discovered value in many of the philosophies she analyzed, some critics have attempted to tie Objectivism to such traditions as rationalism, materialism, or existentialism.[6] What her critics failed to grasp was that she was working toward a new synthesis, which required that she use established categories in the process of transcending them. She both accepted and rejected significant principles within each of the polar traditions which she analyzed. Consequently, by abstracting particular aspects from the totality of her thought, one can see elements of rationalism *and* empiricism, idealism *and* materialism, liberalism *and* conservatism. Rand explains: "Most men hold mixed premises; most schools of thought are full of contradictions. One may find some elements of value, of truth and of rationality in many people and schools. This does not make them Objectivist."[7]

Part 2 examines the distinctiveness of Objectivism, even as it traces significant parallels between Rand's thought and others in the history of philosophy. But in dissecting the content of Objectivism, much of the following discussion may sometimes obscure the broad fundamentals of Rand's worldview. Rand herself was once asked to identify the central tenets of her system. Her identification, in each of the major branches of philosophy, is worth recalling:

> 1. *Metaphysics*: Objective Reality. 2. *Epistemology*: Reason. 3. *Ethics*: Self-interest. 4. *Politics*: Capitalism. If you want this translated into simple language, it would read: 1. "Nature, to be commanded, must be obeyed" or "Wishing won't make it so." 2. "You can't eat your cake and have it, too." 3. "Man is an end in himself." 4. "Give me liberty or give me death."[8]

The Rejection of Cosmology

Rand's revolt against formal dualism first manifested itself in the realm of metaphysics or ontology.[9] Metaphysics, for Rand, refers to that branch of philosophy which "deals with the fundamental nature of reality."[10] Metaphysics involves the widest abstractions pertaining to existence as such.[11] Whereas the special sciences separate a part of existence and investigate it thoroughly, metaphysics is concerned with the ultimate context of reality and knowledge, that is, "being qua being."

Rand's approach to the ontological foundations of philosophy was mini-malist. In fact, beyond the general axiomatic proposition of existence, Rand refused—on principle—to commit herself to any a priori judgments about the ultimate constituents of reality. She believed that epistemology was the crux of philosophy because it related to the means of knowledge and was the base of all special sciences. Rand herself considered ontology and epistemology inseparable, and argued that each therefore implied the other (Peikoff 1976T, lecture 4). Thus her axioms serve as the foundation for her theories both of being and of knowing.

Having been schooled in ancient philosophy by Lossky, Rand was well acquainted with the classical Greek thinkers. In the area of ontology, she generally celebrated the accomplishments of antiquity, most particularly the works of Aristotle. But she viewed the inclusion of cosmology in ancient metaphysics as an error that had had disastrous effects throughout intellec-tual history. Cosmology sought to define the *specific* nature of the universe. For Rand, the specific nature of the universe was a scientific question. The legitimacy of philosophy depended on its ability to provide the ontological and logical foundations for all forms of inquiry. Philosophy was metascien-tific.

Rand identified Thales, the father of Western thought, as the first philosopher to define the nature of the universe in cosmological terms. Even though Thales was groping toward a unified view of existence and knowl-edge, he argued that the universe consisted of water, air, and fire. By concluding "that water was the primary metaphysical (or cosmological) element," Thales pretended to an omniscience that was impossible to the human mind. Such an approach was profoundly rationalistic because it dogmatized science by reifying the available knowledge into a self-sufficient whole. It made metaphysics dependent upon "every new discovery of physics."

Rand believed that such rationalism had been duplicated many times throughout the history of philosophy. Later empiricists were correct to repudiate this approach. However, Rand argued that Thales, Plato, and the ancient cosmologists were, in fact, "arrested empiricists" because they had formed conclusions about "the ultimate constituents of the universe" by "taking partial knowledge as omniscience."[12] The cosmologists had pro-jected epistemological conclusions into their metaphysical foundations. But if the rationalists were "arrested empiricists" for reifying their current state of knowledge, then empiricists displayed a "Hegelian or Rationalistic" tendency to dogmatize their empirical conclusions. Both alternatives depend on the same fundamental error. They

> advance conditions for what that primary has to be. . . . You cannot say philosophically what conditions you will ascribe to that which is not known. We cannot know by what means we will grasp something not known today. . . . And yet in making any kind of conclusions about the ultimate stuff of the universe, you are necessarily committing that error. You are prescribing conditions of what something not known to you now has to be. ("Appendix," 292–93)

In Rand's rejection of cosmology, then, there is an important grasp of the origins of dualism in the history of Western thought. Rand argues that the inclusion of cosmology in the body of philosophy necessarily generated antinomic tensions. Cosmology contributed to the belief that the universe could be defined in terms of two separate spheres of reality. This led to the development of reductionistic, monistic alternatives in which one sphere is emphasized to the detriment of the other. In her journal, Rand wrote: "'Cosmology' has to be thrown out of philosophy. When this is done, the conflict between 'rationalism' and 'empiricism' will be wiped out—or rather, the error that permitted the nonsense of such a conflict will be wiped out."[13]

Rationalists and idealists, empiricists and materialists have traditionally embraced one polar principle over another. Each has sought to identify the primary "stuff" of the world. Rationalists identify the basic substance as spiritual or ideal; empiricists, as atomistic and material. The former view matter as a manifestation of the spirit, whereas the latter see consciousness as a pure epiphenomenon of material elements. The former affirm the identity of consciousness, but reject the material basis of reality, and the latter accept the reality of the body, of the physical world in general, but doubt the ontological integrity of the mind. Such traditions cut "man" in two,

> "Setting one half against the other. They have taught him that his body and his consciousness are two enemies engaged in deadly conflict, two antagonists of opposite natures, contradictory claims, incompatible needs, that to benefit one is to injure the other. . . . They have taught man that he is a hopeless misfit made of two elements, both symbols of death. A body without a soul is a corpse,

a soul without a body is a ghost—yet such is their image of man's nature." (*Atlas Shrugged*, 1026)

Both Rand and Peikoff argue that in the history of philosophy, it was the Pythagoreans who first conceptualized this dualism in their distinction between this world and the world of numbers. Their orphic cults taught that the body was the tomb of the soul. Plato absorbed this Pythagorean legacy and distinguished between the world of particulars and the world of universals or Forms.[14] Augustine christianized this dualism and argued that there was an incommensurability between this world and the next (Peikoff 1972T, lecture 7). It was not until Aquinas resurrected Aristotelianism that philosophers began seeing existence as singular, albeit one in which there was a natural, hierarchic totality ascending to God (lecture 8).

Rand contended, however, that at the birth of modern philosophy, dualism reared its ugly head in a more sophisticated form with Descartes, who saw the physical world and human consciousness as two distinct, unrelated spheres. By beginning with the metaphysical assumption that the spiritual and the physical are independent of each other Cartesian philosophy creates the problem of mind-body interaction.[15]

By banishing cosmology from the realm of metaphysics, Rand sought to provide a highly delimited, ontological foundation for philosophy. For Rand, *whatever* the "ultimate stuff" of the universe is, it will have identity—it will be something definite. To this extent, ontology is metascientific. Rand seeks the reconciliation of philosophy and science. Philosophy cannot depend on a changing physics for its ontological foundations. Rand argues, however, that genuine science *must* depend on philosophy to validate its modes of inquiry.

But the relationship between philosophy and science is *not* one of logical dependence. It is *not* a strictly causal relationship. It is an internal relationship in which there is some reciprocity between elements, even though the relation is fundamentally skewed toward the primary element.[16] This *asymmetric internality* preserves both hierarchy and interdependence, and prevents vicious circularity. As Harry Binswanger (1990) explains:

> Some empirical content is and must be contained in philosophical theories. On the other hand, philosophical theories should not be subject to the rise and fall of purely scientific hypotheses, since those hypotheses may come to be rejected in the light of new evidence. Moreover, since science builds upon basic philosophical principles

(e.g., the basic axioms, the law of causality, the principles of logic), there is the danger of employing circular reasoning in using science to support philosophical conclusions. (174)

Since knowledge is rooted in the evidence of the senses, all of the principles of philosophy and science must ultimately depend on observation and inference. Even though Rand's metaphysical axioms can be grasped implicitly by the mind of the infant and the adult alike, they are conceptually identified as primary facts of reality, embracing the entire field of human awareness. As such, the axiomatic concepts serve as the foundation of ontology, epistemology, logic, objectivity, and science itself.

Rand's metaphysic then is both highly abstract and extremely narrow. It is summed up in the axiomatic propositions of identity and causality. For Rand, "Philosophy tells us only *that* things have natures, but *what* these natures are is the job of specific sciences. The rest of philosophy's task is to tell us the rules by which to discover the specific natures."[17]

Thus it is not the task of philosophy to validate the theory of natural selection or to hypothesize about the evolutionary origins of consciousness (Peikoff 1980T, lecture 8). Philosophy is concerned with the broad nature of existence. It must leave to science the assessment of the ultimate nature of life, the ultimate relationship between matter and consciousness, mind and body. Even if Rand assumed an organic unity of elements within the totality of a single universe, she refused to reflect on the basis of the interrelationships of these elements. Such cosmological speculation depends on an imaginary omniscient standpoint. As Peikoff emphasizes, Rand's Objectivism makes a distinction between metaphysics and fantasy.[18] There can be no purely deductive attempt to reveal the ultimate substances of reality (Peikoff 1972T, lecture 10).

Philosophy, then, begins with the knowledge of everything-in-general. It begins with that which exists. Physics, by contrast, requires greater particularity. Like all theories, the hypotheses of physics may change with the growing context of knowledge. Even the Heisenberg Uncertainty Principle leaves Rand undaunted. For Rand, the inability to predict a subatomic event does not prove that causality does not apply to subatomic particles. Our current inability to measure the simultaneous position and momentum of subatomic particles does not show that in reality such events are causeless. Epistemological ignorance does not disprove ontology. In Rand's view, scientific explanation (or the lack thereof) does not erase the reality it seeks to explain.[19]

Thus Rand's Objectivism accommodates all scientific theories.[20] Furthermore, although Rand criticized some of the epistemic foundations of contemporary "pseudo-science,"[21] she did not feel threatened by the nearly anarchic variation within modern theoretical science. As Tibor Machan (1992) notes, Rand's Objectivism is based on "an open-minded ontological pluralism, and an (almost) anything goes, (almost) Feyerabendian, laissez-faire attitude toward the methods of empirical investigation" (53).

Axiomatic Concepts

For Rand, ontology must begin with much more basic, prescientific, fundamental propositions about existence, *axioms* that can be grasped even implicitly by primitive peoples ("Appendix," 247–48). Rejecting cosmology, Rand argues that reality is what it is independent of what people think or feel and that consciousness is the faculty of perceiving and understanding reality. As her protagonist John Galt exclaims in Atlas Shrugged: "Existence exists—and the act of grasping that statement implies two corollary axioms: that something exists which one perceives and that one exists possessing consciousness, consciousness being the faculty of perceiving that which exists" (1015).

Existence *and* consciousness are axioms at the base of knowledge. Such axioms are contained in every fact, perception, observation, statement, proof, explanation, and utterance of any human being, whether it is formally acknowledged or not. An axiom is not a meaningless tautology; it identifies "a primary factor of reality, which cannot be analyzed, i.e., reduced to other facts or broken into component parts" (*Introduction*, 55). An axiom is so fundamental that even those who refuse to recognize its veracity must "accept it and use it in the process of any attempt to deny it" (*Atlas Shrugged*, 1040).

By articulating the axioms of existence and consciousness, Rand did not embrace a dualistic perspective on reality.[22] She merely identified the foundations that lie at the base of all philosophical inquiry. As Peikoff (1991b) explains, these axioms "cannot be sundered. There is no consciousness without existence and no knowledge of existence without consciousness" (149–50). And yet, as a philosophical realist, Rand emphasized the primary axiom of existence. She affirms the *primacy* of existence. In a sense, existence and consciousness are internally, but asymmetrically related.

Existence exists; it does not depend upon consciousness and would continue to exist if every last form of conscious life were obliterated from the universe. The universe simply is; there is nothing outside, prior to, or at the culmination of existence. Existence cannot be derived from any prior certainty of consciousness, nor is it the product of divine will. There is no first cause or teleological design. There is only existence as such.

By contrast, consciousness is radically dependent on existence for its contents. It is metaphysically passive and, as Kelley (1986) explains, "radically noncreative" (27). This metaphysical passivity does not imply epistemological passivity. People are capable of creativity; they are able to selectively reorganize the mind's contents and to project imagination. The radical noncreativity of consciousness refers to the fact that the mind does not create or constitute the objects it perceives. They exist independent of consciousness. Consciousness as such is purely *relational*, and what it relates to is objective reality. In Rand's view, "A consciousness conscious of nothing but itself is a contradiction in terms: before it could identify itself as consciousness, it had to be conscious of something" (Atlas Shrugged, 1015). Every phenomenon of consciousness derives from an awareness of existence. Rand writes:

> Some object, i.e., some *content*, is involved in every state of aware-
> ness. Extrospection is a process of cognition directed outward—a
> process of apprehending some existent(s) of the external world.
> Introspection is a process of cognition directed inward—a process of
> apprehending one's own psychological actions in regard to some
> existent(s) of the external world, such actions as thinking, feeling,
> reminiscing, etc. It is only in relation to the external world that the
> various actions of a consciousness can be experienced, grasped,
> defined or communicated. Awareness is awareness of something. A
> content-less state of consciousness is a contradiction in terms.[23]

Rand's emphasis on the primacy of existence is equally a recognition of the fundamentality of ontology in the hierarchy of philosophy. In this regard, Rand may have learned much from her Marxist professors at Petrograd University, who emphasized the primacy of existence over consciousness. The "objectivist" strain in Marxism was particularly apparent in the Leninist worldview, which dominated early Soviet intellectual life. Rand's metaphysic echoes the Marxist preoccupation with "the world as it is," what Scott Meikle (1985) has described as "the recognition of the primacy of ontology over epistemology" (174).

Marx also rejected cosmology and endorsed the ontological view of logic. He writes:

> Who begot the first man, and nature as a whole? I can only answer you: Your question is itself a product of abstraction. Ask yourself how you arrived at that question. Ask yourself whether your question is not posed from a standpoint to which I cannot reply, because it's wrongly put. . . . When you ask about the creation of nature and man, you are abstracting, in so doing, from man and nature. You postulate them as *non-existent*, and yet you want me to prove them to you as *existing*. Now I say to you: give up your abstraction and you will also give up your question. Or if you want to hold on to your abstraction, then be consistent, and if you think of man and nature as *non-existent*, then think of yourself as non-existent, for you too are surely nature and man. Don't think, don't ask me, for as soon as you think and ask, your *abstraction* from the existence of nature and man has no meaning. Or are you such an egoist that you conceive everything as nothing, and yet want yourself to exist?[24]

Rand would certainly have taken issue with Marx's solipsistic characterization of egoism. But she too rejected "creation" questions as vestiges of a cosmological perspective. Rand would have greatly appreciated Marx's reaffirmation of the primacy of existence through denial. Indeed, Rand argued vociferously against those who attempted to disprove the existence of something for which there was no evidence. As Peikoff explains: "The onus of proof is on him who asserts the positive."[25] Objectivists rely heavily on this polemical style of argumentation, utilizing variations of the "boomerang" principle.[26] This is apparent in Rand's critique of the "stolen concept fallacy" and the "reification of the zero."

It was Aristotle who first employed the technique of reaffirmation through denial when he asserted that nobody could reject the laws of logic without relying on them in the process. Aristotle viewed these laws at the base of all human activity, reasoning, and language. For Aristotle, such principles were both ontological *and* logical, grasped intuitively and without need of proof.

Rand's teacher, Lossky ([1917] 1928, 8), had used a similar argument in his clash with the atomistic materialists. He claimed that even those who denied the organic structure of the world, implicitly accepted it in their every pronouncement. Since every utterance and action depends on the wholeness and predictability of reality, such organicism could not be escaped. Even though the world is composed of many different elements, each of these elements belongs to the same reality. The organic structure of reality is a metaphysical given which makes the world knowable. Knowledge is never constructed out of wholly independent elements. Rather, these elements are part of an all-embracing network of relations that can be analyzed on different levels of generality.

Although Rand would not have seen the organic structure of reality as strictly axiomatic, she did reproduce the form of Lossky's argument. Just as it is a logical error to use what you are trying to prove, the so-called fallacy of "begging the question," it is equally an error to use what you're trying to disprove. Rand calls the latter the fallacy of the stolen concept.[27] As Nathaniel Branden explains, all of knowledge has a hierarchical structure. Hence, "When one uses concepts, one must recognize their genetic roots, one must recognize that which they logically depend on and presuppose." For Branden, as for Rand, one does not have a logical right to use "*a concept while ignoring, contradicting, or denying the validity of the concepts on which it logically and genetically depends.*"[28]

Rand argued that most philosophers treated higher-level concepts as first-level abstractions, tearing them from their appropriate place in the hierarchy of knowledge, denying their epistemological roots, and ultimately detaching them from reality (Peikoff 1991b, 136). This practice has had far-reaching implications and is one of the symptoms of modern anti-conceptualism.

Rand's view of hierarchy is purely epistemological. In reality, all facts are simultaneous. Rand explains: "Regardless of what a given man did chronologically, once he has his full conceptual development, a very important test of whether a concept is first-level would be whether, within the context of his own knowledge, he would be able to hold or explain or communicate a certain concept without referring to preceding concepts" ("Appendix," 214).

Though Rand rejected the vicious circularity of the stolen concept fallacy, she grasps that circularity per se is not necessarily wrong. Many of her own arguments have an element of what Rasmussen has called "just" circularity. This grows out of the starkly dialectical character of Rand's worldview. For instance, Rand saw the aging process as integral to mortality. Though we may never know what ultimately causes people to age, mortality *implies* aging, just as aging itself indicates mortality. This is circular and tautological. Aging is internal to mortality, which is internal to aging. But in "just" circularity, the reciprocal relationship between terms does not invalidate the statement. Indeed, it merely underscores the relational unity these facts have with other facts. Each element of the whole must both support and imply the others. There is a necessary interrelationship of the parts within the totality (Peikoff 1983T, lecture 9).

By contrast, Rand rejects what Rasmussen (1980) has called, "vicious" circularity. In the "vicious" case, there is "reasoning from some principle in order to demonstrate that very principle" (68). For Rand, using an arbitrary assertion to confirm itself or a valid principle to deny itself are instances of vicious circularity.

Adopting the language of internal relations, one could say that such circularity is illegitimate because it is based on arbitrary assertions that attempt to circumvent the hierarchically structured totality of knowledge. Those who make such arbitrary assertions are attempting to make themselves *external* to an epistemological totality that necessarily involves connections between and among concepts. Those who would deny the truthfulness of an axiomatic concept repudiate principles *internal* to every other concept in their usage. Such axioms are at the base of, and form the context for, all concepts. Those who would deny them by exempting themselves from the totality within which all others think and act, are trying to attain a synoptic perspective on the whole. This is an attack on the metaepistemological principles that make knowledge possible.

In Rand's view, the "reification of the zero" is one of the most notorious attempts to achieve such an internal contradiction. In this fallacy, the speaker regards " 'nothing' as a *thing*, as a special, different kind of *existent*." But for Rand, existence and nonexistence are not metaphysically equal. Nonexistence can only be defined *in relation to* existence. The concept "nothing" cannot be removed from the context that gives it meaning; it cannot be reified as a separate thing. Apart from its relational usage, "nothing" is a concept without validity (*Introduction*, 60–61). There is no such thing as "pure" negation apart from that which it negates. Those who attempt to prove the existence of a negative, or to deny an axiom, step outside the bounds of logic and ontologic, and are defeated by their own denials.

Ontology and Logic

Having articulated the two basic axioms, Rand distinguishes a third, which is a corollary of existence and internal to all elements of reality and knowledge. It is the principle of identity, "A is A," a variation on Aristotle's law of noncontradiction.[29]

In the *Metaphysics*, Aristotle argues that permanent negation is not possible. There is an ultimate principle at the base of reason which is both ontological and epistemological. It is not a hypothesis, but a principle that is "true of being *qua* being." It is a principle that is "the most certain of all. . . . It is, that the same attribute cannot at the same time belong and not belong to the same subject and in the same respect. . . . it is impossible for any one to believe the same thing to be and not to be."[30]

Like Aristotle, Rand believes that logic is inseparable from reality and knowledge. She states: "If logic has nothing to do with reality, it means that the Law of Identity is inapplicable to reality" (*Philosophy*, 17). But, as Peikoff (1985) explains: "The Law of Contradiction . . . is a necessary and ontological truth which *can* be learned empirically" (185). Aristotle believed that people learned this principle by intuitive induction (198).[31] Peikoff (1985) maintains that, for Aristotle, "the Law of Contradiction has . . . a twofold epistemological character: it is at once an experiential-inductive principle and an intuitive first principle. This characteristic Aristotelian union of the 'empirical' and the 'rational' is, in one or another form, fundamental to the whole subsequent Aristotelian tradition" (196).

Peikoff, undoubtedly, sees Rand as having inherited significant elements of this Aristotelian tradition. And although it is true that the ontological conception is explicit in Aristotle's text, it is also true that both Russian Marxist-Leninism and Russian neo-Idealism adhered to this view. Lenin himself had proposed an "objectivist" ontology and realist epistemology which echoed the Aristotelian themes.[32] And Lossky, who introduced Rand to the study of Aristotle, was also an advocate of the ontological conception. He wrote: "Logical principles are merely that part of metaphysical principles which has significance both for the structure of being and for the structure of truth" (Lossky [1917] 1928, 183). Thus the laws of logic are at the base of both ontology and epistemology (Lossky [1906] 1919, 409). Rejecting the eleatic monists and the Heracliteans, Lossky (1951) argues that stasis and change are not a violation of the law of identity, for "both movement and rest belong to the body in different respects" (288). Thus, "The laws of identity and of contradiction, if properly understood, are absolutely inviolable" (290).

Rand's Objectivism embraces a similar view. Logic is certainly a law of thought, insofar as it is "the art of *non-contradictory identification*." But logic is true in thought only because contradictions cannot exist in reality. Rand writes:

"An atom is itself, and so is the universe; neither can contradict its own identity; nor can a part contradict the whole. No concept man forms is valid unless he integrates it without contradiction into the total sum of his knowledge. To arrive at a contradiction is to confess an error in one's thinking; to maintain a contradiction is to abdicate one's mind and to evict oneself from the realm of reality." (*Atlas Shrugged*, 1016–17)

Moreover, the law of identity is not a static tautology. Identity includes change and transformation. A *is* A, but dynamism and process are inherent in A's development.[33] In Binswanger's view, "the law of identity does not attempt to freeze reality. Change exists; it is a fact of reality. When a thing is changing, that is what it is doing, that is its identity for that period. What is still is still. What is in process is in process. A is A."[34]

Yet to state that "A is A" is not sufficient. Rand has not reified "existence" as something separate from the things that exist. She links her discussion of identity to *specific* existents: "To exist is to be something, as distinguished from the nothing of non-existence, it is to be an entity of a specific nature made of specific attributes. . . . A thing is itself" (*Atlas Shrugged*, 1016).

Rand's characteristic formulation is that "Existence is Identity" (ibid.). Rand does *not* state that Existence *has* identity (Peikoff 1991b, 6); rather, existence and identity are simultaneous and indivisible. The only "difference" between existence and identity is in their conceptual context and purpose (Peikoff 1990–91T, lecture 1). For Rand,

> The distinction between these two is really an issue of perspective. "Existence" is the wider concept, because even at an infant's stage of sensory chaos, he can grasp that something exists. When he gets the concept "identity," it is a further step—a clearer, more specific perspective on the concept "existence." He grasps that if it exists, it is *something*. Therefore, the referents of the concept "identity" are specific concretes or specific existents. And, you see, even though it is the same concept, the whole disaster of philosophy is that philosophers try to separate the two. ("Appendix," 240–41)

Thus existence and identity are one fact described from two different vantage points. Existence means that something *exists*; identity means that *something* exists (Peikoff 1991b, 7). Rand rejects the view that existence and identity are *aspects* of real existents. Rather, existence and identity *"are the existents."*

Similarly, Rand argues that if existence is identity, "Consciousness is Identification" (*Atlas Shrugged*, 1016). Since consciousness exists, it too, has a specific identity. It is not simply an attribute of a certain state of awareness within living organisms. It *is* the state of awareness. Consciousness is inherent in a person's grasp of existence.

Those who see consciousness as an epiphenomenon of material factors would criticize Rand for her belief that it is an irreducible primary. But Rand preserves the integrity of the whole by asserting that even if consciousness can be explained by a constellation of specific material factors, it is still not reducible to any of its constituent elements.[35] As Robert Efron argues, scientists cannot assert that consciousness is reducible to the laws of physics and chemistry, when these laws are still not yet known in their entirety. Like all cosmologists, "the mechanists insist upon omniscience." They also commit the fallacy of the stolen concept by smuggling the facts of consciousness into their analysis, since they must use volition in the process of denying its efficacy.[36]

Rand's affirmation of the identity of existence and consciousness implies that entities which exist are limited, finite, and knowable. The Greeks believed that such limitation was inherently good. In Greek thought, the unlimited was both indefinable and unknowable. By contrast, the Christian metaphysic moved away from the realism of the Aristotelian tradition and elevated the infinite above the finite. Peikoff argues that this sparked a mystical rebellion against identity which culminated in the irrationality of modern philosophy. Objectivism attempts to recapture the profound realism of the Aristotelian worldview.[37]

Rand believed that the three axioms at the base of ontology and epistemology were significant in several ways. First and foremost, she believed that knowledge depended on the recognition of certain basic foundations. The axioms provided such an ultimate context, an irreducible secular grounding for epistemological continuity, guidance, and objectivity ("Appendix," 260–61). They are the preconditions of all knowledge (Peikoff 1983T, lecture 9).

Second, she did *not* consider these axioms the foundation for a rationalistic science. Peikoff argues that to present Objectivism as a step-by-step deduction from first principles is to reconstitute it as a form of monism.[38] Like Theodor Adorno, Peikoff admits that in the history of philosophy the articulation of axioms has sometimes led to rationalist authoritarianism.[39]

Rand rejected monism as the acceptance of one polar principle over another. She repudiated cosmology and tried to avoid the kind of dogmatism that has plagued other ontologists.

Moreover, Rand did not limit her axioms to the point of exclusion. Though existence, identity, and consciousness are the basic irreducible fundamentals in her system, Rand recognized that other concepts have an axiomatic character too. In their primary usage, such concepts as "entity," "the validity of the senses," and "free will" exhibit all of the irreducible, simultaneous qualities of axioms.[40] Even though Rand provides broad validation of these concepts, she argues that none of them can be proven by reduction to sensory data because each is the basis of proof.

Having emphasized the axioms of existence, identity, and consciousness, Rand traces their implications. The first "self-evident" consequence, or corollary, of identity is the law of causality. Rand's approach to causality is a continuation of her critique of mechanistic materialism. Like the Marxists who reject "vulgar" materialism, Rand views entities as organic wholes that are more than the mere sum of their parts.[41] Rand's teacher, Lossky, also rejected the materialist and positivist conception of causality. He argued that in modern science, events are causally linked to preceding events. The world is studied purely in terms of actions and reactions. Lossky (1952, 372) believed that such materialism obscured the causal links between the entity and its actions. For Lossky, causality implies a teleological dimension in which the "substantival agent" causes and determines its own actions.

The problem with Lossky's "personalist" critique of materialism is that it ascribes a teleological character to every "potential" person, in both inorganic and organic nature. Even atoms, molecules, and electrons are endowed with the potential for causal efficacy.[42] Rand rejected this approach. The concept of final causation applies *only* to human action. It applies to the work of a conscious rational entity who chooses a purpose and proceeds to effect this purpose through specific means. Rand used to joke that the extent to which any individual is an object of efficient causation, rather than final causation, is the extent to which he needs a therapist. Such a person, unmotivated by ends, is a pure reactive being (Rand 1958T, lecture 3).

Thus Rand rejected both the materialist-mechanist and the idealist-personalist versions of causality. She argues: "The law of causality is the law of identity applied to action. All actions are caused by entities. The nature of an action is caused and determined by the nature of the entities that act; a thing cannot act in contradiction to its nature."[43]

The law of causality is as all-encompassing as the law of identity. All the elements of the universe, "from a floating speck of dust to the formation of a galaxy to the emergence of life—are caused and determined by the identities of the elements involved."[44] Since each entity has a specific nature, it is the entity's nature that is the cause of its actions. But actions have a context. The entity itself acts within a given set of circumstances. As an application of the law of identity, the law of causality states that the same entity under the same circumstances must behave in the same way. Causality applies to the relationship between entities and their actions, not between disembodied actions and reactions (Peikoff 1976T, lecture 2).

In conjunction with her rejection of cosmology, Rand rejected the view that the universe itself has a cause. As Nathaniel Branden explains: "Causality presupposes existence, existence does not presuppose causality: there can be no cause 'outside' of existence or 'anterior' to it. The *forms* of existence may change and evolve, but the *fact* of existence is the irreducible primary at the base of all causal chains."[45]

Everything that happens has a cause. Events are determined by the circumstances within which they occur, and these circumstances include both the antecedent events and the nature of the entities that act (Kelley 1985aT, lecture 2). Causality "is a law inherent in being qua being. To be is to be something—and to be something is to act accordingly" (Peikoff 1991b, 17).

The Entity as a Cluster of Qualities

In discussing the nature of an entity, Rand continued to emphasize that philosophy is metascientific. We may never know an entity's ultimate constituents. We may never know if entities are reducible to matter or to some as-yet-undiscovered form of energy. We may never know if our perceptual level is even capable of discovering the ultimate nature of entities in the universe ("Appendix," 290–95). None of this has any philosophic significance.

The only important philosophical conclusion that can be made about the nature of any entities in the universe is that *each* has identity. For Rand, as for Aristotle, " 'Entity' means 'one' " (198–99). This is not an ineffable One, but a *particular* one. Rand was committed to metaphysical pluralism. Since everything that exists in the universe is a particular, particularity is inherent in existence as such. Every entity that exists is something in particular.[46]

But metaphysical pluralism for Rand is *not* atomism. Just as Rand rejected metaphysical, organic collectivism, she also repudiates metaphysical atomism. In her emphasis on the ontological priority of individuals, Rand did not dissolve reality into wholly independent entities. Reality is an interconnected system of interacting entities governed by the laws of identity and causality (Peikoff 1976T, lecture 2). And since in a certain context, the universe itself can be thought of as an entity, it too has identity. It is something specific and finite. Like Aristotle, Rand argued that the concept of "infinity" is applicable only as a methodological tool; it does not apply to the universe as a whole. Such a metaphysical application is pure reification.[47]

Moreover, Rand grasped that the concept of "order" is epistemological, and not metaphysical. The order of the universe is its identity (Binswanger [1987] 1991T, lecture 2). She states: "There is no such thing as a disorderly universe. Our whole concept of order comes from observing reality and reality has to be orderly because it's the standard of what exists. Contradictions cannot exist" (1979aT).

Since order is internal to the universe, Rand contended that in knowledge, as in reality,

> Everything is interrelated. . . . [S]ince reality is not a collection of discrete concretes which have nothing to do with each other, since it is actually an integrated, interrelated whole, the same is true of our conceptual equipment. We cannot begin to use it until we have enough interrelated concepts to permit us, beginning with a small vocabulary, to reach higher and higher distinctions. Observe that all concepts on the first, perceptual level are enormously interrelated. And it would be impossible to say that we have to conceptualize tables first or chairs first. Or inanimate objects in the room before persons. There would be no rule about it. ("Appendix," 180)

Even though our knowledge is hierarchical, in reality, everything is simultaneous. Unlike Lossky, the arch personalist, Rand does not place greater existential emphasis on any particular elements of reality. Atoms are not lower or higher than chairs; chairs *are* atoms. Although people characteristically grasp the entity of "chair" before the "atoms" that comprise it, chairs and the atoms are on equal metaphysical footing (Peikoff 1990–91T, lecture 8).

This whole realm of inquiry leads us to question the status of internal relations as an ontological doctrine in Objectivism.[48] From a metaphysical standpoint, Rand refuses to speculate on whether a thing's identity includes its relations to other things. For Rand, this is a scientific question and as such is outside the province of philosophy proper. However, although Rand offers no doctrine explicating the actual nature of the relationship between the constituent elements of reality, she defends the organic integrity of an entity. She argues that each entity is constituted by qualities from which it cannot be legitimately separated. Indeed, the entity's properties are internal to its identity.

And yet traditional philosophy distinguishes the constitutive from the dispositional properties of an entity. Constitutive properties are part of the entity. They include such qualities as "weight" and "height." Dispositional properties, on the other hand, refer to the entity's capacity for action and interaction. For example, "fragility," a dispositional quality, depends on a relationship between a breakable glass and a concrete floor.

Rand was once asked the following question: if the glass's fragility cannot be defined except in terms of its relations to another entity (i.e., the concrete floor), would the definition of the glass necessarily contain a reference to an entity other than itself? This would seem to imply that there is an interpenetration of two entities in which one enters into the definition of another. Does this not violate identity?

Rand argued, in response, that traditional philosophy had created an "artificial dichotomy" between constitutive and dispositional properties. Rand begins by asking, "What is the nature of the entity?" She does not divide the entity into subcategories. Such qualities can be abstracted epistemologically once the nature of the entity has been determined. But the qualities themselves cannot be separated ontologically from the entity. By focusing on one group of properties to the exclusion of others, traditional philosophy attempts to edit reality by defining "what an entity is on a partial, selective basis."

Rand emphasizes the structure and nature of the entity as consequential to its form of action. The *identity* of the entity implies causality, that certain effects will occur in its interactions with other entities and with the world at large. The potential of an entity to act in a particular way is inherent in its composition and its physical and chemical properties. A dispositional property is one that belongs to a causal relationship. By distinguishing between constitutive and dispositional properties, traditional philosophy divorces the constituent elements of an entity from its potential for action. It simultaneously divorces the entity's potentiality for action from its fundamental characteristics.[49]

For Rand, *all* properties are constitutive of the entity. But no entity can "take an action which is not possible to it by its constituent nature. . . . [O]ne cannot claim causeless actions, or actions contrary to the nature of the interacting entities . . . actions cannot be inexplicable and causeless. If the cause lies in the nature of an entity, then it cannot do something other than what its nature makes possible" ("Appendix," 288).

Rand extended this analysis to her examination of the entity and its attributes: "An attribute is something which is not the entity itself. No one attribute constitutes the whole entity, but all of them together are the entity—not 'possessed by' but 'are' the entity" (276).

The attributes name the same existential fact as the entity itself, from a different vantage point. The entity and its attributes are not two different things. Their relationship is not merely reciprocal, it is identical; "the attributes are the entity, or an entity *is* its attributes."[50] One cannot separate attributes from the entity and reify them as separate existents. Ontologically, each of an entity's characteristics has the same status and is a part of the entity. Because we are not omniscient, we discover the properties of the entity through study, observation, and validation. Even though some of the entity's aspects may be unknown to us presently, this does not mean that such characteristics are excluded from our conceptual identification of the existent. The existent is what it is independent of what people think or feel. Our conceptual designation is open-ended and contextual; it is expandable to include the known and the not-yet-known (*Introduction*, 98–99).

Thus the entity cannot be isolated from its characteristics, nor can its characteristics be taken apart from its being.[51] The entity's attributes are indivisible. Further, just as there are no attributes or actions without entities, so there are no relationships apart from the entities that are in relation to one another.[52] "Length," for instance, does not exist in reality as a disembodied Platonic Form. It exists as an inseparable attribute of concrete, material entities. People establish units of length through abstraction, but this does not disconnect the concept of length from the entity that embodies it ("Appendix," 278).

Attributes are what can be separated mentally from the entity. "Parts" Rand defined somewhat more narrowly. A "part" is something that can be separated materially from the whole. In cutting off the legs from a table, for instance, the legs are parts that are no longer connected to the table top. Hence, the table is no longer what it once was.[53] But Rand preserved the integrity of the whole. The entity is the "sum" of its characteristics. Rand does not mean "sum" in a literal fashion ("Appendix," 265–66). A "sum" is an *integrated* sum. As Nathaniel Branden ([1969] 1979, 16) observes, the organism is "not an aggregate, but an integrate." Hence, although the parts of someone can be viewed as separate and distinct, Rand admonishes us never to drop "the context that they are vital organs of a total entity which is a human being" ("Appendix," 270).

In rejecting the bifurcation of the entity and its attributes, Rand presents an integrated view that is also sensitive to the context within which an entity exists. Entities, like concepts and words, cannot be fully understood when disconnected from their context. Peikoff explains, for instance, that words and concepts are not external or "neutral" to the totality; they often take on the connotation of the context within which they are used.[54] So, too, an entity must be understood in terms of its conditions of existence, which are partially comprised by the entity's dynamic relationship to other entities. This principle is duplicated in Rand's social analysis, wherein no single social problem can be resolved apart from related problems, or apart from the system which they jointly constitute—and perpetuate.

The Metaphysical versus the Man-Made

Rand's simultaneous emphasis on the ontological priority of individual entities and the integrated nature of each entity has immediate implications for her social ontology. Rand did not use the term "social ontology." But it characterizes her view of the nature of humanity, human action, and social institutions. For Rand, the person is an *individual, human, being*, with each of these factors essential to our understanding of his or her nature—*not* an abstraction but a *real* entity. As an entity, the person is an *individual*, a particular. And as a particular kind of entity, the person has a distinctive species identity—*human*. The bulk of Rand's philosophy is an examination of what it means to be *human*.

Within the present context, it should be mentioned briefly that Rand saw free will as one of humankind's most distinctive characteristics. But the power of volition does not enable people to alter that which Rand described as the "metaphysically given."[55] Though people can rearrange the elements of reality to serve human needs, they cannot alter the laws of identity and causality. For Rand, there is no contradiction between inability and the fact of human volition. Rand reaffirmed Bacon's insight that human beings cannot command nature unless they discover the properties of the elements they seek to control, as well as the rules by which volitional consciousness functions. Indeed, for human beings to initiate and direct the actions of consciousness, they must obey the rules of cognition. Though they are free to evade or subvert their own perceptions of reality, they cannot escape the existential consequences of such willful cognitive distortion.

Rand made a crucial distinction between those elements in reality which are metaphysically given, and those objects, institutions, procedures, or rules of conduct made by human beings (33). She refers to this distinction as the "metaphysical versus the man-made": "It is the metaphysically given that must be accepted: it cannot be changed. It is the man-made that must never be accepted uncritically: it must be judged, then accepted or rejected and changed when necessary. Man is not omniscient or infallible" (ibid.).

In essence, Rand rejected those who reify human institutions as unalterable metaphysical facts. Such a practice preserves the status quo, while sanctioning those injustices which happen to exist (Peikoff 1991b, 26). Although "the metaphysically given is, was, will be, and had to be," Rand argued that "nothing made by man *had to be*: it was made by choice."[56]

Rand equated those who would uncritically accept the products of human action with those who would rebel against nature in an attempt to negate existence. In either case, people did not grasp the difference between what *can* be changed and what cannot.

And yet by creating such a distinction between the metaphysical and the man-made, Rand seemed wholly ignorant of what Hayek called the unintended consequences of human action. In Hayek's view, cultural traditions are largely the result of inarticulate social practices. Hayek argued that spontaneously emergent social institutions are the historical product of human interaction but not of deliberate design. The attempt to alter these evolved institutions by will is one of the hallmarks of utopianism. Those who seek to control the delicate fabric of social life ultimately destroy the very forces that generate order. Hayek condemned these utopians as "constructivist rationalists." His critique of utopianism was simultaneously a powerful indictment of the efficacy and propriety of state planning. Ironically, Marx also recognized the tacit dimension in social reality. But unlike Hayek, Marx projected a future communist society in which people were no longer the playthings of history, but the conscious creators of their own destiny.[57]

Rand versus Kant

Rand's commitment to realism in philosophy penetrates to the root of her metaphysics. Objectivism begins with the axioms of existence, identity, and consciousness and proceeds to a defense of the primacy of existence in each of its ontological moments. Rand argued that most philosophies advocate either the primacy of existence or the primacy of consciousness.[58] As Kelley (1986) explains:

> In Ayn Rand's terms, it is a question of the primacy of consciousness versus the primacy of existence: do the objects of awareness depend on the subject for their existence or identity, or do the contents of consciousness depend on external objects? . . . Realists claim that the objects exist independently of the subject. Awareness is non-constitutive, the identification of things that exist and are what they are independently of the awareness of them. Idealists, on the other hand, claim that the object of cognition does depend on some constitutive activity of the subject—even if, with Kant, they allow that some independent noumenal realm also exists. (8, 27)

In Rand's view, Kant's grand and far-reaching synthesis was the philosophy most responsible for promulgating the view that consciousness is ontologically prior to existence. Kant attacked objective reality and the efficacy of the mind on a *metaphysical* level. While a full discussion of Rand's anti-Kantianism is beyond the scope of this book, it is valuable to briefly examine the similarities and differences between the two thinkers. Such an exploration provides additional evidence of Rand's Russian intellectual roots.

George Walsh, a distinguished Objectivist philosopher, criticizes Rand and other Objectivists for their wholesale rejection of Kant's metaphysics and epistemology.[59] Walsh argues persuasively that Rand exaggerated her differences with—and misinterpreted—some of Kant's central positions in these basic fields of philosophy. It is Walsh's view that both thinkers adhere to many of the same basic propositions.

Fig. 5. George Walsh. (Courtesy of Karen Reedstrom)

Kant accepted Aristotle's definition of metaphysics as the study of being qua being. He asked whether metaphysical knowledge is possible and identified the solution of this problem as the aim of his *Critique of Pure Reason*. He divided metaphysics into *ontology*, which studies existing things and events separately, including whether every event has a cause, and *cosmology*, which studies the totality of existence, including whether the universe as such has a cause. Kant concluded that ontology is possible as knowledge since people can visualize causality between events. But cosmology is not possible as knowledge, because the universe as a whole cannot be treated as an entity. Viewing cosmology as knowledge leads to unwarranted conclusions in some cases and to outright contradictions or "antinomies" in others. The only legitimate function of cosmology is to "regulate" science in the direction of broader, more general theories. But for Kant, since no completely general theory can ever be attained, cosmology can never qualify as knowledge.

Like Kant, Rand accepted Aristotle's definition of metaphysics as the study of being qua being. She implicitly acknowledged the conventional division of metaphysics into ontology and cosmology, but rejected cosmology as illegitimate. Whereas ontology or metaphysics can establish *that* there are entities which have natures, and *that* only finite concretes exist and interact causally, it is the job of science to study the *specific* nature of these entities, to discover *what* they are and the laws of their interaction.

Cosmology extends to the whole universe the empirical laws that have been reached at any given moment. For Rand, as for Kant, such cosmological speculation can be defended only by an appeal to some sort of mystical insight. But whereas Rand categorically rejected such "mysticism," Kant provided a defense of faith and intuition as the central means for dealing with fundamental noumena.

This difference, however, does not constitute the central criticism that Rand leveled against Kant. According to Walsh, the principal—and least tenable—point of Rand's critique was her mistaken assumption that Kant had disqualified the efficacy of consciousness precisely because the mind possessed identity. Rand ascribed to Kant the doctrine that knowledge is a "distortion" or "collective delusion." She claimed that Kant derived this conclusion from the premise that the mind possesses a specific identity.

Walsh argues, however, that Kant made no such argument. Kant contended that all knowledge falls necessarily under the forms of space, time, and the categories (which as knowledge are tied to space and time). These forms cannot be the properties or relations of things as they are in themselves, for, if they were, we would know them a posteriori, whereas in fact we know them a priori (Walsh, 14 October 1993C).

For Kant, the mind, with its definite structure or identity, is the only source that originates the formal element in knowledge. This is not Kant's basic premise, but his ultimate epistemological *conclusion*. Walsh argues that Rand has misinterpreted this aspect of Kant's thought; Kant does not believe that the mind must have *some* identity or *other*, and that this identity, *as such*, distorts the objects of its knowledge. As a transcendental Idealist, Kant argues: "All objects of any experience possible to us, are nothing but appearances, that is, mere representations which, *in the manner in which they are represented, as extended beings, or as a series of alterations*, have no independent existence outside our thoughts."[60]

Kant provided a means of distinguishing objective truth from error. He distinguished illusions and delusions from "empirical reality" by systematically applying criteria of order and regular sequence. In Walsh's opinion, Rand cannot dismiss Kant's view that the mind imposes forms of space and time upon percepts without putting in serious question the validity of her own theories of perceptual relativity. As we shall see in Chapter 6, Rand believed that percepts come to us arrayed in forms, such as color, determined by the interaction of our sense organs with appropriate stimuli. How can Rand criticize Kant when her own view suggests that sensory "processing" does not in itself, grasp the "ultimate constituents of the universe," even if these are the "casual primaries" behind our percepts? The only difference between the Randian and Kantian approaches is that for Rand, science may one day discover the properties of the "ultimate constituents," whereas for Kant, such knowledge of things-in-themselves is impossible *as such*. In Walsh's opinion, Rand's critique of Kant's epistemology as radically distort-ive, dualistic, and delusory ought to be qualified. For Walsh, even in Kant's account of knowledge, "empirical reality," once known, may indeed, be obeyed and commanded.

Walsh submits that Rand's misinterpretation of Kant rests on her misun-derstanding of the term "appearance." The word in German that Kant uses is *Erscheinung* which means "manifestation" or "showing." Kant ([1781/1787] 1933) warns us explicitly against confusing this with *Schein*, which means "sham" or "illusion" (B69). Rand's chief predecessor in ignoring this warning is the nineteenth-century irrationalist and romanticist Arthur Schopenhauer, who praised Kant's distinction between the "delusions" of phenomenal appearance and the unknowable noumenal realm: "Kant's greatest contribution is the distinction between *Erscheinung* (appearance) and things-in-themselves . . . that the world presenting itself to the senses has no true being . . . and that the grasp of it is delusion rather than knowledge."[61] Rand's interpretation is comparable, but whereas Schopen-hauer praised Kant for this alleged doctrine, she condemned him.

Yet in my view, it is far more likely that Rand's anti-Kantianism was an outgrowth of her exposure to Russian thought, rather than with any possible acquaintance with Schopenhauer's view. Whereas Schopenhauer celebrated the Kantian metaphysical distinctions, most Russian philosophers rejected Kant because they believed that he had detached the mind from reality. As I suggest, such thinkers as Solovyov, Chicherin, and Lossky were aiming for an integration of the traditional dichotomies perpetuated by Kant's metaphysics. Chicherin, for instance, argued that in Kant's system, pure concepts of reason are empty, and experience is blind. Kant's view makes "metaphysics without experience . . . empty, and experience without metaphysics blind: in the first case we have the form without content, and in the second case, the content without understanding" (Lossky 1951, 135–36).

Interestingly, Rand's own view of the rationalist-empiricist distinction, and of Kant's critical philosophy, is deeply reminiscent of Chicherin's parody. For Rand, rationalists had embraced concepts divorced from reality, whereas empiricists had "clung to reality, by abandoning their mind" (*New Intellectual*, 30). Kant's attempt to transcend this dichotomy failed miserably because his philosophy formalized the conflict. Rand writes: "His argument, in essence, ran as follows: man is *limited* to a consciousness of a specific nature, which perceives by specific means and not others, therefore, his consciousness is not valid; man is blind, because he has eyes—deaf, because he has ears—deluded, because he has a mind—and the things he perceives do not exist, *because* he perceives them" (39).

Rand's teacher, Lossky, was the chief Russian translator of Kant's works. He too had criticized Kant's contention that true being (things-in-themselves) transcends consciousness and remains forever unknowable. Lossky sought to defend the realist proposition that people could know true reality through an epistemological coordination of subject and object. In this process, the real existents and objects of the world are subjected to a cognitive activity that is metaphysically passive and noncreative. Lossky rejected Kant's belief that the mind imposes structures on reality. Such Kantian subjectivism subordinates reality to knowledge, or existence to consciousness. It resolves phenomena in subjective processes that are detached from the real world and distortive of objective reality (Lossky [1906] 1919, 402–3).

Furthermore, Lossky criticized Kant for invalidating metaphysics as a science. Since Kant held that the mind perceives things not as they are but "as they *seem* to me," he institutionalized a war not only on metaphysics, but on the very ability of the mind to grasp the nature of reality.[62]

Though there is no evidence that Rand studied Kant formally while at the university, it is conceivable that her earliest exposure to Kant's ideas occurred in her encounters with the celebrated Lossky. Her distinguished teacher was among the foremost Russian scholars of German philosophy. Lossky's rejection of Kantianism was essential to his ideal-realist project. It is entirely possible that Rand absorbed inadvertently a Russian bias against Kant.

6 Knowing

In conjunction with her view that philosophy is not a deductive system, Rand based her theory of knowledge on observation and induction.[1] Rand refused to rewrite reality; she rejected any attempt to force facts into a preconceived conceptual scheme.[2] She constructed an epistemological theory that drew from her understanding of the history of knowledge, mathematics, and science and of the nature of language (Peikoff 1980T, lecture 9). She realized that epistemology is the crucial element of any philosophical system, because it articulates the very methods by which people can know reality (Peikoff 1987T, lecture 6). Rand wrote in her journal: "*Philosophy is primarily epistemology*—the science of the means, the rules, and the methods of human knowledge."[3] Hence, her system of thought could not be complete without a fully developed epistemological foundation.

Rejecting Epistemological Dualism

Rand's epistemology is a species of philosophical realism. And yet Rand was deeply critical of traditional realist and idealist perspectives. In attempting to bridge the seemingly insurmountable gap between reality and consciousness, classical realists and idealists often totalized one realm while suppressing the other. Rand rejected this dualistic antagonism at its root. She argued that like every existent in reality, consciousness has an identity. But for Rand, there can be no conflict between a this-worldly, natural human faculty and the reality it perceives.

Rand's attack on traditional realism and idealism was certainly not the only one of its kind. Thinkers as diverse as Adorno, Derrida, Foucault, Gadamer, Heidegger, Husserl, and Wittgenstein also rejected both realist "objectivism" and idealist "subjectivism." Many of these thinkers criticized the Platonic realist conception of knowledge because it separated concepts from human life. But they were equally displeased with contemporary subjectivist alternatives, which emphasized the primacy of the cogito.[4]

Recognizing that classical realism was often characterized as an "objectivist" formulation, Rand was compelled to distinguish her own Objectivist epistemology from the traditional view. She eventually developed the term "intrinsicism" to describe the classical realist perspective.[5] According to Rand, intrinsicism was the defining characteristic of both extreme and moderate realism. These realists had regarded "the referents of concepts as *intrinsic*, i.e., as 'universals' inherent in things (either as archetypes or as metaphysical essences), as special existents unrelated to man's consciousness—to be perceived by man directly, like any other kind of concrete existents, but perceived by some non-sensory or extra-sensory means" (*Introduction*, 53).

The realists attempted to preserve the primacy of existence by denying the identity of consciousness. They converted concepts into perceptual concretes that could only be absorbed by the mind through intuition or other supernatural means (ibid.). This was pure mysticism in Rand's view. Rand defined mysticism in epistemological terms, as "the acceptance of allegations without evidence or proof, either apart from or *against* the evidence of one's senses and one's reason."[6] Rand argued that at the base of traditional realism was this paradoxical commitment to mystic revelation, a belief that the mind was an ineffable substance, attaining "true" knowledge through direct contemplation of the world.[7]

It is no accident that Rand was able to identify this intrinsicist paradox. Her earliest encounter with the realist-mystic integration was in the teachings of her philosophy professor, Lossky. For Rand, Lossky's thought must have provided a perfect embodiment of the virtues *and* vices of traditional realism. Deeply influenced by both Plato and Aristotle, Lossky had argued that God was "the primary and all-embracing intrinsic value." Hence, each substantival agent created by God was endowed with intrinsic, enabling qualities that could be actualized in the real world. For Lossky (1951, 258), being, love, beauty, truth, and freedom were among the "absolute intrinsic values" constituting God's organic whole.

Just as Lossky's mystical premises were readily apparent, so too were the realist elements of his philosophy. It was Lossky's aim "to investigate . . . the process of knowledge . . . in man as a knowing subject."[8] For Lossky ([1906] 1919, 413), the mind was engaged in the "modest activity of discriminating and comparing" the elements of reality. This limited cognitive function regarded "the whole material of knowledge as *given* in immediate experience." Lossky regarded his own realism as profoundly empirical in its orientation. He argued that cognitive activity was "*least of all creative,* but based more than any other activity upon *data passively received.*" This metaphysical passivity and radical noncreativity was a "most important condition for the acquisition of an adequate knowledge of the world."

Moreover, Lossky had reacted against subjectivists and Kantians for their attempts to conflate the mode of awareness and the content of the mind.[9] He had opposed the skeptics whose claims "that 'there is no truth'" were contradicted "by that very statement," since one could not maintain "the truth of the non-existence of any truth" without vicious circularity (Lossky [1917] 1928, 177). And though Lossky insisted on the metaphysical passivity of cognition, he also recognized that the mind could be creative in many of its epistemological activities. Extreme originality could be illustrated in the human ability to choose appropriate methods of investigation, and to reconstruct the world in the imagination (Lossky [1906] 1919, 413).

Although Rand would have agreed with the essential thrust of Lossky's view, it is clear that she would have adamantly rejected the other aspects of his epistemology as profoundly "intrinsicist" and "mysticist." For Lossky, all the objects of the universe, both real and ideal, are given to the mind by "direct contemplation."[10] Lossky seems to suggest that perceptual concretes and conceptual abstractions are equally accessible to the mind by such contemplative activity. The mind grasps the existential reality of universals as if by ineffable osmosis. True Reason is expressed in

> the complete unity of the universe which renders it possible for the individual both to represent to himself cosmic purposes and to apprehend intuitively the contents not only of his own life but of other lives in the world. Such unity can only be possible if the ground of the world be a super-individual Reason that coordinates with one another all the various aspects of the life of the universe. (Lossky [1906] 1919, 412)

Thus in her primary contact with Lossky, Rand would have been exposed to a seemingly inseparable link between traditional realism and mysticism. And since Lossky was the first to instruct Rand on the contributions of Plato and Aristotle, it is possible that Rand's own interpretation of both extreme and moderate realism was influenced by his perspective. These factors may have enabled Rand to discover a remarkable ambiguity in the realist tradition: that realists so thoroughly committed to the existence of an objective reality were deeply imbued with mysticism at their epistemic core.

It is no great surprise, then, that nominalists and conceptualists alike would reject the realist perspective and its mystical elements. But the nominalists and conceptualists who repudiated realist "objectivism," had merely substituted an equally one-dimensional subjectivism in its place. Rand argues: "The nominalist and the conceptualist schools regard concepts as *subjective*, i.e., as products of man's consciousness, unrelated to the facts of reality as mere 'names' or notions arbitrarily assigned to arbitrary groupings of concretes on the ground of vague, inexplicable resemblances" (*Introduction*, 53).

In a sense, these subjectivists attempt to counteract the mysticism of intrinsicist epistemology by emphasizing the primacy of consciousness. By totalizing the subjective and suppressing the objective, the subjectivists view concepts and mental integrations as arbitrary and unrelated to reality (53–54). Whereas intrinsicism culminates in mysticism, subjectivism engenders skepticism. For Rand, these antagonists in the history of philosophy had merely embraced two different sides of the same dualistic coin:

> Men have been taught either that knowledge is impossible (skepticism) or that it is available without effort (mysticism). These two positions appear to be antagonists, but are, in fact, two variants on the same theme, two sides of the same fraudulent coin: the attempt to escape the responsibility of rational cognition and the absolutism of reality—the attempt to assert the primacy of consciousness over existence. (79)

While intrinsicists claim to uphold the absolutism of reality, they ultimately rely upon mystic revelation, an epistemic union with the supernatural that assists them in the intuitive grasp of existents. Subjectivism rejects such mysticism. But subjectivists embrace the *primacy of their own consciousness* as partially or wholly constitutive of reality itself.

Interestingly, this was precisely the charge leveled against subjectivism by

Rand's teacher. For Lossky, the fact that a person was conscious suggested three interacting moments: the self, the object (or content of the mind), and the relation of "having" between the self and the content. The self is conscious, and the content is that which the self is conscious of. Kant perpetuated the view "that the contents of consciousness must necessarily be mental states of the individual," rather than something derived from objective reality. For Lossky, a fact is ontologically real. When it is grasped by the knowing subject as part of the content of judgment, it is logically necessary.[11]

For Rand, as for Lossky, Kant's subjectivist approach was to be repudiated. Both Rand and Lossky would have agreed that Kant's system invalidated the objectivity of human perception. Both Rand and Lossky rejected such distinctions as analytic and synthetic, logical and experiential, necessary and contingent, a priori and a posteriori.[12] But Rand went beyond the intrinsicist critique of her teacher. For Lossky, the objective content of judgment is not a fully processed, human form of perceived reality, but reality itself. Ontology and logic nearly collapse. Rand argues, by contrast, that Kant's distinction between things-in-themselves and things-as-they-are-perceived perpetuates a gulf between reality and consciousness. Whereas Lossky as an intrinsicist believed that we grasp "things-in-themselves," Kant maintained, in Rand's view, that we only grasp things as they appear to our consciousness, which imposes a structure on reality. Rand rejected both alternatives. For Rand, there is nothing in the world that can be discussed as "reality in itself," if by such a designation is meant that we can somehow grasp reality external to a human perspective. Similarly, even if there were an omniscient being, that being would still perceive reality by divine methods of perception from which he, she, or it could not escape.

Rand maintained that the subject's means of perception are not a disqualifying element in the grasp of the object ("Appendix," 193–94). The means of perception and the process of cognition do not invalidate or subjectify the reality that is perceived. Rand argued that the Kantian credo "is a revolt, not only against being conscious, but against being alive," since every aspect of life involves *processing*. There is no such thing as "unprocessed knowledge," for this would imply that people could acquire information about the real world without cognitive means. For Rand, every living organism must process the physical and mental elements that sustain it. Our modes of breathing, eating, and knowing are the human means of processing and appropriating elements in objective reality. Rand states:

No one would argue (at least, not yet) that since man's body has to *process* the food he eats, no objective rules of proper nutrition can ever be discovered—that "true nutrition" has to consist of absorbing some ineffable substance without the participation of a digestive system, but since man is incapable of "true feeding," nutrition is a subjective matter open to his whim, and it is merely a social convention that forbids him to eat poisonous mushrooms. (*Introduction*, 81–82)

Hence, just as it is illegitimate to subjectify the digestive process, it is equally incorrect to view perception and cognition as subjective.

Rand explained that in the history of philosophy, the dominance of one polar position ultimately created conditions for the resurgence of its alleged opposite. But intrinsicism and subjectivism, mysticism and skepticism, differ only "in the form of their inner contradiction."[13] The intrinsicist subverts the human mode of awareness in an effort to preserve the objectivity of the mind's contents; the subjectivist denies the objectivity of the mind's contents in an effort to preserve the human mode of awareness. Neither school grasps the *identity* of human consciousness or the *objective* nature of concept formation. Each school totalizes a different polar principle while suppressing its opposite. Each school is the mirror image of its adversary. Rand explains:

Philosophically, the mystic is usually an exponent of the *intrinsic* (revealed) school of epistemology; the skeptic is usually an advocate of epistemological *subjectivism*. But, psychologically, the mystic is a subjectivist who uses intrinsicism as a means to claim the primacy of *his* consciousness over that of others. The skeptic is a disillusioned intrinsicist who, having failed to find automatic supernatural guidance, seeks a substitute in the collective subjectivism of others. (*Introduction*, 79)

Rand's critique of intrinsicism and subjectivism illustrates a highly dialectical exposition, a style common to such thinkers as Aristotle, Marx, and many Russian philosophers, including Solovyov and Lossky. Rand conceptualized not one, but *two*, false alternatives that share a common error. She viewed these antinomies as embodying inner contradictions that must be transcended simultaneously. She recognized an interpenetration between intrinsicism and subjectivism in that each duplicates the psycho-philosophical tendencies of the other. Each school of thought, in its partiality and one-sidedness, perpetuates a distorted view of human consciousness. In both cases, Rand argued, the identity of the mind has not been fully understood or appreciated.

It is not quite accurate to say that Rand actually *constructed* her resolution out of the debris of these false alternatives. To be sure, Rand affirmed and repudiated half of each tradition, preserving only those aspects essential to a genuinely "objective" alternative. But her "Objectivist" resolution is not merely an amalgam of its predecessors; rather, it seeks to transcend their inherent limitations. For Rand, genuine objectivity cannot be validated without grasping that every human attribute and faculty, including mind and body, is subject to the law of identity. If people are to acquire knowledge of the world, they must discover proper *human* methods of cognition. As she put it: "Just as man's physical existence was liberated when he grasped the principle that 'nature, to be commanded, must be obeyed,' so his consciousness will be liberated when he grasps that *nature, to be apprehended, must be obeyed*—that the rules of cognition must be derived from the nature of existence and the nature, the identity of his cognitive faculty" (ibid.).

Perception

Rand considered consciousness axiomatic. But she understood the term "consciousness" in several different, though interrelated, ways. Consciousness is not only a *faculty* of awareness, the faculty of perceiving that which exists. Consciousness is also a *state* of awareness. It is a vital organ or attribute of specific living entities. Consciousness is a *process* of awareness marked by two essential aspects: differentiation and integration (*Introduction*, 5). The human form of consciousness is a repository of multiple constituents, all of which are inseparably linked: perception, volition, focus, reason, abstraction, and conception. Moreover, for Rand, the mind *is* the ego, the self, the I.[14]

Hence, though Rand characterizes consciousness as metaphysically passive—that is, as nonconstitutive in the perception of reality—she views the mind as epistemologically active. Consciousness involves three distinct and interactive levels of awareness: sensation, perception, and conception. Each of these levels *is* a relation between consciousness and existence. There is no such thing as a disembodied mind. Every aspect and process of consciousness has a physical, material component.[15] Rand continues in the grand tradition of Aristotle and Aquinas; she argues that consciousness operates under conditions of materiality and sensuous corporeality.[16]

Furthermore, Rand argues that every faculty, state, or process of awareness involves two essential attributes: "content and action—the content of awareness, and the action of consciousness in regard to that content" (*Introduction*, 29–30). Every sensation, perception, and conception, then, is constituted by the content of awareness, derived from reality, and an action of consciousness—automatic or volitional—in regard to the mind's contents. There is no such thing as a content-less consciousness just as there is no such thing as a fully inactive consciousness.[17] Content and action necessitate one another.

According to Rand, on the first level of awareness, sensations must be recognized as irreducible primaries produced by sensory stimuli. They are irreducible because they cannot be reduced to or analyzed in terms of simpler units (Peikoff 1991b, 52). But she argued that sensations are not at the base of knowledge, for the mind cannot retain sensations in memory. The foundation of epistemology lies on the perceptual level of awareness. Rand defined a "perception" as "a group of sensations automatically retained and integrated by the brain of a living organism, which gives it the ability to be aware, not of single stimuli, but of *entities*, of things."[18]

Hence, knowledge does not begin with isolated, atomistic sensations, but with an automatic *integration* of sensations in the form of a percept. People are unable to reduce perceptions to their sensorial units. In one integrated moment, we can perceive something in five sense modalities: we *see* the ocean, we *hear* its waves against the shore, we *feel* the coolness of the water, we *smell* and *taste* its salt content. This perception is automatically retained and integrated by our brain. We do not break up each of these sensations as components of the perception. The perception is a relational totality. Our ability to abstract each of the sensory moments of a single perception is not a perceptual task; it is a scientific and conceptual capacity that we acquire much later in life (*Introduction*, 5).

Rand's Objectivism opposes the diaphanous view of perception. Our consciousness is not a mirror reproducing the objects of the world free from the influence of our sensory organs. We perceive objects in a specific form. The form of our perception is a relational product of the object, our sense modalities, and the environmental conditions in which our sensory organs operate.[19] We have no purely perceptual way of distinguishing between the object and the form in which it is perceived. Indeed, the form of our

Fig. 6.   David Kelley. (Courtesy of David Kelley)

perception cannot be separated from the object and reified into a separate thing (Kelley 1986, 90). Subjects *are* perceptual systems. They cannot perceive objects external to their sensory means. They cannot attain a synoptic view that abstracts from the form. Their human sense modalities are *internal* to the process of perception (Kelley 1985bT, lecture 2). Peikoff (1972T, lecture 5) has called this a process of "dual actualization" in which the perception is a product of both the sense organ and the object. David Kelley (1991) explains: "Perception is a form of contact with the world, a real relation between subject and object, between the perceiver and what he perceives" (171–72).

Rand's distinction between the form of the object and the object itself is not a separation of appearance and essence, of things-as-they-appear and things-in-themselves. The form of our perception is *not* subjective; it is as much the product of reality as the object itself.[20] It is an outgrowth of the *identity* of the object and the *identity* of the sense modalities involved in perception. A percept is not object alone or subject alone, but the object-as-perceived by the subject in a specific form (Peikoff 1991b, 46). A straight stick that appears bent in water is a form dictated by our sense modalities in conjunction with the object and the specific media and conditions of our perception. A color-blind person who sees gray where there is red has not made a mistake; he has perceived a color patch that is *internal* to *his* specific sense modalities. Rand defends the validity of the senses as an axiomatic proposition, for our sense organs have no capacity to misrepresent the facts of reality. As George Smith explains, the organs of perception "simply transmit sensations according to their physiological characteristics, which our brains then automatically integrate into percepts. We may *misinterpret* the basic data given to us, but there can be no question about the validity of the data *per se.*"[21]

Rand recognized that a scientific examination of perception *can* help to distinguish between those aspects which are generated by our particular sense modalities and those which are products of the object itself. But in keeping with her injunction against hypothetical (and "cosmological") speculation, Rand maintained that the ultimate relationship of form and object is a purely scientific question with no philosophical significance (Peikoff 1991b, 47–48).

It is for this reason, for instance, that Rand refused to accept any distinction between primary and secondary perceptual qualities. Traditional philosophy defines primary characteristics as those which are *intrinsic* to the object. Secondary characteristics are those which are *intrinsic* to the subject's perception of the object. Rand maintained, however, that to distinguish between these two categories, one would need to identify the irreducibility or primacy of a given physical attribute. This is a scientific question which has yet to be fully resolved (464 n. 3). It is illegitimate, in Rand's view, to arbitrarily choose a primary characteristic such as extension, since science may yet discover that more basic causes are manifested in the form of extension as perceived by human sensory organs (Peikoff 1972T, lecture 12). Rand maintained that every attribute we perceive, including color and length, is perceived by some means. Even taste involves an interaction between certain chemical elements in the object and the nerve endings of the tongue ("Appendix," 279–80). Those who attempt to identify—once and for all—the primary and secondary qualities of perception are engaging in what Kelley (1986) calls the "Cartesian quest for an infallible type of knowledge," a form of perception that is somehow free from the conditions and limitations of the sensory apparatus (168).

None of these Randian arguments should suggest that human perception takes place in a vacuum. As people grow to maturity, they begin to apply their conceptual knowledge to the act of perception. Perception itself is guided by our conscious purposes, cognitive history, particular interests, and psychological factors (147). Within the broader social context, Kelley explains, even symbolic objects "have evolved culturally to serve as perceptible bearers of meaning" (254). Yet any differences in perceptual (and conceptual) classifications across cultures do not invalidate the objectivity of the cognitive process. For instance, Kelley observes that although the basic terms of "color" may vary across cultures, the focal instances are not arbitrary, and can be translated from one language into another. Different cultural partitions are no more a proof of subjectivity than are the use of different languages. [22]

Volition and Focus

Having analyzed the first and second levels of awareness, Rand knew that she had to investigate more deeply the third level of awareness distinctive to human cognition. Both animals and human beings are capable of experiencing sensations and perceptions. Human beings however, exhibit volitional, self-conscious, and conceptual awareness. [23] Rand characterized volition as another philosophic axiom. Volition is the choice "to think or not to think," and it is a causal primary in cognition. [24] Such a choice has existential, epistemological, and ethical significance. But "to think or not to think" is Rand's poetic expression for an even broader cognitive choice: whether or not to apply one's ability to focus.

Focusing is the most fundamental choice underlying and conditioning every other aspect of consciousness. It is more fundamental than the ability to choose among competing ideas or alternative courses of action. It is a constituent relation of *cognition* primarily. One cannot think, act, or desire without having volitionally "set" the mind into focal awareness in a general way. [25]

The act of focusing is manifested in a variety of cognitive activities. [26]

There is a *continuum of awareness* such that the mind can move from near unconsciousness to peripheral awareness to focused awareness, with no inherent barriers between states. Focus is much broader than the processes of deduction and induction. It can include meditation, relaxation, and even creative daydreaming.[27] The most advanced categories of focal awareness will involve supreme clarity of mental content, a highly abstract level of cognitive activity, and the recognition of context. In all cases, the mind must initiate and sustain this process volitionally.[28] In the Objectivist view, no antecedent, deterministic factors can explain why people choose or do not choose to focus.[29] Rand recognized, however, that volitional focusing is automatized through habitual methods of thinking such that it would take a special effort for people to *un*focus the mind.[30]

Rand's emphasis on the primary choice "to focus" does not imply that she was oblivious to the conditions, both existential and social, that can assist or block the acquisition and maturation of cognitive skills. These conditions form the broad context within which focal choices are made. This context is necessary but not sufficient to prompt human action.[31] It does not strictly determine the ability of an individual to raise the level of his own focal awareness. Nor does the context invalidate the methods of cognition that must be used by all individuals in their attempts to gain knowledge of reality. But an individual's interests, values, knowledge, and inborn capacities cannot be ignored in judging the efficacy of his focal choices (Peikoff 1991b, 65–66).

For instance, certain inborn physical and cognitive differences make it more difficult—or easier—for some individuals to develop their cognitive skills. Children who are born blind and have their vision restored in later years at first must expend effort to raise their level of visual awareness. Previously, their powers of perception were developed through alternative sense modalities (such as touch). Once their vision is restored, they initially experience visual sensations but cannot see objects.[32] However, the presence of innate disabilities or innate intelligence does not alter the fact that there are specific, objective means of cognition that each person must follow in the quest for knowledge. It is for this reason that Rand saw such innate differences as *epistemologically* insignificant.

Nevertheless, certain *social* practices influence the development of cognitive skills. These practices have epistemological significance because they can facilitate or obstruct a child's cognitive development. This is not an argument for social determinism; it is Rand's way of tracing the interconnections between epistemology and cultural institutions, that is, between the development of cognition and the social practices that can accelerate—or destroy—it.[33]

Reason

One of the most striking aspects of Rand's conception of human consciousness is her refusal to fragment the constituent relations that compose it. Her hostility toward dualism is manifested especially in her antipathy toward a bifurcated, fractured view of consciousness. Consciousness, as such, includes moments of perception, volition, focus, reason, abstraction, and conception. For Rand, these are not separate faculties. Each is both a component part of the others and a distinct aspect of a single, integrated totality.[34] In fact, there are times when Rand's definition of a single constituent of consciousness incorporates all of the other identified moments.

But Rand sometimes identified consciousness with a single attribute. In her early journal entries, for instance, she argued that "all consciousness is reason" and "all reason is logic," creating a virtual identity between reason, logic, and consciousness.[35] These one-dimensional identities were formulated as a reaction against religion—which, in Rand's view, fractured the relationship between consciousness and logic. She saw religion (i.e., faith) as a "disease," a "departure" from reason, logic, and consciousness that necessarily undermined an individual's cognitive contact with the world.[36]

As Rand grew to intellectual maturity, her conception of reason transcended this one-sided emphasis on logic. Ultimately she embraced what Barry (1987) has described as "a particularly expansive concept of 'reason'" (106). In *Atlas Shrugged*, Rand defined reason as the faculty of awareness, that is, "the faculty that perceives, identifies and integrates the material provided by [the] senses" (1016). In this definition, Rand incorporated the moments of perception, identification, and integration, preserving the hierarchical structure of cognition. But she refused to identify reason as a purely logical faculty. Nor is reason a faculty of perception. It is all of these things and more. Though Rand abstracted these aspects in order to examine their distinctiveness, she refused to reify them into separate faculties (Peikoff 1990–91T, lecture 10). For Rand, reason is an integrative faculty, combining analysis with synthesis and applying logic to experience. These characteristics are distinctions within an organic unity. Reason is at once a logical and a practical capacity. It enables the differentiation and integration of experiential data. It guides action and makes it possible to evaluate the consequences of action.

Hence it is particularly disconcerting to read the claims of critics such as Hazel Barnes and Randall Dipert, who argue that Rand's view of reason is one-dimensional. In Barnes's illuminating study, *Existentialist Ethics*, she includes a provocative comparison of the works of Rand and Sartre. According to Barnes, Rand embraced an Aristotelian view of human beings as rational animals that is considerably narrower than Sartre's view of human nature. For Sartre, reason is only one part of human being, not the totality, and self-awareness is what distinguishes humans from all other living organisms. Barnes criticizes Rand for equating such self-consciousness with the rational faculty. In Barnes's view, Rand totalized reason while suppressing the other aspects of consciousness. Barnes suggests that Rand's view of reason is strictly limited to its purely logical functions.[37]

By contrast, Dipert argues that whereas Marx embraced an expansive, practical conception of reason, Rand endorsed a view of the mind as entirely passive.[38] For Marx, as for Aristotle, reason includes both theoretical and practical abilities, the capacity to contemplate, plan, deliberate, intend, and act. However, Rand does not deny any of these constituent aspects of the rational faculty. Dipert erroneously collapses Rand's understanding of the moment of perception into her view of reason. He confuses Rand's concept of reason, which necessarily involves cognitive *activity*, with her view of the metaphysical passivity of perceptual processes.

For Rand, reason embodies epistemological and practical activity. This is a reflection of the seamless unity of mind and body. Since reason is the faculty for knowing reality, and since it functions through the corporeality of the senses, it must also be the faculty that guides action. For Rand, this relationship between reason and action was demonstrated unequivocally by the Industrial Revolution (Peikoff 1991b, 195). Prior to the emergence of capitalism, the connection between knowledge and praxis was not fully appreciated. It was only with the application of reason to the production of material goods that human beings began to recognize the inseparable link between the conceptual faculty and survival.[39]

Rand argued that the faculty of reason guides and directs human consciousness, in a process she once dubbed "front-seat driving." Reason is an engine of active, purposeful thinking. As an integrative faculty, it transcends the purely passive, associational methods of perception, even as it incorporates perception as one of its distinct moments.[40]

Rand's view of the relationship between reason and action is more specifically a conception of the link between an *individual's* reason and actions. The faculty of reason is not a faculty of "pure rationality" disconnected from the individual who possesses it. Rand tied her epistemological perspective to her emphasis on the ontological priority of individuals. For Rand, the mind "is an attribute of the individual. There is no such thing as a collective brain. . . . The primary act—the process of reason—must be performed by each man alone. . . . No man can use his lungs to breathe for another man. No man can use his brain to think for another. All the functions of body and spirit are private. They cannot be shared or transferred" (*Fountainhead*, 680).

Rand recognized that knowledge itself is a product of conceptual thought. It can be transmitted socially and intergenerationally. But the rational faculty itself is not transferable. The individual can perform cognitive functions only in the isolation of his own mind, "rationally grasping every step in the process" as a means of comprehending the whole. People may share *what* they have learned, but they cannot share *how*—the actual means by which—they think. People may be able to articulate the methods of cognition, but they cannot share the epistemic processes, which are performed individually.[41]

Abstraction and Conception

Rand regarded perception as a nonvolitional process integrating sensations into a single unit. She regarded this integration as a primitive relational form at the base of knowledge. In her view, human beings transcend the purely perceptual level of awareness. The volitional ability to focus and reason—in short, the capacity to think—constitutes and is constituted by a distinctly human, *conceptual* level of awareness. The difference between conception and perception, then, lies in the character of the relation. Perception is a relational integration of sensations performed *automatically* by the mind. It is awareness of concrete entities, rather than of isolated sensations. Conception, by contrast, is a relational integration of perceptions performed *volitionally* by the mind. The ability to regard perceived entities as relational units is distinctive to this human mode of cognition. Rand explains: "The building-block of man's knowledge is the concept of an 'existent'—of something that exists, be it a thing, an attribute or an action" (*Introduction*, 5). The concept of "existent" is implicit in every percept. The mind makes a transition from an awareness of existents to an awareness of their specific identity. The ability to discover the "identity" of an existent emerges from the perceptual ability to distinguish among entities. It is the capacity to differentiate entities from one another.

Thus, to grasp an "existent" and its "identity" is to move from perception to perceptual judgment. But to link the identified existent to other similar or different existents is the crucial, primary epistemological step in the conceptual process. This view of an entity as existing in certain relationships with other entities is an awareness of the existent as a relational unit. Rand states: "*The ability to regard entities as units is man's distinctive method of cognition,* which other living species are unable to follow" (6).

Rand defined a unit as "an existent regarded as a separate member of a group of two or more similar members." To identify such units in reality, a person must engage in "a selective focus" (6–7). This selectivity is based on objective criteria of classification. For instance, things exist. Attributes exist. The thing is its attributes. But the attributes can be separated from the thing in an act of mental isolation. The abstracted unit cannot be reified into a separate thing, but it does enable a person to bring the elements of the real world within the range of consciousness. Rand explained: "*Units are things viewed by a consciousness in certain existing relationships.*" The unit helps us to classify objective existents according to observed, real characteristics. Thus, in her concept of "unit," Rand bridges metaphysics and epistemology, the existence of the thing and our knowledge of it as a relation (7).

For Rand, the formation of relational units is the essential foundation of concept formation. A "concept" integrates two or more perceptual concretes—or units—which are isolated by a process of abstraction according to specific characteristics and united by a specific definition.[42] A concept means the existential referents it signifies, or the existents it identifies. This understanding of concept formation involves many distinct and interrelated epistemological aspects.

The first moment of the conceptual process is the ability to abstract. Rand would have agreed with the Marxist theoretician Bertell Ollman, who explains that the necessity of abstraction is

> [a] simple recognition of the fact that all thinking about reality begins by breaking it down into manageable parts. Reality may be in one piece when lived, but to be thought about and communicated it

must be parceled out. Our minds can no more swallow the world whole at one sitting than can our stomachs. . . . "Abstract" comes from the Latin, *abstrahere*, which means "to pull from." In effect, a piece has been pulled from or taken out of the whole and is temporarily perceived as standing apart. (Ollman 1993, 24)

Likewise, for Rand, this process of abstraction is "a selective mental focus that *takes out* or separates a certain aspect of reality from all others" (*Introduction*, 10). Abstraction is a necessary moment of the conceptual process because the mind cannot deal at once with all of the complexities of the totality. People are not omniscient; they function neither as gods nor like Aquinas's angels. Rand explained that in the Thomistic view, each of the angels embodies the form of a different species. Lacking corporeality and human consciousness, the angels are conceived as being capable of grasping all the instances of every universal Form in existence by a single act of contemplation. Rand warned that human beings cannot attempt to operate like Aquinas's angels (Peikoff 1972T, lecture 8).

The human mode of awareness limits how much can be grasped in a single cognitive act. By abstracting units from the totality, people make the world knowable and manageable. These units form the basis of open-ended concepts, each of which incorporates a recognition of context and change. Our abstractions enable us to "chew" the pieces of a complex totality in an effort to make them cognitively digestible.

Thus, abstraction is necessary, according to Rand, because people cannot deal with the whole of reality, or the totality of their own knowledge in a single, simultaneous instant of cognition ("Appendix," 172). Abstraction enables us to reduce the information at our disposal to manageable cognitive units. In this sense, a human being is no different from a crow; each has a limited ability to discriminate beyond a certain number of units. The difference between a human and a crow, however, is that humans are capable of conceptualizing relational units which internalize innumerable variations within a specified range. Thus, though human cognition is also limited by the "crow epistemology," humans are able to transcend these limits by a conceptual process condensing the number of units with which they must grapple (*Introduction*, 63). As Kelley (1984a) explains, the unit economy inherent in concept formation "is a way of treating discriminable things as if they were identical. This has the advantage of filtering out a mass of information that is irrelevant to most cognitive tasks" (19).

Abstraction is a necessary first step in concept formation, but it is not the culmination of the process. Those who would abstract a unit without reintegrating it into a cognitive totality create a distorted, partial, or segmented view of reality. The totality cannot be ignored.[43] Rand would have agreed with Lossky ([1906] 1919) that our ability to abstract "separates out from . . . reality some fresh aspect, of which we become aware precisely as an aspect of, or an element in, the part of reality under investigation" (230). For Rand, the part can never be reified as a separate whole. If we are to avoid such reification, the abstracted units must be blended or synthesized into a single, new mental entity. This new unit of thought is a concept, which is denoted by a word.[44]

The concept can be reduced to its component parts whenever analysis is required. Indeed, the integrated units of a concept can be expanded or contracted depending on the cognitive context. But our integration of the units into a concept is not an arithmetic sum. One does not merely add such units as "mind," "arms," "legs," and "heart" and achieve a concept of human being. Rand preserved the integrity of the conceptual whole. She viewed concept formation as closer to an algebraic formula in which the concept itself stands for a limitless number of concretes of a specific kind (*Introduction*, 10). The consequent blending of the abstracted units "is not a mere sum, but an inseparable sum forming a new mental unit." It is an *integration*.[45]

Thus the second moment of concept formation is integration. The process of abstraction necessitates the process of integration. These two are inseparable; neither aspect is possible without the other ("Appendix," 138, 144). Breaking up and "chewing" the pieces of reality is an analytical process that must be followed by synthesis, so that the pieces are reconnected to the larger totality.[46] A fully human method of thinking requires us to "dance back and forth" between concretes and abstractions. Physical concretes and conceptual units must never be disconnected. And abstractions must never be left floating in disregard of the existential reality that gives them meaning. By integrating concretes and abstractions, units and concepts, human beings unify the elements of body and mind, existence and consciousness (Rand 1958T, lecture 5).

To abstract and to conceptualize, human beings must expend cognitive effort. As a dialectical thinker, Rand would have agreed with Ollman (1993), who argues that "most people are lazy abstractors, simply and uncritically accepting the mental units with which they think as part of their cultural inheritance" (26). Rand implored us to stop thinking in a preconceived square, to name our primaries, to identify our starting points, to recognize the hierarchical structure of our arguments and knowledge.[47] For Rand, this necessity to check our premises is the hallmark not only of a fully human epistemology but of *radical* thinking as well. Radicals go to the root; they refuse to be locked into the ideological boundaries set by others. Indeed, they question their *own* assumptions and strive to articulate their basis in reality as well. As in her distinction between the metaphysical and the man-made, Rand rejected the reification of the status quo as transhistorical and natural. *Every* issue, event, thought, desire, and action must be understood through a process of articulation.

Once the mind has achieved the tasks of abstraction and integration, the formation of a concept is complete. Rand saw each concept as an open file. A concept becomes an instrument for knowing reality. Our initial concepts allow us to grasp new elements of knowledge. With each epistemological expansion, we can return to our original concepts and enrich their meaning. Such integration of old and new knowledge enables us, over time, to subtly change our vantage point on the totality.[48] As Rasmussen (1983a) explains, a concept is "not a closed, a-contextual, repository of omniscience which provides a non-empirical path to knowledge. . . . The 'rich' character of a concept's cognitive content results from the fact that its significance . . . is not limited by what the knower explicitly considers when using a concept" (525–26). Thus, our understanding of each concept grows extensively and intensively with each advance in knowledge.

Rand explains that concept formation is an essentially mathematical process.[49] Since every existent is part of the same reality, each is measurable. The standards of measurement may vary.[50] For Rand, *everything* is measurable, either cardinally or ordinally. Our concept formation process incorporates this reality in the very act of abstraction. In abstracting two or more units from the totality, we differentiate within a specific context according to those characteristics which are commensurable. Our conceptual classifications omit specific measurements and intensities, while retaining the commensurable characteristic(s) that unites the identified cognitive units.[51]

In forming the concept "dog," for instance, we need not be aware of every dog on earth. We omit the variations within the species, forming a classification that comprises all of the diversities within a specific range. As our knowledge deepens from observation and scientific investigation, we are able to sharpen our *definition* of the dog's essential characteristics, without changing our concept of the existent, "dog."

The wide range of the concept "dog" incorporates every dog that has ever lived and will live, from Chihuahuas to Great Danes. But it does not include any cats. The concept "dog" omits the measurements (the various kinds of dogs), but retains those characteristics shared by all dogs. Abstracted characteristics enable us to distinguish "dogs" from "cats," and "dogs" and "cats" from "tables." As our context changes, however, so can our cognitive classifications (*Introduction*, 13–14). Ultimately, *everything* that exists can be integrated by the axiomatic concept "existence," since all things belong to the same reality. But for the purposes of concept formation, indeed, for the purposes of *human* knowledge, we engage in a primary inductive process in which characteristics are isolated according to perceptual similarities. As our knowledge grows, we begin to classify newly discovered instances of established concepts. This interaction of inductive and deductive moments makes possible the movement toward more specific differentiation and wider integration (19, 28).

Rand's theory of measurement omission leads to an interesting paradox. Though the process is crucial to conceptualization, it is not wholly directed by the faculty of volition. Rand argued that most people do not realize that they are engaging in any kind of measurement or measurement omission when they are forming concepts. But from the very first moments of abstraction, our ability to differentiate *is* an ability to distinguish between larger and smaller entities, hotter and colder states, brighter and darker colors, weaker and more intense emotions. Each of these differentiations involves *implicit* measurement. One does not have to measure the exact wavelengths of light that distinguish the color red from the color blue. We perceive differences even though we are not aware of measuring these differences at the time of concept formation. Science and mathematics can help us to articulate the actual measurements that are involved in this process, but explicit quantification is *not* typical or necessary.

Thus Rand saw an interaction in the conceptualization process between conscious volitional actions, such as focusing, logical reasoning, and abstraction, and nonconscious, tacit, habitual operations of perception, perceptual judgment, and measurement omission. As Peikoff explains, this ability to omit measurements is a natural cognitive function. That people may be unaware of the actual mechanism does not invalidate the theory. Rand sought to grasp *how* people form concepts—that is, the process by which the mind creates relational, objective conceptual classifications. Rand sought to identify these methods, not to direct the process, but to analyze a largely inarticulate epistemological mechanism. In articulating its tacit aspect, Rand aimed to validate the reality-based means of human cognition. She wished to preserve the integrity of objective conceptualization, in contradistinction to those intrinsicists and subjectivists who saw concept formation as a product of metaphysical revelation or arbitrary social convention.[52]

Internal Relations Revisited

In her theory of concepts, Rand navigated between the polarities of atomistic individuation and organicist integration. As I explained in Chapter 2, these extremes are integral to externalist and internalist perspectives. The doctrine of external relations faces a problem of integration. Since every thing has an identity strictly external to its relations, the externalist endorses an atomistic conception of reality. The externalist argues that the choice of a single attribute as an essential characteristic is a linguistic exercise largely dependent on social conventions. Since we can never fully know an entity's nature, our definitions of its essence are purely arbitrary. In fact, countless definitions of an entity are all equally valid.

Thus externalism cannot distinguish essential characteristics from nonessential ones. It arbitrarily multiples the number of legitimate classifications that can refer to the same entity. Without the ability to integrate such classifications objectively, the externalist achieves cognitive anarchy and epistemological *dis*integration.

By contrast, the doctrine of internal relations faces a problem of individuation and abstraction. In strict internalism, the nature of an entity is often dissolved into the relationships that constitute it. And yet, paradoxically, in the attempt to define a concept, the internalist, like the externalist, fails to provide any distinction between essential and nonessential characteristics. The internalist reasons thus: since the definition of an entity must reflect the ontological status of its constituent relations, and since *every* relationship is essential to the thing's identity, it follows that *no* essential distinctions can be made. In a fully coherent system, where every element is an extension of every other element, abstraction and definition are agents of distortion. It is no coincidence that the ultimate internalist sees everything as One. Metaphysical plurality gives way to mystical Totality. Individualism gives way to Totalitarian Collectivism.

For Rand, internalism and externalism are both to be rejected. The internalist sees all characteristics as *intrinsically* essential, whereas the externalist argues that the identification of essentiality is entirely *subjective* or socially arbitrary. Ultimately, internalists view *everything* as essential, whereas externalists argue that *nothing* is essential. Thus the internalist is typically an intrinsicist, and the externalist is often a subjectivist. Neither can select an essential characteristic that would make possible an objective definition. Whereas the externalist multiplies concepts *"beyond necessity,"* the internalist integrates concepts in *"disregard of necessity"* (*Introduction*, 72). Rand argues that definitions are neither subjective conventions nor "a repository of closed, out-of-context omniscience" (67). In Rand's view, "A definition is a statement that identifies the nature of the units subsumed under a concept. . . . The purpose of a definition is to distinguish a concept from all other concepts and thus to keep its units differentiated from all other existents" (40).

The definition implies *all* of the concepts' differentiated units. But a definition is only an identification that satisfies the cognitive need for "unit-economy"; it is not a description. Since people cannot grasp every characteristic of every existent in a single act of consciousness, they must utilize definitions that focus on essence within a specific context or level of generality. Rand attempted to avoid the pitfalls of internalist intrinsicism and externalist subjectivism by switching the focus of the debate from the realm of ontology to the realm of epistemology.[53]

Like the internalists, Rand accepted as given the proposition that since everything belongs to one reality, everything is related. But she added the proviso that everything is related *in some sense*. She refused to speculate on the ontological character of these relationships. This does not mean that it is impossible to conceptualize existential relationships. It merely underscores the fact that human beings are not omniscient. They cannot establish "the relationship of a given group of existents to everything else in the universe, including the undiscovered and unknown." They cannot adopt such a synoptic vantage point.

But human beings must show a scrupulous regard for cognitive clarity and precision in their definitions. How can they achieve such exactness, when at any given moment they do not know all the constituent relationships in which an entity may be involved? How can they pick an "essential" characteristic on which to base a definition, when they would have to know everything about the existent in order to know anything about its "essence"?

Rand rejected the view that everything must be known before anything can be classified or analyzed. The internalists and the externalists accept the same nonhuman standards by which to judge cognition, and then indict people for not living up to them. The internalists argue that since everything is intrinsically essential, no definition is fully valid because it is partial. The externalists argue that since nothing can be classified as objectively essential, no definition is fully valid because it is arbitrary. In both cases, the internalist and the externalist focus on essence as a metaphysical category divorced from the contextuality of knowledge.

For Rand, definitions must be "*contextually* absolute" since they must "specify the known relationships among existents (in terms of the known *essential* characteristics)" (*Introduction*, 47). The emphasis here is on what is essential within the context of knowledge. Definitions may change with the growth of knowledge. Hence, the distinction between essential and nonessential characteristics is neither intrinsic nor subjective. A definition identifies an existing characteristic of an entity as essential within a specified context of knowledge. This essential characteristic not only distinguishes the entity from other entities, but also explains the greatest number of other characteristics (45). The identification of an "essential" characteristic serves as a cognitive device enabling people to classify, condense, and integrate the elements of their knowledge (52).

Hence, "*all definitions are contextual*," according to Rand. As our knowledge grows, we may select different essential characteristics by which to define an entity. But Rand emphasized that as our classifications become more advanced, they do not necessarily contradict more primitive definitions (43). Indeed, as Kelley and Krueger (1984) argue, the concept is an expandable relation. Over time, it incorporates "*all* the shared properties which science discovers in its investigation of the kind" (61). This dynamic definitional process views essences within a changing context. At no time does a change in definition signify a change in the referent. The same referent takes on different meanings depending on the context in which it is discussed.

For example, a "human being" might be defined by primitive peoples as "a being who talks." Aristotle identified human beings as "rational animals." Modern scientists have defined them as "bi-pedal mammals," "rational primates," or "Homo sapiens" (Peikoff 1994T, lecture 10). Each of these definitions is valid. But each is based on a different cognitive context.[54] And in no case does the changing definition alter the concept, which refers to an existential referent. The referent remains the same, only our definition of the referent changes according to context. That a concept (i.e., a referent) receives different definitions in various contexts does not mean that these alterations are arbitrary or subjective (Peikoff 1991b, 103). They depend on the conditions of our knowledge (*Introduction*, 73).

Rand further argued that since a definition is based on contextually identified, essential characteristics, a concept and its definition are not interchangeable ("Appendix," 233–34). For example, though human beings may be defined as "rational animals," human nature comprises more than rationality and animality (*Introduction*, 39). They also have thumbs, stand upright, and so on. In reality, all these facts are simultaneous. To identify one characteristic, reason, as essential, is to focus on the cognitive faculty, which fundamentally differentiates human from nonhuman life forms.

Moreover, when Rand stated that "reason" is humanity's "essential" characteristic, she did not mean to imply that rationality best "explains" other inborn traits, such as the distinctively human digestive system. But upon closer inspection, Rand's expansive concept of "reason" may help us to understand that even the most "nonrational" of human characteristics can be deeply affected by the mind. Indeed, such a fundamental insight is central to holistic and psychosomatic medicine. When Rand attempted to transcend the dichotomies of reason and emotion, mind and body, her integrated, dialectical resolution preserved the centrality of the rational mind, even as it traced the reciprocal effects of the emotional and the somatic.

In her theory of definition, Rand admitted that there are some existents that may be difficult to classify or conceptualize. She called these "borderline cases." Such existents may share some characteristics with the referents of a given concept, but lack others. Certain organisms, for instance, may be classified as either animals or plants. For Rand, the choice of classification is optional. One can make the borderline case a subcategory of either concept, or one can draw approximate dividing lines, or merely identify it descriptively. Since no definition is based on an unchanging, metaphysical essence, Rand did not consider her conclusions threatened by such borderline cases. Ultimately, by altering the level of generality, essential differences are bound to surface, and appropriate classifications will be generated (72–74).

What makes an essential characteristic "objective," rather than intrinsic or subjective, is that it is a product of "a volitional relationship between existence and consciousness" (Peikoff 1991b, 113). Rand explained that metaphysically, objectivity is

> the recognition of the fact that reality exists independent of any perceiver's consciousness. Epistemologically, it is the recognition of the fact that a perceiver's . . . consciousness must acquire knowledge

of reality by certain means (reason) in accordance with certain rules (logic). This means that although reality is immutable and, in any given context, only one answer is true, the truth is not automatically available to a human consciousness and can be obtained only by a certain mental process which is required of every man who seeks knowledge—that there is no substitute for this process. . . . Metaphysically, the only authority is reality; epistemologically—one's own mind. The first is the ultimate arbiter of the second.[55]

Thus Rand's epistemology does not endorse intrinsic essences as found in traditional internalism. But neither does it endorse the subjectively identified essences typical of externalism. Rand argued that the relations one traces in reality must be connected to a specific cognitive task. Every characteristic of an entity is potentially relevant to our grasp of its meaning. And each existent is potentially relevant to everything else that exists in the universe. But this relevance must be ascertained *within a specific context*. As Peikoff explains, every blade of grass is potentially relevant to human life, because *within a specific context*, an attempt to count these blades must be related to a particular human purpose. The context helps us to determine relevance and essence (Peikoff 1989T). The meaning we attach to such counting is internally related to our actions, purposes, and knowledge. The meaning, the concept we form, constitutes a relationship between existence and consciousness.

While these principles have obvious application to the sphere of epistemology, they also have broader theoretical and methodological significance. In her social analysis and in her theory of history, Rand recognized a vast network of interrelationships between and among various, seemingly separable factors. Ultimately, she viewed these factors as she would those relational properties that organically constitute any *single* entity. She focused on the *internal* relationships between identifiable components within a single social totality. Whereas a nonradical would analyze social problems as if they were disconnected from one another, Rand was not unlike other *radical* theorists (e.g., Marx) in her emphasis on a kind of *asymmetric* internality between elements. Thus the singular issue of racial discrimination, for instance, cannot be disconnected from broad epistemic, psychological, ethical, political, and economic factors. Likewise, in her theory of history, she placed greater emphasis on the role of philosophy, even as she simultaneously recognized a form of organic, reciprocal interaction between many causal factors.

7   Reason and Emotion

In recent studies of Rand's philosophy, little attention is paid to her reflections on psychology. Peikoff's systematic presentation of Objectivism, for instance, is purely and self-consciously philosophical; he avoids, on principle, any discussion of the extensive implications for psychology of Rand's epistemology and ethics (Peikoff 1990–91T, lecture 13). Merrill (1991, 179) indicates his own unwillingness to discuss these aspects of Rand's thought because their "status" in Objectivist literature is somewhat uncertain. Such themes as "psycho-epistemology," "the psychology of self-esteem," and "social metaphysics" were a theoretical outgrowth of Rand's interaction with her chief intellectual protégé, Nathaniel Branden, prior to their break in 1968. Since that time, many of these important issues have been left largely unexplored.

Merrill correctly notes that Rand never repudiated the pre-1968 writings of Nathaniel and Barbara Branden. Because Rand refused to sanction any of their later work, however, Objectivist scholars have been reluctant to deal with the Brandens' contributions. However, I believe that it is as legitimate to examine the works of the Brandens as those of Binswanger, Kelley, Peikoff, and other Objectivists and neo-Objectivists. Each owes an enormous intellectual debt to Rand. One cannot possibly assess the intellectual implications and historical impact of Objectivism without discussing the contributions of others whom Rand directly influenced. Indeed, in several instances where Rand's initial formulations were one-sided, her successors have developed a more comprehensive response to dualism that is completely consistent with Objectivist philosophy.

In this chapter I explore themes in Rand's philosophical psychology, particularly those pertaining to the relationship between reason and emotion. Peikoff (1972T, lecture 1) once defined "philosophical psychology" as the theoretical application of metaphysics and epistemology to human nature. "Philosophical psychology" considers those topics in epistemology which have implications for psychology. It deals with the intersection between philosophy and psychology, and further illuminates the radical antidualism of Rand's Objectivism.

The Nature of Emotions

Accepting Aristotle's definition of human beings as "rational animals," Rand did not reduce human "being" to rationality and animality. The

Fig. 7.   Ayn Rand and Nathaniel Branden in the mid-1950s. (Courtesy of Nathaniel Branden)

definition serves the need for unit economy by isolating an essential characteristic distinguishing the human from the nonhuman. But such a definition does not capture the full complexity of the existent. In any study of the totality of human nature, it is important to consider both those aspects that are essential and those which are not essential to the definition. Hence, to define human beings as rational animals is not to deny that they have emotions.

For Rand, reason is an essential characteristic because it helps to explain seemingly nonrational aspects of human nature. In Rand's view, human beings have an emotional capacity that is largely dependent on their distinctive rational character. Whereas any dog or cat can experience a "feeling" arising from associational perceptions, only humans are capable of experiencing emotions that are the complex product of their conceptual awareness.[1]

Rand did not consider emotions to be primaries. They are not tools of cognition; they are not instruments for the acquisition of knowledge. They must be clearly distinguished from thought, even if they are a component of consciousness (New Intellectual, 55). For Rand, emotions are the "automatic result" of value judgments previously integrated by the subconscious mind. They are lightning-like estimates "of that which furthers man's values or threatens them, that which is for him or against him."[2]

In Rand's epistemology, reason is as basic as "existence" is in her ontology. Just as consciousness is asymmetrically internal to existence, so, too, is emotion asymmetrically dependent on the rational faculty for its content, even though it has reciprocal effects on mind and body. Those who would stress the primacy of consciousness or of emotion inevitably embrace a form of subjectivism or emotionalism that denies objectivity in cognition. Rand's emphasis on the primacy of existence and the centrality of reason does not nullify either consciousness or emotion. Rand argued that consciousness is the faculty of perceiving that which exists; it cannot be in conflict with existence. So, too, reason is the human means of knowledge; it is not, properly, in conflict with emotion.

From her very earliest philosophical reflections, Rand rejected the view that reason and emotion were natural antagonists. Rand saw the dichotomy between the heart and the mind as a vestige of religious thought. Those who see emotions as the enemy of reason or vice versa perpetuate an erroneous dichotomy between two aspects of consciousness. By emphasizing "faith" as the means to knowledge, the religionists had, in actuality,

proclaimed that their own "mystic" feelings were ineffable cognitive instruments, and declared war on reason.

Rand refused to regard reason as the enemy of the emotions. She refused
to accept the view that "feelings," "emotions," and "instincts" are beyond
rational control or understanding. In a 1934 journal entry, exploring
whether the belief in such a dichotomy was the result of training, she wrote:
"Why is a complete harmony between mind and emotions impossible?"[3]
She asked: "Is there—or should there be—such a thing as emotion opposed
to reason?" For Rand, emotion is not a mystical endowment external to the
reality-based means of knowledge. In Rand's view, it is "a form of undeveloped reason," a species of the conceptual faculty that may be comprehended
through a process of psychological articulation.[4]

It is no coincidence that these first reflections on the nature of emotion
take place within the context of Rand's condemnation of religion. Rand's
denunciation of religious thought was partially due to her exposure to
Russian mysticism. Russian religious philosophy, like much of Russian
culture, had rejected the "Western" emphasis on reason as an absolute.
Even Rand's own teacher, Lossky, had stressed the intuitive basis of
knowledge. Lossky's hierarchical personalism was a deeply mystical vision
in which all entities are One with the Kingdom of God.

Rand's insistence on the centrality of reason is in many ways an outgrowth
of her antipathy toward such mysticism. *Rand's stress on the role of reason
cannot be fully appreciated apart from this Russian context.* For Rand, anything
that even hinted at a devaluation of the rational faculty was to be rejected
and criticized. In her view, reason was the *only* spiritual endowment.[5]

By 1946, Rand had begun to develop a more explicit theory of the
relationship between reason and emotion. She wrote in her notes for
Atlas Shrugged:

> The basic process of a man's life goes like this: his thinking deter-
> mines his desires, his desires determine his actions. (Thinking, of
> course, is present all along the line, at every step and stage. His
> desires are a combination of thought and emotion (the "production"
> and the "consumption" sides being involved), and all his emotions,
> of course, are determined by his thinking, most particularly by his
> basic premises.) . . . This is the basic pattern, or "circle," of man's
> life on earth: from the spirit (thought) through the material activity
> (production) to the satisfaction of his spiritual desires (emotions).
> (He must eat in order to think; *but* he must think in order to eat.
> And he must think first.)[6]

This theme guided Rand in nearly every aspect of her mature philosophic vision, including her ethics, politics, and theory of history. A person learns to utilize the conceptual faculty through various moments of awareness. From focal awareness to logical reasoning, thinking is set into motion—and sustained—volitionally. Thinking determines one's goals. Goals are achieved by human action. Thinking, then, is not purely contemplative. Rand saw it as praxis-oriented, akin to "production." It is a vital, creative activity aiming for the satisfaction of both material and spiritual needs. Thinking is the distinctive *activity* of human existence. Cognitive *activity* is translated into material *activity*.[7] The "basic pattern" Rand discerned is between "production" and "consumption"; the productive, creative act of thought aims for the consumption and enjoyment of deeply spiritual and material needs. At once, Rand creates a link between spiritual and material concerns. She sees a movement from creative thought to material produc-tion to exalted spiritual satisfaction. But at the core of this "circle" is the prime mover of human action: the ability to think.[8]

By the time Rand wrote *Atlas Shrugged*, she had fully formulated her theory of emotions. Her protagonist, John Galt, states in the novel: "Emotions are inherent in your nature, but their content is dictated by your mind" (1021). For Rand, emotions are natural, this-worldly phenomena whose content derives from our cognitive contact with reality. In the novel, she presents characters who are rational creatures with the capacity to experience ecstasy. As a paean to integrated human being, *Atlas Shrugged* presents a union of reason and emotion, cognition and evaluation. The novel is filled with tirades against "whim-worshipers" who act without thought or principles, and who view their own subjective emotions as axiomatic guides to practice. But the novel does not reject emotions as subjective per se; it attempts to link human emotional capacity to the conceptual faculty. One of Rand's characters states: "Feelings? Oh yes, we do feel, he, you and I—we are, in fact, the only people capable of feeling—and we know where our feelings come from. But what we did not know and have delayed learning for too long is the nature of those who claim that they cannot account for their feelings" (783).

This is crucial to Rand's understanding of emotions: truly *human* beings do not supplant their ability to feel with their ability to reason. They do not seek to conquer, rule, or direct their emotions. Rather, they seek to set into motion a process in which emotions and reason are brought into harmony. They seek to articulate the cognitive basis of emotions by introspecting. Extrospection is an outwardly directed epistemological process. It answers the typical questions of epistemology: "What do I know?" and "How do I know it?" Introspection, by contrast, is an inwardly directed epistemological process. It attempts to answer the questions: "What do I feel?" and "Why do I feel it?" Introspection seeks to identify explicitly that which is merely implicit ("Appendix," 262). Though we experience emotions as immediate primaries in our awareness, the introspective person does not accept them as axiomatic. Fear, anger, guilt, shame, joy, arousal are emotions with both mental and somatic effects. But no emotion is without causal antecedents. Every emotion is a complex, derivative, integrated sum.[9]

Nathaniel Branden explains that in our experience of an emotion, we move through a series of psychological events: from perception (of an external or internal event) to evaluation to emotional response. The entire sequence is not immediately apparent, however, for we are aware only of the movement from perception to emotion. Training ourselves to introspect is one of the most important epistemological tasks because it enables us to isolate, through a process of abstraction, the actual moments of the emotive cycle.[10]

Branden explains further that each feeling is experienced as a totality, that is, as a union of two inseparable aspects of the evaluation that they imply: content and intensity.[11] The content of the emotion refers to the implicit evaluation: is that which I have perceived "for me" or "against me"? The intensity of the emotion refers to the implicit judgment: "to what extent?" Thus, we never feel any emotion without content or intensity. We can be slightly angry, or in a state of rage. We can like somebody, or be deeply in love with them. In all cases, the content and the intensity of the emotion will have implications for the course of action, or inaction.[12]

To understand the causal antecedents of a specific emotion then, one must assess it within a complex conceptual context (Peikoff 1991b, 156–57). Rand's Objectivism focuses on understanding this context in order to achieve an efficacious mind. She advocated the same epistemological precision for the introspective articulation of emotions as she did for the extrospective identification of existents. No emotion can be fully understood if it is abstracted from the context that gives it meaning. And no emotional response can be changed without a fundamental alteration of the cognitive context that generates it. The possibilities of self-deceit, evasion, repression, and rationalization are enormous in the introspective process. In Rand's words:

If men identified introspectively their inner states one tenth as correctly as they identify objective reality, we would be a race of ideal giants. I ascribe ninety-five percent or more of all psychological trouble and personal tragedies to the fact that in the realm of introspection we are on the level where savages were (or lower) in regard to extrospection. Men are not only not taught to introspect, they are actively discouraged from engaging in introspection, and yet their lives depend on it. Without that, nothing is possible to them, including [proper] concept-formation. [13]

Since "we can be under the sway of forces we do not recognize or understand," Nathaniel Branden affirms, only introspective self-monitoring can make possible genuine change and personal evolution. [14] Because "we know far more than we are aware of knowing," we must strive toward a fuller integration of the conscious and subconscious elements of mind (N. Branden 1983b, 165).

On this basis, Objectivism rejects the principle of an essential antagonism between reason and emotion. Any conflict between these two spheres reveals a contradiction between two principles—one articulated, the other tacit and subconscious—that has manifested as an emotional response. The fact that a struggle can exist between reason and emotion does not make them interchangeable. Objectivism views the relationship between cognition and evaluation, thought and feeling, the conscious and the subconscious, as causal, even if it allows for reciprocal effects. [15] In this relationship, evaluation emerges from cognition, feeling arises from cognitive contact with reality, and the subconscious stores elements derived from conscious awareness. Reason and emotion can be reconciled only if one initiates an introspective, therapeutic process that ultimately changes one's underlying premises and the consequent emotions. [16]

Though Rand's theory moves toward the integration of reason and emotion, it nevertheless generates some tensions of its own. At times, Rand tended to evaluate reason and emotion somewhat monistically, *purely from the vantage point of reason*, paying less attention to the reciprocal effects of evaluation on cognition, feeling on thought, the subconscious on the conscious. It is as if the tension between these two spheres could be dissolved by viewing emotion as merely an unarticulated form of thought that is amenable to change. Rand ([1976] 1992T) once boasted that she had never experienced an emotion that clashed with her intellect for more than a day—suggesting that she was able to articulate and fully grasp every emotion she had ever experienced, and that it was relatively easy to identify and alter the context from which an "inappropriate" emotional response emanated. Her assertion has several implications: that in a clash between one's reason and emotions, it is usually the premises behind one's emotions that are in need of change, because the emotion is judged to be "inappropriate," "irrational," or "immoral." Indeed, it is apparent from some of Rand's early journal entries, that she did view certain desires as "immoral," even if later published works by Rand and others have clearly stated that emotion in and of itself is *non*moral and *non*rational.[17]

Branden's Critique

Nathaniel Branden has provided a much-needed reassessment of Rand's view of the relationship between reason and emotion. Though he continues to accept many of the Objectivist formulations, since their break in 1968, Branden has argued persuasively that Rand's fictional works in particular convey mixed messages to the reader. To weigh his evidence thoroughly would involve textual analysis and interpretation beyond the scope of the present study. But many other commentators have similarly perceived a bias against emotion in Rand's philosophy, and their criticism extends beyond isolated passages in Rand's novels to constitute a serious indictment of Objectivism. These criticisms must be examined as a fundamental challenge to my contention that Rand's philosophy is inherently nondualistic.

Branden (1989T) claims that in Rand's fiction, her characters exhibit a tendency to disown or repress negative emotions. Howard Roark in *The Fountainhead*, for instance, repudiates his own pain throughout the novel. This device conveyed one of Rand's themes—that pain is not a metaphysical necessity of life on earth. In her notes for *Atlas Shrugged*, outlining the nature of the novel's protagonist, Rand reiterates this theme. She wrote that joy is present in Galt's soul, "*even when* he suffers." Indeed, "the worship of joy as against the worship of suffering" is what motivates Galt's very being.[18] But for Branden, Rand's emphasis on undiluted joy even when the character is suffering suggests to many of her readers that negative emotions should be repressed rather than fully acknowledged, experienced, and ultimately transcended.

Part of the problem, Branden argues, is that Rand's characters are portrayed in such broad moral abstractions that no understanding of their developmental psychology is offered. We never grasp the *process* by which these characters *learned* to live the moral life. Significantly, Branden recognizes that Rand was a profoundly Russian novelist, whose characters were created as the embodiment of specific abstract principles. The psychological growth of her characters was of little interest to her. Like Dostoyevsky, Rand paid much greater attention to the dialectical interplay of ideas in the action of the novel.

The problem, according to Branden, is that many Objectivists attempt to realize in their own lives the abstractions presented in Rand's novels, without understanding that it is very difficult to change one's emotional responses by changing the underlying thinking. In many cases, major areas of childhood repression must be confronted before an individual can alter his emotional responses (N. Branden [1971] 1978, 45, 51). None of Rand's characters face such psychological obstacles.

In fairness to Rand, however, it must be stated that one of her most memorable characters, Hank Rearden in *Atlas Shrugged*, experiences internal conflicts between his consciously accepted convictions and his inarticulate emotions. In the area of sexual psychology, for instance, Rearden responds to Dagny Taggart, Rand's heroine, with a fervor that "should" be reserved for his wife. But through a process of articulation, Rearden realizes that his emotions are speaking to him, telling him something that his conscious thoughts have obscured. Rearden's initial guilt emerges from a conflict between the irrational societal values he has been taught and the rational value premises that he has internalized inadvertently. Rearden begins to realize that his wife does not share his sense of life, and that his seemingly inexplicable sexual responses toward Dagny are an outgrowth of their mutual values. Rearden struggles to understand this and many other ideational conflicts throughout the novel. His integration of these lessons into the fabric of his existence is one of the most insightful portraits of psychological growth in all of Rand's fiction. It also presents evidence that Rand was not entirely ignorant of the "language of emotions" as sometimes superior to the articulated "language of thought."

Nevertheless, Rearden seems to be the exception to the rule. Most of Rand's "ideal" characters are beyond further *psychological* development.[19] Galt, for instance, is presented as a fully integrated individual, with a great willingness to experience joy and an equally strong impulse to repudiate pain, anger, and fear. Branden suggests that Galt is the exemplary representative of a "very powerful bias against emotions" in Rand's novels. Branden acknowledges that he shared in this error in his early years, and "perpetuated it," encouraging his Objectivist students "to fear their own emotions, to distrust themselves."[20]

Rand seemed to hold that certain emotions are "inappropriate" to a rational psychology. According to Branden, she tended to blur the distinction between "reason" and the "reasonable." Branden differentiates between the rational process per se and that which any person or group of people regards as "reasonable" in a given instance. Reason is the faculty of awareness peculiar to human beings. That which is "reasonable" is culturally and historically specific. Rand often dismissed her critics as "mystics" and "irrationalists" without comprehending that they were operating with a different model of the "reasonable," not exhibiting a bias against reason as such (N. Branden 1982T).

> The temptation to equate our particular model of reality with "reason" is so powerful that we are very prone to dismiss as "irrational" or "anti-scientific" any line of thought, any speculation, or *even any data* that our model cannot accommodate. . . . A clash between mind and emotions is a clash between two judgments, one of which is conscious, the other of which might not be. We do not follow the voice of emotion or feeling unthinkingly; rather, we try to understand what it may be telling us. (N. Branden 1983b, 217–18)

Branden argues that Rand did not pay significant attention to "the voice of emotion." One of his most important post-Randian works, *The Disowned Self* (N. Branden [1971] 1978), is largely an attempt to redress this balance. In this regard, Branden appears to move away from his earlier view that Rand was "a master of motivational psychology,"[21] who had provided a definitive synthesis of reason and emotion. In some ways, Branden seems to have moved closer to Rand's early critics, such as Hazel Barnes and Albert Ellis.[22] Barnes (1967) charged that Objectivism regarded "*feelings* . . . with utmost disdain" (130), lacking any appreciation for how "emotions must come to the aid of reason in all fully conscious and significant living" (137). Ellis argued that the Objectivist ideal of the "unbreached mind" was a fantasy. The human ability to alter emotions is not limitless, in Ellis's view. Such alteration is far more difficult than a mere cerebral dissection of the emotive sequence (Ellis 1968, 16).

Eric Mack has also criticized Rand's "promulgation view of proper desires." Unlike Barnes and Ellis, Mack was deeply influenced by Rand. But Mack rejects Rand's suggestion that "appropriate" emotions should be rooted in rational judgments, and that emotions springing from "nonrational judgments" are antithetical to the objective interests of the agent. For Mack, most desires do not result from rational judgment. Like Ellis, Mack argues that reason has a strictly limited capacity to modify the "rich fabric of desires and interests" motivating human action. Mack argues that Rand's promulgation theory seems to contradict the actions of her own fictional characters, who never attempt to deduce their values and desires from the rule of reason. And yet, for Mack, this is precisely what Rand's theory of emotions seems to require.[23]

Barbara Branden (1986) has voiced a similar objection to Rand's understanding of the relationship between reason and emotion. She is critical of Rand's attempt to reduce emotions to "a set of intellectual conclusions that we may then accept or reject according to their rationality. . . . We are not omniscient, not about the world outside us, and not about the vast complexity of our own mental content and processes" (195).

The preceding criticisms raise many interesting issues. First, all of these critics seem to agree that Rand tended to regard the distinction between these two spheres primarily from the vantage point of reason. Though her characterization of Rearden offers evidence that she understood the epistemic role of emotions, in most cases, she assumes that the conflict can be resolved solely through rational deliberation. In addition, several critics are uncomfortable with the implication that certain emotions and desires are "proper," whereas others are "improper." This was a far more religious way of thinking than Rand realized.[24]

Rand's successors have moved beyond the monistic implications of some of her early writings without contradicting her initial formulations. They have integrated new insights into the body of Objectivism, embracing a more explicitly nondualistic, non-monistic interpretation of the relationship between reason and emotion. In the remainder of this chapter, I will outline these developments and show that Rand's own understanding of the distinction was far more complex than might appear at first glance. What emerges is an integrated view of reason and emotion that has startling and revolutionary implications for Rand's project.

The Conscious and the Subconscious

Two concepts are especially significant in Objectivist philosophical psychology: "sense of life" and "psycho-epistemology." Both pertain to the interaction between the conscious and the subconscious mind.

As early as 1947, Rand regarded the "subconscious" as an automatic integrator of the mind's contents, which themselves were derived from the individual's perceptions of reality.[25] In 1970, Rand analyzed the connection between these mental processes more thoroughly. In her essay, "The Comprachicos," she argued that the conscious mind registers and perceives relationships between experiences. The subconscious stores these conscious observations and integrates the connections. The subconscious thus meets the requirements of the "crow epistemology." Since human beings cannot deal with the totality of knowledge in a single frame of consciousness, their minds automatize that knowledge and make it available as it is needed. A mind's efficiency in processing the elements of reality largely depends on how well integrated, automatized, and unrepressed this subconscious context is.

From a very early age, children begin to self-program their minds. Childhood "experiences, observations and sub-verbal conclusions" determine and shape the course of this cognitive development. In assessing a child's cognitive skills, neither the content of the mind nor the mind's methods of functioning can be evaluated in isolation from the other. The methods of acquiring and processing knowledge cannot be fully understood apart from the content of the mind. And the content of the mind cannot be fully appreciated by abstracting it from the process—the particular methods of awareness—that make it possible (Peikoff 1985T, lecture 1). According to Rand, "the interaction of content and method establishes a certain reciprocity: the method of acquiring knowledge affects its content, which affects the further development of the method, and so on."[26] Rand therefore placed great emphasis on the social context within which children develop their cognitive skills. The significant adults in a child's world, the methods of education, and the culture itself "can accelerate or hamper, retard and, perhaps, destroy the development of his conceptual faculty" (195).

Thus, how an individual deals with the facts of reality is a function of the interaction between the content and the methods of his or her consciousness. The content is not always articulated, however. The subconscious integrates the mind's contents and serves as the repository of an inarticulate "sense of life." In her earliest published discussion of this concept, Rand defined a "sense of life" as "a pre-conceptual equivalent of metaphysics, an emotional, subconsciously integrated appraisal of man and of existence. It sets the nature of a man's emotional responses and the essence of his character."[27]

In their initial dealings with the world, children begin to form generalized impressions about the nature of reality, of the self, and of others. Growing up in loving households, children might form a benevolent sense of life, see themselves as worthy of affection, and be able to both give and receive love. Children who are victims of abuse, on the other hand, might form a malevolent sense of life, be distrustful of people, and be handicapped by a poor self-image. The range of subconscious integrations between these two extremes is enormous.

A sense of life, then, is formed by a tacit process of emotional abstraction. The subconscious classifies things and events, people and places, all of the contents of the mind, "according to the emotions they invoke" (27). Relationships are established by subconscious associations and emotional connotations. These subconscious integrations become the emotional equiv-alent of what Rand characterizes as "metaphysical value-judgments" (28). Such judgments pertain to the general nature of being. They are what Edith Packer has called "core evaluations" of the self, the world, and other people.[28]

A sense of life is not a logically derived emotional sum. In fact, no emotions are "deduced" through rational deliberation. Rand does not present a promulgation theory of the origins of emotion. True, she holds that emotions are the result of conscious contact with the world. But they are not the product of explicit or deliberate deduction. A sense of life is formed from the earliest moments of childhood as an unintended conse-quence or by-product of the child's contact with reality.

For Rand, a sense of life is essentially the form in which most people hold their "philosophy." It is an "unidentified philosophy" for most people, but serves as a kind of philosophy nonetheless. A child's sense of life will affect its value choices, actions, emotional responses, and, especially, its conscious convictions. As children grow into adulthood, their sense of life continues to deeply influence their approach to living.[29] Rand and Nathaniel Branden explain that a person's sense of life is rarely explicitly articulated. In our relationships with others, our sense of life is communicated tacitly by our manner "of moving, talking, smiling,"[30] our ways "of standing, of moving, of expressing emotions, of reacting to events . . . by the things said and by the things not said, by the explanations it is not necessary to give, by sudden, unexpected signs of mutual understanding."[31]

Since this tacit dimension permeates nearly every facet of our personality, Branden argues that an individual's sense of life, once formed, is "remark-ably tenacious and resistant to change." Indeed, even if the adult acquires a great deal of knowledge through observation and learning, his or her sense of life is liable to remain unaffected (N. Branden 1980, 99). Rand likewise observed that the great majority of people remain at the mercy of their tacit sense of life.[32]

Speaking as a philosopher, Rand denied that a person could be judged by his or her subconscious premises, since these premises cannot be known explicitly by the observer (Peikoff 1976T, lecture 12). Consciousness can be perceived and evaluated only by its "outward manifestations," its expressions in action. The task of evaluating the subconscious is a psychological, rather than a philosophical, endeavor. Psychology regards the individual agent as a medical "subject," to be evaluated according to standards of mental health and cognitive competence, not moral worth.

Nonetheless, a psychologistic element is evident in many of Rand's commentaries.[33] In addition, it has been observed that Rand psychologized and moralized in her own dealings with people.[34] Rand was philosophically opposed to such practices, however. She stated: "Just as reasoning, to an irrational person, becomes rationalizing, and moral judgment becomes moralizing, so psychological theories become *psychologizing*."[35]

Though Rand holds that a psychologist should not pass judgment on the "proper" or "improper" desires of the patient, it is clear that she has a definite conception of what is "proper" to human being. Mack and others are correct to note that her entire vision of the good colored her understanding of what is healthy and unhealthy in human emotional response. But for Rand, it is not the emotion per se that is immoral or irrational; it is the underlying judgment that must be assessed.[36] Since only the conscious mind is subject to direct control, only conscious actions are subject to moral judgment.[37] And only the guiding hand of reason can enable individuals to articulate their subconscious premises and achieve a more integrated union with their conscious beliefs and actions. When this integration occurs, it is, according to Rand, "the most exultant form of certainty one can ever experience." In Rand's view:

> The transition from guidance by a sense of life to guidance by a conscious philosophy takes many forms. For the rare exception, the rational child, it is a natural, absorbing, if difficult, process—the process of validating and, if necessary, correcting in conceptual terms what he had merely sensed about the nature of man's existence, thus transforming a wordless feeling into a clearly verbalized knowledge, and laying a firm foundation, an intellectual roadbed, for the course

of his life. The result is a fully integrated personality, a man whose mind and emotions are in harmony, whose sense of life matches his conscious convictions.[38]

Rand recognized that this articulation process was fundamentally therapeutic. Individuals who tend to guide their actions by subconscious and emotional factors must be trained to articulate *conceptually* their fundamental base. In a journal entry written in the 1950s, Rand clearly understood that one could not "simply forbid" such individuals from living by the guidance of their tacit minds. The individual must be taught to build "his conceptual files by a constant process of verbalizing and defining, teach[ing] him to analyze his emotional selector when he catches it in action." The purpose of such a therapeutic process is to train individuals to discover the "deeper and deeper reasons" of their emotions, enabling them "to remove more 'onion skins,' and ultimately to reduce [their] emotional premises down to their philosophical primary base."[39]

Rand emphasized, however, that such an articulation process does not mean that the subconscious mind ceases to function. An articulated philosophy does not supplant an inarticulate sense of life. A sense of life, like all subconscious mechanisms, continues to operate as an engine of automatization. But as individuals move toward the clearer articulation of their thoughts and emotions, they learn to derive value judgments conceptually, rather than as mere by-products of a subconscious sense of life. Rand recognized that for many people this articulation process remains dormant or stunted. In such cases, they may experience a clash between their conscious convictions and their "repressed, unidentified (or only partially identified) sense of life." In a clash of this nature, an individual's sense of life cannot be changed volitionally. It can be altered gradually only after a long, difficult process of "psychological retraining."

But Rand also argued that it is not always necessary to change one's sense of life, that sometimes the tacit dimension is more consistent with the facts of reality than an individual's conscious convictions are. "Ironically enough," states Rand, "it is man's emotions, in such cases, that act as the avengers of his neglected or betrayed intellect."[40]

Thus Rand's philosophy does not tend toward a rational construction of feelings, but toward an integrated understanding of mind and of its constituted unity of reason and emotion. In such an organic unity, we grasp the cognitive basis of emotion, and the subconscious-emotive components of our understanding. In Rand's view, it is neither possible nor desirable to conceptualize every experience, action, emotion, and thought. As Packer explains, mental health does not require the articulation of *everything* that is subconscious; it only requires that there be no obstacles to retrieving relevant information held subconsciously.[41] Hence, the freely functioning subconscious can be enlisted in the service of awareness and creativity. Indeed, a "sense of life" governs the creative process and the response to art.[42] Artistic creation itself rests on the ability of the subconscious to integrate everything relevant to a specific context defined by the creator. An act of inspiration is the product of an automatized subconscious integration triggered by an observation of a new fact in its relationship to established knowledge. Creators work "intuitively," allowing their subconscious to integrate evidence that not even their conscious minds grasp immediately.[43] As Nathaniel Branden argues:

> Mind is more than immediate explicit awareness. It is a complex architecture of structures and processes. It includes more than the verbal, linear, analytic processes popularly if misleadingly described sometimes as "left-brain" activity. It includes the totality of mental life, including the subconscious, the intuitive, the symbolic, all that which sometimes is associated with the "right brain." Mind is all that by means of which we reach out to and apprehend the world.[44]

None of these observations contradict Rand's fundamental belief in the centrality of reason. Rather, they are entirely consistent with her expansive concept of consciousness.

Thus far I have explored Rand's conception of the interrelationship between mental content and method primarily from the vantage point of content. In this aspect of her analysis, Rand focuses on the automatized content of the subconscious as expressed in the individual's sense of life. But Rand's investigation goes further. She is also concerned with the automatized, habitual *methods* of consciousness. "Psycho-epistemology" pertains to the interrelationship between content and method from the vantage point of method. In her earliest published statement on this topic, Rand identified "psycho-epistemology" as "a man's method of using his consciousness" (*New Intellectual*, 21). Nathaniel Branden ([1969] 1979, 98 n. 29) states that Rand was the first philosopher to use this term in print. The concept itself was originated by Barbara Branden, who in the 1950s persuaded Rand of its importance. In later years, Rand expanded her understanding of the concept "psycho-epistemology" as "the study of man's cognitive processes from the aspect of the interaction between man's conscious mind and the automatic functions of his subconscious."[45]

Nathaniel Branden's articles on "psycho-epistemology" from the early 1960s suggest that the study of cognitive methods entails an examination of the relationship between the volitional and nonvolitional aspects of consciousness. By examining the link between "*the conscious, goal-setting, self-regulatory operations of the mind, and the subconscious, automatic operations,*" Rand and Branden sought to understand how certain habitual methods of awareness could internalize errors that would distort cognitive functioning.[46] Psycho-epistemology seeks to discover—and correct—these errors by articulating the methods people use to process the content of their minds (Peikoff 1976T, lecture 6). And yet Objectivism recognizes that a person's habitual method of awareness is just as difficult to change as a person's sense of life. Peikoff (1983T, lecture 12) observes, for instance, that the older a person is, the more likely it is that his or her psycho-epistemology will remain entrenched.

Nathaniel Branden argues that there are three basic cognitive habits. These alternative habits are often practiced by children in what Rand describes as "a continuum of degrees" between two extremes.[47] As children grow, they learn to activate and sustain different levels of focus. The clarity of this focus will deeply affect the clarity of their mental contents. Next, children learn to perform independent acts of analysis in assessing the validity of any issue. Their acceptance of an idea's truth or falsity can result from critical inquiry or from uncritical passivity. Finally, children must learn to distinguish between the functions of their reason and the functions of their emotions. They learn to direct their consciousnesses by making explicit, logical deductions and inductive generalizations (N. Branden [1969] 1979, 112). But they can also learn to attend to their subconscious emotions in such a way that their emotions serve as psycho-epistemological aids. *This* Brandenian insight serves as the springboard for a far more dialectical interpretation of the reason-emotion distinction.

Psychological Integration

Having briefly discussed Rand's concepts of "sense of life" and "psycho-epistemology," we can now return to a more informed discussion of the relationship between reason and emotion. As I have suggested, Rand was certainly aware of the possibility that an individual's inarticulate, emotional, and subconscious mechanisms could be more consistent with the facts of reality than an individual's conscious convictions. Even if she tended to focus on the side of reason, she would have agreed with Nathaniel Branden (1971b) that "reason and emotion must function in integrated harmony, or distortions result in both spheres" (8). Whereas Rand and Peikoff emphasize the dictum, "Think, and you shall feel" (Peikoff 1991b, 229), Branden (1983b) argues that we must also *"feel deeply . . . to think clearly."* Branden rejects any "notion that thinking and feeling are opposed functions and that each entails the denial of the other" (159). In this belief, he reaffirms the essence of Rand's nondualistic view. He transcends any emphasis on reason alone. He proclaims that as integrated organisms, individual persons who become disconnected from the reality of emotional experience cannot preserve the clarity of their thinking. For Branden ([1971] 1978, 7), just as an abdication of thought will result in *emotional* privation, so too, a denial of feeling will result in *intellectual* impoverishment.

Branden examines the cognitive distortions that follow from the severing of reason and emotion. An individual who is alienated from his or her inner experiences rationalizes rather than thinks. Rand too recognized this danger. She had argued: "Rationalization is . . . a process of providing one's emotions with a false identity, of giving them spurious explanations and justifications—in order to hide one's motives, not just from others, but primarily from oneself." She acknowledged that in any attempt to subvert one's emotional processes, one risked hampering, distorting, and ultimately, destroying the efficacy of cognition. By rationalizing, individuals become disconnected from the reality of their inner experience.[48]

In a journal entry from the 1950s, Rand grasped too that the process of articulating emotions cannot be rushed; an individual who attempts such articulation must initiate and sustain it gradually and volitionally. Individuals cannot achieve emotional self-awareness by memorizing "formulas and dogmas which [they do] not fully understand."[49] Branden has called this a process not of "rationalizing," but of "intellectualizing." In "intellectualizing," individuals respond to personal problems by spouting floating abstractions with no relevance to the concrete issues of their own lives. Both rationalizing and intellectualizing pervert the purpose of thought, which is the apprehension of reality. By cutting their thought processes off from both external and internal reality, individuals sabotage their capacity to experience the full range of their emotions. Thus, for Branden, intellectualizers are just as dissociated from their inner emotional experience as the most fervent "whim-worshipers" who indulge in a few disconnected feelings (N. Branden [1971] 1978, 7, 24–25). Intellectualizers repress their emotions and escape into the realm of the abstract, undermining their awareness of both inner experience and external reality. "Whim-worshipers," equally threatened by their own inner states, escape into the realm of random emotionalism. In both cases, repression and emotional self-indulgence are a means of undercutting objectivity and separating the conscious from the subconscious aspects of the mind.[50] Having bifurcated reason and emotion, cognition and evaluation, an individual has no recourse but to engage in blind action. Branden ([1971] 1978) observes: "In all such instances, the motive is *avoidance*—avoidance of some aspect of reality" (4–5).

In Branden's view: "*Awareness moves freely in both directions—or it moves freely in neither.*" The integration of reason and emotion is simultaneously a means to the union of mind and body. As persons struggle toward psychological maturity, they begin with the knowledge that the body is part but not all of the self. All too often, however, as a person's consciousness evolves toward a more comprehensive sense of self, the mind may become disconnected from the body. Many people begin to view their own bodies not as an aspect of the self but as a *nonself*. Branden argues that such alienation from the physical is simultaneously alienation from the emotional, because it is through the body that one's emotions are felt. Every emotion has both a spiritual and a somatic component. Hence, estrangement from emotion is, by extension, estrangement from the body. By cutting themselves off from the data that the body provides, many people damage their ability to integrate thought and emotion. Seeing a clash between their thoughts and feelings, they view reason as a means of conquering threatening emotional signals. In an effort to preserve the autonomy of their own minds, they continue to subvert the integrity of their emotional mechanism, and by consequence, they cripple the very rational faculty they wish to sustain. Like Wilhelm Reich before him, Branden argues that "unblocking the body—unblocking feelings—is unblocking consciousness." Our autonomy demands the inseparable union of the physical and the spiritual, the emotive and the cerebral; "it involves our entire being."[51]

Rand was fully aware of this mind-body unity. She recognized that even bodily sensations provide people with "an automatic form of knowledge" based upon the natural pleasure-pain mechanisms of the organism.[52] She also maintained: "Cognitive processes affect man's emotions which affect his body, and the influence is reciprocal."[53] But she did not examine this reciprocal interaction at length.

By contrast, Branden analyzes the elements of the mind-body connection, viewing the issues developmentally. He focuses on how parents "teach" their children to "disown" their feelings. Examining a variety of deadening family situations and relationships, Branden (1992) maintains that "most of us are children of dysfunctional families." He examines how parents can create severe obstacles to the child's cognitive and emotive development (3). In such circumstances, children may unwittingly adopt defense techniques that numb their awareness of unacceptable or painful impulses, feelings, ideas, and memories. As they mature, they may genuinely seek to dissolve their unarticulated guilt, fear, anger, and internal conflicts. But such emotional repression cannot be merely commanded out of existence by sustained logical reasoning. No amount of persistent analysis can overturn the wreckage brought about by long-term cognitive and emotional subversion. Branden argues that in such cases, the individual must first practice the art of "owning" his emotions, of bringing the aspects of his inner experiences into full awareness. Whereas lifelong evasion and repression engender cognitive *dis*integration, the removal of obstacles to the experience of one's emotions reignites the mind's integrative processes (N. Branden [1971] 1978, 42, 87, 102–3). Thus, for Branden: "Therapeutic understanding represents an integration of intellect and emotion, cognition and experience, thought and feeling—not either/or, but always both together" (109).

Many of Branden's post-Randian writings center on the techniques he has developed to aid the self-disclosure of "unrecognized attitudes and patterns." Branden (1983a, 131) uses a sentence-completion method, in which the individual subject spontaneously completes a sentence stem presented to him or her by a qualified therapist. While an assessment of these techniques is beyond the scope of the present study, I believe that Branden has provided Objectivism with the equivalent of a "depth hermeneutics" similar in spirit to that pioneered by Jürgen Habermas.[54] Habermas focused on the process by which the individual could be liberated from "distorted communication." He utilized Freudian psychoanalysis as a means of transcending distortions in communicative interaction brought about by self-deceit and interpersonal manipulation. As Thomas McCarthy (1978) has observed, Habermas's "depth hermeneutics" aims to translate "what is unconscious into what is conscious," igniting "a process of reflection, a reappropriation of a lost portion of the self" (200). This therapeutic process is as important to Habermas's project as it is to Objectivism. The full implications of this parallel will be explored in Chapter 11.

Branden is not the only theorist to redress the imbalance of reason and emotion implicit in some of Rand's formulations.[55] Peikoff, too, has stressed the importance of somatic and emotive aspects of experience. Since he views the individual as a unity of mind and body, reason and emotion, Peikoff explores how emotions serve as crucial psycho-epistemological agents. For Peikoff, although emotions are not means of cognition, they provide an important tie to concretes. They enable individuals to maintain their contact with internal and external reality, concretizing their abstractions and contributing enormously to their creativity.[56]

Like Branden, Peikoff further maintains that there are culturally related differences in how men and women deal with their emotions. In this culture, women are encouraged to exercise their emotions, whereas men are encouraged to intellectualize them. The tendency to equate femininity with intellectual self-alienation and masculinity with emotional self-alienation is disastrous to both women and men in their quest for genuinely human relationships.[57] Peikoff inherits from Rand an antipathy toward the cultural bias to keep women "in their place." Rand characterized sexism as "an ancient, primitive evil, supported and perpetuated by women as much as, or more than, by men."[58] In her view, women had accepted and sustained their own victimization, subverting their need for independence. Her novels present female protagonists who are strong-willed and autonomous, reflecting her own success in a male-dominated intellectual world.

Nevertheless, Rand characterized herself as an ardent "anti-feminist" and "man-worshiper."[59] She dissociated herself from modern feminism because she believed that it had embraced biological egalitarianism and collectivist statism. Both Rand and the early Nathaniel Branden emphasized the anatomical and biological differences between men and women that served as the basis for their respective sex roles as "aggressor" and "responder."[60]

But in his work since 1968, Branden is far more concerned with the need to transcend *culturally induced* dualism in gender relations. Branden (1986, 241) observes that whereas men tend to disown tenderness, sensuality, and the capacity to nurture, women tend to disown strength, assertiveness, sexuality, and self-reliance. He argues that the most creative individuals are those who can integrate both "male" and "female" aspects of personality. By not conforming to cultural stereotypes, such men and women "are more open to the totality of their inner being."[61]

In this regard, Branden and Peikoff agree, surprisingly, with modern feminist methodology. Lynda Glennon, for instance, emphasizes the need for "synthesism" in the human personality. The male-female duality, according to Glennon, violates the wholeness of human nature, splitting men and women into half-people. In her view, "culturally specific connotations of 'masculine/feminine' as opposite categories is, then, but one more variation on the dualism that pervades everyday life and thought."[62]

It is fitting that both Peikoff and, to a larger extent, Branden, in their movement toward a fuller integration of alleged opposites, such as reason and emotion, the masculine and the feminine, have reaffirmed the tendency toward synthesis that Rand had absorbed from her Russian ancestors. This reaffirmation is all the more significant because it bears a subtle resemblance to the ideas of the Russian Symbolists. As noted in Chapter 1, Merezhkovsky had viewed the sexual act as the highest form of unity, since each body is interpenetrated by the other. For Merezhkovsky, true human being involves a synthesis of the womanly aspect in man, and the manly aspect in woman (Lossky, 1951, 337–41). While Peikoff and Branden would not embrace Merezhkovsky's indivisible androgyne as a moral ideal, they are clearly engaged in a similar revolt against culturally induced sexual dualism. This revolt has become more apparent as Peikoff, Branden, and others have separated themselves from some of Rand's personal attitudes, which had been codified by both her followers and detractors as part of the corpus of Objectivism. Rand's traces of cultural conservatism, as expressed in her opposition to the candidacy of a woman president and her disapproval of homosexuality, were sometimes mistakenly elevated to the status of philosophical principle.[63]

The issue of homosexuality, in particular, dramatically illustrates the contrast between Rand and her successors. In 1971, during a question-and-answer session following her Ford Hall Forum lecture "The Moratorium on Brains" (1971T), Rand asserted that although every individual has a right to engage in any consensual sexual activity, homosexuality is a manifestation of psychological "flaws, corruptions, errors, unfortunate premises," and that it is both "immoral" and "disgusting." Ignoring factors of social environment and/or genetic-biological endowment, Rand viewed homosexuality as a moral issue, based on her implicit assumption that it was a consciously chosen behavior. Whereas behaviorists see human beings as primarily products of social conditioning and the psychoanalysts see them as primarily creatures of internal drives, Rand emphasized the volitional aspects of consciousness.[64]

Rand's bias against lesbians and gays has been challenged by both Peikoff and Packer. Though these thinkers continue to regard homosexuality as a psychological detour from the norm, they are less inclined to moralize about it.[65] Branden, too, has exhibited much growth in his view of homosexuality. He formerly maintained that the polarity between man and woman most fully fosters each individual's awareness of his or her male and female aspects. He therefore saw both homosexuality and bisexuality as a "detour or blockage on the pathway to full maturity as an adult human being" (N. Branden 1980, 94). More recently, however, Branden has argued that many factors contribute to our integration as psychological and physical beings: genetic endowment, maturation, biological potentials and limitations, life experiences, explicit knowledge, conscious philosophy, and subconscious conclusions form a complex interrelated totality that cannot be easily reduced to any of its component parts.[66] Indeed, science has yet to discover the roots of sexual orientation. Thus, Branden argues against moralizing about homosexuality, for it is not within the realm of conscious choice and cannot possibly be a moral issue. Allan Blumenthal, a psychotherapist working within the Objectivist tradition, has expressed the same opinion.[67]

Such developments among Objectivist and neo-Objectivist thinkers suggest that they have appropriated from Rand a highly dialectical view of human psychology. In extending Rand's legacy, these thinkers have reaffirmed inadvertently her dialectical Russian roots. They have even exhibited a willingness to distinguish between Rand's personal attitudes and the philosophy of Objectivism. Although Rand's revolt against Russian mysticism sometimes led her to a one-sided emphasis on reason, her successors have more fully realized the integrative character of her philosophy. They have moved toward a conception of psychological integration that builds upon Rand's insights while transcending their limitations.

8 Art, Philosophy, and Efficacy

Throughout Rand's writings, one can find a persistent emphasis on the process by which human beings articulate the tacit dimensions of consciousness. This theme is implicit in Rand's theories of concept formation and emotion. The concept formation process is largely dependent on an act of measurement omission, which takes place in the mind whether people are aware of it or not. By articulating the tacit principles by which people form concepts, Rand attempted to provide an objective foundation for human knowing. She suggested that even though measurement omission is a tacit process, it is necessary to make explicit its reality-based principles in order to defend the objective integrity of our knowledge.

The Objectivist theory of the relationship between reason and emotion stresses a similar articulation process. By delving deeply into the inarticulate contents of the mind, and the habitual methods by which the subconscious integrates these contents, we can make explicit that which is implicit. Rand sought to provide an objective account of human emotional response. Even though we may be unaware of the cognitive roots of many of our emotions, she argued, it is both possible and desirable to initiate a therapeutic articulation process.

Thus both in concept formation and in emotional discernment, Rand's Objectivism aims to bring implicit elements of consciousness into more thoroughly explicit, articulated form. She suggested that knowledge and

Fig. 8. Ayn Rand in the driveway of her ranch in the San Fernando Valley in the 1940s. (Courtesy of Barbara Branden)

emotions are not mysterious, ineffable phenomena beyond our comprehension and control. Understanding the components of our consciousness enables us to better integrate—and alter, if necessary—the contents and methods of awareness.

Rand extended this impulse toward articulation into the realm of aesthetics and ethics. She attempted to show how the interaction of the conscious and the subconscious can move people toward acts of spiritual and material creativity.

The Function of Art

In this section, I am concerned with Rand's view of the fundamental nature of art and its function in human life, rather than with Rand's personal artistic tastes, or her specific views on literature, painting, music, aesthetic judgment, or beauty.[1]

One of the most distinctive aspects of Rand's theory is her belief that "the source of art lies in the fact that man's cognitive faculty is *conceptual*."[2] For Rand, the central function of art is not social, but epistemological. Certainly art reflects the cultural milieu, but its *essential* function pertains specifically to the nature of human consciousness. The mind grasps the infinite complexity of the world by reducing the number of units with which it must grapple. As we have seen, concept formation and definition also serve this cognitive need for unit economy. By abstracting various aspects from a totality and forming relational units, our minds synthesize an infinite number of similar concretes under a particular concept, designated by a particular word. The efficiency of our cognitive processes depends upon how well we have automatized and integrated these units.[3]

Art is the product of a comparable tacit process in which the artist's "metaphysical value-judgments" are concretized. As we have seen, such metaphysical abstractions pertain broadly to the nature of existence. They are usually held subconsciously, in an implicit form, as a component of our sense of life. Metaphysical value judgments are core evaluations of the self, the world, and other people. For most people, they are not consciously deduced judgments, but are an unintended, emotionally charged consequence of innumerable life experiences, from the earliest moments of childhood on.

While an art work, like every human creation, involves the application of both explicit and implicit knowledge, articulated and tacit skills, it remains far more dependent on the artist's subconscious integrations than on any conscious philosophical convictions. And "since artists, like any other men, seldom translate their sense of life into conscious terms," they are just as likely to produce works of art that project all of the tensions and contradictions of their inner worlds.[4]

Rand defined art as "*a selective re-creation of reality according to an artist's metaphysical value-judgments*" (*Romantic Manifesto*, 19). Guided by their sense of life, artists automatically isolate and integrate those aspects of reality which epitomize their unique views of the world. Their creations therefore emphasize the aspects they regard as important. Since the building blocks of knowledge derive, in Rand's view, from perception, art completes the epistemic circle by bringing one's most important metaphysical abstractions back to the perceptual level. Every art form fulfills this same function. An artist's metaphysical abstractions can be concretized in a variety of material, visual, or auditory forms, in literature, sculpture, painting, or musical composition. Rand argued that despite technological innovations, the basic art forms have remained constant since the prehistoric period because they depend on sensory, perceptual, and conceptual means of consciousness that are innate to the human species.[5]

Rand's understanding of the creative process was informed by her introspection into her own literary craft. In writing, Rand argued, authors draw on the knowledge stored in the subconscious mind. The capacity to summon such knowledge must be so automatized that the author "just knows" what to do as if by "instinct." In constructing plot and character, authors can program their subconscious minds to direct their conscious thoughts.[6] Authors achieve a "feel" for their craft that follows from the logic of their own literary context. Harking back to an Aristotelian aesthetic, Rand argued that in the totality of the author's creation, the parts and the whole generate and imply each other.[7] Rand explained that in her own writing, she created descriptions on four distinct, though interrelated, levels: the literal, the connotative, the symbolic, and the emotional. While she never calculated these interconnections consciously, she presented the reader with a totality—an integrated, emotional sum that provoked a corresponding emotional response.[8]

According to Rand, the artist and the responder enter into a communicative interaction.[9] The artist begins with a broad abstraction that he or she concretizes in the art work. The responder perceives and integrates the particulars, grasping the abstraction concretized by the artist. The communicative circle is completed through two interacting psycho-epistemological moments. The first resembles a process of deduction, in which there is a movement from a broad, general abstraction to a specific, concrete, artistic expression. This is a movement from the artist's core evaluation to an aesthetic, concrete embodiment in literary, visual, or auditory form. The second moment of the circle resembles a process of induction, in which there is a movement from the artist's concrete forms to the responder's emotional experience. This experience in turn, reflects the responder's own sense of life.[10]

The responder experiences not only the content of an artist's work, but the artist's style as well. Both the content and style reflect the artist's sense of life. Artists choose subjects that manifest their metaphysics, their views of existence, what they believe to be worthy of contemplation. An artist's style reveals his or her psycho-epistemology; it is the manner in which the artist presents the subject.[11] Artists may choose to present the heroic or the mediocre, the triumphant or the vanquished. They may do so in stark, precise terms, or in blurred abstractions (40–41). Every aesthetic choice made by the artist, every aesthetic experience of the responder, is a psychological confession (N. Branden 1967T, lecture 18). While Rand presumptuously claimed that she could pinpoint the exact nature of the confessions involved, she admitted that it can be very difficult to infer the basis of these choices and responses because there are many cross premises at work in the human psyche (in Peikoff 1976T, lecture 11). Nevertheless, when one responds positively to a work of art, one experiences a certain congruence with the artist's sense of life. When one responds negatively to a work of art, one's sense of life is at odds with the artist's projections.[12] Thus, an art work will confirm or contradict the responder's fundamental outlook on reality.[13]

Though Rand analyzed this communicative interaction between artist and responder in epistemic terms, she recognized that every art work has cultural implications. Each individual's psycho-epistemology and sense of life, developed mainly in early childhood, is influenced by the dominant values and ideas of the culture in which he or she lives.[14] A culture may stress the importance of independence or obedience, of reason or religion. Just as an art work is a reflection of the artist's soul, so, too, it is a barometer of the culture. However, Rand did not posit strict cultural determinism.[15] She did not believe that the individual artist slavishly mimics the values of the culture at large. But most artists, like most individuals, tacitly absorb the dominant ideas of their age. Although a few artists may rebel against the dominant views, the vast majority will give material expression to a culturally specific sense of life.[16]

In absorbing dominant artistic and cultural fashions, the majority also tends to accept the dominant moral trends. It is for this reason perhaps that Rand conjoined her aesthetic and ethical visions. Although all art fulfills a fundamental epistemic need to concretize humanity's broadest abstractions, Rand argued that literature in particular can serve as a means of communicating a moral ideal as well. From the sacred texts of religion to the pages of *Atlas Shrugged*, the most abstract moral codes have found concrete literary expression. Through literature, Rand hoped to provide an image of things not as they are but as they "ought to be." Whereas an ethical code can enunciate abstract moral principles, only literature can create a concretized model for their application in the realm of human action. In Rand's words, "Art is the technology of the soul."[17]

Rand's literary credo can be made the subject of a book in itself.[18] Yet it must be mentioned that Rand saw herself as promulgating a new Romantic literary tradition. She was influenced by such nineteenth-century Romantic writers as Hugo, Dostoyevsky, Schiller, and Rostand. Like these writers, she was deeply concerned with the realm of moral values. She argued that the Romantic movement celebrated the individual as an efficacious being of free will. It partially and implicitly affirmed the Aristotelian sense of life and the individualist culture of nineteenth-century capitalism. But the Romantic movement was, she points out, full of inner contradictions. Its brand of individualism was antimaterialist and emotionalist. As the movement collapsed under the weight of its internal conflicts, its writers were criticized for presenting escapist novels bordering on fantasy.[19] The Romantics were opposed by the Naturalists, who accepted the premises of determinism. Viewing human beings as puppets of their environment, the Naturalists set their stories in more contemporary, "realistic" settings. In keeping with her dialectical impulses, however, Rand rejected the traditional Romantic-Naturalist dichotomy and viewed herself as a "Romantic Realist."[20] As a Romantic, Rand aimed to project a vision of the ideal man. As a Realist, she presented her moral vision almost exclusively in a contemporary, this-worldly context.[21]

Like other aspects of her thought, Rand's literary aesthetic was an outgrowth of her Russian intellectual roots. As both novelist and philosopher, Rand remains true to the rich Russian literary tradition. Dostoyevsky, Tolstoy, and the Symbolist poets all strove to integrate literature with philosophy. Having grown up in the Silver Age, Rand was exposed to the

Symbolist's Nietzschean imagery. The Symbolists, such as Blok, Bely, and Merezhkovsky, believed that the artist should be a Promethean superman, aiming for the "transvaluation of values." Like Nietzsche, the Symbolists were both poets and philosophers. Beginning with the facts of the real world, rather than in the realm of fantasy, they aimed to transform that world. In Bely's words: "Art finds its support in reality. The reproduction of reality is the goal of art or its point of departure. Reality is like food in relation to art, without which its existence is impossible" (Shein 1973, 311).

If the Symbolists saw reality as the basis of art, they saw art itself as the essential creative human activity. Art was the means of creating a new culture that would transcend the limitations of the old. Literary artists were exalted for their desire to solve existential questions and to achieve the Ideal.[22]

While Rand would have opposed the explicitly Dionysian ideal of Russian Symbolism, she appears to have fully absorbed its impulse to transform culture through art. Though Rand had argued that *"art is not the means to any didactic end,"* she acknowledged that one of its most important "secondary consequences" is its ability to educate and influence.[23] In this regard, Rand's Romantic Realist credo is similar in spirit to Socialist Realism. The Socialist Realists believed that art was a positive, constructive, political activity. The artist served as a critic of the social order, projecting a dialectical resolution. When Stalin described the writer as the "engineer of the human soul," he echoed the beliefs of the Nietzschean Marxist God-builders, who saw art as the prime mover of this social transformation.[24] The new Soviet man was projected as an integrated being of theory and practice, a thinking man of action. In characterizing art as the "technology of the soul," Rand projected a different ideal achieved through similar literary means.

Rand's literary method of actualizing this ideal was fully Russian. Like Dostoyevsky and other writers of the Golden Age of Russian literature, Rand created characters based on the ideas they embodied. This method sometimes lacks the depth of an approach in which the characters' psychological development is detailed. It seeks conflict resolution in the interactions of characters who embody key principles (N. Branden 1989, 88).

In writing her fiction, Rand began with the real-concrete, that is, with the world as perceived by her in all of its particularity. Through inductive reasoning and abstraction, she broke down the whole into concepts. Her characters became thought-concretes, reconstituted on the basis of her abstraction. She stated: "My characters are persons in whom certain human attributes are focused more sharply and consistently than in average human beings."[25] These characters embody *essential* principles. Their actions arise from ideas that inform their identity. Rand omits the accidental and the contingent from her characterizations, while she emphasizes primary motivations. In the novel, as in life, Rand was "interested in philosophical principles only as they affect the actual existence of men; and in men, only as they reflect philosophical principles. An abstract theory that has no relation to reality is worse than nonsense; and men who act without relation to principles are less than animals" (107–8).

Rand concretized her abstractions in the characters of her creation. In *The Fountainhead*, for instance, she isolated and identified the principles, stages, and variations of what she called the "diseased ego." Based on this broad abstraction, Rand created a range of characters representing "second-handers"—those who lived *through* others, rather than by their own effort.[26]

Rand believed that her literary method was an instance of the creative process in general. In her view, "the creative process is, in a way, the reverse of the learning process." Both learning and creativity constitute a cycle in which there is a movement from the "concrete to the abstract to the concrete." In creating her characters, Rand first derived abstractions from concrete instances. She then concretized the abstraction "in order to achieve [her] own purpose (in the concrete)." In her notes for *Atlas Shrugged*, she wrote:

> In order to think at all, man must be able to perform this same cycle: he must know how to see an abstraction in the concrete and the concrete in an abstraction, and always relate one to the other; he must be able to derive an abstraction from the concrete . . . then be able to apply this abstraction both as guide for his future specific actions and as standard by which to judge the specific ideas or actions of others.[27]

In Rand's view, those who accept one part of this cognitive cycle, but not the other, are doomed to partiality and distortion. "The cycle *is* a cycle," Rand emphasized. The cycle is "unbreakable; no part of it can be of any use, until and unless the cycle is completed" and rationally grasped by the mind. Rand compared the process to an electric circuit, which must remain unbroken if it is to generate a current. A circuit "does not function in the separate parts," Rand wrote. Indeed, "the parts, in this case, are of no use whatever, of no relevance to the matter of having an electric current" (6).

But in describing the reciprocal relationship between these two modes, Rand emphasized the primacy of learning. For Rand, "the first, basic principle (a kind of first sub-purpose) preceding every other specific purpose is the purpose of gaining knowledge." This principle stems from her conviction that *existence*, not consciousness is primary. Although learning and creativity cannot be bifurcated, Rand preserved their asymmetric internality. She explained: "The process of learning has as its purpose to acquire knowledge. The process of creation is the process of applying one's knowledge to whatever purpose one wishes to achieve" (4). Knowledge must always precede creation. Rand's literary inventions are not floating abstractions cut off from reality. Her fictional characters are intensely one-sided representations of principles and phenomena that *exist*, though not usually in pure, isolated form.

Both cognition and creation involve *"the rational process."* In drawing abstractions from acquired knowledge, or in concretizing these abstractions back into specific concrete embodiments, Rand saw the same principle at work. Cognition and creation constitute a "completed cycle," which is characteristic not merely of literary method, but of all human activity. Rand suggested that human activity *as such*, is creative, for in all of their activities, people concretize their abstractions in the achievement of their distinctive purposes.

In each of her novels, Rand's characters are the kinds of one-sided concretes she wants them to be.[28] In their partiality, these characters interact as constituents of the organic unity that is the novel. The logic of the principles motivating each character unfolds through concrete actions, events, and circumstances, through interrelationships and conflicts that Rand created from the synthesis of her imagination.

But Rand realized that her fictional depiction of the truth of certain ideas was no substitute for fully articulated thought guiding efficacious social action. Since the artist creates and the responder experiences art in terms of sense of life, it is the sense of life that must be understood and, ultimately, influenced. Unlike the Russian Symbolists, Rand proposed a cultural revolution involving far more than just a Promethean aesthetic. Her cultural revolution would require philosophical articulation.

The Function of Philosophy

Much of this discussion has focused on the tacit dimensions of consciousness. For Rand, concept formation, emotions, sense of life, and even our habitual methods of thinking are based on subconscious integrations of which we are largely unaware. But such processes are not the only means by which the mind functions. Rand argued that there is an inescapable human need for philosophical articulation.

In order to appreciate the full meaning of Rand's theory, it is valuable to contrast her views with those of F. A. Hayek. Rand did not fully approve of Hayek's works. She believed that Hayek was not a pure enough advocate of capitalism, and that his understanding of reason was much too limited.[29] Given this antipathy toward Hayek's works, it is regrettable that Rand did not take his contributions more seriously, because she would have found that Hayek was critical of a particular conception of reason, rather than of the rational faculty per se. In many ways, both Hayek and Rand exhibit a similar disdain for traditional rationalism. I explore these parallels later in this chapter.

What needs to be discussed here is the distinction that Hayek and others have made between "knowing how" and "knowing that," between tacit and articulate epistemological dimensions. This is a distinction that Rand never made in these formal terms, but which is apparent in many aspects of her thought. Appropriating these concepts from the works of Gilbert Ryle and Michael Polanyi, Hayek argued:

> Men may "know how" to act, and the manner of their action may be correctly described by an articulated rule, without their explicitly "knowing that" the rule is such and such. Of course, once particular articulations of rules of conduct have become accepted, they will be the chief means of transmitting such rules; and the development of articulated and unarticulated rules will constantly interact.[30]

For Hayek, skills and habits, customs of thought and action are instances of our "knowing how" to do something without necessarily being aware of exactly what we are doing. Even as we articulate rules, we reduce and shift the tacit elements of our knowledge, but we can never entirely eliminate them. Polanyi ([1958] 1962) argued, for instance, that we may "remain ever unable to say all that we know" just as "we can never quite know what is implied in what we say" (56). Each of our statements may have an infinity of unspecifiable connotations (250).

Both Hayek and Polanyi maintained that we do not know why certain customs or taboos exist, except that some of them seem to embody an unarticulated "wisdom of the ages." Skills and crafts are passed on for generations without the craftspeople being able to articulate exactly what it is that they do. They may for instance, "know how" to use a tool, steer a boat, or play an instrument. But they may not be able to explain the actual creative process at work. They may not understand the physical or physiological principles involved in the continued reproduction of the skill. Should they come to recognize and articulate such principles, their very definition of the principles incorporates linguistic rules that guide their thought, though they have not explicitly formulated or articulated these rules either. As Hayek observed, "The ability of small children to use language in accordance with rules of grammar and idiom of which they are wholly unaware" is a striking instance of this phenomenon. As with language, so with moral values, "Man has more often learnt to do the right thing without comprehending why it was the right thing, and he is still more often served by custom than by understanding" (Hayek 1981, 157).

Rand recognized that most people accepted rules of social conduct tacitly as if by cultural osmosis. But she rejected emphatically the claims of evolutionists like Hayek, who assessed the efficiency of moral codes by their relative ability to sustain the cultures that embraced them. Cultural longevity was an insufficient standard for evaluating the morality of a given rule of conduct.

In addition, Rand acknowledged that there is a significant tacit dimension in concept formation, subconscious integration, emotional response, sense of life, and psycho-epistemology. She recognized that skills and creativity involve important tacit elements. But Rand hated the phrase "know how," much as she rejected the view that human beings exhibit an "instinct of tool-making" that could not be fully comprehended (Peikoff 1990–91T, lecture 12).

What must be understood is that Rand did not seek a synoptic identification of all that is tacit in the mind. It is true that every statement we utter carries with it certain implicit premises and conclusions of which we "may not necessarily be aware." To grasp the consequences of that which is merely implicit in our statements requires "a special, separate act of consciousness" ("Appendix," 159). Indeed, to understand the meaning of an emotion, the essence of our sense of life, and the actual methods by which we think, we must train ourselves in the art of knowing. To say what we mean and mean what we say is an epistemological achievement in which we become aware of the implications of our statements by the clarity of our own thinking (Peikoff 1980T, lecture 1).

Like Habermas, Rand argued that a rational reconstruction is needed to render explicit the structure and elements of our "know-how." This does not mean that someone playing the piano must simultaneously grasp the physiological processes that make this playing possible. The pianist need not be omniscient before performing a sonata. But there are many areas where self-understanding is desirable. An awareness of one's own emotions, an appreciation of one's own values, is as essential as technical proficiency to one's creativity. The extent to which one automatizes and integrates this knowledge will deeply affect the efficacy of one's actions. Rand would have agreed with Polanyi, who stressed that the context determines the appropriate level of focus. Thus, a pianist may be aware of playing the piano without being *focally* aware of the movement of each finger. Beginners must focus on each successive strike of a different piano key, but their ability to automatize these motions raises them to a higher level of proficiency. For the mature pianist, the fingering process is largely automatized. Polanyi ([1958] 1962) explains: "If a pianist shifts his attention from the piece he is playing to the observation of what he is doing with his fingers while playing it, he gets confused and may have to stop. This happens generally if we switch our focal attention to particulars of which we had previously been aware only in their subsidiary role" (56).

Rand would not have disagreed with any of these observations. She recognized that consciousness is, by its nature, finite and limited. Indeed, as Peikoff (1991b, 125) suggests, no mind can hold in the "flash of a synoptic insight" all of the ideas and skills that are relevant to a particular task. And Branden ([1969] 1979) states further that no individual "can achieve exhaustive knowledge of the nature and laws of mental activity, merely by introspection" (9).

But to state that human beings are not omniscient or that they cannot gain complete knowledge of their own minds through introspection is *not* to suggest that certain epistemic elements are fundamentally inexpressible. What Rand opposed in Hayek and Polanyi was their tendency to view skills, ideas, and morals as ineffable.[31] Even though Hayek and Polanyi did not object to the post hoc attempt at a rational reconstruction of a tacit act, they believed, nevertheless, that there are certain epistemic components that cannot be articulated in principle.

By contrast, Rand viewed the tacit components of knowledge as articulable in principle, even if these components had yet to be fully understood. Rand did not believe that it was a requirement of human survival to articulate *every* tacit practice.[32] But for Rand, the articulation process was not only possible, but *essential*, especially in the realm of morality, because it enabled individuals not only to "do the right thing" but to know *why* it was the right thing to do. Philosophy, she maintained, holds the key to such articulation.

To live, human beings must act efficaciously. To act, they must choose. To choose, they must define a code of values. To define values, they must know their own natures and the nature of the world around them. No one can escape from this need to act, choose, value, and know. Rand argued that for the individual the "only alternative is whether the philosophy guiding him is to be chosen by his mind or by chance."[33] The only alternative is whether to act on the basis of rational conviction and articulated understanding or on the basis of raw emotion and tacit sense of life. In Rand's view, an articulated philosophy is a necessity for efficacious living. It is "the foundation of science, the organizer of man's mind, the integrator of his knowledge, the programmer of his subconscious, the selector of his values."[34]

How could Rand make this statement when she had already acknowledged that most people are moved by tacit factors they have never fully grasped or articulated? If people begin by acting on subconsciously held metaphysical value-judgments, is the formation of explicit philosophical convictions nothing but an exercise in rationalizing the implicit? No. For Rand, articulation is *not* rationalization. Our core evaluations of ourselves, of others, and of the world may be wrong, but by not relying on the conclusions of our conscious minds, we are left at the mercy of inarticulate impulses that are largely the result of emotional and perceptual associations. Appropriate, efficacious action is based on the integration of the conscious and the subconscious. It may require alterations in our subconscious premises or, alternatively, in the explicit philosophical principles we have accepted. As Rand put it:

> You have no choice about the necessity to integrate your observations, your experiences, your knowledge into abstract ideas, i.e., into principles. . . . A philosophic system is an integrated view of existence. As a human being, you have no choice about the fact that you need a philosophy. Your only choice is whether you define your philosophy by a conscious, rational, disciplined process of thought and scrupulously logical deliberation—or let your subconscious accumulate a junk heap of unwarranted conclusions, false generalizations, undefined contradictions, undigested slogans, unidentified wishes, doubts and fears, thrown together by chance, but integrated by your subconscious into a kind of mongrel philosophy

and fused into a single, solid weight: *self-doubt*, like a ball and chain in the place where your mind's wings should have grown.[35]

As people learn to define the fundamental principles of their actions, they begin to accept a philosophy by choice. Their conscious convictions program their subconscious minds, rather than being mere rationalizations for the values they have accepted tacitly. Those who are led by conscious thinking are more aware of their values and the premises of their emotions and are far more likely to lead integrated, efficacious, and empowering lives. This does not mean that every person must be an intellectual innovator. But it does mean that each individual must judge ideas critically and choose appropriately correct courses of action.[36] The nature of the conceptual faculty is such that we are not equipped to survive without some kind of comprehensive view of our existence. Whatever the level of our intelligence, we need to integrate our knowledge, project our actions into the future, and weigh the consequences contextually.

Rand argued that throughout human history this need was served by religion. The necessity for a comprehensive understanding of existence led even the most primitive peoples to embrace some form of religious belief.[37] And yet no form of faith or mystic revelation could take the place of rationally dictated principles. Although religion attempted to fulfill this need, its very methods and many of its teachings undercut the ability of people to live and act in a moral and rational manner.[38] Rand's rejection of religion is not a repudiation of ethics. It is an affirmation of a supremely secular need that people have to make their lives knowable, understandable, and efficacious. It is the nature of this "will to efficacy" which must be examined in greater depth.

The Will to Efficacy

In both her ethics and her epistemology, Rand preserved the centrality of reason because she saw it as an individual's chief means for achieving efficacy. Such efficacy is essential to human survival. But it is also internally related to an individual's self-concept. By preserving the ability to think and the will to understand, the individual achieves the self-esteem necessary for psychological and existential well-being (N. Branden [1969] 1979, 117).

In his early essays while he was associated with Rand, Nathaniel Branden explains that to the extent that individuals are committed to the goal of awareness, their mental operations will tend toward cognitive *efficacy*. To the extent that they fail in this commitment, they will achieve cognitive *inefficacy* (111–12). Efficacy is the conviction that one is capable of producing the desired effects in one's actions. A consistent ability to translate thought into action leads to a sense of cognitive control over one's life that is essential to living. Whereas Nietzsche spoke of the "will to power," Objectivism aims to legitimate and affirm what Branden has called, the *will to efficacy* (123). Psycho-epistemologically, Rand's Objectivism reverses the Cartesian cogito. It begins with the fact of existence and defends the necessity of the conscious apprehension of both internal and external reality. In effect, Rand argued: "I am, therefore I will think" (B. Branden 1962T, lecture 10). Branden too emphasizes that we, as volitional beings, must engage in a consistent practice of awareness. We must grasp the cognitive roots of our emotions and the somatic-emotive contexts that condition our understanding. To the extent that our awareness is unobstructed, we will tend to achieve, in action, the goals that we have rationally sought and emotionally desired.

An unobstructed awareness is achieved through both a generalized or "metaphysical" efficacy and a specific or "particularized" efficacy. Metaphysical efficacy, Branden explains, pertains to a person's fundamental relationship to reality. The degree of a person's metaphysical efficacy is a reflection of the reality-oriented nature of that person's process of awareness. Particularized efficacy, by contrast, refers to a person's ability to achieve desired results through the mastery of specific practices. Such efficacy can only be affirmed through the expansion of knowledge and skills. The relationship between metaphysical and particularized efficacy is reciprocal.[39] Specific achievements will fuel a person's feeling of basic cognitive self-control, and such fundamental efficacy will promote the further mastery of practical skills.

Both Rand and Branden might be subject to the criticism that their belief in the human need for psycho-epistemological competence is specific to Western culture. Both of these thinkers recognize that "the individual" and "the self" are phenomena that have existed for thousands of years, though it was not until the development of industry and the rise of capitalism that such concepts were explicitly articulated. Yet, Rand would have agreed with Branden (1992) that the need for cognitive efficacy

> is not the product of a particular cultural "value bias." There is no society on earth, no society even conceivable, whose members do

not face the challenges of fulfilling their needs—who do not face the challenges of appropriate adaptation to nature and to the world of human beings. The idea of efficacy in this fundamental sense (which includes competence in human relationships) is not a "Western artifact." . . . We delude ourselves if we imagine there is any culture or society in which we will not have to face the challenge of making ourselves appropriate to life. (19–20)

It might be said that the need for cognitive efficacy is a part of the identity of the human species. But the kinds of social practices that affect human efficacy *are* a reflection of the culture within which people develop and thrive. Culturally specific political institutions, the family, the school, and the workplace will encourage, reinforce, or, alternatively, thwart the development of the efficacious mind. Branden argues that in our society, there are dysfunctional families, dysfunctional schools, and dysfunctional organizations.[40] One might say that Rand's critique of statism, which I explore in Part 3, is an examination of a *dysfunctional* social formation that places institutional obstacles in the path of human efficacy, values, and life itself.

If "efficacy" is the ability to achieve the effects one desires, then "inefficacy" is its opposite. Does the Objectivist notion of efficacy imply that people are inefficacious if they are unable to actualize their intentions? Is Rand's understanding of efficacious action excessively rationalistic?

Rationalism and Empiricism

Since Rand's project stresses the efficacy and centrality of reason, several critics have placed her in the rationalist tradition.[41] In order to assess the validity of this criticism, it is essential first to explore the extent to which Rand separated herself from both rationalism and empiricism. In this regard, Rand reaffirmed the nondualistic intellectual tendencies of her Russian predecessors.[42]

For Rand, the genuinely philosophical mind is critically objective; it requires an active, passionate, engaged commitment to the pursuit of truth and knowledge as "of crucial, personal, *selfish* importance" to each human actor.[43] Rand's indictment of rationalism and empiricism is, in many ways, a component of her broader critique of "the *unphilosophical* mind." The

unphilosophical mind is representative of contemporary, antirational culture. It consists of an "indiscriminate mixture of floating abstractions and
momentary concretes, without the ability (or the need) to tie the first to
reality, and the second to principles."[44] While Rand's repudiation of
rationalism centers on its penchant for glorifying floating abstractions, her
rejection of empiricism focuses on its essentially anti-conceptual character.

In Rand's view, the inability of post-Renaissance philosophy to solve the
problem of universals ultimately led to the development of two schools of
thought: "those who claimed that man obtains his knowledge of the world
from concepts, which come from inside his head and are not derived from
the perception of physical facts (the Rationalists)—and those who claimed
that man obtains his knowledge from experience, which was held to mean:
by direct perception of immediate facts, with no recourse to concepts (the
Empiricists)."[45]

This division between rationalists and empiricists was a reflection of the
mind-body dualism deeply ingrained in Western philosophy. Each tradition
embodied a distortion; each was half-right and half-wrong. For Rand,
knowledge was the product of a conceptual integration of the facts of reality.
It could not be achieved by severing concepts from percepts, thought from
reality, or abstractions from concretes.

Rand's analysis of rationalism and empiricism is not restricted to their
post-Renaissance historical incarnations. Rand maintained that both rationalism and empiricism are employed as methods of inquiry by contemporary
social scientists. Such modes of investigation must lead inevitably to a
fragmentation of knowledge.

Both Rand and Peikoff argue that rationalism begins with a truth: human
awareness is distinctively conceptual. But by cutting concepts from their
perceptual roots, rationalists base their analyses on floating abstractions.
From these dogmatic, acontextual premises, rationalists typically engage in
deduction as the means to knowledge. They claim that to achieve certainty,
one must be fully comprehensive. Such a proposition, however, translates
into a version of strict organicity; rationalists cannot explain anything
without knowing everything. They exhibit an almost neurotic compulsive-
ness for systematization and order. Paradoxically, in their quest for totalistic
knowledge, they are led toward more concrete-bound methods of inquiry.
Rationalism is the basis of compartmentalization in modern social science.
The desire for absolute specialization is the desire to know everything about
minutiae. The tinier the fragment, the greater the potential for more
"complete" knowledge of it. Each discipline becomes fractured from the

totality. "Full" knowledge of the abstracted part is achieved, but the context and conditions from which the part emerges, is ignored. Rationalists are left with the study of disconnected concretes, mirroring their empiricist counterparts (Peikoff 1983T, lecture 7).

Peikoff emphasizes further that rationalism, by celebrating reason, embodies an abiding contempt for emotions. Rationalists equate feelings with subjectivism. They believe that feelings must be ruthlessly suppressed in the quest for objective knowledge.[46] As such, rationalism becomes a *rationalization* for emotional repression that can only distort the objectivity it seeks to achieve (Peikoff 1983T, lecture 10).

Empiricism, by contrast, begins not with floating rationalistic abstractions, but with the "hard" facts of reality. Empiricists adopt an inductive, observational method, which Rand agreed is the necessary foundation for all knowledge. But empiricists are suspicious of abstraction. They reject the rationalist-organicist tendency toward synthesis. They reject axioms and are frequently philosophical skeptics, atomists, subjectivists, and emotionalists. Their approach is at root anti-conceptual; it focuses on the perceptual, historical, statistical, or psychometric (lecture 8). Rand argued that the anti-conceptual mentality of the empiricist

> treats the first-level abstractions, the concepts of physical existents, as if they were percepts, and is unable to rise much further, unable to integrate new knowledge or to identify its own experience—a mentality that has not discovered the process of conceptualization in conscious terms, has not learned to adopt it as an active, continuous, self-initiated policy, and is left arrested on a concrete-bound level, dealing only with the given, with the concerns of the immediate moment, day or year, anxiously sensing an abyss of the unknowable on all sides. (*Introduction*, 76)

Such a mentality is unable to make clear, conceptual distinctions between thought and emotion, cognition and evaluation, observation and imagination, essential and nonessential characteristics, object and subject, existence and consciousness.[47] It tends to "accept consequences while ignoring their causes." It regards as self-evident the complex products of thought, while not comprehending their preconditions and interrelations.[48]

In her journals in the 1950s, Rand speculated on the psycho-epistemological factors that might predispose an individual to what she later termed "anti-conceptual" methods. She initially characterized such anti-conceptu-

alism as a form of " 'memory-storing' epistemology." She maintained that
someone who "thinks" by such methods does not store "*conceptual* conclusions and evaluations in his subconscious." Rather, he or she "stores *concrete
memories* plus an emotional estimate" of their meaning. "Concrete events"
and "automatic emotional reactions" coalesce to form a "montage" of
"unanalyzed 'gestalts' " within the individual's mind. Such "thinking" short-
circuits the individual's ability to fully perceive and understand reality:

> Since man needs a system of *symbols* to deal with the enormous
> complexity of his experiences, since he has to condense and simplify
> every new event by means of its *essentials*, since he cannot treat
> every new event as if it were an undifferentiated, unprecedented first
> in a baby's blank consciousness, but must integrate (or at least relate)
> it to the context of his past knowledge, this method substitutes an
> *emotion* for the *perception* and *selection* of an *essential*.[49]

In effect, Rand believed that this "emotional" approach to knowledge
was the psycho-epistemological root of anti-conceptualist empiricism and its
modern social science derivatives: pragmatist and positivist methodologies.
Such approaches view facts as "single and discrete," unrelated to each other
or to the context from which they arise (*New Intellectual*, 43–44). By tearing
an idea from its context and treating it as "a self-sufficient, independent
item," the anti-conceptual mentality fractures the connection between
concept and context (Peikoff 1976T, lecture 5). It exhibits passivity with
regard to the formation of concepts and fundamental principles. It focuses
on the "empiric element in experience," and "treats abstractions as if they
were *perceptual* concretes."[50]

Ultimately, empiricism, like rationalism, fuels the contemporary tendency toward compartmentalization. By collecting endless hard data within
a narrowly defined subdiscipline, empiricists engage in specialization without
integration (Peikoff 1983T, lecture 9). Thus the methods of empiricism and
rationalism interpenetrate such that each school achieves similar analytical
distortions (Peikoff 1980T, lecture 2). They make radical thinking and
radical solutions impossible because they disconnect events from issues,
social problems from their antecedent historical conditions, and political
policies from their inexorable consequences.

Moreover, both rationalism and empiricism adhere to an infallibilist
fallacy.[51] In their quest for dogmatic absolutes, the rationalists feign omniscience. In their battle against dogmatic absolutes, the empiricists claim

that certainty is impossible. Both of these schools accept omniscience and infallibility as the standards for knowledge. The rationalists "pretend to have it," and the empiricists "bemoan their lack of it." But as Peikoff explains, the very notion of omniscience must be discarded. Knowledge and certainty are contextual. There is no validity to an absolute, acontextual truth.[52] As Rand explained it: "Man is neither infallible nor omniscient; if he were, a discipline such as epistemology—the theory of knowledge— would not be necessary nor possible: his knowledge would be automatic, unquestionable and total" (*Introduction*, 78).

Rand was not the first philosopher to question the rationalist-empiricist dichotomy (Machan 1971, 104). Hollinger argues persuasively that Rand's critique bears some similarity to those of Nietzsche and Husserl.[53] Even Sartre (1963) laments "the separation of theory and practice which [has] resulted in transforming the latter into an empiricism without principles; the former into a pure, fixed knowledge" (22). But the most readily available parallels can be drawn between Rand and her Russian predecessors. As I suggested in Chapter 1, the rejection of rationalism and empiricism was central to Solovyov's philosophy. Solovyov argued that the empiricists, in their emphasis on sensualism, reduced the world to simple and subjective sensory data. Rationalists, by contrast, viewed the world strictly in terms of concepts and ideas. These traditions dichotomized experience and reason, practice and theory, and achieved distorted partiality. Although Solovyov embraced a mystic resolution, his antidualism greatly influenced the development of Russian philosophic thought. The most important twentieth-century Russian adherent to this approach was Lossky.

As we have seen, Lossky's first major work in epistemology rejected the rationalist-empiricist distinction. For Lossky, rationalism and empiricism led to the fragmentation of an indissoluble unity between subject and object. Both empiricism and rationalism dissolve into a form of subjectivism. In empiricism, sensory data is ultimately *subjective* sensory data. In rationalism, reality dissolves into the *subjective* processes of cognition. Lossky ([1906] 1919) hoped to achieve a coordination of subject and object by transcending the negative and absorbing the positive aspects of these false alternatives:

> In relation to the older ways of thought, our theory is chiefly characterised by the fact that it rejects their negations, but preserves their positive contentions, and seeks to supplement the latter by new truths. It would not, then, overthrow the old systems, but aim rather at bringing them to life again in a new form; it would free

them from their old exclusiveness, and so prepare a way for their reconciliation and union. (402)

Though her resolution differed considerably from Lossky's "epistemological coordination," Rand reproduced the dialectical form of her teacher's critique. She recognized in empiricism and rationalism the same partiality that she saw in subjectivism and intrinsicism. In each of these interconnected polarities, there is one-sidedness and distortion. The Objectivist alternative repudiates the common infallibilist premise of both its opponents, while reuniting previously bifurcated categories. Rand's Objectivism preserves the indissoluble connection between percepts *and* concepts, experience *and* logic, emotion *and* reason. It seeks to end the compartmentalization of the social sciences and the atomistic fragmentation of knowledge, aiming for an organic view of society that is both critical and revolutionary.

Rand and Hayek

Given Rand's antipathy to rationalism especially, it is extremely valuable to compare her views to those of Hayek. There are two reasons for this comparison: First, it helps to place Rand closer to the *non*rationalistic tradition of libertarian thought of which Hayek is a part, and second, it helps to elucidate the full implications of Rand's critique for the issue of human efficacy.

Though Rand and Hayek are opposed on many philosophical and social questions, they generally agree on the desirability of a free market. But Hayek's hostility toward central planning was an outgrowth of his opposition to "constructivist" rationalism. According to Hayek, state interventionism attempted to override the unintended consequences of human action by subordinating the spontaneous order of free exchange to an abstract social construction.

Norman Barry (1986, 15) notes correctly that in Rand's social theory, the Hayekian category of "unintended consequences" is virtually excluded. In my discussion of Rand's social ontology, I noted that Rand had formulated only two basic categories: the metaphysical and the man-made. The metaphysically given elements of objective reality could not be altered, whereas man-made objects, institutions, traditions, and rules of conduct should never be accepted uncritically. But within the category of the man-made, Rand did not distinguish between those objects, institutions, or procedures which people *intended* to make, and those which were the unintended consequences of their actions.

And yet, in recognizing that there are articulated and tacit dimensions of thought and action, Rand seems to have accepted the very distinction she did not explicitly endorse. For Rand, emotion is one such tacit component. No one *intends* to feel a certain emotion. A specific emotional response develops within the mind as an unintended by-product of habitual subconscious integrations. Traditions and customs are also the long-term by-products and manifestations of habitual practices.

Rand never belabored the issue of unintended consequences because it appeared somewhat obvious to her. As Binswanger argues: "Even at a very primitive state of knowledge one can observe that one's actions have two very different kinds of consequences; those which are *intended* and those which one [*sic*] did not." The intended consequences are those which one foresees or anticipates. The unintended results of human action are accidental by-products which were not the basis of the agent's motivation.[54]

Like Marx, Rand believed that an obsessive emphasis on unintended consequences came dangerously close to their reification as transhistorical constants.[55] For Rand, every human institution and practice is ultimately capable of change. This is completely consistent with her view that emotions, habitual methods of awareness, and sense of life are equally open to modification—despite their resilience. However, Rand was not naive; she recognized that for most individuals the process of change was extremely difficult.

Nevertheless, by not focusing extensively on unintended consequences, Rand neglected an aspect of social inquiry that was central to Hayek's worldview. Hayek was influenced by the writings of both classical conservatives, like Burke, and the classical liberals of the Scottish Enlightenment. These thinkers opposed the notion that one can step outside the historical process and redesign the civil order from its first elements through the "infinite" powers of reason. Hayek inherited this legacy and propelled it to a deeper epistemological level.[56] As he put it:

> The picture of man as a being who, thanks to his reason, can rise above the values of his civilization, in order to judge it from the outside or from a higher point of view, is an illusion. It simply must be understood that reason itself is part of civilization. All we can ever do is to confront one part with the other parts. Even this

process leads to incessant movement, which may in the very long course of time change the whole. But sudden complete reconstruction of the whole is not possible at any stage of the process, because we must always use the material that is available, and which itself is the integrated product of a process of evolution.[57]

Since we are unable to get a synoptic view as impersonal, detached social actors, we have it in our power to "tinker with parts of a given whole" but never to "entirely redesign it" (Hayek 1976, 25).

It is within the larger totality—the cultural context—that Hayek situated the mind. He maintained that the mind is inscribed in a cultural setting. It is wrong to apply one-way causal notions to either. The mind and culture developed concurrently. They are internally related. "It is probably no more justified to claim that thinking man created his culture," argued Hayek (1981), "than that culture created his reason" (155). Nonetheless, many thinkers have represented Reason ("with a capital R")[58] as "the capping stone" of evolution that enabled human beings to design culture. But this concept of reason is highly abstract and *rationalistic*. It obscures the interpersonal, social process in which the reasoning individual both absorbs and transmits cultural values. Hayek stated, in almost Marxian fashion, that social theory must start "from [those] whose whole nature and character is determined by their existence in society" (6). Moreover, social interaction creates effects which are greater than any individual mind "can ever fully comprehend" (7).

Hayek's central objection to rationalism is that it obscures the internal relationship of mind and culture. The rationalist conception of reason sees the rational faculty as external to the culture from which it springs. This is an inherently dualistic approach to social reality. Hayek argued that the Cartesian rationalists, in particular, promoted this arrogant interpretation of reason's power. He called these rationalist thinkers "naive" or "constructivistic."[59] They assume that institutions which benefit humanity have "in the past—and ought in the future to be invented in clear awareness of the desirable effects they produce" (85). Constructivism presumes that human beings can design (or "construct") social institutions as if they were outside the context of history, using the infinite powers of Reason. Constructivism is the "fatal conceit" endangering the future of wealth, morals and peace.[60] It is "an abuse of reason based on a misconception of its powers, and in the end leads to a destruction of that free interplay of many minds on which the growth of reason nourishes itself."[61]

Hayek contrasted constructivist rationalism with a legitimate alternative, which he called, "critical rationalism" (94). He believed that "reason properly used" is a faculty that acknowledges its own limited potential. Hayek criticized socialists precisely for their constructivist attempts to invert the structure of social order. Socialism embodies a mechanistic approach to human affairs; it sees social order as a form of arrangement and control. The central planners believe that they can gain access to all those facts which may facilitate social directioning (Hayek 1988, 66). But central planning requires knowledge of relative scarcities, information that cannot be disconnected from the context—the dynamic market process—that generates it.

By contrast, Hayek saw capitalism as an extended order of human cooperation, an emergent, spontaneous product of social interaction. What makes the market so unappealing to the socialist is that most of its institutions are not the product of explicit design. Socialists reject the "anarchy" of capitalism because it appears both "unreasonable" and "unscientific" (ibid.).

For Hayek, there are aspects of social reality which are not subject to direct control. There are many unintended consequences that arise from the process of social interaction. These consequences are not a sign of human inefficacy; they are a natural, social product. Constructivism requires people to step outside the social and historical process, grasping its modus operandi through a synoptic identification of the totality. This attempt at omniscience is an abuse of reason, according to Hayek, because it fails to grasp the actual structure of knowledge, which includes both articulate and inarticulate components.

The constructivist rationalists embrace what Hayek (1973) describes as a "synoptic delusion" (14). A synoptic delusion represents a false belief that one can consciously design a new society as if one had possession of holistic knowledge. Holistic knowledge involves grasping the complex interrelations of the society which are necessarily constituted by both articulate and tacit social practices. Such knowledge ultimately requires omniscience. Omniscience, in turn, implies human infallibility. This infallibility would even have to extend to knowledge of the structure and processes of one's own mind. Hayek stated: "There will always be some rules governing a mind which that mind in its then prevailing state cannot communicate, and that, if it ever were to acquire the capacity of communicating these rules, this would presuppose that it had acquired further higher rules which make the communication of the former possible but which themselves will still be incommunicable."[62] Hayek believed that the idea of a mind explaining itself is a logical contradiction. Its impossibility should help us curb our intellectual hubris.[63] Human fallibility and the inherent contextual limits of knowledge are then the strongest factors militating against a fully imposed or designed rationalist order. The attempted imposition of order dislocates the very processes that make order possible.

Clearly, there are enormous differences in the Randian and Hayekian perspectives. But it is possible to see some significant parallels between them. On an immediate level, Rand would have agreed with Hayek that one cannot explain the rules of mental operation by a process of infinite regress. Moreover, as Binswanger (1989T, lecture 1) argues, we cannot use our own minds to step outside of and judge those very minds. There is no such thing as a "supraconscious" that enables one to "stand above" oneself.

But far more important, Rand and her intellectual allies would have agreed with Hayek's assessment of the historical roots of constructivist rationalism. Hayek argued that just as the Western concept of rationality is the product of both Enlightenment thought and market capitalism, so constructivism is an inappropriate extension of the Enlightenment faith in Reason.[64] Though Rand celebrated the Enlightenment's contribution to the secular defense of liberty, she also argued that the Enlightenment perpetuated a fallacious view of reason.[65]

This critique of Enlightenment rationalism was not peculiar to Rand or Hayek. Thinkers in the hermeneutic and Frankfurt school traditions have all exhibited a similar tendency to criticize the "instrumentalist" view of reason at the heart of Enlightenment thought. John Caputo (1988) explains that these thinkers aimed to redefine reason

> in a more reasonable way and to rescue it from the Enlightenment distortion of rationality. For the Enlightenment subjected reason to the impossible ideal of unconditioned rationality and absolute indubitability, and then, in the hope of meeting such impossible standards, turned reason over to the rule of a rigorous method and systematicity. . . . [W]e have learned to stop blaming reason for the failure to meet these standards and to start blaming the Enlightenment. (5)

This is precisely the crux of both Rand's and Hayek's critique. The failure of rationalism was not a failure of reason. By ascribing to human beings the attributes of an omniscient deity, and then condemning human reason for not fulfilling this ideal, rationalists attack the genuine legitimacy of human cognition. Rand argued that this destructive pattern is reproduced by the advocates of altruism, who erect an impossible, self-abnegating standard of morality and then indict humanity for not being able to live up to it.

Whereas Hayek concentrated on the social and cultural context of the capacity to reason, Rand focused on the identity of the rational faculty. By ascribing to human beings an infallibility that is, in fact, unattainable, rationalists disconnect the will to efficacy from any realistic understanding of its meaning.

But the will to efficacy is not simply a capacity to produce a desired effect. It is the conviction that one is competent *in principle* to think and act. Although such efficacy is expressed in particularized skills, it is not confined to skill. Nathaniel Branden ([1969] 1979) writes: "It is applicable to, and expressible in, every form of rational endeavor" (128). But efficacy is not a purely cerebral experience. Rand's expansive concept of consciousness translates into an equally expansive notion of what it means to be efficacious. Genuine efficacy results from a fully integrated constellation of reason, emotions, values, actions, conscious convictions, and subconscious sense of life, with no dichotomy presumed between any of the constituent elements. In Chapter 9 I explore the Objectivist conviction that labor—productive work—is central to the achievement of such efficacy because it "is the distinctively *human* mode of action and survival" (129). Productive work expands our particularized efficacy, our replication and knowledge of skills, our understanding of tasks, our ability to grasp principles of action.

Rand's recognition of these interrelationships provides a basis for comprehending the nature and guiding purpose of the constructivist rationalism that both she and Hayek condemned. *Such rationalism fractures the constituent elements of consciousness, and abstracts reason from its integrated context.* Rationalism attempts to satisfy the human need for efficacy by a one-sided emphasis on Reason, not human reason, but an abstract, narrow, disconnected, and unintegrated conception of reason.

Rationalism emerges from an error of abstraction, an isolated focus on the apparently limitless capacity of the human rational faculty. In proposing an all-powerful Reason with no limits, rationalists project a Reason with no identity. The rationalist sees the capacity to know as infinite, in the sense that the knowledge of one fact presupposes that a person can attain knowledge of a second fact, a third fact, etc. This knowledge series can be (potentially) extended to infinity. But Rand observed that infinity is only a mathematical or methodological concept; it is not valid as a concept pertaining to human epistemological potential.[66] People are neither immortal nor omniscient. At any point in time, a person's actual capacity and knowledge is both finite and contextual. Rationalism collapses the distinction between potential knowledge and actuality. It deifies the human ability to know and embraces a concept of reason that is epistemologically invalid.

We think within a definite structure. Our senses perceive real things and processes in the universe, and our rational faculty apprehends their structural and logical interrelationships. We achieve the cognitive efficacy that is requisite to survival by acting in accordance with the laws of logic to produce the desired effects. All of natural science is an attempt to systematize our knowledge of consistent and predictable relationships. Science charts certain courses of action initiated by particular entities with distinctive natures, producing specific effects. But as Hayek emphasized, and as Rand would not have denied, one person's attempt to generate a desired effect is tempered by the reality of other people who are engaging in similar actions. The result is often a product that no one intended. To a rationalist, this is incompatible with our need for predictability and certainty. The rationalist wishes to create a social laboratory in which people are made to act with the same predictability as the law of gravity.

Such rationalism is rooted in a deep psycho-epistemological fear. As Branden emphasizes, people can develop a fear of the risks of acting on their own fallible judgments. This is a fear not of action per se, but of action in a universe in which success is not always guaranteed.[67] There are two diametrically opposed ways in which we can respond to this fact of fallibility. There are innumerable variations in behavior between these two extremes. We can accept the possibility that we might make mistakes. We can accept that there will be many unintended consequences to our actions. Or we can revolt against this fact. We might seek to escape from the responsibility of thinking and acting (N. Branden 1980, 100). Alternatively, as Packer (1986T) suggests, we might be neurotically obsessed with planning and structuring every minute detail of our existences in a compulsive and misbegotten effort to conquer life's uncertainties. If we do that, we have replaced our will to efficacy with an illusory quest for omniscience.

In Rand's view, the rationalist assault on reason has "two interacting aspects" that must be examined. The primary aspect is individual since, ultimately, it is the individual who must choose "to think or not to think." Hence, any doctrine that attacks the mind's efficacy must be judged by its effects on our willingness or ability to raise the focus of our awareness. Rationalism subverts an individual's psycho-epistemology because it proposes a standard that no one can live up to. Those who accept this doctrine live in perpetual guilt for their alleged failures.

But Rand recognized that there was a second interacting aspect that needed to be explored. This "contributory cause" is always social. The "social environment can offer incentives or impediments; it can make the exercise of one's rational faculty easier or harder; it can encourage thinking and penalize evasion or vice versa." For Rand, contemporary statist society "is ruled by evasion—by entrenched, institutionalized evasion—while reason is an outcast and almost an outlaw."[68]

What makes Rand's analysis so powerful is her ability to trace the effects of a philosophic doctrine on many different levels of generality. For Rand, rationalism was but one particular form of epistemological perversion with negative consequences for values, culture, education, politics, and human relationships.

9 Ethics and Human Survival

Rand's ethics is a direct application of her theory of knowledge. In her emphasis on the centrality of reason, Rand enunciates both an epistemological and normative principle. If reason is how we gain knowledge, it is simultaneously how we (as human beings) survive. That is, we *should* use our rational faculty *if* we choose to live. In Rand's ethics, life, as an ultimate value, cannot be separated from reason, purpose, and self-esteem.

The issues involved in Rand's ethical theories are enormous, complex, and controversial. Indeed, no other aspect of Rand's thought has received as much scholarly attention as her defense of egoism.[1] Rand herself believed that in addition to her theories of concept formation and politics, her ethics were among her most important philosophic contributions (in Peikoff 1976T, lecture 8). It is impossible to convey the depth of Rand's ethics here. Once again, I focus chiefly on the nondualistic elements of Rand's approach.

Beyond Fact and Value

As we have seen, Rand's emphasis on reason cannot be fully understood without appreciating her antipathy toward Russian mysticism. Most Russian religious philosophers had elevated faith and revelation to a status equal—or superior—to reason. But Russian philosophy was distinctive, in both its religious and Marxist incarnations, for its rejection of the Western-positivist separation of fact and value.[2] Rand's repudiation of this very distinction is a reflection of her Russian roots.

But Rand opposed the typically Russian attempts to synthesize fact and value through statist or supernatural means. In their efforts to combat the bifurcation of fact from value, Russian thinkers fell victim to monistic reductionism. Both Bolshevism and Russian orthodoxy aimed for a union that emphasized a different element of the polarity. For Rand, communism was a form of materialism that attempted to transcend the fact-value dichotomy by a monistic emphasis on the factual. Rand characterized communists as "mystics of muscle," who saw all values as epiphenomena of material forces. They stressed a change in the material "base" as a means to the transformation of human values. Inevitably, the base could not be altered without the violent intervention of the secular, totalitarian state.

By contrast, Rand interpreted religion as a form of spiritualism in which the fact-value distinction was resolved by a one-sided emphasis on spiritual values to the detriment of material reality. The religionists, or "mystics of spirit," saw all things in the world as infused with intrinsic worth or divinity. Ultimately, their dogmatic definition of absolute values translated into an equally authoritarian statism of the theocratic form.

Both the Bolsheviks and the Russian mystics were the paradigm for Rand's rejection of materialism and idealism. Both perpetuated the bifurcation of existence and consciousness. In essence, the materialists "believe in existence without consciousness," and idealists "in consciousness without existence." In *Atlas Shrugged*, Rand wrote: "Both demand the surrender of your mind, one to their revelations, the other to their reflexes. No matter how loudly they posture in the roles of irreconcilable antagonists, their moral codes are alike, and so are their aims: in matter—the enslavement of man's body, in spirit—the destruction of his mind" (1027).

The religionists had embraced a kind of intrinsicism. In epistemology, such intrinsicism emphasizes metaphysical essences grasped by intuitive revelation. In ethics, it sees the good as inherent in things or actions regardless of their context or consequences. Intrinsicism separates the concept of "value" from the valuer and his distinctive purposes. It sees the good as good "in, by, and of itself," part of reality, and totally independent of consciousness. It tends toward dogmatism and authoritarianism.

Not surprisingly, aspects of this intrinsicist approach to ethics were exemplified in the works of Lossky. Lossky saw facts and values as part of the same reality. For Lossky ([1917] 1928): "Values do not constitute a separate realm of their own, distinct from existence" (178). It was the goal of human beings to discover those absolute values which inhered in reality, as a means to a communion with God. Like Solovyov before him, and most Russian neo-Idealists, Lossky proposed an ethic that was profoundly mystical and altruistic. Lossky believed that egoism entailed the human separation from the Kingdom of Harmony. As such, selfishness was the "*primary* evil, giving rise to all kinds of derivative evil" (Lossky 1951, 262). In this regard, Lossky echoed the central themes of Russian ethical thought. In the writings of Kireevsky, Khomyakov, Solovyov, and the Russian Symbolists, the notion of *sobornost'* suggested the transcendence of conflict between the individual's selfish interests and the common interests of society. In practice, such harmony could only be achieved by the individual's self-subordination to the whole. This conciliar union allegedly preserved the individual's uniqueness, while achieving an integrated totality. But whereas the religious philosophers sought a mystic organic unity, the Bolsheviks appropriated the communal *sobornost'* in their legitimation of the One State.

In Rand's view, such individual subordination was typical of all altruistic doctrines. In both Russian religious and political thought, altruism—the creed of self-denial, self-sacrifice, and self-abnegation—served as a rationalization for the individual's subjugation. By placing God, the Collective, or the State above the self, altruism aimed for a "culturally-induced *selfless-ness*."[3] Its goal was not benevolence or the relief of suffering.[4] Rather, its purpose was to prey on peoples' sense of guilt and inadequacy.[5] The religionists had mastered the technique of guilt-manipulation by focusing on Original Sin. By positing an inherent human evil outside the province of choice, the religionists had perpetuated a Big Lie to serve their own authoritarian impulses (*Atlas Shrugged*, 1025).

Rand argues that in the post-Renaissance world, such mystical concepts as Original Sin were being undermined by reason, science, and individualism. Yet instead of overturning medieval mysticism, Western civilization internalized a lethal contradiction. According to Rand, the West attempted to sustain a culture of reason on an altruistic and neo-mystic philosophic foundation. Rand argued that this contradiction was at the heart of Kant's thought. In Kant's system, there is a fatal split between fact and value. Reason is given domain over the material world, whereas faith is recognized as the master of the spiritual sphere. Kant separated reason from "the choice of the goals for which material achievements are to be used." He provided a philosophical justification for the belief that human goals, actions, choices, and values could only be determined by faith.[6] He secularized religious morality, fracturing the tie between self-interest and virtue. He argued that action could not be moral if performed from personal inclination (Peikoff 1970T, lecture 3). In the end, Kant's deontology had rescued faith and the altruist ethic from the onslaught of reason.[7]

Kant was certainly not the first philosopher to doubt the possibility of a rational morality of self-interest. Even before Hume questioned the likelihood of deriving an "ought" from an "is," the history of philosophy was replete with attacks on ethical egoism. Peikoff (1972T, lecture 2) argues that even in the pagan, humanistic culture of ancient Greece, the Sophists had identified egoism with subjectivity and brutality. But in Western thought, strong egoistic themes were to be found in the works of Aristotle, Spinoza, and Nietzsche.[8] Rand was most probably influenced by certain Aristotelian and Nietzschean themes in the creation of her own concept of egoism.

It was Nietzsche's critique of altruism that made a huge impact on the Symbolists of the Russian Silver Age, and on Rand's early intellectual development. Nietzsche had criticized altruism as a slave morality that sanctioned the dominance of the herd. In the altruist's view, according to Nietzsche ([1886] 1966), "Everything that elevates an individual above the herd and intimidates the neighbor is henceforth called *evil*; and the fair, modest, submissive, conforming mentality, the *mediocrity* of desires attains moral designations and honors" (114).

By contrast, Nietzsche described a master morality in which all that was deemed evil by the altruist code became a source of virtue. He rejected abject selflessness and asceticism. He repudiated the altruist penchant to celebrate a nonexistent God by crucifying human beings. He aimed for the "transvaluation of values," such that the virtues of the slave morality would be overturned by its vices, that is, by the virtues embodied in the master ethos.

Though Nietzsche's writings are open to widely divergent interpretations, there is much evidence to suggest that his tribute to human greatness, to a "blessed *selfishness*, the wholesome, healthy selfishness, that springeth from the powerful soul" (Nietzsche [1883–85] 1905, 211) was rooted in his exposure to the works of classical antiquity. Walter Kaufmann argues persuasively that Nietzsche's projection of the reverence of the "noble soul," the very quotation that Rand placed in her introduction to the twenty-fifth anniversary edition of *The Fountainhead*, emerges from an Aristotelian base. Kaufmann cites sections of Aristotle's *Nicomachean Ethics* dealing with the "great-souled man." As a lover of self, the "great-souled man" rarely asks for the assistance of others. He is a being of self-esteem, caring "more for the truth than for what people think."[9] Nietzsche appropriated these very themes in his own paean to individual excellence.[10]

Rand drew from this Aristotelian and Nietzschean constellation. In one of her earliest journal entries, she wrote: "The true, highest selfishness, the exalted egoism, is the right to have one's own theoretical values and then apply them to practical reality." For Rand, ethics must begin from the self, not from society, the mass, the collective, "or any other form of selflessness."[11] Rand would come to see that an attack on "selfishness" was simultaneously an attack on the integrity of an individual's self-esteem (*Virtue of Selfishness*, xi). She believed that her "*most important job is the formulation of a rational morality of and for man, of and for his life, of and for this earth.*" Such an ethical achievement was a necessary aspect of Rand's philosophical project, because it would affirm the possibility of a secular, moral existence free of religious imperatives and categorical altruistic duties.[12]

Defending the need for morality against religious intrinsicism, Rand argued that a rational approach could not embrace the other, subjectivist side of the same dualistic coin. Her chief objection to "Nietzschean" egoism was its tendency to regard any action as good if it was intended to satisfy one's own desires (*Virtue of Selfishness*, x). Rand's interpretation of Nietzsche's ethos as "subjectivist" may have taken root in her exposure to the Russian Symbolist movement. Despite their tendencies toward synthesis, the Symbolists had unabashedly embraced Nietzsche's Dionysian principle, the orgiastic celebration of emotions, as far superior to Apollonian rationality. It was against this kind of Nietzschean subjectivism that Rand reacted with a fervent hostility. For Rand, while the intrinsicist endorses a view of the good as inhering in reality, external to human consciousness, the subjectivist argues that the good is the product of subjective feelings or desires, bearing "no relation to the facts of reality."[13]

Such subjectivism characterized most conventional theories of egoism. In Rand's view, traditional altruist and egoist alternatives shared the same collectivist premise. Much like Marx, who rallied against "vulgar" idealists and "vulgar" materialists, Rand criticized many thinkers in the individualist tradition who merely substituted the sacrifice of the many for the self-sacrificial creeds they fought: "It is in their statements on morality that the individualist thinkers have floundered and lost their case. They had nothing better to offer than vulgar selfishness which consisted of sacrificing others to self. When I realized that that was only another form of collectivism—of living through others by ruling them—I had the key to *The Fountainhead* and to the character of Howard Roark."[14]

More than this, Rand had begun to articulate the basis of her own, unique understanding of the "virtue of selfishness." For those who had formulated a concept of selfishness solely "in terms of sacrificing others to oneself," there was an apparent "psychological confession about the nature of their own desires" (*New Intellectual*, 56). Rand excoriated such thinkers as "counterfeit" individualists, whose view of human survival oscillated between conquest and defeat, exploitation and submission.[15] In Rand's view: "The man who is willing to serve as the means to the ends of others, will necessarily regard others as the means to *his* ends."[16]

Despite this two-pronged rejection of conventional morality, several critics have argued that Rand's definitions of altruism and egoism are "untenable and slanted." O'Neill believes that Rand maintains "a totally artificial dichotomy between *egoism* and *altruism*."[17] Ellis (1968, 28) agrees that both altruism and selfishness are "taken to rigid and one-sided lengths" in Rand's thought. And Barnes (1967) argues further that Rand's "altruistic" villains frequently aim to satisfy their own welfare, while utilizing the veneer—or rationale—provided by the traditional ethos of self-sacrifice. Barnes believes that such a cynical use of altruism does not adequately define its essence as a moral doctrine (135).

But none of these commentators recognize Rand's critique of altruism as a simultaneous rejection of *conventional* egoism. Inherent in traditional ethics was an interpenetration of sacrificial credos, a duality involving both giving and taking. As Robert Greenwood (1974) explains: "A person who is expectant, even in the pragmatic sense, and counts on receiving the unearned, may be said to countenance altruism, to practice it passively, as it were, in the transactional sense, as receiver, not giver" (46).

Rand's resolution, by contrast, seeks to transcend one-sided "giving" and one-sided "taking." She argued that such distortions are not proof of human immorality, but of the kinds of moralities that people have been taught. In Rand's view, people have tacitly obeyed these cultural and moral ideals. They have divided themselves into masters and slaves, while being united by their reciprocal dependency.[18] She proposed to transcend such dualism by looking once again at the fact-value distinction. She did not envision the absorption of all values into facts, or all facts into values. She argued instead that values are a kind of fact emerging from an objective relation between existence and human consciousness. Just as she preserved the internality of existence and consciousness, so she preserved the internality of fact and value. In both cases, she emphasized the primacy of existence and the primacy of fact, which leads to the necessity for values. As she put it:

> The *objective* theory holds that the good is neither an attribute of "things in themselves" nor of man's emotional states, but an *evaluation* of the facts of reality by man's consciousness according to a rational standard of value. (Rational, in this context, means: derived from the facts of reality and validated by a process of reason.) The objective theory holds that *the good is an aspect of reality in relation to man*—and that it must be discovered, not invented, by man.[19]

Values cannot be separated from the valuer and the valuer's purposes. Conventional ethics fracture the relationship between "actor and beneficiary." Rand sought to unite these elements, reasserting the *"right to a moral existence."* She argued that only morality can serve as a guide to the achievement of one's ultimate goals. For Rand, we *"must be the beneficiary of [our] own moral actions,"* because it is only through such principles that we can survive and flourish as human beings (*Virtue of Selfishness*, viii–x).

Life and Value

At the foundation of her ethical system, Rand remained true to her dialectical roots. She traced an internal relationship between life and value, such that neither phenomenon is possible in the absence of the other. The pursuit of values is not possible without the context provided by life, which is both the existential basis—and the ultimate value—constituting the relationship.

While preparing *Atlas Shrugged*, Rand wrote in her journal, that we are born as abstractions with our reason serving as our guide. Our lives are a process in which we concretize and create our selves through our own efforts. For Rand, life and self-preservation were synonymous. Since everything in the universe has identity, a person's nature encompasses capacities and needs that are specific to the human character. To perform the activity of living as human beings, we must pursue our own self-preservation by the means distinctly available to us. The individual must live consciously, Rand explained, since "the essence and tool of his life is his mind."[20] Thus, an epistemological insight serves as the departure for ethical theory.

Rand argued that in the history of normative philosophy the primary question of ethics has usually been: What values ought one to pursue? But for Rand, to begin ethical inquiry with this question is to commit the fallacy of reification. Rand explained that most philosophers have taken the existence of ethics for granted, reifying the historically given codes of morality, but never considering their existential foundation.[21]

Ethicists cannot debate the value alternatives without asking a more fundamental question: Why are values necessary for human existence? Rand began her investigation by exploring the epistemological roots of the concept of "value." She defined a value as "that which one acts to gain and/ or keep." The concept itself is not axiomatic; it is both relational and contextual. It requires an answer to the twofold question "of value to whom and for what?" The concept "presupposes an entity capable of acting to achieve a goal in the face of an alternative. Where no alternative exists, no goals and no values are possible."

The basic alternative that every living organism must face is its own existence or nonexistence. The sustenance of life requires activity on the part of the organism. Life as such "is a process of self-sustaining and self-generated action. . . . It is only the concept of 'Life' that makes the concept of 'Value' possible. It is only to a living entity that things can be good or evil."[22]

In this formulation, Rand traced the internal relations between three conceptual couplings: life and value, life and action, value and action. Just as life and value entail each other, so too do life and action. Binswanger explains that the relationship between life and action is reciprocal. Not only is the survival of life contingent upon the action of an organism, but action is itself conditional upon life; "A dead organism cannot act."[23] This same reciprocal dependency is noted between the categories of value and human action. As Nathaniel Branden ([1969] 1979) argues: "Value and *action* imply and necessitate each other" (26). The achievement and maintenance of a value requires a specific course of action, while the motive and purpose behind a consciously initiated action is the achievement and maintenance of a value.

The specific actions and goals an organism must undertake to achieve the sustenance of its own life are determined by the specific kind of entity that the organism is. Plants, animals, and human beings have distinct needs dictated by their distinct identities. The ultimate context—and goal—that

Fig. 9. Ayn Rand on Madison Avenue in New York City after *Atlas Shrugged* was accepted by Random House for publication, 1957. (Courtesy of Barbara Branden)

conditions the needs and actions of the entity is the entity's life. Just as existence cannot be validated by reference to anything beyond itself, neither can life be sustained by reference to a standard that transcends it. Since life is not the means to a supernatural realm, it is the means to its own end. It is "an *end in itself.*" Life "makes the existence of values possible." It is an ultimate value because people must act to gain and keep it by a process that only life makes viable. In Rand's view: "Metaphysically, *life* is the only phenomenon that is an end in itself: a value gained and kept by a constant process of action. Epistemologically, the concept of 'value' is genetically dependent upon and derived from the antecedent concept of 'life.' To speak of 'value' as apart from 'life' is worse than a contradiction in terms."[24]

Rand transcended the fact-value dichotomy by claiming that "the fact that a living entity *is*, determines what it *ought* to do." Rand affirmed the Aristotelian belief that actuality precedes potentiality.[25] What a thing *is* determines what it can and will become. Just as Rand's ontology dictates that "to be" is "to be something," so her ethics demand that for something "to be," it must act in accordance with what it is—that is, in accordance with its specific nature. And as Rand's epistemology views human beings as entities possessing free will, so her ethics demand that for human beings "to be" human beings, they must *choose* to act rationally. But unlike other organisms, human beings *can* act against their nature; they can act irrationally.

Beginning with an integrated, expansive concept of human reason, Rand attempted to develop and validate a rational code of values. She argued that there is in fact an awareness of "good" and "evil" even on a primitive, sensorial level. In the pleasure-pain mechanism, we first become aware of those things which are "for" us and "against" us. Our sensations and perceptions are the foundation of our cognitive and evaluative development. But sensations of pleasure and pain are automatized responses, "an automatic form of knowledge," which a human consciousness cannot avoid experiencing. Our distinctive modes of sensual, perceptual, and conceptual awareness are our integrated means of surviving in the world. And since we have free will, we must choose to think and raise our mental focus if we are to sustain our lives.[26]

Thus the science of ethics is "an *objective, metaphysical necessity of . . . survival*" (23). It satisfies a practical need that we cannot avoid. By accepting a code of principles to guide our actions, we consciously—or tacitly—accept a code of morality. In Rand's system, a genuinely objective moral code emerges from ontological and epistemological premises. The standard of an objective morality is "man's *life*, or: that which is required for man's survival qua man. Since reason is man's basic means of survival, that which is proper to the life of a rational being is the good; that which negates, opposes or destroys it is the evil" (ibid.).

Just as Rand proposed an expansive concept of reason, so too, she proposed an expansive concept of what it means to live as a rational being. One cannot evaluate her concept of good and evil outside this context. For us to survive as human beings, we must not aim for "a *momentary* or a merely *physical* survival." Nor can we survive through purely sensual or perceptual means. We have a *conceptual* consciousness, which shapes the "terms, methods, conditions and goals" that our survival requires, "in all those aspects of existence which are open to [our] choice." Thus the abstract standard of value—our lives as human beings—is concretized on the individual level, as each of us pursues his or her own life as the ethical purpose of our existence. To survive, to fulfill and enjoy our own lives as integrated "continuous whole[s]," each of us must choose among actions, values, and goals according to the objective standards that our lives as human beings require (24).[27]

At this point, it is necessary to examine Rand's proposed link between life and value in much greater detail. Her theory has been the subject of extensive scholarly discussion. Nozick, O'Neill, and other philosophers have not focused extensively on Rand's main contention that the choice to live necessitates a guiding code of values.[28] Rather, the critics question why anyone *should* choose to live. Why could not "death" be the ultimate standard of value? Such Rand-influenced thinkers as Nathaniel Branden and John Hospers have responded to this query in a similar manner: To choose death as the ultimate standard of value distorts the very concept of value. Since value is that which one acts to gain and/or keep, death cannot qualify as a value per se. Death does not require any action at all; it demands nothing active. Thus issues of morality cannot be discussed if they are divorced from the very concept of life that provides the context for values. It is life that gives the notion of value any meaning.[29]

And yet even among those who are inclined to accept Rand's contention, there is the belief that this argument is marred by a form of circularity. Merrill, for instance, argues that Rand seems to be using the concept of value in her understanding of the concept of life itself. At the base of her ethics, Rand seems to employ the same "stolen concept" arguments that are apparent in her defense of ontological axioms. By challenging the principle that life is the standard of moral values, one must be alive in order to raise the objection. If life were not the standard of morality, then the critic would be involved in a logical contradiction by questioning that which he implicitly accepts by the very fact of his continued existence (Merrill 1991, 101).

But Rasmussen has argued further that the mere presence of a logical contradiction in the critic's challenge begs the question of why a person ought not to commit contradictions. Rasmussen wonders too: "Is life a value because we choose it, or do we choose it because it is a value?" For Rasmussen, the choice to live seems to be based on an arational commitment, outside the province of Rand's ethics.[30]

It appears that even the friendly critics have pinpointed a difficult problem at the foundation of Rand's ethical system. But such theorists as Gotthelf, Peikoff, and Binswanger have each argued that these questions are not fatal to the Objectivist approach. Gotthelf answers Rasmussen's questions directly. He argues that in strict terms, life is not a value because we choose it, nor do we choose life because it is a value. For Gotthelf, as for Rand, there are no human values apart from human choice. But this does not imply that life is an ultimate value simply because we have chosen it to be so. It is in the nature of life that an individual's choice to live simultaneously concretizes that person's own life as the only rational, ultimate value within his or her grasp. In Gotthelf's opinion:

> The whole point of Ayn Rand's derivation of "ought" from "is," as it applies to humans, is that *if* you choose to exist, *then* you can consistently pursue that choice, and any other particular choice, only by holding life as your ultimate value—because life, by its nature, requires a specific course of action; only that fact about life gives point to any act of evaluation, any reason to choose—any basis for a *concept of value*. But that fact about life has no implication for action to beings who choose not to exist. The choice to live and the nature of life *together* ground the status of one's life as one's actual, and only rational, ultimate value.[31]

Peikoff (1991b, 244, 248) argues further that the choice to live is indeed a metaethical commitment. It is a choice that both precedes and underlies the need for morality. But such a choice is not arbitrary. Rather, it is an affirmation of a human being's willingness to accept the reality of his or her own existence. Binswanger concurs that the choice to live is what gives a person a stake in his or her own actions. Such a choice engenders the need for evaluation. Binswanger agrees with Peikoff that the choice to live establishes the context for ethics. In choosing to live, a person has chosen the only *consistent* alternative. By choosing not to live, a person has rejected the entire realm of values and has no alternative but to die. To actualize his or her potential for life, an individual must choose to live and pursue those values that are requisite to survival.[32] Those who deny this proposition are guilty of a contradiction; their very ability to deny is proof that they are alive, that they continue to choose life, and that such a choice is tacitly affirmed in their every commentary.

Rand's argument that there is an inseparable link between life and value is in fact circular. But it is not a vicious form of circularity. Such circularity is inherent in any internal relationship. When Rand stated that "metaphysically, life is the only phenomenon that is an end in itself," she was *identifying* both life and value. Life *is* the ultimate value. It entails value in its very identity. Life is internally related to value because it could not be what it is in the absence of this relation. To attempt to separate life and value would be to evade the meaning of both concepts. Life and value are conditional upon each other. One can no more refer to life without value, than to value without life. Thus Rand maintained that their bifurcation is "worse than a contradiction." Rand did not see the relationship of life and value in strictly linguistic terms. She did not deduce the concept of value from the concept of life. Her arguments for their internal relationship are inductive. They are based upon an observation of a fact of reality. Epistemologically, Rand recognized that the concept of life is prior to the concept of value. But ontologically, the two are simultaneous. The very existence of life depends on the pursuit and achievement of values; the very phenomenon of value depends on the existence of life.[33]

In this internal link, Rand was not offering an immediate defense of any particular value system. She was merely observing that life and value cannot be separated from each other. To say that the choice to live is metaethical is to acknowledge that it is a fact inherent in the conditional nature of human life itself. A person's continued existence is predicated on his or her choices. None of these choices can have any meaning if they are disconnected from the most basic choice to live. It can be said that even if someone pursues contradictory values inimical to survival, he or she may still be affirming the will to live. Subjectively, these choices may appear to have short-term survival value, even if they objectively threaten long-term survival interests.[34] Rand's critique of altruism is at once her explicit articulation of the means by which people unwittingly accept a death premise on which to base their actions. Just as the principle of altruism is based on a self-sacrificial death premise, Rand proposed that those who attempt to practice it will, in fact, subvert their own ultimate survival. One cannot consistently engage in self-sacrifice without negating the basic choice at the foundation of ethics. Those who consistently live by self-abnegating principles achieve literal suicide.

Rand acknowledged that one's conceptual awareness is governed by cognitive concepts and evaluative choices that are often subconscious and tacit. Thus she suggested that even the primary choice to live is implicit. As a child learns to distinguish between right and wrong, it may not be making a calculated decision "to live." Indeed, it may not even know *why* certain actions are good and others are bad. Even as its consciousness evolves toward full conceptual maturity, it is more likely to take for granted the moral principles governing its actions as it follows certain traditional precepts by habit (Rand 1946, 9). In most cases, the choice to live becomes apparent in the everyday pursuit of life-sustaining material and spiritual values. In Rand's view, it is the task of ethics to objectively validate values that confirm this most basic choice to live through the conscious, articulated, principled pursuit of goals that make *human* living both possible and desirable.

Rationality and Virtue

Having traced the relationship between life and value, and having enunci-ated an objective ethical standard, Rand argued that there is an inseparable link between the moral and the practical. Moral principles are the means by which a human being—a being of integrated mind and body—survives *practically* on this earth. Everything that a human being needs to sustain life must be discovered by his or her mind. A rational being survives by thinking and by applying thought to action. Rand identified those derivative values and virtues which serve as the means to this genuinely *human* survival: "*Value* is that which one acts to gain and/or keep—*virtue* is the act by which one gains and/or keeps it. The three cardinal values of the Objectivist ethics—the three values which, together, are the means to and the realiza-tion of one's ultimate value, one's own life—are: Reason, Purpose, Self-Esteem, with their three corresponding virtues: Rationality, Productive-ness, Pride."[35]

These values and virtues have both theoretical and practical, intellectual and existential aspects. Recalling the ethos of classical antiquity, Rand saw Virtue as One. No values and no virtues can be thoroughly abstracted from the ethical totality they constitute. Though Rand analyzed the virtues separately, she emphasized that they form an indissoluble whole (Peikoff 1991b, 250). For instance, just as Rand saw reason as the source of productive work, and pride as the result of achievement, she recognized that each component nourishes—and is nourished by—the other elements in the totality. Successful production enables a person to attain his or her rational purposes. Both reason and production contribute to a sense of accomplishment. The ability to realize goals contributes to a sense of self-efficacy. Pride in one's accomplishments fosters a continuing policy of rationality and productive work. Each of these moments is in reciprocity with its constituent relations. Each is both the source and product of the other. Each is part of an organic unity.

Nevertheless, as in most aspects of Rand's thought, there is an asymmetric internality among the constituent elements of the whole. In other words, though the elements are reciprocally related, there is a skewed emphasis on one factor. In keeping with her epistemic focus, Rand argued: "Rationality is [the] basic virtue, the source of all . . . other virtues." Rationality entails the raising of one's level of mental awareness. A volitional, cognitive activity serves as the basic moral virtue because it affirms the mind as the human being's only means of knowing reality and of surviving on earth. In exercising rationality, human beings validate, choose, and derive their convictions, values, goals, desires, and actions from a process of thought.[36]

While this formulation suggests a one-sided focus on the rational to the detriment of other constituent factors of consciousness, it must be remembered that Rand's conception is essentially expansive. As we have seen, Rand's emphasis on the centrality of reason does not negate the role of emotions or the automatized integrations of the subconscious. By focusing on rationality as the chief virtue, Rand was *not* devaluing the nonrational and nonconscious elements of the mind. Certainly there is evidence that as someone who scorned Russian religious culture, Rand was deeply hostile toward all things irrational. At times this translated into an antipathy toward emotionalism. But the thrust of Rand's Objectivist philosophy is toward the transcendence of dualism. The virtue of rationality does not mean that one *rationalizes* one's actions, values, goals, and desires. Rather, it entails the conscious *awareness* and *articulation* of rationally derived goals, the *articulation*—and long-term, therapeutic alteration, if necessary—of one's emotions and desires.

Rationality as articulation is how people grasp the metaphysical value judgments they have tacitly absorbed and integrated into their subconscious. Such core evaluations are not rationally derived; they are formed tacitly from a very early period in a child's life. Thus a child raised in a loving, predictable household may achieve a benevolent sense of life, internalizing the values and virtues that Rand identified as objective. But Rand believed that an individual could not act consistently and efficaciously over the long run on the sole basis of unarticulated premises. Likewise, a child raised in a nightmare universe, the victim of verbal, emotional, and physical abuse, may acquire a malevolent sense of life that reflects its experiences. If the child internalizes a view of itself as worthless and evil, or if it practices evasion, or if it represses its anger, hurt, and pain, it stunts its development toward full efficacy. For Rand, rationality is the moral choice—regardless of one's metaphysical value judgments—because it compels the child to augment its introspective focus and to grasp the experiential roots of its emotions and subconsciously held values. Rationality is the means to an unobstructed and integrated awareness. It is the means to articulating that which is implicit, serving the need for conceptualization which is crucial to genuinely human survival.

As derivatives of rationality, Rand cited several subsidiary virtues.[37] Each of these virtues is a reality-oriented means to a rational end. The virtue of independence means that one must have the responsibility to form one's judgments based upon one's own perception of reality. Integrity is the virtue of never sacrificing one's rationally derived judgments to the wishes or opinions of others. Honesty is the virtue of never faking reality in any manner. Justice is the virtue of recognizing and evaluating people based on objective criteria.

Rand emphasized that none of these virtues is intrinsically absolute. Each constitutes an objective *relation* between the faculty of consciousness and reality. Each is *contextual*. Practicing honesty, independence, and integrity in one's life requires existential conditions that make such practices efficacious. There is no virtue to being honest with a kidnapper who has abducted your child. And there is little possibility of being independent in a social system that makes the exercise of one's rationality ineffectual. Rand's critique of culture suggests that statism subverts the consistent practice of virtue. Indeed, the practice of these virtues without regard to context can prove fatal.

This contention is most dramatically illustrated in Rand's depiction of a totalitarian society in *We the Living*. Her protagonist, Kira, seeks to secure material benefits for her sick lover, Leo, by lying to, and manipulating

Andrei, an idealistic and influential communist. Kira's dishonesty is necessary, and yet it involves her in a romantic triangle that inevitably destroys all three characters. The fault lies not in Kira's dishonesty, as much as it does in a system that penalizes virtue. At the culmination of the novel, each of the three main characters has been literally or figuratively destroyed. Rand wished to show that such a system is anathema to the achievement of human life and values. From the time of this early novel, Rand was making explicit connections between morality and the sociopolitical conditions that make its practice both necessary and desirable.

Productive Work

Rand did not merely deduce the practical power of reason from ontological and epistemological axioms. Her observations of history helped to provide the foundation for her philosophical approach. Rand recognized that her own identification of ethical principles would not have been possible without the Industrial Revolution. Though the ancient Greeks had celebrated the human being as a rational animal, even thinkers such as Aristotle saw contemplative knowledge as superior to practical knowledge.[38] Industrialization brought the practical power of reason to fruition. It offered an uncontestable historical display of the connection between thought and reality, thinking and activity, theory and practice, science and technology, reason and production.[39]

Rand's validation of the virtue of productive work is as much an outgrowth of historical specificity as it is of objective necessity. For Rand, labor is a concrete expression of rationality. It is the "process by which man's mind sustains his life." Productive work, in Rand's view,

> is the road of man's unlimited achievement and calls upon the highest attributes of his character: his creative ability, his ambitiousness, his self-assertiveness. . . . It means the consciously chosen pursuit of a productive career, in any line of rational endeavor, great or modest, on any level of ability. It is not the degree of man's ability nor the scale of his work that is ethically relevant here, but the fullest and most purposeful use of his mind.[40]

Productive labor is a constellation of both mental and physical activity. Every productive *human* endeavor involves the translation of thought into a specific material form. Although the proportion of mental and physical activity will vary depending on the relative level of skills required, Rand argued that every human productive process is an outgrowth of mental effort.[41] For Rand, "Production is the application of reason to the problem of survival."[42]

Productive work is the distinctive means by which human beings attain purpose in their lives. It is also the means by which they concretize their species identity as goal-directed beings. The purposive character of human action is manifested in production. By mastering production techniques and skills, they gain a sense of particularized efficacy. By integrating their goals and achieving their purposes over a period of time, they enhance their generalized sense of control over both the material world and their own lives.[43] In optimizing a person's sense of efficacy, productive work also brings forth all of the rational and creative impulses in the human spirit. This is essential to Rand's expansive conception of labor. Labor is a synthesizing activity, involving both spiritual and material aspects. It is not the application of a purely instrumental rationality. It is constituted by a creative process, one that involves the full integration of reason and emotion, the conscious and the subconscious, articulated and tacit dimensions of mind.

It is possible that Rand's tribute to the role of productive labor in human life was influenced by her exposure to the works of Marx while she was a student at Petrograd University. Though there is no journal evidence that can corroborate this contention, it is clear that the entire Russian intellectual and cultural atmosphere was suffused with Marxist theory. And though Rand was deeply critical of Marx, both thinkers exhibit a quasi-Aristotelian respect for human praxis. For Marx, as for Rand, persons are rational, productive beings with inherent potentialities.[44] Both thinkers viewed labor as causally efficacious, as enabling the actualization of specifically human powers and needs.[45]

In Marx's thought, as in Rand's, labor is not purely instrumental or mechanical. Marx argued that labor is a process "in which man of his own accord starts, regulates, and controls the material re-actions between himself and Nature" (Capital, 1:177). The labor process concretizes the human "species-character," which is exemplified by "free, conscious activity" (Marx, Manuscripts, 113). Productive work transforms both the external world and the laborer's internal world. Human beings affirm themselves objectively as they appropriate nature's substances to human requirements (140). By acting on material reality, human beings change it and actualize their own nature as conscious and social animals. In Capital, Marx expressed a profound respect for the integrated nature of human labor, its synthesizing effect on mind and body, its distinctively *human* character:

> A spider conducts operations that resemble those of a weaver, and a bee puts to shame many an architect in the construction of her cells. But what distinguishes the worst architect from the best of bees is this, that the architect raises his structure in imagination before he erects it in reality. At the end of every labour-process, we get a result that already existed in the imagination of the labourer at its commencement. He not only effects a change of form in the material on which he works, but he also realises a purpose of his own that gives the law to his modus operandi, and to which he must subordinate his will. And this subordination is no mere momentary act. Besides the exertion of the bodily organs, the process demands that, during the whole operation, the workman's will be steadily in consonance with his purpose. This means close attention. (1:177)

It is fitting that Marx used the example of the architect as the paradigmatic case for specifically human, productive work. Howard Roark, Rand's protagonist in *The Fountainhead*, reflects everything in Marx's passage and more. He epitomizes the creative architect and laborer, integrating the material and spiritual in each of his productive efforts. In Roark's architectural blueprints, form follows function. In his design of the Stoddard Temple for instance, Roark spiritualizes the secular, giving material form and objective visibility to his exaltation of humanity's noble soul; he "thought that a place built as a setting for man is a sacred place" (356).

While Rand shared with Marx a view of productive work as the distinctive, conscious, practical activity of the human species, she celebrated the creative spirit embodied by the labor process. It is this integrated creativity which enables people to take pride in their achievements.

The Virtue of Selfishness

For Rand, pride is one of the spiritual consequences of productive work. But it is also a by-product of consistent reality-oriented practices. It is based on the premise "that as man must produce the physical values he needs to sustain his life, so he must acquire the values of character that make his life worth sustaining—that as man is a being of self-made wealth, so he is a being of self-made soul" (*Atlas Shrugged*, 1020).

Rand distinguished between pride and conceit. A proud man holds himself as his own highest value.[46] A conceited man is a "pretentious mediocrity." The conceited judge themselves by a comparative standard that frequently places them in positions of superiority or inferiority relative to other people. In Rand's view, a person engaging in offensive boasting is as self-abasing as a person who practices humility.[47] For Rand, humility and presumptuousness are two sides of the same dualistic coin.[48] Nathaniel Branden has argued further that those who arrogantly boast of their worth to others are implicitly acknowledging their own shortcomings (N. Branden and E. D. Branden 1983, 28). Narcissists are not proud. Their excessive self-absorption is unhealthy because it "arises from a deep-rooted sense of inner deficiency and deprivation" (N. Branden 1987, 146).

In attempting to draw this distinction between genuine pride and the false alternatives of humility and conceit, both Rand and Branden inadvertently affirmed elements of the Aristotelian ethos. Aristotle argued that virtuous behavior was the golden "mean between two vices, the one involving excess, the other deficiency."[49] Pride is the "crown of the virtues," enhancing the other virtues of a person's character and forming an inseparable unity with them. A proud person's claims to greatness are strictly in accordance with his or her actual merits.[50] The proud are neither boastful nor humble. As lovers of self, the proud have "nobility and goodness of character." A proud person refuses "to make his life revolve round another, unless it be a friend; for this is slavish."[51]

In recognizing Aristotle's perceptiveness, Peikoff argues, however, that it is incorrect to conceptualize pride as a mean on the same continuum as the vices it opposes. In most cases, the vices that Aristotle typically identifies are different not in degree, but in *kind* from the virtuous "mean." The proud are *essentially* different from the boastful and the obsequious.[52] In keeping with the nondualistic thrust of Objectivism, Peikoff suggests that Aristotle has actually identified a pair of false alternatives, each of which is a variation on the other. Both the humble person and the braggart share the premise of self-doubt, while the genuinely proud individual is self-reliant, self-respecting, and self-accepting.[53]

Rand recognized pride as a virtue, an ambitious dedication to the achievement of one's highest potential. But Objectivism also distinguishes between the virtue of pride and the *value* of self-esteem. Branden ([1969] 1979) explains:

> The two are related, but there are significant differences in their meaning. Self-esteem pertains to a man's conviction of his fundamental efficacy and worth. Pride pertains to the pleasure a man takes in himself on the basis of and in response to *specific* achievements or actions. Self-esteem is confidence in one's capacity to achieve values. Pride is the consequence of having achieved some particular value(s). Self-esteem is "I can." Pride is "I have." (125)

This is an important distinction. Pride is an aspect of one's particularized efficacy grounded in the genuine mastery of certain skills and practices. Self-esteem pertains more to a person's generalized or metaphysical efficacy. Both Rand and Branden see self-esteem as a fundamental human need. Branden defends the concept of "need" in the same manner that Rand defends the concept of "value." A need arises from the "conditional nature of life. . . . Without the concept of *life*, the concept of *need* would not be possible. . . . 'Need' implies the existence of a goal, result or end: the survival of the organism. Therefore, *in order to maintain that something is a physical or psychological need, one must demonstrate that it is a causal condition of the organism's survival and well-being*" (19).

But self-esteem is not like other human needs. It seems less "real" than say, the need for food, clothing, or shelter. And yet, self-esteem is mind-esteem.[54] In Rand's original formulation, it is a man's "inviolate certainty that his mind is competent to think and his person is worthy of happiness, which means: is worthy of living" (*Atlas Shrugged*, 1018). To achieve self-esteem is not a purely cerebral accomplishment. It is more than the mere conviction that we are worthy. It is earned by consistently applying thought to action. It is experienced through praxis, and is both the source and product of human efficacy.[55] It is a human need not because people would die without it, but because it has survival value that impinges on their very capacity to think, act, and live *as* human beings (N. Branden and E. D. Branden 1983, 11).

Drawing from Rand's initial formulations, Nathaniel Branden has made a lifetime profession of exploring the meaning and applications of self-esteem.[56] He argues that self-esteem has two internally related aspects: a sense of personal efficacy and a sense of personal worth.[57] Just as we cannot escape the need to evaluate the facts of external reality, so we cannot escape the need for self-evaluation. By achieving our goals, we gain a sense of self-confidence and control over our existence that fuels our further achievements, as well as our practical competence. To be the beneficiary of our achievements, we must also feel that we deserve these benefits. By living

(1) consciously and (2) purposively, and by practicing the arts of (3) self-acceptance, (4) self-responsibility, (5) self-assertiveness, and (6) personal integrity, we achieve a generalized feeling of self-worth, which is as necessary to our practical competence as the mastery of any technical skill.[58] Neither Rand nor Branden deny the effects of internal and external factors on the development of self-esteem. Indeed, as Branden emphasizes, our sense of identity does not evolve solipsistically. It emerges in the context of our relationships, which contribute to the sense of self we acquire. In human interaction, each person expresses that which is internalized in his or her consciousness, the many complex consequences of past encounters and experiences (N. Branden 1983b, 40). Our relationships to parents, teachers, significant others, organizations, and the culture greatly impact upon our evolution toward independence and autonomy. The ideas, beliefs, and practices that we accept, either consciously or tacitly, can prove fatal to our self-image, and to our very existence (N. Branden 1992, 94–95).

What must be emphasized at this stage is that this exalted view of self-esteem is the essence of Rand's ethical egoism. When Rand advocated *rational selfishness*, she was not projecting the ideal of a savage, club-wielding caveman. She argued that the virtue of selfishness is inseparable from the virtue of rationality. When we exercise our minds to the fullest extent of our ability, we are being rational. By applying our thought to the achievement of material values, we are being productive. By benefiting from our own rational efforts, we are being selfish in the most benevolent sense of that word. None of these virtues is separable from the others.

By realizing our purposes and reaping the benefits of our efforts, we acquire the values necessary to survival. For Rand, such an achievement does not require the sacrifice of others to the self or the sacrifice of the self to others. Objectivism sees no inherent conflict of interest among people who *earn* the values of their existence and who deal with one another by trading value for value. Rand argued that such free, voluntary, uncoerced trade is the only rational and moral principle for all human relationships, whether personal or social, private or public, spiritual or material. This trader principle recognizes neither masters nor slaves in human relations.[59] It acknowledges no polarization between the individual and the society in which that individual lives, *if* that society is genuinely *human*. Indeed, the greater a person's self-esteem, the more likely it is that he or she will engage in social relationships marked by mutual respect, kindness, and generosity. The deeper a person's self-doubt, the more likely it is that he or she will view others with fear and distrust (N. Branden 1987, 147).

At this juncture, it is important to grasp why Rand used the word "selfishness" to connote something beneficent. She argued in *The Virtue of Selfishness*, that she used it for the very reasons that make people afraid of it (vii). She claimed that conventional morality creates a conceptual "package-deal" in which only two alternatives are possible: the sacrifice of the self to others (traditional altruism) or the sacrifice of others to the self (traditional egoism).[60] Convention equates altruism with benevolence and egoism with brutality. In both cases, however, the spirit of benevolence is sabotaged and the practice of brutality is made inevitable.

In Rand's view, the conventional alternatives obscure the true meaning of the word "selfishness," which is: *"concern with one's own interests."* Such a definition is morally neutral, according to Rand.

It is debatable whether Rand pinpointed the actual definition of "selfishness." Most dictionaries define "selfishness" as "concern *only* with one's own interests," which is not neutral. In any event, the major obstacle for Rand is not philological, but philosophical. By transposing the concept of "selfishness" into a nondualistic context, Rand aimed to alter its conventional meaning (*Virtue of Selfishness*, vii). To effect this metamorphosis of meaning, Rand had to transcend the limitations of the very categories she was using. This is a difficulty faced by most dialectical thinkers: utilizing terms whose meaning has been tainted by a vastly different, one-dimensional philosophical context. To avoid such terms entirely, Rand would have been compelled to invent wholly new terms at the risk of becoming incomprehensible. By using known terms, she might appear to have actually endorsed one pole of a duality. Thus, in the conflict between egoism and altruism, for example, she was an egoist. In the conflict between capitalism and socialism, she was a capitalist. But such a one-sided characterization profoundly distorts Rand's philosophical project. She was not a *conventional* egoist. Her ethics constitutes a rejection of traditional egoism and traditional altruism alike. Likewise, she was not a *conventional* capitalist. As I will discuss further in Chapter 10, Rand defended capitalism as an *unknown* ideal. If we fail to grasp these important distinctions, we risk viewing Rand as a monist. In actuality, Rand's approach to ethics is but another illustration of her revolt against formal dualism.

Love and Sex

Rand's ethics are internally related to every other aspect of her developed worldview. It is impossible to comprehend the extent and depth of her vision in a single chapter or study. But there are immediate ramifications that further illustrate the essentially nondualistic tenor of her philosophy. In no area of ethics or psychology is this more apparent than in the Objectivist perspective on love and sex. These issues highlight Rand's understanding of the connections between the conscious and the subconscious, the mind and body.[61]

Rand's integration of the material and the spiritual is central to her concept of productive work. But it is equally essential to her examination of love and sex. Rand traced a philosophical link between those who deny the spiritual roots of production and those who believe that sex is a purely mechanical function. In production, the materialist engages in promiscuous acquisition devoid of principles, and the idealist excoriates material values. In sex, the materialist engages in literal promiscuity, and the idealist extols the virtues of Platonic love. Rand ([1976] 1992T) warned that the cultural treatment of sex as a bathroom function would lead to a Victorian backlash. She maintained that this swinging from one pole to another was an inevitable by-product of the materialist and idealist bifurcation of mind and body.

Rand argued that just as material production emerges from cognitive and creative activity, so too, sexual choices will reflect consciously or subconsciously held convictions. As a distinctively human activity, sex involves the exploration of all of our sense modalities and spiritual values (N. Branden 1980, 90–92). Ideally, it is the expression of romantic love. Such an integration of love and sex is neither exploitative nor submissive. It "is the most profoundly selfish of all acts," because it celebrates the self as an object worthy of desire and appreciation (*Atlas Shrugged*, 489–90). It requires self-assertion, self-responsibility, self-respect, and above all, self-esteem. Indeed, as Rand explained through Roark, "To say 'I love you' one must know first how to say the 'I' " (*Fountainhead*, 377).

In a passage from *Atlas Shrugged*, Rand describes an encounter between Dagny Taggart and Hank Rearden which expresses the fully integrated nature of the sex act:

> She knew that what she felt with the skin of her arms was the cloth of his shirt, she knew that the lips she felt on her mouth were his, but in the rest of her there was no distinction between his being and her own, as there was no division between body and spirit. . . . The course led them to the moment when, in answer to the highest of one's values, in an admiration not to be expressed by any other form

of tribute, one's spirit makes one's body become the tribute, recasting it—as proof, as sanction, as reward—into a single sensation of such intensity of joy that no other sanction of one's existence is necessary. He heard the moan of her breath, she felt the shudder of his body, in the same instant. (252)

Of course, Rand's belief in the full integration of mind and body does not mean that romantic partners are *morally obligated* to have a simultaneous orgasm. Rather, Rand argued that in all relationships of affection, from friendship to romantic love, the partners incorporate the welfare of each other into their hierarchy of values.[62] In romantic love, the interpenetration of each body is a synthesis of both spirits (N. Branden 1980, 120). Sex, however, is not a primary. One cannot generate self-esteem through sexual conquest and adventure. For Rand, only the "rationally selfish," are capable of giving and receiving love. People who do not value themselves first are incapable of valuing anything or anyone.[63]

From the time of his association with Rand, Branden developed the deeper implications of the Objectivist view in his examination of the principle of psychological visibility and its relationship to self-esteem and romantic love.[64] Branden argues that a person's self-concept is constituted by "a cluster of images and abstract perspectives on his various (real or imagined) traits and characteristics." Like any broad, metaphysical abstraction, this cluster of images cannot be held in full conscious awareness at any particular moment. We are tacitly aware of our self-concept in each of our activities, but we never perceive it, as such (N. Branden [1969] 1979, 200). Branden argues that even though we can come to experience ourselves in terms of higher-level concepts, it is only in our interaction with another consciousness that we can experience ourselves perceptually.

This Brandenian argument mirrors Rand's own insights into the creative nature of production and art. Rand suggested that human productive activity as such is essentially objectifying, creative praxis. In concretizing their goals, people make visible not only their explicit production designs, but the implicit values that propel them toward achievement. So too, art enables a person to experience his or her broadest, metaphysical abstractions in objective, perceptual form. By creating an art work, an artist makes visible a tacit sense of life. The artist objectifies materially that which is internal to consciousness. This process is duplicated by the responder. By articulating the basis of his or her aesthetic responses, the responder's own core evaluations become self-visible. In this communicative interaction with an artist's creation, the responder's subconsciously held values are objectified for contemplation. A positive aesthetic experience will suggest a congruence between artist and responder that is mediated through the art work.

Branden recognizes that the experience of objectification and visibility is augmented exponentially in the context of human relations. Just as art allows one to grasp valuational concepts with the ease of perceptual focus, so human relationships permit people "to perceive [themselves] as [entities] in reality—to experience the perspective of objectivity—through and by means of the reactions and responses of other human beings."[65]

Branden's articulation of the principle of psychological visibility emerged initially from his interactions with his dog, Muttnik. He acknowledged that a human being could experience visibility even with a nonhuman consciousness. By playing aggressively with Muttnik, Branden noticed that the dog responded in a fully appropriate manner. Muttnik's response seemed to objectify Branden's actions in a way that mirrored his playful intentions.[66]

The experience of visibility allows us to view ourselves as objective existents. Branden (1980) states somewhat cryptically: "The externalization of the objectification of the internal is of the very nature of successful life" (74). What Branden means is that to the extent that we articulate and make explicit that which is within our own consciousness, we can experience ourselves as objectified beings in the eyes of another. To be genuinely visible to others, we must also be willing to be self-visible. To the extent that we have articulated and grasped our own convictions and values, we will optimize our visibility to others. To the extent that these convictions and values are shared with others, we will maximize the possibility for genuinely intimate relations. In our relations, we can achieve an "expanded awareness of self" (79).

In romantic love, the highest form of human visibility, the relationship constitutes a dynamic system (211). Since no one is a static entity, and since each "is engaged in a constant process of unfolding," the self-visibility of each and the visibility of each to a significant other will evolve over time (N. Branden 1983a, 260). The dynamism inherent in the interpenetration of two selves creates a new universe that is unlike that occupied by either person alone. The result is an intermingling of many complex conscious and subconscious factors, including biological elements that science has yet to fully understand.[67]

Romantic love, then, is the concrete expression of human integration. It is *not* infatuation. An infatuation is a distortion based on the reification of one or two aspects of a person's character. When we are infatuated with another person, we abstract these selected qualities from the totality and respond to the person as if these characteristics constituted the whole (N. Branden [1969] 1979, 210). Romantic love eschews such one-dimensionality. It is a synthesis of body and mind, sense modalities and spirituality, self-visibility and objectification. It is a totalistic and mutual response that preserves the independence of the lovers, even as it heightens their sense of unity. In Rand's fiction, lovers may be willing to die for one another, but they refuse to live for one another. Even in unity, each person retains the self-actualizing values and virtues consonant with their individual, human survival.[68]

Like Rand, Branden recognizes that this conception of self-esteem and romantic love is a product of historical evolution. It is profoundly individualistic, egoistic, secular, and rationally selfish and stands in stark opposition to all premodern and religious theories. Such a conception would not have been possible without the accomplishments of the Industrial Revolution. Industrialization engendered the rise of a middle class that reached beyond its purely material needs and embraced an ideal of romantic love that was revolutionary in its impact (N. Branden 1980, 37). Both Rand and Branden suggest that the implications of this concept have yet to be fully appreciated or understood.

Eudaemonia

It should be apparent by now that Rand's ethics are as expansive as her epistemology. In Rand's epistemology, reason is constituted by many interrelated practices. Reason is consciousness. Consciousness is mind. But mind includes articulated, conscious convictions and tacit, subconscious integrations, the capacity for logical deduction and inductive inference, as well as the ability to evaluate, to feel, and to create. And the mind cannot be abstracted from the body, without losing the totality of what it means to be human. Rand does not identify reason with emotion or thought with action. Her system seeks their integrated and organic unity, such that no part is in fundamental conflict with the other parts or the totality that gives it meaning.

It is this expansive, multidimensionality that is reproduced within Rand's ethical theories.[69] And yet a number of thinkers have criticized Rand because they believe that she never fully explained the exact nature of her standard of moral values. For instance, Mack notes that "man's life qua man" as the standard of moral values seems to incorporate rationality and productivity into the fabric of human survival. Mack wonders why Rand did not make pleasure and happiness partially constitutive of this standard. He asks if Rand valued rationality and productivity instrumentally, as means to the goal of human survival, or if these virtues are constituent elements of that ultimate goal.[70] Henry Veatch is also perplexed by Rand's use of "life" as the ultimate end, since she gives no precise indication of what "man's life qua man" might be.[71]

Many of these criticisms are rooted in actual—ambiguous—passages in Rand's writings. For instance, in the course of three pages in her essay "The Objectivist Ethics," Rand presents three distinct *purposes* as central to a person's life. She argues that everyone's life is his or her own ethical purpose, and that this is the means of concretizing the abstract standard of value, "man's life qua man." But she also states that in the context of a "man's life qua man," productive work is the central purpose, a value that integrates other values. She simultaneously links productive work to rationality, whose function is also primarily integrative. Rationality and productive work, then, seem to fulfill similar requirements of integration. But Rand complicates these themes further when she states, as a social principle, that every person is an end in him- or herself, and not a means to the ends of others. It is *"the achievement of his own happiness [that] is man's highest moral purpose."*[72]

How can one's own life, productive work, and happiness all be *central* to one's highest moral purpose? Was Rand equivocating, or does her argument have its own inner logic? This requires some further exploration.

For Rand, happiness is to living as logic is to thought. Just as logic is the "art of non-contradictory identification," so happiness is the "state of non-contradictory joy" (*Atlas Shrugged*, 1016, 1022). Logic requires the integration of one's basic premises and experience, with an understanding of context. Happiness emerges from the integrated achievement of one's values. It is not merely a fleeting pleasure or a momentary feeling. It requires an acceptance of one's context and a grasp of one's own long-term interests.

However, Rand remarked that though happiness is the *purpose* of ethics, it is not the standard.[73] This suggests a distinction between life as the standard and happiness as the purpose of life. Rand distinguished between these categories in order to criticize hedonism. She maintained that hedonism views pleasure and happiness as moral standards. The good is anything that gives people pleasure and/or happiness, and the evil is anything that gives people pain and/or unhappiness. In Rand's view, however, happiness is an emotional state, proceeding from one's values and convictions. Since values ultimately determine what makes you happy, and since each individual's values arise from a confluence of conscious and subconscious factors, the emotion of happiness is a complex, integrated derivative. It cannot serve as an ultimate standard because it is not an end in itself. Nor is it strictly a means to the end of life. It is an emotional experience of pleasure and joy in being as such. It is a form of pleasure, Branden suggests, which "is a metaphysical concomitant of life, the reward and consequence of successful action."[74]

Rand explained further that the relationship between virtues and values is a relationship between means and ends. She maintained that our virtues enable us to achieve life and happiness. Thus, "Virtue is not an end in itself. Virtue is not its own reward. . . . *Life* is the reward of virtue—and happiness is the goal and reward of life" (*Atlas Shrugged*, 1022).

Rand seems to be saying that virtues do not constitute the values they actualize. And yet how can rationality and productive work constitute the value of life if they are a means to life's achievement? How can the practice of any virtue be a constituent element of the one ultimate value it aims to consummate? How can happiness be the goal of life when life is the ultimate value itself? How can Rand be involved in such a quagmire of apparent ambiguity?

The issue here, I think, is that Rand was being true to her dialectical roots. The circularity indicates that there is an identity between *human* life and all the virtues (reason, purpose, self-esteem) and values (rationality, honesty, integrity, independence, justice, and pride) Rand enunciates. The virtues are the means to life. However, the standard of moral values is not mere survival, but the life proper to a rational being. Life *is* self-sustaining *action*. *Human* life as the standard of value entails the *actions* that are necessary for its achievement.

Despite her emphasis on axioms and derivatives, Rand did not think in terms of strict logical dependence, or one-way causality, i.e., that A leads to B which leads to C. Rather, she thought in terms of reciprocal causation and mutual reinforcement: A leads to B which leads to C, with each of the elements being both the precondition and consequence of the others. Such an integration allowed Rand to view the sex act, for instance, as simultaneously, a celebration of life, an expression of happiness, a manifestation of self-esteem, and a product of human values. The constellation here cannot be understood in its abstracted units, but only in its organic unity.

True, Rand recognized an asymmetry among the elements of the totality. In her ethics, life is the source of value—just as existence is prior to consciousness; just as reason, albeit expansively conceived, is the root of the individual's distinct evaluative and emotive mechanisms. But the relationships between these pairs is reciprocal and integrated. We cannot know existence without consciousness. We cannot understand life without grasping the necessity of valuation in human survival. We cannot remain fully conscious, reasoning animals without articulating our emotions and integrating our subconscious values and conscious convictions; such is the essence of an unobstructed awareness.

Rand's integrated approach is clearly reflected in her statement: "To hold one's own life as one's ultimate value, and one's own happiness as one's highest purpose are two aspects of the same achievement."[75] While happiness depends upon the standard of life, it is also a constituent aspect of genuinely human survival. But so are all the values and virtues that Rand has enunciated. To hold the life of a rational being as the standard of value, is simultaneously to endorse a view of *what* a rational life is. Not surprisingly, it comprises the very derivative values and virtues that make *human* life possible. In Peikoff's words: "The moral, the practical, and the happy cannot be sundered. By their nature, the three form a unity: he who perceives reality is able to gain his ends and thus enjoy the process of being alive."[76]

Peikoff (1976T, lecture 7) argues that at the core of Objectivism is a belief in the actualization of human potentialities. In this regard, Objectivism follows the Aristotelian conception of eudaemonia as the human entelechy. For Aristotle, the proper end of human action is the achievement of "a state of rich, ripe, fulfilling earthly happiness."[77]

Branden too applauds Aristotle's eudaemonic worldview. He argues that human life involves the expansion of "the boundaries of the self to embrace all of our potentialities, as well as those parts that have been denied, disowned, repressed." The actualization of human potential is a form of transcendence, an ability "to rise above a limited context or perspective—to a wider field of vision." This wider field does not negate the previous moments; it is a struggle "from one stage of development to a higher one, emotionally, cognitively, morally, and so forth" (N. Branden 1983b, 114, 244).

This teleological strand in Objectivism has led Den Uyl and Rasmussen to view Rand's philosophy as fully within the Aristotelian eudaemonic tradition.[78] They suggest, quite persuasively, that Rand, like Aristotle, saw human life in terms of personal flourishing. The principles that guide people toward their own fulfillment "are both productive of the condition and expressive of it" (Den Uyl and Rasmussen 1991, 59–60).

This "flourisher" interpretation of Rand's ethics is not without its critics. In the Objectivist literature, the "flourishers" are opposed by the "survival-ists."[79] Kelley (1992c), for instance, argues that to regard "flourishing" as a constituent of the ultimate value of life, is to put the cart before the horse. According to Kelley, every value and virtue in Rand's ethics has a bearing on self-preservation. To incorporate these values and virtues into the ultimate value, life, escapes the need to prove that they are a "necessary *means* to that end" (54, 58). For Kelley, Rand has established a strictly causal relationship:

> The alternative of existence or non-existence is what bridges the is-ought gap, it is what all values have to be tied back to, and that means literal survival or death. I think if you're going to ground your ethics in facts, you have to trace everything back to survival or non-survival, because that's where you face the fundamental alternative. Or you have to develop a new theory, some other connection between facts and values, in addition to or instead of the one Ayn Rand proposed.[80]

But as I have suggested, Rand endorsed a form of reciprocal connection. She did trace the necessary links between virtue and survival, but she also argued that survival is specifically *human* survival, an integrated existence. Her virtues serve the goal of human life, even as they are necessary constituents of the goal itself. If, as I have argued, Rand is profoundly dialectical in her methodology, then the "survivalist" interpretation of Rand's ethics is fundamentally flawed.

Morality and Moralizing

In this chapter I have presented a rather exalted view of Rand's approach to ethics. I have yet to focus on Rand's concept of immorality or on her own reputation for "moralizing." While I will have the occasion to explore her view of evil later, it is impossible to leave this chapter without a brief discussion of these themes. The primary reason for addressing these issues at this time, relates to the leitmotif of this book. If Rand's ethics are inherently nondualistic, does her definition of evil reintroduce dualism into the framework of her philosophy? Furthermore, does her alleged penchant for moralizing undermine the rich, integrated conception that I have reconstructed in this chapter?

As a novelist and lecturer, Rand presented her otherwise integrated perspective in stark terms, which often did violence to the complexities and subtleties of her philosophy. This was perhaps an unavoidable by-product of her popular expositional style. It was an approach that made her famous, and which very much reflected the immoderate tendencies inherent in the Russian literary tradition.

Rand advocated "a black and white view of the world" since one could not "identify anything as gray, as middle of the road," without knowing "what is black and what is white, because gray is merely a mixture of the two."[81] While she defined rationality as the basic virtue, she regarded irrationality as the basic vice.[82]

In order to understand Rand's notion of irrationality, it is important to grasp her distinction between an error of knowledge and a breach of morality (*Atlas Shrugged*, 1059). Rand recognized that people are not infallible or omniscient. A person who makes an error of knowledge may be in full mental focus, but may either lack sufficient information, or make a mistake. Such a person is not irrational. By contrast, a person who breaches morality commits the equivalent of a "cardinal sin," in Rand's view, a "sin" that makes all other vices possible. For Rand, the essence of such a breach is willful evasion of the facts of reality.

Rand recognized that evasion can become habitual in a person's psycho-epistemology. Such evasions may inevitably contribute to a form of psychological repression that blocks an individual from being aware of certain uncomfortable facts. Though repression is outside the realm of conscious control, and thus, extra-moral, Rand condemned the sustained practice of willful evasion. A person who consciously evades the facts of reality acts against the means of his or her own survival. Such irrationality cannot be practiced with impunity; it must engender consequences that undermine a person's self-preservation.

Rand believed in a kind of Gresham's law of morality. Just as bad money drives out good money, so bad moral principles have a tendency to drive out good ones. She argued that most people internalize a mixture of both rational and irrational premises, but that unless the irrational ones were fully articulated and transcended, people risked poisoning even their good principles (Peikoff 1987T, lecture 6). Knowledge is an integrated totality. To evade one fact is to introduce a contradiction into one's consciousness, which, if left unchecked, must engender further contradictions, and the ultimate disintegration of one's cognitive and evaluative mechanisms. Rand compared the process to government intervention in the economy. She argued that unless the irrationality (or intervention) is examined and entirely eliminated, it requires further irrationality (or intervention) in a misbegotten attempt to overturn the deleterious consequences.[83] The result is disastrous in both cognitive and social spheres. Ultimately, Rand's analysis of statism is a radical critique of systemic irrationality.

Rand argued that rationality, the good, has nothing to gain from irrationality, the evil. Rand believed that evil is impotent because those who engage in sustained evasion cannot realize the potentialities distinctive to human being. Because evil is fundamentally impotent, it can only succeed by the default of those rational and moral people who do not recognize its basic irrationality. In a clear articulation of principles, irrationality is defeated. By obscuring these principles, the irrational gain a certain leverage in social relations they do not naturally possess.[84] It is for this reason that Rand rejected any compromise on basic principles of right and wrong.

This ethical stance had political implications. While Rand viewed "indiscriminate tolerance" and "indiscriminate condemnation" as variants of the same error, she asserted that in an "irrational society," a rational person must never fail to pronounce moral judgment.[85] Any failure to do so would constitute an implicit moral sanction of evil. Since evil is a destructive force, and reason is fundamentally creative, a single appeasement is morally reprehensible and has potentially fatal long-term consequences. Still, a person's context might determine the appropriateness of a specific moral response; it has been alleged that Rand and many of her followers engaged in endless tirades and denunciations where polite conversation and orderly debate might have been more effective.

This intolerance was reflected in many of Rand's positions in the area of situational ethics. Though Rand saw restitution as a means of earning forgiveness of a moral breach (Peikoff 1991b, 289), her uncompromising view of the world left little room for moral reform. And while Rand did not deny the legitimacy of charity as a means of helping those who were unfortunate victims of circumstance, she most certainly did not give enough attention to the issue of private, voluntary assistance in human affairs. Typically, Objectivists would answer those who inquired about the plight of the poor and the handicapped, with a flippant, "If you want to help them, we will not stop you."[86]

These flashes of insensitivity cannot be taken completely out of context. In Rand's opinion, the institutional poor were a consequence of statist economy. Peikoff (1987bT, questions, period 1) argues too that if people were to let orphans starve in a genuinely free society, they would be so malevolent and corrupt that freedom could not last for any length of time. Indeed, voluntary, mutual aid has survival value (N. Branden 1983b, 225n). Rand recognized that a rational individual never forgets the fact that *life* is the source of value, that there is "a common bond among living beings," and that other individuals are potentially capable of achieving the same virtues of character.[87]

While Rand's situational ethics are tempered by enlightened self-interest, the evidence suggests that in her own personal relationships, she was a fervent moralizer. This "religious" streak in Rand's approach has been noted variously by a number of commentators.[88] Nathaniel Branden argues that Rand exhibited a kind of "Manichaeism."[89] Manichaen thought is inherently dualistic. Paul Thomas (1980) explains that the Manichaens saw good and evil as "two independent, co-equal principles, so that evil *as evil* is required if the good is to establish itself" (384n).

Strictly speaking, Rand was *not* a Manichaen. Rand did *not* posit a radical separation of good and evil precisely because evil is not coequal with good. She defined evil *negatively*, as rooted in a revolt against rationality. Evil has no power without the sanction of good. It cannot exist on its own, and depends upon the default of the good for its sustenance. Evil can only destroy, it cannot create. It requires that others create before it can expropriate their values. Good does not require the presence of evil, but evil is a parasite on the moral host. Rand skewed the relationship in terms of the good and the rational, not in terms of their negations.[90]

And yet it is entirely possible that Rand did integrate elements of the Manichaen perspective into her psychology. As a child of Russia's Silver Age, Rand may have inherited the Symbolists' belief in the polarity of good and evil. Merezhkovsky had in fact endorsed a Manichaen view, and even the dogmatic communists saw the world in terms of a ruthless, apocalyptic struggle between polar opposites.[91] Rand's intolerance echoes these immoderate Russian tendencies. If anything, this suggests that it is not possible to escape the limitations of one's past completely or remake oneself entirely. In Rand's struggle against dualism, she may have retained aspects of a

Manichaen worldview in her own psychology. But in speculating so freely on the roots of Rand's alleged moralizing, I risk committing an equally dangerous psychologistic error. The more important question is whether such intolerance is endemic to any totalistic philosophy.

It is apparent, however, that the history of the organized Objectivist movement is replete with stories of "authoritarianism in the name of reason." Those "students of Objectivism" who displayed "inappropriate" behavior were condemned for having committed "an offense against an abstraction called 'morality' " (N. Branden [1969] 1979, 246 n. 48). Nathaniel Branden admits to having fueled such intolerance. In later years, he recognized that this use of moralistic judgment only obscured an understanding of a person's specific circumstances and context. As a psychologist, Branden (1987) sees human beings engaged in a struggle for adaptation and self-preservation: "Even if the path we choose is mistaken, even if *objectively* we are engaged in self-destruction, *subjectively* at some level we are trying to take care of ourselves—as in the case of a suicide who seeks escape from intolerable pain" (79).

For Branden (1973), neurotic behavior can be understood as an individual's attempt to protect his self-esteem and to assure his own "*survival by self-destructive (reality-avoiding) means*" (8). But there is a subtle distinction here between psychological and ethical egoism. Psychologically, every action seems to embody self-interested motivation *subjectively* defined. Ethically, however, the achievement of values that are objectively and rationally selfish frequently requires a dedicated, personal struggle of momentous proportions.[92] Psychology and the therapeutic process provide an individual with a technology that facilitates the practice of virtue and the actualization of value (N. Branden 1982T).

Branden is not the only post-Randian theorist to grapple with moralism. Peikoff himself has argued that moralizing is a product of rationalism. As we have seen, rationalism begins with a list of intrinsic truths. Ethically, the rationalist applies these dogmatic principles with authoritarian ruthlessness. Peikoff explains that in "rationalist" interpretations of Objectivism, there is a one-sided emphasis on a "morality" abstracted from the context and concrete circumstances that give it meaning. The rationalist tends to be as severe on himself as he is on others.[93]

As the post-Randian theorists move away from the premise that they are bearers of holy truth, they move toward a kinder, gentler Objectivism. The essence of Rand's ethos lies not in her alleged moralizing, but in her ecstatic vision of extraordinary human creativity. This normative vision cannot be fully understood if removed from the broad social context that gives it existential meaning. While Rand believed that it was possible to live a rational life in an irrational society, her ethical theory beckons toward a polity that makes the practice of virtue fully efficacious.

10 A Libertarian Politics

In this chapter I examine Rand's libertarian politics as an outgrowth of her ontology, epistemology, and ethics, the culminating moment of a nondualistic philosophical totality. She aimed to transcend the polarities between anarchism and statism, atomistic individualism and organic collectivism. She defended laissez-faire capitalism as the only social formation consonant with fully integrated human being. Most important, she stressed an inextricable link between the personal and the political.

In my characterization of Rand as a libertarian thinker, I am using this word somewhat broadly. "Libertarianism" is a twentieth-century political ideology that carries on the eighteenth- and nineteenth-century classical liberal legacy. Its adherents advocate free-market capitalism and the rule of law, and they oppose statism and collectivism. They include individual-rights advocates such as Ayn Rand, Murray Rothbard, Tibor Machan, Douglas Den Uyl, and Douglas Rasmussen, but also those who depart from the rights perspective, such as Ludwig von Mises, F. A. Hayek, and Milton Friedman. It is incorrect to view these thinkers as constituting a monolith, since there are significant differences between and among them. Though Rand praised Mises, for instance, she frequently derided others in the libertarian tradition for their lack of purity, or their inconsistency.[1] In fact, she despised the word "libertarianism," and often identified it with those who advocated "anarcho-capitalism." She characterized these individualist anarchists as "hippies of the right."[2] Her critique of anarchism was a crucial component of her own nondualistic defense of the free market.

And yet despite her protestations, Rand's politics is essentially libertarian. Her defense of individual rights, limited government, and laissez-faire capitalism constituted an invaluable contribution to the reemergence of classical liberal ideology in the twentieth century. Even though her approach is broader than most of her free-market contemporaries, it is fully within the libertarian tradition.

The Individual and Society

In stressing the ontological priority of individuals, the centrality of reason, and the necessity of ethical egoism, Rand provided the philosophical foundation for her defense of capitalism. Just as we achieve psychological visibility and an expanded awareness of self in our interactions with other human beings, so too, can we best actualize our unique potentialities in a social context. But for Rand, the full development of human capacities

Fig. 10.   Ayn Rand and Frank O'Connor. (Courtesy of John Hospers)

requires a *specific* social context. A social system must be consistent with our species identity and with the requirements of *human* survival.

While Rand acknowledged the sociality of human being, much of her politics is designed to clarify the very meaning of the concept "social." Throughout her writings, it is possible to find vastly different connotations attached to it. At times, Rand exhibited an almost knee-jerk reaction against the very notion that we have a "social" nature. From her earliest journal entries, she questioned whether human beings are born "social," and whether they must remain so. She asked: "If man started as a social animal—isn't all progress and civilization to be directed to making him an *individual?*"[3] In later years, her polemical tracts insist that "there is no such entity as 'society,' " and that "society" is merely "a number of individual men."[4] And although she most emphatically rejected solipsism, she denied on one occasion that human beings are social animals. Society as such does not make us distinctly human, since it is possible to find communal living even among apes (N. Branden 1967T, lecture 13). Rand argued instead that the human being "is a *contractual* animal," who must plan long-range, make choices, and trade with other individuals on the basis of reliable voluntary agreements.[5]

Abstracted from the totality of Rand's works, these statements reek of reification. Indeed, by characterizing a human being as a "contractual" animal, Rand conjured up images of vulgar, "economic man" as a transhistorical constant. And yet Rand never ceased to criticize society and social institutions. From a purely methodological vantage point, Rand clearly believed that the concept of the "social" was a legitimate abstraction. Rand saw "society" as a relational concept, as peoples' "relations to each other . . . men in relation to men."[6] In such a relational construction, Rand committed neither the fallacy of composition nor division. In composition, we discover a fact that is true of a part, and mistakenly conclude that it is also true of the whole as the whole.[7] Division, by contrast, applies what is true of the whole to each of its individual constituents taken separately (Peikoff 1974T, lecture 3). Objectivism recognizes that both the part and the whole have analytical integrity within a specifically defined context. In Rand's view:

> You are permitted to regard as an entity, for purposes of study, a collection of human beings such as a society, but you are not permitted then to say that metaphysically it is an organism, tied together by some ineffable means. You cannot say it is anything

other than a group of a certain kind of entities, living beings, and you regard them as one entity only from a certain aspect. ("Appendix," 272)

Thus, for Rand, society has no autonomous existence apart from the individuals who compose it.[8] By stressing the ontological priority of individuals, Rand rejected the metaphysical basis of organic collectivism.

Rand's opposition to organic collectivism was a by-product of her Russian youth. In its thrust toward dialectical synthesis, the history of Russian philosophy centered on the conflict between the individual and society. But in contrast to the Western-Hobbesian view that people must be forced into a social whole to avoid the war of all against all, most Russian thinkers resolved the conflict through mysticism. Nearly every major Russian philosopher, from Solovyov to Lossky, embraced the theme of *sobornost'*. This Russian concept accommodated the interests of the individual and of the collective through a mystical conciliarity. In their unity, each person was both the source and product of the whole. Each person reflected the organic social whole while being an inseparable constituent of it. This union was typically achieved through an ineffable, mystical process. Many Russian Marxists absorbed the collectivistic thrust of *sobornost'*, and sought to achieve unity through the coercive power of the state.

It is within this context that we can understand Rand's hostility toward most things "social." Outside of its analytical usefulness, the "social" became a euphemism for the subordination of the individual, the dissolving of the unique human personality into an undifferentiated mass. In all of Rand's early writings, there is a sustained attack against this social determinism, whether of a religious or secular variety. By the 1940s and 1950s, Rand was swimming against the currents of modern Western sociology. She had unabashedly rejected what Dennis Wrong would call the "oversocialized conception of man."

Wrong's famous essay scolded contemporary sociologists for their "one-sided" view of man as a "disembodied, conscience-driven, status-seeking phantom." Most sociologists projected an image of human beings as fully pliable, disciplined automatons whose chief goal was conformity and stability. Wrong (1961, 183, 190) argued that sociology had merely replaced one dualistic view of human being with another. In place of the hedonic, utilitarian calculus of bourgeois, economic man, sociology had created another undialectical, one-dimensional, "reified abstraction." For Wrong, human sociality did not mean that human beings were entirely the product of socialization.

Rand anticipated Wrong's thesis by many years. But she recalled a more classically oriented view of human sociality. Like Aristotle, Rand saw ethics and politics as mutually supplementary. For Aristotle, the good man and the good citizen are identical.[9] When Aristotle saw the individual as "by nature a political animal," he was expressing the conviction that human beings lived naturally in a polity, or political community, and that these existential conditions were necessary for their personal flourishing.[10] Rand inherits this classical impulse. She sees human beings neither as solipsists nor as socialized automatons. As Nathaniel Branden (1980) emphasizes:

> There are a thousand respects in which we are not alone. . . . As human beings, we are linked to all other members of the human community. As living beings, we are linked to all other forms of life. As inhabitants of the universe, we are linked to everything that exists. We stand within an endless network of relationships. Separation and connectedness are polarities, with each entailing the other. (61)

In Rand's thought, social existence enables us to actualize most fully our distinct potentialities. Rand stated, through a character in *Atlas Shrugged*, that "man *is* a social being, but not in the way the looters preach."[11] As social beings, we need to live in a rational social world, to bring our goals to fruition, to exchange the products of our effort, and to cooperate in a free association with one another. Our growth and creativity—our very survival—depends upon appropriate social and existential conditions that make such growth possible.[12] By extension, Rand argues that there are social practices and conditions that are inimical to our survival as *human* beings. For Rand, it is the initiation of physical force that is anathema to genuinely human existence.

Force

To fully appreciate Rand's opposition to the initiation of physical force, it is necessary to reiterate some of her basic epistemological assumptions. She believed that we have free will. The essence of our free will is our ability to raise the level of our focal awareness by an act of cognitive volition. If freedom is an aspect of consciousness, it *must* also be an aspect of human existence. There is no mind-body duality.

Rand argued that the mind cannot work under compulsion or threat. If we are to grasp reality, we cannot subordinate our perceptions and knowledge to the orders, opinions, or wishes of another. The cognitive mechanism can be hampered or destroyed, but it cannot be forced to function in a way that compromises its basic nature.[13] In *Atlas Shrugged*, Rand enunciated this principle:

> "To interpose the threat of physical destruction between a man and his perception of reality, is to negate and paralyze his means of survival; to force him to act against his own judgment, is like forcing him to act against his own sight. Whoever, to whatever purpose or extent, initiates the use of force, is a killer acting on the premise of death in a manner wider than murder: the premise of destroying a man's capacity to live. . . . Force and mind are opposites; morality ends where a gun beings." (1023)

In Rand's view, this is the basic contradiction at the root of nonobjective ethics. To impose an abstraction of the Good on our lives is to attack our cognitive and evaluative capacities, to invalidate and distort our very ability to be moral. An objective value is contextual; it must relate to an individual's life and knowledge, specific needs and distinctive goals. A moral action is a chosen action. Outside of this context, action loses its ethical import.

Intrinsicism and subjectivism each subvert the possibility of objective valuation. The religionist-intrinsicist, for instance, identifies a "higher" good and typically sanctions the use of force to compel people to accept their categorical duties. The secular-subjectivist properly denies the reality of such mystic values. But subjectivism is the credo of most contemporary collectivists, who substitute the "intersubjective" for the objective, divorcing values from their existential basis. Rand acknowledges that these opposing ethical orientations may originate with "mistaken conviction," but that ultimately, "both serve as a rationalization of power-lust and of rule by brute force, unleashing the potential dictator and disarming his victims."[14]

Rand focused on the impact that the initiation of physical force has on human cognitive efficacy. She argued that in all historical periods, people have lived by projecting their goals and taking the requisite actions to actualize them. Such efficacious action takes place in a spatiotemporal dimension. People must operate on the conviction that their goals are capable of attainment. This is necessary whether they are primitive hunters and gatherers, farmers, or industrial producers. The need for efficacy is necessary for proper functioning as a conceptual being, regardless of the mode of production. Yet, progress in production techniques requires corresponding evolution in the integrative capacity of the mind. Rand explains: "Agriculture is the first step toward civilization, because it requires a significant advance in men's conceptual development: it requires that they grasp two cardinal concepts which the perceptual, concrete-bound mentality of the hunters could not grasp fully: *time* and *savings*."[15]

Time and savings are the "stock seed" of all forms of production. Farmers save their seed to support themselves through bad harvests and to expand the scope of production. The maintenance and expansion of this productive capacity enables them to improve their material welfare and, inevitably, to trade with others. This advancement in production is marked by a further elevation of human conceptual abilities. It requires sustained cognitive effort, which some people seek to avoid. Predation, rather than production, becomes their modus operandi. Historically, such people have seized the products of others by the use of force. Protection against predation remains the fundamental social problem in human existence, and was the ultimate rationale for the establishment of tribal, feudal, and modern governing associations.[16]

Defense against the initiation of force is not merely a material necessity. By interfering with a person's material production and consumption, the initiation of force also cripples a person's cognitive efficacy. By nullifying a person's material efforts and threatening his or her body, the initiation of force achieves a corresponding nullification of the mind. It ruptures the connection between thought and action, ends and means, action and beneficiary, life and value. If our actions are not based on the judgments of our own minds, our survival is in jeopardy. And if, under the threat of force, we choose to act independently, we have also placed our survival at risk (Peikoff 1991b, 314). Force creates a lethal *cognitive* contradiction.

There is an inseparable link then, between rationality and freedom, just as there is an internal relation between faith (i.e., irrationality) and force. For Rand, "reason and freedom—are corollaries, and their relationship is reciprocal." Rand does not posit strict, one-way causality, or logical dependence here. Together, reason and freedom form an organic unity. Each is internal to or constitutive of the other. Rand views freedom as a direct consequence of reason, and reason as a natural result of freedom. Consciousness is volitional. So too, is the capacity for action. We must be able to attain our rational goals free from the interference of other people. Reason is free, conscious activity. Freedom is a condition of rational cognition. Existentially, freedom is also a necessary, though not sufficient, condition for human survival. Throughout history, "when men are rational, freedom wins; when men are free, reason wins."[17]

Ironically, Rand projects a view that is similar, at least in some respects, to the Hegelian synthesis. While Hegel's view of Reason cannot be disconnected from his exhaustive history of consciousness, there are some parallels between Rand and Hegel concerning the relationship between reason and freedom. In tracing the development of consciousness toward philosophy, or "Absolute Knowledge," Hegel ([1807] 1977) states: "In thinking, I am *free*" (120). In Hegel's philosophy, as Marcuse ([1941] 1960) explains:

> Reason presupposes freedom, the power to act in accordance with knowledge of the truth, the power to shape reality in line with its potentialities. The fulfillment of these ends belongs only to the subject who is master of his own development and who understands his own potentialities as well as those of the things around him. Freedom, in turn, presupposes reason, for it is comprehending knowledge, alone, that enables the subject to gain and to wield this power. (9)

Whereas Rand projected a corresponding connection between reason and freedom, she proposed that the relationship between irrationality and force is also reciprocal. Faith and force "are corollaries." Each is constitutive of the other. The initiation of force is a natural consequence of the reliance on faith. And the perpetuation of faith and irrationality is a direct by-product of the initiation of force. In Rand's view, "every period of history dominated by mysticism was a period of statism, of dictatorship, of tyranny."[18] Force is irrational; it subverts the very capacity to be rational. It seeks legitimation in mystic creeds and collectivist ideologies. It fragments the requirements of human life, and is a crucial foundation for the proliferation of social dualism. Each of these themes is significant to Rand's developed critique of statism and culture.

Individual Rights

Having traced the anticognitive effects of the use of physical force in human relations, Rand began her social ethics with a libertarian nonaggression principle: "No man may *initiate* the use of physical force against others."[19] This principle is not an endorsement of pacifism. Rand fully recognized that people have the moral right to defend themselves, and to use force in retaliation against aggressors. She also acknowledged that force may not necessarily entail violence, and that fraud and extortion are subspecies of force, since they involve the appropriation of a person's property under false pretenses or by coercive threats.

The nonaggression principle has immediate consequences, which Rand explored in her conception of individual rights. The notion of "rights" has had a long intellectual history, emerging from the natural-law prescriptions of antiquity and reaching its apex in Lockean political philosophy.[20] Criticism of individual rights has had an equally impressive intellectual history. From Bentham, who saw the doctrine as "nonsense upon stilts," to Marx, who saw it as a peculiar manifestation of bourgeois economy, the individual-rights perspective has been greatly disparaged. So it is not surprising that Rand's own contribution to this debate has incited several critical commentaries.[21]

Rand's approach, however, differs from the rights doctrines of classical liberalism because it is self-consciously derived from a broader theory of ethics. Whereas some libertarian thinkers, such as Rothbard, *begin* their defense of rights with an "axiom" of nonaggression, Rand's theory is the *culmination* of a full-bodied system of thought. Rand approached her philosophical totality from a variety of vantage points. Since a social existence is necessary for the flourishing of the individual, Rand's defense of rights is her consideration of this totality from the perspective of social relations. Everything she wrote about being, knowing, ethics, life, survival, reason, and the integrated nature of human beings is internal to her concept of individual rights.

In 1946, in one of her first published discussions of the subject, Rand argued: "A right is the sanction of independent action." She endorsed a traditional Lockean-Jeffersonian view that the individual has the right to life, liberty (including property), and the pursuit of happiness. Having already written *The Fountainhead* as a tribute to the human ego, Rand was insightful enough to see this last right as a celebration of the individual's ability to choose and pursue "his own private, personal, individual happiness and to work for its achievement, so long as he respects the same right in others." For Rand (1946, 5–6, 8–9), criminal activity is not an affront to "society," but an infringement on the rights of *individuals*.

In later years, Rand expanded on her earlier formulations and integrated these into the corpus of her fully developed philosophy. She argued that the concept of "rights" provides a moral bridge between individual ethics and social relations. It "preserves and protects individual morality in a social context," and is *"the means of subordinating society to moral law."*[22] Just as life provides the standard of morality, so, too, the right to life provides the basis for all other rights. For Rand, "the right to life means the right to engage in self-sustaining and self-generated action—which means: the freedom to take all the actions required by the nature of a rational being for the support, the furtherance, the fulfillment and the enjoyment of his own life."[23]

Rights have both positive and negative aspects. They sanction the freedom of voluntary, uncoerced action, even as they include the provision that each individual abstain from violating the corresponding rights of others. But Rand argued that all rights are indivisible. There is no distinction between the right to life and the right to property, just as there is no duality between mind and body. The right to life cannot be abstracted from its material manifestation. Just as the virtue of productive work derives from the value of *human* life, so too, the right to keep the products of our labor is the means by which we sustain our own lives. Property rights are a material corollary of the right to life. Since we must appropriate the products of our own efforts in order to survive, "The man who produces while others dispose of his product, is a slave" (94).

In economic terms, Marx endorsed a similar view. He argued that the capitalists' extraction of surplus value from the laborer's product is in essence an act of expropriation. Rand, however, rejected this Marxian conviction and maintained that it is the initiation of force that constitutes the fundamental means of nullifying an individual's ability and right to sustain his or her life.

At this juncture, it is valuable to consider some of the immediate implications of Rand's formulation. Den Uyl and Rasmussen (1991, 111–15) have argued that Rand's conception of rights is "ambiguous," since it is not clear if rights are "normative principles" counseling individuals in their social conduct, or if they are "meta-normative principles," which provide guidance in the creation of a constitutional order and legal system that protects the individual's "self-directedness." They recognize that for Rand, rights *include* the normative provision that an individual is obliged to respect the self-directedness of others. They argue, however, that rights are metanormative principles. To this extent, rights provide a broad framework for a legal system that applies fundamental criteria to the definition of *specific* obligations.

The evidence suggests that Rand's conception of rights is indeed, meta-normative, even though it has some obvious normative implications. If rights provide a link between individual morality and a society's law codes, clearly, they are broad principles that serve as guides for specific legal applications. It was not Rand's goal to define these applications; this is a social task that relates general abstractions to a specific context.

But in another sense, Rand's system of thought moves toward the fusion of metanormative and normative considerations. For Rand, an individual has the right to choose between life-affirming and self-destructive courses of action, *as long as the latter do not infringe on other peoples' rights to do the same.* The first provision of this formulation is just as important as the second. She made a distinction between what a person has a *right* to do, and what is the *right* course of action for a person to take in the pursuit of the ultimate value of life. The most important ramification of Rand's theory is her view that rights provide a social sanction of the individual's quest for a moral existence. Crucial to Objectivist epistemology and Objectivist ethics is the human ability to choose. Rand may show contempt for certain individual practices, but this hostility does not translate into a denial of the legal rights of the religious worshiper, the gambler, the drug pusher, the drug taker, or any person engaging in unconventional, consensual sexual activities.

Hence, individuals have the right to pursue even anti-life activities, as long as these activities do not infringe on the corresponding rights of others. In a sense, individuals have the right to pursue suicidal actions, but not homicidal ones. But this is not the whole story; for Rand refuses to disconnect her notion of individual rights from the broader ethical theory of Objectivism. Since Rand believed that certain actions were immoral, her approach sought to understand and articulate the cognitive and social roots of such behavior as a means to their transcendence. For Rand, the more interesting question was not whether or not a person had the right to poison his or her own body with lethal drugs, but *why* someone would seek to escape from reality through drugs.

In this regard, Rand's approach echoes the dimensions of the Marxian perspective. Marx opposed the concept of rights because it seemed to create a dualistic distinction between form and content. The rights doctrine endorsed the form of liberation, namely, free, conscious, human activity, by abstracting it from the content or context within which choices are made. Thus, bourgeois "freedom of conscience" merely tolerates religion, rather than liberating the human soul "from the witchery of religion."[24] For Marx, human beings created religion as the "heart of a heartless world."

They will not transcend mysticism until they abandon "*a condition which requires illusions.*"[25]

Rand would have agreed with the thrust of Marx's perspective. She viewed religious practices as not much different from drug addiction. Such practices were manifestations of a broader, anti-conceptual cultural bias, social conditions that have engendered a profound sense of alienation. Rand's exploration of this issue links her libertarian politics to a critical, secular, humanist perspective.

Rand's ability to rise above the strictures of previous rights theories is indicative of her fundamentally *dialectical* methods of inquiry. And yet, while Rand shared this integrated approach with Marxism, she departed significantly from Marx's political orientation. According to Marx, the doctrine of individual rights was based on an atomistic conception of humanity. Private property defined the limits within which someone could enjoy his own possessions, seeing "in other men not the realisation but the limitation of his own freedom." Marx wrote: "The right of man to freedom is not based on the union of man with man, but on the separation of man from man. It is the right of the limited individual who is limited to himself. . . . The right of man to property is the right to enjoy his possessions and dispose of the same arbitrarily, without regard for other men, independently from society, the right of selfishness."[26]

Whereas Rand would have proudly affirmed property as "the right of selfishness," it is obvious that Marx spoke disparagingly of this phenomenon. In this regard, Rand was actually closer to Hegel than to Marx. In Rand's philosophy, individualism has ontological, ethical, political, and psychological components. The concept of rights does not depend on the reified, atomistic individual of bourgeois economy. Rand's individualism does not view any person as a means to any end, rather, it views each person as an end in him- or herself. It holds that each of us should value nothing higher than our own autonomous thinking and judgment. The rights to life, liberty, property, and the pursuit of happiness are the social expression of the individual's quest for self-realization.[27] Since property is the material means of sustaining life, it is crucial to the actualization of the human potential.

It should be emphasized that Rand defined property broadly; it does not necessarily entail land ownership. Property is the product of a person's labors. It refers to all of the material assets he or she has created, earned, exchanged, and legitimately appropriated for survival as a rational being. Much like Hegel, who saw property in an ontological relation to the person, Rand viewed the right to property as a sanction of human ability to appropriate nature for the purposes of self-development. As Den Uyl and Rasmussen suggest, this conjunction of property and personhood is so intimate that one cannot separate the creator from the creation without obliterating the integrated view of human existence that Rand projected.[28] In Rand's conception, people have the potential to engage in empowering social activities. They can pursue their goals unarbitrarily, with reason, creativity, purpose, and pride. And while an individual's rights may be threatened by others, the Randian vision points toward a social order based on voluntary, mutually beneficial interaction. Rand's philosophy aims for a free association of persons united *by their own choice*.

Rand's concept of rights has many other specific implications that are outside the scope of this book. But it is valuable to mention some of these briefly. Rand did not believe that rights were applicable to fetuses or to nonhumans; she fervently advocated the right to abortion and opposed the animal-rights movement.[29] She supported the extension of rights into the realm of intellectual property. She defended the right of inheritance, voluntary association, incorporation, free trade, and immigration.[30] She believed that apart from some tangential public property linked to narrowly defined governmental functions, all property should be privately owned. For Rand, the notion of "public property" undermined individual responsibility, since everyone and no one was held liable for their actions. In Rand's view, privatization should be extended to the forests, the oceans, and the airwaves as a means of introducing accountability into law.[31]

Rand's doctrine of individual rights was also in stark opposition to modern welfarism. Rand believed that the entitlement mentality had manufactured all sorts of illegitimate "rights," such as the "right" to food, clothing, shelter, employment, and medical care. No one could have a right to goods or services abstracted from the process that makes them possible. Rand asks, "*At whose expense*" are such goods to be provided? To postulate that some people are rightfully entitled to goods which they have not earned, is to *force* those who have achieved legitimate values into supporting others by unchosen obligation.[32] This was not a resistance to voluntary charity, but it was a moral condemnation of the coercive redistribution that characterizes the welfare state.

Anarchy and Government

John Robbins (1974, 123, 125) argues that Rand's undiluted concept of individual rights logically entails an endorsement of anarchy. Despite her dissociation from anarchism, Rand, like Marx, incorporated some basic anarchistic elements into her political theory. Murray Rothbard, the contemporary libertarian, credited Rand with having convinced him of the theory of natural rights.[33] But he too believed that Rand's injunction against force must necessarily translate into a moral opposition to the state as such. In Rothbard's view, the state is force incarnate.[34]

While Rand would have vehemently disagreed with Robbins and Rothbard on this issue, her understanding of the nature of government does in fact sublate and preserve elements of anarchist theory. Just as Marx seems to have endorsed an anarchistic utopia in the final stages of communism, so Rand assimilated anarchistic elements in her vision of the ideal government. The reasons for this provocative parallel between Marx and Rand are strategic and methodological.

First, within their respective political movements, both thinkers had to deal with dissenting factions. Marx dealt strategically with the followers of Proudhon, Stirner, and Bakunin; Rand, with the Rothbardian anarcho-capitalists. The anarcho-capitalists were forging a new, vibrant ideology in their synthesis of Austrian-school economics, natural rights, New Left historical revisionism, and an indigenous brand of American individualist anarchism in the tradition of Tucker, Spooner, and Nock. Against such opposition, Marx and Rand developed remarkably similar theoretical responses to anarchism.

This is not to say that the Marxian and Randian critiques of anarchism are instances of mere political strategy. Their opposition to anarchism was primarily the expression of their distinctive dialectical methods. Marx had opposed the anarchists because they advocated a dualistic worldview in which the state was distinguished from civil society. They emphasized the voluntarist principles of the latter to the detriment of the former. But this anarchist approach was ahistorical. The history of capitalism, according to Marx (Grundrisse, 885), was replete with "state influences." Indeed, the state was endemic to the genesis and development of capitalism, the source of primitive accumulation, and the financial fulcrum of the business cycle. Marx maintained that capitalism had never existed in its purest form and that it would take a historical movement to dispense with both the market and the state.

In Marx's view (Capital, 1:356), within the capitalist mode of production, aspects of statism and anarchism exist side-by-side in organic conjunction. Capitalism merges "anarchy in the social division of labour and despotism in that of the workshop" where these principles "are mutual conditions the one of the other." Socialism will resolve the conflict by transcending both anarchy and despotism, by subjecting the social production process to conscious human control, and by freeing the worker from the exploitation of capital. Paul Thomas observes that for Marx, statism and anarchism, "like blind obedience and blind destruction—have in common a certain specific form of false consciousness. . . . [They] are opposite sides of the same idolatrous coin."[35]

While the content of Rand's critique of anarchism differs considerably from that of Marx's, the *form* of her analysis is just as dialectical. It is for this reason perhaps that Rand (1971T) had much greater respect for Marxists than she did for anarchists. She adamantly opposed the attempts of some libertarians who sought to conjoin her theories with anarchist principles and make her a "Marcuse" of the right. Rand believed that anarcho-capitalism had a much closer affinity with the outer fringes of the collectivist movement than with her own Objectivist philosophy.[36] She argued that she was not primarily an advocate of capitalism or egoism. She maintained that her endorsement of the supremacy of reason provided the necessary epistemological basis for egoism in ethics and capitalism in politics. This was a hierarchy that could not be reversed. Politics was the final moment of a huge philosophical totality. Socially too, it was the product of a country's dominant intellectual trends (1089). The anarcho-capitalists had attempted to invert this structure, and to establish a social system without any concern for historical reality or cultural context.

In the Objectivist view,[37] these libertarian anarchists applied the principle of competition to the sphere of government. They were free-market advocates who sought to end the coercive monopoly of the state, and to institute a system of decentralized governing units. Such agencies would compete for the provision of defense and legal services, within the broad context of a universally accepted Libertarian Law Code.[38] Rothbard maintained that such a Law Code would enshrine the basic "axiom" of self-ownership and nonaggression. In a genuinely voluntarist world order, this Law Code would sanction a plethora of alternative lifestyles. Some communities would opt for collectivistic communes; others would be individualistic. Some would maintain religious values; others would be oriented toward secular humanism. Some would submit to voluntary racial separatism and segregation; others would promote racial integration. For Rothbard, variations in culture and individual moral codes are irrelevant to the establishment of a libertarian society.[39] His libertarian ethos seeks to protect the peaceful coexistence of all value systems within any cultural context.

Rand opposed the anarcho-capitalist attempt to fracture the intimate relationship between personal morality and social ethics. But she also opposed the anarchists because they had embraced a dualistic distinction between state and market. In this regard, anarcho-capitalism was the same as totalitarian statism. Both the anarchists and the statists saw fundamental and irreconcilable antagonism between the state and the market. The statists attempted to resolve the tension between these two spheres by placing a monistic emphasis on the state to the detriment of the market; the anarchists attempted to resolve this tension by placing a similarly monistic emphasis on the market to the detriment of the state. In the statist resolution, the state absorbs the market (or "civil society") completely. In the anarchist resolution, the market absorbs the state, providing for all "public" goods, such as defense, and judicial services.

For Rand, this anarchist construction was "a naive floating abstraction," a rationalist device for implementing a disjointed notion of liberty without the requisite foundations.[40] Anarchists were guilty of committing the "fallacy of the frozen abstraction." They observed that established states had always initiated the use of force and equated this historically specific model with the concept of government as such. They abstracted and reified historical instances and failed to grasp the true nature of government because they presumed that all governments must necessarily violate individual rights.[41] In Rand's view, a free society could not survive without the presence of crucial moral, cultural, and psycho-epistemological preconditions, all of which are integrated and organically linked. Rand writes:

> Accepting the basic premise of modern statists—who see no difference between the functions of government and the functions of industry, between force and production, and who advocate government ownership of business—the proponents of "competing governments" take the other side of the same coin and declare that since competition is so beneficial to business, it should also be applied to government.[42]

For Rand, such a competition in the retaliatory use of force would spell practical disaster. And yet the evidence suggests that Rand's own view of the nature of government incorporates significant anarchistic elements that cannot be ignored.

Rand's political theory is highly abstract. Like her ethical system, Rand's politics was geared toward defining broad principles that needed to be adapted to concrete circumstances. Consequently, one will not find in

Rand's political theory any extensive, specialized discussions of particular legal applications, constitutional principles, or legislative procedures. Nor can one find any kind words for democracy in Rand's writings, since she believed that a majoritarian system would degenerate into mob rule in the absence of legally enforced rights, republican constraints, and a system of checks and balances (Peikoff 1991b, 368). Her definition of government is standardized Weberism, since she views it as an agency established within a certain geographical area, holding a monopoly on the power to enforce rules of social conduct.

However, Rand's political theory is distinct in its emphasis on a nondualistic conception of government, one that is neither anarchistic nor statist in its orientation. Rand argued: "*Government is the means of placing the retaliatory use of physical force under objective control*—i.e., under objectively defined laws."[43] Individuals necessarily delegate their right of self-defense to such an agency for the purposes of maintaining the orderly rule of law. In Rand's view, government has a highly limited scope. Its proper functions are to provide police, armed services, and law courts for the protection of individual rights and the adjudication of disputes (107–12). No government has the right to move beyond these strictures. One can presume that any functions that transcend these narrow limits must necessarily violate individual rights, which government was designed to protect.

This characterization suggests that no existing government on earth has moral legitimacy, since, to varying degrees, each violates its citizens' rights. And yet practically speaking, Rand did view certain governments as morally superior to others. She believed that since its inception, the United States was the only moral society in human history, despite how its evolution had progressively undermined its original libertarian principles. In the contemporary world, Rand was most apt to condemn those governments that had sustained one-party rule, executions without trial, punishment for political offenses, nationalization and expropriation of private property, and censorship.[44]

But it must be emphasized that Rand's vision of a genuinely moral government is considerably different from all established institutions in political history. In league with her own injunction against the initiation of force, Rand opposed such standard government practices as taxation and the draft. She viewed taxation as theft, the coercive expropriation of justly acquired property. She saw conscription as a form of slavery.[45] Her ideal government would retain a monopoly on the coercive use of force, but this monopoly itself would be constituted by a voluntary association of citizens who contributed freely toward the maintenance of appropriate government functions. Rand offered several blueprints for such a system, including generalized charges on government-enforced contracts, and a lottery system of financing.[46]

What is most clear is that Rand viewed government as a necessary component of any social system. She argued: "A social system is a set of moral-political-economic principles embodied in a society's laws, institutions, and government." These principles are usually not articulated, but they determine the social relationships and terms of association within a specific geographical area.[47] The fundamental issue faced by every social system is its orientation toward individual rights. In Rand's view, capitalism is the only social system that fully recognizes the rights of the individual. It is the only social system consonant with the rational nature of human beings.

The question remains, however, that if "government" is a concept, then presumably, like other concepts, it must have existential referents. But if Rand's ideal is anticipatory, then how can she claim any validity for such a concept when it has *no* legitimate past or current referents?[48] In actuality, Rand created an "ideal-type" by abstracting liberal referents from historical states, while disregarding nonliberal factors that have been internal to every state in history. For Rand, such concepts as "government" and "capitalism" are socially transformative; their "ideal" character is latent in currently distorted social forms.

Thus, what is most striking about Rand's conception of government is its ahistorical character. Despite Rand's affection for the American, republican form of government, her own vision is less a description of historical reality than it is the projection of an ideal that has yet to be realized. Like capitalism, Rand's voluntary political association remains an *unknown* ideal.

Capitalism

Rand's defense of capitalism is similar in form to her defense of "selfishness." In fact, Rand titled her collection of essays in social theory, *Capitalism: The Unknown Ideal*, for much the same reasons that she titled her collection of essays on morality, *The Virtue of Selfishness: A New Concept of Egoism*. Both "capitalism" and "selfishness" have had such a negative conceptual history that Rand needed to reclaim these concepts and to recast them in a new and nondualistic framework. Branden remarks that he had told Rand of his preference for the word "libertarianism" as an alternative to "capitalism," since the latter term had been coined by anticapitalists.[49] For Branden, "libertarianism" signified a broader, philosophical characterization and addressed the issues of social, political *and* economic freedom (Branden 1978, 60). But Rand refused to renounce the concept of "capitalism," just as she rejected any attempt to couch her ethos of rational selfishness in more neutral terms.

In addition to such nominal problems, Rand was faced with the fact that her defense of "capitalism" differed considerably from other theoretical justifications. Rand's approach is not Weberian; she did not view capitalism as an expression of the Protestant work ethic. Nor did she view capitalism as compatible with Roman Catholicism or any other form of religion.[50] Though she accepted the empirical and theoretical arguments of Austrian-school economists who see the market as the most efficient and productive mechanism in history, she refused to defend capitalism on purely utilitarian grounds.[51] And while Rand celebrates the record of economic growth under Western capitalism, she believes that the historical reality diverged radically from a pure, unadulterated laissez-faire system. While the nineteenth-century United States best approximated this system, its progress was severely undermined by massive government intervention in the areas of finance and banking, and in the bolstering of monopolies through land grants and industrial privileges. Marx himself had viewed this nineteenth-century system as only an approximation of full capitalism, since it was "adulterated and amalgamated with survivals of former economic conditions" (*Capital*, 3:175). For Rand, as for most Marxists, this "mixed" system reached its twentieth-century climax in the neofascist and corporativist policies of the U.S. welfare-warfare state.

Rand argued that the underlying reason for this failure to achieve systemic purity was moral and cultural. Capitalism as a social system was an implicit by-product of an Aristotelian philosophical base, one that celebrated the rational, the secular, and the egoistic. And yet capitalism was historically distorted because the cultures within which it evolved had not fully emerged from the influence of mysticism, altruism, and collectivism.[52] Rand saw capitalism and altruism as "philosophical opposites" that could not "co-exist in the same man or in the same society."[53] The modern age was fractured by an "inner contradiction" because it tried to combine the concept of eudaemonic man with the notion that human beings were sacrificial animals.[54] It was for this reason that Rand was extremely apprehensive about the introduction of capitalist markets into primitive cultures. She argued that capitalism required a predominantly rational and secular orientation, and that industrialization could not "be grafted onto superstitious irrationality" without massive distortion in the evolving structure of production.[55] Though the United States achieved the greatest progress because it was the most secular Western country, it too had preserved significant elements of altruism and collectivism in its cultural base. And it was paying the price.

Curiously, Rand spoke in terms of a cultural and philosophical "base." This view differs considerably from the Marxist formulation, which sees culture and philosophy as components of a social "superstructure," a by-product of a *material* "base." These opposed characterizations have disparate consequences for both the theory of history and the nature of social revolution; however, what must be explored at this stage is Rand's understanding of capitalism as an *unknown ideal*. In Rand's view, the nature of capitalism is so inherently radical that its historical, philosophical, and cultural implications have yet to be fully comprehended. Rand unabashedly proclaims that Objectivists "are *radicals for capitalism* . . . fighting for that philosophical base which capitalism did not have and without which it was doomed to perish."[56] Once again, Rand's project is geared toward articulation. She aimed to articulate those premises which underlie the daily practices and institutions of a historically emergent but not yet fully realized social system.

Following her literary methods, Rand seems to have extracted and emphasized those principles which, she believed, distinguish capitalist society from all previous social formations. She began with the real concrete circumstances of the historically mixed system, breaking down its complexity into mental units. She constituted her vision of capitalism on the basis of such abstraction, having isolated and identified those precepts which are *essential* to its systemic nature. In this way, she eliminated the accidental and the contingent in order to focus instead on the philosophical ideals of the capitalist revolution. Such a revolution was incomplete because its principles had never been fully articulated and implemented. Rand viewed her own project as the first successful attempt to articulate the *moral* nature of the capitalist system, *ideally understood*, thus making possible its historical fulfillment.

Without access to all of Rand's journals, it is difficult to ascertain the point at which she actually began to defend capitalism as part of her developing philosophical synthesis. It seems clear that by the time she had published *The Fountainhead*, her political convictions were fully formed. In the 1930s and 1940s, she enjoyed cordial relationships with several individualist and free-market thinkers, including Ruth Alexander, Henry Hazlitt, Rose Wilder Lane, Ludwig von Mises, Albert Jay Nock, and Isabel Paterson. Stephen Cox suggests that it was Paterson who introduced Rand to most of the individualist works in economics, philosophy, history, and politics. In later years, Rand favorably reviewed Paterson's *God of the Machine* for N.B.I.'s book service. Despite their eventual estrangement, it was clear that Rand felt a certain debt of gratitude for Paterson's tutelage.[57]

Another important intellectual influence on Rand's developing free-market perspective was Mises, the father of the modern Austrian school of economics. Mises had taught such economists as the Nobel laureate, F. A. Hayek, the distinguished Israel Kirzner, and the libertarian anarchist, Murray Rothbard (B. Branden 1986, 163–67, 188–89). Later, it was through Rand's lectures and writings, and through the Nathaniel Branden Institute (N.B.I.) and the N.B.I. Book Club, that Mises's works began to enjoy a wider and more popular audience.

Though Rand criticized Mises and other Austrians for their "Benthamite" utilitarianism, she had largely accepted their extensive demonstrations of the superiority of markets (1961T). Throughout Objectivist literature, there are many Austrian-flavored discussions of the gold standard, business cycles, monopolies, labor unions, public education, and child labor.[58] Like the Austrians, Rand rejected the positivistic, mechanistic, and statistical methods of mainstream economics. And while she acknowledged competition as a natural by-product of the market process, she repudiated the standard neoclassical models of "perfect competition" as a vestige of rationalist, Platonic Idealism with no relevance to the real world.[59]

For Rand, while the Austrians had provided a profoundly important theoretical, *economic* defense of the free market, they had failed to articulate an appropriate moral base for the capitalist system they championed. Peikoff (1983T, lecture 8) argues, for instance, that Mises, like most Austrians, had rejected socialism because it did not actualize the alleged goals of its practitioners. This method of criticizing socialism on the basis of its internal inconsistencies was insufficient. One cannot simply reject socialism or accept capitalism based on rationalist polemics or purely empirical evidence. Such approaches, though effective in certain contexts, could not bypass the need for a principled defense of the moral superiority of capitalism.

In Rand's view, most social theorists were guilty of reification. Political economists in particular had observed that people were producing goods and services, and trading with one another. They assumed that human beings "had always done so and always would." They saw these facts of economic life as "given, requiring no further consideration," and merely addressed themselves "to the problem of how to devise the best way for the 'community,' to dispose of human effort." Most contemporary theorists approached the study of economics on the macrolevel, without ever focusing on the individuals that constituted the social whole. Like their counterparts in sociology, they endorsed a conception of humanity as an undifferentiated, aggregated collective. This was a kind of methodological "tribalism" that began the study of society without defining the nature of the entities involved in social practices and institutions. Reiterating her objection to this oversocialized conception, Rand writes: "A great deal may be learned about society by studying man; but this process cannot be reversed: nothing can be learned about man by studying society—by studying the interrelationships of entities one has never identified or defined."[60]

It is ironic that Marx and Engels leveled a similar, though opposite, charge against those liberal thinkers who viewed capitalism as a logical derivative of the "eternal laws of nature and of reason."[61] The "Robinsonades," as Marx called them, dissolve society "into a world of atomistic, mutually hostile individuals," who are self-interested and isolated from one another.[62] Whether he was commenting on Locke or Smith, Marx (*Grundrisse*, 83) argued that the bourgeois vision of civil society as "natural" and "normal" was typical of each epoch in its quest for transhistorical legitimacy. Marx condemned this vision as a product of "vulgar economy" and "bourgeois narrow-mindedness" to counter the liberal defense "in doctrinaire fashion" of those categories of explanation which were historically specific to the capitalist mode of production.[63]

For Marx, as for Rand, political economists expressed capitalist social relations as a given, without grasping the conditions that made them possible. In Rand's view, such an approach was one-dimensional and abstract. It obscured any understanding of human species identity and failed to grasp either the nature of capitalism, or the philosophical, psychoepistemological, moral, cultural, and social conditions that make capitalism possible.

This parallel between Rand and Marx, however, cannot erase their very different assessments of the capitalist system. One of the most important distinctions between Rand and Marx lies in their alternative conceptions of the relationship between capitalism and dualism. Since I have described Rand as a nondualistic, dialectical thinker, it is extremely valuable to consider her response to the Marxian view that capitalism, as such, engenders an array of dualistic tensions in social life that only socialism can resolve.

Marx views capitalism as a historical and organic totality, one that generates a "dualism between individual life and species-life, between the life of civil society and political life" (*Jewish Question*, 225, 231). According to Marx, the capitalist labor process stunts the development of integrated human being. Such fragmentation is endemic to capitalist social relations. Whereas in previous social formations, the laborer unites within himself multiple functions, the development of capitalism leads to a corresponding differentiation in the relations of production. The division of labor is the turning point. Products are no longer the result of individual labor; they are social products produced by the cooperation and combination of many laborers, each of whom performs a different task (*Capital*, 1:508).

Previously combined branches of production become separated, even as each branch internally differentiates its own operations (*Surplus-Value*, 3:288–89). In capitalist commodity production, "*separation* appears as the normal relation" (1:409). The manufacturing process develops the natural endowments of the laborer in a one-dimensional manner. The laborer becomes a perfectionist in his limited tasks and one-sided specialties (*Capital*, 1:363).

The division constitutes and is constituted by a dual dynamic. First, according to Marx, it cripples the laborer by pitting the functions of his body against the functions of his mind. The organic unity of body and mind is fractured, as the laborer's particularized, mechanical abilities are developed to the detriment of his cognitive, creative abilities. Second, it expresses the basic alienation of the laborer who becomes estranged from the product of his labor as he is forced to sell that product, and his own labor-power as a product, on the market.

The market, itself, exists by virtue of the distinction between the product and the producer. The laborer's product becomes externalized and objectified. The early Marx focused on this process as one "of self-sacrifice" and "mortification" (*Manuscripts*, 108). The later Marx stressed that alienated labor-power is the basis of commodity exchange. On the market, dualism takes the form of a division between purchase and sale or the exchange of commodities for money, and the exchange of money for commodities (*Grundrisse*, 148, 146). Money, itself, spontaneously emergent in precapitalist society, comes to dominate bourgeois life.

Marx recognized that the evolution of exchange is a chief means for the

individuation of human society. "It makes the herd-like existence superfluous and dissolves it" (496). But its progressive character is subverted because
capitalism robs people of the ability to consciously plan their own fate. The
emergence of more substantive notions of human freedom is coupled with
"the most complete suspension of all individual freedom, and the most
complete subjugation of individuality under social conditions which assume
the form of objective powers, even of overpowering objects—of things
independent of the relations among individuals themselves" (652).

Rand proceeded upon entirely different assumptions. She celebrated the
division of labor and saw the exchange of knowledge and goods as two of
the most important values of human social existence.[64] In Rand's view,
specialization of labor does not symbolize fragmentation; it is how a laborer
develops his particularized efficacy through the mastery of certain skills and
practices. What makes capitalism distinct from all previous systems is its
expansion of the avenues for human social advancement. Capitalism liber-
ates the laborer from all former institutional constraints on his mobility. No
laborer is compelled to remain frozen in a guilded caste. The laborer can
rise as high as his ambition and knowledge will take him, enabling him to
pursue his chosen goals and to actualize his unique potentialities without
the interference of religious or political authorities.

Rand's defense of capitalism traces the moral meaning of every essential
market category, including trade, money, the law of supply and demand,
and the objective value structure which the system embodies. She argued:
"*Capitalism is a social system based on the recognition of individual rights,
including property rights, in which all property is privately owned.*"[65] According
to Rand, the market is a dynamic, continuous, upward process "that
demands the best (the most rational) of every man and rewards him
accordingly." Trade—the voluntary exchange of value for value—is the
central form of social relation under capitalism. Such trade is founded on a
delineation of rights that bars the initiation of physical force in human relationships.

One of the most important categories of capitalist economy is money.
The predominant role of money in market society is not a fact that Rand
laments. As one of her characters in *Atlas Shrugged* explains:

> "Money is a tool of exchange. . . . Money rests on the axiom that
> every man is the owner of his mind and his effort. Money allows no
> power to prescribe the value of your effort except the voluntary
> choice of the man who is willing to trade you his effort in return.

. . . Money permits no deals except those to mutual benefit by the
unforced judgment of the traders. . . . Money is your means of
survival. . . . Money is so noble a medium that it does not compete
with guns and it does not make terms with brutality. . . . Money is
the root of all good. . . . When money ceases to be the tool by
which men deal with one another, then men become the tools of
men. Blood, whips and guns—or dollars. Take your choice—there is
no other—and your time is running out." (410)

In this passage, Rand does not deny that money can be used in a distorted
or corrupted fashion.[66] But it must be remembered that Rand here is
describing money within the context of capitalism, the unknown ideal. The
current mixed system features an interpenetration of statist and market
categories, such that it becomes very difficult to distinguish between the
genuine money-makers and the money-appropriators, between those who
trade legitimate values and those who use money as a tool of expropriation.

In Rand's conception of the free market, however, she reserves for the
dollar sign the same reverence that Christians project in the sign of the
cross. It is interesting that in the above passage, Rand implies an identity
between reason and money. She states that "money is your means of
survival," recalling her epistemological conviction that *reason* is one's means
of survival. While Rand emphasizes that money is a material means for
human sustenance, she is also tracing a much more profound connection
between money and the rational process, which underlies its accumulation
and use. For Rand, money "is a frozen form of productive energy," and
cannot be severed from the rational activities that make its existence possible.[67]

The role of money in capitalist economy is crucial, in Rand's view,
because it is both a tool of exchange and a tool of savings, enabling people
to delay their own consumption, and to purchase time for all future
production. While consumption is the final cause of the production process,
savings is its efficient cause. Savings represent future goods that have yet to
be produced and consumed. The dynamism of the process is driven by the
law of supply and demand. This economic law embodies a normative
principle since it involves the same people in two different, though inseparable capacities, that of producer and consumer. While a producer can support
a limited number of nonproducers, Rand argued: *"The man who consumes
without producing is a parasite, whether he is a welfare recipient or a rich
playboy."*[68]

Interestingly, Rand enunciated a principle that Marx would have accepted in starkly different terms. For Marx, capitalist "exploitation" is a direct outgrowth of the separation of the product from the producer. In the production process, the laborer endows the product with its value and receives in return only enough for his or her own subsistence. The extraction of surplus value makes possible capitalist accumulation. But it is symptomatic of a condition in which the capitalist consumes value without producing it. In this regard, Marx views the capitalist qua capitalist as a parasite on the production process.

Paradoxically, Rand's criticism of the Marxian doctrine of exploitation illustrates her own endorsement of a form of the labor theory of value. Rand presents a caricature of the classical labor theory, when she argues that in Marx's view, "the material tools of production" (that is, "machines"), determine thinking, and that it is "muscular labor" which "is the source of wealth" (New Intellectual, 33). As we have seen, Marx's conception of human labor was far richer than Rand presumed. Nevertheless, Rand criticized Marx for obscuring the intellectual praxis at the foundation of production. For Rand, an innovation, an idea, is the creative force behind the production of material values. The implementation of creative ideas are a permanent benefit to the day laborer, much more valuable than the hourly expense of merely physical work that extends no further than the range of the immediate productive process.

Rand presented a view of the capitalist as creator, inventor, and entrepreneur.[69] It is the creator who stands at the top of the intellectual pyramid of ability, contributing "the most to all those below him," but receiving far less in material payment than his or her innovations make possible. In Rand's view, even though day laborers contribute their energy to the production process, they would starve outside the wider social context because they depend for their employment on the innovations introduced by those above them. Even the machines that laborers use are "the frozen form of a living intelligence," expanding the potential of the laborers' lives by raising their productivity (Atlas Shrugged, 1064–65).

Contrary to Rand's assumptions, Marx did not endorse a vulgar version of the labor theory of value. Marx postulates all sorts of complex labor-time derivatives, such that the labor-time expended by a skilled worker, even by a capitalist in his capacity as a skilled innovator, is a multiple of simple labor-time. And for Marx, it is obvious that the material forces, the "machines" as Rand puts it, do not strictly determine consciousness. In Marx's view, "Nature builds no machines, no locomotives, railways, electric telegraphs, self-acting mules, etc. These are products of human industry; natural material transformed into organs of the human will over nature, or of human participation in nature. They are *organs of the human brain, created by the human hand*; the power of knowledge, objectified" (*Grundrisse*, 706).

Rand grossly distorted the mature Marxian perspective. But in contrast to Marx, she offered a more sophisticated view of the creative process. As I have suggested in previous chapters, Rand saw creativity as a constellation of rational and emotional, conscious and subconscious, articulated and tacit elements that cannot be quantified as complex multiples of simple labor-time. Creativity is the lifeblood of human action. It is the very fuel of the capitalist system. It is an expression of the individual's integrated nature as a rational being, and it is the source of values for human consumption and enjoyment. Indeed, as Barry (1983, 109) remarks, there are times in which Rand seems so awestruck by the creative qualities of the innovator and the entrepreneur that she occasionally "slips into a crude intentionalist explanation of the free economy; as if it were the virtues of capitalists that produced the system." This, however, is not Rand's view, but it does underscore Rand's conviction that capitalism as a social system *rewards* such virtues, raising people to a higher standard of living, and challenging them to greater knowledge and greater achievement. Such a system enriches the efficacious, self-esteeming individual. It promotes the mastery of particular skills, even as it beckons the laborer to expand his or her capacities and earn the values that sustain life.

This creativity-driven conception of the capitalist production process is also manifested in Rand's discussion of the objective value structure that the system embodies. She argued that market trade is never disconnected from the essential question of objective value theory: "of value to whom and for what?" Economically, the value of an individual's work is determined by the voluntary consent of those who choose to exchange their work or products in return. Prospective participants evaluate the exchange on the basis of those values which they seek for their own benefit. There is an intimate connection here between the actor and the action, such that the actor benefits from the exchange. Hence, Rand's ethical egoism finds social expression in the simple act of trading value for value, as evaluated by each actor within his or her own specific context.

But Rand emphasized that the market itself cannot be separated from the culture in which it functions. The market can perpetuate a kind of duality between "philosophically objective values" and "socially objective values." The market value of a product reflects the latter. A "socially objective value," in Rand's view, is "the sum of the individual judgments of all the men involved in trade at a given time, the sum of what *they* valued, each in the context of his own life."[70] Hence, if people sought to purchase cocaine for their own enjoyment, the "socially objective" market value would be reflected in the relative supply and demand for that product. But Rand argues that it is reality that will serve as the "ultimate arbiter" of human decisions on the market. For if people en masse choose to purchase narcotics within the context of their own goals, they will ultimately pay the price of their irrationality. While capitalism can be accused of leaving people free to indulge their irrational whims, such "whim-worship" cannot be pursued with impunity. In Rand's view, the market *localizes* the self-destructive implications of irrational action. Rather than rewarding irrationality, capitalism leaves to individuals the choices that only they must make.

The market process, however, does make possible the discovery of "philosophically objective values." Rand maintains that such a value is "estimated from the standpoint of the best possible to man, i.e., by the criterion of the most rational mind possessing the greatest knowledge, in a given category, in a given period, and in a defined context."[71] Since nothing is a value-in-itself, and since values are not the result of subjective fancy, the free market will tend to enrich those individuals who see the wider context in the long run, and who introduce radical innovations that benefit human life.

This distinction between the socially and the philosophically objective focuses attention on Rand's conviction that no economic system can be extracted from the wider cultural totality within which it functions. An *unimpeded* market that rewards astrologers, coke dealers, and prostitutes is not Rand's goal. A culture that enriches such self-destructive behavior has a profoundly anti-conceptual, anti-life orientation. No social system on earth could survive such irrationality. *This* is why Rand argues that self-esteem is a precondition of freedom. *This* is why Rand refuses to abstract her political theory from its foundations in ontology, epistemology, psychology, and ethics. *This* is why Rand sees an inseparable relation between the personal and the political, between reason and freedom.

In Rand's view, capitalism is the only social system that makes possible a triumph over social fragmentation. Dualism is as old as recorded history. The bifurcation of mind and body, the moral and the practical, the spiritual and the material predates capitalism by thousands of years. Capitalism is the first social system in history that points toward a genuine integration of human being. It makes the actor the beneficiary of his actions. It spiritualizes the secular and materially rewards the creative synthesis of innovative rationality. *This* is capitalism, ideally understood. But it is also the radical potential that lies dormant in a contemporary social system that mixes elements of freedom and unfreedom. For even in this unstable mixture, capitalist principles have exhibited their revolutionary and progressive character.

Part Three

The Radical Rand

11 Relations of Power

The synthesis of theory and practice has been one of the most significant themes in the history of Russian thought. Nearly every great Russian writer embraced a critical praxis as the central, motivating task of philosophy. Theoretical contemplation was considered incomplete and one-dimensional; it required consummation in the quest for truth-justice (*iskaniye pravdy*). This cultural predisposition toward political criticism and action provided fertile ground for the implantation of Marx's revolutionary doctrine, encapsulated in the credo: "The philosophers have only *interpreted* the world in various ways; the point is to *change* it" ([1845] 1967, 401–2).

Ayn Rand gave full expression to this radical impulse in Russian thought. She recognized that philosophical contemplation was insufficient. Her initial theoretical musings emerged as a response to the dualities she confronted in the Russia of her youth. Her positive formulations constituted a critical revolt against Russian religious mysticism and communist politics. Just as Marx's dialectical method was "in its essence critical and revolutionary,"[1] Rand's dialectical sensibility led her toward a comparable, radical resolution. But Rand's project was neither theocratic nor communist in its political implications; it was profoundly secular, humanistic, and libertarian.

Like her dialectical forebears, Rand refused to disconnect any part from the totality that gave it meaning. Rand's critical method recognized the fundamental relatedness of all social phenomena. She adamantly opposed reification in social inquiry. Where some attempted to universalize a historically specific concrete, Rand saw "frozen abstractions." Where others asserted certain premises as true and without need of proof, Rand saw "frozen absolutes" and "false axioms." Where still others sought to combine two or more issues that needed to be analyzed and considered separately, Rand saw "package-dealing." She rejected the modern tendency to "think in a square," the contemporary disposition to accept a constricted, narrow definition of a social problem without understanding the principles underlying the issue, or the various links between issues.[2] Everywhere Rand looked, she attempted to identify the principles that unite seemingly separate and fragmented spheres of human existence. She observed facts, identified the essential issues, integrated the data from diverse areas of inquiry, and articulated the basic principles at work.[3] Her dialectical methods uncovered startling connections between economics, psychology, sex, art, politics, and ideology.

In her political theory, Rand suggests that the initiation of force is a crucial component in the genesis of social dualism. Force creates a lethal contradiction between the mind and reality, thought and action. But in Rand's view, just as freedom and reason presupposed each other, so too do force and faith. Faith (that is, irrationality, unreason) produces the same lethal contradiction between the mind and reality, thought and action. Force and faith, like dictatorship and determinism, "are reciprocally reinforcing corollaries." In Rand's view, enslavement requires an attack on the validity of human volition. Those who see reason as impotent necessarily accept the rule of force in its stead.[4] For Rand, while the initiation of force nullifies an individual's cognitive capacity, human inefficacy is both the precondition and by-product of sustained coercive action. Though Rand recognizes the initiation of force as the only existential practice that can violate rights, she focuses just as much attention on the cognitive practices and conditions that subvert individual autonomy and predispose us to accept our own subjugation.

Rand's assault on contemporary statist relations of power focuses attention on these theoretical and existential components. Her social criticism follows in the footsteps of her formal philosophy by repudiating dualism in all of its cultural incarnations. Her analysis can be comprehended on three distinct levels. While it is possible to abstract and isolate these various aspects, it must be understood that they are interrelated constituents of a single totality.

Diagram 1. Ayn Rand's Multilevel Analysis of Power Relations

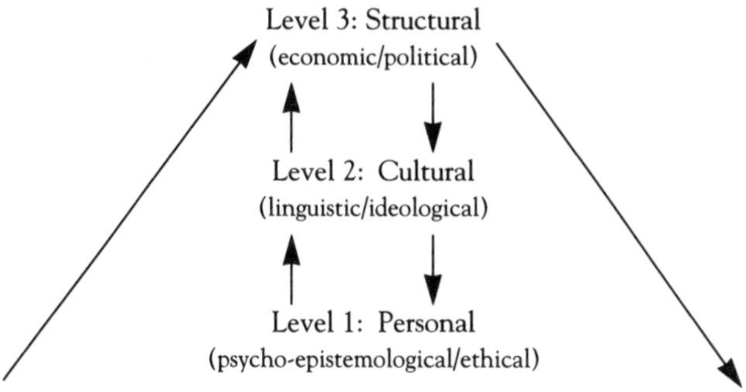

Level 3: Structural
(economic/political)

Level 2: Cultural
(linguistic/ideological)

Level 1: Personal
(psycho-epistemological/ethical)

On Level 1, Rand examined relations of power between persons. She focused on the psycho-epistemological and ethical principles at work in exploitative interpersonal relations. The psycho-epistemic and normative aspects are two, coextensive vantage points on the same phenomenon. These aspects are so closely related that they constitute a double-edged sword. On this first level of analysis, Rand comprehended the significance of the master-slave duality and the "sanction of the victim." Within this context, important constructs are integrated into the Objectivist corpus, including "pseudo-self-esteem," "social metaphysics," and "alienation."

On Level 2, Rand considered many of these distortions in social interaction as by-products and reflections of cultural practices. She argued that modern intellectuals have mounted an assault on the integrity of concepts and language that has had the effect of ideologically legitimating social, political, and economic exploitation. She traced the impact of such conceptual and linguistic subversion on every area of culture, including art, literature, music, education, religion, sex, and race.

On Level 3, Rand reviewed exploitative social relations within the structural context of statist interventionism.[5] The relations of power at this level are mediated through a variety of economic and political structures and institutional processes. Rand examined the essential role of the predatory state in creating conditions of economic dislocation, class (or intergroup) struggle, social fragmentation, and brutality.

Each of these three levels of analysis seeks to uncover another facet of modern statist power relations. Each is internally related to and implicit in the others. Each level incorporates personal, cultural, and structural dimensions. Each level is a relation between real people. Thus:

- The codependency relationship (master and slave) of Level 1 is reproduced on the cultural and structural levels.
- The distortion of concepts and language (Level 2) provides ideological
  legitimation for the codependency relationship (Level 1) and for the
  structural context within which it occurs (Level 3).
- The sustenance of the predatory state (Level 3) requires individuals
  whose autonomy has been fundamentally thwarted (Level 1) and whose
  conceptual and linguistic practices have been distorted (Level 2).

What must be emphasized is that for Rand, the goal of all social analysis
is emancipation. In each aspect of her developed critique, change and
transcendence beckon. Rand proudly declared that she was a philosophical
"innovator" and a "radical" for capitalism, with everything that this implied.
She wore these labels as terms "of distinction . . . of honor, rather than
something to hide or apologize for" (Rand, 1964b, 15). In keeping with her
revolutionary fervor, she sought to uncover the "fundamental" roots of
contemporary social problems, "boldly proclaiming a full, consistent, and
radical alternative" to the status quo.[6]

Master and Slave

As we have seen, *The Fountainhead* provided Rand with the first opportunity
to present a complex psychological portrait of those individuals whom she
described as "second-handers." As she puts it, speaking through Roark:
"The second-hander acts, but the source of his actions is scattered in every
other living person" (607). The second-hander seeks fame and admiration,
a greatness in the eyes of others. The second-hander's existence is partial,
incomplete, and fundamentally dependent on those who possess self-suffic-
ing egos. Whereas creators necessarily think and work alone, second-
handers live through other people. They must rob, exploit, and rule others
upon whom their sustenance depends. As parasites of both body and mind,
they exist "through the persons of others" (606–7, 683). In attempting to
rule others, they subjugate their victims by keeping them on a spiritual
leash. But "a leash is only a rope with a noose at both ends." Rand
recognized that exploitation ultimately destroyed both the slave *and* the
master, both the victim *and* the executioner (683, 661).

At this stage in her intellectual development, Rand did not fully recognize the extent to which the creators participated in their own destruction. She argued that the second-hander's attempt to exploit the creator required a legitimating ideology. As Toohey observes, those who seek to rule the creators don't "need a whip." The creators will often provide their own "and ask to be whipped" (636). Such self-subjugation was achieved through psychological manipulation. Roark exclaims: "When the first creator invented the wheel, the first second-hander responded. He invented altruism" (684).

The creed of self-sacrifice provided the second-hander with a veneer of moral action. But Rand warns us, "Don't bother to examine a folly—ask yourself only what it accomplishes." While this dictum is uttered by Toohey, one of Rand's grand-villains, it expresses Rand's own views about the political utility of certain culturally accepted ethical doctrines. Toohey tells Keating, one of his victims:

> "Every system of ethics that preached sacrifice grew into a world power and ruled millions of men. Of course, you must dress it up. You must tell people that they'll achieve a superior kind of happiness by giving up everything that makes them happy. You don't have to be too clear about it. Use big vague words. 'Universal Harmony'— 'Eternal Spirit'—'Divine Purpose'—'Nirvana'—'Paradise'—'Racial Supremacy'—'The Dictatorship of the Proletariat.' . . . It stands to reason that where there's sacrifice, there's someone collecting sacrificial offerings. Where there's service, there's someone being served. The man who speaks to you of sacrifice, speaks of slaves and masters. And intends to be the master."[7]

What is crucial about this statement is Rand's grasp of altruism as a tool of exploitation used by political and religious forces alike. She conflated several images that are ordinarily kept separate and distinct: the religious fundamentalist, the Nazi racist, and the Bolshevik agitator. Each of these historical figures was involved in a similar game of spiritual or material exploitation. Each used the language of sacrifice to a "higher" purpose. Altruism destroys creators by duping them into putting their virtues at the service of their destroyers. Altruism institutionalizes what Rand would later call, the "sanction of the victim."[8]

The most subversive political implication of *Atlas Shrugged*, is that individual freedom is possible only to those who are strong enough, psychologically and morally, to withdraw their sanction from any system that coercively thrives off their productive energies. In the novel, Rand examined the process by which the creators tacitly collaborate in their own enslavement by granting moral legitimacy to their exploiters. The exploiter must count upon the virtue of his subject and "use it as an instrument of torture." He practices "blackmail with the victim's generosity as sole means of extortion," in which "the gift of a man's good will" is transformed "into a tool for the giver's destruction" (465). Rearden recognizes that the political authorities who choose to deal with him "by means of compulsion," do not fully realize that they need his voluntary cooperation in order to succeed in their tasks. One of his most revelatory experiences is grasping that it is the victim's own volition that makes the exploiters' survival possible. Rearden tells his enslavers:

> "Whatever you wish me to do, I will do at the point of a gun. If you sentence me to jail, you will have to send armed men to carry me there—I will not volunteer to move. If you fine me, you will have to seize my property to collect the fine—I will not volunteer to pay it. If you believe that you have the right to force me—use your guns openly. I will not help you to disguise the nature of your action." (479)

Rearden refuses to participate in his own martyrdom. He refuses to condone the seizure of his property, and lays bare the naked aggression of his enslavement.

Though Rand developed her notion of the "sanction of the victim" and of the reciprocity between master and slave in her own unique style, these concepts were not entirely new to intellectual history. As far back as 1577, Étienne de la Boetie wrote *A Discourse on Voluntary Servitude*, which argued that political tyranny ultimately rested on popular consent. La Boetie believed that most citizens obeyed authority out of sheer habit and custom, duped by the tyrant who promoted a benevolent view of his rule.[9] But even before La Boetie, hints of the master-slave duality could be found in Aristotle, who recognized that each term is "reciprocally connected with that in relation to which it is defined." For Aristotle, such "correlatives" as "master" and "slave" must "come into existence simultaneously."[10]

In the history of philosophy, however, it was Hegel who dealt most explicitly with the codependency of master and slave. As Heilbroner explains, this definition of the master and slave each in terms of its "contradiction" or "negation" is not a violation of Aristotelian logic: "The *logical* contradiction (or 'opposite' or 'negation') of a Master is not a Slave, but a 'non-Master,' which may or may not be a slave. But the *relational* opposite of a Master is indeed a Slave, for it is only by reference to this second 'excluded' term that the first is defined."[11]

For Hegel, the emergence of master and slave (Hegel uses the terms "lord" and "bondsman") is a component of the evolution of consciousness. Hegel sketches the development of selfhood from the first confrontational moments between one self and another. In this initial encounter, the Self seeks to assert its own existence by annihilating the Other. Ultimately, however, each Self manifests a form of dependency. The master and slave use each other in their attempts to achieve self-consciousness. The master sees in the slave an instrument for the achievement of his or her own goals, while the slave sees the master as someone who will care for his or her needs. Masters need slaves to maintain their status as masters, whereas the servant requires the master to perpetuate his slavery. Each is in *"reciprocal self-surrender"* to the other. In their self-alienation, each fails to achieve genuine independence (Hegel [1807] 1977, 134).

At first, masters appear to be independent. They seem to live only for themselves, whereas slaves appear to live only for their masters. But in reality, the conditions of each consciousness interpenetrate the other. The master's self is "mediated" through the slave's consciousness. The master appropriates the material products of the slave's labor and depends on the slave for survival. As such, masters fail to recognize slaves as legitimate persons, and deprive themselves of the mutual recognition that their consciousnesses require.

By contrast, the slave seems to be an abject dependent. And yet, as slaves master their crafts, they objectify themselves through material production. It is they who most adequately anticipate "the *truth* of the independent consciousness." By consummating their purposes in the production of material goods, they become conscious of what they truly are. Even as the master reaps the benefits, and alienates the product of the slave, it is the slave who moves gradually toward the full integration of a genuinely human consciousness (115–19).

For Hegel, the slave does not achieve independence by merely negating the existence of the master. The reciprocal relationship of authority and obedience cannot be broken by reproducing the structure of codependency. It is only in the final phase of Universal Self-Consciousness that slaves stop tying their will to the authority of the Other. They attain full independence, appropriating the products of their own efforts and seeing in others a full, mutual recognition of Self.[12]

Hegel's insights served as the model for Marxian theory. In Marx's view, the worker is the slave for the capitalist master. Capitalists expropriate the worker's products for their own use, as workers are forced to sell their alienated labor-power on the market. For Marx, communism replaces Hegel's Universal Self-Consciousness. The communist society is one in which workers realize their potential as producers, emerging as fully integrated, self-conscious, social beings in mutual, benevolent interrelations with others.

There is currently no available evidence to suggest that Rand absorbed any of Hegel's or Marx's explicit contributions to this area of social thought. Rand was probably exposed to the Marxian thesis while at Petrograd University. In her intellectual evolution, it would seem that she switched the focus from capitalism to statism. For Rand, the market economy was an outgrowth of voluntary association with trade. Modern statism had introduced an element of coercion into the system of exchange, reproducing, in many insidious forms, the relationships of obedience and authority. But even if Rand did not consciously use Hegelian or Marxian categories in her analysis of the codependency relationship, her dialectical approach would have led her toward a similar assessment of the nature of power.

In Rand's view, there is no legitimate choice between the self-sacrifice of the slave or the domination of the master. Each is the other side of the same dualism. As Roark argues, there is only the choice between independence or dependence. The independent man "is the man who stands above the need of using others in any manner. He does not function through them. . . . He does not exist for any other man—and he asks no other man to exist for him." Independence is the only basis for relationships among equals, "the only pattern for proper cooperation," and "the only form of brotherhood and mutual respect possible between men."[13]

In contrast to both Hegel and Marx, Rand focused greater attention on the psychology of power. Her notion of the second-hander, and her acceptance of several key Brandenian concepts, was an attempt to explain the psycho-epistemological roots of codependency relationships. Ultimately, Rand tied this psychological dimension to a broader systemic context, emerging with a full-bodied critique of contemporary statism.

During his association with Rand, Branden provided a psychological counterpart to Rand's own view of the "second-hander." In his concepts of "pseudo-self-esteem" and "social metaphysics," Branden sought to synthe-size Rand's understanding of the codependency relationship with a psycho-logical dynamic. It was an exposition that Rand fully endorsed.

Central to Objectivism is a vision of human efficacy that entails the full integration of mind and body, reason and emotion, the conscious and subconscious, the articulate and tacit. Rand's ethos is essentially epistemic. It emphasizes the achievement of reason, purpose, and self-esteem as the basis for and reflection of human efficacy. Rand writes: "The relationship of reason and morality is reciprocal: the man who accepts the role of a sacrificial animal, will not achieve the self-confidence necessary to uphold the validity of his mind—and the man who doubts the validity of his mind,

Fig. 11. Nathaniel Branden. (Photo by E. Devers Branden, courtesy of Nathaniel Branden)

will not achieve the self-esteem necessary to uphold the value of his person and to discover the moral premises that make man's value possible" (*New Intellectual*, 37–38).

Branden accepted Rand's formulation and argued further that since every person must have confidence in his mind in order to act efficaciously, some self-doubting individuals will develop a pretense at self-efficacy and self-worth. Such a pretense is a necessary survival technique for those who fail to achieve genuine epistemological self-confidence. Branden defines "pseudo-self-esteem" as "a non-rational, self-protective device to diminish anxiety and to provide a spurious sense of security—to assuage a need of authentic self-esteem while allowing the real causes of its lack to be evaded."[14]

Branden explains that pseudo-self-esteem is maintained by the evasion, repression, or rationalization of those ideas and feelings which may adversely affect an individual's self-appraisal. In such instances, the individual seeks to derive his self-efficacy from experiences that are less demanding of his ability. Persons of pseudo-self-esteem are motivated by fear. They adopt a host of defense mechanisms as anti-anxiety devices. They may seek solace in religious faith or in the manipulation of others.

Branden extends his analysis by developing a second crucial concept: "social metaphysics."[15] Branden (1983b, 50) recognizes that as social beings, persons seek visibility in their interactions with others. But individuals who attempt to tie their self-assessment to the opinions of others place themselves in a humiliating subordinate position. Such individuals are parasites on human consciousness. Their frame of reference is not reality, but their own fantasies about the ideas inside the minds of others (Branden 1989, 128). They live not in a universe of facts, but in "a *universe of people*." People mediate reality and become the prime tool of their survival. Branden ([1969] 1979) writes: "*Social metaphysics is the psychological syndrome that characterizes a person who holds the minds of other men, not objective reality, as his ultimate psycho-epistemological frame of reference*" (179–80).

Branden maintains that social metaphysicians lack a firm sense of objective existence distinct from "the judgments, beliefs, opinions, feelings of others." They experience a metaphysical inefficacy, a basic helplessness, and a malevolent sense of life. Their pseudo-self-esteem is dependent upon the responses of significant others whom they fundamentally fear (185). Social metaphysicians organize their lives "around the desire to please, to be taken care of, or, alternatively, to control and dominate, to manipulate and *coerce*" others. They seek "completion and fulfillment through domina-

tion or submission, through controlling or being controlled, through order-
ing or obeying." But ultimately, they experience a "fundamental sense of
emptiness" and a lack of authenticity. Their individuation process stunted,
they fail to assimilate the basic fact of their aloneness (N. Branden
1980, 111).

Branden ([1969] 1979, 185–95) identifies certain dominant trends among
social metaphysicians. He creates typological classifications that in reality,
often coexist within a single consciousness:

- Conventional types are pure conformists. They fear independent value
  judgment and action and are unquestioning in their loyalty to the social
  "mainstream."
- Spiritual types seek social position in a culture or subculture of mysticism. As religious fanatics, they claim to possess an ineffable, superior
  soul visible only to God. Their faith in God and adherence to ascetic
  rituals serve to bolster an illusory sense of personal worth. They seek
  the protection and blessing of God because God is, allegedly, the only
  Other of any significance in their lives.
- Independent types reject the status quo, not on principle, but in
  an attempt to project a defiant rebelliousness. Such "counterfeit"
  individualists define themselves not in terms of their conformity to
  others, but in terms of their opposition to others.[16]
- Ambivalent types exhibit "a significant degree of intellectual sover-
  eignty," even as they conform tacitly or indifferently to the values
  of society.

Of greatest relevance to the current discussion, however, is the Power-
seeking social metaphysician. Branden accepts Rand's view that "power-
lust" is "a manifestation of helplessness, of self-loathing and of the desire
for the unearned."[17] For Rand, as for Branden, "power-lust is a psycho-
epistemological matter."[18] Power-seekers have a basic fear and hatred of
both themselves and other people. They attempt to quell their anxiety and
to promote a sense of pseudo-efficacy by attempting to control others,
especially those who are genuinely efficacious (N. Branden [1969] 1979,
189). Their deep sense of inferiority leads them to deceive, manipulate, and
coerce other people, even as they struggle to command their respect,
obedience and love. Such types may be found in all professions, but they
are attracted principally to politics and the military. In a statist social order,

they reproduce "in startling numbers." Their desire to manipulate others is at root a desire to make their whims efficacious (188–90).

Branden (1980, 172–73) maintains further that a high proportion of such Power-seekers experience peaks of sexual intensity in sadomasochism. The ability to inflict and/or endure pain is internal to their psychology. Branden (1983b, 128) argues, however, that symbiotic dependency is not an adequate model for human relationships. He agrees with Rand that the moral life is not a choice between sadism or masochism.[19]

There is a period style in Rand's and Branden's interest in such issues, which was influenced significantly by the popular, contemporaneous writings of the leftist intellectual, Erich Fromm.[20] Fromm similarly opposed the duality of sadism and masochism as an outgrowth of the master-slave relationship. Fromm argued that in striving toward domination and submission, the sadist and the masochist seek to escape from their "unbearable aloneness." Masochists exhibit inferiority, powerlessness, and insignificance. They belittle themselves in the company of their oppressors. Alternatively, sadists seek to exploit, humiliate, embarrass, and use their partners. They seek to inflict mental and physical harm. But just as the masochist is dependent upon the sexual dominance of the sadist, so too, the sadist is dependent upon "the object of his sadism." Each derives a sense of fulfillment from the other. Each seeks to escape from the burdens of independence, responsibility, and freedom. In their "symbiosis," there is a mutual loss of integrity and authenticity.[21]

Despite this parallel between Fromm's portrait and the Objectivist conception, there are significant differences between them: Rand and Branden endorse capitalism; Fromm does not. Fromm argues that the perpetuation of sadism and masochism in human relationships is a reflection of the unbearable freedom engendered by the emergence of capitalism. Capitalism destroys the human spirit because it constitutes and is constituted by a spontaneous order that is beyond the control of any human actor. It maximizes material wealth and political freedom even as it undermines the individual's sense of efficacy. Its institutions are impersonal and not amenable to social control. In essence, it is the cause of modern man's alienation.

It was largely in response to Fromm's theories, that Branden wrote his essay "Alienation." Branden saw alienation as the problem of "the disowned self."[22] Individuals who had failed to develop self-sufficient egos were incapable of experiencing themselves as responsible for their own actions. Branden argues in dialectical fashion: "The problem of alienation and the problem of personal identity are inseparable. The man who lacks a firm sense of personal identity feels alienated; the man who feels alienated lacks a firm sense of personal identity."[23]

Branden agrees with Fromm that alienated individuals achieve "a splintered sense of self, a self broken into unintegratable fragments" (291). They engage in flights from reality and from their selves. Most important, they attempt to flee "from the responsibility of a volitional (i.e., self-directing) consciousness" (294). But they cannot escape from the necessity to choose in the cognitive and evaluative realms. Those who default on the responsibility to think and judge inevitably fracture the integrated requirements of their own survival. They achieve crippling guilt and anxiety in their day-to-day lives.

Both Rand and Branden saw capitalism as the only social system that can provide the existential context for the transcendence of alienation. Capitalism is based upon the primacy of existence, the efficacy of reason, and the necessity of freedom. Freedom is not sufficient in itself for human fulfillment, but it is a necessary social requirement. Although self-doubting individuals cannot escape from the cognitive freedom that is inherent in their species-identity, they can escape from freedom on "the existential or social level." Political freedom can be rejected by those social metaphysicians who seek to escape the responsibility of directing their own lives. Branden declares: "The psychological root of the revolt against freedom in one's existence, is the revolt against freedom in one's consciousness. *The root of the revolt against self-responsibility in action is the revolt against self-direction in thought.* The man who does not want to think, does not want to bear responsibility for the consequences of his actions nor for his own life" (295).

Branden ([1971] 1978) later remarked: "A concentration camp guard is the ultimate example of alienated man" (139). No thinker in the Objectivist tradition has written more about the tragedy of the concentration camps than Leonard Peikoff. Peikoff's discussion sheds further light on the Objectivist contention that the use of force necessarily invalidates self-responsibility and self-direction. But it is not Peikoff's particular analysis that is pivotal here. What is most significant is the utility of the Objectivist framework for analyzing certain kinds of human experience.

Peikoff's book *The Ominous Parallels* explores some of the similarities between the rise of Nazism in Germany and contemporary U.S. culture. Mirroring the efforts of the early Frankfurt school theorists such as Theodor Adorno, Max Horkheimer, and Herbert Marcuse, Peikoff expends considerable energy trying to make sense out of the madness of Auschwitz.[24] Drawing from the works of Bruno Bettelheim and Hannah Arendt, Peikoff (1982, 255) argues that the camps were created to inculcate unconditional obedience. Their goal was "psychological destruction," the obliteration of the human "capacity to function independently" (258).

The relations of power were reproduced on every scale within the concentration camp structure. The camps aimed to control both victims and killers. "The victims had to become robots, slavishly obedient to the guards; the guards had to become robots, slavishly obedient to the Führer" (259).

The camps destroyed their victims' self-efficacy and self-worth. As their faculty of volition was assaulted, the degraded prisoners were denied their essential personhood. Their ability to grasp existence was slowly eradicated. Their focal choices were made irrelevant to their survival. If they attempted to raise the level of their focal awareness, their minds could not make sense of the reality of mass extermination. If they attempted to shrink the level of their focal awareness in an effort to insulate themselves from existential terror, their minds were invalidated as tools of survival. Living in a nightmare universe, the prisoners learned ultimately "to suppress any outward signs of perceptiveness." They were forced to "implicate [themselves] in evil" regardless of the choices they made. The prisoners were made accessories to their own destruction as the camps blurred the distinction between victim and executioner (267–68). Peikoff (1980T, lecture 6) emphasizes that under such conditions, the question of the sanction of the victim was beside the point. The victims were spiritually destroyed before they were physically exterminated.

But the conditioning did not end with the victims. The camp guards too "received a certain kind of 'reinforcement' or processing" that slowly eradicated their cognitive independence. They were part of a hierarchic system of military terror in which superiors inflicted capricious punishments on all their subordinates. The guards were "well-clothed, well-fed and ideologically trained" to "question nothing and carry out anything." As prisoners learned to submit to power, the guards learned "to *wield* it, with everything this requires, and destroys, in the wielder." With each atrocity they committed, the guards negated their own moral sense. Most of the executioners turned to alcoholism. Like their victims, they schooled themselves in nonawareness (Peikoff 1982, 268).

For Peikoff, the camps had frustrated "man's most abstract, delicate, spiritual . . . *philosophical* requirements," revealing "the need by means of starving it" (274). Yet, while the Holocaust has been viewed as an aberration, Branden (1983b) has argued that the abdication of personal responsibility and autonomy "is inherent in our methods of child-rearing and education." Branden draws from the experiences of the celebrated Milgrim experiment, in which an individual subject was prompted by a supervisor to administer electric shocks to a student for each incorrect answer to a question. Unbeknownst to the individual subject, the electric shocks were fake, and both the student and the supervisor were trained actors. And yet an alarming number of individual subjects administered increasing levels of shocks to their students when ordered to do so by the supervisor. Frequently, they pushed buttons marked as activating dangerous and life-threatening dosages of electricity, despite the screams of the student-actors.

Branden maintains: "Most of us have been trained to push those buttons since the day we were born." The educational system often distorts the development of the individual's moral autonomy. The individual is taught to follow rules, and "to respect the voice of others above the voice of self." Virtue is equated with compliance, conformity, social adaptation, and obedience. The self is subordinated to the society or God (132–35). When a social system is established on the basis of such premises, it is ultimately inimical to the requirements of human life. Under such social conditions, "psychological and physical disaster" is the inevitable result.[25] Branden adds: "It is not freedom but the lack of freedom—brought about by the rising tide of statism, by the expanding powers of the government and the increasing infringement of individual rights—that produces in man a sense of powerlessness and helplessness, the terrifying sense of being at the mercy of malevolent forces."[26]

Both Rand and Branden recognized the systemic factors (Level 3) that provide the broad context for the master-slave duality, the sanction of the victim, and modern alienation (Level 1). But Rand argued that statism was both the outgrowth of and the basis for exploitative power relations. These relations embody and engender the very system within which they occur. They are manifested in both the psycho-epistemological and existential realms, in both the personal and the political dimensions of human life. They can even be found in the modes of communication and language (Level 2).

A Linguistic Turn

To say that Rand's critique takes a linguistic turn is not to imply that her approach is deconstructionist. The "linguistic left" takes its cue from

Nietzsche, who saw grammar as restricting thought and genuinely radical alternatives.[27] Such thinkers as Derrida and Foucault aim to deconstruct the structures of language and knowledge as a means of revealing their internalized power relations. Objectivists have generally criticized such approaches, which seem to postulate that no one controls language, but that language, in its culturally inherited forms, controls both communication and thought. Peikoff (1990T) has argued, for instance, that such a deconstructionist method makes the objective judgment of a text's validity impossible.

And yet despite this antipathy toward the linguistic left, Objectivist critique suggests a similar concern for the power relations implicit in contemporary language usage. Rand was always suspicious of the linguistic biases in social dialogue. She challenged the distorted cultural constructions of such concepts as "selfishness" and "capitalism." She sought to remove these concepts from their traditional context and to cast them in an entirely nondualistic light. She did not argue that oppression was rooted in language per se. But on Level 2 of her analysis, Rand recognized that language was an institution that perpetuated social exploitation especially in its modern anti-conceptual incarnations. Her discussion of such issues in public discourse exhibits a provocative similarity to the dialogical theories of Jürgen Habermas. This brief linguistic turn in Rand's analysis was not fully developed. But it illustrates the profundity of Rand's dialectical mode of inquiry while pointing to a thoroughly non-Marxist, radical resolution.

The Habermasian project grows out of the critical tradition of the Frankfurt school of sociology. Habermas integrates the contributions of Marxism, phenomenology, psychoanalysis, and hermeneutics in a wide-ranging critique of contemporary social relations. He views all social systems "as networks of communicative actions" (Habermas [1976] 1979, 98). For Habermas, a society's reified institutions of power are reflected in distorted patterns of communication. He aims for a condition in which political discourse is made intelligible by the progressive elimination of manipulative dialogical forms.[28]

Drawing from the works of Hans-Georg Gadamer, Habermas believes that mutual understanding cannot arise in the absence of an intersubjective "fusion of horizons." Persons involved in social discourse bring with them certain constellations of expectations and norms. Genuine communication is not possible if the dialogical partners habitually engage in deceitful or distortive practices. The partners can become more competent at communication only if they learn to translate between their distinctive ways of viewing the world. In Habermas's view, such a dialogue anticipates an "ideal speech situation," a community in which distortion and manipulation is barred from human relationships.

Habermas maintains that it is possible to achieve undistorted social communication through a process of rational reconstruction. Accepting Ryle and Polanyi's distinction between articulate and tacit knowledge, Habermas recognizes that each speaker performs a variety of dialogical activities without grasping the explicit linguistic rules upon which such communication is based. A meaningful exchange of ideas can be achieved as each speaker draws from his or her articulate and tacit knowledge. Rational reconstruction requires that each speaker render explicit that which is implicit. Such a process requires adherence to the universal validity foundations of speech, which Habermas ([1976] 1979, 3–5) characterizes as "universal pragmatics." It requires each speaker to select propositional content that reflects real facts and experiences; that expresses the meaning of his or her intentions accurately; that recognizes honesty and truthfulness in communication. The speech act is successful only if it is comprehensible to both speaker and hearer alike (2–3).

Comprehension is undermined by "strategic" forms of communication, such as lying, misleading, and manipulating one's dialogical partner. Such exploitative forms are "parasitic," for every attempt to distort or deceive must rely on the logic of ideal speech. Even "intentional deception" is ultimately oriented toward truth, since it is truth that it seeks to usurp (Habermas [1971] 1973, 17). For Habermas, "*systematically distorted communication*" is a negation of ideal speech. It results when the participants are engaged not only in interpersonal deception, but in self-deception as well. Such self-deception involves, at least partially, the obscuring of one's own strategic behavior from oneself.[29]

In Habermas's view, ideal speech is an achievement that demands increasing self-reflection on the part of each participant. Rational consequences cannot emerge unless the participants free themselves from distorting influences and self-deceptions that block genuine understanding. Habermas embraces a Freudian "depth hermeneutics" in which participants become more visible to themselves and to their dialogic partners. It is a therapeutic process of translation in which one brings the unconscious into conscious awareness and reappropriates a lost portion of the self.[30] Such self-reflection enables each partner to clarify misunderstandings within the context of accepted norms. The ideal speech situation is one in which each participant has an equal opportunity to engage in symmetrical, reciprocal, nonexploitative and comprehensible acts of communication. Such discourse "is intended to render inoperative all motives except solely that of a cooperative readiness to arrive at an understanding."[31]

Although Rand would have vehemently rejected Habermas's emphasis on "intersubjectivity" and the social consensus of norms, she fully understood the exploitative nature of "strategic" forms of communication. As we have seen in our discussion of Objectivist ethics, Rand viewed honesty as a contextual virtue dictated by the requirements of human survival. Honesty for her is not primarily a social relationship; it is a relationship between the mind and reality.[32] Nevertheless, Rand understands that deceptive practices introduce elements of distortion into social relations. Dishonesty is a constituent of the master-slave duality. As Rearden states in *Atlas Shrugged*:

> "People think that a liar gains a victory over his victim. What I've learned is that a lie is an act of self-abdication, because one surrenders one's reality to the person to whom one lies, making that person one's master, condemning oneself from then on to faking the sort of reality that person's view requires to be faked. And if one gains the immediate purpose of the lie—the price one pays is the destruction of that which the gain was intended to serve. The man who lies to the world, is the world's slave from then on." (859)

In such circumstances, liars are not the masters of their fates, but slaves to unreality, and to those whom they attempt to dupe. They attain the status of social metaphysician, with a stake in the victim's gullibility. They focus not on reality but on the consciousness of their victims. The victim's consciousness as such is given primacy over objective reality (Branden [1969] 1979, 168).

Rand recognized that honesty is an essential component of rational human relations. In all forms of spiritual and material discourse, we count explicitly or implicitly on the rationality, honesty, and integrity of our partners.[33] The purpose of all communicative exchange—in love, in art, or in trade—is to elicit a suitable response to the content communicated.[34] Branden argues that in verbal exchange in particular, communication consists of far more than what a person says explicitly. Tone of voice, facial expression, gesture, and behavior will tend to support a person's statements or undermine them (N. Branden and E. D. Branden 1983, 59–60). Honesty, then, involves an integrated response of articulate and tacit factors. Honest communication is a microcosm of genuinely human relationships which "have a mutually enhancing effect on feelings of self-worth"

(N. Branden 1983b, 47). Peikoff (1980T, lecture 7) states further that such honest interpersonal communication will lead each participant to greater self-clarity and mutual understanding. By not entering into such a dialogical process, the participant is less likely to comprehend the implications of his or her own views.

But the Objectivists emphasize again that the primary issue is not the interpersonal character of the lie. Since honesty constitutes a relationship between the mind and reality, it is *self*-deception that is at root, the most distortive of an individual's efficacy and communicative competence. Self-deception, however, is not necessarily the result of a conscious process of evasion. In fact, it is most often the result of a habitual, subconscious process of repression, which "forbids certain ideas, memories, identifications and evaluations to enter conscious awareness." Branden ([1969] 1979) states further: "Repression is an *automatized avoidance reaction*, whereby a man's focal awareness is involuntarily pulled away from any 'forbidden' material emerging from less conscious levels of his mind or from his subconscious" (78–79).

The repressed individual may show emotional constraint or whimsical self-indulgence, but in reality, these extremes "are merely two sides of the same coin." Disconnected from the reality of his or her inner experience, the repressed individual ultimately undercuts "the clarity and efficiency of his [or her] thinking" (87, 93). Such individuals can restore themselves to "biologically appropriate functioning" through a therapeutic process of de-repression,[35] the Objectivist equivalent of a "depth hermeneutics." Mental health is constituted by an "*unobstructed capacity for reality-bound cognitive functioning*." The individual consciousness is healthy to the extent that it is "unobstructed" and "integrated," unencumbered by fear, guilt, depression, pathological anxiety, neurosis, or pain (N. Branden [1969] 1979, 99–100).

Branden's therapeutic methods are not the subject of the current study, but they center on a "sentence-completion" technique of "directed association." Though Branden relies on a host of complementary methods, he seeks to engage the patient in a process that draws "upon implicit meanings for explicit statements." Patients are given sentence stems that they complete spontaneously. Stem-completions enable individuals to meditate on their conclusions, not to rationalize them, but to "allow subconscious understandings to find their way into articulate speech." By disclosing "unrecognized attitudes and patterns," the sustained technique of directed association engenders a process of self-healing and self-clarification that aims for integration on both a conscious and subconscious level.[36]

This emphasis on communicative truthfulness, self-awareness, and "de-repression" is as crucial to the Randian project as it is to Habermasian discourse theory. Rand grasped that many of the distortions in communicative interaction can be traced to a systematic attack on the integrity of concepts and language launched by intellectuals who consciously or tacitly serve the modern predatory state. Rand argued that such intellectuals have confounded social discourse by "the destruction of language—and, therefore, of thought and, therefore, of communication—by means of anti-concepts."[37]

The "anti-concept" is but one symptom of a modern social formation that is steeped in negation. Rand describes the culture as "anti-reason," "anti-mind," "anti-man," and "anti-life." Its art is "anti-art," its ideology is "anti-ideology." Its "mixed" economy constitutes an "anti-system." Its hegemony is bolstered by a proliferation of "anti-conceptual" social practices and institutions. Rand's study of such negation is a crucial component of her radical critique.[38]

Rand defines an "anti-concept" as "an unnecessary and rationally unus-able term designed to replace and obliterate some legitimate concept." Just as, in contemporary literature, the antihero is a creation designed to eradicate heroes, and the antinovel is intended to destroy the novel form, so "anti-concepts" are formulated to annihilate real concepts. While rational concept formation renders explicit the meaning of an existential referent, "the use of anti-concepts gives the listeners a sense of *approximate* understanding."[39] An anti-concept sounds like a real concept, but it is formed illegitimately. It is constructed not through a process of abstraction and integration, but through a process of "package-dealing," in which "disparate, incongruous, [and] contradictory elements [are] taken out of any logical conceptual order or context," and united by a nonessential characteristic. The use of anti-concepts undermines the speaker's and the listener's conceptual clarity and precision, making social discourse unintelligible.[40] The anti-concept comes to have any number of contradic-tory meanings, depending on who uses it. Frequently, it serves as a euphemistic device, sanitizing an offensive condition or action. Or it may serve as an "anti-euphemism" to denigrate a "great and noble" fact.[41] The purpose of such linguistic obfuscation is ideological rationalization.

Rand does not suggest that anti-concepts are deliberately designed by a power elite and foisted on an unsuspecting populace. Indeed, the use and acceptance of anti-concepts is often tacit. For Rand, what is supremely significant is the tendency for anti-concepts to proliferate in a statist culture of unreason, distorting or obscuring the real nature of power relationships.

Rand analyzed several instances of the use of anti-concepts in contemporary discourse. In the 1960s and early 1970s, in the midst of the Vietnam war and growing political corruption, there was much focus on the "credibility gap" in U.S. politics. In the face of protests and civil unrest, a premium was placed on the value of social unity. Establishment policymakers criticized intellectual "polarization" as detrimental to the formation of a social consensus. They bandied about disingenuous assertions that individuals had a "duty" to serve the "common good." Such terms had an "elastic, undefinable, mystical character" that obscured the reality of a foreign policy that drafted young men to die in a war in which no compelling national interest was at stake.[42] The paean to the "public interest" was a cover-up for political conditions that favored the interests of some groups to the detriment of others.[43]

"Duty" was, in Rand's view, "one of the most destructive anti-concepts in the history of moral philosophy."[44] In its religious, psychological, and political usages, it destroyed legitimate concepts of morality. Indeed, the concept was a pure "product of mysticism," since it projected categorical imperatives without regard to context. It sanctioned obedience to authority and severed the connection between values and choice, thus crippling the individual's ability for self-directed moral action.

Rand also criticized the Establishment for using the term "polarization" derisively in hopes of quelling public debate on important issues of policy and deflecting or preventing any discussion or definition of fundamental principles. Whether they attacked the Goldwater Right or the New Left, they characterized the political pursuit of unequivocal principles as inflexible and impractical. They sought to bar such "extremism" from public life. Rand argued that in conforming to an artificial social consensus, each public speaker or writer

> struggles to hide his meaning (if any) under coils of meaningless generalities and safely popular bromides. Regardless of whether his message is good or bad, true or false, he cannot state it openly, but must *smuggle* it into his audience's subconscious by means of the same unfocused, deceptive, evasive verbiage. He must strive to be *misunderstood* in the greatest number of ways by the greatest number of people: this is the only way to keep up the pretense of unity.[45]

The dominant trend in the culture of consensus is anti-ideology.[46] Whereas a genuine political ideology projects a program of long-term action guided by fundamental principles, anti-ideology shrinks "men's minds to the range of the immediate moment, without regard to past or future, without context or memory." The anti-ideologists, the pseudo-intellectuals and lobbyists, claim to have no attachment to "inflexible" principles, but they nonetheless rely on spurious principles of their own. They disarm their opposition by switching the terms of the debate whenever it is expedient. In this manner, they distort public discourse to suit the strategic purposes of the pressure groups in whose interests they serve.[47]

If people do not explicitly define the nature of the debate, or the nature of their goals, Rand asked, how can genuine social unity ever be achieved? Since efficacious action is not possible in the absence of principles, how can public debate encourage rational negotiation and compromise when "the intentions of the various men or groups involved are not revealed?" How can anyone ascertain the desirability of any political deal without reference to the explicit principles at work?

Under such conditions of public discourse, "men begin to regard social relationships not as a matter of dealing with one another, but of putting something over on one another." By assaulting "the precision—of public communication (and its precondition: the freedom of public information)," the system necessarily breeds an atmosphere of mistrust and bitterness. Fostering an illusory intellectual unity, the system engenders the growth "of divisiveness or *existential* polarization" through the mass proliferation of conflicting pressure groups. Each group unites not by loyalty to an idea, but on the basis of race, age, sex, religious creed, or common hatred of another group. The unity within each group is motivated "not by choice, but by terror."[48] And just as the Establishment uses anti-concepts to legitimate its own foreign and domestic initiatives, so each group uses anti-concepts in its quest for political power. For Rand, "any ideological product of the mixed economy . . . is a vague, indefinable, approximation and, therefore an instrument of pressure group warfare."[49] Rand asked: "What sort of unity can one establish between victims and executioners?"[50]

In abandoning the necessity of clearly defined principles, people are unable to plan for the long term or engage in comprehensible social discourse. The absence of principles obscures any understanding of "the context, causes, consequences or solutions" of any given social problem. The "brute physical force" of the state becomes the "ultimate arbiter of disputes."[51]

Like Habermas, Rand envisioned a genuine, truthful, public discourse. She favored real intellectual "polarization" in which dialogical participants enter into constructive debate, bringing to the "cultural atmosphere an all-but-forgotten quality: honesty with its corollary, clarity." The unintelligible would be transcended as rational people grasped "their own stand and that of their adversaries." Out of this dialogue would emerge a genuine social unity, a unity that would be "a consequence, not a primary," one based on the triumph of "fundamental principles, rationally validated, clearly understood and voluntarily accepted" (4).

But unlike Habermas, Rand defended capitalism, "the unknown ideal," as the only social system capable of establishing the necessary conditions for free human discourse.[52] Unlike any other radical theorist of her generation, Rand linked a multilevel, dialectical analysis to a libertarian politics.

The Antirational Culture

Rand recognized that radical social change could not emerge solely on the basis of an honest public dialogue. In Rand's view, such honesty is anathema to statist society. The existing culture and the political system were, she thought, profoundly "antirational."[53] As she saw it, the system itself expressed and perpetuated a fundamental irrationality that punished virtue and rewarded vice. To this end, culture and politics were "two mutually reinforcing manifestations of the same philosophy."[54]

Before examining the dimensions of cultural irrationality that Rand condemned, it is important to grasp what she meant by "culture." Rand interpreted the social sphere in a manner that reflected her own view of the individual sphere. Every society, like every individual, acts on the basis of a certain articulated or tacit philosophic view of the world. Our survival as human beings, the integrated direction of our lives, and the efficacy of our chosen courses of action ultimately depend on the principles we accept, either consciously or tacitly. Likewise, a society's economic, political, and cultural trends are ultimately set by its implicit, dominant philosophical premises. (Whether Rand's theory of history borders on a kind of philosophical determinism is a contention I explore later.)

What must be emphasized at this juncture is Rand's view of society as an organic totality. Rand refused to see the social whole as a hodgepodge of unrelated tendencies. These tendencies form a *system*, for better or for worse. The system shapes each of its constituent parts. And the parts both generate and reflect the system they jointly constitute.

Rand proposed an equivalence between social and individual structures. She sees a basic correspondence on three tiers (Diagram 2).

The vertical links between these three tiers are not what interests us here. For Rand, the factors within the vertical relationship of each sphere can both mutually support and undermine one another. Moreover, she sees a one-to-one horizontal correspondence between the respective social and individual spheres.

Vertically, in the social sphere, a nation's politico-economic trends and policies (Tier 3) cannot be abstracted from its cultural forms and practices (Tier 2), or from the sense of life of its people as expressed in their predominating social practices and attitudes, loosely defined as their "life-style" (Tier 1).[55] Culture (Tier 2) is explicitly manifested in the works of intellectuals and artists in such areas as letters, manners, painting, sculpture, music, and science (Peikoff 1991b, 129). Taken collectively, such cultural forms express the dominant ideas, values, and attitudes of a given age.

Rand recognized that intellectuals and artists constituted a small minority in any given national population. In the case of the United States, Rand saw a stark contrast between the purveyors of culture (Tier 2) and the people, specifically, between the intellectuals and artists' sense of life and the predominating sense of life of the American people (Tier 1). This conflict can be better understood when placed in a horizontal relationship with the individual sphere.

On Tier 3, a society's political and economic policies correspond to an individual's course of action. They are not implemented in a vacuum. Just as an individual's course of action cannot be abstracted from his conscious convictions, so a society's political and economic policies cannot be ab-

Diagram 2. Parallel Spheres: Social and Individual

The Social Sphere		The Individual Sphere
Political trends	◄──── Tier 3 ────►	Individual's course of action
Culture	◄──── Tier 2 ────► (articulated)	Individual's conscious convictions
Sense of life ("lifestyle")	◄──── Tier 1 ────► (inarticulate/tacit)	Sense of life (subconscious)

stracted from its cultural trends. Thus, on Tier 2, the culture, as manifested in explicit intellectual and artistic products, is analogous to an individual's conscious convictions. The culture embodies a society's dominant philosophy.

On Tier 1, Rand created an analogy between the nation's sense of life as expressed in its "lifestyle," and the individual's sense of life. The nation's "lifestyle" is represented in its predominating social practices and attitudes, which constitute a general emotional atmosphere, an integrated encapsulation of the values that most people hold.[56] These practices and attitudes serve "as the leitmotif of a given age, setting its trends and its style."[57] It becomes possible to identify "national characteristics" because the great majority of people will tacitly absorb and express values, attitudes, and traditions that have been habitually reproduced by successive generations. They tend to develop "the essentials of the same subconscious philosophy" from the earliest impressions of their childhood.[58]

Branden has echoed this Randian view. He argues that if one does not overtly identify accepted cultural values and practices, one cannot call these into question, "precisely because they are absorbed by a process that largely by-passes the conscious mind." Branden maintains that such a "cultural unconscious"[59] encompasses implicit beliefs about nature, reality, human beings, masculinity and femininity, good and evil. These beliefs reflect the context of a given historical time and place. Though there will be ideational differences among people within a specific culture, Branden argues "that at least some of these beliefs tend to reside in every psyche in a given society, and without ever being the subject of explicit awareness" (287–88). Recognizing that "cultures do not encourage the questioning of their own premises," Branden, like Rand, grasps the crucial necessity of critical thinking in the struggle for personal and social change (303).

Rand emphasized that a society, like an individual, will tend to see its inarticulate beliefs, practices, and attitudes (Tier 1) as natural and self-evident. But these beliefs cannot be reified; they must be analyzed as by-products of complex evaluations made by many people over a long period of time and reflecting a fundamental view of human nature.[60] Just as Rand aimed for the articulation of values and attitudes within each individual as a means toward his or her rational integration or alteration, so too, did she aim to grasp a society's implicit values and attitudes as a means toward their explicit articulation or transcendence.

Rand argued that within both the individual and social spheres, there can be a pronounced conflict between tacit and articulated dimensions, between Tier 1 and Tiers 2 and 3. The social world, like the individual's inner world, is not constituted by a hegemonic unity; it is frequently a sphere in contradiction with itself. She wrote:

> Just as an individual's sense of life can clash with his conscious convictions, hampering or defeating his actions, so a nation's sense of life can clash with its culture, hampering or defeating its political course. Just as an individual's sense of life can be better or worse than his conscious convictions, so can a nation's. And just as an individual who has never translated his sense of life into conscious convictions is in terrible danger—no matter how good his subconscious values—so is a nation. (252)

The political trend (Tier 3) in the United States is statist. Its cultural trend (Tier 2) is "directed at the obliteration of man's rational faculty."[61] The prime psychological effect of Tiers 3 and 2 on most people is "the erosion of ambition." In Rand's view, the political goal presupposes these two dominant cultural and psychological tendencies. Statism requires docility, hopelessness, and stagnation. Since "thinking men cannot be ruled," and since "ambitious men do not stagnate," statism had to institutionalize the antirational.[62] Whereas previously there had been an Age of Reason and an Age of Enlightenment, contemporary U.S. culture had brought about an Age of Envy, which expressed "*hatred of the good for being the good.*"[63] In nearly every aspect of culture, a fundamental malevolence sought to annihilate every desirable human good *because* it was good. In the Age of Envy, there was a social function to every cultural idea that opposed success or ambition.

The egalitarian-intellectuals, for instance, attacked human uniqueness and turned "equality . . . into an anti-concept." They switched its meaning from a political to a metaphysical context, and proposed to invalidate the physical and spiritual distinctions among individuals through the coercive power of the state. In actuality, they wished to achieve "an inverted social pyramid, with a new aristocracy on top—*the aristocracy of non-value*" (165). Such policies penalized the truly intelligent. But they also destroyed every individual, "each in proportion to his intelligence." Under such conditions, the average person did not possess the genius's resilience and self-confidence, and was much more apt to abdicate his mind, "in hopeless bewilderment, under the first touch of pressure."[64]

The modern egalitarians seek to replace self-responsibility and earned achievement with a psychology of entitlement and victimization based on claims of illusory rights and metaphysical equality (N. Branden 1994, 297–305). Their ultimate weapon is the altruist morality. Rand argued: "It makes no difference whether they embraced altruism as a means to their ulterior motives or the motives grew out of their altruistic creed." These "two elements are mutually reinforcing."[65] Even if the egalitarians' motivations were sincere, their doctrine of self-sacrifice, self-immolation, and self-abnegation inculcated a sense of guilt and worthlessness in other people. Historically, philosophically, and psychologically, altruism was used as a rationalization "for the most evil motives, the most inhuman actions, the most loathsome emotions."[66]

However, Rand believed that the nation's "sense of life," upheld by the majority of Americans (Tier 1), was in stark contradiction to this primordial cultural-intellectual trend. Though most Americans had "mixed" premises, they had internalized a fundamentally Aristotelian sense of life that was reality-oriented, progressive, technological, and defiant. But the United States could not long survive on the basis of a tacit benevolence. Without the full articulation and objective definition of rational values, American society was doomed.[67] Its sense of life (Tier 1) was gradually being corrupted in an atmosphere of explicit cultural (Tier 2), and political (Tier 3) irrationality as manifested in most social institutions and practices.

Rand's critique duplicates the comprehensive, integrated character of the Marxian analysis of culture. Certainly there is an important distinction in emphasis: Rand saw social phenomena in terms of their philosophical roots, whereas Marx focused on their material roots. Yet both thinkers examine the extent to which a dominant philosophical or material mode is reproduced in nearly every aspect of social life.[68] Rand presented a view of systemic irrationality that encompasses everything from art and religion to politics and pedagogy.

In many ways, Rand's approach bears an even closer resemblance to the vision of Antonio Gramsci, the Italian Marxist. Gramsci (1971) argued that philosophy (or culture), politics, and economics "are the necessary constituent elements of the same conception of the world, [hence] there must necessarily be, in their theoretical principles, a convertibility from one to the others and a reciprocal translation into the specific language of each constituent element. Any one is implicit in the others, and the three together form a homogeneous circle" (403).

Gramsci developed an expansive definition of power relations that was reflected in each of the constituents he identified. He maintained that the phenomenon of power pervaded all social structures and institutions. As a Marxist, Gramsci developed the concept of "hegemony" to describe how capitalist relations achieved predominance in both the political and social spheres of action. He emphasized that power structures were not exclusively state formations. Most of them, in fact, reside in "civil society." The "ideological state apparatuses" include institutions of religion, education, family, law, communication, and culture, as well as political parties and trade unions, all of which are expressive of "bourgeois" power relations. His vision of proletarian revolution required the formation of parallel institutions, a "counter-hegemony," or "bloc of historical forces," which would develop "within the womb of the old society," negating every manifestation of capitalist relations. This was not primarily a "top-down" political revolution, but a "bottom-up" cultural transformation.[69]

Like Gramsci, Rand grasped the expansive nature of power relations. She recognized the presence of oppressive forces in culture, politics, and economics and believed too that any genuine revolution in the political sphere would be preceded necessarily by a cultural renaissance. Unlike Gramsci, however, Rand argued that it was not capitalist hegemony that needed to be transcended. Capitalism was an unknown ideal, a social system not fully realized, undermined by antirational, ancient cultural practices. The aesthetic images in the contemporary "mixed" economy were a "*concretized* reality" of the tribalist and mystic philosophical premises at work in modern culture.[70] For Rand, "Just as modern philosophy is dominated by the attempt to destroy the conceptual level of man's consciousness and even the perceptual level, reducing man's awareness to mere sensations—so modern art and literature are dominated by the attempt to disintegrate man's consciousness and reduce it to mere sensations, to the 'enjoyment' of meaningless colors, noises and moods" (97).

The culture mirrored such philosophical bankruptcy. In literature and motion pictures, writers had dispensed with structured plot progression. They were unconcerned with projecting an ideal man or woman, and frequently presented a clash between two variations of evil. The antihero became the central focus. In modern music, atonalism replaced melody and harmony. Mindless sounds and noises were introduced into composition as a deliberate attack on musical integration and structure.[71] In painting and sculpture, artists presented formless blotches of a nonobjective and nonrepresentational nature.[72] They distorted perspective, space, shape, color, and the human figure.

In the face of such cultural nihilism, Rand believed that the individual was deprived "of conceptual stimulation and communication." There was an absence of "value experiences" in modern culture that had the effect of lowering human expectations under the pressure of an omnipresent irrationality.[73] In such a cultural context, many people turned to religion as a panacea. Rand recognized that "mystic fantasies" helped to explain those things which people failed to understand.[74] But even in contemporary religion, Rand saw the progressive abandonment of rational, Thomistic theology in favor of fundamentalism, cults, astrology, and reincarnation.[75] Most people respond to mysticism out of loneliness, hurt, and pain, eager to find inspiration in a moral ideal projected in the God-concept. Tragically, such people view existence as hopeless. They doubt their own efficacy and become victims of what Branden called a mystic "protection racket," which fuels people's fear of death—and of life on earth.[76] But faith was no antidote. It was, in Branden's view, "a tool of distortion"; religion by its nature fostered a bias against the mind.[77]

Although purportedly secular, the public educational system exhibits this same antirational bias. Rand suggested that modern education has internalized the "ideology of socialization (in a neo-fascist form)" which was "floating, by default, through the vacuum of our intellectual and cultural atmosphere."[78] Rand characterized modern educators as "the comprachicos" of the mind. Adopting this phrase from Hugo's *Man Who Laughs*, Rand explains that the comprachicos bought and sold children. They made the children into physical monstrosities, degrading and deforming them to complete "the task of political suppression."

The comprachicos of the mind degrade and deform the child's cognitive faculty toward the same end. From the very earliest moments of his education, the child is stunted by "militantly anti-cognitive and anti-conceptual" pedagogical methods, through rote memorization, repetition, and concrete-bound association, rather than understanding, isolation of essentials, or conceptual integration. A premium is placed on social adaptation and adjustment, inculcating "the supremacy of the pack." In Rand's view, the Progressive nursery schools do not foster independent thinking. They attempt to socialize the child into conformity. And yet they defeat the very possibility of genuine social integration, since it is only "the thinking child" who is "fit for social relationships." In elevating "the rule of mediocrity," the system undermines the child's intelligence and autonomy. Such pedagogical methods fuel fear and self-doubt and reproduce within education an "Establishment of Envy." The child's self-doubt pertains to a fundamental uncertainty over the efficacy of his mind and the rightness of his actions. The adults, teachers, and class "goons" in a child's life contribute to his "moral emasculation."[79]

It must be remembered that Rand was intimately aware of Progressive "activity methods of teaching." In her youth, at the university, she witnessed the disastrous results as the Petrograders of Narkompros introduced Deweyite pedagogy into class instruction. While much of the disarray was to be blamed on how poorly many instructors were oriented to the Progressive credo, Rand believed that these methods were fundamentally anti-conceptual. But she also credited herself with being able to rise above the chaos.

Rand recognized, however, that not all children are as fortunate, especially those who are victimized by Progressive pedagogy from an early age. The child's "early programming may become indelible at a certain point," such that it becomes nearly impossible for the child to master the complex skills that his existence requires.[80] As such, the child attempts to quell his own self-doubt by following the rituals and beliefs of the group as a guide to action. His loyalty is primarily to the group and to its members, not to ideas or to principles. The group binds all of its members "by the same concretes."[81] It is such anti-conceptual tribalism that serves as the psycho-epistemological root of pressure-group warfare, especially in its racist incarnations.

Rand argued that the educational "system is self-perpetuating: it leads to many vicious circles."[82] As the student moves into the higher grades, his concrete-bound methods of functioning are matched by an equally concrete-bound, compartmentalized curriculum. The curriculum militates against system-building and the integration of knowledge.[83] But the teachers are not much better off than the students, since they too, are "products of the same educational system in its earlier stages."[84] As Branden (1994) emphasizes, many of these teachers "lack either the self-esteem or the training or both to do their jobs properly. These are teachers who do not inspire but humiliate. They do not speak the language of courtesy and respect but of ridicule and sarcasm" (202).

In the universities, the anti-cognitive, anti-conceptual methods are perpetuated.[85] The major difference is that on this level of education, the students are spoon-fed theories of modern philosophy that provide an intellectual sanction for their own stunted cognitive skills. Rand saw the universities as the source and center of contemporary "philosophical corruption."[86] She explained: "Whether the theories of modern philosophy serve merely as a screen, a defense-mechanism, a rationalization of neurosis or are, in part, its cause—the fact remains that modern philosophy has destroyed the best in these students and fostered the worst."[87]

The universities continue the policy of educational fragmentation and intellectual disintegration, as each course requires the students to master a different language and method of thinking. With each subject torn from the larger context, the material that is taught in one class frequently contradicts the lessons of another (251).

The educational and economic systems reinforce each others' "moral nihilism . . . range-of-the-moment pragmatism . . . [and] anti-ideological ideology" (254).[88] The concrete-bound, anti-conceptual mentality serves a useful function in the maintenance of power relations on the structural level (Level 3). Those who function by means of disconnected concretes do not question the principle of government control, but only "the 'good' or 'bad' character of government officials."[89] They accept as self-evident the premise that the government will solve social and economic problems, "somehow." Rand writes: "As Nathaniel Branden pointed out in a lecture, 'somehow' always means 'somebody.' "[90]

The epistemological method of the modern statist focuses on "single, concrete, out-of-context, range-of-the-moment issues," militating against any consideration of basic principles or long-term consequences. The purpose of this anti-integrative, "verbal fog" is to obscure the predatory nature of state power.[91] The ultimate product of American education was the "archetypical citizen of a mixed economy: the docile, pliable, moderate Milquetoast who never gets excited, never makes trouble, never cares too much, adjusts to anything and upholds nothing."[92]

Given this scathing attack on the staleness of contemporary American education and its relationship to the statist Establishment, it seemed odd that Rand would express an equally venomous hostility toward those who *did* get excited and *did* make trouble—the student rebels of the 1960s. Rand did not condemn the activists for their excitement; she believed that their goals were fundamentally misguided. Her analysis of the student movement is distinctive, both methodologically and historically.

Rand criticized the student movement for its acceptance of Hegelian and Marxian theoretical constructs;[93] however, Rand recognized that many students ran to the Marxist camp because it was more intellectual and systematized than its social science counterparts (N. Branden 1989, 47). She claimed that if the students had been offered the *Wall Street Journal* and Southern racism as examples of capitalist politics, they were correct to sense hypocrisy and to move further to the left.[94] But the New Left did not embrace the more reputable Marxist synthesis, which had retained some respect for reason, science, and technology. The New Leftists rejected ideological labels, and proclaimed the supremacy of emotionalism and immediate action. Nourished on a poisonous diet of Kantianism, pragmatism, logical positivism, linguistic analysis, and existentialism, the New Left mounted an anti-ideological assault on a system that was fundamentally anti-ideological as well.[95]

Methodologically, Rand's critique of the New Left was profoundly dialectical. Rand refused to detach even a seemingly radical rebellion from the social totality in which it emerged. The New Left was as much an outgrowth of the antirational as the culture it had rejected. While the "hippies" were to be commended for their repudiation of the Establishment, they failed to recognize their own place in it. The students were the "most consistently docile" archetypes of the System they condemned. They had internalized every major premise of the liberal Establishment and every major tenet of the altruist morality. Their rebellion was a symptom of "cultural disintegration . . . bred not in the slums, but in the universities." They were, by and large, "middle-class savages."[96]

For Rand, the counterculture, like the culture-at-large, had celebrated the superiority of faith, emotion, and instinct. In their indiscriminate, promiscuous, group sexual activity, and in their efforts to merge the self with the communal herd, there was but another manifestation of the cultural collectivism that had seeped into the pores of the social totality. Their use of drugs was an attempt to escape from their own unbearable inner lives, a "quest for a deliberately induced insanity" that invalidated their rational faculties.[97] Rand proclaimed: "They are the distilled essence of the Establishment's culture, they are the embodiment of its soul, they are the personified ideal of generations of crypto-Dionysians now leaping into the open."[98]

This characterization of the New Left counterculture as "crypto-Dionysian" gives us a further clue into Rand's historical savvy. As I suggested in Chapter 1, Rand had witnessed the same emotionalist, orgiastic, Dionysian elements in the Russian Symbolist movement of the Silver Age. In their exaltation of the cultic loss of self, the Symbolists had internalized the flagrant mysticism and collectivism of the Russian cultural milieu. Despite a revolutionary aesthetic, the Symbolists reflected their Russian roots. In Rand's view, the New Left was no different. It was a pure by-product of its cultural context.

On Level 1 and Level 2 of her analysis of power relations, Rand had traced the broad effects of psychological, ethical, linguistic, cultural, and pedagogical practices on the autonomy and efficacy of the individual. Rand saw these factors in terms of their organic conjunction; each was both a precondition and a consequence of the other. Her dialectical sensibility helped her to project an all-encompassing, multilevel, non-Marxist, radical resolution. But Rand's task was not complete. In challenging the implicit, antirational premises at work in modern culture, Rand mounted a simultaneous assault on the explicit antirational economic, social, and political structures and policies of the modern predatory state.

12 The Predatory State

On Level 3 of her analysis, Rand focused on the relations of power as mediated through statist structures and processes. She emphasized the role of the predatory state in perpetuating social dualism and fragmentation. She recognized that power relations at this level simultaneously incorporate and depend on the interpersonal and cultural conditions she explored on Levels 1 and 2.

The Mixed Economy

It must be remembered that Rand's political theory was an attempt to enunciate and defend the underlying social principles of capitalism. The capitalist system, ideally understood, was based on the volitional exchange of values. Within such a system, "economic power is exercised by means of a *positive*, by offering men a reward, an incentive, a payment, a value" for their labors.[1] In a pure capitalist system, Rand saw no inherent dualism between the state and the market. She rejected the anarchist resolution because it reified a dualism between state and market that was historically specific to statism. Individualist anarchists typically sought resolution by proposing the market's absorption of all political functions.

The anarchists were responding, no doubt, to the brutality of statism. Statism had created a violent antagonism between state and market. It sought to reconcile their opposition by the complete political absorption of the economic sphere. The organizing social principle of statism was "political power," which "is exercised by means of a *negative*, by the threat of punishment, injury, imprisonment, destruction." The trader deals in a market of values, but the statist deals in fear, authority, and obedience (48). In Rand's view, statism concentrates extensive economic, political, and social controls in the state at the expense of individual rights. It is the negation of every rational and moral principle of social organization. It is a structural formation of legalized looting, "a system of institutionalized violence and perpetual civil war, that leaves men no choice but to fight to seize power over one another."[2]

As a twentieth-century social critic, Rand witnessed some of the most flagrant state brutality in human history. In keeping with her revolt against formal dualism, Rand opposed both fascism and communism as "two variants of the same political system." Despite their apparent ideological and sociological differences, both systems were fundamentally statist. They enslaved the poor and expropriated the rich "in favor of a ruling clique." The struggle between fascists and communists and each of their political derivatives obscured the central issue of contemporary politics, the clash not between rich and poor, but between the individual and the state, between capitalism and statism.

While Rand did not live to see the death of communism, she was convinced that the danger to the West lay within. For Rand, Soviet communism was morally, culturally, and economically bankrupt. The West's social, economic, and political crises were not an outgrowth of external clashes with the Eastern bloc, but of its own internal contradictions, its attempt to combine elements of freedom and slavery under the rubric of the so-called, "mixed" economy. Rand argued: "A mixed economy is an explosive, untenable mixture of two opposite elements, which cannot remain stable, but must ultimately go one way or the other."[3]

Rand recognized that throughout history, all societies were "a kind of mixture," since neither the principles of freedom nor those of slavery were "observed consistently."[4] Twentieth-century social formations differed only in their relative mixtures. Western economies were typically skewed toward capitalist principles of organization, while Eastern-bloc economies were predominantly statist in their orientation.

In merging the fundamental principles of two opposing systems, the mixed economy leads to a complex interpenetration of social practices, making it extremely difficult to distinguish the "real producers of wealth" from the "pseudo-producers." Rand argues that the genuine producers are "money-makers," in the exalted sense her political theory champions. The money-makers constitute a very small minority of businessmen. They are innovative entrepreneurs and creators who translate their discoveries into material goods. By contrast, government officials and the vast majority of businessmen are pseudo-producers or "money-appropriators." The money-appropriator is a looter. He is a parasite on the wealth created by others. He becomes rich not through a process of symmetrical trade, but "by means of *legalized force*," through government favors, privileges, subsidies, and franchises.[5] While the authentic producer earns money as a means to his distinctive ends, the pseudo-producer seeks social-metaphysical prestige by flaunting "his money in vulgar displays of ostentation." For the money-appropriator, the accumulation of money is an end in itself, a gauge of his pseudo-self-esteem (7–8).

Rand's distinction between producers and pseudo-producers, money-makers and money-appropriators, is consistent with the classical liberal and modern libertarian traditions. Such thinkers as Nock, Paterson, and Mises had proposed similar distinctions.[6] Like her contemporaries, Rand attempted to trace historically those economic developments rooted in free production and exchange, and those rooted in government intervention-ism.[7] She argued, however, that as each business became entangled in a network of government regulations and controls, the objective distinction between the earned and the unearned, between the money-makers and the money-appropriators was blurred. The "mixed economy" was "a society in the process of committing suicide."[8] Genuine producers were compelled to seek government assistance, participating in a political process that was destructive of their ultimate aims, while some pseudo-producers entered the realm of production to bolster their "public image" (*New Intellectual*, 48). As the economy muddled through one crisis after another, statist ideologists continued to ascribe to "capitalism" the abuses that were a direct outgrowth of government intervention.[9]

Economic Dislocation

Rand's analysis of the political roots of economic crisis and dislocation is derived from the teachings of Austrian school theory, specifically the contributions of Ludwig von Mises. The modern Austrian school offered sophisticated theories of monopoly and the business cycle that focused on the interrelationships between state and market. While a full presentation of Austrian theory is beyond the scope of the current study, it is important to explore several key Austrian themes that Rand reiterated in her structural critique of statism.

For Rand, capitalism was a historically emergent system that was hampered from its earliest moments by a variety of cultural forces. Attacked by both the feudal right and the socialist left, capitalism inherited mass poverty but laid the basis for a revolutionary and progressive transformation (N. Branden 1967T, lecture 14). It slowly eradicated the economic necessity for child labor and enabled women to earn their own living and to move away from the social drudgery and stagnation of family life. [10]

And yet capitalism has been blamed for vast inequalities of wealth, the emergence of monopolies, and wild swings of inflation and unemployment. In Rand's view, such chaotic social and economic tendencies were not an inexorable product of the free and unimpeded market. Following the Austrian theorists, Rand argued that these structural aberrations were an outgrowth of state intervention in the market process.

The Objectivist view of the genesis of monopoly is a case in point. Alan Greenspan, drawing from Austrian theory, and writing for Objectivist periodicals, argues that the essential precondition for the establishment of any monopoly is a legal obstacle to market entry. [11] The Austrians enumerate the various institutional mechanisms that cause monopolistic price and wage rigidities, structural unemployment, and the restriction of the free flow of labor and capital. These include governmental grants of franchise, license, and subsidy; compulsory cartellization; price controls; output quotas; certificates of convenience and necessity; compulsory unionization; product control through standards of quality and safety; tariffs; immigration restrictions; minimum wage laws; maximum hour laws; conscription; conservation laws; and the use of eminent domain. Even government prohibitions on narcotics, prostitution, and gambling engender monopolistic control of black markets. [12]

In her quest to distinguish between genuine producers and pseudo-producers, Rand referred rhetorically to "big business" as "America's persecuted minority." But one of her central historical contentions constituted an indictment of big business. Rand traced the emergence of coercive monopolies to a historical movement initiated by businessmen in their struggle to exempt themselves from the rivalrous competition of the market:

"The attempts to obtain special economic privileges from the government were begun by businessmen, not by workers, but by businessmen who shared the intellectuals' view of the state as an instrument of 'positive' power, serving 'the public good,' and who invoked it to claim that the public good demanded canals or railroads or subsidies or protective tariffs."[13] Such business organizations as the National Association of Manufacturers and the various chambers of commerce had done more than any other groups in U.S. history to establish a neofascist, corporativist form of statist collectivism (Rand 1971T). The United States was racing "toward a plain, brutal, predatory, power-grubbing, de facto fascism . . . a random, mongrel mixture of socialistic schemes, communistic influences, fascist controls, and shrinking remnants of capitalism still paying the costs of it all—the total of it rolling in the direction of a fascist state."[14]

Grants of monopolistic privilege produced a modern, rigidified caste system. The statist ideologists defended this system by claiming that a business-government "partnership" was essential to industrial and technological progress. But in Rand's view, to call such an incestuous relationship a "partnership" was to engage in an anti-conceptual "linguistic corruption." The neofascist ideology saw no distinction between production and predation. It regarded "force as the basic element and ultimate arbiter in all human relationships." Such a "partnership" created an aristocracy of political pull, which benefited "the worst type of predatory rich, the rich-by-force, the rich-by-political-privilege, the type who has no chance under capitalism, but who is always there to cash in on every collectivist 'noble experiment.' "[15] This aristocracy of pull enabled private groups to wield governmental power, without the responsibility it entailed.[16] Dishonesty was "inherent in and created by the system."[17]

Just as business initiated the movement toward monopoly, it was also responsible for the nineteenth-century passage of the antitrust laws as a means of quelling competition.[18] Rand viewed antitrust legislation with particular disdain because it invariably benefited the inefficient at the expense of the efficient. It introduced an element of dictatorial caprice into U.S. law. For Rand, the brutality of a dictatorship was not due to its enforcement of strict and rigid rules. Dictatorships enforce rules in an unpredictable, incomprehensible, and irrational manner. Their goal is to undermine human efficacy by creating social conditions of "chronic uncertainty."[19] The antitrust laws were implemented in the same arbitrary manner. They were a mass of contradictions that could penalize any businessman for pricing his products too low, too high, or at the same level as his competitors. By complying with one law, a businessman risked criminal prosecution under another.[20]

Rand's analysis of American neofascism occurred at a time when revisionist scholars of the left academy were engaging in a similar critique. Such historians as Gabriel Kolko and James Weinstein documented the extent to which big business, faced with the rivalrous rigors of the competitive market, turned to the federal government to establish the industrial consolidation that they were unable to achieve by strictly economic means. Kolko argued that the market, with its decentralizing tendencies and falling relative prices, constantly thwarted the efforts of big business to achieve monopolistic control over the economy. The relatively freer markets of the nineteenth century had generated a vast productive capacity that threatened the economic status of established businesses and ushered in an era of innovation and technological growth. The "political means" were used by each industrial interest in its search for industry-wide cartellization and rationalization. Monopolistic practices were legally sanctioned through the regulatory agencies of the federal government, affecting nearly every industry, including railroads, trucking, farming, communications, iron, steel, oil, medicine, pharmaceuticals, insurance, and banking. With the emergence of "war collectivism" and the welfare-warfare state of the post–New Deal era, the establishment of American corporativism was complete.[21]

While Rand would have adamantly rejected Kolko's anticapitalism, her own Austrian-derived analysis provided a provocative complement to the revisionist historical investigations.[22] Rand viewed the genesis and persistence of monopolies as a significant component of the statist structure of power. It is no surprise then that Rand saw the creation of the banking monopoly as the single most dangerous statist intervention into the economy, the root of the trade cycle. Once again, Rand's critique draws heavily from the Austrian tradition.

The Austrian theory of the business cycle is built on the insights of Mises and Hayek. These thinkers engaged in pioneering work on the nature and use of knowledge in the market economy. The market process, in Austrian theory, is a dynamic mechanism for transmitting information. Prices transmit knowledge of relative scarcities. Entrepreneurs make decisions based on the informational content of market price signals. Prices alert entrepreneurs to discrepancies and disequilibria, offering profit opportunities for capital investment and economic growth. Rand explains:

> An industrial economy is enormously complex: it involves calculations of time, of motion, of credit, and long sequences of interlocking

contractual exchanges. This complexity is the system's great virtue
and the source of its vulnerability. The vulnerability is psycho-
epistemological. No human mind and no computer—and no planner—can grasp the complexity in every detail. Even to grasp the
principles that rule it, is a major feat of abstraction. This is where
the conceptual links of men's integrating capacity break down:
most people are unable to grasp the working of their home-town's
economy, let alone the country's or the world's.[23]

Rand shares the Austrian view that system-wide discoordination in the
structure of relative prices is the outgrowth of an inflationary expansion of
the money supply. Rand recognizes that the preconditions and distortive
consequences of inflation are primarily "psycho-epistemological" (159).
Inflation dupes the producers into extending investment capital, what Rand
calls "the stock seed of industry," because of an artificial lowering of the
interest rate. Whereas genuine interest rates reflect people's time preferences, inflation makes it appear that more money, or greater savings, is
actually available for investment purposes. By distorting the signals for
entrepreneurial decision-making and generating a systemic discoordination
of relative prices, inflation prompts entrepreneurial investments that do not
reflect the actual savings-investment ratios. When the boom is completed,
malinvestments must be liquidated as the market reasserts its genuine
consumption patterns. A massive cluster of error can only be eliminated if
the market is allowed to enter a necessary phase of depression.

Rand argues that this boom-bust cycle is the direct result of political
intervention in the market. As the gold standard is eroded and fiduciary
media are introduced into the economy through state-sanctioned fractional-
reserve banking, it becomes easier to inflate the currency in a process of
legalized counterfeiting. With the cartellization of the banking industry
through the Federal Reserve System, inflation became a structural component of the political economy, a by-product of sustained, massive credit
expansion through the state-banking nexus. This inflationary dynamic sets
the boom-bust cycle into motion.

Interestingly, Rand and the Austrians shared this view of the political
roots of economic crisis with Marx. Though Marx theorized on the basis of
assumptions significantly different from those of the Austrians, he too, saw
the state's central bank as the "pivot" of the credit system. For Marx,
the state's artificially induced monetary expansion engenders an illusory
accumulation process in which "fictitious money-capital" distorts the struc-

ture of prices. This leads to overproduction and overspeculation. Real prices—those that reflect actual supply and demand—appear nowhere, until the economy begins the necessary corrective measures.[24]

One of the major differences between Marx and the Austrians lies in their respective resolutions. Marx saw the boom-bust cycle as destructive, but historically progressive because it magnified class struggle and facilitated socialized control of production and capital investment.[25] By contrast, Rand and her Austrian contemporaries saw the trade cycle as retrogressive, necessarily benefiting some groups at the expense of others.

Rand recognized that sustained government intervention in the market was partially designed to quell the deleterious effects of boom and bust for which it was ultimately responsible. But continued political intervention thwarted the reassertion of genuine price patterns. Ultimately, the state-banking nexus enables the government to free itself from the limits of its revenues and to engage in deficit financing of its various welfare and warfare schemes. Stepping far beyond its legitimate functions, cutting "the connection between goods and money," the government becomes a parasite on the private economy, consuming its "stock seed."[26]

While the emergence of the welfare state attempts to deal with structurally generated poverty, its primary task is to dilute growing discontent by creating classes of politically privileged dependents. The actual welfare recipients become the "visible profiteers" of institutional altruism. But they "are part victims, part window dressing for the statist policies of the government." As the government increases the scope of its interventions, it establishes a bureaucratic system of subsidized consumption for the benefit of proliferating pressure groups and economic interests (161–62). The predatory rich wish to rule, while the victimized poor wish to be ruled.[27] Rand argues that "morally and economically, the welfare state creates an ever accelerating downward pull" serving the needs of the groups making demands and the needs of those in power "who require a group of dependent favor-recipients in order to rise to power."[28]

But Rand argues that the predatory rich, the pseudo-producers, are the predominant material beneficiaries of the welfare-statist expansion. Welfarism froze the status quo and perpetuated "the power of the big corporations of the pre-income-tax era, placing them beyond the competition of the tax-strangled newcomers."[29] Having initiated the policy of government interventionism, businessmen became ever more dependent on a political, rather than an economic, process of accumulation. Like Hayek, Rand maintained that the more the state came to dominate social and economic life, the more political power became the only power worth having.[30]

Rand believed that organized labor was potentially a bulwark against state expansion because it often recognized the differential economic and political benefits that certain businesses derived from interventionism. But the organized union movement sought to counter pro-business controls with pro-labor controls. Though labor was "much more sensitive to the long-range implications" of statist interventionism than business, it too, was involved in an internal contradiction.[31] Although Rand supported the right of voluntary union association, the use of the boycott, and the strike, she opposed compulsory unionism. She argued that unions had joined in the statist game of their business counterparts, fueling structural unemployment by forcing wage rates above their market levels.[32] In Rand's view, both business and labor were perishing in an orgy of mutual self-sacrifice. She warned: "He who lives by a legalized sword, will perish by a legalized sword."[33]

The welfare state and its widening cartellization did not cease at the nation's borders. Rand maintained that economic dislocation leads to an expansion of interventionism at home and abroad. Government begins to subsidize foreign investment through direct assistance, the United Nations, and the World Bank. Business sells its products to foreign nations, which pay for them with money received from foreign aid. Ultimately, however, in the face of economic chaos, statists resort to their "favorite expedient . . . in times of emergency: a war."[34]

In Rand's view, there is an organic link between statism and militarism. The government that does not respect the rights of its own citizens will not respect the rights of others living in foreign lands. Just as the rule of physical force comes to predominate in statist domestic policy, so too does it determine the direction of statist foreign policy. Statism "*needs* war." It "survives by looting." It makes war both possible and necessary. Moreover, it creates a context that benefits those pseudo-producers who are unable to survive on a free market. Such businessmen amass huge fortunes by means of colonialist conquest and foreign exploitation.[35]

But the neofascist mixed economy could not conduct a reckless foreign policy without further intrusions into the lives of its citizens. Rand maintained that a genuinely free society would rely upon an all-volunteer force to defend its legitimate self-interest. Under conditions of freedom, few would volunteer to become cannon fodder in the pursuit of irrational foreign policy goals. Statism often requires the institutionalization of a military draft. Rand believed that the draft is the worst statist violation of individual rights. It is based upon the premise that a citizen's life belonged to the state. It allows the state to sacrifice its citizens in wars, such as Korea and Vietnam, that have no clear bearing on national self-defense.[36]

Rand offered a radical assessment of the relationship between the state and militarism. And yet, as a social critic, she sometimes endorsed foreign policy positions that were closer to traditional conservatism. Rand was generally an isolationist in foreign policy; she questioned U.S. involvement in World War I, and by extension, in World War II, and advocated a U.S. withdrawal from the United Nations.[37] In addition, her immense hostility toward the Soviet Union made her less likely to question the structural effects of continued U.S. defense build-ups and police actions.[38] In a speech to West Point cadets, for instance, she argued that "the military-industrial complex" is "a myth or worse."[39]

But Rand was certainly not oblivious to the damaging consequences of statist militarism. *Atlas Shrugged* depicts a statist society in which there is a deadly alliance between government, science, and big business.[40] In the novel, the creation of "Project X" by the state-science nexus illustrates Rand's conviction that only the state can breed weapons of mass destruction. Under statism, "the progress of science is a threat to the people."[41]

Like the Frankfurt school theorists who decried scientism and instrumentalism, Rand warned of the lethal barrier that modern statists had built between science and ethics. For Rand, Western scientific civilization was dominated by an altruist morality of "prehistorical savagery." This was "a ghastly spectacle," in Rand's view, because it divorced means from ends, process from substance.[42] This dualism was a central implication of Kantian philosophy, which had allowed "man's reason to conquer the material world," even as it eliminated "reason from the choice of the goals for which material achievements are to be used." Consequently, contemporary scientists, slurping at the public trough, proposed strictly technical solutions to human problems, never asking how people *should* live.[43]

In Rand's view, state-sponsored scientific research was necessarily politicized. Whether it attempted to restrict or alternatively, to promote, certain forms of technology, the state introduced massive distortions into the structure of production. Rand saw the problem of pollution control, for instance, as one that could be ameliorated by the internalization of market "externalities" through privatization. Ultimately, she believed that pollution could be controlled through technological and scientific progress that state intervention would only undermine. In restricting technology, state planners acted as if they were omniscient. They had no way to ascertain the consequences of any given restrictions on future technological innovation.[44] As Rand explained:

> Technology is applied science. The progress of theoretical science and of technology—i.e., of human knowledge—is moved by such a complex and interconnected sum of the work of individual minds that no computer or committee could predict and prescribe its course. The discoveries in one branch of knowledge lead to unexpected discoveries in another; the achievements in one field open countless roads in all the others. The space exploration program, for instance, has led to invaluable advances in medicine. Who can predict when, where or how a given bit of information will strike an active mind and what it will produce?[45]

But if space exploration contributed to medical advances, it was also true that the state-funded space program, much like the state-funded railroad expansion of the nineteenth century, introduced discoordinating changes into the delicate network of the social economy. Though Rand celebrated the symbolism of the lunar landing, she did not see scientific research as a legitimate governmental function. Rand claimed: "The 'conquest of space' by some men . . . [was] accomplished by expropriating the labor of other men who are left without means to acquire a pair of shoes."[46]

The intervention of the state into scientific research also had far-reaching effects on the structure and content of U.S. education. Rand had opposed compulsory public schooling on moral grounds; she saw state-controlled education as consistent with the Nazi or communist worldview. But government intervention had created a disaster even in private education. The voluntary contributions that sustained private universities were eroded by ever-increasing taxes and rising inflation. Most universities became dependent upon government research projects as their prime source of income. Inevitably, government controlled the direction of research and created an official orthodoxy and privileged elite. Typically, such research perpetuated anti-conceptual compartmentalization. Moreover, it forced the taxpayers to support ideas that were often inimical to their own beliefs.[47]

In her analysis of the effects of statist intervention, Rand followed her Austrian contemporaries in their belief that government controls create "economic disclocations, hardships and problems, which—if the controls are not repealed—necessitate further controls, which necessitate still further controls, etc."[48] Each intrusion into the market becomes both the precondition and the consequence of every other intrusion. Each intervention is a precondition because it necessitates further interventions; each is a consequence because it is brought about by previous interventions. In this regard, Rand's analysis of the statist spiral resembles the dialectical formulations of Marx in his examination of the production process: "Each pre-condition of the social production process is at the same time its result, and every one of its results appears simultaneously as its precondition. All the *production relations* within which the process moves are therefore just as much its products as they are its conditions" (*Surplus Value*, 3:507).

Like Marx, Rand recognized an organic conjunction, a mutual reinforcement of factors within a self-perpetuating system. And also like Marx, Rand recognized that the "chain reaction" is far more insidious because it embodies internecine warfare between social groups. Each intrusion into the market process leads the victimized groups to seek a form of "redress by imposing controls on the profiteering groups, who retaliate in the same manner, on an ever-widening scale." Employing the master-slave analogy on this structural level of her analysis, Rand wrote: "If a nation cannot survive half-slave, half-free, consider the condition of a nation in which every social group becomes both the slave and the enslaver of every other group." The neofascist mixed economy institutes a "cold civil war" in which "every social group is destroying every other."[49] In its persistent use of physical force to achieve its policy goals, the statist system engendered massive social fragmentation.

Social Fragmentation

Rand argued that in a free society, there are no inherent conflicts of interest among rational individuals, but in a nonfree society, there *are* inherent conflicts of interest among individuals—whether they are rational or not.[50]

In this proposition, Rand suggested a grasp of class dynamics in contemporary statism. But Rand did not develop a theory of class struggle because she did not believe that statism benefited any one social group *structurally*. In this regard, her exploration of power relations on Level 3 applied the master-slave analysis of Level 1 with ruthless consistency. Statism made masters and slaves of every social group. All were "victims and losers," even if some gained differential benefits at the expense of others (Rand 1962). Each group was tied helplessly to the government in some fashion (1971T). In her view, statism required "a class of beggars."[51]

Under statism, the rule of force is a corrupting influence, since it creates institutional means for legalized predation. Rand states: "If *this* is a society's system, no power on earth can prevent men from ganging up on one another in self-defense—i.e., from forming *pressure groups*."[52] Pressure-group warfare was an inexorable by-product of the mixed economy.[53] It was for this reason that Rand characterized statism as an "anti-system." Just as statism emerged from and perpetuated the antirational and the anti-conceptual, so too did it constitute an "anti-system," which militated against genuine social integration and unity. It reproduced social fragmentation on a grand scale, fostering the cult of compromise in material, spiritual, and intellectual affairs. Initially, however, the statist anti-system fragments the nation into economic groups that fight offensive and defensive political battles for their own self-preservation. The mixed economy is "an amoral, institutionalized civil war of special interests and lobbies, all fighting to seize a momentary control of the legislative machinery, to extort some special privilege at one another's expense by an act of government—i.e., by force."[54]

The mixed economy is "amoral" because it makes honest and just decision making irrelevant to the legislative process. No legislative decisions can be morally justified when each act of law necessarily sacrifices some groups to others.[55] Every group, regardless of the merits of its cause, becomes "a potential threat to everyone," holding the power, not merely to disagree, but to destroy.[56] Each legislative action is a by-product of predatory lobbying in which groups participate in strategic forms of communicative interaction. Social courtesies, parties, favors, threats, bribes, and blackmail consume the process. Rand insists: "If parasitism, favoritism, corruption, and greed for the unearned did not exist, a mixed economy would bring them into existence."[57] But Rand maintained that none of the respective groups constituted a monolithic class. Even as each social class preys on adversarial classes, the "real warfare" of the mixed economy occurs within classes, not between them. The pseudo-producers within each class prey on the genuine producers of their own class as a means to the enforcement of an unearned, stagnant economic equality. Such a process of intragroup annihilation must ultimately destroy the authentic producers, the money-makers, in all classes and professions.[58]

As the mixed economy careens from one crisis to another, warfare between and within pressure groups intensifies. In this social context of wild uncertainty, each group attempts to deal with perceived threats to its efficacy by relying on the state. State action provides an illusory sense of control, since in the long run, political intervention necessarily undermines the stability and efficacy of every social group and every individual.[59] Rand was adamant in this regard: she maintained that *every* discernable group was affected by statist intervention, not just every economic interest. *Every* differentiating characteristic among human beings becomes a tool for pressure-group jockeying: age, sex, sexual orientation, social status, religion, nationality, and race. Statism splinters society "into warring tribes."[60] The statist legal machinery pits "ethnic minorities against the majority, the young against the old, the old against the middle, women against men, welfare-recipient against the self-supporting."[61]

Racism

In Rand's view, racism is the most vicious form of social fragmentation perpetuated by modern statism. Racism is not a mere by-product of state intervention; it is a constituent element of statism.

Rand's critique of racism is a good illustration of her three-level analysis. On Level 1, she examined racism in terms of its psycho-epistemological and ethical implications. On Level 2, she explored the linguistic and conceptual subversion that institutional racism requires. On Level 3, she linked her discussion to the broader, structural context of contemporary statism. Each level is a precondition and reciprocal implication of the other.

Nathaniel Branden claims that despite Rand's antagonism toward racism, she was reluctant to write on the subject because it had been monopolized by the left. But Branden (1989, 335) persuaded Rand to contribute her first essay on racism in the September 1963 issue of *The Objectivist Newsletter*. Rand argued initially from a psycho-epistemological and ethical standpoint. She wrote: "Racism is the lowest, most crudely primitive form of collectivism." It negated the uniqueness of the individual, his reason, choice, and values by "ascribing moral, social or political significance" to his "genetic lineage." It judged each individual solely on the basis of "his internal body chemistry . . . not by his own character and actions, but by the characters and actions of a collective of ancestors." Psychologically, it emerged from the "racist's sense of his own inferiority." It was "a quest for the unearned," "a quest for automatic knowledge," and "a quest for *an automatic self-esteem* (or pseudo-self-esteem)." In evaluating people by a racial criterion, racists attempt to by-pass the need to rationally judge the facts of a person's character. They seek moral distinction not in their own actions, but in the actions and beliefs of their forebears.[62] They struggle "to induce *racial guilt*," by punishing people for the sins—real or illusory—committed by their ancestors.[63]

The racist has an associational, perceptual psycho-epistemology that stores concrete memories and emotional estimates of isolated incidences. Such a mentality is incapable of thinking in terms of principles or abstractions (Rand, quoted in B. Branden 1962T, lecture 6). Racism, in all of its forms, was a "manifestation of the anti-conceptual mentality." The fear of foreigners (xenophobia), the group loyalty of the guild, the ancestor worship of the family, the blood ties of the criminal gang, and the chauvinism of the nationalist were all examples of anti-conceptual tribalism. Tribalism was "a reciprocally reinforcing cause and result" of the various caste systems throughout history.[64]

Rand argued: "Philosophically, tribalism is the product of irrationalism and collectivism." Though some people denigrate the efficacy of reason, they cannot dispense with the need for a comprehensive view of their own existence. They cannot dispense with the need for self-efficacy and self-worth. Such people will seek an illusory efficacy and worth by latching on to any group that provides them with a frame of reference. The group seems to possess a kind of "knowledge" the individual lacks, a "knowledge" acquired by an effort-less, ineffable process. People find that the easiest group to join is that to which they belong by virtue of birth—their race.[65]

Moving toward Level 2 of her analysis, Rand recognized that the individual's awareness of himself in racial terms was not always a cause for concern in the multicultural, contemporary society. Rand did not object to the need of individuals to take pleasure in their familial or ancestral backgrounds. Commenting on Alex Haley's *Roots*, for instance, Rand (1977T) recognized that African Americans had been robbed of a historical past. Having been torn forcibly from their culture, they needed to project "moral heroes." Haley's book, in Rand's view, created a useful mythology, an exalted, "enormously compelling and very beautiful" image of how people in despair could preserve their human dignity.

What Rand objected to was the practice of those who sought to substitute their lineage for an authentic self-esteem. Self-efficacy and self-worth cannot be derived from others—past or present. In the twentieth century, the most notorious—and murderous—practitioners of such racial worship were the Nazis. Nazi ideology had obliterated the core of individualism by ascribing notions of good and evil to whole groups of people based upon their alleged blood ties (Peikoff 1982). Following Rand, Peikoff argued that nationalism was in essence a form of tribalism and racism. It was not a rationally patriotic loyalty to the principles on which a country was based. Rather, it extolled and defended the Volk, the nation, on the grounds of racial purity.[66]

Rand recognized that contemporary racist doctrines were frequently disguised as celebrations of "ethnicity." In Rand's view, "ethnicity" was an anti-concept that concealed the individual's racism. The advocates of "ethnicity" conform to their ethnic groups' traditions. They see language not as a conceptual tool but as "a mystic heritage." Their "hysterical loyalty" to subtle differences of dialect and ritual provide them with an illusory sense of self-esteem derived from the blood collective to which they belong.[67]

Such tribalism had engulfed Europe for centuries. Rand argued that in such a tribalist atmosphere, not even collectivistic Marxism could succeed. For Rand, Marxism was false and corrupt, but "clean" in comparison to the tribalist anti-conceptual mentality:

> Marxism is an *intellectual* construct; it is false, but it is an *abstract* theory—and *it is too abstract for the tribalists' concrete-bound, perceptual mentalities.* It requires a significantly high level of abstraction to grasp the reality of "an *international* working class"—a level beyond the power of a consciousness that understands its own village, but has trouble treating the nearest town as fully real. (126)

Such ethnic tribalism seriously undermined the Soviets' attempts to establish a communist hegemony.[68]

Perhaps it was Rand's experiences in the Soviet Union that influenced her hostility toward quotas. Though Rand benefited from the abolition of educational restrictions on Jews and women students, she bore witness to the reinstatement of quotas by the Bolshevik regime. Just as the czars had practiced institutional racism, the Bolsheviks attempted to boost the participation of "proletarian" students through open admissions, relaxed educational standards, and a mass purge of "bourgeois" scholars and pupils. Unqualified students were advanced on the basis of their proletarian background. It was this experience perhaps that led Rand to see all "affirmative action" programs as humiliating and degrading to the individual's talents and abilities.

Indeed, for Rand, the notion of "affirmative action," was but another anti-concept to hide the reinstitutionalization of race as a criterion of judgment. Quotas embodied an internal contradiction. They attempted to use racism in order to combat racism. They categorized all members of a given racial group as identical. This stereotyped collectivization of all minority group members was achieved first in the eyes of those who did not gain from quotas and who resented the beneficiaries. But even those who benefited from quotas were humiliated by the stigma of helplessness and victimization.[69]

The imposition of quotas by the state could only inspire more "blind, interracial hatred."[70] Just as the state's financial inflation caused the debasement of the currency, so too did the state's "moral inflation" cause the debasement of genuine morality. By multiplying countless forms of injustice, in the name of justice, the state ultimately enriched itself and its dependents (312). Rand argued that racism could not, therefore, be explained on the sole basis of the tribalists' psycho-epistemology or on the basis of ideological utility. Racists had a vested interest in their biases (Rand, quoted in B. Branden 1962T, lecture 6). Moving toward Level 3 of her analysis, Rand recognized that tribalism, irrationalism, and collectivism had been present throughout history. She sought to explain their rebirth in the modern era, their historically specific manifestations in contemporary statism.

Rand argued that the relationship between statism and tribalism was reciprocal. The tribal premise was the ideological and existential root of statism. Statism had arisen out of "prehistorical tribal warfare." Once established, it institutionalized its own racist subcategories and castes in order to sustain its rule.[71] The perpetuation of racial hatred provided the state with a necessary tool for its political domination. Statists frequently scapegoated racial and ethnic groups in order to deflect popular disaffection with deteriorating social conditions.[72] But if tribalism was a precondition of statism, statism was a reciprocally related cause. Racism had to be implemented politically before it could engulf an entire society: "The political cause of tribalism's rebirth is the *mixed economy*—the transitional stage of the formerly civilized countries of the West on their way to the political level from which the rest of the world has never emerged: the level of permanent tribal warfare" (123).

In Rand's view, the mixed economy had splintered the country into warring pressure groups. Under such conditions of social fragmentation, any individual who lacks a group affiliation is put at a disadvantage in the political process. Since race is the simplest category of collective association, most individuals are driven to racial identification out of self-defense. Just as the mixed economy manufactured pressure groups, so too did it manufacture racism.[73]

And just as the domestic mixed economy made racism inevitable, so too did the global spread of statism. Rand saw the world fracturing into hostile ethnic tribes with each group aiming to destroy its ethnic rivals in primitive conflicts over cultural, religious, and linguistic differences. Rand called the process one of "global balkanization." In 1977, in a statement of prophetic significance, she observed that the situation in Czechoslovakia and Yugoslavia was symptomatic of the larger, global trend. The "Balkan tribes . . . never vanished," Rand wrote, "they have been popping up in minor explosions all along, and a major one is possible at any time."[74]

In her critique of racism, however, Rand focused most of her attention on American race relations. She argued that the utter devastation in the African American community was a historical product of statist brutality. Slavery was the complete negation of individual rights and dignity. In the United States, it predominated in the agrarian-feudal South. Rand agreed with those Marxist historians who argued that it was the capitalist North that destroyed the slavery of the noncapitalist South. For Rand, however, the destruction of slavery illustrated the virtue of the capitalist system, which left "no possibility for any man to serve his own interests by enslaving other men." Only capitalism, with its free trade and free immigration, could squelch the rebirth of domestic and global tribalism.[75]

However, the post-slavery period in U.S. history did not eradicate the problem of racism. In Rand's view, racism continued especially "among the poor white trash" of the South whose support of this apartheid was a reprehensible by-product of their own sense of inferiority.[76] But Rand opposed forced segregation *and* forced integration. She argued that racism could not be forbidden or prescribed by law. And while she supported social ostracism and economic boycott as powerful weapons in the struggle for racial equality, she asserted that racism could not be defeated in the absence of a genuine philosophical, cultural, and political revolution.[77]

Rand and other Objectivists, such as George Reisman, traced the social disintegration in the African American community to persistent political intervention. Those African Americans who migrated north were victimized by zoning laws, rent control, public housing and education, urban renewal, municipal health and sanitation services, franchise and licensing laws.[78] Each of these institutional mechanisms blocked their entry into the semi-competitive market and ghettoized their communities. Intergenerational welfare became the only recourse for a disproportionate number of African Americans, since their low wages were often competitive with welfare allowances. The welfare system, funded by grand-scale extortion of the taxpayer, severed *"economic rewards from productive work."*[79] This institutional duality between values and action, money and effort, had long-term deleterious psychological effects on the victims of welfare statism.

Rand argued that in many circumstances, the civil rights leaders only perpetuated the problem by advocating enforced economic egalitarianism as a panacea. Since the psychology of victimization was "a precondition of the power to control a pressure group," many of these leaders sought comfort in the notion that their own constituency was a "passive herd crying for help." Many condemned the achievers in their own communities as "Uncle Tom's."[80] They exploited the despair of their constituents by offering them jobs, subsidies, or expanded welfare privileges. Invariably, the only beneficiaries of such schemes were the group leaders, the welfare bureaucrats, and the politicians who derived electoral strength from blocks of ethnic support.[81]

The cultural predominance of the altruist morality and the educational system's perpetuation of concrete-bound pedagogical methods served to reinforce intolerable African American repression. Children were raised in a social atmosphere that kept them in a state of mental inertia not all that different from the mentality of slaves.[82] In an effort to escape from such conditions, many turn to drugs and crime as a way of life.[83]

For Rand and her followers, even though the plight of African Americans was historically unique, it was symptomatic of the larger illness affecting U.S. society and the world. Just as the mixed economy bred racial conflict between black and white, it perpetuated racism in nearly every cultural institution. The statist society required fragmentation, compartmentalization, and tribalism. It is within this context that Reisman has characterized the multicultural movement in education not as a paean to ethnic pride, but as a "racist road to barbarism."[84] The growing racial and ethnic strife in U.S. society has made the further fragmentation of the academy inevitable.

Conservatism versus Liberalism

Rand's fundamental antipathy toward racism was a contributing factor in her rejection of political conservatism. She observed that many conservatives claimed to be defenders of freedom and capitalism even though they advocated racism at the same time.[85] Such a combination was lethal, in Rand's view, because it served to discredit capitalism. It was for this reason that Rand reserved her most vicious rhetoric for the conservative racists. In 1968, she characterized George Wallace's American Independent Party as a crude, openly fascist movement that combined racism, primitive nationalism, militant, populist anti-intellectuality, welfare statism, and a reliance on state coercion as a means to the resolution of social problems.[86]

But Rand's wrath toward conservatism extended equally to its representatives in the major political parties and in the media. She (1964b, 13–14) considered William Buckley's "*National Review* the worst and most dangerous magazine in America," and attacked the conservative alliance of capitalism with faith, tradition, and depravity.[87] Strategically, Rand distanced herself from conservatives because she believed that it was dangerous to have political allies who shared some of her free-market and anticommunist opinions, but based these on irrational philosophical premises (in Peikoff 1976T, lecture 5). On the prospect of Ronald Reagan's election, for instance, Rand said that she was "glad to be old," and wished for her own death if such a cataclysmic event took place (in lecture 7). Though she believed that Reagan was sincere in his "folksy sentimentality," she argued that he was a moral monster. Reagan's ties to the "militant mystics" of the Moral Majority and his opposition to abortion portended an "unconstitutional union of religion and politics."[88] Rand had even denounced Aleksandr Solzhenitsyn, despite his heroic expose of the Gulag, for this same integration of religion and politics. She argued that Solzhenitsyn had rejected Marxism, not for its statist and anticapitalist character, but for its "western" atheistic focus. Rand derided Solzhenitsyn as a "Slavophile" and a "totalitarian collectivist" who would have merely substituted a Russian orthodox theocracy for the communist state (1976T). In Rand's view, no inspiration was to be found "in the God-Family-Tradition swamp."[89]

Rand maintained that the conservative obsession with the "Family" was at root, a vestige of tribalism: "The worship of the 'Family' is mini-racism, like a crudely primitive first installment on the worship of the tribe. It places the accident of birth above a man's values, the unchosen physical ties of kinship above a man's choices, and duty to the tribe above a man's right to his own life."[90]

Though Rand recognized the crucial importance of the parent-child relationship, she argued that the Family was a cultural institution that frequently undercut the individual's independence and autonomy, breaking "a man's or a woman's spirit by means of unchosen obligations and unearned guilt."[91] Devotion to the Family was a con game in Rand's view, in which the weaker and irresponsible family members are dependent on those who are stronger. Frequently, the relations within the family mirror those of master and slave. Just as the stronger members are exploited, they are also obeyed. For Rand, these family figures become "mini-dictator[s]" (in Walker 1992T).

Beginning with her rejection of conservatism, Rand became disillusioned with the two major alternatives in U.S. politics. Whereas the conservatives sought to perpetuate the tyranny of the Family, the liberals sought to make the nation one huge Family, dedicated to the exploitation of the producers for the benefit of the money-appropriators. As early as 1962, Rand suggested that U.S. electoral politics had offered the citizens two major political parties dedicated to the preservation of the status quo. Whereas the Democratic liberals sought to "leap" into the abyss of statism, the Republican conservatives preferred to crawl "into the same abyss." Elections were contests in which voters casted their ballots not *for* a particular candidate or program, but merely *against* the politician or proposed policy changes that they feared most.[92]

It was this early observation on the futility of U.S. politics that led Rand to a more thorough consideration of the conservative-liberal distinction. Prompted by Supreme Court decisions on censorship and pornography, Rand's dialectical analysis of the dualism in contemporary thought was a microcosm of her genuinely radical alternative.

Rand was a principled civil libertarian. Though she abhorred pornography, she opposed all legal and judicial attempts to censor it.[93] And yet Rand believed that the censorship controversy revealed the essence of the conservative-liberal duality.[94] In the nineteenth century, the classical liberal was an anti-authoritarian advocate of individual rights and laissez-faire capitalism, while the classical conservative had advocated state authority and tradition. Modern American politics achieved a near total inversion, offering "a choice between 20th century liberal statism and 19th century conservative statism."[95]

The polarity between modern conservatives and liberals was based on their dualistic metaphysical assumptions. Both schools of thought embraced different sides of the same mind-body dichotomy. The conservatives tended to advocate freedom of action in the material realm of production and business, but favored government control of the spiritual realm through state censorship and the imposition of religious values. The liberals tended to advocate freedom of action in the spiritual realm of ideas, the arts, and academia, but favored government control of the material realm in their adherence to economic regulation and welfare statism. Rand explains: "This is merely a paradox, not a contradiction: *each camp wants to control the realm it regards as metaphysically important: each grants freedom, only to the activities it despises.*"[96]

The conservatives are "mystics of spirit," metaphysical idealists, seeking to use the power of the state to control the spiritual products of the human mind. Epistemologically, the conservatives are intrinsicists and advocates of faith. The liberals are "mystics of muscle," metaphysical materialists seeking to use the power of the state to control the material products of the human mind. Epistemologically, the liberals are subjectivists and advocates of emotionalism. Each ideological group is united with its apparent opposite in rejecting reason, and the freedom that the mind requires (228–29).

As a child of Russian culture, Rand had seen this same political dualism before: in the opposition between the religious idealists and the Bolshevik materialists. The idealists, like modern-day conservatives, opposed Bolshevism with their own visions for a theocratic utopia. The Bolsheviks, like modern-day liberals, were thoroughgoing economic statists. Both sides had accepted different forms of the same collectivist tyranny.

Rand's resolution was directed toward the union of the "homeless refugees" in contemporary politics: the nontotalitarian liberals and the nontraditional conservatives.[97] Her radical alternative aimed to transcend dualism in each of its personal, cultural, and structural manifestations.

13 History and Resolution

Ayn Rand's philosophical project comprises successive negative and positive moments of inquiry. It began as a historically constituted critique of the Russian duality of religion and statism. It embraced a positive synthesis, seeking to transcend false alternatives by integrating categories traditionally kept separate and distinct. Given her critical view of dualism and her vision of the ideal individual and the ideal society, Rand was faced with the typical problem of all radical thinkers: how to move from theoretical prescription to practical implementation. Like most radical thinkers, Rand looked to history for instruction.

Attila versus the Witch Doctor

Though her view of history was far more complex than some of her essays suggest, Rand's popularized exposition projects an almost apocalyptic battle between good and evil. Rand's conception reflects her Russian roots. In Russia, the two main philosophic fashions of the Silver Age proposed conflicts in similar apocalyptic terms. The mystical Symbolists warned of the impending doom of the old order; the materialist Bolsheviks posited a life-and-death struggle between communism and capitalism.

Rand's apocalyptic imagery, however, is less a clash between good and evil than one between good and two interpenetrating versions of evil. Rand relied upon symbolic metaphors to dramatize the historical opposition and mutually beneficial support that mystics and materialists derived from each other. Rand understood the value of symbolic figures as an "adjunct to philosophy." She appreciated Nietzsche's aesthetic distinction between Apollo and Dionysus because it enabled people "to integrate and bear in mind the essential meaning of complex issues."[1] Following Nietzsche, Rand's symbols were designed to achieve the same clarity and integration. They encapsulate her repudiation of mysticism and statism, each of which requires the other in order to survive. They formalize the organic relationship between the "man of faith" and the "man of force":

> These two figures . . . are philosophical archetypes, psychological symbols and historical reality. As philosophical archetypes, they embody two variants of a certain view of man and of existence. As psychological symbols, they represent the basic motivation of a great many men who exist in any era, culture or society. As historical reality, they are the actual rulers of most of mankind's societies, who rise to power whenever men abandon reason. (New Intellectual, 14)

Drawing from a designation made initially by Nathaniel Branden, Rand identified these archetypes as Attila and the Witch Doctor.[2] Attila rules by brute, physical force, whereas the Witch Doctor rules by mysticism. Like other dualities, these archetypes "appear to be opposites," but they are united by a pronounced hostility to the conceptual level of consciousness.

Attilas seek to achieve physical domination by ruling the bodies of their subjects and seizing their material products. They regard people "as others regard fruit trees or farm animals." They exhibit a "perceptual mentality," which is as close to "an animal 'epistemology' . . . as a human consciousness can come." Attilas are the anti-conceptual mentality incarnate. They do not understand the cognitive roots of production. They see no need to comprehend "how men manage to produce the things [they covet]" (New Intellectual, 14–16). In modern social science, Atillas contribute to the fragmentation of knowledge and the compartmentalization of the disciplines. They view the problems of social life in a piecemeal, concrete-bound fashion, rejecting all forms of "system-building" as "irrational, mystical and unscientific" (43–44).

In the face of such anti-conceptualism, it is little wonder that people are drawn psychologically to the Witch Doctor. Rand argues that human efficacy requires a comprehensive view of the world. The Witch Doctor attempts to fulfill this need. But the Witch Doctor's attempt at comprehensiveness is saturated with mysticism. By manipulating floating abstractions, the Witch Doctor "seeks to rule . . . men's souls." A Witch Doctor views his or her own consciousness as an "irreducible primary," obliterating "the distinction between consciousness and reality, between the perceiver and the perceived." The Witch Doctor damns the material world, the body, and the self as evil, asserts an ineffable grasp of a higher reality and proposes to lead people to paradise. The Witch Doctor achieves spiritual domination through the "lethal opposition of the *moral* and the *practical*," reducing people to sacrificial animals by attacking their self-esteem (16–18).

Thus, whereas Attilas prey on peoples' bodies, Witch Doctors prey on their souls. Whereas Attilas focus on "concretes unintegrated by abstractions," Witch Doctors accept "floating abstractions unrelated to concretes." Both of these figures "are incomplete parts of a human being who seek completion in each other: the man of muscle and the man of feelings, seeking to exist without *mind*" (19). Their historical opposition—and alliance—is "based on mutual fear and mutual contempt" (20). It is a synthesis of apparent opposites brought about by the poverty of each.

Rand argued that the dominance of Attila and the Witch Doctor was fundamentally challenged from the beginning of Western civilization by the genesis of philosophy. From the time of ancient Greece, as people were provided with a modicum of political freedom, the first rumblings of a rational view of reality were felt. Though Witch Doctor metaphysics were reproduced in the works of most of the early Greek philosophers, including Plato, it was Aristotle who became "the world's first *intellectual*, in the purest and noblest sense of that word" (22). By providing human beings with an objective view of reality, and by articulating the laws of logic, Aristotle challenged the mystic creeds of his day. For Rand, the history of philosophy was largely a duel between the secular rationality of Aristotelianism and the mysticism of Plato. Despite the achievements of Greek culture, early Western civilization was dominated by the predatory rule of statist empires and feudal tribalists. The Attilas often aligned themselves with Witch Doctors, who provided their rule with mystical, ideological legitimation. But after centuries of brutality, the reign of Attila and the Witch Doctor was fundamentally undermined by the rebirth of secular philosophy. The reintroduction of the Aristotelian worldview into Western culture, via Thomas Aquinas, was the philosophic precursor that made possible the

Renaissance, the Industrial Revolution, and capitalism. Though it took nearly four hundred years to secularize the Western mind, the release of body and soul from the domination of Attila and the Witch Doctor led to a burst of scientific discovery and invention, material production and creativity (Peikoff 1976T, lecture 12).

These historical developments brought forth thinking and acting men and women, demonstrating in a definitive manner the efficacy of the mind in the production of goods and services for human survival on earth. The newly emergent, though "mixed," capitalist systems "wiped out slavery in matter and in spirit," and introduced two new historical archetypes: "the producer of wealth and the purveyor of knowledge—*the businessman and the intellectual*" who flourished in their respective marketplaces of goods and ideas (*New Intellectual*, 25). The businessman is the conduit of science, translating technological discoveries into material products for human consumption. The intellectual is the conduit of philosophy, translating philosophic abstractions into ideational products for human consumption (26–27).

Like Marx before her, Rand saw the professional businessman and the professional intellectual "as brothers born of the industrial revolution" (13).[3] But even as the Attilas and the Witch Doctors were kept at bay, they were not completely eliminated as historical forces. The Attilas began to use ever more sophisticated methods of predation to feast on the enormous productive power unleashed by the reasoning mind. The Witch Doctors began to infiltrate secular philosophy and to undercut the efficacy of reason by couching their mysticism in technical and scientific verbiage. The great philosophical turning point was achieved by Kant, who formalized dualism, pitting mind against body, reason against reality, morality against practicality. Nearly every major modern school of philosophy derived from this Kantian irrationality (*New Intellectual*, 30–34).

Capitalism as a social formation was made possible by the rebirth of reason. But just as reason made political freedom possible, it required political freedom for its sustenance. Capitalism "was the last and (theoretically) incomplete product of an Aristotelian influence." Before it reached structural maturity, it was undercut by a resurgent tide of mysticism in a culture that had never totally abandoned the mind-body distinction and the tribal premise. In the absence of an articulated moral base, capitalism remained stillborn, forever an unknown ideal.[4]

Under capitalism, the businessman and the intellectual were archetypically involved in a process of free trade and free expression. But as the state came to dominate social life, most businessmen became modern-day Attilas, just as most intellectuals became modern-day Witch Doctors. Businessmen turned to the state to achieve consolidation and expansion. They typically scorned the realm of ideas as idealistic, impractical, and inconsequential. The intellectuals by contrast scorned the realm of production as materialistic and greedy. They provided the ideological rationale for the very predatory practices they often condemned. Their explicit and implicit attacks on rationality and freedom ideologically bolstered the power of the state. Frequently, they too depended on the state for material support of their research.

Capitalism did not make this dualism possible; it had inherited it. Capitalism had challenged dualism *radically*, but its revolution remained unconsummated. Whereas the Renaissance and the Enlightenment had made capitalism possible, modern philosophy made the death of capitalism inevitable. It could not survive in a culture so thoroughly committed to the obliteration of the mind. Rand believed that it was a "tragic irony" that businessmen and intellectuals, "the sons of capitalism," were perishing in a struggle of mutual contempt. She argued: "If they perish, they will perish together." But for Rand, "the major share of the guilt will belong to the intellectual" (*New Intellectual*, 13).

The Primacy of Philosophy

Rand's contention that the major share of the guilt would belong to the intellectual requires detailed explanation. Recall the "tier" in Diagram 2 of Chapter 11. I have recast that figure here with interconnecting arrows to emphasize the point that there is no one-way causality between any two tiers (Diagram 3).

As Diagram 3 shows, Tier 1 does not *lead to* Tier 2, and Tier 2 does not *lead to* Tier 3. Rather, each tier is a precondition and context for the other two. The political and economic systems of a given society cannot be abstracted from the culture, nor can these be abstracted from the "lifestyle" of the majority of people. Hence, it is illegitimate to discuss "capitalist" political and economic institutions as external to the culture within which they reside. Unlike Marx, Rand did not see culture as a "superstructure" of capitalist relations. Closer to the Weberian paradigm, she saw culture as a "base" that provides the broad context for political and economic relations.

Diagram 3. Reciprocal Causation in the Social and Individual Spheres

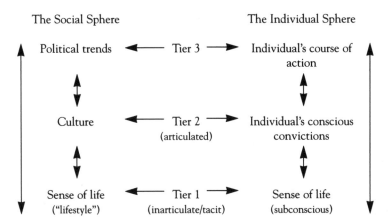

For example, Rand would have rejected the postcommunist Russian attempt to graft capitalist institutions onto an indigenous noncapitalist base. Russian culture lacked sufficient commitment to individualism and reason. Even if Russia rejected communism, its culture was constituted historically by a profound mysticism and tribalism that would necessarily undercut the effective achievement of even a Western-style mixed economy,[5] much less a purely capitalist one.

Because most people have tacitly absorbed the values of their age, Rand recognized that, in the United States, the last remnants of an Aristotelian sense of life were being eradicated under the weight of systemic irrationality. The essence of the "mixed" economy was not merely its structural mixture of the principles of capitalism and statism but its corresponding mixture in each person's soul, what Rand called "the 'mixed economies' of the spirit."[6] There were conflicting philosophic cross-currents in U.S. culture and social psychology. After two hundred years of retrenchment, secular Aristotelianism, in Rand's view, had been relegated to the cultural unconscious, as expressed in the predominating lifestyle of the American people (Tier 1). Explicit culture (Tier 2) was dominated by antirational practices, values, and ideas.

How were such antirational practices, values, and ideas transmitted culturally? Let us examine the constituent human components of Tier 2 (Diagram 4).

In Rand's view, the "philosophic system-builders" set the ultimate trends of an age or a nation's culture.[7] The ideas of the system-builder filter

Diagram 4. Tier 2: Culture

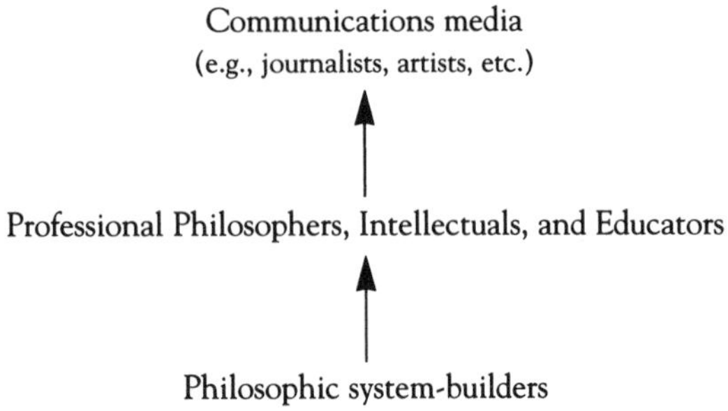

Communications media
(e.g., journalists, artists, etc.)

↑

Professional Philosophers, Intellectuals, and Educators

↑

Philosophic system-builders

through the culture as the adherents to the philosophy begin to derive implications from the innovator's teachings. Rand used military terminology to describe the crucial role of the intellectuals in this regard; the intellectual is "the field agent of the army whose commander-in-chief is the *philosopher*" (*New Intellectual*, 26–27). The intellectual proceeds to apply the system-builder's principles to a variety of subdisciplines. The central tenets are transmitted through the educational establishment to those who will become scientists, businessmen, workers, politicians, journalists, and so on. These practitioners further transmit ideas through the communications media, art, literature, and music.[8] As Kelley (1990, 28) suggests, in time, such ideas become "an element in the dominant psychology of an age, predisposing people to accept the kinds of art, behavior, and institutions that are consistent with the idea."

Rand did not believe that every single individual must accept a specific philosophic idea in order for it to qualify as a dominant trend. In any given historical period, there will be many philosophic cross-currents. But intellectual life, expressed in the normative, aesthetic, political, and economic sciences, will ultimately constitute a dominant philosophic paradigm. The key to comprehending the logic of history is to render explicit the dominant paradigm implicit in a variety of cultural forms. History, in Rand's view, is "*not* an unintelligible chaos ruled by chance" but something that can be comprehended, predicted, and shaped.[9]

Peikoff maintains that one of the prime reasons for Rand's majoring in history was her conviction that it was impossible to develop theories about the human species unless one could distinguish historically specific fashions from transhistorical elements. In Rand's view, the study of history is a prerequisite to all theoretical developments in the humanities. It is the laboratory and workshop of the social sciences; it is where the theorist discovers the role of basic factors in human evolution (Peikoff 1985T, lecture 4).

This view of history as a comprehensible, predictable, and malleable process is central to the Marxist historiography to which Rand was exposed while at Petrograd University. In contrast to the Marxist materialists, Rand argued that historical prediction is possible because each "society's existential conditions are preceded and determined by the ascendancy of a certain philosophy" among the intellectuals and purveyors of culture (*New Intellectual*, 28). The historical events of a given period will derive from the ascendant philosophy of the preceding age. Just as an individual's actions are the consequence of past thoughts, so too, a society's history is a logical unfolding of the philosophical premises it has internalized.

The primacy of philosophy in history derives from the centrality of reason in individual life. Rand constantly repeated the phrase: "Check your premises." It was the title of her column in *The Objectivist Newsletter* and appeared in countless forms throughout her writings. Rationality involves a process of both internal and external articulation. To check one's premises is to articulate the causal antecedents of one's ideas, feelings, and actions. The integrated individual does not experience any conflict between these spheres. He or she sets into motion a process in which each is brought into harmony with the other.

But by placing emphasis on the primary choice "to think or not to think," Rand avoided vicious circularity in the relations between thought, feeling, and action. It is our ability to *think* that separates us from other living organisms. If we must eat in order to think, even if we must be willing to *feel* in order to think clearly, it is thinking that constitutes our distinctive mode of survival. The *human* production of goods and the *human* experience of emotions are ultimately related to—and derived from—this primary *human* cognitive choice.[10]

This epistemological principle is instantly related to Rand's theory of history. Since we must think in order live, the *content* of our thought is deeply significant to our *individual* survival; it will direct our emotions and our actions. And since every act of material and cultural production ultimately derives from the human ability to think, the *content* of a historical period's dominant philosophic trends—internalized by the majority of people—will be just as deeply significant to their *social* survival.

Thus, in both individual and social spheres, Rand attempted to render explicit the implicit. In her theory of history, she sought to understand the philosophical roots of social policies, ideological doctrines, and the broad emotional atmosphere of contemporary culture (*New Intellectual*, 28). Just as she admonished us to check our premises, so she checked the premises of her own society. She refused to reify the tacit dimensions of consciousness or culture. She wished to inspire people to analyze their own mixed premises, and the mixed premises of the culture in which they live. She sought to push the individual and the social spheres toward a nondualistic resolution in which Tiers 1 through 3 become an integrated, rational totality.

Just as philosophy "is a necessity for a rational being,"[11] providing the individual with an essential, comprehensive view of existence, so too, does it serve an essential function in the life—and death—of a given society. She wrote: "There is only one power that determines the course of history, just as it determines the course of every individual life: the power of man's rational faculty—*the power of ideas*. If you know a man's convictions, you can predict his actions. If you understand the dominant philosophy of a society, you can predict its course. But convictions and philosophy are matters open to man's choice."[12]

Given that Rand was a deeply dialectical thinker, such a formulation seems oddly one-dimensional. Rand seemed to embrace a philosophic version of determinism that mirrors the vulgar materialist view that "the material mode of existence" is the "primary agent" in history. Yet both Marx and Engels understood the difficulties involved in identifying a singular cause within a dialectical totality. Though Engels was later accused of "revisionism," he argued persuasively in the 1890s that vulgar economism was not Marx's historiograpical credo. Engels recognized that he and Marx were "partly to blame" for the predominance of an economistic interpretation of Marx's historical method. But, he explained: "We had to emphasize the main principle *vis-à-vis* our adversaries, who denied it, and we had not always the time, the place or the opportunity to give their due to the other factors involved in the interaction."[13]

The key word here is "interaction." Sophisticated Marxist methodology incorporates a thoroughly organic understanding of historical causality, which traces the reciprocal interconnections between economic and noneconomic factors. Marx gave priority to the material mode of existence because it is production, in his view, that is most responsible for the sustenance of human life. In Marx's view, productive labor "is a necessary condition, independent of all forms of society, for the existence of the human race; it is an eternal nature-imposed necessity, without which there can be . . . no life" (*Capital*, 1:42–43). Engels argued however, that Marx did not intend for this material emphasis to become "an excuse for *not* studying history."[14] Political, ideological, philosophical, religious, racial, literary, artistic, legal, and other factors may all play a part in the human drama. All of these factors "react upon one another and also upon the economic base," but it is this base of material existence that "in the last resort," "in the last instance," must assert its primacy.[15]

Rand did not respond to this materialist conception by embracing a reified notion of the Idea as a causal agent in world history. She accepted Marx's view that production is necessary to human sustenance, but she believed that *thinking* is the essential root of human production and survival. Hence, it is thinking, the ideas that people accept and practice in their daily lives, that is the primary causal factor in human historical development. And if certain philosophic ideas lead to specific historical consequences, Rand argued nonetheless that "there is no such thing as historical determinism," for ultimately, ideas are formulated and accepted *volitionally*. People do not have to be subject to forces beyond their understanding or control.[16] For Rand, the articulation of mixed premises is an activity of critical praxis, because it makes people more conscious of tacitly accepted principles, even as it pushes them toward action by *conscious* conviction.

If Marx emphasized material causality in his historical method as a response to his Idealist adversaries, Rand came to prominence at a time when many sociologists and historians projected an image of the individual as a puppet of material forces.[17] Rand's emphasis on the power of ideas may appear as a one-dimensional response to this "oversocialized" conception of humanity, but such a characterization would suggest that she was ignorant of the reciprocal forces in historical development. This is most definitely not the case.

For Rand, ideas are not disembodied causal agents. Ideas are part of a wider totality; their genesis cannot be completely abstracted from a certain material, historical, and psychological context. First, Rand repudiated those who would dichotomize ideas and material goods. Such a distinction

> is a product of the mystics' mind-body dichotomy, which holds that ideas belong to some higher, "spiritual" dimension of reality, while goods belong to an inferior, material dimension: this earth. But, in reality, there is only one reality; man is an integrated entity of mind and body, and neither can survive without the other. Man's mind (his *ideas*) is as crucially necessary to the production of goods as the translation into a material form (into speech or print) is to the development of ideas.[18]

Second, Rand recognized that every idea emerges within a historical context. She argued that her own ethical theories could never have been fully articulated in preindustrial, precapitalist historical periods. Just as the first glimmerings of a rational philosophy emerged in Athenian society, with its "comparative degree of political freedom" (*New Intellectual*, 22), so too, the completion of the Aristotelian project was not possible until the Industrial Revolution demonstrated definitively the efficacy and practicality of reason. Based on this understanding, Rand was less judgmental of altruistic ethical and political conceptions that were fashionable in premodern cultures. For example, the anti-wealth views of St. Ambrose, who lived in the fourth century, are "explicable, if not justifiable" within the context of his culture, which lacked an appropriate philosophical understanding of the role of property in human life. Rand was not as generous to those who adopted the Ambrosean credo in the nineteenth and twentieth centuries.[19] But she was extremely realistic about the progressive acceptance of a rational philosophy; she rejected the ahistorical view that people would simply read Aristotle or Aquinas or her own works and become true believers.[20]

Aside from her recognition of the importance of an appropriate context of knowledge and culture, Rand also acknowledged that the development of ideas required a certain psychological predisposition on the part of the innovator. Peikoff argues that frequently there is a close relationship between the philosophy and the psychology of the theorist. A person with a benevolent, positive outlook on life would be less apt to author a philosophic system with death and pain as its standard than a person with a malevolent sense of life.

Peikoff has examined the relationship between philosophy and psychology in history, and concludes that ultimately, the distinction is one between an explicit conscious conviction and an implicit idea. Since Objectivism roots psychological factors, such as emotions, the subconscious, and sense of life, in certain consciously or tacitly accepted ideas, Peikoff argues that it is the absorption of certain implicit philosophic premises that will shape the individual's psychology. Thereafter, the development of philosophical and psychological factors will be concurrent.[21] The acceptance of a philosophy that sanctions obedience and authority gives rise to a psychology of dependence. The psychology of dependence requires such a philosophy. Philosophy, in this context, is not a mere rationalization of the relations of dependence; it is a causal antecedent. Philosophy will not determine the specific applications of an idea, the speed of their dissemination and proliferation into the culture, or the various consequences of progressive acceptance of a given principle. Rather, philosophy provides the broad context that predisposes a culture to accept as normal those relations which may be patently irrational (Peikoff 1991b, 452).

It is on this basis that Peikoff rejects the argument that Hitler, for instance, used altruistic slogans as a cover-up for his brutality. In the Objectivist view, altruism *is* brutality. When Hitler advocated the sacrifice of the individual to the Volk, he was being true to his altruistic roots. Had the Nazis used the notion of individual rights to justify their policies of genocide, they could never have succeeded. Peikoff does "not believe that hypocrisy is a factor in history."[22] The Attilas and the Witch Doctors have practiced what they have preached; the critical role of philosophy lies in *comprehending* the essence of their ideas in order to transcend them.[23]

"What Can One Do?"

Because Rand was a radical social thinker, she faced the difficulty of trying to chart a moral course of action for those who lived in an antirational, immoral culture. Every one of her major fictional characters—from Kira Argounova to Equality 7-2521 to Howard Roark to John Galt—accepts the Herculean task of trying to live a rational life in an irrational society. Ultimately, it is only Galt who removes himself from a collapsing social order, eventually retiring to the mountains of Colorado, and founding a "utopia of greed" based on individualist and capitalist precepts.[24] Yet most of Rand's characters—and many of her followers—were deeply alienated from the culture in which they lived.[25]

Rand rejected the founding of utopian communities as a solution to systemic irrationality. The utopia of *Atlas Shrugged* is a fictional device that projects an ideal society composed of ideal people. It is not a prescription for the future. Rand (1964b) remarked that she "was interested in politics for only one reason—to reach the day when [she] would not have to be interested in politics" (14). Though Rand advocated broad principles on which to build an ideal society, she refused to construct a detailed, futuristic blueprint. She stated unequivocally: "I am not a government planner nor do I spend my time inventing Utopias" (12). In this regard, she was not much different from Marx, who refused to concoct a "doctrinaire recipe" "for the cookshops of the future."[26]

But still Rand asks the question, "What can one do?" in the face of massive statist repression and cultural bankruptcy. Her question is the Objectivist equivalent to Chernyshevsky's and Lenin's query, "What is to be done?"[27] It encapsulates the difficulty of advocating any reforms under prevailing social conditions, the problem of moving toward a new context from a position within the status quo.

First and foremost, Rand argued that no individual can fight a political battle without challenging the basic philosophic premises on which contemporary conditions have been built. Rand reiterated that philosophy is ultimately responsible for the current state and that only philosophy can lead to a cultural and political renaissance (*New Intellectual*, 50). Therefore, any political changes must be preceded by a cultural revolution.[28] Considering the depth of her project, Rand acknowledged that "there's only so much that one person can do." She (1974T) stated, amusingly: "You don't expect me also to be some kind of woman on the barricades and lead an army on Washington; it's much too soon for that." Even if every politician disappeared, the problems of the neofascist mixed economy would remain. Genuine change encompasses personal, cultural, and structural transformation.

Personally, an individual can begin the process of altering cultural trends by focusing on his or her own struggle for enlightenment (Rand 1962T). As Nathaniel Branden (1983b) emphasizes: "One of the core meanings of *enlightenment* is liberation from false and spurious value attachments that blind the individual to his or her true essence" (91). But even as each individual struggles toward the articulation and integration of subconscious and conscious elements, *some* personal political action may be possible—and necessary—within the current context.

In broad terms, Objectivists argue that the goal of freedom cannot be served by fighting the battle on the statist's terms.[29] Statism compels people to accept their status as "sacrificial victim or moral cannibal."[30] And yet Rand believed that the victims of statist expropriation have the right, when necessary, to accept government jobs, research grants, public scholarships, unemployment compensation, social security, and welfare assistance, based on the premise of restitution. Only those who oppose state intervention have a right to such restitution, in Rand's view. Those who support statism have no such right, because it is they who perpetuate a system of codependency and institutionalized poverty.

This "paradox" is dictated by the inner contradictions of the system. The victims of statism do not advance the cause of the free society if they leave "their money, unclaimed, for the benefit of the welfare-state administration." As taxation, inflation, and deficit-spending crowd out the avenues for advancement, individuals are left with little choice but to enter into the government sphere in order to sustain their own lives. Rand recognized, however, that government welfare expenditures are a "bribe" to co-opt the support of those who are injured by statist policies. She cautioned the victims not to accept any government jobs that would demand their ideological compromise or their participation in the enforcement of "non-objective laws." In most circumstances, however, Rand believed that statism makes it impossible for individuals to determine a moral course of action. The "fundamental irrationality and immorality" of the system forces people into relations of dominance and submission. In their daily activities, individuals face persistent tests of their integrity. Rand warned that such a system leads to "a gradual, imperceptible, subconscious deterioration" in each individual's mind. People are driven inevitably to compromise, evade, or submit to dehumanizing conditions of existence (44–45).[31] Just as certain ideas generate structural conditions of repression, these structures perpetuate repression on a personal and cultural level.

Rand offered another strategic technique by which the victims of statism can milk the inner contradictions of the system. She proposed a "fairness doctrine" for U.S. education. Such a doctrine would accept the statist premise that public or quasi-public institutions (e.g., the universities, the airwaves, etc.) should grant equal time to all sides of a controversial issue. Since nearly every aspect of U.S. education has become dependent on the government, Rand believed that the fairness doctrine could temporarily impede the perpetuation of intellectual monopolies. It would require that public universities offer courses from unconventional perspectives. Such a doctrine might benefit communists, religionists, multiculturalists, and astrologists, but it would also lead to courses on Aristotle, Austrian economics, Montessori education, and Romantic literature. Rand suggested that the Establishment could be bested at its own game, even if it did not fundamentally alter its faculties and administrations.[32]

The Objectivist Society

Rand's proposals for utilizing statist policies and doctrines to lessen their distortive impact were mere exercises in political technique. Rand recognized that the mixed economy, just like the person of mixed premises, must move toward some kind of resolution as the internal contradictions of the system become apparent. But Rand offered no inexorable laws of motion. Though she believed that the imposition of controls would necessitate further interventions, she argued that people could opt out of the process and choose the path to freedom.

But this choice was only possible within the context of a philosophic and cultural revolution. Without such a change, people would have neither reason nor desire to embark on the path toward freedom. Rand saw revolution as "the climax of a long philosophical development." Justified as a response to tyranny, "it is an act of self-defense against those who rule by force."[33] While Rand admitted the possibility that people, "in sheer anger and despair," would resort to violence and mass civil disobedience, she did not view these political techniques as primaries.[34] She argued that ultimately, it was the cultural base that provided individuals with a specific menu for social change. Within the context of a massive cultural transformation, people could choose political alternatives that were radically different and realistically attainable.

But in keeping with her theory of history, Rand believed that such a cultural revolution depended on a new intellectual movement, led necessarily by a small minority,[35] a kind of intellectual vanguard. The philosophic system-builder is the source of revolution. The system-builder presents a compelling philosophic alternative and a structure of analysis that answers the human need for a comprehensive view of existence.[36] Over a long period of time, the essential ideas of the philosophic system-builder are grasped and perpetuated by intellectuals who pass on the doctrine in education, art, and the communications media. As the purveyors of ideas, these human actors generate conditions favorable for personal, cultural, and structural change.

In Diagram 5, Rand is presented as a new philosophic system-builder, akin to Plato, Aristotle, and Kant. Rand believed that the Objectivist paradigm offered a radical intellectual shift away from the dominant trend of the anti-mind, anti-man, anti-life culture. Though Rand believed that Objectivism had global implications, she emphasized its applicability to the American context, which was the subject of her social critique (Peikoff 1991b, 460). She knew that American society would not adopt her program in a month, a year, or even a century (1971T). She hoped to be the fountainhead of a philosophical renaissance that would culminate in the establishment of a society based upon the principles of laissez-faire capitalism, individual rights, and nonexploitative social relations. She instructed her followers to break from the culture, the schools, and most important, the ideas that were destroying American society; they were "to be the creators of a new culture" (1961T) (Diagram 5).

In Rand's view, an Objectivist society could emerge only *after* the dominant philosophic trend was fundamentally Objectivist. The political and economic institutions would reflect this cultural base. Self-directed thought and self-responsible action would be confirmed as efficacious in the dominant philosophy and psychology of the new age. In aesthetics, the dominant trend would be Romanticism, though many schools of art would continue to exist. The projected aesthetic ideals and values would be contemplated and appreciated by individuals whose sense of life matched their rational, conscious convictions.[37]

In an Objectivist society, the socialization process would aid, rather than hinder, the development of maturity, rationality, and self-responsibility. Parents and teachers would treat children with respect, encouraging them to think, rather than to evade. They would not deliver moral ultimatums or religious injunctions, but present the child with reasons and explanations within the context of his knowledge, for every rule (Rand [1964] 1993bT).

The development of human cognitive and evaluative capacities would turn the tide away from modern anti-conceptualism. Whereas the anti-conceptual mentality treats "the passage of time, the four seasons, the institution of marriage, the weather, the breeding of children, a flood, a fire, an earthquake, a revolution, a book [as] phenomena of the same order," genuinely conceptual beings would distinguish between those things that were open to human choice and those that were metaphysically dictated by the nature of reality.[38] People would not act on the basis of an uncritical

Diagram 5. Tier 2: The New Cultural Movement

Communications media
(e.g., journalists, artists, etc.)

↑

Professional Philosophers, Intellectuals, and Educators

↑

Ayn Rand
as
Philosophic system-builder

acceptance of traditions and/or of tacit rules of behavior (48). They would understand the nature of their actions and the implications of their beliefs. They would develop a sense of identity that would be reinforced by a sense of self-efficacy and self-worth. Accepting their own uniqueness and potential, such people would have a benevolent attitude toward one another.[39] Human communication, sexual relations, spiritual commitments, and material exchanges would not be marked by strategic lying and deceit, but by mutual trust and respect.

Thus, in seeking to overturn the dynamics of power, an Objectivist movement would spark a revolution on each of the three levels in which power is manifested: the personal (Level 1), the cultural (Level 2), and the structural (Level 3). Rand's multilevel analysis of power relations (see Diagram 1 on page 299) becomes a model for Objectivist social relations.

Rand believed that only reason and freedom could defeat faith (i.e., irrationality) and force. In statism, irrational power relations are apparent on each of three levels. In the Objectivist society, rational and free social relations would be manifested across the same personal, cultural, and structural dimensions. Rand argued that an Objectivist revolutionary movement would seek first to consummate reason and freedom on the personal and cultural levels, before seeking their realization on the structural level.

On Level 1 (the personal), the practice of a rational psycho-epistemology and a rational ethical code would simultaneously confirm and perpetuate the primacy of existence and the identity of consciousness, which is, in its essence, volitional (i.e., free). People would relate not as masters and slaves, but as independent equals, trading value for value.

On Level 2 (the cultural), the forms of culture and of language would simultaneously confirm and perpetuate the objective validity and necessity of rational and free discourse.

On Level 3 (the structural), the achievement of a libertarian political and economic ideal would end the domination of statist brutality. Rand envisioned an identity between the rational and the free social order. The genuinely rational society *is* free. The genuinely free society *is* rational.

Finally, Rand linked each of these levels with the others in an organic unity such that "*intellectual* freedom cannot exist without *political* freedom; political freedom cannot exist without *economic* freedom; *a free mind and a free market are corollaries*" (*New Intellectual*, 25).

Thus, self-responsible, free-thinking individuals would rise from all social groups and "initiate a process, not of chaining one another, but of trading de-control for de-control."[40] Statism, with its intrusive regulatory, warfare, and welfare machinery, would be replaced by the rule of objective law. The deregulation of economic and social life could not be accomplished over-night (Rand [1964] 1993cT). Nor could it be realized within the current constitutional context. Rand envisioned a legal system in which the government is severely limited to the protection of individual rights through the police, an all-volunteer army, and the courts. The state's power of eminent domain and its authority to regulate interstate commerce would be eliminated. All property—the roads, the airwaves, the forests, the oceans, even outer space—would be homesteaded and privatized.[41] As the state is separated from the banking industry, and as a strict gold standard is introduced, the boom-bust cycle would come to an end. Structural and economic dislocation would be a thing of the past. Peace and prosperity would ensue. The welfare bureaucracy would be dismantled gradually, and state intervention would end in religious, educational, scientific, and aesthetic affairs.

As a final reform, in the very distant future, Rand advocated the abolition of taxation. With minimal government services, payment for their provision would be voluntary. Citizens in a fully free society "would (and should) be willing to pay for such services, as they pay for insurance." Rand suggested several possible alternatives, including a government lottery, and the pay-ment of fees to the government as a means of enforcing contractual agreements. Such voluntary financing would be progressively "proportionate to the scale of an individual's economic activity," with "those on the lowest economic levels . . . virtually exempt."[42]

God-Builder?

In her introduction to The Romantic Manifesto, Rand wondered if she would live to see an aesthetic renaissance in her time. She added: "What I do know is this: anyone who fights for the future, lives in it today" (Romantic Manifesto, viii). Rand's statement has significance for her philosophic project as well.

Those who fight for the future must understand and integrate its guiding precepts into their everyday lives with full knowledge of the implications of their beliefs and the consequences of their actions. Those who fight for a future society in which fully integrated people interact with one another freely, must aim for that integration in their own lives now. The leaders of the renaissance will be the New Intellectuals, people who "discard the basic premise . . . [of] the soul-body dichotomy." The New Intellectual "will discard its irrational conflicts and contradictions, such as: mind *versus* heart, thought *versus* action, reality *versus* desire, the practical *versus* the moral. He will be an *integrated man*, that is: a thinker who is a man of action. He will know that ideas divorced from consequent action are fraudulent, and that action divorced from ideas is suicidal" (*New Intellectual*, 51).

The New Intellectuals conquer dualism and reunite the prodigal sons of capitalism: the intellectual and the businessman. In the realm of the intellect, they will be practical thinkers. In the material realm, they will be philosophical business leaders. Whatever their areas of specialization, New Intellectuals will be radical "in the literal and reputable sense of the word"; they will grasp the fundamental philosophic roots of the current crisis as a means to its transcendence. Rand declared: "Let those who do care about the future . . . realize that the new *radicals* are the fighters for capitalism" (51–54).[43]

Rand's concept of the New Intellectual is the historical counterpart of her fictional ideal man. It must be remembered that Rand's major literary goal was the projection of this human ideal. John Galt in *Atlas Shrugged* was perfection incarnate, because he was simultaneously "a philosopher and inventor . . . a thinker and a man of action." Rand described him as "the *perfect* man, the perfectly integrated being."[44] It was toward this aesthetic end that Rand defined the social conditions within which ideal people would live and flourish. Her concept of the free society is a convergence of psychology, ethics, and politics.[45] Aesthetic ideal is wedded to psychological independence, ethical egoism, and political libertarianism. Ultimately, as Alvin Toffler (in Rand 1964b) observes, Rand offered "radical proposals for changing not merely the shape of society, but the very way in which most men work, think and love" (16).

Since Rand used the novel form as a vehicle for the presentation of her ideal, many critics have assumed that Objectivist society would require everyone to attain the heights of a John Galt or a Howard Roark. Barry (1986) asserts that Rand's

> Aristotelian version of liberalism depends almost entirely on a level of human excellence that it may well be impossible for men as we know them to achieve. . . . There is no reason why capitalistic institutions—private property, money, and the market—may not themselves be regarded as permanent threats to the full flowering

of the human personality, just as Rand regards socialist ones to be. (15–16)

Indeed, the Russian Marxists saw communism, not capitalism, as providing the necessary social context for the full actualization of the human potential. Trotsky ([1924] 1960) maintained that under communism, human beings would transcend all forms of dualism. They would be fully efficacious, self-worthy, self-respecting, autonomous, and cultured:

> Man at last will begin to harmonize himself in earnest. . . . He will try to master first the semi-conscious and then the subconscious processes in his own organism. . . . Man will make it his purpose to master his own feelings, to raise his instincts to the heights of consciousness, to make them transparent, to extend the wires of his will into hidden recesses, and thereby to raise himself to a new plane, to create a higher social biologic type, or, if you please, a superman. . . . Man will become immeasurably stronger, wiser, and subtler; his body will become more harmonized, his movements more rhythmic, his voice more musical. The forms of life will become especially dynamic. The average human type will rise to the heights of an Aristotle, a Goethe, or a Marx. And above this ridge, new peaks will rise. (254–56)

In this passage, Trotsky, the supreme Russian Marxist, internalizes Nietzschean imagery in his characterization of the new communist "superman." But the similarity to the Randian project is startling. The new communist man, like the New Intellectual, triumphs over dualism. Thus for Trotsky, "man" will "master . . . the semi-conscious and then the subconscious processes in his own organism." He will "master his own feelings." For Rand, this mastery entails the rational articulation of the cognitive roots of emotion and the tacit dimensions of the subconscious mind, including "sense of life" and "psycho-epistemology." Also, for Trotsky, "man" will "raise his instincts to the heights of consciousness." From her earliest philosophical reflections, Rand too, refused to accept the view that human "instincts"—and she uses this word—are beyond rational control.[46] Ultimately, she saw emotions, feelings, and "instincts" as components of the conceptual faculty. Like Trotsky, Rand projected the extension of reason into the "hidden recesses" of the mind as a means toward a fully integrated consciousness. And while Rand abandoned the Nietzschean notion of the "superman," her own concept of the ideal man poses as an equivalent Objectivist formulation. Also, for Trotsky, "man will become more harmonized, his movements more rhythmic, his voice more musical." Can there be any doubt that Rand's ideal man lacks such harmony and grace? In her descriptions of Howard Roark and John Galt, Rand projected an image that combines consummate will with physical strength, passionate sensuality with the ease of movement.[47]

The major difference between Rand's and Trotsky's vision is that she does not assume that all people "will rise to the heights of an Aristotle, a Goethe, or a Marx." Rand respected the creators as unique and uncommon. She emphatically denied the "Marxist" and "utopian" proposition that everyone in the ideal society would have to be supremely rational and moral. The formation of rational character is not guaranteed by an Objectivist social order (Rand [1964] 1993bT). Rand respected the infinite variety of humanity, and expected fully that her society would benefit the average and the superior, the ordinary and the extraordinary. Yet this qualification does not in any way, shape, or form pertain to the fictional utopia of Galt's Gulch, where the rule of mediocrity is transcended, and each individual is of great talent and excellence.

None of these parallels is meant to imply that Rand simply transferred Nietzschean, Marxian, or Trotskyian concepts to her own philosophic context. But it must be remembered that Trotsky himself was influenced by the Nietzschean themes of the Silver Age. The Nietzschean Marxists, the so-called God-builders, deified human strength and potentialities. They argued that under socialism, each individual would be the master of his or her destiny. Rand was exposed to these very themes from a fairly young age. Her literary and philosophic representations of the ideal man—or the New Intellectual—were comparable in tone. Such an integrated conception of human being was central to the Randian project because it signified the triumph over dualism. The "God-builders" sought a similar dialectical unity, even if they embraced a political ideal that ultimately undermined their goals.

The Communitarian Impulse

In Rand's view, however, the political ideal of the Russian synthesis was to be rejected in both its mystic and statist incarnations. The Nietzschean

Symbolists and the Idealists of the Russian religious renaissance sought to bridge the gap between the real and the ideal through a conflict-free mystical union. Rand's teacher, Lossky, summarized the essence of this mystical conception in the Russian concept of *sobornost'*. It is worthwhile to look at this ideal once again:

> The world of harmony is a perfect creation of God. . . . Plurality in this Kingdom is conditioned only by the ideal distinctions between its members, i.e. by individualizing opposition without any conflicting opposition and consequently without hostility of one being to another. There is no selfish isolation there, no mutual exclusion. Each part of this Kingdom exists for the whole, and the whole exists for each part. Moreover, owing to a complete interpenetration of all by all, the distinction between part and whole disappears: every part is a whole. The principles of organic structure are realized in the completest way possible. It is a wholly perfect organism. (Lossky [1917] 1928, 81)

Russian religious thinkers of that time viewed this organic whole as One with the mystic body of Christ, a freedom-in-unity and a unity-in-freedom. The Russian Marxists rejected this mysticism and secularized the concept of *sobornost'*. In the words of Bogdanov, the individual "man was organically fused with the whole, with the group or commune, as cells are fused together in living tissue." In such a social order, the state would wither away and "coerceive norms which regulate the conflict of those ends will become superfluous" (Kline 1969, 179).

In essence, Rand rejected such *sobornost'* as a vestige of mystical, organic collectivism and statism. But several critics have charged that Rand's wish to remake the social totality amounted to another form of totalitarianism. Kingsley Widmer (1981) sees Randian individualism as "patently narrow in its puritanical and rationalistic constructivism" (13), while Norman Barry believes that Rand's emphasis on objective morality is a pretext for the authoritarian inculcation of virtue. On this basis, Barry fears that Rand's social philosophy will gradually disintegrate "into a certain kind of statism."[48] And though Milton Friedman credits Rand for developing a popular libertarian following, he too believes that Rand's "utopian" moral streak is "productive of intolerance."[49]

As I have suggested, there is evidence that such intolerance was endemic to the organized Objectivist movement. In a bizarre twist, many "students of Objectivism" deified their charismatic leader and embraced a messianic cultism not much different from that exhibited by the extremist Russian cultural and political movements of Rand's youth. Moreover, Rand and many of her followers allegedly engaged in destructive moralizing and psychologizing. Some observers have remarked that it was a great irony that a so-called individualist philosophy had driven many of its followers into despair and emotional repression.[50] At least one book has been written about the tyranny of an "Objectivist" psychotherapist who attempted to assist one of his patients in her struggle for greater autonomy—only to intimidate and sexually abuse the woman in the process (Plasil 1985). This is especially significant even if the psychotherapist himself was not actually a genuine Objectivist. Since the uprooting of "bad" premises requires a psychotherapeutic process in Rand's approach, it is easy to imagine how an emphasis on philosophical reeducation, emotional articulation, and de-repression could dissolve into an authoritarian nightmare. Ellis argues that under such circumstances, Objectivist ideological "training" would be insufficient. Ellis (1968, 16) believes that the unobstructed consciousness of the New Intellectual is an illusory notion requiring the "biological reconstruction" of the human species.

Would an Objectivist notion of "mental health," for instance, be but another construction of the medical profession designed to control the nonconformists? Would the victory of Objectivism involve a quasi-Maoist cultural revolution? Is such a totalitarian tendency inherent in any philosophy that proposes a totalistic transformation? Is there an identity between methodological totalitarianism and political totalitarianism?

Rand never answered any of these crucial questions directly. What must be emphasized here, however, is that Rand's proposed cultural renaissance is not equivalent to a state-directed Maoist cultural revolution. Such a renaissance would seek to undermine statism, not bolster it. It would not be a tool of the state. It would lead to a cultural "counterhegemony," to use a Gramscian phrase. By overturning the antirational premises of culture in each of its forms, it would create a broad context and necessary base for political change.

Once achieved, it is doubtful that an Objectivist society would use a form of psychological "conditioning" to control its citizens. Given Rand's profound individualism and antistatism, she adamantly opposed the state's involvement in medicine and mental health. Both Branden and Rand applauded the libertarian psychiatrist, Thomas Szasz, who fought against the involuntary institutionalization of mental patients. Psychiatry, stripped of its incestuous ties to the state, would be far less lethal.[51] Rand suggests that an Objectivist society would not seek to reproduce these repressive structures in the new age of freedom. It would leave people free to be irrational, even as it would deny them the structural means to violate the rights of others. More important, the Objectivist society would leave rational people free to discover and earn their own contextually objective values.

The central issue here is whether Rand's vision of a totalistic revolution would necessarily translate into another form of totalitarianism. Like many classical liberals, Popper ([1962] 1971, 133–34) has argued persuasively against any philosophy that seeks to collapse the "critical dualism" between "facts and standards." He states that without this dualism, there is a tendency to "identify present might and right," or "future might and right." Those who claim to have discovered an objective ethos attempt to impose it on other people. Moreover, such an attempt is an inevitable by-product of any "grandiose philosophic system," because such a system seeks to remake the totality in its own image.

Popper believed that Marx was the last, great philosophic system-builder. He hoped that Marx's totality would never be replaced "by another Great System" seeking to achieve "monolithic social ends" (393). Such systems spell "the death of freedom: of the freedom of thought, of the free search for truth, and with it, of the rationality and the dignity of man" (396).

Popper's identity of methodological and political totalitarianism is a stern warning, one that Rand would have respected. As I suggest in Chapter 9, Rand's repudiation of theocratic and secular collectivism was based on her belief that each had collapsed the dualism of facts and values by monistically emphasizing one sphere over another. Rand did not identify an a-contextual "intrinsic" or "social" good, nor did she seek to impose a vision of the good on an unsuspecting populace. The good was an aspect of reality in relation to man. It had to be defined within a specific context and related to the specific purposes of an individual beneficiary. Most of the great philosophic system-builders attacked the ontological priority of individuals and attempted to achieve a notion of the good that was unrelated to reason or reality. In Rand's view, it was Aristotle who laid the foundation for a genuinely rational alternative based upon the primacy of existence and the necessity of reason. Rand believed that Objectivism would complete the Aristotelian revolution.

Rand's philosophical system combined an emphasis on methodological totality with a commitment to individualist libertarianism. Since Rand never lost sight of the totality or the context, her individualism never dissolved into atomism. But her repudiation of *sobornost'* was not a repudiation of the concept of community. Even as she revolted against the Russian *sobornost'* in its mystical and Marxist incarnations, she sustained a belief in a conflict-free society of individuals united by their common love for the same values. Rand achieved a dialectical *Aufhebung*—a sublation of dualities that simultaneously abolished and absorbed, transcended and preserved elements of the Russian communitarian vision. In this respect, Rand's philosophic project is infused with a communitarian impulse; a communitarianism that is neither mystical nor statist, but founded on the moral autonomy of the individual.

The integration of individual and social harmony in Rand's thought has been noted by a number of commentators, including Tibor Machan, Douglas Den Uyl, and Antony Flew. Machan notes correctly that in Rand's moral vision, "both aspects of each individual's life," "humanity and individuality," are conjoined "equally and inseparably."[52] Den Uyl notes further that in Rand's ideal society, much like in Plato's *Republic*, the soul of the city is in harmony with the soul of the individual.[53] For Flew, Rand was "like Marx" in her belief "that human nature and the human condition are such as to make possible a conflict-free utopia."[54] Each of these commentators has pinpointed significant communitarian themes in the Randian project.

In Rand's view, the integrated, rational individual, living in a fully free society, will not experience any inherent conflicts with other people. This does not mean that all people will have the same personal tastes, opinions, desires, or thoughts. But it does mean that if people live consciously and rationally, they will recognize no inherent conflicts between one another. This is a controversial contention in Objectivism that merits a study of its own.

Rand argued that genuinely integrated human beings do not detach their emotions from their thinking, nor do they detach their thinking from reality. Reality-based awareness means that people will not seek or desire the attainment of a contradiction. Rational persons pursue goals that are appropriate to the context of their knowledge. They do not divide their short- and long-run interests. They do not seek goals without considering the means of their achievement. They accept the responsibility of considering the interests and lives of other human beings. They accept that their decisions and actions will have consequences on the lives of others. They recognize that nothing in life can be achieved without effort.

Within the context of a free society, in which social relations are nonexploitative, Rand argued that there is no inherent conflict between two people seeking the same job, or the same romantic partner. If employers make decisions based on rational criteria, they will choose the most capable person for a given job. Persons not chosen have not been sacrificed. They will not be psychologically damaged by the rejection, and will have ample opportunity to search for other jobs for which they will be qualified. Likewise, in spiritual matters, a rational person who enters into a relationship with one individual does not sacrifice the interests of others who are not so engaged. Rand argued: "Love is not a static quantity to be divided, but an unlimited response to be earned." The love of one friend does not compromise the love of another friend. And a rational individual who chooses one romantic partner rather than another, makes that choice not on a comparative basis, but within the context of his or her own interests and happiness. Rand observed: "The 'loser' could not have had what the 'winner' has earned."[55]

What must be stressed is that such decisions are nonsacrificial only among rational people living in a free society. In a free society, it is possible to avoid those who are irrational. Rand emphasized that none of these observations pertain to human relations "in a nonfree society." Under statism, "no pursuit of any interests is possible to anyone; nothing is possible but gradual and general destruction" (56).

Here, the validity of Rand's formulations is not at issue. But it is difficult to grasp the Randian ideal if only because today's world is composed of many different types of people, many—if not most—of whom are *not* rational. This observation, however, only underscores the extraordinary radicalism of Rand's project. Rand envisions a society that banishes the master-slave duality on every level of human discourse—in personal, cultural, and structural relations among individuals.

For Rand, the social world is necessary to human flourishing. People naturally seek and give visibility to those whom they love and with whom they communicate. Independence breeds benevolence. Individuality breeds sociality. Those who are not afraid to show their excitement, passion, and integrity will encourage others to do the same. As Nathaniel Branden (1983b) explains, to honor the self is to provide the foundation for a community of individuals who honor one another: "Individualism is not the adversary of community but its most vital pillar" (143).

In the Objectivist society, voluntary, mutually beneficial relations among autonomous individuals is indispensable to the achievement of a genuinely *human* community. Rand wrote: "National unity, like love, is not a primary, but a consequence and must come voluntarily or not at all." One does not engender communal benevolence by forcing people into social relations they seek to avoid. The predatory use of force creates and perpetuates social fragmentation and dualism. Politically, the doctrine of individual rights is the only moral vehicle for peaceful "human coexistence," because it bars physical force from social relations. It sanctions a plethora of voluntary material and spiritual exchanges by which people earn the values that sustain their lives.[56] The "Universal" brotherhood is not achieved on the sole basis of species identity or even kinship ties, but on the basis "of holding the same values."[57] Despite her differences with modern communitarian critics of liberalism, such as Alasdair MacIntyre, Rand recognizes similarly that a free society is not merely a voluntary association of disparate individuals; it is a "community of values" that is the necessary ingredient "of any successful relationship among living beings."[58]

I close this chapter—and this book—with one final, lengthy passage written by Ayn Rand, the novelist and philosopher. It is from *The Fountainhead.* It portrays, in a single instant of time, the Randian ideal of the human community. On trial for destroying a public housing project, Howard Roark takes the oath. As he prepares for his self-defense, Roark stands before his peers:

> He stood by the steps of the witness stand. The audience looked at him. They felt he had no chance. They could drop the nameless resentment, the sense of insecurity which he aroused in most people. And so, for the first time, they could see him as he was: a man totally innocent of fear.
>
> The fear of which they thought was not the normal kind, not a response to a tangible danger, but the chronic, unconfessed fear in which they all lived. They remembered the misery of the moments when, in loneliness, a man thinks of the bright words he could have said, but had not found, and hates those who robbed him of his courage. The misery of knowing how strong and able one is in one's own mind, the radiant picture never to be made real. Dreams? Self-delusion? Or a murdered reality, unborn, killed by that corroding emotion without name—fear—need—dependence—hatred?
>
> Roark stood before them as each man stands in the innocence of his own mind. But Roark stood like that before a hostile crowd—and they knew suddenly that no hatred was possible to him. For the flash of an instant, they grasped the manner of his consciousness. Each

asked himself: do I need anyone's approval?—does it matter?—am I tied? And for that instant, each man was free—free enough to feel benevolence for every other man in the room. (678–79)

Ultimately, it is this exalted moment of human benevolence that Rand's project seeks to universalize.

Epilogue

Some of you may know the story of the four travelers who on a moonless night chanced upon an elephant and came away separately convinced that it was very like a snake, a leaf, a wall, a rope. Not one could persuade any other to change his mind, for each had touched a different part. Not one could resolve their differences for none of them knew the entire elephant.

The moral of the story is not the inevitability of subjectivism. Rather, it is a lesson in the fallacy of reification. Each traveler abstracted a part of the whole and reified that part into a separate entity, which was identified as the totality. Reification is possible because no one—and no human being—can achieve a synoptic vantage point on the whole. Our definition of what is *essential* depends on a specific context.

I have approached Ayn Rand's legacy in a self-consciously one-sided fashion, with an emphasis on its historical roots. I do not have the intellectual hubris to propose that my perspective is the *only* legitimate vantage point on Objectivism. But as scholarship on Rand's thought progresses, different perspectives will necessarily bring into focus aspects formerly obscured from view.

The importance of Objectivism then, in this context, does not lie merely in its repudiation of formal dualism or its insistence on the primacy of existence. Objectivism is a seamless conjunction of method and content—of a dialectical method and a realist-egoist-individualist-libertarian content.

This synthesis is Rand's most important contribution to twentieth-century radical social theory.

The Randian project overturns traditional assumptions about the relation-ship between dialectical method and specific political content. In contempo-rary intellectual history, the dialectic has been identified almost exclusively with the Hegelian and Marxian traditions. In 1919, for instance, the philosopher and literary critic Georg Lukács actually declared that the dialectic *is* Marxism, and that even if research disproved each and every one of Marx's individual theses, that would not detract from the veracity of his method. Just as Marx identified capitalism with dualism, Lukács identified Marxism with the dialectic. And as we have seen, liberal thinkers such as Karl Popper would agree. For Popper, what saves capitalism from tyranny is its dependence on a "critical dualism" between facts and standards. Whereas Lukács sees the dialectic as the means by which theory becomes "a vehicle of revolution,"[1] Popper sees it as the methodological moment of political totalitarianism.

Based on this identification of Marxism with dialectics, it may seem odd to view Objectivism partially in terms of its dialectical sensibility. Either Lukács's identification is incorrect, or Ayn Rand was a Marxist. The former is far more likely. Rand affirmed the dialectical connection between critique and revolution, but her revolutionary credo is thoroughly non-Marxist. Marx did not have a monopoly on the dialectic. Aspects of this approach have been employed by many diverse thinkers, including Aristotle, Hegel, Marx, Lossky, and as I have documented, Ayn Rand. Peikoff recognizes correctly that such a relational view is not distinctive to Objectivism, even though it is a hallmark of the philosophy.[2]

By articulating the methodological elements of Objectivism, I have discovered a host of provocative intellectual links that previously went unnoticed. We can now view Objectivism in historical terms—not only as an heir to Aristotelianism, as Rand would have had it, but as a by-product of her Russian past. Objectivism is as much defined by what Rand accepted from the Russian cultural milieu as by what she rejected.

What Rand accepted was the dialectical revolt against formal dualism. This dialectical method was at the heart of the Russian tendency toward synthesis. Such a tendency was endemic to Russian culture; it was expressed not only in the articulated statements of her teachers, but in the very intellectual air she breathed.

What Rand rejected was the mystical and statist content of Russian philosophy and culture. On this basis, Rand built a philosophical edifice that was simultaneously integrated and secular, dialectical and capitalist. In Rand's project, there is reciprocity in the interaction between content and method. Her method of processing the data of the world affected the content of her theories, while the content affected the further development of the method. In its critical, negative aspects, Rand's Objectivism is a grand revolt against formal dualism in each of the major branches of philosophy and in each of the institutions of modern statism. In its revolutionary, positive aspects, Rand's Objectivism is a grand projection of the ideal person and the ideal society—the autonomous, integrated individual and the benevolent *human* community. Neither moment can be abstracted from the other. Both constitute the historic essence of Objectivism.

I characterize my approach as "hermeneutical" because the investigation of Objectivism should not merely reproduce Rand's words, but produce further implications that neither Rand, nor her followers, nor her critics, nor I had foreseen. This proposition goes beyond Rand's admission that the elaboration of her philosophy was a task that no one individual could finish in a lifetime (Rand [1976] 1992T). It goes beyond the validity of any of Rand's philosophic formulations or critical commentary. It relates specifically to the task of Rand scholarship. In my own research, I have found that there is so much serious scholarly work that still needs to be done. In *literary studies*, an investigation is needed of the relationship between Nietzsche and Rand; the use of symbolism and mythological imagery in the Randian novel; and, Rand's literary method and its relationship to nineteenth-century Russian literature. In *philosophy, social theory, and intellectual history*, an exploration of the parallels and distinctions between Objectivism and contemporary philosophies (e.g., phenomenology, pragmatism, existentialism, and so on) with regard to such ontological and epistemological issues as the nature of being, relations, consciousness, thinking, and acting; the convergence of psychology and ethics in Objectivist theory; the links between Aristotelian, Nietzschean, and Objectivist ethics; the intellectual relationship between Rand and other twentieth-century individualists, such as Isabel Paterson and Ludwig von Mises; and, the political and cultural impact of Rand's thought.

I have suggested here only a few prospects for the future course of Rand scholarship. In each of these potential areas of study, it is my hope that critically minded scholars will have at their disposal all of Rand's private papers and journals. For now, it is my hope that this book has contributed to a serious dialogue on the profound importance of Ayn Rand's intellectual legacy.

Fig. 12. Ayn Rand in her New York City apartment, 1967. (Courtesy of Barbara Branden)

Notes

Introduction

1. Gladstein (1984, 110) lists accessible translations. Among the newest is a Russian translation of several of Rand's essays and literary excerpts, published in English as *The Morality of Individualism* (Rand 1992).

2. Rand capitalized "Objectivism," perhaps to distinguish it from conventional "objectivism" (which Rand characterized as "intrinsicism"). I continue that policy here.

3. *Library of Congress News*, 20 November 1991, 1.

4. Rand [1926–38] 1984, [1945] 1986, [1966–67] 1990, 1982, 1989, and 1991. Also Baker 1987, B. Branden 1986, and N. Branden 1989. As of this writing, several books are forthcoming from Penguin: an "authorized" biography; *Letters of Ayn Rand*, edited by Michael Berliner; an expanded edition of *The New Left*; Rand's journals; and a collection of the author's comments written in the margins of her books (ARI Impact 1994). Rand [1926–38] 1984 is hereafter cited as *Early Ayn Rand* by page number in text and notes.

5. See Binswanger 1980–87, vols. 1–8; Gladstein 1984; and Schwartz 1979–94, vols. 1–8. Binswanger and Schwartz are hereafter cited by volume, issue, and page number in both text and notes. I cite Schwartz for ease of reference. In fact, *The Intellectual Activist* was edited by Schwartz from 1 October 1979 to 3 September 1991, Linda Rearden from November 1991 to May 1994, and Robert W. Stubblefield from July 1994 to the present.

6. The following textbooks, used in introductory philosophy and political theory courses, include selections and/or discussions of Rand's thought: Rachels 1986; Pojman 1990, 1992, and 1994; Bowie, Michaels, and Solomon 1992; Feinberg 1992; and Hoover 1994. Articles on Rand's thought have appeared in the *American Journal of Economics and Sociology*, *American Philosophical Quarterly*, *Aristos*, *Cognition and Brain Theory*, *Critical Review*, *Indian Political Science Review*, *Journal of Applied Philosophy*, *Journal for the Theory of Social Behavior*, *Monist*, *Organizational Behavior and Human Decision Processes*, *Personalist*, *Perspectives in Biology and Medicine*, *Reason Papers*, and *Theory and Decision*.

7. These include the Ayn Rand Institute, founded in 1985, directed by Michael Berliner; the Ayn Rand Society, founded as an affiliate of the Eastern division of the American Philosophical Association in 1989, headed by Allan Gotthelf; and the Institute for Objectivist Studies, founded in 1990, directed by David Kelley.

8. The "inner circle" around Rand, playfully called the Collective, included many relatives and friends of Nathaniel Branden (formerly Nathan Blumenthal) and Barbara Branden (formerly Barbara Weidman). Rand and the Brandens shared a Russian Jewish ancestry, as did Nathaniel Branden's cousins, the Blumenthals, and Barbara Branden's cousin, Leonard Peikoff. B. Branden 1986, 254; N. Branden 1989, 16, 134.

9. Rand (May 1968), "To whom it may concern," in Rand [1966–71] 1982, 453. I cite "Rand [1966–71] 1982" for ease of reference. In fact, The Objectivist was edited by Rand and Branden from January 1966 to April 1968, and Rand from May 1968 to September 1971. Rand [1966–71] 1982 is hereafter cited as Objectivist by page number in both text and notes.

10. Peikoff (April 1989), "Foreword to the second edition," in Rand [1966–67] 1990, 127. Rand [1966–67] 1990 is hereafter cited as Introduction by page number in both text and notes.

11. Rand (June 1968), "A statement of policy," in Objectivist, 471.

12. Rand (February 1980), "To the readers of The Objectivist Forum," in Binswanger 1.1.1.

13. Rand parodied the process by which certain philosophic books generate whole industries of scholarship. "Within a few years of the book's publication," she wrote, "commentators will begin to fill libraries with works analyzing, 'clarifying' and interpreting its mysteries." These interpretations will differ and contradict one another, but "within a generation, the number of commentaries will have grown to such proportions that the original book will be accepted as a subject of philosophical specialization, requiring a lifetime of study—and any refutation of the book's theory will be ignored or rejected, if unaccompanied by a full discussion of the theories of all the commentators, a task which no one will be able to undertake." Rand (29 January–26 February 1973), "An untitled letter," in Rand 1982, 142–43. Rand 1982 is hereafter cited as Philosophy by page number in both text and notes.

14. Rand (February 1980), "To the readers of The Objectivist Forum," in Binswanger 1.1.2.

15. W. W. Bartley, "Knowledge is a product not fully known to its producer," in Leube and Zlabinger 1984, 27.

16. Ricoeur (1971), "The model of the text," in Dallmayr and McCarthy 1977, 316–34.

17. Machan, 16 March 1994C. "C" will be used throughout to indicate correspondence and personal communication.

18. The ongoing publication in various media of several of Rand's private papers, journals, and lectures has not occurred without editing. Although the public availability of these papers should be lauded by scholars, it is equally important that they be made available in unedited form. For a discussion of Library of Congress efforts to place Rand's personal papers in a central repository, see Reedstrom 1993b, 8.

19. This institution was called "Petrograd University" until early 1924. Prior to World War I, it was "St. Petersburg University."

20. To identify all religious thought with "mysticism" would strike some as odd, especially since mysticism is usually equated with specific esoteric or occult practices signifying a direct contemplative union with a deity. George Kline (18 August 1993C) notes, however, that whereas the Russian thinkers, Solovyov, Frank, and Lossky are indeed mystics, Tolstoy, Shestov, Leontyev, and Rozanov are not, "at least not in the same sense." Rand ignored these differences. She rejected all Russian religious thought as mystical. My use of the terms "mysticism" and "mysticist" reflects Rand's own, which referred not to esoteric practices or ideas, but to the general method by which such practices or ideas were upheld. Rand saw "mysticism" as "the claim to some non-sensory, non-rational, non-definable, non-identifiable means of knowledge, such as 'instinct,' 'intuition,' 'revelation,' or any form of 'just knowing.' " Rand (17 February 1960), "Faith and force: The destroyers of the modern world," in Philosophy, 75.

21. Shein 1967, 86. Lossky has also been recognized as the "dean of the emigre philosophers," one of the leading "philosophers in exile" from the prerevolutionary Russian period who emigrated to the West in the early 1920s. Edie, Scanlan, and Zeldin 1965, 141.

22. The phrase, "revolt against dualism," was used by Arthur Oncken Lovejoy (1930). Lovejoy sees this revolt as a rejection of dichotomies, particularly ontological (e.g., mind and body), and epistemological, dualities. I use the phrase in a much wider and more formal sense.

23. Rand in Peikoff 1976T, Lecture 6.

24. B. Branden 1986, 311. Hospers (1990), in an intellectual memoir of his conversations with Ayn Rand, writes that "in time I realized that she read almost no philosophy at all. And I was amazed how much philosophy she could generate 'on her own steam,' without consulting any sources" (47).

25. Ollman (1993, 17) notes that many "dialectical" thinkers make such broad generalizations, and often "miss the trees for the forest" by moving too quickly to the bottom line of an argument and by not giving enough attention to the complex interactions of various factors over time.

26. Hollinger, "Ayn Rand's epistemology in historical perspective," in Den Uyl and Rasmussen 1984, 55. Hollinger notes certain viable similarities between Rand and Dewey, Rorty, Wittgenstein, Gadamer, and other thinkers in the hermeneutic tradition, all of whom can claim to be legitimate heirs of Aristotle's philosophy.

27. N. Branden 1989; Kelley 1990, 74.

28. Peikoff (1983T) criticizes this reification of Rand's fictional characters, describing it as a "rationalist" fallacy (Lectures 7–9). In Chapter 8, I explore the Randian critique of such "rationalism" as a form of dualism.

29. On Rand's attitudes toward facial hair as symptomatic of "a spiritual defect," see B. Branden 1986, 208. Though one might dismiss Rand's dislike of facial hair as a matter of personal taste, it is interesting to note that the wearing of the beard had deep significance in Russian cultural history. Modeled after the icons of the saints, the wearing of the beard was a traditional practice of Orthodox religious ritual. When Peter the Great ushered in an era of Westernization, he introduced laws against such Orthodox beards. In 1705 Peter imposed taxes and license fees on those who chose to remain unshaven. The cultural battle between the "beards" and the "non-beards" was a battle between the Orthodox-Slavophiles and the Westernizers. Willis 1977, 686; Wallace 1967, 156, 161. Rand's preference for a clean-shaven appearance may have reflected her general esteem for the Westernizers.

30. Rand (1 January 1973), "To dream the noncommercial dream," in Rand (1989), 259. Rand 1989 is hereafter cited as *Voice of Reason* by page number in both text and notes.

31. Rand 1961, 33. In *The Fountainhead* (Rand [1943] 1993), there are instances in which Rand ridicules dialectical materialism; see pages 292, 554, and 638. Rand [1943] 1993 is hereafter cited as *Fountainhead* by page number in text and notes; Rand 1961, similarly, as *New Intellectual*.

32. Popper ([1940] 1963) criticizes dialectics.

33. See, for instance, Novack [1969] 1971, 17. Novack unnecessarily polarizes two very compatible philosophical positions. The source for such polarization is Hegel himself, who at times viewed dialectics as both incorporating and transcending the Aristotelian laws of logic. There are passages in Hegel's writings—see *The Science of Logic*, particularly bk. 2, sec. 1, chap. 2C—in which, for example, motion is described as an "existing contradiction." Hegel [1812–16] 1929. Engels also employed such terminology in *Dialectics of Nature* ([1882] 1940). Thanks to Walsh (19 April 1994C) for this observation. Given such terminological confusion, it is understandable how Rand would have rejected "dialectics" as a repudiation of formal logic. The many usages of "dialectics" are discussed in Thorslev 1971.

34. Aristotle, *Rhetoric* 1.2.1355b26–27, in Aristotle 1941, 1329. In this context, "dialectics" also suggests a type of metaphysical reasoning from first principles. Thanks to Rasmussen in Kelley 1993T for this observation.

35. For this point, thanks to Gotthelf (29 April 1994C).

36. Nevertheless, Irwin (1988) argues that Aristotle uses a form of dialectics in negative demonstration, in which one proceeds from premises that one's opponent cannot reject (174–78). This "strong dialectic" is an aspect of Aristotle's defense of "first principles" or ultimate truths. Thanks to Rasmussen (19 April 1994C) for bringing this to my attention. Rand's ontology also makes use of negative demonstration.

37. Engels [1878] 1947, 29, 29n; Marx [1867] 1967, 59, 408. Marx [1867] 1967 and [1894] 1967 are hereafter cited as *Capital* by volume and page number in text and notes.

38. Lenin (1914–16), "On Aristotle's *Metaphysics*," in Selsam and Martel 1963, 361.

39. Thanks to Walsh (19 April 1994C) and to Gotthelf (29 April 1994C), who notes too that some of this technique can be found in Aristotle, though less systematically.

40. In the history of philosophy, it was not Hegel who enunciated the triadic formulation. One can find hints of this terminology in Kant's discussion of the antinomies, but it is used most extensively by Fichte [1794] 1970, in *The Science of Knowledge* (*Wissenschaftslehre*).

41. This is most true of "reductionist" monists. Ontologically, dualists posit two basic and different "stuffs" in existence, for example, the "mental" and the "physical." The "reductionist" monists express the basic "stuff" in terms of a single attribute, that is, as *either* "mental" *or* "physical." By contrast, "neutral monists" argue that there is one basic "stuff" in existence of which the "mental" and the "physical" are attributes. There are many variations on these positions. For clarifying these issues, thanks to Rasmussen (interview, 15 March 1994). A critique of "neutral monism" is provided in Lossky 1952. Interviews, unless otherwise cited, were conducted by the author on the date indicated.

42. Dialectical method transcends neither logical "contradictions" nor "contraries." This distinction was proposed by Aristotle in the seventh chapter of *De Interpretatione* (*On Interpretation*), in Aristotle 1941, 43–45. Thorslev (1971) explains: "Contradictory propositions cannot both be true, and they cannot both be false: they are exclusive, and between them they exhaust the field of discourse. Contraries, on the other hand, cannot both be true, but they may both be false; they are exclusive but not exhaustive"(50). Typically, the dialectical thinker sees opposing perspectives as neither "contradictory" nor "contrary" per se, but rather as "partial" or "one-sided," combining elements of truth and elements of falsity. By examining opposition within a wider context, the dialectical. thinker often views the two alternatives as *neither* exclusive *nor* exhaustive, since they *both* share a common premise *and* restrict the field of possible alternatives by reifying their limitations.

43. This raises an interesting question concerning the ontology that underlies the dialectical approach, something which I do not address in this book. It can be said that dialectics recognizes the reality of "relation"—not as substance—but as a category that cannot be reduced to any other. Rasmussen (19 April 1994C) suggests that Rand's understanding of the "objective" is, in fact, based on her refusal to collapse what is relational into its terms, what she calls "intrinsic" and "subjective." If Rand recognized the reality of "relation," this would suggest that she was not as fully "Aristotelian" as she maintained. I do not believe that Rand had an identifiable ontological doctrine of "relation." However, there are significant elements of relationalism in every branch of Objectivism.

44. Thorslev 1971, 50. Thorslev criticizes the "Both-And-Syndrome" as one of the "dangers of dialectic thinking." In some instances, however, Thorslev confuses dialectics with formal dualistic and monistic alternatives.

45. Rand (March 1966), "Art and sense of life," in Rand 1975b, 40. For this observation, thanks to Kamhi (interview, 23 May 1994). Rand 1975b is hereafter cited as *Romantic Manifesto* by page number in both text and notes.

46. Thanks to Kelley in Kelley (1993T) for this observation. Thorslev (1971) suggests that insofar as dialectics attempts to define "polar opposites," it is a method that "is at least as old as philosophy—indeed, Claude Lévi-Strauss has suggested that it is basically characteristic of all

human thinking whatever, and that it is this which we moderns have in common with the savage" (45–46). See also Lévi-Strauss 1966. As I have defined it, dialectics is not merely an attempt to *define* "polar opposites," but to *transcend* them in a nondualistic, nonmonistic manner, based on an awareness of their organic unity.

47. I have personally encountered this view among Rand enthusiasts in several Objectivist forums.

48. Thanks to Gotthelf (15 February 1993C) for reiterating this observation.

49. This is *not* my opinion; Rand did not merely synthesize previously developed philosophic doctrines. It is my conviction that she developed not only an original synthesis, but an original, nondualistic defense of egoism and capitalism.

50. Rand (July 1966), "Introduction to *Capitalism: The Unknown Ideal*," in Rand 1967, vii. Rand 1967 is hereafter cited as *Unknown Ideal* by page number in both text and notes.

51. In Sciabarra 1988a and 1995, I argue that Hayek exhibits a similar dialectical sensibility.

52. Nietzsche's dictum on "muddy waters" appears in his *Thus Spake Zarathustra* ([1954] 1970, 240). A similar statement appears in sec. 173 of *The Gay Science* ([1887] 1974). Thanks to both Kline (8 September 1993C) and Enright (22 December 1993C) for their assistance in locating these references.

Chapter 1. Synthesis in Russian Culture

1. The name appearing on Rand's dossier at Leningrad University is Alissa Zinovievna Rosenbaum (Leningrad University Archives, 06.08.92). Rand's middle name, or "patronymic," suggests that her father's name was Zinovy. This is confirmed by Binswanger 1994T, who lists Rand's father's name as Zinovy Zakharovich, and her mother's name as Anna Borisovna. In Barbara Branden's biography (1986), however, the father's name is listed as "Fronz," which is not typically Russian. "Zinovy," though not very common, is fully *Russian*. Perhaps "Fronz" was Rand's nickname for her father. Thanks to Kline (20 October 1992C) and B. Lossky (17 September 1992C) for clarifying these issues.

2. Rand (June 1969), "Introduction," in *Romantic Manifesto*, vi.

3. *Sobornost'* can also be translated as "communality," and *sobornyi*, the adjectival form, as "communal." But *sobornost'* is better translated as "conciliarity," and *sobornyi*, as "conciliar." Kline (26 February 1994C) notes that the word "communal" is more secular than the original Russian meaning, which suggests church councils (*sobory*). Kline's translation gives these terms a more appropriately religious flavor.

4. Hessen (1978), writing for an Objectivist periodical, praises Tibor Szamuely's *Russian Tradition*, which demonstrates that nearly all aspects of Russian culture, including moral and political philosophy, rejected the concept of individual rights, affirming the ideal of self-sacrifice to the collective and/or the state.

5. Rosenthal (15 November 1993C) suggests that Rand probably reacted against the mystic, occult doctrines that were popular in the late Russian and early Soviet period. Nathaniel Branden (1982T) argues that the Russian mystical context of Rand's youth often made her "quick on the draw" concerning any theories that hinted of "mysticism," such as hypnosis, telepathy, ESP, or associated "altered states" of consciousness, which might have a natural, rather than supernatural, basis.

6. Leibniz in fact, served as an adviser to Czar Peter. Since Russia was both a European and Asian country, it absorbed influences from both West and East. Though Russian religious philosophy owes much to Greek Orthodox and Byzantine traditions, it also mirrors many mystic Eastern and Asian traditions that stress—like their more secular Western, dialectical counterparts—a form of

holistic unity and relational identity. Unfortunately, Rand and her Objectivist successors have largely ignored Eastern philosophy. See Walsh 1988T for some interesting analysis.

7. For this observation, thanks to Walsh (interview, 22 April 1994).

8. Copleston 1986, 60–61. Echoing this view, see Marcuse [1941] 1960, 40–42.

9. Despite their common organicism, these thinkers should not be taken as a single unit. See Lossky 1951, 59–78.

10. Lossky 1951, 62. Lenin ([1903] 1969) appropriates Chernyshevsky's question in discussing the movement for Russian social change.

11. In contrast to his later writings, Solovyov's earlier work is far more critical of Hegel. Kline (1974) argues persuasively that Solovyov owed much of his philosophical and metaphilosophical system to Hegel.

12. Lossky 1951, 142. Chicherin is one of the very few Russian philosophers to defend property rights. For this observation, thanks to Rosenthal (15 November 1993C).

13. For what follows, I owe a great intellectual debt to Bernice Rosenthal. See Rosenthal 1975, 1980, 1986, 1990 (with Bohachevsky-Chomiak), 1991a, 1991b, and 1994.

14. Rosenthal and Bohachevsky-Chomiak 1990, 25. In opposition to the Symbolists, even the Russian futurists embraced aspects of Nietzsche's philosophy. The futurists celebrated the machine age, while emphasizing the Dionysian elements of change and flux. They rejected transcendentalism and dualism. They were among the first artistic groups to support the revolution, though not all were Bolshevik sympathizers. Rosenthal 1991a.

15. Rosenthal, "Introduction," in Rosenthal 1986, 18. Not all Symbolists advocated a libertine sexual ideal.

16. Kline (18 August 1993C) observes that unlike the Symbolists, Nietzsche envisioned the emergence of the supermen only after thousands of years of cultural change.

17. Rosenthal, "Introduction," in Rosenthal 1986, 10; Rosenthal 1994.

18. Rand (December 1969–January 1970), "Apollo and Dionysus," in Rand 1975a: 58. She also employs Apollonian-Dionysian imagery in Rand (February 1970), "The left: Old and new," in Rand 1975a: 82–95. She credits the Old Left with attempting "to maintain an Apollonian mask" of reason in its defense of socialism and describes the New Left as having abandoned all pretense to rational justification. Rand 1975a is hereafter cited as *New Left* by page number in both text and notes.

19. Rand calls Blok's "sense of life" "ghastly," but Blok himself "a magnificent poet" (in Peikoff 1976T, Lecture 11). A representative of "pre-October" Russian culture, Blok was praised by Trotsky ([1924] 1960) for his poem, "The Twelve."

20. Evelyn Bristol, "Blok between Nietzsche and Soloviev," in Rosenthal 1986, 150; Rosenthal and Bohachevsky-Chomiak 1990, 291.

21. Rosenthal, "Introduction," in Rosenthal 1986, 20.

22. Most conceptions of *sobornost'* stress its anarchistic character.

23. Rosenthal, "Introduction," in Rosenthal 1986, 39–40.

24. Ibid., 35–37.

25. Mihajlov, "The great catalyzer: Nietzsche and Russian neo-Idealism," in Rosenthal 1986, 132. The full impact of Nietzsche on Russian neo-Idealism has not been studied. Mihajlov's essay provides an introduction to this topic.

26. Rand believed that Dostoyevsky was unequaled "in the psychological depth of his images of human evil." Rand (May–June 1969), "What is romanticism?" in *Romantic Manifesto*, 114. She greatly appreciated his technique, and listed him among her favorite fiction writers. Rand [1958] 1986T, Lecture 12, and (April 1977), "Favorite writers," in Rand 1991. Rand 1991 is hereafter cited as *Column* by page number in both text and notes.

27. Not all neo-Idealists sought to overcome the Kantian distinction. Some are traditional neo-Kantians. Berdyaev (1951), for instance, sees an impenetrable split between physical nature and

spirit. For Berdyaev, human beings are dual entities who live in both phenomenal and noumenal worlds. Berdyaev liked Nietzsche, but had no great sympathy for Hegelianism. For a time, he tried to synthesize Marxism and Kantianism and admitted to a "tendency to dualism" (127).

28. Frank wrote *Marx's Theory of Value and Its Significance*, which was influenced by the early Austrian economists like Boehm-Bawerk. Rosenthal 1991b, 60. This early Austrian school was a precursor to the Mises-Hayek Austrian tradition of the twentieth century.

29. Mihajlo Mihajlov, "The great catalyzer: Nietzsche and Russian neo-Idealism," in Rosenthal 1986, 133–34.

30. Kline (1967) sees three groups of Russian Marxists: Nietzschean, orthodox (including the Marxist-Leninists), and neo-Kantian. I do not survey the many Russian Marxist derivatives.

31. Copleston 1988. On the inherent problems of trying to integrate Slavophile and Marxist perspectives, see Peikoff (July 1992), "Some notes about tomorrow, part one," in Schwartz 6.4.4. Peikoff argues that Russian Marxism tried to offer "the essence of the Slavophile mentality under the veneer of being western, worldly, scientific." According to Peikoff, the Marxist concept of "class" is too abstract for the Slavophile mentality, which appeals to tribal notions of race and nationality. With the collapse of the Marxist paradigm, nationalism has erupted with a vengeance within the former Soviet Union. John Ridpath (1987T) provides another Objectivist analysis of the messianic roots of Bolshevism. In a comparable vein, Pipes (1994), a non-Objectivist, has argued that Soviet totalitarianism was a distinctive outgrowth of both Marxism and the Russian "patrimonial heritage."

32. The integration of Russian Marxism and Kantianism was very short-lived.

33. Nicolaus (1972), "Foreword," in Marx [1857–58] 1973, 7; Kamenka 1967, xlvi–l. Marx [1857–58] 1973 is hereafter cited as *Grundrisse* by page number in text and notes.

34. Copleston 1986, 300–12. Rosenthal (15 November 1993C) suggests that the shaping of Marxist ideology during this period was as much the product of Lenin's polemics as it was of his political power.

35. Lenin (1908), *Materialism and Empirio-Criticism*, in Selsam and Martel 1963, 140–41.

36. Nietzsche ([1883–85] 1905) decries the "*immaculate* perception of all things" (132).

37. Much of Lenin's approach falls outside the tradition of Russian philosophy. Yet despite the materialist and spiritualist distinctions between Leninist and Russian traditions, both approaches retain a formal opposition to dualism.

38. Merrill (1991) argues: "Zamiatin lived in Petrograd during the 1920s, at the same time as Rand; prominent in literary circles, he was a leading anti-Bolshevik intellectual. Rand must surely have been familiar with his work" (168 n. 6). It is not entirely clear that Rand was familiar with *We*. The book *may* have been written as early as 1920. It *may* have circulated unofficially in Petrograd, Moscow, and Berlin. An official reading of the book was given in 1924, at a Russian Writer's League meeting. Except for early English translations, and abridged Russian versions circulated in 1927 by a Prague-based liberal émigré periodical, Zamiatin's work was not published in its original language or form until the 1950s, by the Chekhov Publishing House in New York. It was published in the Soviet Union around 1988. Guerney 1960, 164–65; Rosenthal, 15 November 1993C. Zamiatin's *We* appears in Guerney's *Anthology of Russian Literature in the Soviet Period: From Gorki to Pasternak* (1960). This "unexpurgated" and "complete" version was published by Bennett Cerf and Donald S. Klopfer of Random House, three years after they published *Atlas Shrugged*. Berberova (1992, 128–29, 141–43, 292–94, 589–90) offers some interesting reflections on Zamiatin's life.

39. Zamiatin (1919–20), in Guerney 1960, 177.

Chapter 2. Lossky, the Teacher

1. Kline 1985, 265–66; Zenkovsky 1953, 657.

2. A privatdocent is a private teacher or unsalaried lecturer who is paid directly by his

students. This practice was especially prevalent in German universities, and is sometimes spelled "privatdozent" to reflect its origins. Hayek (1992, 23–24) discusses the life of the privatdocent in "The Economics of the 1920s as seen from Vienna."

3. Peikoff (September 1964), "Books," in Rand and Branden 1962–65, 3:36, 40. Rand and Branden 1962–65 is hereafter cited as *Objectivist Newsletter* by volume and page number.

4. The translator, Natalie Duddington, called the English version of *Obosnovanie intuitivizma*, *The Intuitive Basis of Knowledge*. According to Kline (18 August 1993C), *The Foundations of Intuitivism* is the more accurate translation of the Russian title.

5. Lossky translated the first Russian edition of *The Critique of Pure Reason* (St. Petersburg, 1907) and the second (1915). His translation of Kant's 1770 dissertation appeared in two editions (1902 and 1910), of Paulsen's *Immanuel Kant: His Life and Doctrine* in 1899 and 1905. In 1975, Rand wrote a critique of Paulsen's 1898 book as a "symptom" of a Kantian "malignancy" which "had spread through Western culture at the dawn of the twentieth century." Rand (October 1975), "From the horse's mouth," in *Philosophy*, 93–99.

6. St. Vladimir's was named for Prince Vladimir of Kiev (956–1015), who in 988 embraced the Eastern Orthodoxy of Byzantium and became the first Christian grand prince of Russia.

7. Rosenthal and Bohachevsky-Chomiak 1990, x. *Voprosy filosofii* is the leading journal of philosophy. *Voprosy literatury* is the leading journal of literature.

8. Lossky's *Vospominaniia* (Memoirs) was published posthumously in 1968, and reissued in 1991, in nos. 10, 11, and 12 of *Voprosy filosofii*.

9. Lossky 1951, 361. In this book, Lossky discusses his own philosophy in the third person.

10. Edie, Scanlan, and Zeldin 1965, 141. The intellectual link between Leibniz and Lossky is most direct. Leibniz influenced Radishchev and Gustav Teichmuller, who was a German philosophy professor in the Russian University at Yurev (Dorpat) in Estonia. Teichmuller taught S. A. Boborov and I. F. Oze, both of whom influenced Aleksei A. Kozlov, a professor at Kiev. Lossky knew Kozlov well; Lossky's own view of substantival agents is similar to Kozlov's.

11. Mihajlov, "The great catalyzer: Nietzsche and Russian neo-Idealism," in Rosenthal 1988, 131.

12. Lossky, "Absolute perfect beauty," in Shein 1973, 274. Lossky's personalism is similar to the approach of James Ward, who rejected materialism and dualism. Though Ward was a spiritualistic monist, like Lossky he accepted the existence of interactive, non-windowless monads. Copleston 1966, 249. Lossky (1952, 382) refers to Ward as an "eminent thinker" in the personalist tradition.

13. Lossky [1917] 1928, 185–90. I cite Natalie Duddington's English translation of Lossky's original text. Duddington states that Lossky made some peripheral additions and modifications in the English edition.

14. Lossky [1917] 1928, 182–83. Lossky addresses the issue of "beauty" in such essays as "Absolute perfect beauty," "The essence of perfect beauty," and "The essence of imperfect beauty," excerpts of which are found in Shein 1973, 272–98.

15. Lossky 1955, 138. For an Objectivist critique of the causal theory, see Kelley 1986, 121–42.

16. On the intrinsicist-subjectivist dichotomy, see Peikoff 1991b, 142–51, 241–48.

17. Rand 1969–71, 141. Rand 1969–71 is hereafter cited as "Appendix" by page number in both text and notes.

18. A detailed analysis of the similarities between the Losskyian and Randian interpretations of Aristotle is beyond the scope of this book. In any event, it would require much more textual evidence than is currently available. Neither author wrote extensively on Aristotle, and the Lossky lectures that Rand may have attended in 1922 are unavailable.

19. Although it is true that standard interpretations of Aristotle's theory emphasize the notion of "metaphysical essences," not all scholars agree with this view. Though Rand saw a clear distinction between the Objectivist and Aristotelian theories of concept-formation, Allan Gotthelf (1988T, Lecture 2) has noted a much closer affinity. He maintains that Aristotle endorsed elements

of "measurement-omission" and contextualism in his theory of definitions, key aspects of Rand's Objectivist epistemology.

20. Objectivism also endorses an ontological view of logic. In addition, Rand praised Aristotle's philosophy as "biocentric." She stated: "Aristotle was the first man who integrated the facts of identity and change, thus solving that ancient dichotomy." Rand (May 1963), "Review of Randall's *Aristotle*," in *Voice of Reason*, 7.

21. Lossky [1906] 1919, 405. In his *Logika* (1923) and his *Logical and Psychological Aspects of Affirmative and Negative Judgments* (1912) Lossky considers the "subjective" and the "objective" aspects of knowledge. Psychology studies the "subjective" component of knowledge, whereas logic deals with the structure of the object itself. Hence, it is "objective." Thus, "a system of logic is the ideal form of the object which is expressed in the functional dependence of its different aspects on each other and other aspects." Excerpts from the above works are found in Shein 1973, 160.

22. Aristotle, *Metaphysics*, in Aristotle 1941, 681–926; Copleston [1946] 1985, 304.

23. Aristotle, *De Anima* (On the soul) 2.2.414a16–28, in Aristotle 1941, 558–59.

24. Gotthelf (1976), "Aristotle's conception of final causality," in Gotthelf and Lennox 1987, 230.

25. Aristotle, *De Partibus Animalium* (On the parts of animals) 1.5.645a31–37 and 2.1.646a27–29, in Aristotle 1941, 657, 659. Aristotle emphasized the ontological priority of particulars, of *things*. Even though he recognized a system of relationships between things, he does not see "relation," per se, as an ontological category unto itself. The whole debate of internalism and externalism, discussed later, would have been foreign to Aristotle's worldview. Aristotle argued too that certain parts are prior to the whole, whereas others are posterior to the whole. Certain parts "cannot even exist if severed from the whole." Thus, "attributes do not exist apart from their substances." Aristotle, *Metaphysics* 7.10.1035b23–24 and 13.2.1077b5, in Aristotle 1941, 799, 891. "Relation" as an ontological category is central to the Hegelian tradition, wherein each thing is a cluster of relations and thus internal to every other thing in the universe. Marx integrated Aristotelian and Hegelian conceptions in his own distinctive approach. See Ollman 1976 and Gould 1978. I discuss Rand's perspective on relations in Chapters 5 and 6.

26. During the Renaissance, many philosophers linked Aristotle to religious scholasticism. In his introduction to Aristotle 1941 McKeon argues that Leibniz and Hegel are exceptions; unlike other post-Renaissance philosophers, they incorporate significant Aristotelian themes in their work (xii).

27. Lossky 1934a, 151. Lossky ([1917] 1928, 78) qualifies Spinoza as another thinker "with a general leaning towards Intuitionism." Lossky is not alone in his appreciation of the Aristotelian element in Hegelian philosophy. Gadamer ([1971] 1976) argues that although Hegel was deeply influenced by Cartesian subjectivism and the Kantian "transcendental dialectic," he appreciated the ancients' method of "bringing out the consequences of opposed hypotheses" (5). Hegel saw Aristotle as "the proper teacher for us all since he is a master at bringing the most various determinations together under one concept. He gathers up all aspects of an idea, as unrelated as he might first find them, while neither leaving determinations out nor seizing first upon one and then upon another; rather, he takes them all together as one" (8).

28. Lossky 1951, 347. Even in Soviet philosophy, there was a gradual abandonment of the assumption that the Hegelian dialectic transcended the "static" and "bourgeois" logic of Aristotle. Kline (1967, 266) reminds us that Soviet philosophers Zinoviev and Kolman reinterpreted Engels's apparent endorsement of objective contradictions, and argued that Marx, Lenin, and Engels did not violate the Aristotelian law of noncontradiction.

29. Edie, Scanlan, and Zeldin 1965, 317; Lossky (1913–14), "Intuitivism," in Edie, Scanlan, and Zeldin 1965, 321–42.

30. Zenkovsky (1953, 669–71) believed that Lossky's attempted reconciliation is "triumphant immanentism, rather than an overcoming of . . . cognitive dualism."

31. Despite his opposition to the Soviets, Lossky's approach to atomism and organicism parallels the Marxist critique. This is to be expected considering their common Aristotelian and Hegelian roots. In tracing the links between Marx, Hegel, and Aristotle, Scott Meikle (1985) contrasts atomistic "reductive materialism" and organic "essentialism," in a way that is reminiscent of Lossky's critique:

> Reductive materialism believes in an ontology of simples, of basic building-blocks lacking complexity, and further believes everything else is reducible to them. Essentialism, on the other hand, admits into its ontology . . . "organic wholes" or "entities," and does not consider them reducible but rather irreducible. . . . The relation between the whole entity and its parts is not the same as that between the constituent simples of an aggregate like a pile of sand. The complexity of an entity is irreducible, and it is what exists. (154)

32. Reviewing Blanshard's *Reason and Analysis* in *The Objectivist Newsletter*, Nathaniel Branden praises Blanshard's critique of logical positivism and linguistic analysis. Though he criticizes Blanshard's Idealist theory of universals, he views the book as "brilliant" and "powerful." N. Branden (February 1963), "Books," in *Objectivist Newsletter* 2:7–8. Blanshard is also praised by Peikoff (1988bT; 1970T, Lectures 7 and 9). These appraisals reflect Rand's own views since everything that was published in Objectivist publications, or presented in Objectivist courses, was approved by Rand.

33. Rorty 1967, 125. The issue is complicated further when we assess not merely an entity's relational properties but its relations with other entities. Internalists might say that entities which appear separate and distinct are actually *defined* by their relations to everything else in the universe. This view of the entity as a cluster of relations blurs the line between the object and the subject; even the table-as-observed-by-me is part of the definition of the table, that is, a feature in the absence of which it would no longer be called a table. For this observation, thanks to Hospers (17 July 1993C). To discuss the vast implications of the internalist-externalist dispute would take me well beyond the scope of this book. See also note 35 to this chapter.

34. In his essay "Historical materialism" (in Mepham and Ruben 1979), Geoffrey Hellman suggests that strict organicity applied to social critique generates a problem of individuation. In a strict organicist perspective, "social systems are so thoroughly interdependent that independently varying variables are not isolable in principle" (161).

35. It is the relation between seemingly separable things within a broader totality that constitutes a central question in the internalist-externalist dispute. Kline (18 August 1993C; 1983) explains that most relations are two-term, but some are three-term. A three-term relation is expressed in the statement: "Philadelphia is between New York and Washington." A two-term relation is expressed in a temporal context, as in the relationship between presently living Person A and his long-dead great-grandfather. Kline stresses that the relationship between Person A and his great-grandfather is not symmetrical or reciprocal. The relationship is internal (or "constitutive") with respect to Person A, and external (or "non-constitutive") with respect to the great-grandfather. That the great-grandfather "was who he was and led the life he led makes a difference to" Person A, but who Person A is and what life he has lead "makes/made no difference" to the great-grandfather. Thus, "In general, if a relation is *internal* ('constitutive') with respect to *one* relatum, it is *external* ('non-constitutive') with respect to the *other*." By contrast Rand viewed internal relations as asymmetric, rather than purely symmetrical.

36. Copleston 1966, 446. Copleston argues that this kind of pure externality is implied in Russell's logical atomism. Peikoff (1970T, Lecture 8) agrees that Russell sees reality as a collection of disparate, disconnected facts.

37. Aristotle, *De Poetica* (Poetics) 8.30–35, in Aristotle 1941, 1463.

Chapter 3. Educating Alissa

1. Rand (June 1982), "To the readers of The Fountainhead," in Binswanger 3.3.4. This letter, written in 1945, was a "general response letter mailed by Bobbs-Merrill or the author in answer to reader enquiries." See Perinn (1990): 69.

2. Kline (18 August 1993C) asks if Rand's reference to the "content of a person's brain" is indicative of reductionist materialism. Rand probably made a category mistake; she means the contents of a person's "mind." I demonstrate later that Rand is neither a vulgar materialist nor a vulgar idealist.

3. B. Branden, "Who is Ayn Rand?" in Branden and Branden 1962, 164.

4. Rand, "About the author," in Rand [1957] 1992, 1170–71. Rand [1957] 1992 is hereafter cited as Atlas Shrugged by page number in text and notes.

5. Unless otherwise indicated, biographical information in this chapter is derived from Barbara Branden's previously cited essay, "Who is Ayn Rand?"; The Passion of Ayn Rand (1986), especially the first five chapters; and interviews and correspondence with Branden herself.

6. Rand 1979bT. Rand recollected that she would read a textbook once and comprehend the entire course.

7. It is common to refer to both February and March of 1917 as the time of the food riots. After their seizure of power, the Bolsheviks changed the calendar from the "old style" to the "new style." Prior to this change, Russia was thirteen days behind the new calendar. For this observation, thanks to Rosenthal (15 November 1993C).

8. Rosenthal (15 November 1993C) remarks that many Russian Jews would have been repelled by the Slavophile literature since it was assertively anti-Semitic in its orientation.

9. In her adult years, Rand (1979bT) recollected that she went to two different schools in two different cities and was the "top" student in each of the respective classes. She does not name either school.

10. B. Branden 1986, 27. Branden (1986) also writes: "I corresponded with Dmitri Nabokov, the son of Vladimir, in an effort to locate and talk to his aunt. I learned from him that his father had had two sisters, one of whom had died; the other one [Helene Sikorski], whom he was kind enough to question for me, had no memory of Alice Rosenbaum; Alice's young friend must have been the deceased sister" (27 n. 1).

11. H. Sikorski, 12 October 1992C. Another classmate of Helene's, Helena Posener Vilga belonged to the 1916–17 class. She does not remember Alissa Rosenbaum. But since Rand may have been in Olga's class, Rand would not have been in Helene's. Special thanks to Boris Lossky (29 May–4 June 1992C) for forwarding to me this information from Madame Vilga. Boris himself attended the Stoiunin school in the academic years 1913–14 and 1914–15. During that time, boys were admitted into the college preparatory classes of the girls' school. Boris does not remember Alissa, but he was registered in the Chidlovsky gymnasium, another coed school, in 1915–16 and 1916–17, the very years that Alissa was friends with Olga. Boris returned to the Stoiunin school in the 1917–18 school year and remained there until 1921–22. By the fall of 1918, Alissa departed for the Crimea with her family. The Nabokov sisters had also left Petrograd. Olga Vladimirovna Petkevich died in 1978.

12. Boyd 1990, 44, 61. Special thanks to Brian Boyd for having put me in touch with Helene Sikorski.

13. Not unlike other Petrograd gymnasiums, the Stoiunin school day probably ran from 9 A.M. to 3 P.M., six days a week from mid-September to late May, with a two-week Christmas vacation between semesters and a one-week Easter break. Boyd (1990, 86) describes the similarly constituted Tenishev gymnasium, in which Vladimir Nabokov was enrolled. In her later years, Rand ([1964] 1993bT) was critical of Nabokov's work.

14. Rand in Peikoff 1980T, Lecture 1.

15. According to Boris Lossky (27 October 1992C), teachers of German and French in the Institutes of Foreign Languages at the Stoiunin school during the period of 1910–22 included Besantux, Gourault, Hartmann, Joue, Kamenskaia, Kiehl, Konioutchenko, Perschre, Raynault, Staatsbaeder, and Tchikhatcheva. Anna Rosenbaum does not appear among the foreign language teachers. There were many other Petrograd gymnasiums in which she could have taught.

16. Baker 1987, 3. Such atheism was a tenet of Russian radicalism well before Marxism. Rosenthal, 15 November 1993C.

17. Rand [1936] 1959 is hereafter cited as We the Living by page number in both text and notes. The 1936 edition is similarly cited, but as We the Living (1936).

18. Guerney 1960, xvii; Rosenthal, 15 November 1993C.

19. Copleston 1986, 313; Rosenthal, "Introduction," in Rosenthal 1986, 34.

20. Ibid. Kline, 18 August 1993C.

21. Friese, "Student life in a soviet university," in Kline 1957, 53.

22. Ivanov, "The training of soviet engineers," in Kline 1957, 162.

23. The trend toward scholastic democratization predates the Bolsheviks. Under the Provisional Government of 1917, the professoriate was able to achieve a degree of autonomy in shaping educational legislation. The czarist regime had barred women from university instruction, though these restrictions were eased in the years prior to the Revolution. But the czarist regime had also set severe quotas on Jews, and gave preference to the graduates of elite classical gymnasiums. Under the Provisional Government, each institution was granted the right to set its own admission policies. Petrograd University, along with other institutions, moved toward eliminating these restrictions. Though the Soviets eventually lifted the restrictions universally, they began to introduce new preferential guidelines for proletarian youth. The professoriate's newly won autonomy was another casualty of revolution. McClelland 1989, 247–55.

24. For this insight, and for his translation of the Leningrad dossier, thanks to Kline (20 October 1992C).

25. Rand quoted in Current Biography 1982, 332.

26. Peikoff 1990–91T, Lecture 7. Peikoff (1985T, Lecture 3) remarks that Rand achieved an excellent university education because she benefited from the instruction of fine teachers, like Lossky and others, who were carried over from the pre-Bolshevik period. Peikoff (1983T, Lecture 4) also argues that Rand's decision to major in history reflected her "inductive method" of formulating concepts through [historical] observation. Once these concepts were formed inductively, Rand deduced the logical implications of the principles involved.

27. Rand, "About the author," in Atlas Shrugged, 1170.

28. Emmons, "Introduction: Got'e and his diary," in Got'e 1988, 21–22.

29. Rand (June 1979), "Questions and answers on Anthem," in Column, 118.

30. Rand quoted in Current Biography 1982, 332.

31. See Shteppa 1962, 33–38, for a more detailed discussion of the history textbooks in use during the early Soviet period.

32. Marxist historiography underwent many transformations during the lifespan of the Soviet Union to conform to the temper of the times. Pokrovsky's Marxist orthodoxy was later overthrown by the patriots and Russian chauvinists during the Stalinist period. Afterward, Marxist-Leninist historiography came back into favor. Shteppa 1962, 380.

33. I would like to thank Boris Lossky for arranging my receipt of this dossier from the Leningrad archivists. The official dossier, stamped by the archivists with the seal of the university, lists Rand's original name as "Rosenbaum, Alissa Zinovievna." It indicates her year of birth (1905), and her enrollment in the Department of Social Pedagogy in the College of Social Sciences. It also includes the date of her admission and the date on which she concluded her studies, thus, finishing the requirements for the degree. The dossier includes no specific information on her actual classes, teachers, or grades. My discussion of her curriculum is gleaned from Rand's reminiscences as

reported to Barbara Branden (1986), and from my own understanding of the structure of study at the university.

34. Thanks to Andrew Lossky, Boris Lossky, and George Kline for assisting me in the reconstruction of the history department's distinguished personnel during the early Soviet period. The following list is not exhaustive, but it constitutes the bulk of historians in the department. The Petrograd history department had a grand tradition of scholarship. Several historians who taught at Petrograd emigrated prior to Alissa Rosenbaum's enrollment, including Michail T. Rostovtsev, who taught ancient history. Despite their political differences, Lunacharsky praised Rostovtsev for his archaeological expertise.

35. Platonov was arrested in January 1930 as part of a supposed plot to restore the monarchy. Emmons, "Introduction: Got'e and his diary," in Got'e 1988, 22. Other teachers in the history department were Olga Antounouvna Dobiach-Rozhdestvenskaia, who taught on the Crusades; Boris Vladimirovich Farmakovsky, who taught on the Hellenistic period of Greek sculpture; Vladimir Vasilyevich Weidle, who lectured in the history of art from 1916 to 1918 and from 1920 to 1924; and Sergei Vasil'evich Rozhdestvensky, best known for his work on sixteenth-century landholding. Rozhdestvensky taught throughout the 1920s and was arrested in October of 1929. Got'e 1988, 369 n. 84.

36. Rand (February 1970), "The left: Old and new," in *New Left*, 85.

37. Meetings between students and faculty were becoming more commonplace during this "progressive" period of university education. Interestingly, Rand models many of her fictional characters in *We the Living* on actual people whom she met while living in Russia. Peikoff indicates that Uncle Vassili was modeled after Rand's father, Kira's mother was like Rand's mother, and Leo was named after Rand's first love. Peikoff and Scott 1988T. In this same novel, there is a character named "Captain Karsavin." Karsavin is a White Army leader who is captured by Andrei Taganov, the idealistic communist soldier. Captain Karsavin is forced to commit suicide. It is possible that Rand modeled the captain after his namesake at the university, who was eventually exiled by the Bolsheviks for his counterrevolutionary ideals. The "Captain Karsavin" episode appears in *We the Living*, 101–3. Another of Rand's early Russian characters, from the screenplay "Red Pawn," is named "Kareyev." Kareyev is the commandant of Strastnoy Island. Rand (1931–32), "Red Pawn," in *Early Ayn Rand*, 111. Likewise, Rand may have taken the name "Kareyev" from Petrograd history professor, Kareev.

38. An English translation of *Thus Spake Zarathustra* was the first book that Rand purchased in the United States. B. Branden 1986, 45.

39. Zielinsky quoted in Curtis, "Michael Bakhtin, Nietzsche, and Russian pre-revolutionary thought," in Rosenthal 1986, 344.

40. Ibid., 345. Zielinsky saw both Nietzsche and Dostoyevsky as modern expositors of the classical Greek influence (348). Rosenthal (15 November 1993C) observes that Zielinsky was also anti-Semitic.

41. Rosenthal, "Introduction," in Rosenthal 1986, 4, 34.

42. Rosenthal (15 November 1993C) suggests too, that the Soviets were deeply critical of Nietzsche's "idealism" and his antimaterialism.

43. B. Branden, interview, 26 January 1992. It is unclear how many courses Alissa would have had to pass for the three-year degree. Degree requirements changed frequently during this period. Nevertheless, Alissa's course load as a history major would have been heavy. As a philosophy minor, she may have been required to take only two or three electives, including Lossky's course.

44. B. Branden, interview, 26 January 1992.

45. Rand did not concede a philosophical debt to Nietzsche, even though, as a child, she had been impressed with aspects of his work.

46. B. Branden, quoted in Reedstrom 1992, 4.

47. B. Branden 1986, 42. In relation to her university studies, Rand (1979bT) recollects one

particularly memorable adage from an ancient "Greek philosopher" whose name she did not remember. When discussing the possibility of her own death, Rand was fond of citing this maxim: "I will not die, it's the world that will end." (I was unable to locate this quotation in the works of any ancient philosophers.) If indeed, Rand encountered this statement at age sixteen, it may have been in the context of Lossky's course on the ancients.

48. B. Branden, "Who is Ayn Rand?" in Branden and Branden 1962, 165.

49. Kline, 28 February 1992C; N. Lossky, 12 February 1992C; A. Lossky, 2 March 1992C; B. Lossky, 4 March 1992C.

50. Thanks to Cox (17 March 1993C) for this suggestion.

51. McClelland 1989, 260; Lossky 1969, 209–10. Lossky wrote his *Memoirs* intermittently between 1935 and 1956, and they were published posthumously, by Boris, in 1968–69.

52. B. Lossky and N. Lossky 1978, 14. *Hylozoism* is the doctrine that matter and life are inseparable. *Vitalism* views life as caused or sustained by a vital principle that is neither chemical nor physical.

53. This question is raised by Boris Lossky (29 May–4 June 1992C; 27 October 1992C). Peikoff (27 May 1992C) has indicated that Rand's Estate is compiling biographical data and, as yet, has not found any relevant information that would shed light on the perplexities of the Lossky-Rand connection.

54. It should be emphasized "that the mere mention of Lossky's name" was never made in public; Rand recorded these recollections privately with her future biographer. Barbara Branden (28 June 1993C) states that she *"never* heard [Rand] mention him publicly."

55. Kline (18 August 1993C) notes that during the period of Lossky's last days, Zenkovsky had sent him a copy of his *Osnovy khristianskoi filosofii* (Foundations of Christian philosophy), which was to be published in two volumes. Apparently, Lossky was much too weak to write anything in Zenkovsky's copy except "Sochuvstvuiu" [I sympathize].

56. B. Branden, interview, 9 October 1992.

57. B. Branden, interview, 26 January 1992.

58. B. Branden, interview, 6 May 1992.

59. There is some evidence substantiating Rand's knowledge of the ancients. She exhibits an understanding of Aristotle and Plato. In her work on epistemology, she also deals briefly with the contributions of pre-Socratic philosophers such as Pythagoras, Protagoras, Zeno, and Parmenides. See *Introduction*, 8, 90, 248, 262. And in her journals, Rand criticized Thales as the father of cosmology. Rand (19 June 1958), "From Ayn Rand's unpublished writings: philosophic notes, 1949–1958," in Binswanger 5.4.7–8.

60. Despite his doubts, Boris Lossky (27 October 1992C) does not question his father's philosophical influence on Rand. He believes that Rand may have been well acquainted with his father's works, even if she did not actually study with him.

61. For this suggestion, thanks to Cox (17 March 1993C).

62. B. Lossky, 29 May–4 June 1992C. Barbara Branden (28 June 1993C) indicates that the temperature readings recorded in her biography were not derived from her taped interviews with Rand. Branden states that the unusual temperature readings were garnered from two separate sources.

63. Rand quoted in *Current Biography* 1982, 332.

64. Central Committee report quoted in Fitzpatrick 1979, 76–77.

65. Solzhenitsyn (1973, 372) reports that there were nearly three hundred prominent Russian humanists who were exiled in 1922. Additional small groups were exiled in 1923.

66. Rand (January 1969), "The 'inexplicable personal alchemy,' " in *New Left*, 117.

67. Rand quoted in *Current Biography* 1982, 332.

68. B. Branden (1986) writes that Rand "graduated from the university with the highest honors" (54). I could not substantiate this claim by reference to the Leningrad dossier on Alissa Rosenbaum.

69. B. Branden 1986, 55; "Who is Ayn Rand?" in Branden and Branden 1962, 165. Also during this period, Alissa enrolled in a Leningrad school for young people who wished to pursue a career in the Russian film industry. She learned useful information on the craft of film that she would later apply to movie scripts. B. Branden 1986, 57.

70. B. Branden 1986, 55–63. Childs (1982) observed that Rand was "in effect one of the first Russian Jewish dissidents" to come to America (33).

71. In *We the Living*, Rand dramatizes how statism destroys the best in people. But she ends the novel on a positive note; although statism destroys the best people *physically*, it is unable to destroy them spiritually. As such, Kira dies smiling that "so much . . . had been possible" (446).

72. B. Branden 1986T. Branden (28 June 1993C) also remarks that the committee never gave Rand the forum they had promised her. Rand was bitterly disappointed that she was denied this opportunity. In the immediate aftermath of her HUAC testimony, Rand, in her "Notes on the Thomas committee" (November 1993), in Schwartz 7.6, argued that Congress had the right to ask questions of fact with regard to Communist Party membership since the organization was committed to criminality. She also lamented that many of the "friendly witnesses" (including Adolphe Menjou and Morrie Ryskind) were blacklisted in the post-McCarthy era. Later, however, Rand argued that in a genuinely free society, "There would be no hearings." B. Branden 1986, 200–203; Rand in Peikoff 1976T, Lecture 6.

73. Rand (20 October 1947), "Ayn Rand's HUAC Testimony," in Binswanger 8.4.1–11; Willis, "Introduction," in Hellman 1976, 1–3.

Chapter 4. The Maturation of Ayn Rand

1. Rand (4 May 1946), quoted in Peikoff 1991a, xiv.

2. Rand (October–November 1963), "The goal of my writing," in *Romantic Manifesto*, 162.

3. Ibid., 163.

4. Rand 1964b, 3. This interview was reprinted in Haley 1993.

5. Rand (September 1971), "Brief summary," in *Objectivist* 10:1091.

6. Some of these stories (e.g., "Her Second Career") do not relate directly to Rand's experiences in Russia.

7. Peikoff, "Editor's preface," in *Early Ayn Rand*, 5.

8. Ibid., 108. One can find a similar disdain for *both* the state *and* the Church in *Thus Spake Zarathustra*, the first book of Nietzsche's that Rand ever read. See Nietzsche [1883–85] 1905, 144.

9. In later years, in Rand (17 February 1960), "Faith and force: the destroyers of the modern world," in *Philosophy*, 85, she argued: "Communists, like all materialists, are neo-mystics." I explore this identity more thoroughly in Parts 2 and 3.

10. Rand (1931–32), "Red Pawn," in *Early Ayn Rand*, 111.

11. Rosenthal (15 November 1993C) remarks that Rand's synopsis deals with a real-life Soviet prison at the Solovetsk monastery.

12. Rand (1931–32), "Red Pawn," in *Early Ayn Rand*, 130–31.

13. Peikoff, "Editor's preface," in *Early Ayn Rand*, 172, writes that this story was cut from the novel, "presumably" because it was unnecessary to the establishment of Kira's character.

14. Rand (1931), "Kira's viking," in *Early Ayn Rand*, 179.

15. Peikoff and Scott 1988T; Reedstrom 1993b.

16. Rand in Peikoff 1976T, Lecture 11.

17. *We the Living*, 446. During World War II, Italian film-makers produced a faithful (if unauthorized) film version of the book, starring Alida Valli as Kira, Rossano Brazzi as Leo, and Fosco Giachetti as Andrei. Directed by Goffredo Allessandrini, the film was initially shown in two parts to cheering Italian audiences. Though it depicted the grim reality of life under communism,

the film may have been banned by Mussolini's government for its implicit attack on all forms of totalitarianism, including fascism. The Nazis may have blocked the film's entry into Germany because they believed that Andrei, the communist idealist, was too sympathetic a character. This is ironic, considering Rand's virulent anticommunism! The film was lost to audiences for many years, until it was rediscovered, remastered, and rereleased in 1988 with English subtitles. The movie is distributed through Duncan Scott Productions. Reviews and different perspectives on the film are provided by Edelstein (1988), Ericson (1988), McGrady (1988), Peikoff and Scott (1988T), Chase (1988), Bradford (1988), Kamhi (December 1988), "Ayn Rand's We the Living," in Torres and Kamhi (1982–94), and Vermilye 1994, 27–28. I cite "Torres and Kamhi (1982–94)" for ease of reference. In fact, Aristos was edited by Torres from July 1982 to September 1991, and Torres and Kamhi from January 1992 to the present.

18. Rand in Peikoff 1976T, Lecture 8.

19. Rand (October 1958), "Foreword," in We the Living, viii.

20. Merrill 1991, 21–40. Merrill observes correctly that Rand's revisions were not extensive. He points out some minor modifications of interest. In the first edition, Leo recites Kant at social gatherings; in the later edition, Leo quotes Spinoza, Nietzsche, and Oscar Wilde. Rand's antipathy toward Kant was obviously not as pronounced in 1930–33 when she worked on the original manuscript. In the 1936 edition, Rand may have used Kant strictly as a Western philosophic symbol. Leo acknowledges Western sources to aggravate his Slavophile associates. Rand also writes that people "looked at Leo as they looked at the statue of Apollo." Apparently, Rand rejected the Dionysian, and embraced the Apollonian, metaphor from an early point in her literary and intellectual development. We the Living, 127–28. Cox (1986) discusses Rand's stylistic revisions.

21. The following passages appear in the first (1936) edition of We the Living (92–95) and in a comparable scene in the second edition (79–80).

22. Hicks 1992, 6. Echoing Rand's own views, Oyerly (1990, 5) argues that Rand's stark condemnation of the masses in the first edition of We the Living, was "poetic metaphor" entirely due to Rand's early linguistic difficulties. Nathaniel Branden (1971b, 13), by contrast, argues that Rand made important philosophical changes in the second edition.

23. Barbara Branden (28 June 1993C) states that in any event, such a "full philosophical explanation" would have been inappropriate in a novel. She suggests that the so-called Nietzschean elements of We the Living are really only features of Rand's youthful, over-dramatized, literary style. In Branden's view, these elements were never an authentic part of Rand's perspective: "In fact, in the years I knew her, she often spoke of her deep respect for 'the common man,' saying that in many ways . . . the American common man had a greater intelligence [and] commitment to reason and individualism than was generally understood."

24. Rand (1934), Ideal, in Early Ayn Rand, 234. Ideal, like Rand's 1939 play, Think Twice, was never performed. She wrote two other plays that were produced on Broadway. An adaptation of We the Living, called The Unconquered, did not have a successful run. Another play, written in 1932–33, originally titled Penthouse Legend, had a fairly successful Broadway presentation. It was published in 1968 as Night of January 16th. The play is a courtroom drama, and it featured a gimmick in which a jury is drawn from the audience. Rand considers the work an example of "Romantic symbolism." She discusses the play's history in Rand (June 1968), "Introduction," in Rand [1933] 1968.

25. Peikoff, "Editor's preface," iin Early Ayn Rand, 181–84.

26. Rand (9 April 1934), "From Ayn Rand's unpublished writings: Philosophic journal," in Binswanger 4.4.2.

27. Ibid., 3. Barbara Branden (28 June 1993C) suggests that the mature Rand would never have published such an antireligious comment. This underscores the fact that Rand's journals were indeed, "thinking on paper," rather than carefully edited for public consumption. Rand believed that she was primarily an advocate of reason, and that once reason won, faith and religion would cease to be issues.

28. Rosenthal (15 November 1993C) observes too, that Chinese also lacks a word for "privacy."

29. Rand (1934), "From Ayn Rand's unpublished writings: Philosophic journal," in Binswanger 4.4.2.

30. Ibid., 5. Torres and Kamhi note that there is a similarity between Rand's concept of "sense of life" and Ortega y Gasset's concept of "metaphysical sentiment" as presented in his work *On Love: Aspects of a Single Theme*. Torres and Kamhi (September 1991), "Ayn Rand's philosophy of art: A critical introduction," parts 3 and 4, in Torres and Kamhi 1982–94, 6 n.12. The "sense of life" concept, which I explore in Chapter 7, has implications for Rand's aesthetics. Though it is clear that Rand read Ortega y Gasset, there is currently no available journal evidence to suggest that she formed this concept as a direct result of his influence.

31. Rand (15 May 1934), "From Ayn Rand's unpublished writings: Philosophic journal," in Binswanger 4.4.5–6.

32. Rand (4 December 1935), quoted in Branden and Branden 1962, 192.

33. Some have assumed that Roark was modeled on Frank Lloyd Wright. For two accounts of the relationship between Rand and Wright, see B. Branden 1986, 140, 172, 189–91, 208–9, and Secrest 1992, 494–98, 510.

34. Saint-Andre (5 August 1993C) notes that in many ways, Rand assigned to Roark the "positive" aspects of the Nietzschean superman (heroic strength of will and defiance of social convention), and to Wynand, the "negative" ones (cruelty and ruthlessness). A very similar technique was used by Gorky in his novel *Klim Samgin* (1925–1936). Gorky assigned "positive" Nietzschean aspects to his heroes and "negative" Nietzschean aspects to his villains. Rosenthal, "Introduction," in Rosenthal 1986, 36. Wynand, of course, is not a villain in *The Fountainhead*, but he is the embodiment of all that Rand believed was wrong with the Nietzschean ethos.

35. See Nietzsche [1886] 1966, 228 [par. 287]. Rand quotes a slightly different translation.

36. Rand (25 December 1935), quoted in Peikoff (March 1992), "Afterword," in *Fountainhead*, 697.

37. Rand (9 February 1936), in ibid., 698–99.

38. Rand (22 February 1937), in ibid., 700.

39. Thanks to Cox (3 May 1993C) for emphasizing this particular aspect of Toohey's character.

40. *Fountainhhead*, 338. Rand was always "haunted" by this metaphor from *Thus Spake Zarathustra*. She lamented later that she felt as though *she* had become a philosophical "fly swatter" in her ongoing critique of contemporary thinkers. She thought Marx was a worthy adversary, but had grown tired of fighting intellectuals such as Freud or Rawls. Rand (November–December 1975), "A last survey, part one," in Rand [1971–76] 1979, 4:382. Rand [1971–76] 1979 is hereafter cited as *Ayn Rand Letter* by volume and page number in text and notes.

41. Rand (27 March 1937), in *Fountainhead*, 702.

42. Rand (22 February 1937), in ibid., 701. Cox (3 May 1993C) reminds me that in the finished novel, Toohey is not quite portrayed as a "repulsive swine." Rand achieves great literary irony by presenting him as a puny character with the "voice of a god."

43. Rand [1937] 1946, 108–10. Rand [1937] 1946 is hereafter cited as *Anthem* by page number in both text and notes.

44. The Greek mythic imagery throughout Rand's fiction could be the subject of a book in itself. In *Atlas Shrugged*, the Promethean metaphor figures prominently: "John Galt is Prometheus who changed his mind. After centuries of being torn by vultures in payment for having brought to men the fire of the gods, he broke his chains and he withdrew his fire—until the day when men withdraw their vultures" (517).

45. The latter two screenplays were adaptations. See Cox 1987 for a fine overview of Rand's writing for the cinema. As of this writing, a remake of *The Fountainhead* is being prepared by Warner Brothers.

46. Rand (1 January 1945), in Peikoff 1991a, x.

47. Though Rand began outlining her novel in 1945, *Atlas Shrugged* is foreshadowed in a question Roark poses in *The Fountainhead*: "What would happen to the world without those who do, think, work, produce? (607). Raimondo claims that Rand's novel, *Atlas Shrugged*, exhibits certain similarities to journalist Garet Garrett's 1922 novel, *The Driver*. Raimondo (1993, 203) concludes that Rand "was influenced by Garrett." I could not find any evidence to link Rand to Garrett, who was, as Raimondo correctly notes, an "exemplar of the Old Right." A rebuttal to Raimondo is provided by Bradford (1994).

48. Chambers 1957, 595–96. Even upon Rand's death, William Buckley (1982a), editor of *National Review*, lamented that she had theologized her atheistic beliefs and had short-circuited her otherwise "eloquent and persuasive" antistatism. However, Berger (1986, 13) calls Rand's philosophy "a vulgarized cross between Adam Smith and Friedrich Nietzsche." Though there are many negative reviews of Rand's works to choose from, it is possible to find an occasionally provocative characterization from an unlikely source. Feyerabend is said to have reported to McCawley (1990, 385 n. 21) that Rand "is much better than most academics." In Feyerabend's view, Rand defended her philosophy in "juicy tales full of sex, industrial espionage, murder, mystery, and at the climax introduces her beloved Aristotle (*Atlas Shrugged*—a story I read with considerable pleasure). And Aristotle, as far as I can see, by far exceeds all existing 'thinkers' in versatility and depth. . . . I prefer her to Derrida and Foucault any time." Rand herself, was not as generous toward Feyerabend. See Rand (March 1970), "Kant versus Sullivan," in *Philosophy*. For another positive review of Rand's work, see Pruette 1943.

49. Rand (20 January 1947), "From Ayn Rand's unpublished writings: Notes for *Atlas Shrugged*," in Binswanger 5.2.2.

50. Rand (31 July 1950), "From Ayn Rand's unpublished writings: Philosophic notes," in Binswanger 5.4.4–5.

51. Rand (6 October 1949), "From Ayn Rand's unpublished writings: Philosophic notes," in Binswanger 5.4.1–2. Rand recognized (through her character Hank Rearden), "that by accepting the mystics' theory of sex I was accepting the looters' theory of economics" (*Atlas Shrugged*, 859). This observation had far-reaching implications that Rand developed later in her assessment of the conservative-liberal duality in U.S. politics.

52. Rand (29 June 1946), "From Ayn Rand's unpublished writings: Notes for *Atlas Shrugged*," in Binswanger 4.6.8–9.

53. Rand (28 August 1949), in Peikoff, "Editor's preface," in *Early Ayn Rand*, 260.

54. Peikoff (1987bT) questions, period 1, explains that Rand could have named her philosophy "rationalism," "existentialism," "realism," or "conceptualism," but these labels were preempted by other traditions. Rand ultimately chose "Objectivism" because it emphasized the "objective" nature of her approach in every philosophic branch.

55. Rand (8 June 1958), "From Ayn Rand's unpublished writings: Philosophic notes," in Binswanger 5.4.7.

56. Hook 1961, 3. Despite Rand's theatrical expository style, some of her critics have praised her ability to capture the essence of other systems of thought. See, for instance, Hollinger, "Ayn Rand's epistemology in historical perspective," in Den Uyl and Rasmussen 1984.

57. The affair ended for a variety of reasons. It has been acknowledged by Barbara Branden (1986), Nathaniel Branden (1989), and Leonard Peikoff (1987aT).

58. Peikoff (1964). Barbara Branden also took courses with Hook. Nathaniel Branden took courses with William Barrett. N. Branden 1989, 115–16.

59. Peikoff 1972T, Lecture 10; 1985T, Lecture 1.

60. Peikoff 1972T, Lecture 12. However, Peikoff (1990–91T, Lecture 15) warns that one cannot simply take any twelve topics in philosophy and thread them together seamlessly. Some issues are more closely related than others.

61. Peikoff 1991b, 4. Peikoff (1983T, Lecture 2) admits that he struggled with rationalism for fifteen years in his understanding of Objectivism.

62. Peikoff (1990–91T, Lecture 5) admits to preferring synthesis over analysis.

63. The most important aspect of Brandenian revisionism is its attempt to transcend the cultic qualities of the early Objectivist movement. Branden accepts most of the responsibility for having generated a virtual cult around Ayn Rand. N. Branden 1989, 402; B. Branden 1990, 51.

64. Branden claims that he has some differences with Rand that relate to her theories of sex and emotions. Branden (1983b, 225n) argues that he tends to emphasize generosity and mutual aid as essential to an ethic that "holds man's/woman's life as its standard" (emphasis added). Even if Branden's formulation seems more "politically correct" than Rand's, it is still within the broad Objectivist tradition. Ironically, in a 1978 lecture, Rand (1978T) claimed that Objectivism had made very little impact on the science of psychology. She stated that she could name exceptions, "but not in print." This is the closest Rand has come to recognizing Branden's post-1968 contributions. In any event, if Nathaniel Branden is the legitimate father of the self-esteem movement, Ayn Rand is its mother.

Chapter 5. Being

1. Rand (June 1970), "The chickens' homecoming," in New Left, 108.

2. Peikoff 1987T, Lecture 1; 1985T, Lecture 3.

3. Peikoff 1991b, 122–23. One crucial question which must be considered is this: If Rand is wrong about a single aspect of her system, does this invalidate the totality? I do not consider this issue in the current study because it relates to the validity of Rand's system-as-such. But it is worth examining.

4. In this regard, Rand's system resembles Marx's system. On Marx's approach, see Meikle 1985, 71.

5. Rand rejected nearly every imaginable dichotomy: mind vs. body; idealism vs. materialism; rationalism vs. empiricism; internalism vs. externalism; intrinsicism vs. subjectivism; concepts vs. percepts; reason vs. emotion; the conscious vs. the subconscious; the articulate vs. the tacit; reason vs. art; fact vs. value; conventional egoism vs. traditional altruism; love vs. sex; anarchism vs. statism; atomistic individualism vs. organic collectivism. A number of other dichotomies are mentioned by Peikoff (1976T, Lecture 1): happiness vs. pleasure; pure vs. applied science; woman vs. man; art vs. business; politics vs. economics; morality vs. science; art vs. entertainment. In his course on logic, Peikoff (1974T, Lecture 3) explains that these dichotomies are all examples of the fallacy of the false alternative. This tendency toward the analysis of the "coincidence of opposites" in the modern world is not distinctive to Objectivism. It is also apparent in the systems of Aristotle, Spinoza, Leibniz, Kant, Hegel, Marx, and Emerson. See Kuntz 1981.

6. Robbins 1974; Barry 1983, 1986; Barnes 1967. Interestingly, Berger (1986) alludes to the similarity between Rand's epistemology and Lenin's dialectical materialism. It is perhaps in this spirit that Tuccille (1972, 16) called Objectivism "a kind of New Marxism of the Right." Robbins argues further that Rand is a philosophic materialist. He believes that her defense of objective reality, sense perception, the open-ended nature of concepts, natural being, and Promethean humanism is virtually "indistinguishable from the general materialist position of the 19th century." He adds: "Both Engels and Lenin rejected the 'vulgar materialist' idea that the brain secretes thought as the liver secretes bile." In this area, Rand, Lenin, Marx, and Feuerbach are opposed only to "the non-dialectical vulgar materialists." Although I disagree with some of Robbins's characterizations, I applaud his ability to see some of the parallels between Rand and the dialectical tradition. See Robbins 1974, 46 n. 100, 48 n. 107, 80 n. 49, 82–83, 85 n. 73, and 87 n. 85.

7. Rand (March 1967), "An answer to readers: About the 'horror file,' " in Objectivist 6:237–38.

8. Rand (17 June 1962), "Introducing Objectivism," in Voice of Reason, 3.

9. Peikoff (1980T, Lecture 9) explains that Objectivism does not make any distinction between

ontology and metaphysics. He (1970T, Lecture 6) also explains that, in contrast to Comte and other positivists who used the word "metaphysical" as a reproach, Rand refers freely to "metaphysics" as the branch of philosophy dealing with the widest existential abstractions.

10. Rand (April 1965), "The psycho-epistemology of art," in *Romantic Manifesto*, 19.

11. Rand (9 February 1961), "The Objectivist ethics," in Rand 1964a, 14. Rand 1964a is hereafter cited as *Virtue of Selfishness* by page number in both text and notes.

12. Rand (19 June 1958), "From Ayn Rand's unpublished writings: Philosophic notes," in Binswanger 5.4.8; "Appendix," 290.

13. Rand (19 June 1958), "From Ayn Rand's unpublished writings: Philosophic notes," in Binswanger 5.4.7.

14. Rand 1962T; Peikoff 1972T, Lecture 1.

15. Peikoff 1972T, Lecture 9; *New Intellectual*, 28–29.

16. Rand did not use the term "asymmetric internality." For a fuller discussion of the differences among asymmetric, causal, and reciprocal relations, especially in Marx's social ontology, see Gould 1978, 89, 92, and 184 n. 22.

17. Rand (19 June 1958), "From Ayn Rand's unpublished writings: Philosophic notes," in Binswanger 5.4.7–9.

18. Peikoff 1972T, Lecture 8. On the need to avoid the "dogmatizing" of science, Peikoff 1990–91T, Lecture 1.

19. Peikoff 1991b, 16–17, 192; 1990–91T, Lecture 10.

20. Rand's perspective has some parallels with modern science. As N. Branden (1980) suggests: "Discoveries in physics and biology have exploded old-fashioned materialism and have led inexorably toward what is frequently described as an *organismic* rather than a *mechanical* model of the universe" (53).

21. Objectivist literature is replete with attacks on the epistemological foundations of what Rand characterized as "pseudo-scientific" movements, for example, environmentalism. See *New Left*.

22. Peikoff (1974T, Lecture 4) explains that in her first two axioms, Rand merely distinguishes between existence and consciousness, metaphysics and epistemology. She rejects the idealist attempt to blend existence and consciousness into an "indeterminate package-deal" in which the crucial differences between them are ignored. Rand (12–26, March 1973), "The metaphysical versus the man-made," in *Philosophy*, 29–30. O'Neill ([1971] 1977, 83) argues that Rand's distinction between existence and consciousness suggests "at the very least, an *operational dualism*" in her ontology. I counter that the distinction is one of "asymmetric internality," which is *not* dualism as I have defined it.

23. *Introduction*, 29. In contemporary philosophical discourse, much work has been devoted to the relationship of consciousness and content by those in the phenomenological tradition, such as Husserl; and to the issue of being vs. nonbeing, as expressed in the works of Heidegger, Quine, Davidson, and Kripke. However, there is no evidence to suggest that Rand was influenced by the thought of any of these figures. Essays by Den Uyl and Rasmussen, and Hollinger in Den Uyl and Rasmussen 1984 discuss Rand's metaphysics and epistemology as they relate to the contemporary context.

24. Marx [1844] 1964, 145. Marx [1844] 1964 is hereafter cited as *Manuscripts* by page number in text and notes. A number of scholars have argued that Marx was not primarily a materialist, but a naturalist and/or an essentialist in the Aristotelian tradition. See Meikle 1985 and Bhikhu Parekh (1975), "Marx's Theory of Man," in Machan 1987, 40–61. Parekh believes that Marx's project integrated radical humanism and naturalism. Marx saw people as a dialectical unity of natural and human being and took a vitalist, Aristotelian view of nature in which each natural being strives toward the actualization of its potential. Furthermore, each being is involved in a network of complex interrelationships. Parekh adds that for Marx, "A non-objective being, a being that is totally self-sufficient, is a non-natural being, and therefore a non-being, a fantasy" (43). Other parallels between Marx and Aristotle are explored in McCarthy 1990 and 1992.

25. Peikoff 1991b, 167; Rand 1979aT.

26. As Phillips (1934–35, 2:36–37) explains, in all axiomatic concepts there is a "boomerang" attribute such that "even though we cast it away from us, it returns to us again." The "boomerang" argument is characteristically used by many Aristotelians and Thomists in their defense of the law of noncontradiction.

27. On the links between "begging the question" and the "stolen concept", see Peikoff 1947T, Lectures 1 and 13.

28. N. Branden (January 1963), "The stolen concept," in *Objectivist Newsletter* 2:2–4.

29. Aristotle defined the law of noncontradiction (also called the law of contradiction), as well as the law of excluded middle (that everything is either A or not-A at a given time or in a certain respect). In *Atlas Shrugged*, vii–viii, Rand employs the various forms of these laws of logic in the titles of three successive parts: "Non-Contradiction," "Either-Or," and "A is A." Peikoff (1972T, Lecture 4) tells us that the law of identity ("A is A") was formally enunciated in the twelfth century, by Antonias Andreas, but it is implicit in Aristotle's law of contradiction.

30. Aristotle, *Metaphysics* 4.3.1005b18–21, in Aristotle 1941, 736.

31. Peikoff states that unlike Aristotle, Aquinas saw the law as a first principle of being. Locke believed it was an inductive principle.

32. See Chapters 1 and 3 herein. Peikoff (1974T, Lecture 1) agrees that Marxists do not detach logic from reality. Though Peikoff recognizes that Marxists retain the ontological view, he argues that this is undermined by their belief in reality-as-contradiction. As I indicated in the introduction to this book (and elsewhere), dialectical "contradiction" is more properly described as *relational*, rather than logical. I return to this issue in Chapter 11. Also see Sciabarra 1988a, 1990a, and 1995.

33. N. Branden 1967T, Lecture 3. Marcuse ([1941] 1960, 40, 42) argues that this dynamic reading of the law of identity was central to the Hegelian ontology. Both Aristotle and Hegel were system builders, unifiers of previous trends. Hegel had rediscovered "the extremely dynamic character of the Aristotelian metaphysic, which treats all being as process and movement." According to Marcuse, this dynamic had been lost in the formalistic Aristotelian tradition, which viewed the law of identity as a static tautology. Hegel had grasped the process orientation of Aristotle's ontology. Hegel, like Aristotle, regarded "being-as-such" as a "process or movement through which every particular being molds itself into what it *really* is." Unlike Aristotle, however, Hegel historicized the temporal dimension.

34. Binswanger (December 1981), "Q&A department," in Binswanger 2.6.14. Binswanger explains that certain concepts, such as motion and location, are purely relational. Peikoff (1976T, Lecture 2) also accepts the Aristotelian explanation of time and space as relational; time exists in the universe, and the universe is eternal. Space applies to definite points within a relational context; it does not apply to the universe as a whole.

35. Peikoff 1990–91T, Lecture 2. Binswanger also recognizes that consciousness may be an emergent property of physical matter, but we do not know this for sure. And in any event, this does not alter the fact that it is an irreducible primary. Binswanger [1987] 1991T, Lecture 2; Peikoff 1972T, Lecture 2.

36. Efron 1966, 499; 1967. Efron 1967 was reprinted in *The Objectivist* in four parts, from February through May 1968.

37. Peikoff 1990–91T, Lecture 9. Peikoff indicates that the three axioms were grasped explicitly at different periods in history: "existence" by Parmenides, "identity" by Aristotle, and "conscious-ness" by Augustine. Displaying a Hegelian flair, Rand remarks: "The human race developed the three axioms in the right order. . . . You know it's been said many times that the human race follows in a general way the stages of development of an individual" ("Appendix," 262–63).

38. Peikoff (1983T, Lectures 7 and 9) criticizes those "rationalistic" Objectivists who try to reduce the three axioms to only one: A is A.

39. Peikoff 1983T, Lecture 7; Adorno [1966] 1983; Kolakowski 1984.

40. Peikoff (1991b, 12; 1990–91T, Lecture 1) emphasizes that a concept such as "entity" is axiomatic, but not basic. Since entity is a category of being, we do not know, on the basis of philosophy, whether it is universal. Primary entities (such as "dog," "cat," etc.) may be the form in which we perceive puffs of metaenergy. Philosophers should not try to answer questions that are properly scientific. "Existence" is a basic axiom because it is universal. Rand did not fully explore the nonbasic axioms. Peikoff 1987T, Lecture 2. They are "undeveloped waters" in Objectivist philosophy. On the simultaneous character of axioms, see Peikoff 1983T, Lecture 5.

41. On the Marxist rejection of such "vulgar" materialist reductionism, see Meikle 1985, 154–63.

42. Peikoff (1972T, Lecture 2) criticizes this very spiritualist-idealist tendency to counteract reductionist materialism by the reverse method of applying psycho-epistemological concepts to electrons.

43. *Atlas Shrugged*, 1037. Peikoff (1990–91T, Lecture 1) believes that Objectivism offers a view of causality in the Aristoletian tradition. Gould (1978, 72–78) argues that Marx's view of causality is just as Aristotelian.

44. Rand (12–26 March 1973), "The metaphysical versus the man-made," in *Philosophy*, 30.

45. N. Branden (May 1962), "Intellectual ammunition department," in *Objectivist Newsletter* 1:19.

46. Peikoff 1991b, 6–7; 1972T, Lecture 5; 1976T, Lecture 8.

47. "Appendix," 148–49; Binswanger [1987] 1991T, Lecture 2.

48. This discussion is based on an exchange which appears in "Appendix," 282–88. In Chapter 6 I discuss the Objectivist *epistemological* perspective on the internalist-externalist debate.

49. "Appendix," 284. Peikoff (May–September 1967, in *Introduction*, 108–9) provides a similar critique of the dichotomy between necessary and contingent facts. Facts merely *are*. To use the term "necessity" is superfluous. Some man-made facts did not have to be, but once they are, they too are necessary. Objectivism stresses not a dichotomy between necessity and contingency, but between the metaphysical and the man-made.

50. "Appendix," 266. Den Uyl and Rasmussen ("Ayn Rand's Realism," in Den Uyl and Rasmussen 1984, 7) argue persuasively that even though Rand would not accept a distinction between form and matter, she does accept one between substance and accident. This is a distinction between primary existents and those things that exist in a relationship to them. Presumably, this would mean that an entity is a primary existent, and that its attributes (accidents) inhere in the entity. This would make the attributes dependent on the existence of the entity.

51. Peikoff (May–September 1967), "The analytic-synthetic dichotomy," in *Introduction*, 105.

52. In Rand (8 March 1947), "From Ayn Rand's unpublished writings: Notes for *Atlas Shrugged*," in Binswanger 5.2.3, she explains that our grasp of "entity" is almost simultaneous with our grasp of "acting entity," even though we must grasp the former before the latter. What is clear is that we abstract the concept of "action" by observing *entities* that act.

53. Rand ("Appendix," 265) uses this example of the table and its legs. Blanshard ([1962] 1964, 475) uses this example, though it involves more substantive issues. Blanshard asks if the "essence" of the table can be present whether or not a book was sitting on its top. If the table is internally related to the book, and to everything else in the universe, we risk dissolving its nature into its relations. This issue of the table's "essence" relates more to the theory of definitions, which I discuss in Chapter 6.

54. Peikoff 1982T, Lecture 7. But this does not imply strict organicity. See Chapter 6.

55. Rand (12–26 March 1973), "The metaphysical versus the man-made," in *Philosophy*, 30.

56. Ibid., 33.

57. Sciabarra 1988a, 1988c, and 1995. Did Rand give any credence to Hayek's concept of the unintended consequences of human action? Can the contributions of Rand and Hayek be reconciled to achieve a more comprehensive grasp of the constructivist fallacy? I address these issues in Chapter 8.

58. Rand (12–26 March 1973), "The metaphysical versus the man-made," in *Philosophy*, 29.

59. Walsh 1992; Reedstrom 1993a, 1–4; Walsh, 14 October 1993C. Among other Objectivist interpreters of Kant is Peikoff; see Peikoff 1982 and 1970T, Lectures 2 and 3.

60. Kant [1781/1787] 1933, A491/B519. A refers to the first (1781) German edition of Kant's *Critique of Pure Reason*, whereas B refers to the second (1787) German edition.

61. Schopenhauer, *Kritik der Kantischen Philosophie*, in Dryer 1966, 499 n.1. In *Introduction to Objectivist Epistemology*, Rand quotes not Schopenhauer, but the nineteenth-century Kantian Henry Mansel. Rand argued that Mansel provides a more explicit statement of the attack on consciousness than Kant himself (80–81).

62. Lossky 1934c, 265–66. For Lossky ([1906] 1919, 112), though Kant is an improvement over his rationalist-empiricist predecessors, he failed to provide any validation for his subjectivism. "Search through the *Critique of Pure Reason* as diligently as you may, you will nowhere find a proof of this important position, but merely assertions to the effect that it must be true."

Chapter 6. Knowing

1. Peikoff 1990–91T, Lecture 5. Despite Rand's contention that her epistemology was based upon induction, some have characterized her theory as rationalistic. Barry (1987, 112), for instance, argues that Rand's epistemology is "a series of rationalist assertions" deduced from authoritarian first principles. I dispute such a characterization.

2. Binswanger (December 1982), "Ayn Rand's philosophic achievement, part four," in Binswanger 3.6.11.

3. Rand (19 June 1958), "From Ayn Rand's unpublished writings: Philosophic notes," in Binswanger 5.4.8.

4. Rasmussen 1984, 330 n. 25; Adorno [1966] 1983; Caputo 1988; Johnson 1990.

5. Peikoff (1972T, Lecture 9) suggests that Rand characterized most classical "objective" or "realist" approaches as intrinsicist, rather than as "objectivist."

6. Rand (17 February 1960), "Faith and force: The destroyers of the modern world," in *Philosophy*, 75.

7. *Introduction*, 80; Peikoff 1983T, Lecture 6.

8. Lossky [1906] 1919, 413. Interestingly, this very same desire was manifested by Rand and other Objectivists. For instance, in *The Evidence of the Senses*, Kelley (1986, 255) aims to provide the foundations for "an epistemology with a knowing subject."

9. On this conflation of the mode of cognition and the contents of consciousness, see Rasmussen 1983b, 85, and 1984, 332, and Den Uyl and Rasmussen 1984, 13.

10. Lossky (1923), in Shein 1973, 25.

11. Lossky (1913–14), "Intuitivism," in Edie, Scanlan, and Zeldin 1965, 321–22, 338.

12. On these philosophical distinctions, see Peikoff (May–September 1967), "The analytic-synthetic dichotomy," in *Introduction*. Lossky too attacks the analytic-synthetic division. See Edie, Scanlan, and Zeldin 1965, 318.

13. *Introduction*, 79. Peikoff (1982, 56; 1976T, Lecture 6) provides a comparable analysis of the "dogmatist" versus the "pragmatist." In eschewing the duality of dogmatism and skepticism, Objectivist analysis is similar to the Nietzschean *metacritique*, which, as Habermas ([1968] 1971, 290) explains, unmasks "the modern form of skepticism . . . as a veiled dogmatism."

14. "Appendix," 251–53; N. Branden [1969] 1979, 6, and 1983b, 29; Binswanger 1990, 193, and (August 1986), "The goal-directedness of living action," in Binswanger 7.4.10.

15. Peikoff 1987bT, questions, period 1; (1990–91T), Lecture 3.

16. Rand is not the only modern thinker to grow out of Aristotelian realism. On the relationship of hermeneutics to the Aristotelian tradition, see Caputo 1988, 5. Copleston ([1963] 1985, 334)

also argues that many modern Thomists and Marxists share an ontological and epistemological realism, even though the latter dismiss the former as idealists.

17. Something that is "unconscious" is *not* conscious. All forms of conscious awareness involve *action*.

18. Rand (9 February 1961), "The Objectivist ethics," in *Virtue of Selfishness*, 19.

19. Kelley 1986, 88–90. Kelley acknowledges that Rand had the greatest impact on his thinking about perception. Though Rand did not write much on this subject, her views on perceptual form are expressed briefly in "Appendix," 279–82; N. Branden 1967T, Lecture 2; Peikoff 1970T, Lecture 11; 1972T, Lectures 5 and 12; 1987bT, questions, period 1; and 1991b, chap. 2; and Binswanger 1989T, Lecture 2.

20. Rand would never have characterized perception as "objective." This is a point which needed clarification since there was a time when Peikoff himself committed the error of applying the objective-subjective-intrinsic trichotomy to the realm of perception. Peikoff was corrected by Rand in later presentations for this misapplication of her theory. Peikoff 1987bT, questions, period 1. Peikoff (1991b, 112, 117) argues that normative terms such as "objectivity" cannot be applied to automatic processes such as perception. Since perception is nonvolitional, it cannot be characterized as "objective" or "intrinsic" or "subjective." Perception "cannot depart from reality." "Objectivity," is volitional adherence to reality "by following certain rules of method based on facts *and* appropriate to man's form of cognition."

21. Smith 1979, 155, 159. Smith acknowledges that his discussion of perception owes much to Objectivist sources. On the issue of hallucinations and illusions, see Kelley 1986, 131–38. On hallucinations, compare Lossky 1957, 42.

22. Kelley 1984a, 15. This applies equally to the analysis of linguistic, grammatical, and idiomatic differences. Though there are many optional methods of application, certain grammatical distinctions are present in some form in every language. And even though an idiom cannot be translated by looking at each of its individual linguistic constituents, its meaning can still be grasped by an equivalent descriptive expression. Linguistic differences—like cross-cultural variations in perceptual classification—are not arbitrary. If we could not grasp different idioms and classifications, people would be condemned eternally to a Tower of Babel. Peikoff 1982aT, Lectures 1 and 7.

23. Objectivists recognize that we are unable to get inside the animal's faculty of awareness. It is entirely possible that certain higher animals have the ability for rudimentary choice. None of this disqualifies Rand's belief that self-consciousness and volition are the essential, defining characteristics of *human* conscious awareness. "Appendix," 161–62, 246, 255–56.

24. *Atlas Shrugged*, 1012. In keeping with Rand's injunction against the dogmatizing of scientific theories, she recognizes volition as a *philosophic* axiom. Even if natural selection can explain volition as a product of evolution, even if science can trace the neurochemical impulses at the base of volitional cognitive processes, volition remains *philosophically*, a causal primary. A scientific explanation does not eliminate the reality it explains. See Kelley 1985cT, Lecture 2, and 1988, 183, on the issue of evolutionary epistemology.

25. Rand in Peikoff 1976T, Lecture 6; N. Branden (January 1964), "Intellectual ammunition department," in Rand and Branden 1962–65: 3. O'Neill ([1971] 1977) argues that Rand's choice to think is similar to Sartre's original choice. Peikoff (1991b, 469 n. 21) disputes this contention.

26. N. Branden [1969] 1979, 41; Peikoff 1991b, 56–57, and 1990–91T, Lecture 4. Peikoff claims that his is the first Objectivist discussion of "focus" in print. But Branden examined the concept of "focus" as early as April 1964 in *The Objectivist Newsletter*, and in N. Branden 1967T, Lecture 5. Branden's discussion in *The Psychology of Self-Esteem* (a work published after his 1968 split from Rand) is an exact duplicate of these previous articles and lectures. However, N. Branden (1983b, 24n) claims that Rand identified the choice to focus exclusively with the choice to think. He claims that his own view is "considerably broader." I strongly suggest that Rand's own concept is as expansive as Branden's.

27. N. Branden 1983b, 21. Peikoff (1976T, Lecture 7) agrees that daydreaming is a valid activity of focusing. There is much that can be gained in observing the actions of the free subconscious.

28. N. Branden (April 1964), "Intellectual ammunition department," in *Objectivist Newsletter* 3:15; N. Branden 1983a, 56.

29. Binswanger (1991), "Volition as cognitive self-regulation," in Locke 1991, 168–70.

30. Peikoff 1991b, 56–57. In Chapter 7 I discuss the subject of habitual methods of awareness.

31. For this observation, thanks to Cox (18 October 1993C).

32. Rand (August–December 1970), "The comprachicos," in *New Left*, 221.

33. Nathaniel Branden, Allan Blumenthal, Edwin Locke, and other Rand-influenced theorists, have argued further that a full understanding of human cognition requires a more complete grasp of genetic, biological, developmental, environmental, and subconscious factors. As the next chapter documents, some of these theorists have gone beyond Rand's initial formulations, and have aimed for a more complex model that is entirely within the Objectivist framework. See N. Branden 1983b, Locke 1991T, and Blumenthal 1992T.

34. Den Uyl and Rasmussen (1984), "Life, teleology, and eudaimonia in the ethics of Ayn Rand," in Den Uyl and Rasmussen 1984, 69; Rasmussen and Den Uyl 1993, 122–25. Peikoff (1990–91T, Lecture 4) argues that Rand's assimilation of will (volition) to reason is one of her most distinctive contributions.

35. Rand (8 March 1947), "From Ayn Rand's unpublished writings: Notes for *Atlas Shrugged*," in Binswanger 5.2.6–7.

36. Rand (15 May 1934), "From Ayn Rand's unpublished writings: Philosophic journal," in Binswanger 4.4.7.

37. Barnes (1967) fails to grasp Rand's contextual view of concepts and definitions, which I examine in the following sections.

38. Dipert 1987, 69. On this topic, see Rasmussen 1992, in which the author integrates Aristotelian, Hayekian, and Randian insights to examine the role that "phronesis" (or "practical reason") plays in capitalism.

39. In contrast to Dipert, Hollinger ("Ayn Rand's epistemology in historical perspective," in Den Uyl and Rasmussen 1984, 54–55) argues that Rand's view of reason, volition, and knowledge is compatible with certain pragmatist and empiricist conceptions of reason as practical activity, as put forth by Quine and Dewey. Objectivism shares with these perspectives the view that "knowledge is routed [sic] in praxis; knowledge is contextual and not judged by reference to a context-free absolute standard."

40. Rand once called such associational thinking, "back-seat driving." N. Branden 1967T, Lecture 6; B. Branden 1962T, Lecture 2.

41. Rand [1945] 1986, 3.

42. This explanation of a "concept" incorporates two different definitions that Rand proposes in two distinct contexts. Rand (9 February 1961), "The Objectivist ethics," in *Virtue of Selfishness*, 20, and *Introduction*, 10.

43. N. Branden 1967T, Lecture 5; B. Branden in N. Branden 1967T, Lecture 6.

44. In Rand's view, words (i.e., language) are the handmaiden of concept formation. Concepts and language are *primarily* tools of cognition, rather than communication. One cannot even think without language; and one cannot communicate without thinking. *Introduction*, 69. Peikoff (1982aT, Lectures 1 and 7) presents an Objectivist view of grammar which steers clear of classicism ("intrinsicism") and the modern ("social/subjective") view. I do not discuss Rand's view of language in the current study.

45. *Introduction*, 10; "Appendix," 153.

46. Peikoff (1983T, Lecture 3) praises Hegel for this emphasis on the moment of integration.

47. This principle has become known as "Rand's razor." Peikoff 1991b, 139, and 1976T, Lecture 5; "Appendix," 251. Peikoff's course "Objective Communication" (1980T) provides valuable

insights on how dialectical thinkers can present highly integrated ideas in a simple manner. He focuses specifically on the moment of exposition.

48. Peikoff 1982aT, Lecture 3; 1987bT, Lecture 1.

49. The mathematical element in cognition is recognized in Rand's view of the concept formation process within this more specific context: *"A concept is a mental integration of two or more units possessing the same distinguishing characteristic(s), with their particular measurements omitted." Introduction,* 13.

50. Rand ("Appendix," 189) argued that it is a scientific question whether or not such standards of measure are "ultimately translatable" or "reducible" to one another.

51. Rand (*Introduction,* 15) referred to the basic commensurable characteristic as a "Conceptual Common Denominator."

52. Peikoff 1991b, 85–86, 111; 1990–91T, Lecture 5. In keeping with the Objectivist rejection of reductionism and epiphenomenalism, Kelley (1984a) writes: "Someday, perhaps, we will have a neurological explanation of the capacity for omitting measurements, and perhaps also an evolutionary explanation for our coming to have it. But I see no way to decompose it further into *cognitive* steps" (356).

53. Kelley (1991) argues that Objectivism provides an empirical foundationalism that incorporates integration and system, and rejects reliabilism and rationalistic coherence.

54. See Peikoff 1991b, 131, and 1974T, Lecture 10. Peikoff observes that the theories of Newton and Einstein do not contradict one another. Each identifies laws within a specific context. Newton could not take into account those issues which preoccupied Einstein, because certain facts had not yet been discovered. An alteration of context does not mean that a more primitive definition is *contradicted* by a more advanced one.

55. Rand (February 1965), "Who is the final authority in ethics?" in *Voice of Reason,* 18. I do not discuss the Objectivist theory of truth in this book. See Peikoff 1991b, 174–79. Rand (in Peikoff 1976T, Lecture 6) opposed the coherence theory of truth, but she also remarked that the traditional correspondence theory is invalid if it depends on mystical, "perfect" correspondence between reality and cognition. Such "perfection" implies noncontextual omniscience. See also Jetton 1993, 96–99.

Chapter 7. Reason and Emotion

1. Peikoff (1990–91T, Lecture 13) remarks that in 1951, Rand told him that an animal's purely physical pleasures become primarily spiritual pleasures for people, because they are filtered through human consciousness.

2. Rand (9 February 1961), "The Objectivist ethics," in *Virtue of Selfishness,* 27. This description does not include an evaluation of *what* is beneficial or harmful to people. I discuss *what* a person *should* value in Chapter 9.

3. Rand (9 April 1934), "From Ayn Rand's unpublished writings: Philosophic journal," in Binswanger 4.4.2.

4. Rand (9 May 1934), in Binswanger 4.4.4. In Rand (15 May 1934), in Binswanger 4.4.7, she used "instinct" and "emotion" somewhat interchangeably. For instance, although she called emotion "a form of undeveloped reason," she described instinct as "a form of unrealized reason." Conversely, she saw reason as "instincts made conscious," which suggests that "the study of psychology" makes possible the articulation of largely tacit "instincts" and "emotions." From a very early point in her intellectual development, Rand saw such introspective articulation as "the base of the reconciliation of reason and emotions."

5. N. Branden (1982T) provides a similar view of the historical context that influenced Rand's attitudes toward mysticism and emotions.

6. Rand (30 April 1946), "From Ayn Rand's notes for *Atlas Shrugged,*" in Schwartz 6.1.3.

7. On the thinking-activity relationship, there are additional parallels between Rand and such American naturalists as Dewey. These are noted by Hollinger, "Ayn Rand's epistemology in historical perspective," in Den Uyl and Rasmussen 1984, 54–55, 58, n. 24, 58 n. 25.

8. Interestingly, Rand shared with Marx a view of reason as internally related to material production. She noted a reciprocal conjunction between the need to eat and the ability to think. But she opted out of any vicious circularity by arguing that people must think *first* in order to commence the process of production.

9. Rand (6 March 1974), "Philosophy: Who needs it," in *Philosophy*, 20–21.

10. N. Branden [1969] 1979, 68–69. This material from *The Psychology of Self-Esteem* appeared first in *The Objectivist Newsletter* and *The Objectivist.* Though I reference the post-1968 book, it is clear that Rand and other Objectivists fully accept these principles. For instance, both Peikoff and Packer, orthodox Objectivists, recognize that each emotion presupposes a sequence of perception, identification, evaluation, and emotional response. Both argue that the cycle is automatized, experienced as a movement from perception to emotional response. The Peikoff-Packer position is almost indistinguishable from that enunciated by Branden in the early Objectivist publications. In fact, orthodox Objectivist thinkers, in writing about most psychological topics, have not diverged significantly from the original formulations of Rand and Branden. On the emotive sequence, see Packer (December 1985), "The art of introspection," in Binswanger 6.6.2, and Peikoff 1976T, Lecture 1.

11. On "content" and "intensity," see *Introduction*, 31.

12. N. Branden [1969] 1979, 71–73, 76. Just because an emotion implies action, that does *not* mean that we *must* act on it. Rational action must be assessed within a broader context, which includes the application of reason. Branden's view of the nature of emotions has remained relatively unchanged throughout his writings. N. Branden 1980, 62; 1983b, 146. He characterizes his system as "biocentric." Like Rand's metaethics, it emphasizes biologically oriented, life-centered methods and principles. N. Branden [1969] 1979, ix.

13. "Appendix," 227. B. Branden (1986, 242) observes that this attitude toward introspection had some unfortunate consequences. For Rand, "behind every statement stood an enormous breadth and complexity of thought and integration." This made some of Rand's associates feel as if they were on psychological trial with every utterance.

14. N. Branden 1983b, 51. Today, Branden (21 June 1993C) prefers terms such as "self-awareness" or "self-examination" since " 'introspection' has a certain intellectual connotation that does not capture the reality of what goes on when we learn to pay attention to our own internal processes."

15. N. Branden (January 1962), "Intellectual ammunition department," in *Objectivist Newsletter* 1:3.

16. N. Branden (1962), "Objectivism and psychology," in Branden and Branden 1962, 73–74.

17. Rand (18 April 1946), "From Ayn Rand's unpublished writings: Notes for *Atlas Shrugged,*" in Binswanger 4.6.2.

18. Rand (29 June 1946), "From Ayn Rand's unpublished writings: Notes for *Atlas Shrugged,*" in Binswanger 4.6.8–9.

19. However, Rand's characters *do* grow intellectually. For instance, in *The Fountainhead*, Roark experiences growth in his knowledge and application of certain principles.

20. N. Branden 1971b, 18. Merrill (1991, 79–84) responds to Branden's critique.

21. N. Branden (1962), "Objectivism and psychology," in Branden and Branden 1962, 78.

22. Despite these similarities, Branden and Ellis have vastly different approaches to psychology and politics.

23. Mack (1984), "The fundamental moral elements of Rand's theory of rights," in Den Uyl and Rasmussen 1984, 146–48.

24. N. Branden ([1971] 1978, 86) argues precisely this point: the characterization of thoughts or feelings as moral or immoral is akin to thinking of them as virtuous or sinful, a religious view inappropriate to Objectivism.

25. Rand (8 March 1947), "From Ayn Rand's unpublished writings: Notes for *Atlas Shrugged,*" in Binswanger 5.2.7.

26. Rand (August–December 1970), "The comprachicos," in *New Left*, 193–94.

27. Rand (February 1966), "Philosophy and sense of life," in *Romantic Manifesto*, 25.

28. Packer (February 1985), "Understanding the subconscious," in Binswanger 6.1.1. Packer links her concept of "core evaluations" to Rand's concept of "sense of life." Core evaluations are "basic conclusions, bottom-line evaluations, that we all hold subconsciously."

29. Rand (22 November–6 December 1971), "Don't let it go," in *Philosophy*, 250–51.

30. Rand (February 1966), "Philosophy and sense of life," in *Romantic Manifesto*, 31.

31. N. Branden 1980, 103. Branden's discussion is a direct outgrowth of Rand's discussion in "Philosophy and sense of life" (see note 30).

32. Rand (February 1966), "Philosophy and sense of life," in *Romantic Manifesto*, 30; Peikoff 1976T, Lecture 11, and 1991b, 427.

33. Peikoff (1974T, Lecture 2) argues that Rand's psychologizing is appropriate in this context, but it is independent of the truth or falsity of the philosopher's viewpoint, which can only be assessed by rational argument.

34. N. Branden (1971b, 12) does not disagree with Rand's insights into the fallacy of "psychologizing." But he believed that she was being "hypocritical," since she often moralized about other peoples' psychologies. B. Branden (1990, 76) observes too that Rand frequently engaged in such psychologizing, and that anything in her writings "that impinges on psychology is really a disaster." In a private correspondence (28 June 1993C), however, Barbara Branden qualifies this sweeping statement: "Much of what Ayn considered to be psychological syndromes were in fact philosophical syndromes, conscious or subconscious errors of thinking about wide general issues. They therefore gave no guidance to the altering of deep-seated errors held only in emotional form."

35. Rand (March 1971), "The psychology of psychologizing," in *Voice of Reason*, 23–24.

36. In the authorized course on Objectivism, one in which Rand participated, Peikoff (1976T, Lecture 4) argues that emotions as such are not moral or immoral. Morality applies only to volitional issues. We have no choice over what we feel, even if we *can* alter, over time, the basic premises of our feelings.

37. Rand (March 1971), "The psychology of psychologizing," in *Voice of Reason*, 29; Peikoff 1989T, Lecture 1, and 1991b, 280.

38. Rand (February 1966), "Philosophy and sense of life," in *Romantic Manifesto*, 29.

39. Rand (January 1994), " 'Memory-storing' epistemology," in Schwartz 8.1.3–4. It is noted that the journal entry was written *"probably in the 1950s."*

40. Rand (February 1966), "Philosophy and sense of life," in *Romantic Manifesto*, 29–30.

41. Packer 1990T; N. Branden 1983b, 180–81.

42. Rand (March 1966), "Art and sense of life," in *Romantic Manifesto*, 34.

43. B. Branden 1962T, Lecture 3; N. Branden [1969] 1979, 81–82.

44. N. Branden 1990, 15. See also Wieder (1988–89), who views the left-brain/right-brain dichotomy as rooted in "the age-old dichotomies of mind versus body." Allan Blumenthal provides an interesting parallel in his discussion of musical conducting. He stresses the notion of the right hand as the "doer" and the left hand as the "dreamer." Blumenthal and Blumenthal 1974T, Lecture 12. If the left side of the brain controls the right side of the body, and vice versa, one can see in the union of right and left hand direction a synthesis of linear and emotive components.

45. Rand (April 1965), "The psycho-epistemology of art," in *Romantic Manifesto*, 18.

46. N. Branden [1969] 1979, 99–100. Branden's original articles on psycho-epistemology appear in *The Objectivist Newsletter*, October–November 1964.

47. Rand (August–December 1970), "The comprachicos," in *New Left*, 195.

48. Rand (6 March 1974), "Philosophy: Who needs it," in *Philosophy*, 20–21.

49. Rand (January 1994), " 'Memory-storing' epistemology," in Schwartz 8.1.4.

50. N. Branden [1969] 1979, 87–88; [1971] 1978, 105.

51. N. Branden 1983b, 141–46. N. Branden (1980, 92n) argues too, that there are "biological forces deep within our organism that speak to us in a wordless language we have yet barely begun to decipher." Though Peikoff (1976T, Lecture 7) has dismissed Eastern philosophy, and though Rand and Branden never formally examined such holistic medical concepts and techniques as chi, biofeedback, or psychosomatic medicine, these perspectives offer interesting nondualistic parallels on the mind-body unity. See Moyers 1993.

52. Rand (9 February 1961), "The Objectivist ethics," in *Virtue of Selfishness*, 17–18; Saint-Andre 1993, 161–63.

53. Rand (April–June 1971), "Art and cognition," in *Romantic Manifesto*, 60.

54. For Branden, psychology provides the crucial link "on 'how to get there from here,' meaning: how to learn to live the Objectivist morality." His post-Randian work "provides something missing [from] and badly needed" by the philosophy of Objectivism. He has "been concerned with devising the means that would enable a person to live consciously, responsibly, productively—and happily." N. Branden, 14 January 1994C; 21 June 1993C; 1994.

55. Redressing the balance of reason and emotion is by no means the chief aim of Branden's post-Randian work. In a personal correspondence (15 June 1993C), Branden explains: "In the years since I left New York, I have had three principal goals which my writing reflects: (1) to develop further my theory of self-esteem; (2) to explore the psychology of romantic love; (3) to design a psychotherapeutic technology for facilitating change and growth."

56. Peikoff 1983T, Lectures 2, 6, and 10, and 1991b, 159–62.

57. Peikoff 1983T, Lecture 2; N. Branden and E. D. Branden 1983, 99.

58. Rand (July–August 1971), "The age of envy," in *New Left*, 173–74.

59. Rand did not repudiate all of modern feminism, only its "collectivist" elements. She responded positively to Friedan's *Feminine Mystique*. Edith Efron (July 1963), "Books," in *Objectivist Newsletter* 2:27. Despite her hostility toward "Women's Lib," several commentators have written of Rand's positive contribution to feminism. Riggenbach argues that Dagny Taggart, the heroine in *Atlas Shrugged*, is an extraordinary female role model, great at everything from engineering to sex. Riggenbach maintains that Rand's message of individual autonomy influenced those whom she would have "disowned," including militant feminists, gay activists, and student rebels. Riggenbach 1979, 1982. Gladstein (1978) explores the "unlikely," but positive alliance between Rand and feminism. Landrum (1994) characterizes Rand as among the most important "creative women who changed the world." And Taylor (1992), who knew Rand in the 1960s, incorporates a number of significant Objectivist themes in her feminist work.

60. N. Branden [1969] 1979, 206–8. In Rand's fiction, especially *The Fountainhead*, there is a pronounced emphasis on the male as sexual aggressor. This aggressiveness, however, is *not* a sanction of rape. Rand uses explosive imagery in her description of sexual acts that are *always* consensual and mutually desired.

61. N. Branden 1983b, 174. Like other psychologists, N. Branden (1983b, 1986, 1987, 1994) argues not only for the integration of the "male" self and "female" self, but of other "sub-selves" or "sub-personalities," including the "child-self," "teenage self," "intuitive self," and "sage self." Livingston (1994, 10) observes that this doctrine was originated in the "therapeutic movement known as Transactional Analysis."

62. Glennon (1983), "Synthesism: A case of feminist methodology," in Morgan 1983, 260.

63. On a woman president, see Rand (December 1968), "About a woman president," in *Voice of Reason*. Peikoff (1985T) claims that Rand's opposition to a woman presidential candidate was not a philosophical issue. Rand wrote the article based upon her personal view of masculinity and

femininity, not as a philosophical distinction. On homosexuality, Rand never wrote an article, but in several instances, exhibited definite homophobia: Rand (July–August 1971), "The age of envy," in *New Left*, 175; and Rand 1971T.

64. On the "nature-nurture" debate, see Rand (1972), "The stimulus and the response," in *Philosophy*, 175, and Peikoff 1991b, 204. On the "determinist" premises shared by behaviorism and psychoanalysis, see Locke (February 1980), "Behaviorism and psychoanalysis: Two sides of the same coin," in Binswanger 1.1.11.

65. Peikoff 1983T, Lecture 11, and 1988aT; and Packer 1985T.

66. N. Branden 1982T and 1983T.

67. N. Branden 1983T; Blumenthal 1992T. Blumenthal argues too that there are certain biochemical factors and physiological complexities that must be taken into account in our understanding of emotions. Since clinical depression and chemical imbalances are not alterable by a therapeutic articulation process, aspects of Rand's theory may need further modification.

Chapter 8. Art, Philosophy, and Efficacy

1. See *Romantic Manifesto* for these more specific applications. For Rand's discussion of music, which employs Helmholz's theories, see Rand (April–June 1971), "Art and cognition," in *Romantic Manifesto*, 50–71, and Blumenthal and Blumenthal 1974T. Though not considered as a component of Rand's aesthetics, a discussion of the nature of beauty is provided by Rand in Peikoff 1976T, Lecture 11 and 1991b, 448. The best critical presentation of Rand's aesthetics is provided by Torres and Kamhi (January 1991–September 1992), "Ayn Rand's philosophy of art: A critical introduction," in Torres and Kamhi 1982–94; (August 1993), "Reader's forum: on 'Ayn Rand's philosophy of art,' " in Torres and Kamhi 1982–94, 4–6. This series is forthcoming as a book. See Torres and Kamhi 1996.

2. Rand (April 1965), "The psycho-epistemology of art," in *Romantic Manifesto*, 16–17.

3. Compare Hayek (1948), who similarly argues that our efficacy is largely a result of how well we perform certain activities without thinking about them.

4. Rand (May–July 1969), "What is romanticism?" in *Romantic Manifesto*, 101.

5. Rand (April–June 1971), "Art and cognition," in *Romantic Manifesto*, 46–47, 73.

6. Rand 1958T, Lectures 1 and 7. On the nature of "creative thinking," see N. Branden [1969] 1979, 81; Smith 1993; and Rand (1940), "The simplest thing in the world: A short story," in *Romantic Manifesto*, 173–85. In this stream-of-consciousness narrative, Rand depicts the inner workings of the mind of Henry Dorn, an author, in his attempt to write a story. Dorn's subconscious integrations direct his conscious thoughts with lightning-like speed.

7. Peikoff 1991b, 446. Though Lossky was not an aesthetician, it was he who taught Aristotle to Rand. Lossky himself argued that each art work is an organic unity in which all elements are "in harmony with, and exist for, one another." Lossky [1917] 1928, 48, 160. Tolstoy was another Russian writer who championed the "completeness, oneness, the inseparable unity of form and contents" in a work of art. Tolstoi [1899] 1913, 96.

8. Rand, in N. Branden (1962), "The literary method of Ayn Rand," in Branden and Branden 1962, 135–40. Cox (1993) examines the extensive integration that Rand achieved in *The Fountainhead*.

9. I use the word "responder" to include viewers (for the visual arts), readers (for the literary arts), and listeners (for music). Thanks to Torres and Kamhi for this suggestion.

10. Rand (March 1966), "Art and sense of life," in *Romantic Manifesto*, 35.

11. In her concept of "style," Rand merged two tacit dimensions: "sense of life" and "psycho-

epistemology." As she put it: "Style conveys what may be called a 'psycho-epistemological sense of life,' i.e., an expression of that level of mental functioning on which the artist feels most at home." *Romantic Manifesto*, 42.

12. Rand (March 1966), "Art and sense of life," in *Romantic Manifesto*, 35.

13. Rand (April 1965), "The psycho-epistemology of art," in *Romantic Manifesto*, 24.

14. Rand (April–June 1971), "Art and cognition," in *Romantic Manifesto*, 63.

15. For raising this issue, thanks to Saint-Andre (5 January 1993C).

16. Rand (January 1965), "Bootleg romanticism," in *Romantic Manifesto*, 129–30.

17. Rand (October–November 1963), "The goal of my writing," in *Romantic Manifesto*, 169.

18. See Cox 1986, in which Cox relates Rand's aesthetic theories to her own literary craft.

19. Rand (May–July 1969), "What is romanticism?" in *Romantic Manifesto*, 99.

20. Rand (October–November 1963), "The goal of my writing," in *Romantic Manifesto*, 167. Among Russian writers, Yuri Carlovich Olesha has also been identified as both a Romantic and a Realist. Guerney 1960, 375.

21. In *Anthem* Rand experimented with futuristic themes. *Atlas Shrugged* also contains elements of science fiction and fantasy.

22. Rosenthal 1975, 15–18, and (1986), "Introduction," in Rosenthal 1986, 46–47.

23. Rand (April 1965), "The psycho-epistemology of art," in *Romantic Manifesto*, 22–23. In this context, Rand argued: "The greater a work of art, the more profoundly universal its theme." Thus, while her own fictional works have a strong propaganda element, they also incorporate themes that transcend a particular time or place.

24. Rosenthal (1986), "Introduction," in Rosenthal 1986, 36–37; Steele 1988, 41. For additional parallels between the "God-builders" and Rand, see Chapter 13.

25. Rand quoted in N. Branden (1962), "The literary method of Ayn Rand," in Branden and Branden 1962, 97.

26. Rand (1943–44), "From Ayn Rand's unpublished writings: A speech to architects," in Binswanger 6.6.13.

27. Rand (4 May 1946), "From Ayn Rand's notes for *Atlas Shrugged*," in Schwartz 6.1.5.

28. Rand (4 May 1946), quoted in Peikoff 1991a, xiv.

29. Rand 1961T. Childs (1993, 46) observed correctly that Rand's writings do not make a single reference to and that the N.B.I. has never carried a single book written by Hayek.

30. Hayek (1968), "The confusion of language in political thought," in Hayek [1978] 1985, 81. The notion of a "tacit" dimension does not originate with Ryle, Polanyi, or Hayek. Livingston (1991, 174) argues that Aristotle's discussion of the "topic or commonplace is roughly the same as Hayek's tacit dimension or tradition."

31. There are many other differences between Rand and Hayek. For example, Rand would have disagreed with Hayek's endorsement of Popper's falsifiability criterion. Gray (1984, 12, 19–21) notes, however, that Hayek's acceptance of a "falsificationist methodology" comes with "massive qualification."

32. In this regard, N. Branden (1994, 288) has suggested a closer affinity with the Hayekian-Polanyian perspective. He argues that every person has a tendency to accept certain cultural beliefs that are never "the subject of explicit awareness. . . . It is not possible for anyone, even the most independent, to make *every* premise conscious or to subject *every* premise to critical scrutiny." Each of us is a being of our time and place. "None of us can entirely escape the influence of our social environment." I discuss these issues further in Chapters 11 and 13.

33. Rand (February 1966), "Philosophy and sense of life," in *Romantic Manifesto*, 30.

34. Rand (October 1975), "From the horse's mouth," in *Philosophy*, 99. Even a thorough "materialist" such as Engels argued for the primacy of philosophy over science: "Natural scientists may adopt whatever attitude they please, they will still be under the domination of philosophy. It is only a question whether they want to be dominated by a bad, fashionable philosophy or by a

form of theoretical thought which rests on acquaintance with the history of thought and its achievements." Engels 1882, in Selsam and Martel 1963, 171.

35. Rand (6 March 1974), "Philosophy: Who needs it," in *Philosophy*, 6.

36. Rand (3 January 1972), " 'What can one do?' " in *Philosophy*, 246.

37. Rand (June 1970), "The chickens' homecoming," in *New Left*, 107.

38. Smith (1979) provides a Rand-influenced defense of atheism.

39. N. Branden [1969] 1979, 127–28. On reciprocal causation, see N. Branden 1987, 41, and 1983b, 60, and Peikoff 1974T, Lecture 9.

40. N. Branden 1994 is Branden's most detailed treatment to date of the impact of cultural institutions on the development of self-esteem and efficacy.

41. See Emmons 1971, and Barry 1983 and 1986.

42. Aside from some references to rationalism and empiricism in *For the New Intellectual*, Rand did not write much on the subject. The material herein discussed is primarily from Peikoff's lectures, which derive from Rand's teachings and from the oral Objectivist tradition.

43. Rand (28 January–11 February 1974), "Philosophical detection," in *Philosophy*, 19.

44. Rand (25 February 1974), "Ideas v. goods," in *Ayn Rand Letter* 3:296.

45. *New Intellectual*, 39. Though there are many different meanings attached to rationalism and empiricism, Rand does not make any distinction between "concept-empiricism" and "judgment-empiricism," or "concept-rationalism" and "judgment-rationalism." "Concept-empiricism" sees all concepts as arising out of experience, whereas "concept-rationalism" denies this. "Judgment-empiricism" views all propositions as either verifiable-in-principle or analytic, whereas "judgment-rationalism" views propositions as synthetic and a priori. Thanks to Hospers (17 July 1993C) for these qualifications. Rand would have probably rejected each of these incarnations.

46. Peikoff 1983T, Lecture 7. This course is described by Peikoff as a product of his own struggle with methodological rationalism. Peikoff (1983T, Lectures 1, 3, and 12) argues that Objectivism cannot be filtered through the dualism of mind and body without causing interpretive distortions. He offers useful guidelines against "rationalist Objectivism."

47. *Introduction*, 76; Rand (30 July 1973), "Perry Mason finally loses," in *Ayn Rand Letter*, 225.

48. Rand (28 January–11 February 1974), "Philosophical detection," in *Philosophy*, 15.

49. Rand (January 1994), " 'Memory-storing' epistemology," in Schwartz 8.1.3.

50. Rand (7–21 May 1973), "The missing link," in *Philosophy*, 45–46.

51. Smith (1979, 133) uses this phrase.

52. Peikoff 1976T, Lecture 6. For Objectivism's contextual view of "certainty," see Peikoff 1991b, 171–82.

53. Hollinger (1984), "Ayn Rand's epistemology in historical perspective," in Den Uyl and Rasmussen 1984, 42, 49.

54. Binswanger 1990, 30–32. Both Rand and Branden argued that human rationality required responsibility—a willingness to accept the intended *and* unintended consequences of one's actions. They were fond of the old Spanish proverb, "God said: 'Take what you want and pay for it.' " Rand (July 1970), "Causality versus duty," in *Philosophy*, 122; N. Branden 1980, 188; N. Branden and E. D. Branden 1983, 148.

55. On the Marxian view, see Flacks 1982, 16. Rand's resolution actually lies somewhere between the optimism of Marx and the conservatism of Hayek. Marx believed that capitalism perpetuated and was constituted by unintended consequences. To focus purely on unintended consequences reified characteristics that were historically specific to capitalism. He envisioned a future society in which people conquered the unintended consequences of their actions. Although Rand did not exhibit such intellectual hubris, her resolution required the emergence of a degree of cognitive efficacy hitherto unseen in human history.

56. Sciabarra 1988a; 1995.

57. Hayek (1970), "The errors of constructivism," in Hayek [1978] 1985, 20.

58. Hayek (1946), "Individualism: True and false," in Hayek 1948, 15.

59. In Hayek (1965), "Kinds of rationalism," in Hayek [1967] 1980, 85, he cites Gladstone as the first person to use the term "constructivism" to describe the "engineering type of mind."

60. Hayek 1981, 129; 1988.

61. Hayek (1965), "Kinds of rationalism," in Hayek [1967] 1980, 93.

62. Hayek (1962), "Rules, perception and intelligibility," in Hayek [1967] 1980, 62.

63. Hayek (1964), "The theory of complex phenomena," in Hayek [1967] 1980, 39.

64. Lavoie (1982, 21–22) has a provocative insight when he writes: "Both Marx and Mises pointed out that rationality as we know it is itself a product of the emergence of market relations." The belief that rationality is internal to capitalism is one held by thinkers as diverse as Marx, Mises, Weber, and Rand. I further explore Rand's conception in Chapters 9 and 10.

65. See her *New Intellectual*. Also see Peikoff 1982. Rand added that it was this fallacious view of pure reason that Kant criticized in a "straw man" argument that undermined a proper understanding of the rational faculty. Rand (17 February 1960), "Faith and force: The destroyers of the modern world," in *Philosophy*, 77–78; Rand 1972T.

66. "Appendix," 148–49. On the concept of infinity, compare Aristotle, *Physics* 3.4.204a34–5. 206a7, in Aristotle 1941, 260–64.

67. N. Branden [1969] 1979, 175. Compare Shaffer 1976, 14.

68. Rand (April–May 1966), "Our cultural value-deprivation," in *Voice of Reason*, 102.

Chapter 9. Ethics and Human Survival

1. Among those articles on Rand's egoism that appeared in the *Personalist*: N. Branden 1970a and 1970b; Emmons 1971 and 1972; Machan 1971; Hospers 1970; Mack 1971; Den Uyl 1975; Dwyer 1972, 1973, and 1974; Bold 1973; and Lugenbehl 1974. Also see Nozick (1971), "On the Randian argument," and Den Uyl and Rasmussen (1978), "Nozick on the Randian argument," both reprinted in Paul 1981.

2. Many Western philosophers, as well, have criticized the fact-value distinction. Peikoff (1970T, Lecture 8) argues that Dewey developed a contextualist ethic that opposed both subjectivism and rationalism as mystical and intuitivist. Despite his disagreements with Dewey, Peikoff acknowledges his effective denunciation of the dichotomy between body and mind and fact and value. Veatch (1992) also discusses the similarity between Rand's critique and the critiques of the "old-line analytic-linguistic philosophies" of MacIntyre, Williams, and Nussbaum.

3. Rand (April 1965), "The psycho-epistemology of art," in *Romantic Manifesto*, 16; (9 February 1961), "The Objectivist ethics," in *Virtue of Selfishness*, 34.

4. Rand (August–September 1967), "Requiem for man," in *Unknown Ideal*, 313–14, and (July–August 1971), "The age of envy," in *New Left*, 163; and N. Branden (July 1962), "Benevolence versus altruism," in *Objectivist Newsletter* 1:27.

5. N. Branden (October 1963), "Intellectual ammunition department," in *Objectivist Newsletter* 2:39.

6. Rand (October 1975), "From the horse's mouth," in *Philosophy*, 96.

7. Rand (17 February 1960), "Faith and force: The destroyers of the modern world," in *Philosophy*, 75.

8. Peikoff 1972T, Lectures 2 and 10; 1970T, Lecture 5.

9. Kaufmann, in Nietzsche [1886] 1966, 138 n. 35, and 228 n. 35.

10. Interestingly, Nietzsche's rediscovery of classical antiquity was foreshadowed by Hegel. Copleston ([1963] 1985, 208) maintains that in Hegelian thought, "the moral agent has a right to seek his own welfare, the satisfaction of his needs as a human being." Hegel appropriated this view

from "Greek ethics as represented by Aristotle." He rejected "the Kantian notion that an act loses its moral value if performed from inclination."

11. Rand (15 May 1934), "From Ayn Rand's unpublished writings: Philosophic journal," in Binswanger 4.4.6.

12. Rand (6 October 1949), "From Ayn Rand's unpublished writings: Philosophic notes," in Binswanger 5.4.2.

13. Rand (November–December 1965), "What is capitalism?" in *Unknown Ideal*, 21–22.

14. Rand (June 1982), "To the readers of *The Fountainhead*," in Binswanger 3.3.5.

15. The phrase "counterfeit individualism" is actually used in N. Branden (April 1962), "Counterfeit individualism," in *Virtue of Selfishness*, 135. Though not in the individualist tradition, there are several Russian thinkers who attempted to transcend the egoist-altruist distinction, including Fedorov and Chernyshevsky, who defended a form of psychological egoism. See Chapter 1, and Lossky 1951, 61–62, 78. Even such nonindividualists as Marx and Engels ([1845–46] 1970, 104–5) projected a transcendence of egoism and altruism. They recognized "that egoism, just as much as self-sacrifice, is in definite circumstances a necessary form of the self-assertion of individuals." Though Marx shows humanistic tendencies, especially in his early works, he is apt to condemn capitalism precisely for its "selfishness."

16. Rand (January 1963), "Collectivized ethics," in *Virtue of Selfishness*, 81.

17. O'Neill [1971] 1977, 201. Whereas O'Neill criticizes Rand's redefinition of "altruism," Steele (1988, 43) criticizes Rand's redefinition of "selfishness" for much the same reason. For Steele, Rand's definition leaves "most of traditional bourgeois morality . . . unscathed."

18. Rand (9 February 1961), "The Objectivist ethics," in *Virtue of Selfishness*, 35.

19. Rand (November–December 1965), "What is capitalism?" in *Unknown Ideal*, 21–22.

20. Rand (8 March 1947), "From Ayn Rand's unpublished writings: Notes for *Atlas Shrugged*," in Binswanger 5.2.4.

21. Rand (9 February 1961), "The Objectivist ethics," in *Virtue of Selfishness*, 14.

22. *Atlas Shrugged*, 1012–13. This is Rand's *description* of life. Peikoff (1990–91T, Lecture 10) explains that Rand never offered a *definition* of life because this was outside the domain of philosophy.

23. Binswanger (August 1986), "The goal-directedness of living action," in Binswanger 7.4.4–5. I do not discuss Binswanger's application of Objectivist principles to the theory of natural selection. Peikoff (1991b, 476 n. 19) explains that because Darwin's theory was a special science, Rand took no philosophical position on it. Nor do I discuss Binswanger's defense of emergentist teleology against the vitalist-teleological and mechanistic positions. See Binswanger 1990, 6, 132, and Binswanger (1992), "Life-based teleology and the foundations of ethics," in Smith 1992, 84–103. Binswanger's "emergentist teleology" is offered as an alternative to the dualism of vitalist teleology versus mechanism. Interestingly, Lossky ([1917] 1928, 154–55) himself rejected mechanistic explanations in favor of teleological ones.

24. Rand (9 February 1961), "The Objectivist ethics," in *Virtue of Selfishness*, 17.

25. Aristotle *Metaphysics* 9.8–9, in Aristotle 1941, 828–33. Rand (1969–71, 285) argued that though she never wrote on the subject directly, she has "referred to actual and potential in any number of ways in any number of articles."

26. Rand (9 February 1961), "The Objectivist ethics," in *Virtue of Selfishness*, 21.

27. Later in this chapter, I argue in favor of the eudaemonic interpretation as consistent with Rand's dialectical approach. In conjunction with the idea that our survival as human beings is no mere, momentary survival, Den Uyl and Rasmussen (1983) maintain that the "eudaemonic individual" does not "view life as a linear succession of discrete moments," rather he or she "lives a time-*integrated* life, whereas the dysdaemonic individual lives a time-differentiated life" (115).

28. O'Neill [1971] 1977, 88; Nozick (1971), "On the Randian argument," in Paul 1981, 206–31.

29. N. Branden (1962), "Objectivism and psychology," in Branden and Branden 1962, 72;

Hospers 1967, 594; Den Uyl and Rasmussen (1978), "Nozick on the Randian argument," in Paul 1981, 232–69; Mack (1984), "The fundamental moral elements of Rand's theory of rights," in Den Uyl and Rasmussen 1984, 123, 128.

30. Rasmussen 1990b; Den Uyl (1992), "Teleology and agent-centeredness," in Smith 1992, 31 n. 18.

31. Gotthelf 1990, 6. Though Gotthelf (5 March 1994C) does not now accept all the formulations of his unpublished paper on "The Choice to Value," I appreciate his permission to cite its key arguments.

32. Binswanger (1992), "Life-based teleology and the foundations of ethics," in Smith 1992, 99–100.

33. As I discussed in Chapter 6, Rand's epistemology endorses a form of contextual internalism. In what sense, then, did Rand define life and value as internally related? For Rand, the concept of "life" serves the same function in ethics as does the axiomatic concept of "existence" in ontology. Even though "existence" is the "ultimate" context for every concept imaginable, Rand did not speculate on the "ultimate" constituents of existence. And even though "life" is the context for value and the ultimate value, Rand did not speculate on the "ultimate" constituents of life either. She did not *define* life, since this is a scientific task; she merely described it. Hence, her identification of a link between life and value occurred on a broad level of generality. By rejecting metaphysical (or "cosmological") conjecture, Rand retained contextuality.

34. Rand does not explicitly make this argument, but N. Branden (1987, 79) suggests it.

35. Rand (9 February 1961), "The Objectivist ethics," in *Virtue of Selfishness*, 25.

36. Rand (9 February 1961), "The Objectivist ethics," in *Virtue of Selfishness*, 25–26.

37. Peikoff (1990–91T, Lecture 4) explains that Rand did not provide an exhaustive list of virtues. Rand focused on basic, broad abstractions. In Peikoff (27 February 1989), "Why should one act on principle?" in Schwartz 4.20.4–5, he remarks that these broad principles serve the epistemic need for unit economy; they reduce the complexity of human choices "to simple, retainable units, telling us which actions support human life and which ones destroy it."

38. Aristotle, *Metaphysics*, book 1, in Aristotle 1941, 689–93.

39. Peikoff 1976T, Lecture 12; Ridpath 1988T; Peikoff 1991b, 195; Kelley 1990, 40. Interestingly, Peikoff (1987bT, questions, period 2) hints at moral relativism. He maintains that because of the contextual nature of knowledge, it is wrong to condemn a primitive person for knowledge that he does not possess. In passing moral judgments, one must take account of the knowledge that is available to a person living within a certain cultural context.

40. Rand (9 February 1961), "The Objectivist ethics," in *Virtue of Selfishness*, 26; Peikoff 1976T, Lecture 8, and 1983T, Lecture 10. Like Rand, Peikoff suggests that the scope of productive work is wide; even motherhood constitutes a profession.

41. Rand (May 1964), "Patents and copyrights," in *Unknown Ideal*, 130.

42. Rand (November–December 1965), "What is capitalism?" in *Unknown Ideal*, 16. Reason as a theoretical and practical activity suggests Rand's implicit awareness of *phronesis* or prudence (practical reason). For an interesting quasi-Aristotelian examination of this virtue, see Den Uyl 1991 and Rasmussen 1992.

43. N. Branden (February 1964), "The psychology of pleasure," in *Virtue of Selfishness*, 62; Rand (1971), "Why I like stamp collecting," in *Column*, 120.

44. An Objectivist discussion of Marx is provided by Walsh [1985] 1990T, Lecture 2. Though Rand had some respect for Marx as a thinker, there are times (e.g. *New Intellectual*, 37) when she grossly simplifies and distorts his project.

45. Ollman 1993, 63. Gould (1978) explores Marx's quasi-Aristotelian view of the efficacious character of labor.

46. Rand (9 February 1961), "The Objectivist ethics," in *Virtue of Selfishness*, 27.

47. Rand (July–August 1971), "The age of envy," in *New Left*, 161.

48. Rand (August 1962), "The 'conflicts' of men's interests," in *Virtue of Selfishness*, 53.

49. Aristotle, *Nicomachean Ethics* 2.9.1109a20–23, in Aristotle 1941, 963; Copleston [1946] 1985, 337.

50. Aristotle *Nichomachean Ethics* 4.2.1123b21–27, in Aristotle 1941 , 991–92.

51. Ibid. 4.3.1124a3–4; 4.3.1125a1–2; 9.8.1169a12, in Aristotle 1941, 992, 994, 1087.

52. Peikoff 1972T, Lecture 5, and 1985T.

53. Also see Wheeler (1984), "Rand and Aristotle: A comparison of Objectivist and Aristotelian ethics," in Den Uyl and Rasmussen 1984, 87.

54. On the relationship of "self" and "mind," see N. Branden 1983b, 29, and *Atlas Shrugged*, 1030, 1057.

55. N. Branden 1980, 124; Peikoff 1991b, 307; Locke (December 1982), "Ayn Rand and psychology, part two," in Binswanger 3.6.13.

56. N. Branden ([1969] 1979, 110 n.31) credits Rand with having provided "a partial anticipation" of the concept of self-esteem he develops at length in his books.

57. Initially, N. Branden ([1969] 1979, 114) identified self-esteem with the two interrelated aspects of "self-confidence" and "self-respect." His most recent formulations (1994) are more fully developed.

58. Branden's identification of six pillars of self-esteem is an expansion of his earlier discussion ([1971] 1978, 155) of the "four pillars of self-esteem," which he identified as: self-awareness, self-acceptance, self-responsibility, self-assertiveness. Branden's newest work identifies these six pillars as both ethical and psychological, involving the virtues of rationality, honesty, independence, productiveness, and integrity. Interestingly, by book's end, Branden (1994, 308) embraces a seventh "pillar" of self-esteem, which he defines as "the motive power" of the others: "the love we have for our own life." These seven interacting principles duplicate—on a psychological level—many of the themes encapsulated by Rand's seven basic virtues: rationality, productiveness, pride, honesty, integrity, independence, and justice. See also N. Branden 1991T.

59. Rand (9 February 1961), "The Objectivist ethics," in *Virtue of Selfishness*, 31.

60. Branden echoes Rand's contention. He argues that in modern culture, the equating of "selfishness" with evil leaves people no way of characterizing as noble that which is self-focused. Branden suggests that by controlling the content of language, modern intellectuals invariably control how people think. N. Branden (n.d.T), *The Psychology of Individualism*, and 1983b, 205–9.

61. Rosenthal (15 November 1993C) suggests that Rand's preoccupation with the integration of love and sex was a major issue for Silver Age thinkers, especially Rozanov. On Rozanov, see Anna Lisa Crone, "Nietzschean, All Too Nietzschean? Rozanov's Anti-Christian Critique," in Rosenthal 1986, 95–112.

62. Rand (February 1963), "The ethics of emergencies," in *Virtue of Selfishness*, 46.

63. Rand (9 February 1961), "The Objectivist ethics," in *Virtue of Selfishness*, 31–32. In his critique of Rand, Emmons (1971, 96) argues that Rand's belief in self-value as a prerequisite to valuing others is rooted in Nietzsche. In fact, this perspective is as old as Aristotle.

64. In later years, Branden criticized a number of Rand's beliefs in the area of love and sex. But he remains in general agreement with her view that love, sex, and values are intimately connected. As has been suggested, Branden sees our sexual choices as far more complex than Rand supposes. He is also far less likely to moralize on issues of sexual psychology. In Branden's view, sex can be a valuable activity in the absence of romantic love. What he objects to is "sex without personal involvement, sex between two people who do not relate to each other as persons and do not care for each other as persons and are not interested in each other as persons." N. Branden 1971b, 9–10; 1983T.

65. N. Branden [1969] 1979, 202. Neither Rand nor Branden explicitly trace the parallel between psychological visibility, productive creativity, and aesthetic experience. This is my own interpretive analogy.

66. Ibid., 200. The Muttnik principle is still employed by orthodox Objectivists. Packer 1988T.

67. N. Branden (1980) remarks: "Biologists have discovered that every person possesses an inherent biological rhythm, determined genetically and only slightly modifiable within the first two or three years of life, almost never thereafter" (118). Two people who are romantically involved and in "sync" with one another, may in fact exhibit the same "bio-rhythm."

68. One of the most poetic statements of this romantic credo occurs in The Fountainhead, when Roark tells Wynand, "I could die for you. But I couldn't and wouldn't live for you" (609). Though there are many different kinds of love, such sentiment might lend some credence to Baker's dubious contention (1987, 55–56) that the Roark-Wynand relationship has a romantic or "nonphysical homoerotic" element. I doubt that Rand ever intended to project such latent homosexuality, given her antigay bias. Nathaniel Branden (12 October 1994C) argues persuasively that Rand most probably endowed Roark and Wynand with her own "female" perspective. He adds that, to his best recollection, in an earlier draft of the novel, Wynand tells Roark: "I love you—in every sense except the one a fool would think of first." Rand eventually cut this line. It should be noted too, that Rand, in Atlas Shrugged, 1091, and in 44–45, (February 1963), "The ethics of emergencies," in Virtue of Selfishness, accepts the possibility of rational suicide, or dying for the one you love. In extreme circumstances, these actions are not self-sacrificial if one's values have been fatally threatened or thoroughly obliterated.

69. Thanks to Saint-Andre (28 February 1993C) for emphasizing the importance of these issues.

70. Mack (1984), "The fundamental moral elements of Rand's theory of rights," in Den Uyl and Rasmussen 1984, 136.

71. Veatch 1992, 64. Though Veatch is critical of Rand, he shares many of her Aristotelian premises. Some Objectivists have praised Veatch's work. Binswanger 1989T, Lecture 1.

72. Rand (9 February 1961), "The Objectivist ethics," in Virtue of Selfishness, 25–27.

73. Rand (9 February 1961), "The Objectivist ethics," in Virtue of Selfishness, 29.

74. N. Branden (February 1964), "The psychology of pleasure," in Virtue of Selfishness, 61.

75. Rand (9 February 1961), "The Objectivist ethics," in Virtue of Selfishness, 29.

76. Peikoff 1991b, 337; Packer (March 1993), "Happiness skills," in Schwartz, 7.2.

77. Peikoff 1991b, 349; 1972T, Lecture 5.

78. Den Uyl and Rasmussen (1984), "Life, teleology, and eudaimonia in the ethics of Ayn Rand," in Den Uyl and Rasmussen 1984, 68; Rasmussen and Den Uyl 1991, 1993; Saint-Andre 1993. Interestingly, Kellner (1989, 32) argues that the Frankfurt school theorist, Max Horkheimer, also embraced a "eudaemonistic ethics." In Chapter 11, I discuss important parallels between Rand and Habermas, who can be considered a member of the Frankfurt tradition.

79. Den Uyl and Rasmussen are among the foremost "flourishers" in this debate. The survivalist argument can be found in Kelley 1992c; Kelley, in Stata 1993; Mozes 1992; Khawaja 1992. For an interesting discussion of the "survivalist" vs. "flourishers" controversy within Objectivism, and an attempted reconciliation, see Bidinotto 1994 and Scuoteguazza 1993.

80. However, Kelley (in Stata 1993, 7) argues that flourishing has validity "in certain contexts, but we need to work out the concept exactly and how it applies."

81. Rand 1964b, 9; (June 1964), "The cult of moral grayness," in Virtue of Selfishness, 75.

82. Rand (9 February 1961), "The Objectivist ethics," in Virtue of Selfishness, 25.

83. Rand (31 July 1950), "From Ayn Rand's unpublished writings: Philosophic notes, 1949–1958," in Binswanger 5.4.4.

84. Rand (July 1962), Doesn't life require compromise?," in Virtue of Selfishness, 68; (January 1964), "The anatomy of compromise," in Unknown Ideal, 147.

85. Rand (April 1962), "How does one lead a rational life in an irrational society?," in Virtue of Selfishness, 71.

86. B. Branden, quoted in Rand (January 1963), "Collectivized ethics," in Virtue of Selfishness, 80. In a communication printed in Commonweal after the publication of Atlas Shrugged, a young

Murray Rothbard (1957, 313) defended Rand's book against those who saw it as embodying an "anti-charity" creed. Rothbard, who was characteristically critical of Rand in later years, argues that despite its rejection of the traditional virtue of "humility," *Atlas Shrugged* does praise "charity *for the sake of virtues*" and not "for the subsidization of vice": "The difference between Miss Rand's concept and the usual Christian morality is that there is compassion for a man's *fight against* suffering, or against unjustly imposed suffering, rather than pity for suffering *per se*."

87. Rand (February 1963), "The ethics of emergencies," in *Virtue of Selfishness*, 46–47.

88. Rothbard 1987; N. Branden 1989, 296; Bidinotto 1989; Kelley 1990, 76; B. Branden 1990, 51; Smith 1991, 218.

89. N. Branden 1989, 296. Branden argues that the "strain of Manichaeism" in Rand's thought is not a "literal" dualism, but a "tendency to see good and evil as essentially separate and opposed principles, and to interpret all human experience in terms of their confrontation."

90. In Rand (September 1971), "Brief summary," in *Objectivist*, 1091, she stated: "One cannot start with or build on a negative; it is only by establishing what is the good that one can know what is evil and why."

91. Rosenthal 1975, 129; B. Branden 1986T. Interestingly, there are passages in Lossky [1917] 1928 which also suggest that evil was not coequal with good, and that it was dependent on good for its existence; see 182–83.

92. N. Branden (September 1962), "Isn't everyone selfish?," in *Virtue of Selfishness*, 60.

93. Peikoff 1983T, Lecture 10. Despite this view, in Peikoff (18 May 1989), "Fact and value," in Schwartz 5.1, he continues the practice of intellectual "purges."

Chapter 10. A Libertarian Politics

1. Rand ([1964] 1993cT) acknowledged that Mises and Hazlitt "are usually called libertarians." She distinguished them from traditional conservatives because they did not defend capitalism on mystical grounds. She also recognized that the libertarians were a loosely defined group of thinkers who came from a variety of philosophical traditions. Though she agreed with libertarians on most political and economic issues, she argued that these issues could not be separated from a more basic philosophical framework.

2. Rand (September 1971), "Brief summary," in *Objectivist* 10:1090.

3. Rand (9 May 1934), "From Ayn Rand's unpublished writings: Philosophic journal," in Binswanger 4.4.4.

4. Rand (9 February 1961), "The Objectivist ethics," in *Virtue of Selfishness*, 15, and (April 1963), "Man's rights," in *Virtue of Selfishness*, 92.

5. Rand (23 October 1972), "A nation's unity, part two," in *Ayn Rand Letter* 2:127.

6. Rand (1 January 1945), quoted in Peikoff 1991a, x.

7. In Rand (January 1963), "Collectivized ethics," in *Virtue of Selfishness*, 81, she suggested that the "fallacy of the frozen abstraction," is a variation on the fallacy of composition, in which one substitutes a "particular concrete for the wider abstract class to which it belongs."

8. N. Branden (February 1962), "Intellectual ammunition department," in *Objectivist Newsletter* 1:7.

9. McKeon (January 1941), "Introduction," in Aristotle 1941, xxvi.

10. Aristotle, *Politics* 1.2.1253a2, in Aristotle 1941, 1129. This Aristotelian predilection reappears even in Locke's state of nature, where individuals compose a polity out of their compelling interests. Replogle 1984, 83. Rasmussen and Den Uyl's (1991) development of Aristotle's social conception is informed by Rand's insights.

11. *Atlas Shrugged*, 747, and Rand 1947.

12. N. Branden (August 1963), "The divine right of stagnation," in *Virtue of Selfishness*, 123; N. Branden and E. D. Branden 1983, 9.

13. Rand (November–December 1965), "What is capitalism?" in *Unknown Ideal*, 16.

14. Ibid., 22–23.

15. Rand (3 June–1 July 1974), "Egalitarianism and inflation," in *Philosophy*, 153.

16. Rand (23 October 1972), "A nation's unity, part two," in *Ayn Rand Letter* 2:125–26.

17. Rand (17 February 1960), "Faith and force: The destroyers of the modern world," in *Philosophy*, 79–80.

18. Rand (17 February 1960), "Faith and force: The destroyers of the modern world," in *Philosophy*, 79–80. A discussion of the reason/freedom and faith/force distinction is provided by Hollinger (1984), "Ayn Rand's epistemology in historical perspective," in Den Uyl and Rasmussen 1984.

19. Rand (9 February 1961), "The Objectivist ethics," in *Virtue of Selfishness*, 32.

20. For an Objectivist view of the development of the concept of individual rights, see Ridpath 1983T.

21. O'Neill 1983; Osterfeld 1983; Den Uyl and Rasmussen 1983; Mack (1984), "The fundamental moral elements of Rand's theory of rights," in Den Uyl and Rasmussen 1984; Nozick 1974, 179n. I dealt with some of the critics' objections to Rand's views in Chapter 9, since most focus on the ethical basis of the theory.

22. Rand (April 1963), "Man's rights," in *Virtue of Selfishness*, 92. Peikoff (1983T, Lecture 6) emphasizes that Rand's theory of rights does not apply to a state-of-nature or a Robinson Crusoe scenario. Rights are strictly applicable to a social context.

23. Rand (April 1963), "Man's rights," in *Virtue of Selfishness*, 93.

24. Marx (1875), "Critique of the Gotha programme," in Marx and Engels 1968, 333–34.

25. Marx [1843] 1963, 44. Marx [1843] 1963 is hereafter cited as *Critique* by page number in text and notes.

26. Marx, [1843–44] 1971, 103, 108.

27. On these issues, see N. Branden (April 1962), "Counterfeit individualism," in *Virtue of Selfishness*, 135; 1980, 51; and 1983b, 230.

28. This parallel between Rand and Hegel was first noted in print by Den Uyl and Rasmussen ("Capitalism," in Den Uyl and Rasmussen 1984, 172, 181 n.25). The authors speculate that Rand could have developed a theory of alienation that would have had obvious similarities to the Marxian view. By coercively appropriating a person's property, the state, through taxation, alienates an aspect of the person. I explore some of these themes in Part 3.

29. On abortion, see Rand (September–November 1968), "Of living death," in *Voice of Reason*, 58–59; Schwartz (June 1980), "Interview with Ayn Rand," in Binswanger 1.3.1–2. On animal rights, see Peikoff 1991b, 358.

30. On intellectual property rights, see Rand (May 1964), "Patents and copyrights," in *Unknown Ideal*. On inheritance, see N. Branden (June 1963), "Inherited wealth," in *Unknown Ideal*, 92. On corporate rights, see Peikoff 1976T, Lecture 9, and Hessen 1979. On removing immigration restrictions, see Rand 1973T.

31. Rand (April 1964), "The property status of the airwaves," in *Unknown Ideal*, and Kelley and Donway 1983. Though in Rand (24 April 1972), "The Shanghai gesture, part three," in *Ayn Rand Letter* 1:68, she saw the "somberly dignified Indian," as one of America's most important self-images, she was, by and large, not very respectful of those Native American cultures which lacked a notion of private property. She was insensitive to the different cultural means through which the notion of property was filtered. On Native American rights, see Rand 1974bT; Peikoff 1976T, Lecture 9; and Binswanger 1991T, Lecture 3. For an alternative view of European–Native American relations, see Franck 1992. His argument against the Spaniard devastation of the indigenous populations is fully within the Objectivist tradition.

32. Rand (April 1963), "Man's rights," and (June 1963), "Collectivized 'rights,' " in *Virtue of Selfishness*.

33. Rothbard, quoted in B. Branden 1986, 413.

34. Rothbard 1973, 15–18. Childs ([1969] 1994) also criticized Rand's position on the nature of government. Though he later changed his views on the subject, Childs utilized key Objectivist concepts in his defense of anarchism. B. Branden, 28 June 1993C.

35. Thomas 1980, 56. Horkheimer observes similarly that "Anarchism and authoritarian statism both belong to the same cultural epoch." Jay 1973, 125.

36. Rand (September 1971), "Brief summary," in *Objectivist* 10:1090.

37. See Schwartz (1986) for an extensive critique of anarcho-capitalism from an Objectivist perspective. Also see Sciabarra 1987.

38. An analysis of anarcho-capitalist ideology is central to Nozick's famed work, *Anarchy, State, and Utopia* (1974).

39. Rothbard (1982) provides an Aristotelian-Thomistic-Lockean foundation for his particular brand of libertarian theory.

40. Rand (December 1963), "The nature of government," in *Virtue of Selfishness*, 112. Rothbard's libertarianism has elicited critical responses from socialists, conservatives, Hayekians, and Objectivists. On this provocative critical convergence, see Sciabarra 1991. Rothbard (1978) is the best introduction to his thought.

41. B. Branden 1962T, Lecture 8; Peikoff 1983T, Lecture 7.

42. Rand (December 1963), "The nature of government," in *Virtue of Selfishness*, 112–13.

43. Ibid., 109.

44. Rand (June 1963), "Collectivized 'rights,' " in *Virtue of Selfishness*, 103.

45. Rand (April–May 1967), "The wreckage of the consensus," in *Unknown Ideal*.

46. Rand (February 1964), "Government financing in a free society," in *Virtue of Selfishness*.

47. Rand (November–December 1965), "What is capitalism?" in *Unknown Ideal*, 18.

48. For raising this issue, thanks to Nyberg (2 December 1993C).

49. It was Hayek (in "History and politics," in Hayek 1954, 15) who first observed that it was somewhat misleading to use the word "capitalism," when it had been closely tied to a socialist interpretation of history.

50. Weber 1930; Novak 1993.

51. Mises ([1949] 1963) defends a "value-free" approach to economics. Hayek (1976, 120, 132) argues that the market economy, governed by the rule of law, will maximize chance opportunities, even though its rewards *"often have no connection with merit."*

52. It is for this reason perhaps that Walsh ([1985] 1990T, Lecture 3) acknowledges that the institutions of Western capitalism were developed in their initial stages by noncapitalist means, which were the only methods available at the time. One commits an ahistorical fallacy if one indicts capitalism as a social system for having utilized methods that were distinctive to the historical period out of which it emerged. On this basis, all of human history is bathed in blood, and nothing on earth is legitimate.

53. Rand (7 December 1960), "Conservatism: An obituary," in *Unknown Ideal*, 195.

54. Rand (April 1963), "Man's rights," in *Virtue of Selfishness*, 95. Rand does not use the word "eudaemonic."

55. Rand (August–September 1967), "Requiem for man," in *Unknown Ideal*, 308. This same apprehension is expressed by Peikoff, in (July 1992), "Some notes about tomorrow, part one," in Schwartz 6.4, in which he analyzes the movement away from communism in the former Soviet Union.

56. Rand (January 1962), "Check your premises," in *Objectivist Newsletter* 1:1.

57. Cox (1993), "Introduction to the Transaction edition," in Paterson [1943] 1993, xix–xx; Rand (October 1964), "Books: *The God of the Machine*," in *Objectivist Newsletter* 1:42–43. Nineteen

forty-three saw the publication of *The Fountainhead* and *The God of the Machine*, as well as Nock's *Memoirs of a Superfluous Man* and Lane's *Discovery of Freedom*. In fact, Paterson's book was published in the same month as *The Fountainhead*. Both books are critical of "the humanitarian with the guillotine." Rand and Paterson differed violently over religion. Without access to Rand's personal journals, it is difficult to ascertain who influenced whom on certain issues. B. Branden (1986, 172, 177, 182) notes that Rand probably learned much about U.S. history and political institutions from Paterson. But in failing to give Rand any credit for some of the ethical ideas expressed in *The God of the Machine*, Paterson disappointed Rand deeply. Also see N. Branden 1989, 123–24.

58. N. Branden, "Common fallacies about capitalism," in *Unknown Ideal*. I will examine some of these Austrian-flavored discussions in Chapter 12.

59. Rand (25 October 1971), "The moratorium on brains, part one," in *Ayn Rand Letter* 1:8; Reisman (August–September 1968), "Platonic competition," in *Objectivist* 7:504; Buechner (August 1982), "Ayn Rand and economics," in Binswanger 3.4.3.

60. Rand (November–December 1965), "What is capitalism?" in *Unknown Ideal*, 12, 15.

61. Marx and Engels (1848), "Manifesto of the communist party," in Marx and Engels 1968, 49.

62. Marx [1843–44] 1967, 247. Marx [1843–44] 1967 is hereafter cited as *Jewish Question* by page number in text and notes.

63. *Capital*, 3:817; Marx [1863a] 1963, 393. Marx [1863a] 1963, [1863b] 1968, and [1863c] 1971 are hereafter cited as *Surplus-Value* by part and page number in text and notes.

64. Rand (9 February 1961), "The Objectivist ethics," in *Virtue of Selfishness*, 32.

65. Rand (November–December 1965), "What is capitalism?" in *Unknown Ideal*, 19.

66. Rand [1976] 1992T.

67. Rand (21 November 1981), "The sanction of the victims," in *Voice of Reason*, 154.

68. Rand (3 June–1 July 1974), "Egalitarianism and inflation," in *Philosophy*, 154.

69. Among non-Marxist theorists, the Austrians have also promoted a theory of capitalist entrepreneurship and creativity as essential to the production process. See Kirzner 1973. Schumpeter ([1942] 1976, 81–86), who was not a fully Austrian theorist, celebrates the entrepreneur as the author of a "process of creative destruction."

70. Rand (November–December 1965), "What is capitalism?" in *Unknown Ideal*, 24–25. Peikoff (1976T, Lecture 10) maintains that Rand's identification of the "socially objective values" is merely a terminological difference with those Austrians who champion the "subjective-value" theory. Peikoff recognizes that the Austrians discuss "subjective" values in their campaign against intrinsicism, or old-style objectivism. Some Austrian school theorists, however, are philosophically subjectivist, since they deny the possibility of any objective valuation.

71. Rand (November–December 1965), "What is capitalism?" in *Unknown Ideal*, 24. Franck (27 July 1993C) observes that there are epistemic problems with this formulation. Despite Rand's contextual proviso, there is the implication that one *can* take the synoptic standpoint of "the most rational mind" in evaluating the "best possible to man."

Chapter 11. Relations of Power

1. Marx (24 January 1873), "Afterword to the second German edition," in *Capital*, 1:20.

2. B. Branden 1962T, Lecture 8; Rand 1969T.

3. Peikoff (June 1987), "My thirty years with Ayn Rand: An intellectual memoir," in *Voice of Reason*, 343–45.

4. Rand (17 July 1972), "Representation without authorization," in *Voice of Reason*, 234–35.

5. To say "structural" is not to imply "structuralism" in Rand's analysis. Though Rand has a structuralist-like interest in examining the reciprocal relations among various factors within a system, she does not eliminate the human element in sociohistorical theory.

6. Rand (July–September 1965), "The cashing-in: The student rebellion," in *Unknown Ideal*, 268; *New Intellectual*, 54.

7. *Fountainhead*, 637–38. While the master-slave dynamic is obvious in the case of Toohey and Keating, it is less obvious in the relationship of Keating and Roark. And yet, there are significant elements of parasitism in their relationship. Roark recognizes that Keating is a pure "second-hander," who has lived off of Roark's achievements as a "parasite" of consciousness. But throughout their academic and professional careers, Roark helped Keating with his architectural designs. This was not an "altruistic" offering; it was motivated by Roark's perfectionism. In the climax of the novel, Roark submits plans for public housing under Keating's name. He soon realizes that he has been a willing participant in a relationship that benefits no one. He states: "It's I who've destroyed you, Peter. From the beginning. By helping you. There are matters in which one must not ask for help nor give it." Roark learns that his assistance, however "nonsacrificial," could never have facilitated the emergence of genuine self-sufficiency in Keating's life. *Fountainhead*, 612–13. This aspect of the Roark-Keating relationship raises a host of fascinating psycho-ethical issues about the nature of "nonsacrificial" assistance. Rand has not resolved this issue: Why would Roark hopefully expect even "nonsacrificial" assistance to facilitate the emergence of genuine self-sufficiency in Keating, unless Roark had the "altruistic" expectation that actions which benefit himself will also benefit Keating? For raising this issue, thanks to Cox (18 October 1993C).

8. Rand foreshadowed her own concept of "the sanction of the victim," in her earlier novel, *The Fountainhead*. Roark defeats Toohey by not granting him any existential or moral validity. Toohey approaches Roark in their only encounter in the novel, and asks him: "Mr. Roark, we're alone here. Why don't you tell me what you think of me? In any words you wish. No one will hear us." Roark responds: "But I don't think of you" (389).

9. La Boetie [1577] 1975. This edition includes an introduction by Rothbard.

10. Aristotle, *Categories* 7.7b1–19, in Aristotle 1941, 20. Lincoln ([1 August 1858?], "Fragment," in Basler 1953, 532) also recognized the organic unity of master and slave, for in a democracy, "as I would not be a *slave*, so I would not be a *master*." Thanks to Franck (27 July 1993C) for this reference.

11. Heilbroner (1981), "The dialectical approach to philosophy," in Machan 1987, 6–8.

12. Copleston [1963] 1985, 183; Marcuse [1941] 1960, and (1936), "A study on authority," in Marcuse 1972, 51.

13. *Fountainhead*, 682–83. For a discussion of the virtue of independence in "the code of the creator," see Kelley 1993.

14. N. Branden [1969] 1979, 144–45. Branden (1992, 36) still employs this concept, which he has recently described as "the illusion of self-efficacy and self-respect without the reality." Orthodox Objectivists also continue to use this concept. Peikoff 1983T, Lecture 9; Packer, in Peikoff 1983T, Lecture 11; Locke (April 1984), "Review of Stanton E. Samenow's *Inside the Criminal Mind*," in Binswanger 5.2.12.

15. Branden's first discussion of "social metaphysics" appeared in print in the November 1962 issue of the *Objectivist Newsletter*. I cite *The Psychology of Self-Esteem*, which reproduces these early entries almost in their entirety. According to both Barbara and Nathaniel Branden, Rand saw "social metaphysics" as an embellishment of and advance over her own concept of the second-hander. B. Branden 1986, 269; N. Branden 1989, 128. In Rand (July 1964), "The argument from intimidation," in *Virtue of Selfishness*, 141, she used the Brandenian concept freely, especially in her pre-schism writings. Barbara Branden argues, however, that the concept of "social metaphysics" was only "a valuable *description* of an aspect of inner behavior . . . not a fundamental motivational principle; it names how some people behave, but it does not name the underlying sources and base of such behavior." In her view, the concept of "social metaphysics" became an instrument of psychological control within Rand's inner circle.

16. Rand saw many of the protesting students of the New Left as Dionysian, "Independent" social metaphysicians and "counterfeit" individualists.

17. Rand (December 1962), "The monument builders," in *Virtue of Selfishness*, 88.

18. Rand (August–December 1970), "The comprachicos," in *New Left*, 227.

19. Rand (9 February 1961), "The Objectivist ethics," in *Virtue of Selfishness*, 30; N. Branden (1962), "The moral revolution in *Atlas Shrugged*," in Branden and Branden 1962, 34–35.

20. For the recognition of a unique "period style," thanks to Cox (18 October 1993C).

21. Fromm [1941] 1969, 163–80. Interestingly, Barnes (1967, 133) notes that Rand's portrait of the "second-hander" bears some resemblance to Fromm's "Market Personality."

22. Branden's essay appears in *Unknown Ideal*, but it also appears in abridged and revised form in N. Branden [1971] 1978. See also N. Branden 1983b, 253.

23. N. Branden (July–September 1965), "Alienation," in *Unknown Ideal*, 289.

24. See Adorno 1950.

25. N. Branden (July–September 1965), "Alienation," in *Unknown Ideal*, 295.

26. Addendum to N. Branden (July–September 1965), "Alienation," in N. Branden [1971] 1978, 237.

27. The phrase "linguistic left" was coined by Hughes (1993).

28. McCarthy 1978, 86, 133; Habermas [1968] 1971; 1970; [1971] 1973; and [1976] 1979. McCarthy presents a very comprehensible summary of Habermas's views.

29. Habermas, "A reply to my critics," in Thompson and Held 1982, 264.

30. McCarthy 1978, 200; Habermas [1968] 1971, 217–36.

31. Habermas [1971] 1973, 18–19; McCarthy 1978, 305, 312.

32. Peikoff 1983T, Lecture 3. To say that honesty is a relationship between the mind and reality is not to say that Rand's theory is solipsistic. Rand seeks to objectify the virtue of honesty.

33. Rand (February 1963), "The ethics of emergencies," in *Virtue of Selfishness*, 52.

34. Rand did not develop the issue of communicative interaction in art, but it is clear that there is a kind of raw, subconscious honesty involved in the "sense of life" relationship between the artist's creation and the responder's experience.

35. N. Branden (March 1963), "Mental health versus mysticism and self-sacrifice," in *Virtue of Selfishness*, 36.

36. N. Branden 1983a, 100, 127, 131; 1986, 21; 1983b, 178–79; 1987; 1994.

37. Rand (11 October 1971), "Credibility and polarization," in *Ayn Rand Letter* 1:1. Rand's identification of anti-concepts should be distinguished from the "anti-conceptual mentality" discussed in Chapter 8. An anti-concept is not simply the linguistic creation of an anti-conceptual mentality. It is at root an illegitimate concept with no clear existential referent. The anti-conceptual mentality, by contrast, is an illegitimate method of cognitive functioning. Thanks to Kelley (20 August 1989C) and Johnson (18 June 1990C) for emphasizing this point. In addition, it should be noted that Objectivists distinguish between an "anti-concept" and a "floating abstraction." An anti-concept is illegitimate, whereas a floating abstraction may be a legitimate concept in need of concretization. Peikoff 1990–91T, Lecture 9.

38. There are some obvious Hegelian overtones in Rand's study of systemic negation. But this parallel should be noted with a caveat: while Rand sees the statist system as a negation of everything rational, her future Objectivist society is *not* the inexorable product of a historical *Aufhebung*.

39. Rand (11 October 1971), "Credibility and polarization," in *Ayn Rand Letter* 1:1.

40. Rand (September 1964), " 'Extremism,' or the art of smearing," in *Unknown Ideal*, 176–77.

41. Rand (25 September 1972), "How to read (and not to write)," in *Voice of Reason*, 131. Rand argues that "atomism" is one such "anti-euphemism," a term which makes offensive the concept of a free, independent, individual.

42. Rand violently opposed the draft on moral grounds, even when a compelling national interest is at stake; she favored instead the all-volunteer army. Rand (April–May 1967), "The wreckage of the consensus," in *Unknown Ideal*.

43. Rand (September 1962), "The pull peddlers," in *Unknown Ideal*, 170; (November–December

1965), "What is capitalism?" in *Unknown Ideal*, 20–21; (December 1969–January 1970), "Apollo and Dionysus," in *New Left*, 61. Rand discusses a host of "anti-concepts" throughout her writings, including "fairness doctrine," "isolationism," "meritocracy," "mixed economy," "xenophobia," and concepts of mysticism, among others. For brief explanations of each of these anti-concepts, see the corresponding entries in Binswanger 1986.

44. Rand (July 1970), "Causality versus duty," in *Philosophy*, 114.

45. Rand (11 October 1971), "Credibility and polarization," in *Ayn Rand Letter* 1:3.

46. Rand (May–June 1965), "The new fascism: Rule by consensus," in *Unknown Ideal*, 203–4.

47. Rand (April–May 1967), "The wreckage of the consensus," in *Unknown Ideal*, 222. Rand viewed "anti-ideology" as a species of philosophical pragmatism. In Rand (9–23 April 1973), "Brothers, you asked for it!" in *Ayn Rand Letter* 2:191, she defined pragmatism as "*power without purpose.*" In this context, Rand used a generic definition of the concept "ideology," which should not be confused with the Marxian construct. In "The Wreckage of the Consensus," she defined "ideology" as "a set of principles aimed at establishing or maintaining a certain social system; it is a program of long-range action, with the principles serving to unify and integrate particular steps into a consistent course." However, in a clearly defined alternative context, Rand attached an opposite meaning to "ideology." For instance, in Rand (3 January 1972), "What can one do?" in *Philosophy*, 248, she denigrated certain groups and movements (such as conservatives and libertarians) as "ideological," because they proclaim "some vaguely generalized, undefined (and, usually, contradictory) *political* goals." She argued that these groups attempt "to reverse the philosophical hierarchy and to sell out fundamental principles." In this context, the "ideological" is an anti-concept. It is not long-range and integrative; it is vague, undefined, and noncontextual. Such contrasting meanings in Rand's thought caused me some expositional problems in Sciabarra 1989. Though I have modified some of the formulations from this earlier article, I still believe that Rand's critique of anti-conceptualism serves a function in her system that is similar to the Marxian critique of ideology. Both notions are intimately connected to the legitimation of power relations. I do not explore these specific parallels here because it requires a more detailed exposition of the Marxian concept. A good, brief discussion of Marx's theory is provided in Ollman [1971] 1976, 227–33.

48. Rand (11 October 1971), "Credibility and polarization," in *Ayn Rand Letter* 1:3.

49. Rand (5 June 1972), " 'Fairness Doctrine' for education," in *Philosophy*, 231.

50. Rand (6 November 1972), "A nation's unity, part three," in *Ayn Rand Letter* 2:131.

51. Rand (11 October 1971), "Credibility and polarization," in *Ayn Rand Letter* 1:3.

52. In his most recent published comments, Habermas (1994, 26) remains critical of state socialism, while adhering fundamentally to the Marxist critique of capitalism. He identifies "radical democracy" as a political ideal, which "includes using welfare state measures to tame capitalism to some point where it becomes unrecognizable as such."

53. Rand (January 1966), "Altruism as appeasement," in *Voice of Reason*, 33.

54. Rand (20 November 1972), "The American spirit," in *Ayn Rand Letter* 2:134.

55. Rand (22 November–6 December 1971), "Don't let it go," in *Philosophy*, 250. Apparently aware of its vague and slang usage, Rand places the phrase "life-style" in quotation marks.

56. Rand (22 November–6 December 1971), "Don't let it go," in *Philosophy*, 250.

57. Rand (July–August 1971), "The age of envy," in *New Left*, 152; (22 November–6 December 1971), "Don't let it go," in *Philosophy*, 252.

58. Rand (22 November–6 December 1971), "Don't let it go," in *Philosophy*, 251.

59. N. Branden 1994, 288. Branden places the phrase "cultural unconscious" in quotation marks. It is similar in form to Jameson's "political unconscious," and highlights the tacit dimensions of culture.

60. Rand (22 November–6 December 1971), "Don't let it go," in *Philosophy*, 250.

61. Rand (July–August 1971), "The age of envy," in *New Left*, 165.

62. Rand (13 March 1972), "Tax credits for education," in *Voice of Reason*, 247.

63. Rand (July–August 1971), "The age of envy," in *New Left*, 153.

64. Rand (August–September 1967), "Requiem for man," in *Unknown Ideal*, 306.

65. Rand (1 January 1973), "To dream the noncommercial dream," in *Voice of Reason*, 245.

66. Rand (July–August 1971), "The age of envy," in *New Left*, 162–63, 165. Aspects of Rand's critique in (January 1963), "Collectivized ethics," in *Virtue of Selfishness*, 81, have a psychologistic tone since she attempts to identify the implicit motivations and intentions of the egalitarian-humanitarian: "The more neurotic [the egalitarian-humanitarian] is or the more conscientious in the practice of altruism (and these two aspects of his psychology will act reciprocally to reinforce each other), the more he will tend to devise schemes 'for the good of mankind' or of 'society' or of 'future generations'—or of anything except actual human beings."

67. Rand (July–August 1971), "The age of envy," in *New Left*, 153; (22 November–6 December 1971), "Don't let it go," in *Philosophy*, 252.

68. Sciabarra (1989) provides additional Marx-Rand comparisons.

69. Gramsci 1971, 432; Bobbio 1979, 41.

70. Rand (July–August 1968), "Basic principles of literature," in *Romantic Manifesto*, 97.

71. Blumenthal and Blumenthal ([1974] 1987T) present an Objectivist view of music theory, history, and performance.

72. Rand (April–June 1971), "Art and cognition," in *Romantic Manifesto*, 76. Tolstoy had also criticized "modern artists" for their "counterfeit art." At the end of the nineteenth century, he argued: "Art, in our society, has been so perverted that not only has bad art come to be considered good, but even the very perception of what art really is has been lost." Tolstoi [1899] 1913, 87, 132.

73. Rand (April 1966), "Our cultural value-deprivation," in *Voice of Reason*, 102, 104.

74. Rand (July–August 1971), "The age of envy," in *New Left*, 162.

75. Peikoff 1976T, Lecture 12. Rand's hostility toward religion did not blind her to the specifically nonreligious achievements of one of the most important saints of the Catholic Church: Thomas Aquinas. In Rand (August–September 1967), "Requiem for man," in *Unknown Ideal*, 315–16, she writes that Aquinas "brought an Aristotelian view of reason (an Aristotelian *epistemology*) back into European culture, and lighted the way to the Renaissance." In Rand's view, "the grandeur of his thought almost lifted the Church close to the realm of reason (though at the price of a basic contradiction)." Interestingly, in her first outlines of *Atlas Shrugged*, Rand included a priest named Father Amadeus, who was to be a positive character. Peikoff (1991a, xiii) remarks that Rand later eliminated the character because she could not make him convincing.

76. N. Branden 1967T, Lecture 4; Rand (April 1966), "Our cultural value-deprivation," in *Voice of Reason*, 106.

77. N. Branden (March 1963), "Mental health versus mysticism and self-sacrifice," in *Virtue of Selfishness*, 38; [1971] 1978, 165; 1983b, 88. Peikoff (1983T, Lecture 12) recognizes that certain religions foster respect for the individual, but this is often undercut by their deeper commitment to faith and sacrifice. Walsh (1988T, Lectures 1 and 3) maintains that people will frequently turn to religion in order to deal with their anxiety over a lack of efficacy. For Walsh, religion will be with us as long as any real or illusory needs can be met by an appeal to the supernatural. Rothbard (1989, 29) argues that the antipathy to religion in Objectivism suggests that "the Randians were fanatically anti-religious" and "that Rand hated God far more than she ever hated the State." However, Rand maintained that her atheism derived from her belief in the centrality of reason, not from her antipathy to religion.

78. Rand (December 1962), "The monument builders," in *Virtue of Selfishness*, 91.

79. Rand (August–December 1970), "The comprachicos," in *New Left*, 190, 210, 213. Also Rand (1966T). Rand argued that both the content and the structure of education should be changed. Though she proposed an alternative system of private education, she recognized the prime importance of changing the approach to learning. There are a number of Objectivist sources that deal with the nature of a proper education: N. Branden (June 1963), "Common fallacies about

capitalism: Public education," in Unknown Ideal, 89–92, which advocates the abolition of the public schools; B. Hessen (May–June 1970), "The Montessori method," in Objectivist 9, which defends the value of Montessori education; Peikoff (15 April 1984), "The American school: Why Johnny can't think," in Voice of Reason, which criticizes the American educational system; and Peikoff 1985T, which offers six lectures that are an Objectivist primer for "rational" education.

80. Rand (August–December 1970), "The comprachicos," in New Left, 204.

81. Rand (7–21 May 1973), "The missing link," in Philosophy, 50.

82. Rand (August–December 1970), "The comprachicos," in New Left, 228.

83. Both Marxists and Objectivists oppose this tendency toward fragmentation in the social sciences. Ollman (1979, 136) notes: "Formal education in America is in large part training in how to think undialectically."

84. Rand (August–December 1970), "The comprachicos," in New Left, 228.

85. In keeping with the Randian tradition of using negative phrases to describe contemporary institutions, Reisman (1990T) characterizes universities as "anti-universities."

86. Rand (21 November 1981), "The sanction of the victims," in Voice of Reason, 153.

87. Rand (July–September 1965), "The cashing-in: The student rebellion," in Unknown Ideal, 250.

88. On the organic link between anti-conceptualism and statism, see Peikoff 1985T, Lecture 5.

89. Rand (22 April 1974), "Ideas v. men," in Ayn Rand Letter 3:319.

90. Rand (August 1962), "The 'conflicts' of men's interests," in Virtue of Selfishness, 54.

91. Rand (August 1962), "Let us alone!" in Unknown Ideal, 141.

92. Rand (September 1964), " 'Extremism,' or the art of smearing," in Unknown Ideal, 182.

93. Rand (July–September 1965), "The cashing-in: The student rebellion," in Unknown Ideal, 266. Interestingly, Riggenbach (1982) has reported that in a nationwide survey of the radical, sixties generation, published in 1979, one in six respondents mentioned Rand as a person whom they admired, or whom they had been influenced by. Rand ranked twenty-ninth out of eighty-one individuals mentioned. The survey indicates that among authors, Rand was tied for sixth place with Greer, behind Vonnegut, Gibran, Wolfe, Sartre, Camus, and Ginsberg, but ahead of McKuen, Hesse, Goodman, de Beauvoir, Mailer, and Jones.

94. Rand (22 October 1973), "Thought control, part three," in Ayn Rand Letter 3:258; (17 May 1970), "From a symposium," in New Left, 97, which repudiates both the New Leftists and their conservative-racist critics, including George Wallace.

95. Rand (February 1970), "The left: Old and new," in New Left, 82–95; (July–September 1965), "The cashing-in: The student rebellion," in Unknown Ideal, 241.

96. Rand (July–September 1965), "The cashing-in: The student rebellion," in Unknown Ideal, 249; (17 May 1970), "From a symposium," in New Left, 97; 1969T. Rand was certainly not the only thinker to condemn New Left counterculture. Even established scholars of the left academy, such as Habermas, criticized the student movement for its infantile, compulsive action, and short-term narcissistic gratification. See Heydebrand and Burris (1982) for a discussion of Habermas's attitudes.

97. Rand (December 1969–January 1970), "Apollo and Dionysus," in New Left, 80; (August–December 1970), "The comprachicos," in New Left, 236. As a political libertarian, Rand (1969T) favored the legalization of drugs. In her view, drug prohibition profited organized crime. She believed that drug prohibition was a vestige of moral puritanism, since the government sought to control substances that gave some people pleasure. She (1976T) also recognized that the use of drugs in some circumstances, was not a moral, but a medical question.

98. Rand (December 1969–January 1970), "Apollo and Dionysus," in New Left, 77.

Chapter 12. The Predatory State

1. Rand (December 1961), "America's persecuted minority: Big business," in Unknown Ideal, 48.

2. Rand (24 June 1962), "War and peace," in *Column*, 8.

3. Rand (September 1964), " 'Extremism,' or the art of smearing," in *Unknown Ideal*, 180–81.

4. Rand (18 June 1946), "From Ayn Rand's notes for *Atlas Shrugged*," in Schwartz 6.1.6.

5. Rand (April 1963), "The money-making personality," in Binswanger 4.1.1–2.

6. Nock ([1935] 1977) distinguishes between the economic and political means of acquiring wealth. Paterson ([1943] 1993) distinguishes between the moral and political means, "producers" and "non-producers." Mises ([1949] 1963) distinguishes between the principles of market exchange and those of central planning. These distinctions are fully within the classical liberal tradition, which championed the society of contract over the society of status.

7. Rand (26 March 1961), "The intellectual bankruptcy of our age," in *Voice of Reason*, 91.

8. Rand (22 July 1962), "The cold civil war," in *Column*, 23.

9. Rand (December 1961), "America's persecuted minority: Big business," in *Unknown Ideal*, 48.

10. Hessen (April, November 1962), "The effects of the industrial revolution on women and children," in *Unknown Ideal*, 112–13. In the current study, I do not examine the Objectivist response to such issues as "comparable worth." See Schwartz (1 September 1981), "The wages of sex," in Schwartz 2.9.

11. Greenspan (September 1961), "Antitrust," in *Unknown Ideal*, 68. Greenspan deals with the ALCOA antitrust suit and distinguishes between "coercive" and "non-coercive" monopolies. The coercive type depends upon legally enforced closed entry; the noncoercive type can emerge in isolated fields, such as the mining of certain minerals. The noncoercive "monopolist," however, does not reap monopoly profits since he must price his minerals competitively. He remains in fierce competition with producers of other, complementary materials. See also N. Branden (June 1962), "Common fallacies about capitalism: Monopolies," in *Unknown Ideal* 75; Rand [1964] 1993aT.

12. N. Branden (June 1962), "Common fallacies about capitalism: Monopolies," in *Unknown Ideal*, 73; Greenspan (August 1963), "The assault on integrity," in *Unknown Ideal*, 118; Mises [1949] 1963, 357–97; Rothbard [1970] 1977, 41–82. In Rand ([1946] 1959), "Notes on the history of American free enterprise," in *Unknown Ideal*, and (17 December 1961), "America's persecuted minority: Big business," in *Unknown Ideal*, Rand focuses especially on the history of American railroads in her analysis of monopolistic distortions. On wage and price controls as a form of "socialism for big business," see Rand (8 November 1971), "The moratorium on brains, part two," in *Ayn Rand Letter* 1:11. On immigration restrictions, see Rand 1973T.

13. Rand (March 1961), "The intellectual bankruptcy of our age," in *Voice of Reason*, 96.

14. Rand (May–June 1965), "The new fascism: Rule by consensus," in *Unknown Ideal*, 213–14.

15. Ibid., 218; Rand 1962.

16. Rand (8 May 1972), "The establishing of an establishment," in *Philosophy*, 205.

17. Rand ([1946] 1959), "Notes on the history of American free enterprise," in *Unknown Ideal*, 108.

18. Rand (May–June 1965), "The new fascism: Rule by consensus," in *Unknown Ideal*, 216.

19. Rand (February 1962), "Antitrust: The rule of unreason," in *Voice of Reason*, 254.

20. Rand (17 December 1961), "America's persecuted minority: Big business," in *Unknown Ideal*, 49.

21. Kolko 1963; Weinstein 1968. For an Objectivist view of the crisis in U.S. medical care, see Peikoff (14 April 1985), "Medicine: The death of a profession," in *Voice of Reason*. Also see Peikoff 1993 and Reisman 1994.

22. Rothbard pioneered an even more explicit synthesis of Austrian theory and New Left revisionism. See Radosh and Rothbard 1972, which provides a useful bibliography of revisionist works. Childs ([1974] 1977) integrates Objectivist, Austrian, and New Left arguments.

23. Rand (3 June–1 July 1974), "Egalitarianism and inflation," in *Philosophy*, 160. See Mises [1912] 1971, and [1949] 1963; Hayek [1929] 1966, and [1931] 1967; and Rothbard [1963] 1975, 1970, [1970] 1977, and 1978.

24. Marx, *Capital* 3:493. Marxism and Austrian economics have had an illustrious adversarial

history, beginning in the nineteenth century with Boehm-Bawerk's critique of Marx's labor theory of value. See essays by Boehm-Bawerk and Hilferding in Sweezy [1949] 1975. Vorhies (1989) provides an interesting comparative analysis of Marxian and Austrian theories of money and credit.

25. Marx [1859] 1970, 119, 148, and *Capital* 3:362, 490.

26. Rand (3 June–1 July 1974), "Egalitarianism and inflation," in *Philosophy*, 161–62.

27. Rand (22 November 1971), "Don't let it go," in *Philosophy*, 260–61.

28. Rand (14 August 1972), "A preview, part two," in *Ayn Rand Letter* 1:99–100. Rand's critique mirrors the analysis of Piven and Cloward (1971).

29. Rand (8 May 1972), "The establishing of an establishment," in *Philosophy*, 207.

30. Rand (8 November 1971), " 'The moratorium on brains,' part two," in *Ayn Rand Letter* 1:10. See Hayek [1944] 1976, 107.

31. Rand (June 1962), "Check your premises: 'The national interest, c'est moi,' " in *Objectivist Newsletter* 1:22.

32. Rand (14 August 1972), "A preview, part two," in *Ayn Rand Letter* 1:100; N. Branden (November 1963), "Common fallacies about capitalism: The role of labor unions," in *Unknown Ideal*, 83, 86.

33. Rand (8 November 1971), " 'The moratorium on brains,' part two," in *Ayn Rand Letter* 1:10.

34. Rand (3 June–1 July 1974), "Egalitarianism and inflation," in *Philosophy* 162; 1965T; N. Branden (August 1962), "Common fallacies about capitalism: Depressions," in *Unknown Ideal*, 83.

35. Rand (June 1966), "The roots of war," in *Unknown Ideal*, 36–37, 40.

36. Rand (April–May 1967), "The wreckage of the consensus," in *Unknown Ideal*, 226; (May 1975), "The lessons of Vietnam," in *Voice of Reason*.

37. Rand (June 1966), "The roots of war," in *Unknown Ideal*, 40–42; 1964b, 14. From a historical perspective, Rand argued that World War II was made inevitable by World War I, and that neither war made the world "safe for democracy." She rooted the modern emergence of U.S. nationalistic imperialism in the ideology of progressivism. Moreover, in Rand (4 November 1962), "Nationalism vs. internationalism," in *Column*, 78, she saw the U.N. as an agency designed to promote "tribal racism."

38. In her opposition to the Vietnam war for instance, in Rand (April–May 1967), "The wreckage of the consensus," in *Unknown Ideal*, she argued that it was against U.S. interests to participate in the conflict, but she stopped short of any structural analysis of the war's effects. Rand's anticommunism was inherited by many of her followers, who were more likely to side with "authoritarian" nations, in any U.S. conflict with the former Soviet Union. Schwartz, for instance, endorsed the conservative's distinction, popularized by Jeane Kirkpatrick in 1980, between "authoritarianism" and "totalitarianism." In Schwartz (29 April 1986), "Foreign policy and the morality of self-interest, part two," in Schwartz 4.6.5, he argues: "There is nothing America need apologize for in associating with authoritarian countries, provided we denounce their tyranny and offer moral support to any budding freedom movements in those countries."

39. Rand (6 March 1974), "Philosophy: Who needs it," in *Philosophy*, 10.

40. This point was suggested by Riggenbach 1982, 58. In the novel, Rand's characters employ the tactics of civil disobedience against this militarist system; one of them engages in the piracy of foreign aid freighters.

41. Rand (14 October 1962), "Our alleged competitor," in *Column*, 72; Binswanger (December 1986–February 1987), "Science under slavery," in Binswanger 7.6 to 8.1.

42. Rand (October 1962), "To young scientists," in *Voice of Reason*, 13; (4 June 1973), "Selfishness without a self," in *Philosophy*, 62; Peikoff 1991b, 442–43.

43. Rand (October 1975), "From the horse's mouth," in *Philosophy*, 96; Rand (1972T).

44. Rand (January–February 1971), "The anti-industrial revolution," in *New Left*, 131, 142, 146; Schwartz 1990T. This emphasis on the unexpected consequences of technological innovation suggests a further convergence of Randian and Hayekian views.

45. Rand (January–February 1971), "The anti-industrial revolution," in *New Left*, 145–46. Rand's opposition to wage and price controls was based on the same epistemological criterion, since no one could possibly predict the effects of an edict controlling the price of a single item within an interrelated network of production. Rand (16 July 1973), ". . . and the principles," in *Ayn Rand Letter* 2:221.

46. Rand (January 1963), "Collectivized ethics," in *Virtue of Selfishness*, 84; (September 1969), "Apollo 11," in *Voice of Reason*, 169.

47. N. Branden (June 1963), "Common fallacies about capitalism: Public education," in *Unknown Ideal*, 89. Compare Paterson ([1943] 1993, 251–61), who is also critical of "progressive" education. Rand (13 March 1972), "Tax credits for education," in *Voice of Reason*, 250–51; (8 May 1972), "The establishing of an establishment," in *Philosophy*, 201–4.

48. Rand (22 July 1962), " 'The cold civil war,' " in *Column*, 23.

49. Rand (22 July 1962), " 'The cold civil war,' " in *Column*, 23–25.

50. Rand (August 1962), "The 'conflicts' of men's interests," in *Virtue of Selfishness*, 56.

51. Rand (August 1969), "Books: Shirley Scheibla's *Poverty Is Where the Money Is*," in *Objectivist*, 8:699.

52. Rand (25 September 1972), "How to read (and not to write)," in *Voice of Reason*, 133–34.

53. Rand (July–August 1971), "The age of envy," in *New Left*, 166. For another, sometimes complementary, view of the fragmenting effects of U.S. political processes, see Roelofs 1976.

54. Rand (May–June 1965), "The new fascism: Rule by consensus," in *Unknown Ideal*, 206–7.

55. Rand (16 July 1973), ". . . and the principles," in *Ayn Rand Letter* 2:221.

56. Rand (July 1963), "Check your premises: Vast quicksands," in *Objectivist Newsletter* 2:25.

57. Rand (September 1962), "The pull peddlers," in *Unknown Ideal*, 168–70.

58. Rand (1 July 1962), "Progress or sacrifice," in *Column*, 11–12. This contention is echoed by others in the modern libertarian tradition, especially Paterson ([1943] 1993). There are other libertarians who accept the contention of intragroup conflict, even as they develop a more structured class analysis, based on an integration of Austrian theory and revisionist history: Rothbard 1983; Grinder 1975; Grinder and Hagel 1975, 1977.

59. This particular thesis was advanced by Childs ([1974] 1977). Childs integrates Branden's theory of neurosis with a neo-Objectivist, libertarian critique of statism.

60. Rand (23 September 1962), "Blind chaos," in *Column*, 61.

61. Rand (16 July 1973), ". . . and the principles," in *Ayn Rand Letter* 2:221; (July–August 1971), "The age of envy," in *New Left*, 175.

62. Rand (September 1963), "Racism," in *Virtue of Selfishness*, 126–28.

63. Rand (8 April 1974), "Moral inflation, part three," in *Ayn Rand Letter* 3:309.

64. Rand (7–21 May 1973), "The missing link," in *Philosophy*, 50–51. In the current study, I do not examine every manifestation of the anti-conceptual mentality. For instance, in Rand (4 June 1973), "Selfishness without a self," in *Philosophy*, 56–57, 60, Rand argues: "All tribalists are anti-conceptual in various degrees, but not all anti-conceptual mentalities are tribalists." She identifies the "tribal lone wolf" as another distinct type of anti-conceptual mentality. The lone wolf is an amoralist who is rejected by the tribe. He avoids commitment to anything, or anyone, and disassociates his "self" "from his actions, his work, his pursuits, his ideas."

65. Rand (10 April 1977), "Global balkanization," in *Voice of Reason*, 117.

66. Peikoff (July 1992), "Some notes about tomorrow, part one," in Schwartz 6.4.4; Schwartz (24 March 1986), "Foreign policy and the morality of self-interest, part one," in Schwartz 4.5.5. It is on these grounds that Binswanger has argued against all forms of protectionism. In Binswanger (April 1987), " 'Buy American' is un-American," in Binswanger 8.2.2, he condemns the protectionist "buy-American" campaign as a form of economic nationalism, collectivism, and tribalism.

67. Rand (10 April 1977), "Global balkanization," in *Voice of Reason*, 118, 122.

68. Peikoff (July 1992), "Some notes about tomorrow, part one," in Schwartz 6.4.

69. Rand (17 July 1972), "Representation without authorization," in *Voice of Reason*, 235–36.

70. Rand (8 April 1974), "Moral inflation, part three," in *Ayn Rand Letter* 3:309.

71. Rand (September 1963), "Racism," in *Virtue of Selfishness*, 128; (June 1966), "The roots of war," in *Unknown Ideal*, 36.

72. Rand (10 April 1977), "Global balkanization," in Rand (1989): 127.

73. Rand (7–21 May 1973), "The missing link," in *Philosophy*, 52.

74. Rand (10 April 1977), "Global balkanization," in *Voice of Reason*, 128.

75. Rand (September 1963), "Racism," in *Virtue of Selfishness*, 128–30; (30 September 1962), "The man-haters," in *Unknown Ideal*, 136; (10 April 1977), "Global balkanization," in *Voice of Reason*, 127–29.

76. Rand (September 1963), "Racism," in *Virtue of Selfishness*, 128. For Objectivist discussions of South African apartheid, see Rand 1978T, and Schwartz (20 January 1986), "Untangling South Africa," in Schwartz 4.4.5.

77. Rand (September 1963), "Racism," in *Virtue of Selfishness*, 130; [1964] 1993dT. The evidence suggests that Rand would have seen contemporary "bias" crimes as one more concession to tribalism. She did not believe that racially motivated crime was worse, morally, than any other crime. For Rand, the smallest minority was the individual. The difference between the murder of a single individual and genocide was quantitative, not moral. Evil ideas, in Rand's view, were dangerous only because other individuals failed to offer a better alternative. Rand (June 1978), "The first amendment and 'symbolic speech,' " in *Column*, 110; Schwartz 1990T.

78. Reisman (27 May 1982), "Capitalism: The cure for racism, part three," in Schwartz 2.17.6; (21 October 1982), "Capitalism: The cure for racism, part five," in Schwartz 3.1.3.

79. Rand (14 August 1972), "A preview, part two," in *Ayn Rand Letter* 1:100–101.

80. Rand (July–August 1971), "The age of envy," in *New Left*, 166–67. Also see Steele (1990) whose book receives an excellent review in the catalogue of Second Renaissance Books. Steele (1994) provides an analysis of "group entitlements" that is compatible, in many respects, with Rand's own views.

81. Rand (7–21 May 1973), "The missing link," in *Philosophy*, 52.

82. Reisman (23 August 1982), "Capitalism: The cure for racism, part four," in Schwartz 2.19.3.

83. Reisman (15 November 1982), "Capitalism: The cure for racism, conclusion," in Schwartz 3.2.4.

84. Reisman 1990. Reisman criticizes the multiculturalists for attacking the values of Western civilization, values which are *not* confined to the West or to white Eurocentrists. He argues: "Western civilization *is a body of knowledge and values.*" See also Hull (November 1993), "A postscript on post-modernism," in Schwartz 7.6; Schwartz 1994T. In the multiculturalist debate, many non-Objectivists have noted similar tendencies toward ethnic fragmentation in education and politics. Magner (1990, A37) observes that at Berkeley, "Words like 'balkanization' and 'tribalism' are being used to describe undergraduate life here. Both refer to a tendency among students to segregate themselves into racial and ethnic enclaves." Krauthammer (1992, 33) argues too that "racial Balkanization [is] so routine" in U.S. politics, that it has become a principle for the gerrymandering of congressional districts.

85. Rand (September 1963), "Racism," in *Virtue of Selfishness*, 131.

86. Rand (June 1968), "The presidential candidates, 1968," in *Objectivist* 7:468.

87. Rand (7 December 1960), "Conservatism: An obituary," in *Unknown Ideal*, 196; [1964] 1993cT.

88. Rand 1981T. This anti-Reagan stance differs significantly from Rand's initial assessment of the former president when he campaigned for Goldwater and was elected governor of California. Rand (April–May 1967), "The wreckage of the consensus," in *Unknown Ideal*, 234–35.

89. Rand (21 November 1981), "The sanction of the victims," in *Voice of Reason*, 155–56. For a complementary critique of religious authoritarianism, see N. Branden 1994, 294–97, and Schwartz (14 October 1987), "Secularism and public schools," in Schwartz 4.13.7.

90. Rand (June 1981), "The age of mediocrity," in Binswanger 2.3.5.

91. Ibid. On the mutual responsibilities of parent and child, see N. Branden (December 1962), "Intellectual ammunition department," in *Objectivist Newsletter* 1:55; Rand 1983T, interview 2; and Rand in Peikoff 1976T, Lecture 9.

92. Rand (18 November 1962), "Post-mortem, 1962," in *Column*, 86.

93. Rand (24 September 1973), "Thought control, part one," in *Ayn Rand Letter* 2:245. Though Rand opposed censorship, it must be emphasized that she saw censorship as an outgrowth of *governmental* action. It was not censorship, in Rand's view, in (June 1963), "Man's rights," in *Virtue of Selfishness*, 98–99, for a private individual or group to refuse to fund projects or to provide a forum for the expression of ideas to which they were opposed. Likewise, Rand opposed *all* government involvement in the arts. The establishment of the National Endowment of the Arts introduced, by necessity, an element of government control over artistic expression. Objectivists endorse the adage: "He who pays the piper, calls the tune." In recent years, they have argued that the debate over who would receive government art subsidies fails to question the legitimacy of granting *any* subsidies to *any* artist. See J. Blumenthal (December 1968), "Art for power's sake, part two," in *Objectivist* 7:563–71; Peikoff (1 August 1981), "The conservative establishment: A report," in Schwartz 1.19.

94. Rand (13 August–10 September 1973), "Censorship: Local and express," in *Philosophy*, 210.

95. Rand (26 March 1961), "The intellectual bankruptcy of our age," in *Voice of Reason*, 86.

96. Rand (13 August–10 September 1973), "Censorship: Local and express," in *Philosophy*, 228–29.

97. Rand (26 March 1961), "The intellectual bankruptcy of our age," in *Voice of Reason*, 88.

Chapter 13. History and Resolution

1. Rand (December 1969–January 1970), "Apollo and Dionysus," in *New Left*, 58.

2. Rand credits Branden for this designation in *New Intellectual*, 14n. Also see Hollinger (1984), "Ayn Rand's epistemology in historical perspective," in Den Uyl and Rasmussen 1984, in which Hollinger relates the Witch Doctor–Attila distinction to Rand's critique of Plato, Descartes, Hume, and Kant.

3. Marx and Engels ([1845–46] 1970, 39–68) saw the division of society into businessmen (the "bourgeoisie") and intellectuals as a by-product of capitalism, a system which thrived on the dualism of material and ideal factors.

4. Rand (November–December 1965), "What is capitalism?" in *Unknown Ideal*, 30–31.

5. See Peikoff (July 1992), "Some notes about tomorrow, part one," in Schwartz 6.4. Compare Hayek (in Geddes 1979), who argues too that the movement toward capitalism "requires a very slow and gradual change in national morals and national customs, which takes a few generations." Without such an evolutionary change, the market economy is "bound to fail."

6. Rand (7–21 May 1973), "The missing link," in *Philosophy*, 53.

7. Rand (October 1975), "From the horse's mouth," in *Philosophy*, 94.

8. Rand (October 1975), "From the horse's mouth," in *Philosophy*, 94; (August–December 1970), "The comprachicos," in *New Left*, 238.

9. Rand (August 1964), "Is Atlas shrugging?" in *Unknown Ideal*, 165. There are some parallels here with Kuhn [1962] 1970. I do not explore these similarities in the current study.

10. Rand (30 April 1946), "From Ayn Rand's notes for *Atlas Shrugged*," in Schwartz 6.1.3.

11. Rand (October 1975), "From the horse's mouth," in *Philosophy*, 99.

12. Rand (August 1964), "Is Atlas shrugging?" in *Unknown Ideal*, 165. The most dramatic, literary presentation of Rand's belief in the power of ideas can be found in *Atlas Shrugged* (605–7) in the description of an inexorable railroad catastrophe.

13. Engels (21–22 September 1890), "Letter to Joseph Bloch," in Marx and Engels 1982, 396.

14. Engels (5 August 1890), "Letter to Conrad Schmidt," in Marx and Engels 1982, 393.

15. Engels (27 October 1890), "Letter to Conrad Schmidt," in Marx and Engels 1982, 397; (25 January 1894), "Letter to W. Borgius," in Marx and Engels 1982, 441. This is not the place to consider the myriad interpretations of Marxist historiography. My own view of Marx's dialectical historical methodology is presented briefly in Sciabarra 1988a and 1995.

16. Rand (April 1977), "Global balkanization," in Voice of Reason, 115.

17. In this same historical context, Paterson formulated a theory of history that also gave credence to the power of ideas. Though there are substantial differences between Rand and Paterson, a study of their important intellectual relationship has yet to be written. Paterson ([1943] 1993, 53) writes: "Ideas precede accomplishment. . . . Every achievement is foreshadowed in fancy; every major disaster is the result of inadequacy, error, or perversion of intelligence." Also see Cox (1993), "Introduction to the Transaction edition," in Paterson [1943] 1993; Rand (October 1964), "Books: The God of the Machine by Isabel Paterson," in Objectivist Newsletter 3:42–43.

18. Rand (25 February 1974), "Ideas v. goods," in Ayn Rand Letter 3:296.

19. Rand (August–September 1967), "Requiem for man," in Unknown Ideal, 299–300.

20. Peikoff 1972T, Lecture 8. See also Peikoff 1985T, Lecture 5, which compares Rand and the conservatives in terms of their respective views on the speed of social change. N. Branden tells a story in his memoirs (1989, 294) that Rand was amused when, in 1957, on the publication of Atlas Shrugged, Peikoff, the youngest member of the inner circle, suggested that Rand's book would convince America to embrace laissez-faire capitalism within a few years. " 'That's not how things happen, or can possibly happen,' she insisted. 'I will have an influence—Atlas will have an influence—but it will be a very slow process. We won't begin to see its concrete results in action for many years. I may not fully see them at all.' " Of course, Peikoff no longer adheres to such ahistorical reasoning.

21. This is an instance of reciprocal causation. Peikoff (1974T, Lecture 9) explains, for instance, that low-caliber movies will contribute to the disintegration of a culture, even as they are symptomatic of it. In such circumstances, each factor mutually reinforces the other. It should be noted that Peikoff's book, The Ominous Parallels (1982), despite its more popularized style of exposition, is the most explicitly developed application of the Objectivist theory of history yet published.

22. Peikoff (October 1985), "Philosophy and psychology in history," in Binswanger 6.5.8. Peikoff's essay is, in many ways, a response to Branden who argues that the Objectivist philosophy of history is in great need of revision. N. Branden (1982T) suggests that Rand's theory of history should incorporate both philosophy and psychology.

23. On the issue of whether or not "good or ill" pertains to an idea or to the practitioners of the idea, there has been a debate within Objectivist circles. The themes discussed in the following sources are wide-ranging and controversial, and symptomatic of a deep division between orthodox and neo-Objectivists, particularly Peikoff and Kelley: Schwartz (27 February 1989), "On sanctioning the sanctioners," in Schwartz 4.20; Peikoff (18 May 1989), "Fact and value," in Schwartz 5.1; and 1989T; Bidinotto 1989; Kelley 1990.

24. In the first two-thirds of Atlas Shrugged, Galt does not remove himself entirely from the social order; he works incognito at Dagny Taggart's railroad, but not in his capacity as an inventor and entrepreneur.

25. Peikoff argues that many Objectivists make a mistake of abstraction. They adopt a quasi-religious perspective, substituting Galt's Gulch for Heaven, and alienating themselves from the culture-at-large. Like the Christians in days of yore, they view suffering as their destiny. Peikoff (1983T, Lecture 12) rejects such "rationalistic" Objectivism.

26. Marx (13 October 1868), "Letter to J. B. Schweitzer," in Marx and Engels 1982, 201; Capital, 1:17.

27. Rand (3 January 1972), " 'What can one do?' " in Philosophy, 245–49. On Chernyshevsky and Lenin, see Chapter 1.

28. Rand (January 1962), "Check your premises: Choose your issues," in *Objectivist Newsletter* 1:1; (October 1966), "A letter from a reader," in *Objectivist* 5:156.

29. B. Branden (June 1963), "Intellectual ammunition department: What is the Objectivist stand on 'right-to-work' laws?" in *Objectivist Newsletter* 2:23.

30. Rand (June 1966), "The question of scholarships," in *Voice of Reason*, 40.

31. See also Rand in Peikoff 1976T, Lecture 10. Peikoff (1983T, Lecture 4) argues further that under statist conditions, one may be justified to lie about age, national origin, etc., in order to gain employment, shelter, and other amenities of life.

32. Rand (5 June 1972), " 'Fairness doctrine' for education," in *Philosophy*, 231–43.

33. Rand (February 1970), "The left: Old and new," in *New Left*, 96.

34. Rand (18 July 1946), "From Ayn Rand's notes for *Atlas Shrugged*," in Schwartz 6.1.6; (July–September 1965), "The cashing-in: The student rebellion," in *Unknown Ideal*, 256–57.

35. Rand (3 January 1972), " 'What can one do?' " in *Philosophy*, 245.

36. See Peikoff 1984T, which discusses systematization and comprehensiveness as two important components of previously successful intellectual movements.

37. Rand 1962T; [1964] 1993bT.

38. Rand (7–21 May 1973), "The missing link," in *Philosophy*, 45.

39. Packer (February 1984), "The psychological requirements of a free society," in Binswanger 5.1.2–5.

40. Rand (22 July 1962), " 'The cold civil war,' " in *Column*, 23–25.

41. Rand (April 1964), "The property status of airwaves," in *Unknown Ideal*. A more detailed Objectivist blueprint for deregulation is presented in Reisman 1986T.

42. Rand (February 1964), "Government financing in a free society," in *Virtue of Selfishness*, 116; [1964] 1993aT. Prominent Objectivists have debated the morality of taxation in the pages of *Full Context*. See especially, articles and letters by Peter Saint-Andre, Tibor Machan, Murray Franck, and others, in Reedstrom 1994.

43. Rand (7 December 1960), "Conservatism: An obituary," in *Unknown Ideal*, 201.

44. Rand (18 July 1946), "From Ayn Rand's notes for *Atlas Shrugged*," in Schwartz 6.1.3.

45. On this convergence, see N. Branden 1983b, 239.

46. Rand (9 April 1934), "From Ayn Rand's unpublished writings: Philosophic journal," in Binswanger 4.4.2.

47. It is no coincidence that Nathaniel Branden (1992, 43–45) projects this same harmonious integration in his description of the fully efficacious individual of self-esteem.

48. Barry 1983, 108–9; 1987, 130.

49. Friedman 1991, 17–18. On the other hand, Rand argued that Friedman was *not* an advocate of capitalism. She characterized him as a "miserable eclectic," and repudiated his "amoral" defense of the fact-value dichotomy in economics. Rand (January–February 1976), "A last survey, part two," in *Ayn Rand Letter* 4:386; 1976T; Peikoff 1980T, Lecture 1.

50. B. Branden 1986; Rothbard 1987, 1; Kelley 1990, 71–72.

51. Though Foucault is most famous for his opposition to the treatment of those individuals labeled as "mentally ill" by the psychiatric profession, it is Szasz among libertarian psychiatrists who has actually fought the practice. Both Branden and Rand have praised Szasz. Though N. Branden (1971b, 6) opposes Szasz's belief that mental illness is a "myth," he applauds the famed psychiatrist's fight against the victimization of mental patients in state psychiatric hospitals. Rand (1976T) considered Szasz a promising advocate of individual rights in this regard.

52. Machan (1984), "Reason, individualism, and capitalism: The moral vision of Ayn Rand," in Den Uyl and Rasmussen 1984, 214.

53. Den Uyl 1973, 7. Rasmussen and Den Uyl (1993, 126–30) provide a quasi-Aristotelian critique of the "moral dualism" that underlies this dichotomy of individuality and sociality.

54. Flew (1984), "Selfishness and the unintended consequences of intended action," in Den Uyl and Rasmussen 1984, 191–92.

55. Rand (August 1962), "The 'conflicts' of men's interests," in *Virtue of Selfishness*, 55–56.

56. Rand (23 October 1972), "A nation's unity, part two," in *Ayn Rand Letter* 2:127–28.

57. Rand (1971), "Why I like stamp collecting," in *Column*, 122.

58. Rand (July–August 1971), "The age of envy," in *New Left*, 157–58. Despite his criticism of such doctrines as "natural rights," MacIntyre's conception is informed by Aristotelian and Thomistic moral theory. He criticizes "the modern liberal attempt to render our public shared morality independent of conceptions of the human good." MacIntyre 1990, 1981. An interesting commentary on MacIntyre is provided in Rasmussen and Den Uyl 1991, 97–101.

Epilogue

1. Lukács (March 1919), "What is orthodox Marxism?" in Lukács 1971, 1–2. More specifically, Lukács identified Marxism with dialectical materialism. Himmelfarb (1994, 52–54) provides an interesting account of the impact of Lukács's book on Marxist scholarship.

2. Of course, Peikoff (1990–91T, Lecture 8) does not characterize the relational view as "dialectical."

References

Books and Articles

Adorno, Theodor W. 1950. *The Authoritarian Personality*. New York: Harper.
———. [1966] 1983. *Negative Dialectics*. Translated by E. B. Ashton. New York: Continuum.
ARI Impact. 1994. News from the Ayn Rand Institute, April.
Aristotle. 1941. *The Basic Works of Aristotle*. Edited by Richard McKeon. New York: Random House.
Baker, James T. 1987. *Ayn Rand*. Edited by Warren French. Boston: Twayne, G. K. Hall.
Barnes, Hazel E. 1967. *An Existentialist Ethics*. New York: Alfred A. Knopf.
Barry, Norman P. 1983. Review article: The new liberalism. *British Journal of Political Science* 13 (January): 93–123.
———. 1986. The concept of "nature" in liberal political thought. *Journal of Libertarian Studies* 8 (Winter): 1–17.
———. 1987. *On Classical Liberalism and Libertarianism*. New York: St. Martin's.
Basler, Roy P., ed. 1953. *The Collected Works of Abraham Lincoln, 1848–1858*. Vol. 2. New Brunswick: Rutgers University Press.
Berberova, Nina. 1992. *The Italics Are Mine*. New York: Alfred A. Knopf.
Berdyaev, Nicolas. 1951. *Dream and Reality: An Essay in Autobiography*. New York: Macmillan.
Berger, Peter L. 1986. Adam Smith meets Nietzsche: Review of Branden's *The Passion of Ayn Rand*. *New York Times Book Review*, 6 July, 13.
Bernstein, Richard J. 1971. *Beyond Objectivism and Relativism: Science, Hermeneutics, and Praxis*. Philadelphia: University of Pennsylvania Press.
Bidinotto, Robert James. 1989. *Facts, Values and Moral Sanctions: An Open Letter to Objectivists*. New Castle, Pa.: Broadsheet.

————. 1994. Survive or flourish?—a reconciliation. *Full Context* 6 (February); 6 (April).

Binswanger, Harry, ed. 1980–87. *The Objectivist Forum.* 8 vols. New York: The Objectivist Forum.

————, ed. 1986. *The Ayn Rand Lexicon: Objectivism from A to Z.* With an introduction by Leonard Peikoff. New York: New American Library.

————. 1990. *The Biological Basis of Teleological Concepts.* Los Angeles: Ayn Rand Institute.

Blanshard, Brand. 1940. *The Nature of Thought.* 2 vols. New York: Macmillan.

————. [1962] 1964. *Reason and Analysis.* LaSalle, Ill.: Open Court.

Bobbio, Norberto. 1979. Gramsci and the conception of civil society. In *Gramsci and Marxist Theory,* ed. Chantal Mouffe. London: Routledge & Kegan Paul.

Bold, David. 1973. A reply to William Dwyer's "The contradiction of 'the contradiction of determinism.' " *Personalist* 54 (Summer): 284–89.

Bowie, G. Lee, Meredith W. Michaels, and Robert C. Solomon, eds. 1992. *Twenty Questions: An Introduction to Philosophy.* 2d ed. New York: Harcourt Brace Jovanovich.

Boyd, Brian. 1990. *Vladimir Nabokov: The Russian Years.* Princeton: Princeton University Press.

Bradford, R. W. 1988. Report: The search for *We the Living. Liberty,* November.

————. 1994. Was Ayn Rand a plagiarist? *Liberty,* May.

Branden, Barbara. 1986. *The Passion of Ayn Rand.* Garden City, N.Y.: Doubleday.

————. 1990. The *Liberty* interview. *Liberty,* January, 49–57, 76.

Branden, Nathaniel. [1969] 1979. *The Psychology of Self-Esteem: A New Concept of Man's Psychological Nature.* Los Angeles: Nash.

————. 1970a. Rational egoism: A reply to Professor Emmons. *Personalist* 51 (Spring): 196–211.

————. 1970b. Rational egoism: Continued. *Personalist* 51 (Summer): 305–14.

————. 1970c. *Breaking Free.* Los Angeles: Nash.

————. 1971a. Comments on Professor Mannison's address. *Personalist* 52 (Spring): 362–67.

————. 1971b. Break free: An interview with Nathaniel Branden. *Reason,* October, 4–9.

————. [1971] 1978. *The Disowned Self.* New York: Bantam.

————. 1973. *An Informal Discussion of Biocentric Therapy.* Washington, D.C.: Libertarian Review.

————. 1978. Thank you, Ayn Rand, and goodbye. *Reason,* May, 58–61.

————. 1980. *The Psychology of Romantic Love.* New York: Bantam.

————. 1983a. *"If You Could Hear What I Cannot Say": Learning to Communicate with the Ones You Love.* New York: Bantam.

————. 1983b. *Honoring the Self: Personal Integrity and the Heroic Potentials of Human Nature.* Los Angeles: Jeremy P. Tarcher.

————. [1986] 1993. *The Art of Self-Discovery.* New York: Bantam. Originally published as *To See What I See and Know What I Know: A Guide to Self-Discovery.*

————. 1987. *How to Raise Your Self-Esteem.* New York: Bantam.

————. 1989. *Judgment Day: My Years with Ayn Rand.* Boston: Houghton-Mifflin.

————. 1990. What is self-esteem? Paper presented at the First International Conference on Self-Esteem, Asker/Oslo, Norway, 9 August.

————. 1992. *The Power of Self-Esteem.* Deerfield Beach, Fla.: Health Communications.

————. 1994. *The Six Pillars of Self-Esteem.* New York: Bantam.

Branden, Nathaniel, and Barbara Branden. 1962. *Who Is Ayn Rand?: An Analysis of the Novels of Ayn Rand*. New York: Random House.

Branden, Nathaniel, and E. Devers Branden. 1983. *The Romantic Love Question and Answer Book*. New York: Bantam. Subsequently republished under the title *What Love Asks of Us*.

Buckley, William F. 1982a. Ayn and Randism recalled. *New York Daily News*, 10 March.

———. 1982b. Isolation affects the manners of Objectivists. *New York Daily News*, 9 May.

Caputo, John D. 1988. Presidential address: Radical hermeneutics and the human condition. In *Hermeneutics and the Tradition*, vol. 62, ed. Daniel O. Dahlstrom. Washington, D.C.: National Office of the A.C.P.A.

Chambers, Whittaker. 1957. Books in review: Big sister is watching you. *National Review*, 28 December, 594–96.

Chase, Chris. 1988. "Living" Ayn Rand's ideal. *New York Daily News*, 30 November, 37.

Childs, Roy A. [1969] 1994. Objectivism and the State: An Open Letter to Ayn Rand. In *Liberty Against Power: Essays by Roy A. Childs, Jr.*, ed. Joan Kennedy Taylor. San Francisco: Fox & Wilkes.

———. [1974] 1977. Big business and the rise of American statism. In *The Libertarian Alternative*, ed. Tibor R. Machan. Chicago: Nelson-Hall.

———. 1982. Ayn Rand: 1905–1982. *Inquiry*, 26 April.

———. 1993. Interview with Jeff Walker: Ayn Rand, Objectivism and all that. *Liberty*, April.

Copleston, Frederick. [1946] 1985. *A History of Philosophy: Volume I: Greece and Rome*. Garden City, N.Y.: Image.

———. [1963] 1985. *A History of Philosophy: Volume VII: Fichte to Nietzsche*. Garden City, N.Y.: Doubleday, Image.

———. 1966. *A History of Philosophy: Volume VIII: Bentham to Russell*. Notre Dame: University of Notre Dame Press.

———. 1986. *Philosophy in Russia: From Herzen to Lenin and Berdyaev*. Notre Dame: University of Notre Dame Press.

———. 1988. *Russian Religious Philosophy: Selected Aspects*. Notre Dame: University of Notre Dame Press.

Cox, Stephen. 1986. Ayn Rand: Theory vs. creative life. *Journal of Libertarian Studies* 8 (Winter): 19–29.

———. 1987. It couldn't be made into a really good movie: The films of Ayn Rand. *Liberty*, August.

———. 1993. The literary achievement of *The Fountainhead*. In *The Fountainhead: A Fiftieth Anniversary Celebration*. Poughkeepsie, N.Y.: Institute for Objectivist Studies.

Current Biography. 1982. Ayn Rand. New York: H. W. Wilson.

Dallmayr, Fred R., and Thomas A. McCarthy, eds. 1977. *Understanding and Social Inquiry*. Notre Dame: University of Notre Dame Press.

Den Uyl, Douglas J. 1973. The new republic. *Reason*, November, 6–11.

———. 1975. Ethical egoism and Gerwirth's PCC *Personalist* 56 (Autumn): 432–47.

———. 1991. *The Virtue of Prudence*. New York: Peter Lang.

Den Uyl, Douglas J., and Douglas Rasmussen. 1983. In defense of natural end ethics: A rejoinder to O'Neil and Osterfeld. *Journal of Libertarian Studies* 7 (Spring): 115–25.

———, eds. 1984. *The Philosophic Thought of Ayn Rand*. Urbana and Chicago: University of Illinois Press.

Dipert, Randall R. 1987. Review essay: Kelley's *The Evidence of the Senses*. *Reason Papers* 12 (Spring): 57–70.

Dryer, D. P. 1966. *Kant's Solution for Verification in Metaphysics*. London: George Allen & Unwin.

Dwyer, William. 1972. The contradiction of "The contradiction of determinism." *Personalist* 53 (Winter): 94–101.

———. 1973. A reply to David Bold. *Personalist* 54 (Summer): 284–89.

———. 1974. The argument against "An objective standard of value." *Personalist* 55 (Spring): 165–81.

Edelstein, David. 1988. Rand's living legacy. *New York Post*, 25 November, 39.

Edie, James M., James P. Scanlan, and Mary-Barbara Zeldin. 1965. *Russian Philosophy*. Vol. 3. Chicago: Quadrangle.

Edwards, Paul, ed. 1967. *The Encyclopedia of Philosophy*. New York: Free Press.

Efron, Robert. 1966. The conditioned reflex: A meaningless concept. *Perspectives in Biology and Medicine* 9 (Summer).

———. 1967. Biology without consciousness—and its consequences. *Perspectives in Biology and Medicine* 11 (Autumn).

Ellis, Albert. 1968. *Is Objectivism a Religion?* New York: Lyle Stuart.

Emmons, Donald C. 1971. Discussion—rational egoism: Random observations. *Personalist* 52 (Winter): 95–105.

———. 1972. Discussion—Professor Machan's observations. *Personalist* 53 (Winter): 71–73.

Engels, Frederick. [1878] 1947. *Herr Eugen Dühring's Revolution in Science*. Moscow: Progress.

———. [1882] 1940. *Dialectics of Nature*. New York: International.

Ericson, Nels. 1988. Ayn Rand's *We the Living* reborn. *New York City Tribune*, 25 November, 16.

Feinberg, Joel. 1992. *Reason and Responsibility*. 8th ed. Belmont, Calif.: Wadsworth.

Fichte, Johann Gottlieb. [1794] 1970. *The Science of Knowledge*. Edited and translated by Peter Heath and John Lachs. New York: Appleton-Century-Crofts.

Fitzpatrick, Sheila. 1970. *The Commissariat of Enlightenment: Soviet Organization of Education and the Arts under Lunacharsky, October 1917–1921*. London: Cambridge University Press.

———. 1979. *Education and Social Mobility in the Soviet Union, 1921–1934*. Cambridge: Cambridge University Press.

Fitzpatrick, Sheila, Alexander Rabinowitch, and Richard Stites, eds. 1991. *Russia in the Era of N.E.P.: Explorations in Soviet Society and Culture*. Bloomington: Indiana University Press.

Flacks, Richard. 1982. Marxism and sociology. In *The Left Academy: Marxist Scholarship on American Campuses*, vol. 1, ed. Bertell Ollman and Edward Vernoff. New York: McGraw-Hill.

Franck, Murray. 1992. An objective view of Columbus's legacy bone and marrow: Neither clay nor marble. *Full Context* 5 (December): 11–12.

Friedman, Milton. 1991. Talk: Say "no" to intolerance. *Liberty*, July, 17–20.

Fromm, Erich. [1941] 1969. *Escape from Freedom*. New York: Avon.

Gadamer, Hans-Georg. [1971] 1976. *Hegel's Dialectic: Five Hermeneutical Studies*. Translated by P. Christopher Smith. New Haven: Yale University Press.

Geddes, John M. 1979. New vogue for critic of Keynes. *New York Times*, 7 May, D1, D7.

Gladstein, Mimi Reisel. 1978. Ayn Rand and feminism: An unlikely alliance. *College English* 39 (February): 680–85.

———. 1984. *The Ayn Rand Companion*. Westport, Conn.: Greenwood.

Got'e, Iurii Vladimirovich. 1988. *Time of Troubles: The Diary of Iurii Vladimirovich Got'e—Moscow: July 8, 1917 to July 23, 1922*. Edited and translated by Terence Emmons. Princeton: Princeton University Press.

Gotthelf, Allan. 1990. The choice to value: Comments on Douglas Rasmussen's "Rand on Obligation and Value." Ayn Rand Society Address, Boston, 28 December.

Gotthelf, Allan, and James G. Lennox, eds. 1987. *Philosophical Issues in Aristotle's Biology*. New York: Cambridge University Press.

Gould, Carol C. 1978. *Marx's Social Ontology: Individuality and Community in Marx's Theory of Social Reality*. Cambridge: MIT Press.

Gramsci, Antonio. 1971. *Selections from the Prison Notebooks of Antonio Gramsci*. Edited and translated by Quentin Hoare and Geoffrey Nowell Smith. New York: International.

Greenwood, Robert. 1974. Ayn Rand and the literary critics. *Reason*, November, 44–50.

Grinder, Walter E. 1975. The Austrian theory of the business cycle: Reflections on some socio-economic effects. Symposium on Austrian Economics, University of Hartford, 22–28 June.

Grinder, Walter E., and John Hagel III. 1975. Towards a theory of state capitalism: Imperialism—the highest stage of interventionism. Libertarian Scholars Conference, 24 October.

———. 1977. Toward a theory of state capitalism: Ultimate decision-making and class structure. *Journal of Libertarian Studies* 1, no. 1:59–79.

Guerney, Bernard Guilbert, ed. 1960. *An Anthology of Russian Literature in the Soviet Period: From Gorki to Pasternak*. Translated and annotated by Bernard Guilbert Guerney. New York: Random House.

Habermas, Jürgen. [1968] 1971. *Knowledge and Human Interest*. Boston: Beacon.

———. 1970. Toward a theory of communicative competence. In *Recent Sociology*, no. 2, ed. H. Dreitzel. New York: Macmillan.

———. [1971] 1973. *Theory and Practice*. Boston: Beacon.

———. [1976] 1979. *Communication and the Evolution of Society*. Translated by Thomas McCarthy. Boston: Beacon.

———. 1994. "More humility, fewer illusions"—a talk between Adam Michnik and Jürgen Habermas. *New York Review of Books*, 24 March, 24–29.

Haley, Alex. 1993. *The Playboy Interviews*. Edited by Murray Fisher. New York: Ballantine.

Hayek, F. A. [1929] 1966. *Monetary Theory and the Trade Cycle*. New York: Augustus M. Kelley.

———. [1931] 1967. *Prices and Production*. New York: Augustus M. Kelley.

———. [1944] 1976. *The Road to Serfdom*. Chicago: University of Chicago Press.

———. 1948. *Individualism and Economic Order*. Chicago: University of Chicago Press.

———, ed. 1954. *Capitalism and the Historians*. London: Routledge & Kegan Paul; Chicago: University of Chicago Press.

———. [1967] 1980. *Studies in Philosophy, Politics, and Economics*. Chicago: University of Chicago Press, Midway Reprints.

———. 1973. *Law, Legislation and Liberty—Volume 1: Rules and Order*. Chicago: University of Chicago Press.

———. 1976. *Law, Legislation and Liberty—Volume 2: The Mirage of Social Justice*. Chicago: University of Chicago Press.

———. [1978] 1985. *New Studies in Philosophy, Politics, Economics, and the History of Ideas*. Chicago: University of Chicago Press.

————. 1981. *Law, Legislation and Liberty—Volume 3: The Political Order of a Free People.* Chicago: University of Chicago Press.

————. 1988. *The Fatal Conceit: The Errors of Socialism.* Edited by W. W. Bartley III. Chicago: University of Chicago Press.

————. 1992. *The Fortunes of Liberalism: Essays on Austrian Economics and the Ideal of Freedom.* Vol. 4, *The Collected Works of F. A. Hayek.* Edited by Peter G. Klein. Chicago: University of Chicago Press.

Hegel, G.W.F. [1807] 1977. *Phenomenology of Spirit.* Translated by A. V. Miller, foreword by J. N. Findlay. Oxford: Oxford University Press.

————. [1812–16] 1929. *The Science of Logic.* 2 vols. Translated by W. H. Johnston and L. G. Struth. London: George Allen & Unwin; New York: Macmillan.

Hellman, Lillian. 1976. *Scoundrel Time.* Introduction by Gary Willis. New York: Bantam.

Hessen, Robert. 1978. Review of Tibor Szamuely's *The Russian Tradition. Objectivist Calendar*, June.

————. 1979. *In Defense of the Corporation*, no. 207. Stanford: Stanford University, Hoover Institution.

Heydebrand, Wolf. 1981. Marxist structuralism. In *Continuities in Structural Inquiry*, ed. Peter Blau and Robert Merton. London: Sage.

Heydebrand, Wolf, and Beverly Burris. 1982. The limits of praxis in critical theory. In *The Frankfurt School Revisited*, ed. Judith Marcus and Zoltan Tas. New York: Columbia University Press.

Hicks, Stephen. 1992. Big game, small gun?: Review of Merrill's *The Ideas of Ayn Rand. IOS Journal* 2 (Fall).

Himmelfarb, Gertrude. 1994. *On Looking into the Abyss: Untimely Thoughts on Culture and Society.* New York: Alfred A. Knopf.

Hook, Sidney. [1936] 1950. *From Hegel to Marx: Studies in the Intellectual Development of Karl Marx.* New York: Reynal & Hitchcock.

————. 1961. Each man for himself: Review of Rand's *For the New Intellectual. New York Times Book Review*, 9 April, 3, 28.

Hoover, Kenneth R. 1994. *Ideology and Political Life.* 2d ed. Belmont, Calif.: Wadsworth.

Hospers, John. 1967. *An Introduction to Philosophical Analysis.* 2d ed. New York: Prentice-Hall.

————. 1970. Ethical egoism: Introduction to Nathaniel Branden's essay. *Personalist* 51 (Spring): 190–95.

————. 1990. Memoir: Conversations with Ayn Rand. Parts 1 and 2. *Liberty*, July, 23–36; September, 42–52.

Hughes, Robert. 1993. *Culture of Complaint: The Fraying of America.* New York: New York Public Library, Oxford University Press.

Irwin, Terence. 1988. *Aristotle's First Principles.* New York: Oxford University Press; Oxford: Clarendon Press.

Jay, Martin. 1973. *The Dialectical Imagination: A History of the Frankfurt School and the Institute of Social Research, 1923–50.* Boston: Little, Brown.

Jetton, Merlin. 1993. Theories of truth—part three. *Objectivity* 1, no. 6 (1993).

Johnson, Gregory R. 1990. Hermeneutics: A protreptic. *Critical Review* 4 (Winter–Spring): 173–211.

Johnson, Gregory R., and Glenn A. Magee, eds. 1991. *Rethinking Foundationalism: Metaphysical Essays. Reason Papers* 16 (Fall)

Kamenka, Eugene. 1967. Communism, philosophy under. In Edwards 1967, 1.

Kelley, David. 1984a. A theory of abstraction. *Cognition and Brain Theory* 7 (Summer/Fall): 329–57.

———. 1984b. Life, liberty, and property. In *Human Rights*, ed. Ellen Frankel Paul, Jeffrey Paul, and Fred D. Miller, Jr. Bowling Green: Basil Blackwell, Social Philosophy and Policy Center.

———. 1986. *The Evidence of the Senses: A Realist Theory of Perception*. Baton Rouge: Louisiana State University Press.

———. 1988. *The Art of Reasoning*. New York: W. W. Norton.

———. 1990. *Truth and Toleration*. Verbank, N.Y.: Institute for Objectivist Studies.

———. 1991. Evidence and justification. In Johnson and Magee 1991.

———. 1992a. Marketplace of ideas: Food for thought. *IOS Journal* 1 (Summer).

———. 1992b. Peikoff's summa: Review of Peikoff's *Objectivism: The Philosophy of Ayn Rand*. *IOS Journal* 2 (Summer).

———. 1992c. Post-Randian Aristotelianism: Review of Den Uyl and Rasmussen's *Liberty and Nature*. *Liberty*, July.

———. 1993. The code of the creator. In *The Fountainhead: A Fiftieth Anniversary Celebration*. Poughkeepsie, N.Y.: Institute for Objectivist Studies.

Kelley, David, and Roger Donway. 1983. *Laissez Parler: Freedom in the Electronic Media*. Bowling Green: Social Philosophy and Policy Center.

Kelley, David, and Janet Krueger. 1984. The psychology of abstraction. *Journal for the Theory of Social Behavior* 14 (March): 43–67.

Kellner, Douglas. 1989. *Critical Theory, Marxism, and Modernity*. Baltimore: Johns Hopkins University Press.

Khawaja, Irfan. 1992. Natural right and liberalism: Review of *Liberty and Nature* by Rasmussen and Den Uyl. *Reason Papers* 17 (Fall): 135–51.

Kirzner, Israel M. 1973. *Competition and Entrepreneurship*. Chicago: University of Chicago Press.

Kline, George L., ed. 1957. *Soviet Education*. New York: Columbia University Press.

———. 1967. Russian philosophy. In Edwards 1967, 7.

———. 1969. "Nietzschean Marxism" in Russia. In *Demythologizing Marxism*. Boston College Studies in Philosophy, no. 2. Boston and the Hague: Nijhoff.

———. 1974. Hegel and Solovyov. In *Hegel and the History of Philosophy*, ed. Joseph J. O'Malley, Keith W. Algozin, and Frederick G. Weiss. The Hague: Nijhoff.

———. 1983. Form, concrescence, and concretum. In *Explorations in Whitehead's Philosophy*, ed. Lewis S. Ford and George L. Kline. New York: Fordham University Press.

———. 1985. Nikolai O. Lossky. In *Handbook of Russian Literature*, ed. Victor Terras. New Haven: Yale University Press.

Kolakowski, Leszek. 1984. The Frankfurt school and critical theory. In *Foundations of the Frankfurt School of Social Research*, ed. Judith Marcus and Zoltan Tar. New Brunswick, N.J.: Transaction.

Kolko, Gabriel. 1963. *The Triumph of Conservatism: A Reinterpretation of American History, 1900–1916*. New York: Free Press.

Krauthammer, Charles. 1992. Balking at our balkanization. *New York Daily News*, 27 September, 33.

Kuhn, Thomas S. [1962] 1970. *The Structure of Scientific Revolutions*. 2d ed. *International Encyclopedia of Unified Science* 2, no. 2. Chicago: University of Chicago Press.

Kuntz, Paul G. 1981. The coincidence of opposites in the modern world. *The New Scholasticism* 55 (Winter): 16–34.

La Boetie, Étienne de. [1577] 1975. *The Politics of Obedience: The Discourse of Voluntary Servitude*. Introduction by Murray N. Rothbard. New York: Free Life.

Landrum, Gene N. 1994. *Profiles of Female Genius: Thirteen Creative Women Who Changed the World*. Buffalo, N.Y.: Prometheus.

Lavoie, Don. 1982. The market as a procedure for the discovery and convergence of inarticulate knowledge. *Center for the Study of Market Processes: Working Paper Series* 100–2, Department of Economics, George Mason University.

Lenin, V. I. [1903] 1969. *What is to be done? Burning Questions of Our Movement.* New York: International.

Leube, Kurt R., and Albert H. Zlabinger, eds. 1984. *The Political Economy of Freedom: Essays in Honor of F. A. Hayek.* Munich: Philosophia Verlag.

Lévi-Strauss, Claude. 1966. *The Savage Mind.* Chicago: University of Chicago Press.

The Library of Congress News. 20 November 1991, 1.

Livingston, Donald W. 1991. Hayek as Humean. *Critical Review* 5 (Spring): 159–77.

Livingston, Kenneth. 1994. To awaken the hero within: Review of Branden's *The Six Pillars of Self-Esteem. IOS Journal* 4 (March).

Locke, Edwin A., ed. 1991. *Theories of Cognitive Self-Regulation,* special issue of *Organizational Behavior and Human Decision Processes* 50 (December).

Lossky, Boris N. 1991. *Historical Almanac: Our Family in the Years of Troubles, 1914–1922,* vol. 12. Paris: Atheneum.

Lossky, Boris, and Nicolas O. Lossky. 1978. *Bibliographie Des Oeuvres de Nicolas Lossky.* Introduction by Serge Levitsky. Paris: Institut D'Études Slaves.

Lossky, N. O. [1906] 1919. *The Intuitive Basis of Knowledge: An Epistemological Inquiry.* Translated by Natalie A. Duddington; preface by G. Dawes Hicks. London: Macmillan.

———. [1917] 1928. *The World as an Organic Whole.* Translated by Natalie A. Duddington. London: Humphrey Miford, Oxford University Press.

———. 1934a. Ideal-realism, part one. *Personalist* 15 (Spring): 148–57.

———. 1934b. Ideal-realism, part two. *Personalist* 15 (Summer): 250–60.

———. 1934c. Our foreign letter—correspondence: Reply to Professor Flewelling. *Personalist* 15 (Summer): 265–67.

———. 1951. *History of Russian Philosophy.* New York: International Universities.

———. 1952. Personalism versus materialism. *Personalist* 33 (Autumn): 366–84.

———. 1955. Psychology with a psyche. *Personalist* 36 (Spring): 129–40.

———. 1957. The conditions of the direct perception of the external world. *Personalist* 38 (Winter): 37–44.

———. 1969. *Vospominaniia: Zhizn' i Filosofskii put'* (Memoirs). Edited by Boris Lossky. Slavische Propylaen, 43. Munich: Wilhelm Fink Verlag.

Lovejoy, Arthur Oncken. 1930. *The Revolt against Dualism: An Inquiry concerning the Existence of Ideas.* Chicago: Open Court; New York: W. W. Norton.

Lugenbehl, Dale. 1974. The argument for an objective standard of value. *Personalist* 55 (Spring): 155–64.

Lukács, Georg. 1971. *History and Class Consciousness: Studies in Marxist Dialectics.* Translated by Rodney Livingstone. Cambridge: MIT Press.

Machan, Tibor. 1971. A note on Emmons' random observations. *Personalist* 53 (Winter): 99–106.

———, ed. 1987. *The Main Debate: Communism versus Capitalism.* New York: Random House.

———. 1992. Evidence of necessary existence. *Objectivity* 1, no. 4.

MacIntyre, Alasdair. 1981. *After Virtue.* Notre Dame: University of Notre Dame Press.

———. 1990. The privatization of good. *Review of Politics* 52 (Summer).

Mack, Eric. 1971. How to derive ethical egoism. *Personalist* 52 (Autumn): 735–43.

Magner, Denise K. 1990. Amid the diversity, racial isolation remains at Berkeley. *The Chronicle of Higher Education,* 14 November, A37–A39.

Marcuse, Herbert. [1941] 1960. *Reason and Revolution: Hegel and the Rise of Social Theory.* Boston: Beacon.

———. 1972. *Studies in Critical Philosophy.* Translated by Joris de Bres. London: NLB.

Marx, Karl. [1843] 1963. *The Critique of Hegel's Philosophy of Right.* In *Early Writings,* translated and edited by T. B. Bottomore; foreword by Erich Fromm. New York: McGraw-Hill.

———. [1843–44] 1967. *On the Jewish Question.* In *Writings of the Young Marx on Philosophy and Society,* edited and translated by Loyd D. Easton and Kurt H. Guddat. Garden City, N.Y.: Anchor, Doubleday.

———. [1843–44] 1971. *On the Jewish Question.* In *Early Texts,* ed. David McLellan. Oxford: Oxford University Press.

———. [1844] 1964. *Economic and Philosophic Manuscripts of 1844.* Edited by Dirk J. Struik; translated by Martin Milligan. New York: International.

———. [1845] 1967. *Theses on Feuerbach.* In *Writings of the Young Marx on Philosophy and Society,* ed. and trans. Loyd D. Easton and Kurt H. Guddat. Garden City, N.Y.: Anchor, Doubleday.

———. [1857–58] 1973. *Grundrisse: Introduction to the Critique of Political Economy.* Translated by Martin Nicolaus. New York: Vintage, Random House.

———. [1859] 1970. *A Contribution to the Critique of Political Economy.* Edited by Maurice Dobb. New York: International.

———. [1863a] 1963. *Theories of Surplus-Value, Volume 4 of Capital, Part One.* Translated by Emile Burns; edited by S. Ryazanskaya. Moscow: Progress.

———. [1863b] 1968. *Theories of Surplus-Value, Volume 4 of Capital, Part Two.* Edited by S. Ryazanskaya. Moscow: Progress.

———. [1863c] 1971. *Theories of Surplus-Value, Volume 4 of Capital, Part Three.* Translated by Jack Cohen and S. W. Ryazanskaya; edited by S. W. Ryazanskaya and Richard Dixon. Moscow: Progress.

———. [1867] 1967. *Capital: A Critique of Political Economy.* Vol. 1, *The Process of Capitalist Production.* Edited by Frederick Engels. Third German edition translated by Samuel Moore and Edward Aveling. New York: International.

———. [1894] 1967. *Capital: A Critique of Political Economy.* Vol. 3, *The Process of Capitalist Production as a Whole.* Edited by Frederick Engels. New York: International.

Marx, Karl, and Frederick Engels. [1845–46] 1970. *The German Ideology.* Edited by C. J. Arthur. New York: International.

———. 1968. *Selected Works, In One Volume.* Moscow: Progress.

———. 1982. *Selected Correspondence, 1844–1895.* 3d rev. ed. Translated by I. Lasker; edited by S. W. Ryazanskaya. Moscow: Progress.

McCarthy, George. 1990. *Marx and the Ancients: Classical Ethics, Social Justice, and Nineteenth-Century Political Economy.* Savage, Md.: Rowman & Littlefield.

———, ed. 1992. *Marx and Aristotle: Nineteenth-Century German Social Theory and Classical Antiquity.* Savage, Md.: Rowman & Littlefield.

McCarthy, Thomas. 1978. *The Critical Theory of Jürgen Habermas.* London: Hutchinson.

McCawley, James D. 1990. The dark side of reason: Review of Paul Feyerabend's *Farewell to Reason.* *Critical Review* 4 (Summer): 377–85.

McClelland, James C. 1989. The professoriate in the Russian civil war. In *Party, State, and Society in the Russian Civil War: Explorations in Social History,* ed. Diane P. Koenker, William G. Rosenberg, and Ronald Grigor Suny. Bloomington: Indiana University Press.

McGrady, Mike. 1988. Review: *We the Living. New York Newsday,* 25 November.

Meikle, Scott. 1985. *Essentialism in the Thought of Karl Marx*. LaSalle, Ill.: Open Court.

Mepham, John, and David-Hillel Ruben, eds. 1979. *Issues in Marxist Philosophy*. Vol. 2, *Materialism*. Atlantic Highlands, N.J.: Humanities.

Merrill, Ronald E. 1991. *The Ideas of Ayn Rand*. LaSalle, Ill.: Open Court.

Mises, Ludwig von. [1912] 1971. *The Theory of Money and Credit*. 3d ed. New York: Foundation for Economic Education.

———. [1949] 1963. *Human Action: A Treatise on Economics*. 3d rev. ed. Chicago: Henry Regnery.

Morgan, Gareth, ed. 1983. *Beyond Method: Strategies for Social Research*. Beverly Hills, Calif.: Sage.

Moyers, Bill. 1993. *Healing and the Mind*. New York: Doubleday.

Mozes, Eyal. 1992. Deriving rights from egoism: Machan vs. Rand. *Reason Papers* 17 (Fall): 87–93.

Nietzsche, Friedrich. [1883–85] 1905. *Thus Spake Zarathustra*. Translated by Thomas Common. Introduction by Mrs. Forster-Nietzsche. New York: Modern Library, Random House.

———. [1886] 1966. *Beyond Good and Evil: Prelude to a Philosophy of the Future*. Translated by Walter Kaufmann. New York: Vintage.

———. [1887] 1974. *The Gay Science*. Translated by Walter Kaufmann. New York: Random House.

———. [1954] 1970. *The Viking Portable Nietzsche*. Translated by Walter Kaufmann. New York: Viking.

Nock, Albert Jay. [1935] 1977. *Our Enemy the State*. Introduction by Walter Grinder. New York: Free Life.

Novack, George. [1969] 1971. *An Introduction to the Logic of Marxism*. 5th ed. New York: Pathfinder.

Novak, Michael. 1993. *The Catholic Ethic and the Spirit of Capitalism*. New York: Free Press.

Nozick, Robert. 1974. *Anarchy, State, and Utopia*. New York: Basic Books.

Ollman, Bertell. 1976. *Alienation: Marx's Conception of Man in Capitalist Society*. 2d ed. Cambridge: Cambridge University Press.

———. 1979. *Social and Sexual Revolution: Essays on Marx and Reich*. Boston: South End.

———. 1993. *Dialectical Investigations*. New York: Routledge.

Ollman, Bertell, and Edward Vernoff, eds. 1986. *The Left Academy: Marxist Scholarship on American Campuses*, vol. 3. New York: Praeger.

O'Neil, Patrick M. 1983. Ayn Rand and the is-ought problem. *Journal of Libertarian Studies* 7 (Spring): 81–99.

O'Neill, William F. [1971] 1977. *With Charity Toward None: An Analysis of Ayn Rand's Philosophy*. Totowa, N.J.: Littlefield, Adams.

Osterfeld, David. 1983. The natural rights debate: A comment on a reply. *Journal of Libertarian Studies* 7 (Spring): 101–13.

Oyerly, David. 1990. We the living: The first edition. In *Practice* 2 (July/August).

Palmer, R. R., and Joel Colton. 1971. *A History of the Modern World—Since 1815*. 4th ed. New York: Alfred A. Knopf.

Paul, Jeffrey, ed. 1981. *Reading Nozick: Essays on Anarchy, State, and Utopia*. Totowa, N.J.: Rowman & Littlefield.

Peikoff, Leonard. 1982. *The Ominous Parallels: The End of Freedom in America*. New York: Stein & Day.

———. 1985. Aristotle's "intuitive induction." *New Scholasticism* 59 (Spring): 185–99.

———. 1991a. Introduction to the 35th anniversary edition of *Atlas Shrugged*. In Rand [1957] 1992.

————. 1991b. *Objectivism: The Philosophy of Ayn Rand.* New York: Dutton.

————. 1993. *Health Care Is Not a Right.* Newport Beach, Calif.: Americans for Free Choice in Medicine.

Peikoff, Sylvan Leonard. 1964. The status of the law of contradiction in classic logical ontologism. Ph.D. diss., New York University.

Perinn, Vincent L. 1990. *Ayn Rand: First Descriptive Bibliography.* Rockville, Md.: Quill and Brush.

Phillips, R. P. 1934–35. *Modern Thomistic Philosophy.* 2 vols. Westminster, Md.: Newman Bookshop.

Pipes, Richard. 1994. *Russia under the Bolshevik Regime.* New York: Alfred A. Knopf.

Piven, Frances Fox, and Richard A. Cloward. 1971. *Regulating the Poor: The Functions of Public Welfare.* New York: Vintage.

Plasil, Ellen. 1985. *Therapist.* New York: St. Martin's.

Pojman, Louis P., ed. 1990. *Ethics: Discovering Right and Wrong.* Belmont, Calif.: Wadsworth.

————, ed. 1992. *Philosophy: The Quest for Truth.* 2d ed. Belmont, Calif.: Wadsworth.

————, ed. 1994. *Philosophy: The Pursuit of Wisdom.* Belmont, Calif.: Wadsworth.

Polanyi, Michael. [1958] 1962. *Personal Knowledge: Towards a Post-Critical Philosophy.* Chicago: University of Chicago Press.

Popper, Karl. [1940] 1963. What is dialectic? In *Conjectures and Refutations.* London: Routledge & Kegan Paul.

————. [1962] 1971. *The Open Society and Its Enemies.* Vol. 2, *The High Tide of Prophecy: Hegel, Marx, and the Aftermath.* Princeton: Princeton University Press.

Pruette, Lorine. 1943. Battle against evil: Review of *The Fountainhead. New York Times Book Review,* 16 May.

Rachels, James. 1986. *Elements of Moral Philosophy.* Philadelphia: Temple University Press.

Radosh, Ronald, and Murray N. Rothbard. 1972. *A New History of Leviathan.* New York: E. P. Dutton.

Raimondo, Justin. 1993. *Reclaiming the American Right: The Lost Legacy of the Conservative Movement.* Burlingame, Calif.: Center for Libertarian Studies.

Rand, Ayn. [1926–38] 1984. *The Early Ayn Rand: A Selection from Her Unpublished Fiction.* Edited and annotated by Leonard Peikoff. New York: New American Library.

————. [1933] 1968. *Night of January 16th.* New York: New American Library.

————. 1936. *We the Living.* New York: Macmillan.

————. [1936] 1959. *We the Living.* New York: New American Library.

————. [1937] 1946. *Anthem.* New York: New American Library.

————. [1943] 1993. *The Fountainhead.* Fiftieth anniversary edition. Afterword by Leonard Peikoff. New York: Bobbs-Merrill.

————. 1944. The only path to tomorrow. *Reader's Digest,* January, 88–90.

————. [1945] 1986. *The Rational Faculty.* New York: The Intellectual Activist.

————. 1946. Textbook for Americanism. *The Vigil.* Motion Picture Alliance for the Preservation of American Ideals. Beverly Hills, Calif.

————. 1947. Screen guide for Americans. *Plain Talk,* November, 37–42.

————. [1957] 1992. *Atlas Shrugged.* 35th anniversary edition. New York: Dutton.

————. 1961. *For the New Intellectual: The Philosophy of Ayn Rand.* New York: New American Library.

————. 1962. The fascist New Frontier. *Objectivist* (December). Ford Hall Forum. Reprint.

————. 1964a. *The Virtue of Selfishness: A New Concept of Egoism.* New York: New American Library.

————. 1964b. Alvin Toffler's *Playboy* interview with Ayn Rand: A candid conversation with the Fountainhead of "Objectivism." *Objectivist* (March). Reprint.

————. [1966–67] 1990. *Introduction to Objectivist Epistemology.* 2d ed., expanded. Edited by Harry Binswanger and Leonard Peikoff. New York: New American Library.

————. [1966–71] 1982. *The Objectivist.* vols. 5–10. Palo Alto, Calif.: Palo Alto Book Service.

————. 1967. *Capitalism: The Unknown Ideal.* New York: New American Library.

————. 1969–71. Appendix: Excerpts from the epistemology workshops. In Rand [1966–67] 1990.

————. [1971–76] 1979. *The Ayn Rand Letter.* Vols. 1–4. Palo Alto, Calif.: Palo Alto Book Service.

————. 1975a. *The New Left: The Anti-Industrial Revolution.* 2d rev. ed. New York: New American Library.

————. 1975b. *The Romantic Manifesto: A Philosophy of Literature.* 2d rev. ed. New York: New American Library.

————. 1982. *Philosophy: Who Needs It.* Introduction by Leonard Peikoff. New York: Bobbs-Merrill.

————. 1989. *The Voice of Reason: Essays in Objectivist Thought.* Edited, with additional essays, by Leonard Peikoff. New York: New American Library.

————. 1991. *The Ayn Rand Column.* Introduction by Peter Schwartz. Oceanside, Calif.: Second Renaissance Books.

————. 1992. *The Morality of Individualism: Essays in the Philosophic Foundations of Capitalism.* Los Angeles: Ayn Rand Institute. Translated into Russian by Marina Slovina under the title *Moral' Individualizma* (Moscow: Igra-Tekhnika, 1992).

Rand, Ayn, and Nathaniel Branden, eds. 1962–65. *The Objectivist Newsletter.* Vols. 1–4. New York: The Objectivist.

Rasmussen, Douglas B. 1980. A groundwork for rights: Man's natural end. *Journal of Libertarian Studies* 4 (Winter): 65–76.

————. 1983a. Logical possibility: An Aristotelian essentialist critique. *Thomist* 47 (October): 513–40.

————. 1983b. Review: *Reality at Risk* by Roger Trigg. *Reason Papers* 9 (Winter): 85–90.

————. 1983c. Rorty, Wittgenstein, and the nature of intentionality. *Proceedings of the American Catholic Association* 57:152–62.

————. 1984. Quine and Aristotelian essentialism. *New Scholasticism* 58 (Summer): 316–35.

————. 1990a. Natural rights, philosophical realism, and Hume's theory of the common life. *Reason Papers* 15 (Summer): 118–36.

————. 1990b. Rand on obligation and value. Ayn Rand Society Address, Boston, 28 December.

————. 1992. Capitalism and morality: The role of practical reason. In *Business Ethics and Common Sense*, ed. Robert McGee. Westport, Conn., and London: Quorum.

————. 1995. Letters of Ayn Rand. Edited by Michael S. Berliner. New York: Penguin Dutton.

Rasmussen, Douglas B., and Douglas J. Den Uyl. 1991. *Liberty and Nature: An Aristotelian Defense of Liberal Order.* LaSalle, Ill.: Open Court.

————. 1993. Reply to critics. *Reason Papers* 18 (Fall): 117–35.

Reedstrom, Karen. 1992. Interview with Barbara Branden. *Full Context* 4 (October).

———. 1993a. Interview with George Walsh. *Full Context* 6 (November).

———. 1993b. Rand's manuscripts scattering: Donations requested. *Full Context* 6 (December).

———, ed. 1994. The morality of taxation: The debate. *Full Context* 7 (September).

Reisman, George. 1990. Education and the racist road to barbarism. Irvington-on-Hudson, N.Y.: Foundation for Economic Education.

———. 1994. The real right to medical care versus socialized medicine. Laguna Hills, Calif.: Jefferson School.

Riggenbach, Jeff. 1979. In praise of decadence. *New York Times*, 24 June, E21.

———. 1982. The disowned children of Ayn Rand. *Reason*, December, 57–59.

Robbins, John W. 1974. *Answer to Ayn Rand: A Critique of the Philosophy of Objectivism.* Washington, D.C.: Mount Vernon.

Roelofs, H. Mark. 1976. *Ideology and Myth in American Politics.* Boston: Little, Brown.

Rorty, Richard. 1967. Relations, internal and external. In Edwards 1967, 7.

Rosenthal, Bernice Glatzer. 1975. *Dmitri Sergeevich Merezhkovsky and the Silver Age: The Development of a Revolutionary Mentality.* The Hague: Nijhoff.

———. 1980. Eschatology and the appeal of revolution: Merezhkovsky, Bely, Blok. *California Slavic Studies* 11:195–239.

———, ed. 1986. *Nietzsche in Russia.* Princeton: Princeton University Press.

———. 1991a. A new word for a new myth: Nietzsche and Russian futurism. In *The European Foundations of Russian Modernism*, ed. Peter I. Barta in collaboration with Ulrich Goebel. Lewiston, Queenston, Lampeter: Edwin Mellen.

———. 1991b. The search for a Russian orthodox work ethic. In *Between Tsar and People: Educated Society and the Quest for Public Identity in Late Imperial Russia*, ed. Edith W. Clowes, Samuel E. Kassow, and James L. West. Princeton: Princeton University Press.

———, ed. 1994. *Nietzsche and Soviet Culture: Ally and Adversary.* Cambridge: Cambridge University Press.

Rosenthal, Bernice Glatzer, and Martha Bohachevsky-Chomiak, eds. 1990. *A Revolution of the Spirit: Crisis of Value in Russia, 1890–1924.* New York: Fordham University Press.

Rothbard, Murray N. 1957. Communications: *Atlas Shrugged. Commonweal*, 20 December, 312–13.

———. [1963] 1975. *America's Great Depression.* 3d ed. Kansas City: Sheed & Ward.

———. 1970. *Man, Economy and State.* Los Angeles: Nash.

———. [1970] 1977. *Power and Market: Government and the Economy.* Kansas City: Sheed Andrews & McMeel.

———. 1973. *For a New Liberty: The Libertarian Manifesto.* New York: Macmillan.

———. 1978. *For a New Liberty: The Libertarian Manifesto.* Rev. edition. New York: Collier.

———. 1982. *The Ethics of Liberty.* Atlantic Highlands, N.J.: Humanities Press.

———. 1983. *The Mystery of Banking.* New York: Richardson & Shyder.

———. 1987. *The Sociology of the Ayn Rand Cult.* Port Townsend, Wash.: Liberty.

———. 1989. Memoir: My break with Branden and the Rand cult. *Liberty*, September, 27–32.

Saint-Andre, Peter. 1993. A philosophy for living on earth. *Objectivity* 1, no. 6.

Sartre, Jean-Paul. 1963. *Search for a Method.* Translated by Hazel E. Barnes. New York: Vintage.

Schumpeter, Joseph A. [1942] 1976. *Capitalism, Socialism and Democracy.* Introduction by Tom Bottomore. New York: Harper Colophon, Harper & Row.

Schwartz, Peter, ed. 1979–94. *The Intellectual Activist.* 8 vols. Lincroft, N.J.: The Intellectual Activist.

————. 1986. *Libertarianism: The Perversion of Liberty.* New York: The Intellectual Activist.

Sciabarra, Chris M. 1984. Toward a critical reconstruction of the philosophic thought of Ayn Rand: A dialectical integration and its implications for praxis. Working paper, New York University.

————. 1987. The crisis of libertarian dualism. *Critical Review* 1 (Fall): 86–99.

————. 1988a. Toward a radical critique of utopianism: Dialectics and dualism in the works of Friedrich Hayek, Murray Rothbard and Karl Marx. Ph.D. diss., New York University.

————. 1988b. Response to Tibor Machan. *Critical Review* 2 (Spring/Summer): 227–29.

————. 1988c. Marx on the precipice of utopia: Review of Brien's *Marx, Reason, and the Art of Freedom. Critical Review* 2 (Fall): 76–81.

————. 1989. Ayn Rand's critique of ideology. *Reason Papers* 14 (Spring): 34–47.

————. 1990. From Aristotle to Marx: Review of Meikle's *Essentialism in the Thought of Karl Marx. Critical Review* 4 (Winter): 61–73.

————. 1991. Rothbard's libertarianism. *Liberty,* January, 56–62.

————. 1995. *Marx, Hayek, and Utopia.* New York: State University of New York Press.

Scuoteguazza, Henry. 1993. Man's life vs. the fulfilled life. *Full Context* 5 (April).

Secrest, Meryle. 1992. *Frank Lloyd Wright.* New York: Alfred A. Knopf.

Selsam, Howard, and Harry Martel, eds. 1963. *Reader in Marxist Philosophy from the Writings of Marx, Engels, and Lenin.* New York: International.

Shaffer, Butler D. 1976. Violence as a product of imposed order. *Studies in Law* 4. Menlo Park, Calif.: Institute for Humane Studies.

Shein, Louis J. 1967. Lossky, Nicholas Onufriyevich. In Edwards 1967, 5.

————, ed. 1973. *Readings in Russian Philosophical Thought: Logic and Aesthetics.* Edited, translated, and annotated by L. Shein. Paris and The Hague: Mouton.

Shteppa, Konstantin F. 1962. *Russian Historians and the Soviet State.* New Brunswick: Rutgers University Press.

Smith, Barry, ed. 1992. *The Monist: Teleology & the Foundation of Value* 75 (January).

Smith, George H. 1979. *Atheism: The Case Against God.* Buffalo, N.Y.: Prometheus.

————. 1991. *Atheism, Ayn Rand, and Other Heresies.* Buffalo, N.Y.: Prometheus.

Smith, Kay Nolte. 1993. "If there is a novel inside of you . . ." *IOS Journal* 3 (November): 6–8.

Solzhenitsyn, Aleksandr I. 1973. *The Gulag Archipelago, 1918–1956: An Experiment in Literary Investigation I–II.* Translated by Thomas P. Whitney. New York: Harper & Row.

Sorokin, Pitirim A. [1924] 1950. *Leaves from a Russian Diary—and Thirty Years After.* Enlarged edition. Boston: Beacon.

Stata, Raymie. 1993. Interview with David Kelley. *Full Context* 5 (June).

Steele, David Ramsay. 1988. Appraisal: Alice in wonderland. *Liberty,* May, 35–43.

Steele, Shelby. 1990. *The Content of Our Character: A New Vision of Race in America.* New York: St. Martin's.

————. 1994. How to grow extremists. *New York Times,* 13 March, Op-Ed.

Sweezy, Paul, ed. [1949] 1975. *Karl Marx and the Close of His System.* Clifton, N.J.: Augustus M. Kelley.

Taylor, Joan Kennedy. 1992. *Reclaiming the Mainstream: Individualist Feminism Rediscovered.* Buffalo, N.Y.: Prometheus.

Thomas, Paul. 1980. *Karl Marx and the Anarchists.* London: Routledge & Kegan Paul.

Thompson, John B., and David Held, eds. 1982. *Habermas: Critical Debates*. Cambridge: MIT Press.

Thorslev, Peter L., Jr. 1971. Some dangers of dialectic thinking, with illustrations from Blake and his critics. In *Romantic and Victorian: Studies in Memory of William H. Marshall*, ed. W. Paul Elledge and Richard L. Hoffman. Rutherford, N.J.: Fairleigh Dickinson University Press.

Tolstaya, Tatyana. 1991. In cannibalistic times: Review of Conquest's *The Greater Terror: A Reassessment*. *New York Review of Books*, 11 April.

Tolstoi, Lyof N. [1899] 1913. *What is Art? What is Religion?* New York: Charles Scribner's Sons.

Torres, Louis, and Michelle Marder Kamhi. 1996. *What Art Is: Ayn Rand's Philosophy of Art in Critical Perspective*. Chicago: Open Court.

————, eds. 1982–94. *Aristos: The Journal of Esthetics*. Vols. 1–6.

Trotsky, Leon. [1924] 1960. *Literature and Revolution*. New York: Russell & Russell.

Tuccille, Jerome. [1971] 1972. *It Usually Begins with Ayn Rand*. New York: Stein & Day.

Veatch, Henry B. 1992. Might "Objectivism" ever become academically respectable. *Liberty*, January, 67.

Vermilye, Jerry. 1994. *Great Italian Films*. Secaucus, N.J.: Citadel Press.

Vorhies, Frank. 1989. Marx on money and crises. *Critical Review* 3 (Summer/Fall): 531–41.

Wallace, Robert. 1967. *Rise of Russia*. New York: Time-Life.

Walsh, George V. 1992. Ayn Rand and the metaphysics of Kant. Ayn Rand Society Address, Washington, D.C., 29 December.

Weber, Max. 1930. *The Protestant Ethic and the Spirit of Capitalism*. Translated by Talcott Parsons; foreword by R. T. Tawney. London: G. Allen & Unwin.

Weinstein, James. 1968. *The Corporate Ideal in the Liberal State: 1900–1918*. Boston: Beacon.

Widmer, Kingsley. 1981. Utopia and liberty: Some contemporary issues within their intellectual traditions. *Literature of Liberty* 4 (Winter): 5–62.

Wieder, Charles G. 1988–89. Education and the left-brain/right-brain model of mind. *Human Intelligence Newsletter* 9 (Summer/Fall/Winter).

Willis, F. Roy. 1977. *Western Civilization: An Urban Perspective*. Vol. 1, *From Ancient Times through the Seventeenth Century*. Lexington, Mass.: D. C. Heath.

Wrong, Dennis H. 1961. The oversocialized conception of man in modern sociology. *American Sociological Review* 26 (April): 183–93.

Zenkovsky, Nicolas. 1953. *A History of Russian Philosophy*. Vol. 2. Translated by George L. Kline. New York: Columbia University Press.

Tapes

Binswanger, Harry. [1987] 1991T. *Selected Topics in the Philosophy of Science*. 2 lectures. Oceanside, Calif.: Second Renaissance Books.

————. 1989T. *Consciousness and Identification: The Nature of Cognition and Concept-Formation*. 3 lectures. Oceanside, Calif.: Second Renaissance Books.

————. 1994T. *Ayn Rand's Life: Highlights and Sidelights*. Oceanside, Calif.: Second Renaissance Books.

Blumenthal, Allan. 1992T. *Nature, Nurture, and Free Will*. Institute of Objectivist Studies Forum, 12 December.

Blumenthal, Allan, and Joan Mitchell Blumenthal. [1974] 1987T. *Music: Theory, History, Performance.* 12 lectures.

Branden, Barbara. 1962T. *Principles of Efficient Thinking.* 10 lectures. New York: Nathaniel Branden Institute.

———. 1986T. *An Evening with Barbara Branden.* New York: Laissez-Faire.

Branden, Nathaniel. 1967T. *Basic Principles of Objectivism.* 20 lectures. New York: Nathaniel Branden Institute.

———. 1982T. *The Benefits and Hazards of the Philosophy of Ayn Rand: A Personal Statement.* Washington, D.C.: Biocentric Institute.

———. 1983T. *Love and Sex in the Philosophy of Ayn Rand.* Washington, D.C.: Biocentric Institute.

———. 1989T. *On Ayn Rand.* New York: Laissez-Faire.

———. 1991T. *The Inside Edge Presents an Edge on the Nineties: The Dynamics of Self-Esteem.* Loew's Hotel, Santa Monica, Calif., 23 March [Video].

———. n.d.T. *The Psychology of Individualism: An Informal Discussion of "Honoring the Self."*

Gotthelf, Allan. 1988T. *Aristotle as Scientist: A Proper Verdict.* 2 lectures. Power of Reason Conference, 1, 3 August. Oceanside, Calif.: Second Renaissance Books.

Kelley, David. 1985aT. *The Nature of Free Will.* 2 lectures.

———. 1985bT. *The Primacy of Existence.* 2 lectures.

———. 1985cT. *Universals and Induction.* 2 lectures.

———, moderator. 1993T. Colloquium on Chris Sciabarra's *Ayn Rand: The Russian Radical.* Sponsored by the Institute for Objectivist Studies, New York, 6 June.

Locke, Edwin A. 1991T. *The Nature of Human Intelligence.* 2 lectures. Oceanside, Calif.: Second Renaissance Books.

Packer, Edith. 1985T. *The Language of Emotions and Introspection.* Oceanside, Calif.: Second Renaissance Books.

———. 1986T. *The Role of Philosophy in Psychotherapy.* Oceanside, Calif.: Second Renaissance Books.

———. 1988T. *Toward a Lasting Romantic Relationship, Part One.* Oceanside, Calif.: Second Renaissance Books.

———. 1990T. *Toward a Lasting Romantic Relationship, Part Two.* Oceanside, Calif.: Second Renaissance Books.

Peikoff, Leonard. 1970T. *Modern Philosophy: Kant to the Present.* 12 lectures. Oceanside, Calif.: Lectures on Objectivism.

———. 1972T. *Founders of Western Philosophy: Thales to Hume.* 12 lectures. Oceanside, Calif.: Lectures on Objectivism.

———. 1974T. *Introduction to Logic.* 10 lectures. Oceanside, Calif.: Lectures on Objectivism.

———. 1976T. *The Philosophy of Objectivism.* 12 lectures. Oceanside, Calif.: Lectures on Objectivism.

———. 1980T. *Objective Communication.* 10 lectures. Oceanside, Calif.: Lectures on Objectivism.

———. 1982aT. *Principles of Grammar.* 8 lectures. Oceanside, Calif.: Lectures on Objectivism.

———. 1982bT. *The Sanction of the Victims.* Oceanside, Calif.: Second Renaissance Books.

———. 1983T. *Understanding Objectivism.* 12 lectures. Oceanside, Calif.: Lectures on Objectivism.

———. 1984T. *The Role of Philosophy and Psychology in History.* Oceanside, Calif.: Second Renaissance Books.

———. 1985T. *Philosophy of Education*. 6 lectures. La Jolla, Calif.: Second Renaissance Books.

———. 1987aT. *My Thirty Years with Ayn Rand: An Intellectual Memoir*. Oceanside, Calif.: Second Renaissance Books.

———. 1987bT. *Objectivism: The State of the Art*. 6 lectures. 2 question periods. Oceanside, Calif.: Second Renaissance Books.

———. 1988aT. *Why Should One Act on Principle?* Oceanside, Calif.: Second Renaissance Books.

———. 1988bT. *Certainty and Happiness*. Conceptual conferences. Oceanside, Calif: Second Renaissance Books.

———. 1989T. *Moral Virtue*. 3 lectures. Oceanside, Calif: Second Renaissance Books.

———. 1990T. *Philosophy and the Real World Out There*. Oceanside, Calif: Second Renaissance Books.

———. 1990–91T. *Objectivism: The Philosophy of Ayn Rand*. 15 lectures. Oceanside, Calif.: Lectures on Objectivism.

Peikoff, Leonard, and Duncon Scott. 1988T. *Benefit Screening for "We the Living."* Oceanside, Calif: Second Renaissance Books.

Rand, Ayn. [1958] 1986T. *Lectures on Fiction-Writing*. 12 lectures. Oceanside, Calif.: Lectures on Objectivism.

———. 1961T. *Faith and Force: The Destroyers of the Modern World*. Purdue University, April. Oceanside, Calif: Second Renaissance Books.

———. [1961] 1992T. *Ayn Rand and the 'New Intellectual': Interview with James McConnell*. University of Michigan Television [Video].

———. 1962T. *Questions and Answers on Objectivism*. Oceanside, Calif: Second Renaissance Books.

———. [1964] 1993aT. *Nineteenth-century Capitalism*. WKCR Interview. Oceanside, Calif: Second Renaissance Books.

———. [1964] 1993bT. *Objectivism and Romantic Literature*. WKCR Interview. Oceanside, Calif: Second Renaissance Books.

———. [1964] 1993cT. *Conservatism vs. Objectivism*. WKCR Interview. Oceanside, Calif: Second Renaissance Books.

———. [1964] 1993dT. *The Role of Education*. WKCR Interview. Oceanside, Calif: Second Renaissance Books.

———. 1966T. *Ethics in Education*. New York: Nathaniel Branden Institute.

———. 1969T. *Apollo and Dionysus*. Oceanside, Calif: Second Renaissance Books.

———. 1971T. *The Moratorium on Brains*. Oceanside, Calif: Second Renaissance Books.

———. 1972T. Interview with Edwin Newman. *Speaking Freely*. New York: NBC-TV, 4 March.

———. 1973T. *Censorship: Local and Express*. Oceanside, Calif: Second Renaissance Books.

———. 1974aT. Interview with James Day—Ayn Rand speaks for herself. *Day at Night*. New York: WNET-TV, 30 April [Video].

———. 1974bT. *Philosophy: Who Needs It*. Oceanside, Calif: Second Renaissance Books.

———. 1976T. *The Moral Factor*. Oceanside, Calif: Second Renaissance Books.

———. [1976] 1992T. *Interview with Ayn Rand*. Oceanside, Calif: Second Renaissance Books.

———. 1977T. *Global Balkanization*. Oceanside, Calif: Second Renaissance Books.

———. 1978T. *Cultural Update*. Oceanside, Calif: Second Renaissance Books.

———. 1979aT. *Interview with Phil Donahue: The Phil Donahue Show*. New York: NBC-TV, 15 May.

———. 1979bT. *Interview with Tom Snyder: The Tomorrow Show*. New York: NBC-TV, 2 July.

———. 1981T. *The Sanction of the Victims*. Oceanside, Calif: Second Renaissance Books.

———. 1983T. *Objectivism in Brief*. 2 interviews. The Raymond Newman Journal. Oceanside, Calif: Second Renaissance Books.

Reisman, George. 1986T. *Toward the Establishment of a Capitalist Society*. Oceanside, Calif: Second Renaissance Books.

———. 1990T. *Education and the Racist Road to Barbarism*. Oceanside, Calif: Second Renaissance Books.

Ridpath, John. 1983T. *The Raymond Newman Journal: History of the Concept of Rights*. Oceanside, Calif: Second Renaissance Books.

———. 1987T. *Lenin: 19th century origins and 20th century impact*. 2 lectures. Oceanside, Calif: Second Renaissance Books.

Schwartz, Peter. 1990T. *The Altruist Connection*. Oceanside, Calif: Second Renaissance Books.

———. 1994T. *The Threats to Freedom: A Philosophic Dissection*. 7 lectures. Oceanside, Calif: Second Renaissance Books.

Walker, Jeff. 1992T. *The Legacy of Ayn Rand*. Narrated by Lester Sinclair. San Francisco: Laissez-Faire.

Walsh, George. [1985] 1990T. *Marxism: Philosophy and Political Ideology*. 4 lectures. San Francisco: Laissez-Faire.

———. 1988T. *The Role of Religion in Human History*. 4 lectures. San Francisco: Laissez-faire.

INDEX